16621   598
15·3·96   Aw

Encyclopaedia of Birds.

THE ENCYCLOPAEDIA OF
BIRDS

Project Editor: Graham Bateman
Editors: Peter Forbes, Bill MacKeith, Robert Peberdy
Art Editor: Jerry Burman
Art Assistant: Carol Wells
Picture Research: Alison Renney
Production: Clive Sparling
Design: Chris Munday

 AN EQUINOX BOOK

Published by:
George Allen & Unwin
40 Museum Street
London WC1A 1LU

Planned and produced by:
Equinox (Oxford) Ltd
Littlegate House
St Ebbe's Street
Oxford OX1 1SQ

British Library Cataloguing in Publication Data
The Encyclopaedia of Birds.
Vol. 3
1. Birds—Dictionaries
I. Perrins, Christopher M., II. Middleton, Alex L. A.
598′.03′21   QL673

ISBN 0-04-500032-8

Origination by Fotographics, Hong Kong; Alpha
Reprographics Ltd, Harefield, Middx.

Filmset by BAS Printers Ltd, Stockbridge, Hants,
England.

Printed in Spain by Heraclio Fournier S.A., Vitoria.

Artwork panels

Norman Arlott
Trevor Boyer
Ad Cameron
Robert Gillmor
Peter Harrison
Chloë Talbot Kelly
Sean Milne
Denys Ovenden
Laurel Tucker
Ian Willis

Left: Spotted catbird fledglings.
Half title: Griffon vulture being mobbed by ravens in Himalayas. Title page: Bee-eater.

CONTRIBUTORS

GWA   George W. Archibald PhD
International Crane
Foundation
Baraboo, Wisconsin
USA

MA   Mark Avery PhD
Edward Grey Institute of Field
Ornithology
University of Oxford
England

PJB   Philip J. Bacon DPhil
Institute of Terrestrial
Ecology
Grange-over-Sands, Cumbria
England

JCB   Jon C. Barlow PhD
Royal Ontario Museum
Toronto, Ontario
Canada

JB   Jack Barr PhD
Guelph, Ontario
Canada

JFB   J.F. Bendell PhD
University of Toronto
Ontario
Canada

BCRB   Brian C.R. Bertram PhD
Zoological Society of London
England

MEB   Michael E. Birkhead DPhil
Edward Grey Institute of Field
Ornithology
University of Oxford
England

TRB   Timothy R. Birkhead BSc
DPhil
University of Sheffield
England

DB   Dieter Blume
Gladenbach
West Germany

MDB   Murray D. Bruce
National Parks and Wildlife
Service
New South Wales
Australia

DFB   Donald F. Bruning PhD
New York Zoological Society
Bronx Park, New York
USA

RWB   Robert W. Burton MIBiol
Great Gransden, Bedfordshire
England

NJC   Nigel J. Collar PhD
International Council for Bird
Preservation
Cambridge
England

PRC   P.R. Colston
British Museum (Natural
History)
Sub-department of
Ornithology
Tring, Hertfordshire
England

FHJC   Frank H.J. Crome BSc
CSIRO, Wildlife and
Rangelands Research
Atherton, Queensland
Australia

TMC   T.M. Crowe PhD
Department of Zoology
University of Cape Town
South Africa

JPC   John P. Croxall PhD
British Antarctic Survey
Cambridge
England

SJJFD   Stephen J.J.F. Davies PhD
Mount Helena, Western
Australia
Australia

WRJD   W.R.J. Dean
Knysna
South Africa

AWD   A.W. Diamond PhD
Canadian Wildlife Service
Ottawa, Ontario
Canada

EKD   Euan K. Dunn PhD
Edward Grey Institute of Field
Ornithology
University of Oxford
England

RME   R. Michael Erwin PhD
Patuxent Wildlife Research
Center
Laurel, Maryland
USA

SME   Stewart M. Evans PhD
University of Newcastle-
upon-Tyne
England

CJF   Chris J. Feare PhD
Ministry of Agriculture,
Fisheries and Food
Worplesdon, Surrey
England

JWF   John W. Fitzpatrick PhD
Field Museum of Natural
History
Chicago, Illinois
USA

HAF   Hugh A. Ford PhD
University of New England
Armidale, New South Wales
Australia

CBF   Clifford B. Frith PhD
Paluma via Townsville
Queensland
Australia

CHF   C. Hilary Fry PhD
University of Aberdeen
Scotland

RWF   Robert W. Furness PhD
University of Glasgow
Scotland

EFJG   Ernest F.J. Garcia DPhil
Guildford, Surrey
England

PJG   Peter J. Garson DPhil
University of Newcastle-
upon-Tyne
England

AJG   Anthony J. Gaston DPhil
Canadian Wildlife Service
Ottawa, Ontario
Canada

FBG   Frank B. Gill PhD
Academy of Natural Sciences
Philadelphia, Pennsylvania
USA

LGG   Llewellyn G. Grimes BSc MSc
PhD
Warwick
England

JH   James Hancock
Winchester, Hampshire
England

JWH   John W. Hardy PhD
Florida State Museum
Gainesville, Florida
USA

MPH   Michael P. Harris PhD
Institute of Terrestrial
Ecology
Banchory, Kincardineshire
Scotland

GJMH   Graham J.M. Hirons DPhil
University of Southampton
England

DTH   David T. Holyoak PhD
University of Nottingham
England

JAH   John A. Horsfall BA DPhil
Edward Grey Institute of Field
Ornithology
University of Oxford
England

RH   Robert Hudson
British Trust for Ornithology
Tring, Hertfordshire
England

AMH   A.M. Hutson
Fauna and Flora
Preservation Society
London
England

JNJ   James N. Jolly MSc
Wildlife Service
Department of Internal
Affairs
Wellington
New Zealand

JK   Janet Kear PhD
Wildfowl Trust
Ormskirk
England

AK   Alan Kemp PhD
Transvaal Museum
Pretoria
South Africa

CBK   Cameron B. Kepler PhD
US Fish and Wildlife Service
Kula, Hawaii
USA

JKi   Jiro Kikkawa DSc
University of Queensland
Brisbane, Queensland
Australia

RWK   Richard W. Knapton PhD
Brock University
St Catherine's, Ontario
Canada

JAK   James A. Kushlan PhD
University of Miami
Coral Gables, Florida
USA

DRL   Derek R. Langslow MA PhD
Nature Conservancy Council
Huntingdon
England

AL   Alan Lill PhD
Monash University
Clayton, Victoria
Australia

HL   Hans Löhrl PhD
Egenhausen
West Germany

ALu   Arne Lundberg PhD
Uppsala University
Sweden

GLM   Gordon L. Maclean DSc
University of Natal
Pietermaritzburg
South Africa

CJM   Christopher J. Mead PhD
British Trust for Ornithology
Tring, Hertfordshire
England

*Tyrant flycatchers and pittas
(Denys Ovenden—see page 320).*

MAO   Malcolm A. Ogilvie PhD
Wildfowl Trust
Slimbridge, Gloucestershire
England

GHO   Gordon H. Orians PhD
University of Washington
Seattle, Washington
USA

TWP   T.W. Parmenter
British Museum (Natural
History)
London
England

CMP   Christopher M. Perrins DPhil
Edward Grey Institute of Field
Ornithology
University of Oxford
England

MWP   Michael W. Pienkowski PhD
University of Durham
England

PAP   Peter A. Prince MIBiol
British Antarctic Survey
Cambridge
England

ASR   Andrew S. Richford DPhil
London
England

MWR   M.W. Ridley DPhil
Edward Grey Institute of Field
Ornithology
University of Oxford
England

HR   Hugh Robertson DPhil
Edward Grey Institute of Field
Ornithology
University of Oxford
England

IR   Ian Rowley B Agr Sc
CSIRO, Wildlife and
Rangelands Research
Australia

DHM   Douglass H. Morse PhD
Brown University
Providence, Rhode Island
USA

JBN   J. Bryan Nelson DPhil
University of Aberdeen
Scotland

IN   Ian Newton PhD
Institute for Terrestrial
Ecology
Abbot's Ripton
Cambridgeshire
England

RAN   Richard A. Noske PhD
Canberra College of
Advanced Education
Australia

EAS   Elizabeth Anne Schreiber BA
Los Angeles County Museum
of Natural History
Los Angeles, California
USA

RWS   Ralph W. Schreiber PhD
Los Angeles County Museum
of Natural History
Los Angeles, California
USA

JAS   James A. Serpell PhD
University of Cambridge
England

GHS   Greg H. Sherley
University of Canterbury
Christchurch
New Zealand

DS-C   Douglas Siegel-Causey PhD
Museum of Natural History
University of Kansas
Lawrence, Kansas
USA

AFS   Alexander F. Skutch PhD
San Isidro
Costa Rica

GTS   G.T. Smith PhD
CSIRO, Wildlife and
Rangelands Research
Australia

BKS   Barbara K. Snow BSc
British Museum (Natural
History)
Sub-department of
Ornithology
Tring, Hertfordshire
England

DWS   David W. Snow DSc
British Museum (Natural
History)
Sub-department of
Ornithology
Tring, Hertfordshire
England

GFvT   G.F. van Tets PhD
CSIRO
Lyneham, A.C.T.
Australia

GT   Gareth Thomas PhD
Royal Society for the
Protection of Birds
Sandy, Bedfordshire
England

AKT   Angela K. Turner PhD
University of Glasgow
Scotland

CAW   C.A. Walker
British Museum (Natural
History)
London
England

CW   Cliff Waller
Blythburgh, Suffolk
England

DRW   D.R. Wells PhD
University of Malaya
Kuala Lumpur
Malaysia

BW   Brian Wood PhD
University College
London
England

RDW   Ron D. Wooller PhD
Murdoch University
Murdoch, Western Australia
Australia

CONTENTS

Cranes and rails
(Sean Milne—see page 144).

PREFACE

Birds apparently arouse more interest among the general public than any other animal group—even including mammals. At first sight it is surprising that mankind should respond like this—after all we are mammals. However, man is an unusual mammal in that most mammals rely on the senses of smell and hearing to a much greater extent than we do. Further, although sight is important in mammals, it tends to be less so than in man since few mammals have color vision. Birds, by way of contrast, share with man a dependence on color vision and sound as their two main senses. Further, in keeping with their color vision they are brightly colored. Finally, the majority of birds are active during daylight hours.

Man can, therefore, perhaps "perceive" more of a bird's world than that of many mammals. Consider for example our most-loved pet, the dog. On a walk, it spends a great deal of its time smelling objects; plainly, it is acquiring a great deal of information about its surroundings. Yet, in spite of our long association with dogs, we really do not begin to understand the olfactory messages that it is receiving. It may be illusory, but it seems easier for us to understand the various activities of birds than it is with most mammals, with the exception perhaps of our nearest relatives, the apes, with whom we share more common sensory perceptions.

In this work, we have tried to provide the reader with an encapsulated but up-to-date account of the world's birds. It has been inevitable that we should deal with them by family rather than by individual species because, depending on the source, between 8,000 and 9,021 species of bird are recognized—more than twice as many as there are mammals. In this volume it is considered there are 8,805 species. A large number of them are virtually unknown; the nests and eggs of many species have not yet been described and, for a number of species, we have inadequate records of their range. The vast majority of these, of course, are species which live in the tropical forests where their ability to fly, their small size and the density of vegetation mean that they remain virtually unobserved.

Nevertheless, at the family level, most groups of birds are adequately known for it to be possible to give a comprehensive review of the colorful and varied array of this fascinating assemblage of animals. In particular, there has been during the last 10 years or so a great increase in the number of detailed studies of the behavior of many of the tropical families which hitherto were poorly known. Although such observations have still been made of only a small handful of species, they range over most of the major families and give at least an indication of how the other related species are likely to live. These studies have not merely filled out what was known before; they have demonstrated the ways in which birds cope with their environment which, we realize as we learn more, is a very complex one. The birds are far more intricately adapted to their ways of life than the casual observer might at first assume; natural selection is a powerful tool.

In particular, recent studies have shown that, in many groups, family life is much more complex than was once thought and there is still much to be learned. Up to 20 years ago, most detailed studies had been conducted in Europe and in North America, where the majority of birds live in simple, monogamous pairs. In contrast, many of the species in the tropics live in "extended families" where six or more birds may share a territory and look after a single nest. While much remains to be discovered about them, the studies to date have greatly increased our understanding—if only in some cases of how much there is still to learn!

The layout of the book follows a fairly simple structure. Each article deals with a single family (often the only member of its order) or several families (sometimes all members of an order, sometimes groupings within an order) which, in most cases, are more closely related to each other than to other families. The book is divided into three parts: 1 Ostriches to Buttonquails, 2 Plovers to Woodpeckers, and 3 The Passerines. It should be noted that there is no clear agreement among taxonomists about the way in which birds should be classified! The sequence of families which is used here is described at the start of each section, on pages 16–17, 160–161 and 304–305. Notes on classification which detail some of the major differences of opinion will be found on ppxiv–xv. For further detail the reader should also refer to the texts which are listed in the Bibliography.

There is a widespread view held by the "man in the street" that the experts should know how many species of birds (or

other animals) there are. This is long way from being the case. It is not even easy to define a species! Perhaps the commonest way to decide whether an animal is a different species from another one is to base the decision on whether or not the populations to which they belong naturally interbreed. However, in many cases animals which can potentially interbreed in captivity may not meet in the wild—they may, for example, live on different, far-distant continents. So one has to decide

LEFT Kingfisher (Ian Willis—see page 268).　ABOVE Red-tailed tropicbird.

(or test) whether or not they would interbreed if their ranges naturally overlapped. There can be no objective view and, not surprisingly, opinions differ widely. Studies of their biochemistry and anatomy are also important in deciding species relationships.

As a result, no two books will necessarily list the same families or the same number of species in each family. Since this book is not primarily a work on taxonomy, we have attempted to avoid undue eccentricity. However, the author of each article is often a leading expert on the group concerned and so we have encouraged them to use the results of their own studies.

Each article gives details, where relevant, of physical features, distribution, evolutionary history, classification, breeding, diet and feeding behavior, social dynamics and spatial organization, conservation and relationships with man.

An information panel precedes the textual discussion of each family or group of families. This provides easy reference to the main features of distribution, habitat, dimension, plumage, voice, nests, eggs and diet. Where a number of families are considered, a supplementary table placed elsewhere in the entry gives this detailed information for each family (or in some cases subfamilies). For each family there is a map of natural distribution (not introductions to other areas by man). Unless otherwise stated this is the global distribution of the family and includes breeding and wintering grounds for migratory birds. In some instances (where stated) only breeding distribution is given. For each family, there is a scale drawing comparing the size of a representative species with that of a six-foot (1.8m) human or a 12in (30cm) human foot. Where there are silhouettes of two birds they are the largest and smallest representatives of the family. Unless otherwise stated, dimensions given are for both males and females. Where there is a difference in size between sexes, the scale drawings show the larger sex. The scientific names of species mentioned in the main text are given in the panels.

Every so often a really remarkable study of a species or behavior pattern emerges. Some of these studies are so distinctive that they have been allocated two whole pages so that the authors may develop their stories. The topics of these "special features" give insight into evolutionary processes at work throughout all birds, and span social organization, foraging behavior, breeding biology and conservation. Similar themes are also developed in smaller "box features" alongside most of the major texts.

Most readers have never seen many of the birds mentioned in these pages, but that does not necessarily mean they have to remain remote or unreal in our thoughts. Such detachment vanishes as these animals are brought vividly to life, not only by many photographs but especially by the color and line artwork. These illustrations are the fruits of great labor: they are accurate in minute detail and more importantly they are dynamic—often each bird is shown engaged in an activity or in a posture that enhances or expands upon points made in the text. Furthermore, the species have been chosen as representatives of their group.

We live in a changing world where habitats are being destroyed at an alarming rate. Although there is now a great deal of interest in conservation in many countries, in others, especially the developing ones, the need for new resources—particularly for the rapidly increasing human populations—make it inevitable that further areas of bird habitat will be lost. Most threatened of the major habitats are the rain forests of the tropics. Sadly, rain forest birds are among the most specialized—they are poorly equipped to cope with living in impoverished habitats. Some special forests in restricted areas—such as the thin strip of coastal rain forest in Brazil—have already almost completely disappeared, taking with them their endemic birds. Many other rain forest species still exist only because of the vastness of the forests. Unless we can call a halt, man is certain to destroy even the most extensive tracts in time.

To date we have lost more species from islands than from rain forests. Island species are threatened for a different reason—they only ever exist in comparatively small numbers since their habitats are restricted in size. Hence such birds are vulnerable to minor, local changes. Doubtless such species will be among those that continue to be lost in greatest numbers in the near future, but over a slightly longer period the wide variety of bird species in the big rain forest blocks must also be considered threatened.

Some 265 species of birds are listed as threatened by the International Council for Bird Preservation's (ICBP) Red Data Book, *Endangered Birds of the World* (second edition as revised 1974–9, and compiled by Warren B. King; third edition in preparation).

In this book the following symbols are used in the information panels and tables of families and species to show the status accorded to entire species by the ICBP: Ⓔ = Endangered—in danger of extinction unless causal factors (eg habitat destruction) are modified. Ⓥ = Vulnerable—likely to become endangered in the near future. Ⓡ = Rare, but neither endangered nor vulnerable at present. Ⓘ = Indeterminate—insufficient information available, but known to be in one of the above categories. (Some species that have become extinct within the last 100 years are indicated by the symbol Ⓔₓ.)

However, not all species listed as threatened by the ICBP are discussed in this book, and information about the total number of threatened species in each family is therefore included as follows: Where all such species are included in the summary panel or table of species devoted to a particular family, no further comment is added. Otherwise a figure for the "total threatened species" is given, either at the end of the list of representative species or, where the list is subdivided (for example into subfamilies, tribes or other groups) at the head of the tabulated information on the family.

It must also be stressed that this list is misleading in another way. For a great many of the tropical species so little is known about them that we are not in a position to say whether or not they are in any danger. Therefore the list should be taken to indicate that the species mentioned are threatened, but not necessarily that a species not listed is not threatened. Unfortunately many tropical species with restricted ranges are also a cause for concern.

Today, no single person could hope to put together a complete summary of bird families without the assistance of the large international team of authors we have used here, whose detailed studies and background knowledge far surpass those of any individual. In addition, the editorial team of Equinox (Oxford) Limited has distilled the contributions to consistency, spiced them with the work of the artists and photographers, and skillfully brought all the parts together. If the final product provides a stimulus for readers to discover more about the fascinating world we live in, then all our efforts will have proved worthwhile.

Christopher M. Perrins
DIRECTOR
EDWARD GREY INSTITUTE OF FIELD ORNITHOLOGY
UNIVERSITY OF OXFORD
ENGLAND

LEFT Barn owl.   OVERLEAF (pxvi) Greater flamingos.

Notes on Classification

A great many different classifications of birds have been proposed. As reference to any series of bird books will make clear, there is no simple agreement. At the present time, some exciting studies of the relationships of the different bird groups are being undertaken. In particular, those involving DNA-hybridization (a method which scores the similarity between the chromosomes of different species) seems to be providing some very promising new views, especially on some of the problematical groups. However, this work is not yet complete and we have here used a widely accepted classification. This is based, with only a few exceptions, on the so-called Wetmore order which is used in *Checklist of Birds of the World* by J.L. Peters and others (Museum of Comparative Zoology, Cambridge, Massachusetts).

Equally, it should be stressed that there is no agreement on the number of species in many of the families. Different interpretations and lack of knowledge on many species, especially those of tropical forests, make it impossible to give totally reliable figures. In general, those used here are based on E.S. Gruson's *A Checklist of the Birds of the World* (Collins, 1976), although we have allowed the specialist author to alter this if he or she felt that this was desirable. Another useful list is *The Number of Species and Genera of Recent Birds: A Contribution to Comparative Systematics* by W.J. Bock and J. Farrand (Publication No. 2703 of the American Museum of Natural History, 1980).

The families and orders dealt with are listed on pp17, 161 and 305. Here we will comment on a few points relevant to the groupings.

In the first section of the volume we will deal with a range of groups, most of which contain large or fairly large birds. Because birds fossilize so poorly, we have a very incomplete knowledge of their evolution; many of these groups are also among the most ancient forms.

The ostrich, rheas, emu, cassowaries and kiwis are a group of four orders and five families (Struthionidae, Rheidae, Dromaiidae, Casuariidae, Apterygidae, respectively) of flightless birds which are sometimes referred to as the ratites. This assemblage also includes the extinct moas (Dinornithidae) and elephant-bird (Aepyornithidae). The term ratites (derived from the Latin *rata*—raft) refers to the flat, unkeeled sternum (breast-bone). Since a keel is only necessary if the bird has large flight muscles—which these flightless birds do not

have—this characteristic could be merely one of convergence, independently acquired by different groups within the ratites during the period when these birds lost the power of flight—they are all clearly derived from ancestors that flew, since they have many characteristics of flying birds. It is not clear what the relationships of the families are to each other and despite superficial appearances they may well not be particularly closely related.

The tinamous (order Tinamiformes/family Tinamidae) are a group of partridge-like birds which have a number of primitive characters and have been linked with the ratites. In many ways their closest relatives seem to be the rheas, which is not surprising since both groups are South American.

The classification of penguins (order Sphenisciformes/family Spheniscidae) has caused difficulties. They were formerly put in a separate superorder (Impennes), but it is now thought they are more closely related to the albatrosses and petrels and to loons and also grebes.

The loons or divers (order Gaviiformes/family Gaviidae) and grebes (order Podicipediformes/family Podicipedidae) are normally placed close together, but they have many differences and may not in reality be closely related.

The order Procellariiformes comprises the albatrosses (Diomedeidae), shearwaters and petrels (Procellariidae), storm petrels (Hydrobatidae) and diving petrels (Pelecanoididae), four families of seabirds which are fairly clearly closely related—all have a long humerus (upper arm) and all have fairly similar breeding biology.

The six families in the order Pelecaniformes—the pelicans (Pelecanidae), gannets (Sulidae), cormorants (Phalacrocoracidae), darters (Anhingidae), frigatebirds (Fregatidae) and tropicbirds (Phaethontidae) are a diverse group of seabirds. They do, however, share a number of characters; all, for example, have totipalmate feet (all four toes joined by webs), although these are much reduced in the frigatebirds.

The Ciconiiformes are a group of fairly large long-legged wading birds. Here they are covered in three sections: (1) the herons and bitterns (Ardeidae), whale-headed stork (Balaenicipitidae) and hammerhead (Scopidae); (2) the storks (Ciconiidae) and spoonbills and ibises (Threskiornithidae); and (3) the flamingos (Phoenicopteridae). The flamingos are the most aberrant group and have sometimes been put in a separate order. They probably form a link between the Ciconiiformes and the ducks and geese.

The ducks, geese and swans (order Anseriformes/family Anatidae) form a fairly cohesive group, but the screamers (family Anhimidae) stand out as different. The latter are thought to be an early offshoot of the main Anseriform branch.

The order Falconiformes is a large group of day-active birds of prey, which is now often split into three separate orders but which is here treated as one. The New World vultures (family Cathartidae) may be put in an order of their own (Cathartiformes), as may the falcons (Falconidae) into the Falconiformes, while the remaining three families (Secretary bird/Sagittariidae, Osprey/Pandionidae and kites, eagles, hawks and sparrowhawks/Accipitridae) may be placed in the Accipitriformes.

The order Galliformes, comprising six families (the megapodes/Megapodiidae, guans/Cracidae, grouse/Tetraonidae, pheasants and quails/Phasianidae, guinea fowl/Numididae and turkeys/Meleagrididae), forms a fairly natural group of "game birds." The hoatzin (family Opisthocomidae) has sometimes been placed in this order, but here has been placed in the Cuculiformes—the cuckoos and allies.

The Gruiformes is a very diffuse and difficult group of families which do not all have much in common to the casual observer. However, all are terrestrial or aquatic; some fly very little and some are flightless. Here they are covered in three sections: (1) the cranes (Gruidae), limpkin (Aramidae), trumpeters (Psophiidae) and rails (Rallidae) which together form the suborder Grues; (2) the bustards (Otididae, suborder Otides); and (3) the button quails (Turnicidae) plus six other families.

In the second section of the book we deal with the other groups of birds that, with those in the first section, make up one of the two main groups of birds, the "non-passerines." Most are medium to small.

Members of the order Charadriiformes have clear associations with an aquatic environment. The order is composed of three main groups—the waders or shorebirds (suborder Charadrii), the gulls and terns (suborder Lari) and the auks (suborder Alcae). Although these groups show some common characters, they apparently diverged a very long time ago. Here we have covered four of the shorebird families—the plovers (Charadriidae), sandpipers (Scolopacidae), avocets and stilts (Recurvirostridae) and phalaropes (Phalaropodidae)—in one section and the remaining eight small families in another. It should be noted that the jacanas (Jacanidae) are perceived to be more closely related to the familiar shorebirds rather than to the rails which they superficially resemble.

The families Columbidae (pigeons) and Pteroclididae (sandgrouse) were once grouped together in the Columbiformes, but the two groups are quite distinct and, as here, some authorities place the sandgrouse in an order of their own. The extinct dodo was a highly aberrant flightless pigeon.

The parrots (order Psittaciformes) form a distinct order of their own.

The order Cuculiformes is considered by some to contain just two major groups—the cuckoos and the turacos. However, some recent classifications (as here) have included the hoatzin as a relative of the cuckoos. This very odd South American bird is of uncertain affinities and has often been considered to be an aberrant member of the game birds (order Galliformes).

The owls (order Strigiformes) form a distinct group, although the two constituent families may not be as closely related as was once thought; they have a number of important differences.

The order Caprimulgiformes is divided into two, the nightjars and others (four families of rather similar birds) and the oilbird, a single species which differs in a large variety of ways, possibly mainly related to its nocturnal, fruit-eating habits.

The order Apodiformes contains two groups of distinct birds, the swifts and hummingbirds. Although their similarities are not immediately obvious, the two suborders have a number of characters in common, including a very short humerus (upper arm).

The orders Trogoniformes (trogons) and Coliiformes (mousebirds) are both small groups of quite distinct families, both of uncertain affinities.

The order Coraciiformes is a difficult group to classify, containing four major suborders and nine families. Here we cover separately the kingfishers, the motmots together with the todies, the bee-eaters, the four families of rollers and hoopoes, and the hornbills. Some authorities take the five species of ground roller (all confined to Madagascar) out of the Coraciidae and put them in a family of their own (Brachypteraciidae).

The Piciformes contains two major suborders—on the one hand the toucans, honeyguides, barbets, jacamars and puffbirds (suborder Galbulae) and on the other the woodpeckers (suborder Pici), a fairly uniform group in just one family. The first group is exclusively New World except for the barbets which are widespread; jacamars and puffbirds are covered here separately from the other three families.

The third section differs from the others in that it contains just a single order of birds, the Passeriformes—often referred to as the passerines (in contrast to all the other birds which are called non-passerines). Passerines lack a simple English name, but they are sometimes referred to as the perching-birds (based on the anatomy of the foot)—a term that is hardly helpful when one looks at the many non-passerines that perch!

This order, which is thought to be of recent origin, contains mainly small birds. Its importance can perhaps best be gauged by looking at the number of species. In this work we estimate that there are 8,805 species of birds in total of which some 5,206 are passerines almost 60 percent of all living species!

There are four suborders of which the broadbills (Eurylaimi) with 14 species and the lyrebirds and scrub-birds (Menurae) with 4 species account for only 18 species between them. This leaves two major subdivisions. One, the Tyranni, contains about 1,065 species in 13 families and is almost exclusively of New World origin, most species being confined to South and Central America. The remaining suborder is the Oscines which has a worldwide distribution of some 4,123 species in 48 families. Again, there are no good English names for these important groups; the Oscines have sometimes been called the songbirds, a name as inappropriate for the suborder as perching birds is for the order.

The taxonomy of the Passeriformes is still under intensive debate and there are many arguments about certain groups. The following notes indicate some of these.

Within the Tyranni two small families—the Sunbird asitys (Philepittidae) and New Zealand wrens (Xenicidae)—are of uncertain affinities. In view of their distribution (restricted to Madagascar and New Zealand respectively), they may well not belong to the Tyranni, which is a largely South American suborder.

The helmet shrikes (Prionopidae) are sometimes included as a subfamily of the shrikes (Laniidae). The Laniidae here includes the Bornean bristle-head (*Pityriasis gymnocephala*), a bird of uncertain affinities.

The vanga shrikes (Vangidae) include the Coral-billed nuthatch (*Hypositta corallirostris*) of Madagascar, which is sometimes given a family of its own. The waxwings (Bombycillidae, including the subfamilies Ptilogonatinae and Hypocoliinae) contain three groups, sometimes (but not here) put into separate subfamilies or even families—the waxwings, silky flycatchers and the hypocolius.

The thrushes and allies (Muscicapidae) are an enormous family containing some 1,394 species in 11 subfamilies, many of which are treated as full families in some classifications. The babblers (subfamily Timaliinae) include here: the wren-tit (*Chamaea fasciata*), although this is the only New World representative of this subfamily and is sometimes put in its own subfamily or even family (Chamaeidae); and the two African rockfowl (*Picathartes*), which are sometimes put in their own subfamily, the Picathartinae. The parrotbills (subfamily Paradoxornithinae) are sometimes called the Panurinae; the parrotbills are sometimes included in the Timaliinae. Included in the Old World warblers (subfamily Sylviinae) are the gnat-wrens, a group of about 12 New World species sometimes put in their own subfamily, the Polioptilinae. The Australasian warblers (subfamily Acanthizinae) are sometimes included in the Malurinae. Within the monarch flycatchers (subfamily Monarchinae) are the African Puff-back flycatchers which are sometimes put in a subfamily of their own, the Platysteirinae.

The nuthatches (Sittidae) here include the Australian sitellas (*Neositta*) and the wallcreeper (*Tichodroma muraria*), both sometimes placed in families of their own. The Holarctic tree creepers (Certhiidae) include the Spotted creeper (*Salpornis spilonotus*), which is given a family status by some authorities. The pardalotes (Pardalotidae) are sometimes included in the flowerpeckers (Dicaeidae). The Australian chats (Ephthianuridae) are sometimes merged into the honeyeaters (Meliphagidae). Here the Australasian Meliphagidae includes the two South African sugarbirds (*Promerops*) which sometimes warrant family status.

The buntings and tanagers (Emberizidae) are a large family which here contain five subfamilies. According to recent research by some American workers the wood warblers (Parulidae) and American blackbirds (Icteridae), which are treated here as separate families, should be treated as subfamilies of the Emberizidae.

The magpie-larks (Grallinidae) include the White-winged chough (*Corcorax*) and the apostlebird (*Struthidea*), sometimes treated as separate families.   CMP

WHAT IS A BIRD?

In 1861, workmen splitting slate in a quarry in Bavaria came across a fossil which they passed on to the local museum. The fossilized creature had obviously been reptile-like, and it had a long tail. Quite large numbers of this sort of fossil were being found, but one thing saved this one from being left to collect dust on the museum shelf: clearly outlined around the fossil in the fine texture of the slate were the unmistakable imprints of feathers! As a result, this small creature instantly aroused the greatest interest and has since become one of the most famous and important fossils of all time. To this day it remains the earliest known fossil bird: *Archaeopteryx lithographica* (literally, "ancient wings in slate").

The slate in which *Archaeopteryx* was found dates from the Jurassic period some 150 million years ago. The species—of which several other specimens have subsequently been found—provides a remarkable "missing link" between the birds and the dinosaur stock from which they are believed to have descended.

Archaeopteryx was about the size of a large pigeon. Apart from its long tail like a lizard's (but feathered), its most obvious differences from modern birds are that it had toothed jaws, front limbs that were modified as wings but still retained claws, and a relatively small breastbone. The feathers—that most obvious characteristic of birds—seem to have been very similar to those of modern birds. The positioning of the tail feathers was odd, because the animal still possessed an "unbird-like" tail, but the number and arrangement of wing feathers were more or less identical to those in modern birds.

Archaeopteryx is thought to have evolved from one of the small dinosaurs of the order Saurischia. Indeed the line of descent is sufficiently clear for some people to claim that the dinosaurs did not become extinct since the birds are their living representatives!

Feathers probably first evolved to keep the animal warm—*Archaeopteryx*, like the early mammals of the same period, would have been warm blooded. Although warm-blooded animals need more food to survive they are at a great advantage over the cold-blooded reptiles in that they can be more active in cold conditions—at night, dawn or dusk, and in temperate climates. It is probable that several groups of dinosaurs developed the ability at least partly to maintain their body temperatures in cold conditions. Other reptiles, probably close to the likely line of evolution of *Archaeopteryx*, had greatly extended, overlapping scales, again probably to help keep the animal warm. Viewed in this light, feathers are best regarded as highly complex derivations of reptilian scales.

Probably as *Archaeopteryx*'s ancestors clambered about in the trees, using the claws on both pairs of limbs, and started to leap from branch to branch, the gradual extension of the scales at the rear of the forelimb and on the tail would have provided an expanded surface area helping the creature to extend its leaps into glides. Natural selection would have favored the evolution of progressively longer and lighter

▶ **Half reptile, half modern bird,**
Archaeopteryx, as seen in an artist's reconstruction. The 150 million year-old ancestor of today's birds was about the size of a large pigeon, clambered around in trees using the claws on all four limbs, and probably glided from tree to tree using its feather-covered wings and tail.

▼ **From reptile to bird.** Skeletons of (1) a thecodont reptile (genus *Euparkeria*) from lower levels of the Jurassic period (195–135 million years ago), (2) *Archaeopteryx*, and (3) a modern bird show the progression of evolutionary changes. Key features in birds are: enlarged eye sockets, reduction of jaws and loss of teeth, reduction and fusion of tail bones, modification of forelimbs as wings, enlargement of the breastbone for the attachment of wing muscles, and increased relative size of the hindlimbs to accommodate bipedal walking.

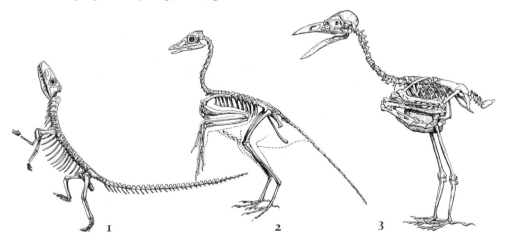

1 2 3

Birds of Prey
Falconiformes (5/80/286)

Game Birds
Galliformes (6/75/263)

Cranes, Rails, Bustards
Gruiformes (12/66/191)

Shorebirds, Gulls, Terns, Auks
Charadriiformes (17/84/317)

Sandgrouse
Pteroclidiformes (1/2/16)

Pigeons
Columbiformes (1/42/300)

Parrots, Lories, Cockatoos
Psittaciformes (1/77/328)

Cuckoos, Turacos
Cuculiformes (3/34/150)

Owls
Strigiformes (2/24/133)

Nightjars, Frogmouths
Caprimulgiformes (5/21/98)

Swifts, Hummingbirds
Apodiformes (3/122/389)

Trogons
Trogoniformes (1/7/37)

Mousebirds
Coliiformes (1/1/6)

Kingfishers, Bee-eaters, Hoopoes
Coraciiformes (9/46/193)

Woodpeckers, Toucans, Barbets
Piciformes (6/63/378)

Passerines
Passeriformes (63/1,085/5,206)

scales for this purpose. Although the wing feathers were long enough for *Archaeopteryx* to have been able to glide a reasonable distance, the lack of a well-developed breastbone suggests that the large muscles required for powered flight may have been missing. In addition, the long tail would have made it somewhat poor at maneuvering in flight compared with the more compact modern birds.

In this one species lies all that we know about the early evolution of birds. No older fossils of animals intermediate in structure between *Archaeopteryx* and its ancestors have yet been found. Most bird carcasses were probably taken as carrion, or disintegrated before they could become fossils, and because of their relatively small size and thin bones, birds fossilize poorly. It is no coincidence that *Archaeopteryx* and most

bird fossils from the later Cretaceous are those of water birds or others that fell into fine muds, for this gives the best chance of them being adequately preserved.

The next fossil birds appear after a gap of some 30 million years in the fossil record, early in the Cretaceous period. They are all obviously similar to modern birds, and include a diver-like bird, *Hesperornis*, whose wing structure shows that its ancestors had been flying birds, although it had already reverted to flightlessness! Hence within a 30-million-year period there must have been a considerable evolution of the birds, but we know next to nothing about it.

By the end of the Cretaceous period 65 million years ago a few birds were beginning to show the characteristics of modern families. However, it was some 65–38 million years ago during the first half of the Tertiary period that the great radiation of birds took place. From the Eocene (54–38 million years ago) we know fossils of at least 30 modern families, including some birds that probably belong to the Passeriformes— the perching birds—that huge order of small birds that dominates our avifauna today. By the end of the Eocene, the birds had truly "arrived."

Size and Energy

Compared with some other classes of animals, birds are a very uniform group, in both structure and size. The mammals, for instance, include horses, lemurs, whales, bats and tigers, to name but a few examples of the range of mammalian representatives. Furthermore, mammals range from tiny bats and shrews to the great whales, a weight ratio of some 1 to 100 million, whereas flying birds range only from some 2.5g (0.09oz) to 15kg (33lb), a ratio of 1 to a mere 6,000.

The reason for this more limited range of size and form in birds may be found in the requirements for flight. (Flightless birds, evolved from the same ancestors, are freed to some extent from these weight restrictions, only to confront other dangers and, often, extinction—see p10.) Flying is, in terms of energy required, an exceedingly expensive method of locomotion, and so it is of paramount importance to do it as economically as possible. Virtually every distinctive characteristic of a bird's anatomy has been evolved as an adaptation for flying.

The size of birds has been constrained for different reasons at the small and large ends of the spectrum. Birds need to be able to maintain a constant warm body temperature—between 41°C (106°F), and 43.5°C (110°F) depending on species—in order to function efficiently. However, with decreasing size, the volume (or weight) of a body is reduced in far greater proportion than its surface area. This is important because a body loses heat at a rate which can be related to the ratio of surface area to volume. As the surface-to-volume ratio increases (ie as objects become smaller) the rate of heat loss increases. So a small bird loses heat relatively faster than a large one. Since the heat which is lost has to be made good by obtaining more food, small birds must eat more, relative to their body size, than large ones. Below a certain size, the time and effort required for energy replacement are so "uneconomic" that survival is not possible.

It is no coincidence that the smallest birds—for example, the Vervain hummingbird (*Mellisuga minima*) of Jamaica which weighs in at about 2.4g (0.08oz)—live in warm parts of the world. Even in the tropics, many hummingbirds go torpid at night to save energy. They have to warm themselves up again at dawn before they can start their day's activities, which include taking up to half their body weight in food.

The upper limit to the size of flying birds also results from problems associated with size and scale. One bird, which has linear dimensions that are twice those of another, will have a surface area which is four times and a volume (and weight) eight times greater. Hence large birds have a heavier weight-to-wing-area ratio than smaller ones: wing loading increases with size. Compared with a small bird, a large one must have relatively bigger wings and/or flight muscles, which in their turn will add further weight.

There is also anatomical evidence that large birds may be more constrained by weight than smaller ones. In the smaller species, only the largest bones may be

hollow (pneumatized), but in larger species more of the bones may be hollow. For example, the Marabou stork not only has hollow leg bones; most of the toe bones are also hollow.

The actual act of taking off is the most energy-demanding moment of flight; the bird must accelerate rapidly to pass stalling speed. This is not a problem for small birds, which just leap into the air and fly away. A large vulture, however, especially one with a full crop, may have to run along the ground to gain sufficient speed to become airborne; a swan may have to do the same on water, and an albatross may have great difficulty taking off at all, unless it can face into a strong headwind.

The upper weight limit in modern flying birds seems to be of the order of 15kg (33lb). It is perhaps no coincidence that the largest birds of a number of different groups approach this weight. For example, the Great bustard may weigh 15kg (33lb), exceptionally even a little more, the largest swans may be about 15kg (33lb), the largest condors about 14kg (31lb), the largest pelicans about 15kg (33lb) and the Wandering albatross about 12kg (26.5lb). However, even for these species such weights are exceptional; most adult individuals are smaller.

This line of argument has one serious flaw: some fossil flying birds were considerably larger! Until quite recently the largest fossils known were mostly birds of the genus *Teratornis*, which are usually thought of as giant condors, although there is considerable doubt about how they really lived. One

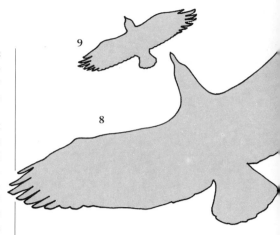

▼ ▶ ▲ **Prehistoric birds.** Seventy million years after *Archaeopteryx*, the diver-like *Hesperornis regaus* (1) still retained the teeth of its reptilian ancestors but had already reverted to flightlessness from a flying ancestor. *Ichthyornis victor* (2) was another bird of the oceans covering what is now the Great Plains of North America.

It was during the Tertiary period 65–2 million years ago that the numbers and variety of birds increased dramatically. The huge, flightless *Diatryma steini* (3) walked 2.2m (7.2ft) tall in Europe and North America in the Eocene (54–38 million years ago) and the late Eocene *Neocathartes* (4) was a forerunner of the New World vultures of today.

From the Miocene (26–7 million years ago) dates another giant flightless bird, *Phororharcos inflatus* (5) from South America, and also the small flamingo-like *Palaeolodus* (6) from Europe. A third species from the Americas was *Argentavis magnificens* (7), the largest-ever known flying bird, which had a wing span of 7m (23ft) or more. The sheer scale of this giant condor is demonstrated by comparing its silhouette (8) with that of the Bald eagle (*Haliaeetus leucocephalus*) of today (9).

of these, *Teratornis incredibilis*, had a wing span of the order of 5m (16ft) and probably weighed well in excess of 20kg (44lb). A less well-known species of marine bird, *Osteodontornis orri*, had a similar wing span. Both pale into insignificance against the remains of another species recently discovered in Argentina. *Argentavis magnificens*, which probably belonged to the same family as *Teratornis*, had a wing span of some 7–7.6m (23–25ft)!

It has been suggested that these giants specialized in riding the upcurrents off hot, open country as do the vultures in East Africa today, but this is speculation. For the biologist attempting to explain how they flew, the giant birds and the gigantic reptilian pterodactyls of an earlier age pose similar problems.

A Body Plan for Flying

The skeleton and musculature incorporate most of birds' major adaptations for flight (that is, apart from feathers). These adaptations achieve two main aims. First, because flight is so expensive in energy, weight has been reduced as far as possible; and second, the need for maneuverability in flight has required the bird to become a very compact unit with as much weight as possible placed close to the center of gravity.

To begin with, the skull has been greatly lightened. The eyes are large and their sockets take up a lot of space in the forepart of the skull, virtually meeting in the middle. A major feature is the reduction of the heavy jaws which other vertebrates possess and the complete loss of teeth. The shape and size of the bill varies enormously, enabling different types of bird to obtain and "handle" a very wide range of foods.

At the other end of the skeleton, the tail's bony elements have been greatly shortened and the bones are fused so that all the tail feathers start at more or less the same place. This has resulted in a structure which is valuable for helping the bird to steer and which is much more effective than the long "floppy" tail of *Archaeopteryx*. Size and form of the tail are varied, matching the flying needs of the bird concerned, even in a few species (woodpeckers, woodcreepers, treecreepers) being stiffened so as to act as a prop during climbing.

The main skeleton has been greatly reduced in weight in many places, by the evolution of bones which are hollow (pneumatized), including the major limb bones, parts of the skull and pelvis. The light ribs have rearward projections (uncinate processes) which overlap the next rib, and give extra rigidity. In some diving birds, such as the guillemots, these are very long, overlapping two ribs and providing extra support to prevent the body cavity being compressed during dives. Many bones have fused, making a rigid frame without the need for large muscles and ligaments to hold the separate bones together.

The forelimbs, and to a lesser extent the hindlimbs, incorporate some of the greatest changes. The forelimbs have become the wings, and associated areas of the body are adapted to provide the attachment areas for the massive flight muscles. The hand has lost two of its digits while the other three are much reduced. The main bulk of the wing muscles is at the base of the wing (close to the center of gravity). Although the downbeat results from the direct pull of the muscle, the upbeat (or recovery stroke) requires the "pulley" action of tendons over the shoulder joint. The joints of the wing are so shaped that there is very little movement possible except in the plane of opening out and closing the wing, so saving the need for muscles and ligaments to prevent "unwanted" movements.

At the base of the upper arm (humerus) there is a broad area for the attachment of the pectoral muscles. These enormous muscles are attached at their other end to the very large keel-like breastbone (sternum). When these muscles are contracted to beat the wings downward, they produce a force great enough to crush the bird's body between the sternum and the wing were these not kept apart on either side by a strong strut-like bone, the coracoid, supported by the wishbone (fused clavicles, or furcula) and shoulder blade (scapula), the ends of which join together and provide a point of articulation for the wing.

Birds are an unusual class of animal in that they use two methods of locomotion, flying (using the forelimbs) and walking and/or swimming (using the hindlimbs). Balance in flight is not a great problem, since the large flight muscles lie close to the center of gravity just below the wings. However, partly because of the presence of these muscles, it would be difficult for the legs also to be positioned close to the center of gravity; in fact the cup-shaped acetabula in the pelvic girdle, which receive the top ends of the upper legs (femurs), lie some way behind the center of gravity. Balance would therefore be difficult for a walking bird supported directly at this point.

Birds have overcome this problem in a unique way. The femur is inserted at the acetabulum in the normal vertebrate

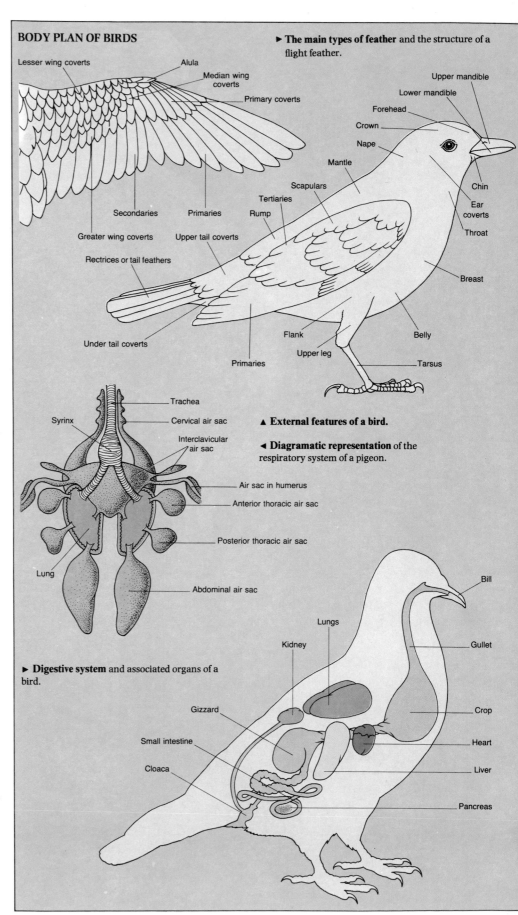

BODY PLAN OF BIRDS

▶ **The main types of feather** and the structure of a flight feather.

Lesser wing coverts
Alula
Median wing coverts
Primary coverts
Secondaries
Primaries
Greater wing coverts
Upper tail coverts
Tertiaries
Rump
Scapulars
Mantle
Rectrices or tail feathers
Under tail coverts
Primaries
Upper leg
Flank
Belly
Breast
Throat
Ear coverts
Chin
Nape
Crown
Forehead
Lower mandible
Upper mandible
Tarsus

▲ **External features of a bird.**

◀ **Diagramatic representation** of the respiratory system of a pigeon.

Syrinx
Trachea
Cervical air sac
Interclavicular air sac
Air sac in humerus
Anterior thoracic air sac
Posterior thoracic air sac
Lung
Abdominal air sac

▶ **Digestive system** and associated organs of a bird.

Lungs
Kidney
Bill
Gullet
Crop
Heart
Liver
Pancreas
Gizzard
Small intestine
Cloaca

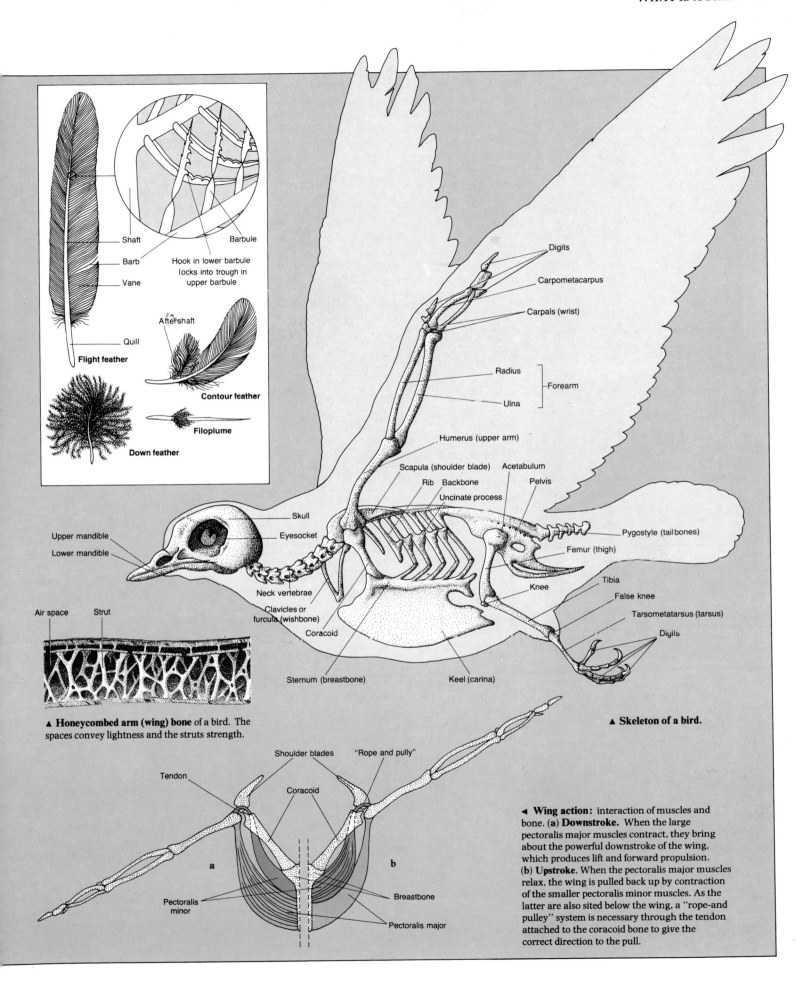

Shaft

Barbule

Barb

Hook in lower barbule
locks into trough in
upper barbule

Vane

Aftershaft

Quill

Flight feather

Contour feather

Filoplume

Down feather

Digits

Carpometacarpus

Carpals (wrist)

Radius ⎤
      ⎬ Forearm
Ulna ⎦

Humerus (upper arm)

Scapula (shoulder blade)   Acetabulum

Rib   Backbone   Pelvis

Uncinate process

Skull

Eyesocket

Upper mandible

Lower mandible

Pygostyle (tail bones)

Femur (thigh)

Neck vertebrae

Tibia

Clavicles or
furcula (wishbone)

False knee

Knee

Coracoid

Tarsometatarsus (tarsus)

Digits

Air space   Strut

Sternum (breastbone)   Keel (carina)

▲ **Honeycombed arm (wing) bone** of a bird. The
spaces convey lightness and the struts strength.

▲ **Skeleton of a bird.**

Shoulder blades   "Rope and pully"

Tendon

Coracoid

a   b

Pectoralis
minor

Breastbone

Pectoralis major

◀ **Wing action:** interaction of muscles and
bone. (**a**) **Downstroke.** When the large
pectoralis major muscles contract, they bring
about the powerful downstroke of the wing,
which produces lift and forward propulsion.
(**b**) **Upstroke.** When the pectoralis major muscles
relax, the wing is pulled back up by contraction
of the smaller pectoralis minor muscles. As the
latter are also sited below the wing, a "rope-and-
pulley" system is necessary through the tendon
attached to the coracoid bone to give the
correct direction to the pull.

▲ **A coat for each season.** The ptarmigan's white winter (ABOVE) and brown summer (BELOW) plumages, as well as providing insulation and lift for flying, help the bird merge into the background and escape the attention of predators.

In spring male ptarmigans molt later than females. The male, still wearing his now conspicuous winter plumage, distracts the attention of potential predators away from the well-camouflaged female, engaged in incubating the eggs on the nest.

manner, but projects forward along the side of the bird's body and has rather little movement, being bound to the body by muscles. In a sense the lower end of this bone (the knee) acts as a new "hip" joint to which the lower leg is attached and which is quite well-positioned with respect to the center of gravity. The two sections of leg which are clearly visible are not comparable with ours: the upper section is the equivalent of our lower leg whereas the lower section or false shin (technically called the tarsometatarsus, or tarsus for short) is formed from parts of the lower leg and sections of the foot bones and has no human equivalent. This explains why the leg appears to bend in the opposite way to the human one—the visible joint is not the knee, but more closely equivalent to our ankle. As with the wing, the leg joints are so shaped that movement in unwanted directions is restricted. Leg movements are controlled—via tendons—by muscles placed near the top of the leg and so close to the center of gravity.

Feathers

Feathers are by far the most characteristic feature of birds, and a major factor in their habits, life-styles and distribution. Keratin, the main constituent of feathers, is a proteinaceous substance which is widespread in vertebrates—the hair and fingernails of mammals are made of it, as are the scales of reptiles. The ancestors of *Archaeopteryx* evolved the basic feather for insulation, and this purpose is well served by the evolution in modern birds of feathers that are light and waterproof, and trap quantities of air so as to slow down heat loss. The principal body feathers consist of a central quill (or rachis) from which the main side projections—the barbs—spread out on either side. These are locked together by barbules (see previous page).

However, feathers have also evolved to serve a number of other functions important to birds. The feathers along the trailing edge of the wing and on the tail have become greatly enlarged, strengthened and specially shaped so that they form the surfaces which provide the lift for flight and for maneuvering. The rest of the visible feathers (contour feathers) which cover the surface of the body add to the efficiency of flying by streamlining the body.

Down feathers, found on young birds and also as an insulating underlayer on many full-grown birds, lack the interlocking barbules and are not organized in one plane, and so look more like shaving brushes. Most

simple of all are the single shafts of the bristles often found around the eyes or at the base of the bill. In many cases these are thought to have a sensory function.

The wide range of colors in feathers also performs a number of valuable functions. On the one hand feathers may camouflage a bird—such as a nightjar—so well that it is difficult for a predator to find it. At the other extreme, in the peacock, hummingbirds, quetzal and other species, feathers provide some of the most dazzling colors found in nature.

Feather colors are produced in one of two ways—or a combination of both. Commonest of the pigments in feathers is melanin, which is responsible for the browns and black. Some pigments are very rare, such as the green turacoverdin found only in some turacos. The other type of color is caused by the physical structure of the feather reflecting only a part of the visible wavelengths of (white) light. Such colors include the metallic blue-green of the starling, and most iridescent colors. Feathers reflecting all light wavelengths look white!

Feathers are not just distributed at random but grow in clearly defined tracts. Each feather grows from a papilla—a special ring of cells. As these cells multiply they produce a series of cells which form into a tube. On one side of this tube is a thickened section, the rachis, and on the opposite side a line of weakness. As the feather grows, it breaks along the line of weakness and spreads out. The individual barbs of the feather also "break apart" at lines of weakness.

Feathers are replaced at intervals. They may be molted because they have become worn and need replacing. Some birds put on a thicker covering of feathers for the winter. Feathers are also changed in order to produce a different colored plumage. Many birds put on bright plumage for the breeding season and change to a duller one for winter. It is thought that the birds need the brighter colors in order to display to one other during courtship; duller, often disruptive, camouflage plumage provides better defense from predators and so birds revert to this at other times of the year.

The ptarmigan's white winter and brown summer plumages help the bird to merge into the background and be more difficult for predators to see. The drakes of many species of duck remain in bright plumage almost the whole year round, but acquire a camouflaged brown plumage for about a month during the summer while they are in full molt and more vulnerable.

▲ **Migrating Snow geese** on their way south from summer breeding grounds in the north of Canada. They winter along the Pacific and Mexican Gulf coasts of the southern USA.

Current migration routes probably date from the end of the ice ages, when birds came to exploit the abundant fast-growing food sources in higher latitudes made accessible by the receding ice. About half the bird species of the world (over 4,000 species) spend their summers and winters in different locations.

Like other migratory birds, the Snow goose is stimulated twice yearly to undertake its journey by changes in daylength. These trigger hormonal changes which result in increased restlessness culminating in departure for the first stage of its 5,000km (3,100m) flight.

For fuel migrating small birds use up fat reserves, up to half the total body weight, that are laid down through feeding on the summer or wintering grounds or on feeding grounds on route.

The mature feather is a dead structure. Its replacement requires energy, and while building the new feathers a bird is less well insulated and may be able to fly less well. Some species, such as ducks and most auks, lose the power of flight altogether during the molt. On the other hand, molting allows damaged flight feathers to be replaced (an advantage over, say, a bat, which cannot mend a badly damaged wing).

Other Adaptations for Flight

In order to be able to fly, birds have to be able to mobilize a large amount of energy very quickly. This requires a very efficient **respiratory system** to supply the necessary large amounts of oxygen. At first sight the lungs of birds do not seem likely to perform this function: they are actually smaller than those of a mammal of similar size. However,

the air capillaries (alveoli) of the avian lung are very small compared with those of mammals, and thus there is a greater surface area for gaseous exchange in a bird than in a mammal.

The bird lung is very efficient, though not more so than that of mammals—at sea level. Its particular advantage is its efficiency at altitude. If mice and sparrows are placed in a chamber containing air at the reduced pressure found at the top of Mount Everest, the mice are soon almost totally exhausted and can barely move around, while the sparrows hop about quite happily—their breathing is not noticeably impaired.

In fact, many birds migrate in a fairly rarefied atmosphere; cranes, ducks and geese such as the Bar-headed goose, often cross high above the Himalayas on their journeys between northern Russia and their winter quarters in India. Although not many have to fly as high as the summit of Everest (8,848m/29,028ft) there have been reports of large birds of prey seen from aeroplanes at this height or even higher.

The respiratory system of birds differs from that of mammals in several important ways. To begin with, birds possess a large number of air sacs throughout the body spaces, some even penetrating into the hollow bones. No gaseous exchange takes place through the thin membranous walls of the air sacs themselves, though they may be important in preventing a bird from overheating.

The importance of air sacs to breathing lies in the fact that the inspired air passes first through the posterior air sacs, then into the lungs proper and finally out of the bird via the anterior air sacs. Air flows in one direction through the lungs instead of the "ebb-and-flow" system found in mammals.

Hence the whole volume of air in the lung can be replaced with each breath, while humans, for example, only change perhaps three-quarters of the volume with each breath, even when breathing deeply.

The blood vessels of the avian lung are very efficient in their uptake of oxygen and disposal of carbon dioxide. Since the airflow is always in one direction, the blood vessels can be arranged so that blood continuously flows in the opposite direction to the flow of air. Blood which is just reaching the lungs, and which is low in oxygen, meets air that has flowed some way through the lungs and has also had its concentration of oxygen lowered; however, there is still enough oxygen there for the blood, with its low concentrations, to be able to take it up. As the blood flows along against the lung wall, it takes up progressively more oxygen, and meets air that contains progressively more oxygen. This system helps to maximize

Flightless Birds

The birds which diverge most markedly from the "typical bird" structure are flightless; in these the restrictions on form required for flight have been relaxed. The most obvious characteristic of flightless birds may be the loss, or great reduction, of wings, but in some species there may also be a considerable increase in size. The ostrich averages some 115kg (253lb) and may attain 150kg (330lb). Males (RIGHT) share care of nest and young of several females (see p19).

All flightless birds are thought to be descendants of flying ancestors. This is fairly obvious in some species, such as flightless rails and coots, which are clearly close relatives of other modern birds that fly. Close examination of other species shows that they have many adaptations for flight, including cavity-filled (pneumatized) bones; in addition, the wing, although sometimes much reduced, is clearly of the form used by flying birds.

A flightless bird is freed from the need to build and carry the very large flight muscles and associated wing structure, and from the energy expenditure of flying. Hence (other things being equal) flying birds would tend to lose out in competition with flightless ones, since the former would need much more food.

The disadvantage of being unable to fly is that the bird is more vulnerable to predators. Flightlessness seems to have evolved where birds were fairly safe from predators, as is often the case on remote islands (eg some rails, the kagu and the kakapo). Such species remain very vulnerable to extinction should the situation change, as may happen when man and his domestic animals arrive—the dodo being just one example.

Another group of birds that have tended to lose the power of flight are water birds, including the penguins, the extinct Great auk

and a number of fossil families. Very large flightless birds form a third group—the ostrich, cassowaries, emus and rheas. Most of these are large enough to defend themselves quite well by either strength or great running speed. Although these birds are large, the giants of the bird world were such as the Elephant bird (*Aepyornis titan*) of Madagascar, which may have weighed as much as 450kg (1,000lb) and several species of moas (family Dinornithidae) in New Zealand. The latter were probably exterminated by the Maoris and the former (perhaps the inspiration for the legendary roc) was probably also exterminated by men only a few centuries ago.

▲ **Birds' most developed senses,** sight and hearing, fit their aerial life-style. The nocturnal owls have good night vision (the Little owl, seen here, is also often seen by day). They are unusual in having forward-facing eyes that provide binocular vision. Even so, hearing remains, for owls, an important means of locating prey.

▶ **Bills for diets.** (1) Upturned bill of avocet for sieving food off water surface with "scything" movements of lowered neck. (2) Skimmer, with longer lower mandible used for scooping up fish from just under water surface. (3) Toucan's large bill brings berries within range of its perch, and may serve in defense and as a social signal. (4) Hummingbird, for nectar feeding at flowers. (5) Bird of prey, for tearing flesh. (6) Pelican, with pouch for holding "catch" of fish. (7) Flamingo, fringed, used upside-down for filter feeding. (8) Finch, for cracking seeds. (9) Mallard duck, fringed for filter feeding on pondweed etc. (10) Heron, for stabbing or seizing fish prey. (11) Spoonbill, used in quest of prey under water surface. (12) Parrot, for shelling nuts, "handling" fruit.

oxygen uptake in a way that is impossible in a mammalian "ebb-and-flow" lung. The same thing happens, in reverse, for the disposal of carbon dioxide.

The **digestive tract** of birds, too, is adapted for flight. The large, weighty jaws, jaw muscles and teeth of reptilian ancestry have been lost (though some birds still have remarkably powerful jaws). Their function of grinding up food is largely taken over by the muscular portion of their stomach, the gizzard. To get food to the gizzard, some birds may use their bill to tear it into small pieces which are then ingested through the wide gape and swallowed.

Once in the gizzard, food is ground down—often with the help of grit which the birds take in for the purpose, though this is only necessary in certain species, for example grain eaters such as sparrows. Fish- and meat-eating birds such as kingfishers and eagles, and insectivores such as swallows and flycatchers do not need grit; their food is comparatively soft, so they manage with their strong digestive juices.

Although many birds eat seeds and fruit, few specialize on leaves, as do grouse, or grass (eg geese and some ducks), at least compared with mammals. Such foods are rather difficult to break down. (In the case of many mammals, for instance the cow, this involves the action of symbiotic bacteria in a very large, very heavy stomach.) Since the gut of birds does not contain these bacteria those that are herbivores have to consume large quantities of material in order to extract their nutritional requirements.

Above the gizzard, many birds—particularly seed eaters—also have a rather thin, extensible side-wall to the oesophagus, the crop. Into it the bird can cram a large quantity of food in a very short time, so that it can retire to a place of safety to digest it. Many seed-eating birds, including finches and pigeons, also take quantities of food to roost in this way, effectively reducing the length of the night's fast. Many species use the crop to carry food to their nestlings.

Birds reduce the amount of water carried in the waste products that are to be excreted, again a weight-saving adaptation. Some birds obtain most of their water from their food. The water is withdrawn from the contents of the hind gut. Urinary products are highly concentrated and are formed primarily of uric acid. The latter becomes mixed with the feces in the cloaca before excretion (birds have no urinary bladder). Some carnivorous species (eg owls) do not digest parts of their prey, which are regurgitated in the form of pellets.

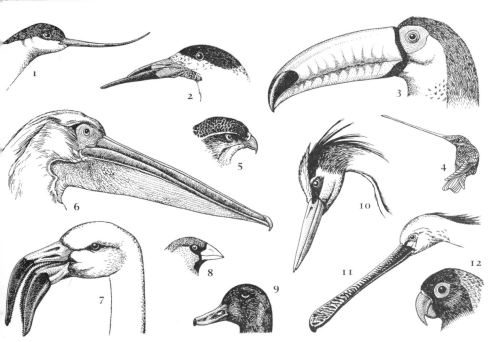

The **reproductive system** of birds also keeps weight to a minimum. For most of the year, sex organs and associated ducts are greatly reduced in size, most markedly in females. As the breeding season approaches, they rapidly develop as gametes are produced. All birds lay eggs, and even those—the great majority—that have a clutch of several eggs only lay one per day; some lay only every other day or less frequently. By laying in this way most bird species are able to produce several relatively large eggs one after the other.

While clutch size ranges from one up to an average 19 eggs in Gray partridges in Finland, the laying bird only carries one fully developed egg in the oviduct at a time (though one or more smaller, developing eggs may be present in the ovary). If the females were to carry all the eggs at the same stage of development (as does a mammal her young) then the size of the individual egg would have to be much smaller or the bird would have to have fewer young.

Egg size as a proportion of adult weight varies from about 1.3 percent in the ostrich to 25 percent in the kiwi and some storm petrels. One advantage of having relatively large eggs is that it shortens the development time in the nest and enables the young bird to be able to fly at an early age (12–14 days in many small species); this, of course, tends to reduce the period of threat from predators when the young are helpless in the nest. (Large species such as swans and eagles may take 4–5 months to reach the flying stage.) Most birds lay their eggs in the early morning. Hence the female does not carry a fully-developed egg during the morning when she needs to be most active while feeding.

The Senses

Most animals rely particularly on just one or two of their senses. Most mammals, in particular night-active ones, rely chiefly on their powers of smell and hearing. Even when sight is important, most mammals seem to rely less on color vision. In birds, however, the power of vision is almost always the most important sense, with hearing second and smell a very poor third; indeed in many birds smell may be hardly used at all. In this respect humans are an exception among mammals; our senses rank in importance in the same sequence as those of birds, and furthermore we, like the birds, have good color vision.

This parallel may explain why birds are so "popular" with people. We rely mainly

on the same senses, and also a pattern of day-time activity, and so can enjoy and appreciate their colors and songs, and to some extent can "share" their lives. By contrast we have a poor idea of what information even such a well-known mammal as the domestic dog or cat obtains from smelling objects; we have little chance of sharing their world in this respect. If we go out into a piece of woodland, we may see lots of birds and almost no mammals, yet there may be more mammals than birds present; they are just less easy for us to perceive, for many are nocturnal, or live underground, or do both.

A bird's is a high-speed aerial life. Sight and hearing are obviously more useful than smell in such conditions. The importance to birds of their eyes is reflected in their size; they fill very large portions of the skull; indeed the eyes of an eagle approach those

◄ ▼ Downy or naked young. Some newly hatched chicks are well developed, covered with downy feathers and have their eyes open. Species that produce such precocious chicks include, for example, the domestic hen and duck, and (LEFT) the Lesser black-backed gull. These species are called nidifugous (literally "nest-fleeting"): they leave the nest within about 24 hours of hatching and usually feed themselves, though most are still guarded and brooded by their parents. In the case of gulls, the young may stay in the nest for a week or two.

At the other extreme are young which hatch blind and naked and are quite unable to move around or gather food for themselves, such as these Bearded tits (BELOW). Most of these nidicolous young (literally, "nest-living") remain in the nest until they are almost fully grown.

To escape predators, well-developed nidifugous young do not have to be able to fly – they can run (or swim) as soon as they are dry. They can also all join in the ever-urgent hunt for food. The chicks need a lot of energy to keep themselves warm and for running about. This means that much food has to be used for "fuel" and so less is available for growth than if the chicks were huddled together in a nest: they have to grow more slowly.

The less developed nidicolous young hatch with relatively large mouths and digestive systems – they are really little more than food conversion units! Needing less energy to keep warm and fuel activity, they grow extremely rapidly, and by 12–14 days many species are able to fly freely. However, until then the nestlings are more dependent on parental care, and totally vulnerable to predators.

of a human in size, although the eagle is much smaller than a human.

The eyes of birds are relatively immobile: the large eye leaves little room in the skull for muscles. However, birds have very mobile necks which enable them to turn their heads easily (eg owls), and their actual field of vision is very wide—some birds may be able to see the whole 360 degrees. A bird such as the woodcock, which has eyes placed very high on the sides of its head, may be able to see both all round and over the top of its head! (To some extent, most birds pay a penalty in that the fields of vision of the two eyes only overlap a small amount, so they have only a small amount of binocular vision. Birds with forward-facing eyes, such as the owls, have good binocular vision.) Birds also have a large part of this field sharply in focus at one moment, perhaps about 20 degrees compared with the 2–3 degrees across which people can focus sharply.

Most birds have good color vision, including those species of owls where it has been tested, though they may see slightly less well at the blue end of the spectrum than we do. The visual acuity of birds of prey and certain other species is perhaps two to three times greater than that of humans, but not more. Some birds, such as the nocturnal owls, have exceptionally good night vision. However, even owls probably depend largely on hearing to locate and catch their prey at night.

Hearing is employed in communication between individual birds, and is particularly valuable in wooded areas where it is difficult to keep in visual contact—hence the striking songs and far-carrying calls of many forest birds, such as the Musician wren and the bellbirds. As with vision, birds and people perceive sounds over a range that is roughly similar, though possibly birds are less good at hearing sounds at the lower frequencies. However, the hearing of birds differs from ours in one important respect. They can distinguish sounds which are very much closer in time than we can. For example, what to us may sound as a single note may by a bird be heard as up to 10 separate notes. A snatch of "simple" bird song may in fact convey to a bird a lot more information than appears possible to our ear.

Many birds seem to lack almost entirely the power of smell, though this is not true of certain groups, such as the nocturnal kiwis, which probe for food on the forest floor and have their nostrils close to the tip of the bill. Smell is also known to be used by the vultures of the New World (though not those of the Old World) as they search for carrion on the forest floor. In some other groups, for example some of the petrels, the olfactory lobes of the brain are well developed, indicating that they too are able to use the power of smell. Taste is by no means strongly developed in all species; the sense of "taste" actually involves olfactory information in birds as in man, and, as we have seen, birds have poor powers of smell.

The tongue of many birds is very horny and would not easily accommodate taste-receptive cells. What taste buds do occur are found toward the back of the mouth, and so birds probably only taste a food item when it is well into the mouth. None the less, birds are capable of distinguishing the four tastes: salt, sweet, bitter and sour.

The sense of touch is well developed in the tongues of many birds and also in the bill tips of many species, especially those such as snipes, godwits and curlews which probe deep in mud for their prey, and birds such as avocets, spoonbills and ibises which "scythe" through water and soft mud with their bill open.

Patterns of Breeding

The two main senses of birds—vision and hearing—are used strikingly in courtship and breeding. Many birds establish breeding territories by use of song, which functions both to repel would-be intruding males and to attract potential mates. Although not all birds have songs, some of those that do produce sounds that to the human ear are the most beautiful sounds in the natural world. The nightingale and European skylark are among the most famous, but others such as the South American Musician wren are also master singers. The songs of some of the non-passerine species, such as the kookaburra, are also remarkable. A few, such as the lyrebirds and the Marsh warbler, show great versatility by being able to mimic the calls and songs of many other species; the cagebirds best at "talking" are mynahs and parrots.

The display of the peacock is legendary, though in some ways the Argus pheasant can put on an even more dazzling performance. The birds of paradise are also among the most impressive. All these species are polygamous, the males attracting females to their display grounds (leks), where mating occurs; the females then go off and lay the eggs, incubate them and rear the young by themselves.

Most birds, however, are monogamous, breeding in pairs—almost all seabirds and birds of prey, for example. It is not understood why, but a very high proportion of the birds that are polygamous are vegetarians—fruit- or leaf-eaters.

It has long been thought that the single pair feeding its young at the nest is the norm for birds. Studies in recent years, however, have shown that in many species it is not at all unusual for there to be several birds attending a single nest. The reason why this habit was overlooked originally is doubtless that most studies were conducted in temperate areas—Europe and North America. Such cooperative breeding is much commoner in birds which live in warmer climates; in particular it is very common among Australian species. The cooperative groups often include young from previous breeding seasons; in many species these are mainly males. It appears that in these species the young females move from their natal territory and are accepted into other territories, young males staying "at home."

In temperate areas, birds are faced with wildly fluctuating food supplies—often great abundances in summer and great shortages in winter. Numbers are cut by starvation in winter, so most of those that survive can find a place to breed in spring. By contrast, bird populations in places which are less seasonal tend to be closer, year-round, to the limit of numbers that the habitat can support. With fewer vacant territories becoming available, it seems to pay a young bird to remain longer within its parents' territory—though perhaps it is always on the lookout for a vacant territory nearby. Indeed it may inherit the territory when its parents die.

Another factor apparently affected by seasonal variation is clutch size. Birds tend to have larger clutches at high than at low latitudes. Again this is thought to be a reflection of the greater abundance of food available in summer in temperate areas.

Bird eggs take a considerable time to develop—between about 12 and 60 days from laying to hatching. During this period, both incubating parent and eggs are very vulnerable to predation. Some birds protect the eggs and young by breeding in colonies. Others hide the nest, in foliage, or in a hole. Species that do not build a nest often lay eggs with camouflage markings.

The simplest nest is a "scrape" made in the ground—no added materials are used. Species which lay their eggs in scrapes include divers, and many game birds and waders. King and Emperor penguins do not even keep their eggs on the ground, but carry them about on the tops of their feet. Some birds, among them most petrels and

Swimming

Of the many different birds that get their food from water almost all depend on swimming to reach it. Swimming birds include penguins, albatrosses and shearwaters, divers, grebes, pelicans and cormorants, ducks, many members of the rail family, gulls, terns, auks and the phalaropes. No passerine has become fully aquatic, though the dippers and the Seaside cinclodes get all their food from the water.

Most of these groups have webbed feet (1) with which they swim. Some, such as the

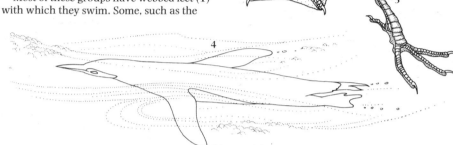

grebes (2), coots, finfoots and phalaropes, have lobed toes rather than webs, and other rails, such as the moorhen, just have a broadened base to their long toes (3) which provides a swimming surface. A few aquatic birds, such as the penguins (4) and the auks, get their main underwater propulsion from their wings, which in penguins (as in the extinct Great auk) have lost the power of flight. One or two flying species, such as the scoters, get some propulsion underwater by use of the folded wing—it is too large to be used fully extended.

For a diving bird, one of the main difficulties is to get below the water. Birds are generally much lighter than water. Most diving birds, by contrast, have relatively high densities and are able to squeeze much of the air (normally important for insulation) out of their feathers as they dive, so helping to reduce their buoyancy. Cormorants have specially wettable feathers which make it easier to lose air—this is why they have to stand with their wings spread to dry off after a fishing session. Grebes are said to increase their specific gravity by swallowing stones.

auks, lay their eggs on the bare rock or the soil of a burrow. Many others, such as hornbills, some pigeons, many birds of prey, and owls, lay their eggs in holes in trees or cliffs without building a nest, though some (eg the woodpeckers, bee-eaters and sand martins) excavate holes in trees or banks.

Other birds build highly complex nests, the most outstanding of which are the intricately woven nests of some weavers and New World blackbirds. They may have entrance tubes 1.5m (5ft) long. Other nest-building skills include those of the tailor birds, which "sew" leaves together, and some swifts and swallows, which build saliva-and-mud nests attached to rock faces.

The degree of development of the hatchling chick varies enormously. Some birds (generally ground nesters) hatch chicks that can fend for themselves straight away. Other newly hatched chicks, blind and helpless, may yet grow to full size within a fortnight. Still others may leave the nest, but remain with their parents for months.

▶ **Hundreds of "eyes"** suddenly flash into sight at the climax of the courtship dance of the male Great crested argus pheasant.

At dawn, in the Malaysian forest that is its home, the adult male gives loud, wailing calls to draw a potential mate to his specially prepared dance floor on top of a hill.

If a female hears the calls and is attracted, the male dances about before her, then, suddenly, throws up his wings into two enormous fan-shapes, revealing the previously hidden 3-D "eyes" on the broad secondary wing feathers.

The successful courtship display will end in mating, after which the female departs, to raise the brood on her own.

CMP

OSTRICHES AND THEIR RELATIVES – THE RATITES

Orders: Struthioniformes, Rheiformes, Casuariiformes, Apterygiformes
Families: Struthionidae, Rheiidae, Dromaiidae, Casuariidae, Apterygidae.
Ten species in 6 genera.
Distribution: see maps and table.

Emu   Rheas   Kiwis

Ostrich   Cassowaries

SEVERAL groups of flightless birds are often grouped together as the ratites. Their most striking common characteristic is the lack of a large keel on the sternum (hence ratites from the latin *rata*, a raft, as opposed to the birds with a keeled sternum, the carinates from *carina*, a keel). However, with the evolution of flightlessness, the need for the large flight muscles and their attachment areas becomes unnecessary. Hence this loss of the keel would be what one would expect with the development of flightlessness and it is not clear whether all these groups are really closely related or not; further fossil finds may help to elucidate this problem.

The **ostrich** is famous for being the largest living bird and for being flightless. Despite the allegation of legend and unflattering popular sayings, no ostrich has yet been observed to bury its head in the sand.

Ostriches are widely distributed on the flatter open low-rainfall areas of Africa, in four clearly recognizable subspecies. The North African ostrich with pink neck inhabits the southern Sahara; the blue-necked Somali ostrich occupies the Horn of Africa; adjacent is the pink-necked Masai ostrich which lives in East Africa; and south of the Zambesi is the blue-necked South African ostrich.

The ostrich is enormous. Its feathers are soft and without barbs. The jet-black plumage of the male makes him highly conspicuous at long distances by day, and his long white outer "flight" feathers (primaries) contrast strikingly. The brownish color of females and juveniles renders them well camouflaged (newly hatched chicks are fawn with dark brown spots and a concealing hedgehog-like cape of bristly down on the back). The neck is long and highly mobile, the head small, the gape of the unspecialized beak wide, the eyes enormous.

Vision is acute. The thighs are bare, the legs are long and powerful, and there are only two toes on each foot. The bird can kick forwards powerfully and can run at about 50km/h (31mph). Ostriches are tireless walkers.

Thanks to their large stride, long neck and precise peck ostriches are highly efficient selective gatherers of the sparsely dispersed high-quality food items in their habitat. They take a very wide variety of nutritious shoots, leaves, flowers and seeds. The takings of many pecks are amassed in the gullet and then pass slowly down the neck as a large ball (bolus) which stretches the neck skin as it descends. Ostriches feeding with their beaks down among vegetation are vulnerable to predators (lions, and occasionally leopards and cheetahs); they periodically raise their heads to scan the landscape for danger.

Breeding seasons vary with locality, but in East Africa ostriches mainly nest in the dry season. A male makes a number of shallow scrapes in his territory. A female (the "major" hen), with whom he has a loose pair bond, selects one of these scrapes. She lays, on alternate days, up to a dozen eggs. Up to six or more other females ("minor" hens) also lay in the nest, but play no other role there. The major hen and the cock share equally, for increasing periods, in first guarding and later incubating the clutch—the female by day, the male by night. Unguarded nests are conspicuous from

► **Representatives of the five families of ratites.** (1) A male South Island brown kiwi (*Apteryx australis australis*) settling on an egg. (2) A One-wattled cassowary (*Casuarius unappendiculatus*) resting. (3) A One-wattled cassowary feeding on fallen fruits, showing a different color variant to (2). (4) A male Masai ostrich (*Struthio camelus massaicus*) chasing two displaying females. (5) Head of a Gray rhea (*Rhea americana*). (6) A male Darwin's rhea (*Pterocnemia pennata*) in an aggressive posture. (7) A male emu (*Dromaius novaehollandiae*) guarding eggs and a chick.

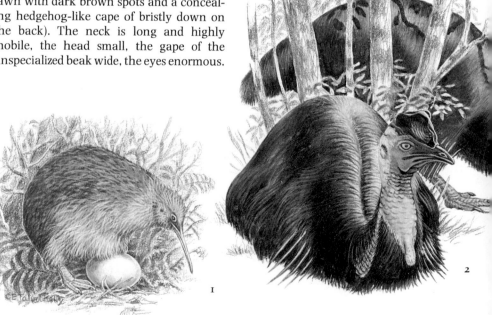

above, and vulnerable to predation by Egyptian vultures which throw stones at the huge eggs to break through their shells (2mm thick). Even guarded nests are at risk from hyenas and possibly jackals. Fewer than 10 percent of the nests started survive the roughly three-week laying period and six-week incubation period.

Ostrich chicks are well developed (precocial). They are accompanied by both male and female who try to protect them from the many threatening raptors and ground predators. Chicks from several different nests usually combine into single large groups, escorted by one or two adults. Only about 15 percent of chicks hatched survive to be one year old, when they will be full height. Females can breed at two. Males start to acquire adult plumage when two, and can breed at three or four. They can probably live to over 40.

Males defend their territories in the breeding season by patrolling and by displaying to and chasing out intruders, and by booming. Their call is surprisingly loud and deep, and is accompanied by inflation of the brightly colored neck skin. Aggressive displays consist of repeated flicking of wings and postures with both wings raised. Breeding males display dramatically yet absurdly to females by squatting and waving their huge spread wings alternately. Females solicit by lowering the head and both wings and quivering the latter. Groups of birds are usually small and not cohesive. Adult ostriches spend much of their time alone.

In few other bird species do some individuals willingly look after the eggs of other individuals, since natural selection usually disfavors such apparently altruistic behavior. The large size of ostriches and the vulnerability of their nests to predation are

The 4 Orders and 5 Families of Ratites

Ostrich

Order: Struthioniformes
Family: Struthionidae
Sole species *Struthio camelus.*
Africa (found also until recently in Arabia). Semidesert and savanna. Size: about 250cm (98in) high, weight about 115kg (253lb); males slightly larger than females. Plumage: males black with white primary feathers on wings and white tail; female earthy brown; neck and thighs bare with skin in males blue or pink, according to subspecies, in females pale pinkish gray. Voice: loud hiss and booming roar. Eggs: 10–40, shiny creamy white; 1,100–1900g (39–67oz); incubation 42 days. Diet: grasses, seeds, leaves, flowers.

Subspeices: **Masai ostrich** (*Struthio camelus massaicus*), **North African ostrich** (*S. c. camelus*), **Somali ostrich** (*S. c. molybdophanes*), **South African ostrich** (*S. c. australis*). The **Arabian ostrich** (*S. c. syriacus*) became extinct early in the 20th century.

Rheas

Order: Rheiformes
Family: Rheidae
Two species in 2 genera.
Darwin's or **Lesser rhea** (*Pterocnemia pennata*): S America in Patagonia and Andes. Scrublands. Size: height 90cm (35in); weight 10kg (22lb); females slightly shorter. Plumage: brown with white flecking throughout. Voice: female voiceless; male has booming call. Incubation: 35–40 days. Longevity: less than 20 years in wild; up to 40 in captivity.

Gray or **Common rhea** (*Rhea americana*): S America from R Amazon S to N Patagonia. Grasslands (both wet and dry). Size: height 1.45m (4.8ft), weight 25kg (55lb); females slightly shorter. Plumage: gray with white under wings and on rump; in breeding season males have a black bib and collar at the base of the neck. Voice: female voiceless; male has booming call. Incubation: 35–40 days. Longevity: less than 20 years in wild; up to 40 in captivity.

Emu

Order: Casuariiformes
Family: Dromaiidae
Sole species *Dromaius novaehollandiae*
Australia, in all areas except rain forest and cleared land; rare in deserts and extreme north. Size: height 1.75m (5.7ft), weight 50kg (110lb); females weigh about 5kg (11lb) more than males. Plumage: dark after molting fading to brown. Voice: grunts and hisses; females make resonant, booming sounds. Incubation: 56 days. Longevity: 5–10 years; longer periods known in captivity.

Cassowaries

Order: Casuariiformes
Family: Casuariidae
Three species of the genus *Casuarius.*
Australia, New Guinea and adjacent islands. Forest (rain forest, swamp forest, montane forest). Plumage: brown in chicks and young birds; black in adults. Voice: croaks, squeaks, howls, grunts and snorts. Incubation: 50 days. Longevity: at least 10 years in captivity. Species: **Bennett's cassowary** or **moruk** (*Casuarius bennetti*), New Guinea, New Britain, Yapen Island, height 1.1m (3.8ft); **One-wattled cassowary** (*C. unappendiculatus*), New Guinea and Yapen Island, height 1.6m (5.3ft); **Southern cassowary** (*C. casuarius*), Australia (Cape York Peninsula), New Guinea, Ceram, Aru Island, height 1.8m (5.8ft).

Kiwis

Order: Apterygiformes
Family: Apterygidae
Three species of the genus *Apteryx.*
New Zealand. Forest and scrub. Eggs: one or two, white, 300–450g (10.5–15.9oz). Incubation: 65–85 days. Diet: invertebrates, including worms, spiders, beetles, insect larvae; plant material, especially seeds and fleshy fruits. Voice: loud, repetitive call, high pitched in all kiwis except female Brown kiwi which has a rasping call. Species: **Brown kiwi*** (*Apteryx australis*), height 35cm (13.8in), weight 2.2kg (4.8lb); **Great spotted kiwi** (*A. haastii*), height 35cm (13.8in), weight 2.3kg (5lb); **Little spotted kiwi** (*A. owenii*), height 25cm (9.8in), weight 1.2kg (2.2lb). Females larger and up to 20 percent heavier than males in all species. Feathers: streaked light and dark brown in Brown kiwi; banded light and dark gray in the other two species. Downy type only on both adults and chicks.

*Three subspecies: **North Island brown kiwi** (*A. a. mantelli*), **South Island brown kiwi** (*A. a. australis*), **Stewart Island brown kiwi** (*A. a. lawryi*).

---

probably the factors allowing it in this species. An ostrich egg is not only the largest bird's egg, but also the smallest in relation to the size of the bird. As a result an ostrich can cover a great many of them, either more than a female can lay or more than is worthwhile her laying herself (with the delays and risks involved in doing so). The skewed sex ratio among breeding adults, with about 1.4 females per male, and the high rate of nest destruction by predators both mean that there are many hens without their own nests to lay in. It obviously benefits them to lay somewhere. The major hen benefits from the presence of extra eggs in her nest, because her own are protected by a dilution effect against small-scale predators (ie her own eggs, probably a dozen among about 20, are less likely to be damaged). If, as frequently happens, more eggs are laid in her nest than she can cover, at the start of incubation she rolls away the surplus into an outer ring outside the nest, where they are not incubated and are doomed. As she is able to discriminate among the many eggs in the nest, she ensures that the eggs she rolls out are not hers. It is an astonishing feat of recognition, for ostrich eggs do not vary much in appearance.

High levels of predator density or of

▲ **New life in the desert.** Many chicks of two species of ostrich (North and South African ostriches) hatch in the desert, in this case the Namib Desert in Southwest Africa. Being well-developed on hatching, the chicks can survive in the harsh conditions and soon be led away in search of water holes and food.

◄ **Brilliant displays.** Huge wings, long neck and legs and great flexibility enable the ostrich to have a great range of highly developed displays. Here a hen attacks with wings full-spread (1), a hen solicits (2), a hen feigns injury (3), and a cock struts about in a threatening posture (4).

human activity make nests unlikely to survive. Delinquent hunting drove the once abundant Arabian ostrich to extinction earlier this century. Ostrich populations today are decreasing with human intrusion into their habitat, but the species is not severely threatened.

Ostrich feathers have long been used by African peoples for adornment, and by Europeans since Roman times. An ostrich feather, being symmetrical, was the symbol of justice in ancient Egypt, where also ostrich brains were a delicacy. Pieces of egg shell are used in necklaces and waistbands, and in some places whole eggshells are believed to have magical properties that protect houses and churches against lightning. More mundanely, the Hottentots used

empty eggshells as water containers.   BCRB

Rheas are large flightless birds frequently called the South American ostrich. Anatomically and taxonomically rheas are quite distinct from the ostrich. Rheas may stand up to 1.5m (5ft) tall, but most never weigh more than 40kg (88lb). Ostriches may reach over 2m (6.5ft) in height and may weigh up to 200kg (440lb). Apart from size the most obvious difference occurs in the feet: ostriches have only two enlarged toes, while rheas possess three toes, as do most other birds.

The Gray or Common rhea was once a common inhabitant of the grassland regions from central and coastal Brazil down to the pampas of Argentina. This species contains three distinguishable subspecies. The smallest, from Brazil, weighs only 20kg (44lb) while the larger Argentinian subspecies may weigh up to 40kg (88lb). The Darwin's or Lesser rhea is also divided into three subspecies. The Darwin's rhea is found on the semidesert grass and scrublands of Patagonia and on the high altitude grasslands of the Andes from Argentina and Chile, north through Bolivia into Peru. Charles Darwin was the first to recognize and describe the difference between the Gray rhea and the Darwin's rhea. One evening in the 1830s as H.M.S. *Beagle* was making its way south along the Patagonian coast Darwin noted a difference in bone structure while eating rhea leg.

Both rhea species tend to congregate in flocks for the winter months and divide into smaller flocks for the breeding season, when

males may become solitary for incubating (see box). Rhea chicks are raised by the males. They feed largely on insects for their first few days, but gradually follow the example of their fathers and begin feeding on vegetation. Male rheas defend their chicks from all intruders, including other rheas—males with chicks are often seen driving females away from the chicks. Male rheas with chicks have been known to attack small planes and regularly charge gauchos (South American cowboys) on horseback. The threat of a rhea charge, which could cause a horse to shy and bolt, is one reason why most gauchos are accompanied by dogs, so they can if necessary scare off or divert the attack of a male rhea. By the end of the summer males, chicks and females gather into large flocks for the winter. In spring, when males

◄ **Food all around,** a solitary male Gray rhea in his habitat. Abundant vegetation in the range of the Gray and Darwin's rheas in South America allows them to remain sedentary, unlike some of their ostrich relatives in Africa and emus in Australia, and exempts them from loss of habitat which threatens the future of many bird species. The main threats to rheas come from the hunting of adults by man and the killing of chicks by predators.

▶ **Male mothers.** The two species of rhea both exhibit reversed sexual roles in rearing young. (1) Each male attempts to gather a harem of 2–12 females with his elaborate courtship displays. The male approaches females with his wings spread. Eventually the females begin to follow the dominant courting male. He then drives off all other males and displays vigorously. Once mating occurs the male proceeds to build a nest consisting of a scrape in the ground surrounded by a rim of twigs and vegetation.

(2) The females now proceed to lay eggs in the nest, each female laying one egg every second day for a week to ten days. On the second or third day the male remains at the nest and starts incubating the eggs. The females return at midday each day to lay their eggs beside the male who carefully rolls each new egg into the nest with his bill. The females move on from one male to another throughout the three-month breeding season. Males regularly incubate 10–60 eggs.

Each male must incubate the eggs and hatch the chicks alone. The chicks synchronize hatching and most hatch within a 36-hour period. (3) The male must now lead the chicks to food, while protecting and brooding them.

◄ **At home in his nest,** a male Darwin's rhea with a newly laid egg.

become solitary and females form small groups, the yearlings usually remain as a flock, which lasts until they are nearly two years old and ready to breed.

Adult rheas are largely vegetarian, feeding on a great variety of plants. The Gray rhea eats some grass but strongly prefers broad-leaved plants and frequently eats even obnoxious weeds, such as thistles. Clover seems to be a favorite. The Darwin's rhea, found generally in a drier or harsher environment, will eat almost anything green, but prefers broad-leaved plants. All rheas eat insects and small animals, such as reptiles, when they have the opportunity.

When rheas have come into contact with humans they have usually been persecuted. They have been hunted for years and are one of the main animals caught with the famous *bolas*. Rhea feathers are used to make feather dusters throughout South America. Rheas and their eggs are regularly eaten by local people or are killed and used for dog food. Rheas can coexist with cattle and sheep ranching even though many ranchers accuse the rhea of competing with cattle or sheep. In actuality competition is probably minimal because rheas eat a lot of unwanted plant species as well as vast numbers of insects. However, once land is put to agricultural use the rheas are eliminated because they will eat almost any agricultural crop. They now thrive only in remote areas, away from man or where they are protected.

The decline of rhea populations has prompted the Convention for International Trade in Endangered Species to list both of the rhea species and all subspecies as either endangered or threatened, thereby requiring permits for their export or import.

In recent times adult rheas have had few natural enemies other than man. The Gray rhea on the pampas of Argentina and in the savanna and riverine grasslands has a virtually limitless food supply. The large predatory cats like the jaguar and Mountain lion do not regularly frequent the vast pampas grasslands and smaller predators cannot readily kill an adult rhea. However, rhea chicks are quite vulnerable to a number of predators, including an array of mammals and birds of prey like the caracara. While protected by the male small chicks are safe; however, small chicks separated from the male, particularly after a sudden thunderstorm, are easily taken by predators. Even the small kestrel-sized chimango can be a successful predator when chicks have become separated from their parent.   DFB

In Australia there is a saying "As stupid as an emu." **Emus**, however, have been resident in Australia for at least 80 million years, ever since it broke away from the great prehistoric antarctic continent, Gondwanaland, and began drifting north. In fact the nomadic emu is well adapted to survive in the harsh Australian environment. Studies show that the way of life of the bird nicely matches the conditions with which it has to come to terms.

Until the late 18th century there were several species and subspecies of emu. The Dwarf emus of King Island (Bass Strait) and Kangaroo Island (South Australia) as well as the Tasmanian subspecies were exterminated soon after Europeans settled in Australia. On mainland Australia the emu remains widespread, taking its place as one of Australia's large native herbivores. It lives in eucalypt forest, woodland, mallee, heathland and desert shrublands and sandplains. In desert areas it is rare, being found there only after heavy rains have induced the growth of an array of herbs and grasses and caused shrubs to fruit heavily. The emu also lives close to Australia's big cities, but is no longer found where native vegetation has been cleared to provide agricultural land. Whatever the habitat, however, the emu must have access to fresh water, usually every day.

Emus are large shaggy birds; their loose double feathers, in which the aftershaft (the secondary feather that branches from the base of the main feather) is the same length as the main feather, hang limply from their bodies. Their necks and legs are long but their wings are tiny, reduced to less than 20cm (8in). After molting the birds are dark,

◄ **Emu wings** are not totally useless. Although hidden by the bird's bushy feathers, the wings can be held out, in hot conditions, to expose the bare "under arm" and its dense superficial blood vessels and thus enable the bird to discharge some heat with ease.

▼ **Protection for survivors.** Until a barrier was erected to keep emus out of wool- and cereal-growing areas of Western Australia the state government encouraged the killing of emus, thus threatening the future of the only emu species to have survived earlier onslaughts.

but as sunlight fades the pigments (melanins) that gave the feathers their brown color, so the birds become paler. Their long legs enable them to walk long distances at a steady 7km/h (4mph) or to flee from danger at 48km/h (30mph). Emus have three toes (differing in this from the ostrich which has only two). Emu chicks are striped longitudinally with black, brown and cream, so they blend easily into long grass and dense shrubbery.

The emu prefers and seeks a very nutritious diet. It takes the parts of plants in which nutrients are concentrated: seeds, fruits, flowers, young shoots. It will also eat insects and small vertebrates when they are easily available, but in the wild it will not eat dry grass or mature leaves even if they are all that is available. It ingests large pebbles, up to 46g (1.6oz), to help its gizzard

grind up its food; it also often eats charcoal. Its rich diet enables it to grow fast and reproduce rapidly, but at a price. Because such rich foods are not always available in the same place throughout the year emus must move to remain in contact with their foods. In arid Australia the exhaustion of a food supply in one place often means moving hundreds of kilometers to find another source of food. The emu shows two adaptations to this way of life. Firstly, when food is abundant it lays down large stores of fat; it is able to use these while looking for more food, so that birds normally weighing 45kg (105lb) can keep moving at bodyweights as low as 20kg (44lb). Secondly, emus are only forced to stay in one place when the male is sitting on eggs. At other times they can move without limitation, admittedly at a slow pace when with small chicks. During incubation the male does not eat, drink or defecate, so he is then independent of the state of the local food supply.

Emus pair in December and January, two birds defending a territory of about 30sq km (11.7sq mi) while the female lays her clutch of 9–20 eggs in April, May and June. Once the male starts sitting many females move away, sometimes pairing with other males and laying further clutches. A few stay to defend the male on the nest, using their characteristic loud booming call. Males are very aggressive when the chicks hatch, after 56 days; they drive the female away and attack approaching humans. The male stays with the chicks, though they lead him rather than the reverse. After 5–7 months the parent–young bond breaks down and the male may then remate for the next season's nesting.

Emus have probably benefitted from man's activities in inland Australia, because the establishment of watering points for cattle and sheep has provided permanent water where there was none before, and so much of Australia is unoccupied or used as open rangeland that the emu is in no danger of extinction. SJJFD

Nomads of the Australian Mainland

The emu's biology centers around its need to keep in touch with its food. In Australia the seeds, fruits, flowers, insects and young foliage that the emu eats become available after rainfall. Emus therefore orient their movements towards places where rain has recently fallen. The orientation seems to depend mainly on the sight of clouds associated with rainbearing depressions, but sound cues from thunder and the smell of wet ground may also be involved. In Western Australia summer rain regularly comes from depressions moving west and south from the north coast, whereas winter rain comes from antarctic depressions moving up from the southwest. Emu movements therefore take on a regular pattern in the western half of Australia. The number of birds involved in a movement may exceed 70,000—a ravaging hoard as far as farmers are concerned. To protect the cereal-growing areas of the

southwest from invasion by movements of emus from the inland a 1,000km (600mi) long fence has been built.

Emu migrations may be a phenomenon generated by man's own actions. The establishment of large numbers of artificial but permanent watering points in the inland, where cattle and sheep are grazed, has enabled emus to expand into places from which they were previously excluded by lack of water.

The total emu population of Western Australia (between 100,000 and 200,000) is therefore larger than before, so that when food runs low many more emus are ready to move. With the regular alteration of weather systems, from the north in summer and the south in winter, very large numbers are sometimes drawn south in winter. By spring, as the crops ripen, they would reach the farms were it not for the barrier fence. SJJFD

There is some of the mystery of the jungle about the **cassowaries**. Many people have seen their footprints, their feces or even heard them call, but glimpses of the birds are rare. For the largest land animals in New Guinea they have kept their secrets well; we still have only the barest outline of their life history.

The three species of cassowaries live in New Guinea. The largest, the Southern cassowary, also inhabits Cape York, Ceram and Aru Island. The One-wattled cassowary,

only slightly smaller than the Southern, is confined to New Guinea. The moruk or Bennett's cassowary, little more than 1m (40in) tall lives in New Guinea, New Britain and Yapen Island.

All three species have sleek, drooping, brown or black plumage. Their wing quills are enlarged, spike-like structures, used in fighting and defense. The three toes on their feet are also effective weapons: the kick of a cassowary has disemboweled many adversaries. In all species the legs and neck are long, and the head is adorned with a horny casque (higher in the female than the male). The neck is ornamented with colorful bare skin and small fleshy flaps (wattles). The sexes are alike. When chicks the plumage is striped brown, black and white, changing to a uniform brown for the first year of life. The glossy black adult plumage begins to grow during the second year and is fully developed at four years. The casque on the head is often thought to be used by the birds to push through the thick jungle. Recently a captive bird was seen using it to turn over soil as it sought food. Perhaps wild cassowaries use the casque to turn over the litter, seeking small animals, fallen fruit and fungi.

Cassowaries feed mainly on the fruit of forest trees, which they eat whole. As the fruit of these trees grows high in the canopy and the cassowaries cannot fly they are dependent on finding fallen fruit. Furthermore they need a supply of fruit throughout the year, so only forests with a good diversity of tree species will sustain a population of cassowaries. Many forests used for timber production no longer retain their primitive diversity, so that in a slow and subtle way they are becoming less capable of supporting cassowaries. The moruk, unlike the other two species which live only in jungle, also has sparse populations in many mountainous parts of New Guinea. In these places it seems to feed on the fruits of those shrubs and heathy plants from which it can take direct. All species will also feed on insects, invertebrates, small vertebrates and some fungi.

Cassowaries are solitary animals, forming pairs in the breeding season but at other times found alone. The male incubates the 4–8 eggs in a nest on the forest floor. He accompanies the chicks for about a year before returning to his solitary life. The bird's most commonly heard call is a deep "chug chug," but during courtship in the Southern cassowary the male approaches the female giving a low "boo-boo-boo" call, circling her and causing his throat to swell

and tremble. Most contacts between wild cassowaries observed outside the breeding season led to fights. It is assumed from their distribution that individuals, at least of the Southern cassowary, are territorial.

Cassowaries need large areas of forest in which to live. Studies of the Southern cassowary on Cape York showed that it ate the fruits of 75 species as well as fungi and land snails. Breeding (in winter) coincided with the period when the maximum amount of fruit was available in the forest. The survival of the cassowaries may therefore depend upon the survival of diverse forests where it is possible for them to obtain food throughout the year.

Individuals of all three species are kept in captivity by the peoples of New Guinea. The birds' plumes are plucked and used for the decoration of headdresses, the quills are

Conserving Kiwis

In New Zealand kiwis have suffered considerably since European settlement began 150 years ago. Large areas were cleared for farming and, in addition, the European settlers introduced mammal predators such as cats and stoats.

The Great spotted kiwi and the Brown kiwi in the South Island and the Brown kiwi on Stewart Island are still widespread and appear to be able to hold their own. In the North Island, however, the Brown kiwi is under threat from land clearance over much of its range. Dedicated catching teams attempt to remove the kiwis before land is cleared but cannot cope with the large areas involved. Fortunately the kiwi has adapted to some man-modified habitats and also lives on in the few large forest reserves within its range.

The Little spotted kiwi has fared the worst and is endangered. The species would be all

▲ **Bird of the night,** a Great spotted kiwi. Though numerous and widely distributed, kiwis prefer bushy habitat in which they can scavenge and are adapted for nocturnal activity. They are famous among birds, but have been seen by few. Much remains to be discovered about their behavior and biology.

◄ **Peculiar and mysterious,** a Southern cassowary. Casque, wattles and "feathers" all provoke questions about origin and function, but few answers are yet available. The wing feathers consist solely of quills and may protect the bird's flanks as it moves through foliage; the casque may provide protection for the head or serve as a tool for digging. But how does one account for the extraordinary combination of colors?

but extinct but for the foresight shown in the transfer of this species to Kapiti Island, a 2,000ha (4,900 acre) island in Cook Strait. It is believed that the island's population, now numbering over 1,000 birds, was established from as few as five liberated birds. The success of the liberation is all the more remarkable because at the time the habitat on the island was in a poor state.

Although Kapiti Island is a reserve, the Little spotted kiwi remains in a critical situation, with only one substantial population on one island. Attempts are being made to breed the species in captivity, both to learn more about its breeding biology and to make birds available for liberation on suitable islands. On Kapiti Island the species' habitat requirements, foods and breeding are being investigated, so that islands can be selected for establishing more populations. This work has led to two further transfers of Little spotted kiwis.   JNJ

used as nose ornaments and the whole animal is finally butchered for a feast. Cassowaries have been traded throughout southeastern Asia for at least 500 years. The populations of the Southern cassowary on Ceram and of the moruk on New Britain probably arose from the breeding of escaped captives, brought from the main island of New Guinea.   SJJFD

Kiwis have taken flightlessness to the extreme. Their tiny vestigial wings are buried in their feathers and their tail has disappeared externally. The kiwi hen lays an egg that is one quarter of her weight and, unlike most other birds, kiwis use their sense of smell rather than their sight to investigate their surroundings.

Kiwis remain fairly widely distributed in New Zealand but have disappeared from large areas, not only where the original native forest has been removed but also from some areas still forested. The North Island subspecies of Brown kiwi has even colonized some exotic pine forests and farmland with mixed scrub and pasture. The South Island brown kiwi and the Great spotted kiwi are confined to the remoter forests and mountains of the western side of the South Island. The Stewart Island brown kiwi occurs in forest, scrub and tussock grassland, and is the only kiwi active in daylight. The Little spotted kiwi, once widespread on both the North and South Islands, is now known on only three offshore islands.

The kiwi is the size of a domestic hen but its body is more elongated and has stouter,

more powerful legs. Its long, curved bill, which has openings for air passages at the tip, is used for probing the ground for food. There is no breastbone (sternum), to which in other birds the flight muscles are attached; other bones that are hollow in most birds (so as to reduce weight for flight) are only partly hollow in kiwis. Although their eyes are small for a nocturnal animal, kiwis can see well enough to run at speed through dense undergrowth.

Compared with its flightless relatives, the ostrich, rheas and emus, the kiwi is a small bird and could probably have evolved only in the absence of mammals. The New Zealand archipelago was formed 80–100 million years ago, before the evolution of efficient land mammals. When mammals appeared there was a sea barrier that prevented them from reaching New Zealand and protected the kiwis, and their ancestors, from their competition and predation. Other flightless birds (the moas) also evolved in New Zealand, but all are now extinct.

The kiwi has invested enormous energy in each large egg rather than in a clutch of many smaller eggs. Its egg is highly nutritious and not only sustains the embryo throughout the long incubation but also provides the newly hatched chick with a yolk sac as a temporary food supply.

After an egg has been laid it is believed that the egg is left unattended for several days, but once incubation begins it is the work of the male. There is some doubt as to whether parents feed their chicks; certainly within a week of their birth the chicks emerge from the nest alone and attempt to feed themselves.

The kiwi is able to detect food by smell, and uses its bill to probe amongst the forest litter, or for thrusting deep into the soil. It picks up food in the tip of its bill and throws it back to its throat in quick jerks.

Kiwis are distributed in pairs and use calls to keep in contact in the dense forest and also to maintain territories. At closer range the kiwi again uses its sense of smell rather than sight, as well as its good hearing, to detect other birds. Nonterritory holders are vigorously repelled. Breeding behavior includes loud grunting and snorting as well as wild running and chasing.

The kiwi has always been an important bird to New Zealanders. To the Maori it provided a source of food and of feathers for highly valued cloaks.

Today the peculiarity of the kiwi to New Zealand is recognized in that it has been adopted as the unofficial national emblem.

                                                   JNJ

TINAMOUS

Order: Tinamiformes
Family: Tinamidae.
Forty-six species in 9 genera.
Distribution: S Mexico S to southern
S America.

Habitat: forest, scrub, grasslands up to 4,000m
(about 13,100ft).

Size: length 20–53cm (8–21in);
weight 450–2,300g (16–81oz).
Females are slightly larger.

Plumage: cryptic, mainly browns and grays;
usually barred, streaked or spotted; two species
have crests. Females are usually brighter,
lighter, or more barred, sometimes with
different leg coloring.

Voice: utters loud, mellow, flute-like whistles
and trills.

Eggs: usually 1–12; glossy green, blue, yellow,
purplish-brown or nearly black. Weight: 21–
68g (0.7–2.4oz). Incubation: 19–20 days.

Diet: mainly fruits, seeds, insects; small
vertebrates also recorded.

Species include: **Great tinamou** (*Tinamus
major*), **Magdalena tinamou** [I] (*Crypturellus
saltuarius*), **Red-winged tinamou** (*Rhynchotus
rufescens*), **Tataupa tinamou** (*C. tataupa*).

[I] Threatened, but status indeterminate.

▶ **Elegant crested tinamou** ABOVE (*Eudromia
elegans*), a species of tinamou almost exclusive
to Argentina. It is often encountered in groups
of 3–5 on the edges of corn fields or running
around on pasture. Hunting and the
destruction of forest habitat threaten the future
of some species, especially the Great tinamou.

▶ **An Undulated tinamou** in undergrowth.
This species (*Crypturellus undulatus*) lives in
forest and scrub in the northern half of South
America (Guyana and southern Venezuela
south to Paraguay and northern Argentina).

THE tinamous are birds restricted to the
forests and grasslands of Central and
South America, where they are thought to
have had their origins. The superficial
resemblance of certain species of this
ground-living group to gamebirds, especially the guineafowl (family Numididae), is
no indication of their true relationship, for
recent analysis of their egg-white proteins,
DNA and bone structure indicates that they
are more closely related to the rheas. Indeed,
it has been suggested that ancient tinamou
relatives actually gave rise to all ratites, even
though the breastbone (sternum) possesses
a well-developed keel, which the ratites lack.

To the casual observer tinamous
outwardly recall the guineafowl in their proportions and carriage, but differ in that the
bill is slender, elongate and slightly
decurved. Further, the rear of the body
appears arched owing to the great development of the rump feathers which normally
obscure the short tail. The legs are thick and
powerful and possess three forward-
pointing toes and one rear toe. The latter is
reduced and elevated, or even absent in
some species. Although the legs are perfectly
adapted for running, the birds soon become
tired when chased and often stumble. Their
flying ability also leaves much to be desired,
for though they have well-developed flight
muscles, their flight is clumsy and they often
collide with obstacles, which sometimes
results in injury or death.

Because of their limited running and flying capabilities, tinamous rely on their protective coloration to avoid detection. They
remain motionless with head extended,
attempting to blend in with the vegetation,
and will creep away from danger using all
available cover. Species living in more open
areas are known to hide in holes in the
ground. At all times they only break cover,
or take to the wing, at the last possible
moment. For these reasons the tinamous are
not the easiest of birds to see in their natural
environment, their presence being indicated
only by their flute-like, whistling calls,
which can be uttered day or night.

Very little detailed information is available concerning the food preferences of any
species. Some crop and stomach contents
have been analyzed, and indicate that they
feed mainly upon fruits, seeds and other vegetable matter such as roots and buds. Insects
and other small animals may also be taken,
especially by species of *Nothoprocta*, while
the Red-winged tinamou may also eat mice.

As in ratites, the sexual roles of the
tinamous are largely reversed, with the
male taking care of the eggs and young,
while the female is the most aggressive
and the main participant in the courtship
display.

Polygamy is common with the tinamous.
It is common for one or more females to lay
eggs in one nest, and occasionally a hen will
deposit her eggs in different nests, which are
being looked after by different males.

Detailed accounts of nesting are very hard
to come by. It is almost certain that the species that live in tropical forests nest in many
months of the year, while others may have
their egg-laying season governed by rainfall
and other climatic factors. What can be said
with certainty is that all are ground nesters
and either lay their eggs directly on the
ground, between roots in a shallow scrape,
or construct a nest of grass and sticks.
Clutches are said to consist of 1–12 eggs,
though the latter figure may be the result
of two females using one nest. The eggs are
relatively large and renowned for their hard,
porcelain-like gloss and vivid clear coloring.
On hatching the chicks are downy and buff
in color with darker stripes and mottles.
They are very well developed, being capable
of running soon after hatching; most species
are able to fly to some degree before they are
half grown.

During the nest period males often
become so tame that they can be picked up
off the nest. In the Tataupa tinamou the
cock will pretend to be lame in order to distract the intruder away from the nest, while
other species may cover their eggs with
leaves as in *Tinamus* species or with feathers
as in *Nothoprocta* species.

Throughout their range, tinamous are
sought after as food. This is because their
meat, although having a strange trans-
lucent appearance, is very tender and full of
flavor.   CAW

PENGUINS

Order: Sphenisciformes
Family: Spheniscidae.
Sixteen species in 6 genera.
Distribution: Antarctic, New Zealand,
S Australia, S Africa, S America N to Peru and
Galapagos Islands.

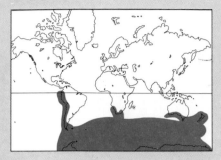

Habitat: sea water, ice, rock, islands and coasts.

Size: ranges from height 30cm
(12in), weight 1–1.5g (2.2–3.3lb)
in the Little blue penguin to
height 80–100cm (32–39in),
weight 15–40kg (33–88lb) in the
Emperor penguin.

Plumage: most are blue-gray or blue-black
above, white below.

Voice: loud, harsh trumpeting or braying calls.

Eggs: one or two, according to genus; whitish
or whitish-green. Incubation: 33–62 days
according to species.

Diet: crustaceans, fish, squid.

Species and genera include: **Adelie penguin**
(*Pygoscelis adeliae*), **Chinstrap penguin**
(*Pygoscelis antarctica*), **crested penguins** (genus
Eudyptes), **Emperor penguin** (*Aptenodytes
forsteri*), **Fiordland penguin** (*Eudyptes
pachyrhynchus*), **Galapagos penguin** (*Spheniscus
mendiculus*), **Gentoo penguin** (*Pygoscelis papua*),
Jackass penguin ⓥ (*Spheniscus demersus*), **King
penguin** (*Aptenodytes patagonicus*), **Little blue
penguin** (*Eudyptula minor*), **Macaroni penguin**
(*Eudyptes chrysolophus*), **Magellanic penguin**
(*Spheniscus magellanicus*), **Rockhopper penguin**
(*Eudyptes crestatus*), **Yellow-eyed penguin**
(*Megadyptes antipodes*).

ⓥ Vulnerable.

▶ **Representative species of penguins.** (1) An
adult Yellow-eyed penguin (*Megadyptes
antipodes*) with two chicks. (2) A pair of
Rockhopper penguins (*Eudyptes crestatus*)
brooding a chick. (3) Little blue penguins
(*Eudyptula minor*) coming ashore. (4) Two
incubating King penguins (*Aptenodytes
patagonicus*), one arranging its egg on its feet.
(5) A pair of Adelie penguins (*Pygoscelis adeliae*)
greeting each other. (6) Adelie penguins
tobogganing, (7) leaping out of the sea,
(8) porpoising. (9) A Jackass penguin
(*Spheniscus demersus*) standing and (10) coming
ashore.

THE name penguin is used for a group of flightless birds of the southern hemisphere whose comical appearance, upright stance and waddling gait belies their abilities as the supreme swimmers and divers amongst birds. It was originally applied to the Great auk of the North Atlantic.

Europeans first heard of penguins after the great exploring voyages of Vasco da Gama (1497–98) and Ferdinand Magellan (1519–22), which discovered Jackass and Magellanic penguins respectively, but many species were not known until the southern ocean was explored in the 18th century in search of the southern continent, to be known as Antarctica.

Penguins breed in habitat ranging from the bare lava shores of equatorial islands to sandy subtropical beaches, cool temperate forests, subantarctic grasslands and antarctic sea ice. They are, however, basically adapted to cool conditions and in tropical areas only occur where cold-water currents exist, eg within the influence of the Humboldt Current along the western coast of South America and of the Benguela and Agulhas Currents around South Africa. Most species occur between 45 and 60 degrees south with the highest species diversity in the New Zealand area and the Falkland Islands; the greatest numbers live around the coasts of Antarctica and on the subantarctic islands. Winter distributions and movements are little known. Tropical and warm temperate species do not migrate.

Although penguins show a wide range in weight and size they are remarkably similar in structure and plumage, being chiefly blue-gray or blue-black above and mainly white below; species distinguishing marks (eg crests, crown, face and neck stripes, breast bands) are chiefly on the head and upper breast, being thus visible while the birds are swimming on the surface. The main chick plumages are gray or brown all over, or have one of these colors along the back and white on the sides and undersurface. Juveniles' plumage is usually very similar to that of adults, only differing in minor ways, eg the distinctiveness of ornamentation. Males are slightly larger than females, those of crested penguins notably so.

Penguins are densely covered by three layers of short feathers. They are highly streamlined, their wings reduced to strong, narrow, stiff flippers with which rapid propulsion through water is achieved. The feet and shanks (tarsi) are short, the legs are set well back on the body and are used, with the tail, as rudders. On land penguins

▲ **Grass for the nest,** carried by a Gentoo penguin. Gentoos often breed a little way inland, forming long-lasting pairs within large colonies or rookeries, which are sometimes situated on low hills. This arrangement entails much walking, in gathering grass and later in carrying food from the sea to the nest. Being adapted for fast swimming, gentoos can only waddle in a somewhat deliberate manner, but ease their task by fixing a route and turning it into a well-trodden track.

▼ **Penguin burrows,** a rookery of Magellanic penguins at Punto Tombo, Argentina.

frequently rest on their heels with their stout tail feathers forming the prop. The short legs induce a waddling gait, but on ice they can move rapidly by tobogganing on their bellies. They have comparatively solid bones and generally weigh only a little less than water, thus reducing the energy required to dive. Bills are generally short and stout with a powerful and painful grip. Emperor and King penguins have long, slightly down-curved bills, possibly adapted for capturing fast-swimming fish and squid at considerable depths.

As well as having to swim efficiently penguins also need to keep warm in cool, often near-freezing waters. For this they have, in addition to a dense, very waterproof feather coat, a well-defined fat layer and a highly developed "heat-exchange" system of blood vessels in the flippers and legs, ensuring that venous blood returning from exposed extremities is warmed up by the outgoing arterial blood, thus reducing heat loss from the body core. Tropical penguins tend to overheat easily, so have relatively large flippers and areas of bare facial skin in order to lose excess heat. They also live in burrows so as to reduce direct exposure to sunlight.

The main prey of penguins are crustaceans, fish and squid, which they chase, catch and swallow underwater. It has been suggested that they may be assisted in prey detection by a form of echolocation based on sounds produced by their swimming movement. Fish are important in the diet of inshore feeders, eg Jackass, Little blue and Gentoo penguins, and also of the deeper diving King and Emperor penguins. Squid may predominate in the food of the King penguin and are frequently taken by Emperor and Rockhopper penguins and some *Spheniscus* species.

Krill are the principal prey of Adelie, Chinstrap, Gentoo and Macaroni penguins and other crustaceans are important to Rockhopper penguins (and probably also to the other crested penguins) and to Yellow-eyed penguins. Krill, like many minute oceanic animals (zooplankton), tend to be absent from surface water during the day, which is when penguins rearing chicks on this food are mainly at sea. However, they may still feed mainly at night (traveling to and from their colony during the day) or use their diving ability to seek prey at depth in daytime.

The Little blue penguin is unusual in feeding its chicks well after nightfall; as the smallest species it will have the shallowest diving capacity and may be more dependent on feeding around dusk when a greater proportion of its prey is near the surface. It may also be avoiding day-active predators by only coming ashore at night. In inshore-feeding species both parents usually bring food to the chick each day. Adelie, Chinstrap and crested penguin parents, however, are usually away at sea for more than a day so the chick only receives one meal per day. King and Emperor penguin chicks are fed large meals at infrequent intervals, seldom more often than every three or four days. Only in large species do meals exceed 1kg (2.2lb) but even quite young chicks of small penguins can easily accommodate 500g (about 1lb) of food. Indeed the capacity of young chicks is astounding and for much of their early growth they are little more than pear-shaped sacks of food, supported by big feet and surmounted by a small head.

Emperor penguins lay their eggs in the fall. King penguin chicks overwinter at the breeding colony but are rarely fed during this period and grow mainly during the previous and subsequent summers (see p38). Otherwise antarctic and most subantarctic and cold temperate penguins breed in spring and summer. Breeding is highly synchronized within and between colonies. Gentoo penguins and the more northerly of the crested penguins have longer breeding seasons and more variable timing. In Jackass and Galapagos penguins there are usually

▲ **Two Rockhoppers preening.** Penguins normally present a placid disposition to the world, and for that they have become endeared. But they can become aggressive, and Rockhoppers are the most aggressive of all.

▶ **Brooding males of the southern seas** OVERLEAF. In this group of King penguins from a rookery males are predominant. Incubating birds are easily identified from the bulges above their feet where they are incubating eggs, tightly held by the birds' flap of skin. As there are neither nests nor territories the birds are unevenly spaced, waddling around with their eggs on their feet.

two main peaks of breeding, but laying occurs in all months of the year. This is also true of most populations of Little blue penguins and in South Australia some pairs are even able to raise broods successfully twice a year. In most penguins, males come ashore first at the start of the breeding season to establish territories where they are soon joined by their old partners or by new birds that they attract to the nest site. Penguins normally mate with the partners of previous years: in a colony of Yellow-eyed penguins 61 percent of pairings lasted 2–6 years, 12 percent 7–13 years and the overall "divorce" rate was 14 percent per annum; of Little blue penguins one pairing lasted 11 years and the divorce rate was 18 percent per annum. In a major Adelie penguin study, however, no pairing lasted six years and the annual divorce rate was over 50 percent.

Macaroni penguins breed first when at least five years old; Emperor, King, Chinstrap and Adelie penguins are at least three (females) or four (males) and Little blue, Yellow-eyed, Gentoo and Jackass penguins at least two years old. In Adelie penguins very few one-year-olds visit the colony; many two-year-olds come for a few days around chick hatching but most birds visit first as three- and four-year-olds. Up to about seven years of age, Adelies arrive progressively earlier each season, make more visits and stay longer. Some females first breed at three years of age, males at four, but most females and males wait another year or two and some males do not breed until eight.

Only Emperor and King penguins lay a single egg; the rest normally lay two. In the Yellow-eyed penguin (and probably generally) age affects fertility so that hatching success in a study colony was 32 percent, 92 percent and 77 percent of eggs incubated by birds aged 2, 6 and 14–19 years respectively. In crested penguins the first egg of the clutch is very much smaller than the second; only in the Fiordland penguin do both eggs normally hatch and only one chick is ever reared—this is an extreme form of a widespread adaptation ensuring that when food is scarce the smaller chick dies quickly and does not prejudice the survival of its sibling. This system may be designed to cope with the high early egg loss resulting from the considerable amount of fighting in the closely packed colonies, which in turn presumably results from sexual selection favoring aggressive males. Alternatively, when both eggs hatch the difference in size of the chicks may ensure that only one survives for long (ie there is a form of brood reduction). Neither explanation is entirely satisfactory. In other penguins hatching is also staggered and this can promote brood reduction, usually by favoring the first hatched chick.

All penguins have the capacity for storing substantial fat reserves (especially before the period of molting and fasting) but only the Emperor, King, Adelie, Chinstrap and crested penguins undertake long fasts during the courtship, incubation and brooding periods. During fasts lasting 110–115 days for brooding male Emperor penguins and 35 days for Adelie and crested penguins up to 45 percent of initial body weight may be lost. By contrast, Gentoo, Yellow-eyed, Little blue and Jackass penguins usually change incubation every 1–2 days. Chicks grow rapidly, particularly in Antarctic species. After 2–3 weeks (6 weeks in Emperor and King penguins) the chicks in open areas form large aggregations or creches (Adelie, Gentoo, Emperor and King penguins) or small ones involving a few chicks from adjacent nests (Chinstrap, Jackass, crested penguins). Once molt is complete chicks usually start going to sea. In crested penguins there is a rapid and complete exodus from the colony (almost all leave within one week) and almost certainly no further parental care. In Gentoo penguins free-swimming chicks return to shore periodically and there obtain food from their parents for at least a further two or three weeks. Some such parental care may occur in other species but it is unlikely that chicks are ever fed by their parents at sea.

In most species, once chicks are independent the parents fatten quickly for a molting and fasting period of 2–6 weeks during which fat reserves are used twice as fast as in incubation. In Jackass and Galapagos penguins the molt period is less defined,

occurring at any time between breeding attempts. Immature birds usually complete molt before breeding birds start and at least in crested penguins the timing of this molt becomes later with age until the first breeding attempt.

Compared with other seabirds, the survival of adult penguins from one year to the next is relatively low, being 70–80 percent for Adelie, 86 percent for Macaroni, 87 percent for Yellow-eyed and 86 percent for Little blue, but 95 percent for Emperor penguins. Penguins are thus not particularly long-lived—records of 19-year-old Yellow-eyed and Adelie penguins being exceptional—and average lifespan is only about 10 years, except for Emperor penguins where it might be double this. Juvenile survival, however, is relatively high in most Antarctic species, except Emperor penguins where only some 20 percent of fledglings are reported to survive their first year, although this may be artificially low due to human interference.

Most penguins are highly social, both on land and at sea, and often breed in vast colonies, only defending the small areas around their nests. Courtship and mate-recognition behavior are most complex in

the highly colonial Adelie, Chinstrap, Gentoo and crested penguins, least so in the species that breed in dense vegetation, such as the Yellow-eyed penguin. Despite living in burrows, Jackass penguins, which usually breed in dense colonies, have fairly elaborate visual and vocal displays; those of Little blue penguins, whose burrows are more dispersed, are more restrained. The social behavior of these penguins is largely nest oriented. In contrast Emperor penguins, which have no nest site, show only behavior oriented to their partners. The great variation in the sequence and patterning of their trumpeting calls provides all the information needed for individuals to recognize each other. In King penguins the incoming bird goes near its nest site and then calls and listens for a response. King and Emperor penguins are the only penguins where the two sexes can easily be distinguished by the characteristics of their calls.

Although flightless, adult penguins have few natural predators on land because they generally choose isolated breeding sites and their beaks and flippers are effective weapons (they are, however, vulnerable to larger introduced mammals). Eggs and chicks are taken by skuas and a variety of other predatory birds. At sea Killer whales, Leopard seals and other seals and sharks catch penguins, but the extent of this predation is at most of local significance. In fact the populations of several species of Antarctic penguins (especially Chinstraps) seem to have increased appreciably in recent decades. This is attributed to the improved food supplies following the massive reduction in stocks of krill-eating baleen whales. Some King penguin populations have also increased, this perhaps being partly a recovery from when they were killed so oil could be extracted from their blubber. In the past many penguin populations were reduced (and colonies eliminated) by egg collecting for human consumption; in most cases this is not a real problem today.

Three species of penguin are presently endangered. Galapagos penguins, with a total population of about 5,000 pairs, breed only on two islands in the Galapagos Archipelago. On one they are now seriously menaced by the presence of feral dogs, although an eradication program has been started. Yellow-eyed penguins have declined to fewer than 5,000 pairs, chiefly because of changing patterns of land use and other human disturbance in the coastal dune systems of New Zealand where they breed. Fortunately populations on off-lying islands, where protection is more feasible,

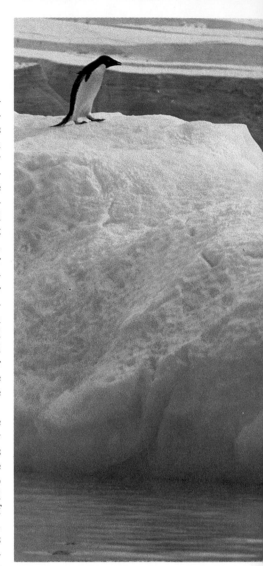

▲ **Penguins in flight.** Evidence of anatomy and behavior suggests that penguins almost certainly developed from a flying bird rather than from a primitive bird that had not yet developed the ability to fly; ie the penguin's flipper is not a modified arm but a modified wing. Penguins in fact have affinities with albatrosses and petrels (order Procellariiformes). The two groups are probably derived from a common ancestor which was able to fly both above and below water (like modern diving petrels). Some members of this primitive species must have opted to perfect underwater flight and in doing so paid for their new skills in losing the ability to fly above water. Today all penguins, such as these Adelie penguins, only "fly" when diving into water.

◄ **An "ecstatic display"** is one of several kinds of displays used by penguins. Performed by males of all species, except Emperors, Little blues and Galapagos penguins, it occurs in rookeries early in the breeding season, for two reasons: firstly to attract unmated hens; secondly to intimidate other males in asserting ownership of territory. This is a Magellanic penguin.

have suffered less. Both the Jackass and the Humboldt penguins occur in highly productive oceanic upwelling systems of nutrients that support large fishing industries. Populations of these species have decreased alarmingly, initially due to egg removal and guano collection, subsequently because of competition for food; the fishing industries off the west coasts of South America and South Africa both depend, as do penguins, on anchovies and pilchards. The survival of these two species therefore depends on compromises between fish-stock exploitation and conservation.

All penguins are highly vulnerable to oil pollution. This is a particularly serious threat to the Jackass penguin, as many Jackass colonies lie near the tanker routes around the Cape of Good Hope. Thousands of Magellanic penguins have died in oiling incidents in the Straits of Magellan. Jackass penguins have been successfully cleaned and returned to their colonies where many have subsequently bred but this is a time-consuming and expensive operation. Commercial fishing practices, whether existing ones for anchovies or developing ones for krill, pose an increasing threat.   JPC

Diving in Penguins

Penguins are probably better adapted for life at sea than any other group of birds. Recently reliable information on their swimming and diving abilities has become available.

Although credited with swimming speeds of up to 60km/h (37mph) all accurate measurements of normal swimming for Emperor, Adelie and Jackass penguins gave speeds of 5–10km/h (3–6mph). In short bursts and particularly when "porpoising" (a swimming motion in which penguins briefly leave the water) faster speeds may well be achieved. The purpose of porpoising is uncertain; it might confuse underwater seal predators, achieve faster speeds by reducing drag when traveling in air or allow breathing without hindering movement at a fast speed.

For Gentoo, Chinstrap and Macaroni penguins dive durations are usually 0.5–1.5 minutes, seldom exceeding 2 minutes. In Jackass and Emperor penguins, however, the mean dive time is 2.5 minutes with maxima of 5 minutes in Jackass and over 18 minutes in Emperors.

Diving depths have been measured, with "pressure-sensitive" recorders, for four species. Six Emperor penguin dives terminated at depths from 45–265m (150–870ft). Of 2,595 King penguin dives half were deeper than 50m (165ft), and two greater than 240m (790ft). By contrast of 1,110 Chinstrap penguin dives 90 percent were shallower than 45m (150ft), 40 percent less than 10m (33ft) and the deepest dive only 70m (130ft). Similarly of 19 Gentoo penguin dives 85 percent were to below 20m (66ft) and only one exceeded 70m (230ft).

How do such relatively small animals as penguins manage frequent deep diving? Diving patterns are influenced by three main factors: firstly submergence time, dictated by how long the breath can be held; secondly, the effect of increased pressure at depth; thirdly, temperature regulation, ie the ability to minimize heat loss. Breath-hold time is determined by the body's oxygen store. Penguins the size of an Adelie use about 100cc of oxygen per minute at rest and their store would be exhausted in a 2.5 minute dive. However, during dives muscles can function on a greatly reduced supply of blood and oxygen, heart beat is reduced from 80–100 beats per minute when resting to 20 beats per minute and the same oxygen store can now sustain a dive of 5–6 minutes.

Human divers who breathe compressed air are vulnerable to inert gas narcosis (the "bends") but in breath-hold diving the inert gas supply is very limited and risks are much less. Penguins on short shallow dives should have no problems but how the Emperors and Kings cope with their long dives to substantial depths is unknown.

Penguins seem well-adapted for reducing heat loss during dives. However, most of their feather insulation is probably due to entrapped air and much of this is expelled under pressure during diving (as a trail of bubbles behind the bird), so penguins may need to remain very active in cold water in order to keep warm.

We know very little about how, and how often, penguins catch prey underwater. Penguins that feed mainly on krill and similar crustaceans have to catch very small prey, usually less than 3cm (1.2in) long. It was calculated that Chinstrap penguins, which averaged 191 dives per day during foraging trips when rearing chicks, need to catch 16 krill (1 every 6 seconds) per average dive. In contrast King penguins would only need to catch a single squid or fish on 10 percent of their 865 dives per trip.

The nature of the prey may also influence dive duration. Penguins feeding on relatively slow-moving, swarming crustaceans can catch many individuals even during short dives. Penguins that pursue fast-moving squid and fish may need to submerge for much longer in order to have a chance of catching them. However, they do not need to succeed often in order to satisfy their food requirements. This could explain the much longer dives of Jackass penguins, which feed mainly on surface-shoaling fish, when compared with the also shallow-diving but krill-eating Gentoo penguin.   JPC

Surviving at the Extremes

Breeding strategies in large penguins

Emperor penguins, when breeding, endure the coldest conditions faced by any bird: the frozen wastes of the Antarctic sea ice, where average temperature is −20°C (−4°F) and mean windspeed 25km/h (16mph), sometimes reaching 75km/h (47mph). Emperor penguin breeding colonies form in the fall (mid May), when courting takes place and females each lay a single egg on the newly formed ice. The males assume the job of incubating the eggs, each holding his partner's egg on his feet for 60 days. When the eggs hatch both parents feed the chicks, from late winter and through the spring, so the young are ready for independence in the summer before the sea ice returns.

This breeding arrangement prompts two questions. Firstly, why do Emperor penguins raise their young at the worst time of year? Secondly how do the penguins survive in the winter conditions?

An answer to the first question seems to be that if Emperor penguins were to breed in the summer (a short season in the Antarctic, only four months long) they would not complete their breeding cycle before the onset of winter. Even when the chicks fledge, in late spring, they are only 60 percent of adult weight, which is the lowest proportion for any penguin, and juvenile mortality is high. The adults, however, are able to breed annually.

The means whereby Emperor penguins survive in harsh conditions are several remarkable physiological and behavioral adaptations, all stemming from the need to minimize the loss of heat and the expenditure of energy.

The body size of Emperor penguins and their shape give a relatively low surface-to-volume ratio and their flippers and bill are 25 percent smaller as a proportion of body size than in any other penguin. Heatloss is further reduced by extreme proliferation of their blood-vessel heat-exchange system (twice as extensive as that of King penguins), by recovering in the nasal passages 80 percent of the heat added to cold inhaled air, and by the excellent insulation provided by very long double-layered, high-density feathers which completely cover the legs.

Because in winter open water lies far away across the ice shelf, feeding is difficult, changeovers at the nest infrequent and long fasts (up to 120 days in males, and 64 days in females) essential. Their large size enables storage of the big fat reserves needed for this. Nevertheless the crucial adaptation is the 25–50 percent reduction in individual heat loss achieved by adults and chicks huddling

in large groups (up to 5,000 birds at 10 per sq m, about 11 per sq yd) and reducing activity to a minimum. The huddle as a whole moves very slowly downwind and windward birds move along the flanks and then into the center until they are once again exposed at the rear, so that no birds are continually exposed on the edge of the group. All this is feasible only because Emperor penguins have developed the ability to move with their egg on their feet and cover it (and the young chick) with a pouch-like fold of abdominal skin. They have also suppressed nearly all aggressive behavior.

King penguins, the other species of large penguins, have a very different solution to the problem of breeding in the short summers. They take over a year for a successful breeding attempt and cannot breed more frequently than two years in three. They have two main laying seasons, November–December and February–March, and most of the time any colony contains adults, eggs and chicks at many stages of molt, incubation and growth respectively. From the eggs laid in late November–early December chicks are reared to 80 percent of adult weight by June and fed sporadically (fasts of two months or so with an overall chick weight-loss of about 40 percent) through the winter until September when regular feeding resumes until the chicks depart in November–December. The adults then have to molt and cannot lay again until February–March. Chicks produced from these eggs are much smaller when the winter comes (and many die), and they do not fledge until the following January–February.　　　　　　　　　　JPC

▲ **An army of Emperors.** As antarctic conditions become severe as many as 6,000 male Emperor penguins huddle together when incubating eggs. If eggs are to hatch successfully they must be protected perfectly by the male's pouch-like fold of skin for about two months. When crossing crevices, for example, the birds have to fall on their chests and push themselves along with their flippers.

▶ **A fat start in life.** By the time King penguin chicks hatch there is not enough time left for the chicks to reach the stage of development at which they can fledge. They therefore sit out the winter and fledge in the spring. During the last weeks of the fall they are fattened by their parents so they may have enough reserves to see them through the harshest part of winter when the parents will only feed them infrequently. By the time winter starts this chick may weigh as much as 13kg (28.6lb).

LOONS OR DIVERS

Order: Gaviiformes
Family: Gaviidae.
Four species belonging to the genus *Gavia*.
Distribution: N America, Greenland, Iceland, Eurasia.

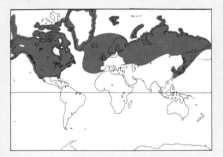

Habitat: in summer, lakes in boreal forest, taiga, tundra; most spend the winter at sea.

Size: ranges from length 53–69cm (21–27in), weight 1–2.4kg (2.2–5.3lb) in the Red-throated loon to length 76–93cm (30–37in), weight 4.4–6.4kg (9.7–14lb) in the Yellow-billed loon. Females are slightly smaller than males.

Plumage: adults of all species have white underparts. Upper parts of Common, Yellow-billed and Arctic loons are basic black with white spots on the back and wings; the Red-throated loon is sooty brown with small light spots. All species have white, vertical stripes on the neck (the pattern differing according to species). The throat of the Red-throated loon is chestnut-red. In winter adults and juveniles have gray upper parts with lighter markings. Newly hatched chicks have dense down, dark gray to black above, white on the belly.

Voice: tremolos, yodels, wails, clucks, mews, cackling. Varies considerably between species.

Eggs: usually 2 (occasionally 1, rarely 3); medium to dark brown to olive with few to many blackish spots or blotches. Weight: for eggs of Common loon 120–170g (4.2–6oz). Size: from 7.3 × 4.5cm (2.8 × 1.7in) for the Red-throated loon to 9 × 5cm (3.5 × 1.9in) for the Common and Yellow-billed loons. Incubation: 24–29 days.

Diet: mainly fish; also crayfish, shrimp, leeches, frogs.

Species: **Arctic loon** or **Black-throated diver** (*Gavia arctica*), **Common loon** or **Great northern diver** (*G. immer*), **Red-throated loon** or **Red-throated diver** (*G. stellata*), **Yellow-billed loon** or **White-billed diver** (*G. adamsii*).

Loons are aquatic predators, so highly specialized for swimming and diving that they are unable to walk properly on land. Apart from penguins of the southern hemisphere, they are the most specialized diving birds. Propelled by foot, they are fast and maneuverable under water where they readily capture fish. They regulate buoyancy by adjusting feathers, the volume of air in air sacs and the amount of air in the lungs. They nest on inland, freshwater lakes in summer. The majority migrate to coastal waters for winter, although some overwinter on large, ice-free lakes in the southern parts of their range.

Loons are mainly associated with clear, oxygen-laden (oligotrophic) lakes of the northern hemisphere, in areas with a past history of extensive glacial coverage. These include thousands of lakes in the northern forests, taiga and open tundra scraped out of rock by retreating glaciers.

Although adult loons cannot walk on land, chicks can waddle upright and have been known on rare occasions to negotiate several hundred meters between tarns or lakes while parents prompted from air or water. Loons are characteristically lone nesters within a large defended territory but colonial nesting has been documented for the Red-throated loon and the Arctic loon. Territories range in size from 6ha to more than 80ha (15–200 acres).

All loons exhibit a strong preference for nesting away from the mainland shore, whether on island, bog islet, stone outcropping or log, although Arctic and Red-throated loons frequently nest in coves or promontories of small tundra lakes that lack islands.

With flight feathers renewed, small groups (packs) of loons may join others and coalesce into flocks of several hundred on certain large bodies of water prior to and during spring and fall migration. Arrival on the breeding ground is usually in singles, pairs (apparently more common in the Arctic loon) or small loosely associated groups. Territories are often reoccupied as soon as sufficient water is ice-free for landing. Loons return to the same territory and often reuse the same nest.

Courtship appears to be a prominent ritualized display only in the Red-throated loon. Copulation is secretive, on shore in the nest area. Both parents may construct the nest, incubate and tend the young. Young loons are well developed (precocial) and leave the nest within a day of hatching, weather permitting. They are brooded on the parents' backs and under a wing if weather is inclement or danger threatens. Loon chicks can dive within a day of hatching, and their expertise rapidly increases. Although chicks peck at and eat small invertebrates such as mosquitoes, black flies and a variety of aquatic insects, they are fed by both parents. Food is fresh-caught (not regurgitated) and comprised of invertebrates or fish (preferred when available) which are taken from the parents' bills. Common loon chicks are weaned from parental feeding between their 8th and 11th weeks, but they occasionally still take fish from parents until they migrate.

Adult nonbreeders and unsuccessful breeders form small social groups (usually 4–12 birds) on many lakes in summer, although certain large lakes seasonally have groups of 80–250 loons. These social groups are frequently joined by the resident parent not tending chicks. Juveniles do not join these groups. In fact they are readily attacked by strange adults.

Although loons can remain submerged for several minutes most dives last less than a minute. Underwater progress is casual while hunting but speed can be sustained while pursuing prey or fleeing. Several hundred meters can readily be traversed underwater and although most foraging occurs in relatively shallow depths with good light, ie

▲ **The streamlined, beautiful head** of an Arctic loon.

◄ **Leg movements in swimming.** Loon legs and feet are completely adapted to swimming. Only the lower part of the leg protrudes, from a position to the rear of the body that gives it great propulsive power which is transmitted by the webbed feet. In each cycle of swimming movements the head and eyes remain almost stationary in relation to the surroundings during the brief period of recovery and thrust of the legs. This allows the loon to see more readily the slightest movement of potential prey. When swimming at a moderate speed this cycle takes 0.8–1.3 seconds.

in the top 10m (33ft), Common loons have become enmeshed in nets at depths greater than 80m (265ft). Loons are visual hunters, and capture fish crosswise in the bill. As with other predators of vertebrates, atypical behavior among prey is quickly singled out for attack. Loons are opportunistic foragers; their prevalent prey is fish, of any species or size that can be captured and ingested, usually less than 15cm (7in) but reportedly even over 40cm (16in). Crustaceans such as crayfish and shrimp, leeches and frogs are also eaten. Loons appear to ingest vegetation only when ill. Digestion in their powerful gizzard is aided by pea-sized stones.

Loons are highly specialized final predators in an aquatic food web composed of complex, interdependent activities among prey and predator, from microscopic plants and animals through fishes to the loons. Hence any degradation of the environment adversely affects loons. In parts of their breeding grounds in North America and Europe they have been reduced in numbers or eliminated because of loss of nesting habitat, disturbances of nesting and brooding areas, excessive aquatic plant growth, unpredictable and extensive water-level fluctuations and toxicity. Large numbers have occasionally succumbed to botulism and considerable numbers are destroyed by oil slicks on coastal waters in winter. Acid rain is also destroying the food chain in thousands of lakes, particularly for the Common loon in eastern North America.

In spite of adversities, loons are reasonably numerous throughout much of their traditional range.   JB

GREBES

Order: Podicipediformes
Family: Podicipedidae.
Twenty species in 6 genera.
Distribution: N and S America, Eurasia, Africa, Australasia.

Habitat: freshwater lakes and marshes; may use coastal waters in winter.

Size: ranges from length 34cm (13.4in), weight 130g (4.6oz) in the Little grebe to length 48cm (18.9in), weight 1,400g (49oz) in the Great crested grebe. Females are slightly smaller.

Plumage: upperparts mostly drab gray or brown shading to white on the underbelly; for breeding the head, throat and neck are often brightly colored. Some species have bright, colored tufts and crests on the head, used in courtship.

Voice: a variety of whistling and barking calls; species living in dense vegetation are often more vocal.

Eggs: usually 2–6; white or cream. Incubation: 20–30 days.

Diet: aquatic insects, crustacea, mollusks and fish.

Species include: **Atitlan grebe** [E] (*Podilymbus gigas*), **Black-necked grebe** (*Podiceps nigricollis*), **Colombian grebe** [E] (*P. andinus*), **Great crested grebe** (*P. cristatus*), **Hooded grebe** [R] (*P. gallardoi*), **Little grebe** (*Tachybaptus ruficollis*), **Madagascar red-necked grebe** [V] (*T. rufolavatus*), **Puna grebe** [R] (*Podiceps taczanowskii*), **Red-necked grebe** (*P. grisegena*), **Silver grebe** (*P. occipitalis*), **Slavonian grebe** (*P. auritus*), **Western grebe** (*Aechmophorus occidentalis*).

[E] Endangered.   [V] Vulnerable.   [R] Rare.

G REBES are an old group, having been inhabitants of lakes and marshes for around 70 million years, and have representative species on all continents except Antarctica.

Thanks to anatomical adaptations grebes are well suited to the rigors of aquatic life and underwater hunting. They have a dense plumage of some 20,000 feathers to keep them dry and warm. Their feet are at the extreme hind end of the body—the tail is reduced to a downy tuft—and have exceptional flexibility in the ankle and toe joints, allowing the feet to pivot in all directions and to be used, simultaneously, as "paddles" and "rudders." The lobes on the toes further aid maneuverability—a diving grebe can move at about 2m (6.6ft) a second and turn extremely quickly. Grebes can sink low in the water by expelling the insulating air from between their feathers and emptying their air sacs (reservoirs of air): this reduces the energy needed to keep them submerged and allows them to dive silently when hunting and to hide submerged when frightened. Dives typically last 10–40 seconds.

Feet placed so far back make even standing difficult: grebes only stand at the nest and, if obliged to reach nests "stranded" by falling water levels, frequently fall when trying to walk; they need a long take-off run across water to become airborne on their long thin wings, but fly quickly with rapid beats and trailing feet; they maneuver poorly in flight. Grebes rarely fly except on migration and a few species are flightless. They may migrate long distances, often flying at night, when they sometimes mistake wet roads for rivers, land on them, and become stranded.

Grebes are carnivorous, eating mainly insects and fish but also some mollusks and crustacea, taking the latter from off and around aquatic water plants or, more rarely, from the bottom. The larger species chase fish, and the Western grebe of North America spears (rather than grabs) fish with its dagger-shaped bill. Grebe species form "guilds" of aquatic carnivores, vying with each other to exploit foods more efficiently.

In Eurasia, for example, the Great crested grebe occurs mostly on open water, eating fish that it usually catches within a few meters of the surface, whereas Little grebes occur on small ponds covered with floating water-plants which they are small enough to dive among. Intermediate-sized species, such as Red-necked and Slavonian grebes, may be restricted to lake habitats where they do not compete with larger species. For

example, the Slavonian is the only grebe that breeds in Iceland and there it eats many fish as well as insects, but in Alaska it restricts its diet largely to insects and fish fry due to competition from the Red-necked grebe; similarly in eastern Siberia and Alaska a long-billed race of the Red-necked grebe has evolved which takes larger fish than its European counterpart which has to compete with Great crested grebes for food.

The courtship behavior of grebes is very striking, involving complex sequences of elaborate, ritualized postures and, particularly in *Podiceps* species, much use of the erectile feather ruffs and tufts on the head. Many elements of these complex sequences are shared by many species and considerable progress has been made both in understanding animal behavior and grebes' evolutionary histories by comparing details of their courtships. Sir Julian Huxley's study of Great crested grebe courtship (1914) was a seminal paper in animal behavior. Detailed studies of the courtship of the recently discovered Hooded grebe (1974) have confirmed its close relationship to Black-necked, Silver and Puna grebes. The crucial role that these displays serve in pair formation has been emphasized by recent findings on the Western grebe: this species occurs in two color variants (morphs) that breed in mixed colonies, but only birds of the same color morph will pair together and this segregation is achieved by each morph using a distinctly different "advertising call" to initiate courtship. An interesting feature of grebe displays is that males and females may reverse their normal roles, even to the extent of reverse mountings.

Most grebes are aggressively territorial, but some species nest in colonies. The timing of breeding is flexible—grebes seem adapted to exploit opportunistically a good food supply rather than being tied to a specific season. In Africa Little grebes may appear and start breeding within a few days of unpredictable rain storms producing temporary flood-ponds. The nests are mounds of aquatic vegetation, usually anchored in emergent waterweeds. The chicks hatch asynchronously and are brooded on their parents' backs, even when their parents dive.

Five species of grebe are listed in the *Red Data Book* including all the localized nonflying South American species: of these the Colombian grebe may well already be extinct, but the threat by a hydroelectric scheme to the only lake on which the Atitlan grebe occurs appears to have recently been lifted. PJB

▲ **Waterborne nest.** Unable to move well on land, grebes nest on water. Their nests are simple: weeds, reeds and other vegetation piled up on aquatic plants or formed so that the nest will float on the water itself. Here a female Great crested grebe incubates her eggs, bearing a recently hatched chick on her back, and is visited by her mate.

▶ **Grebe of the north.** There are three kinds of grebe distributions: very restricted ranges, large ones encompassing latitudes from high north to low south, and intermediate ones covering large areas but restricted in latitude. The range of the Slavonian grebe belongs to the latter, the bird being restricted to northern latitudes.

◀ **Complex displays** occur when grebes are courting, though the composition of sequences differs from species to species. In the Great crested grebe mating includes: (1) the discovery display; (2) the head-shaking display; (3) preening; (4) the weed ceremony.

ALBATROSSES AND PETRELS

Order: Procellariiformes
Families: Diomedeidae, Procellariidae,
Hydrobatidae, Pelecanoididae.
Ninety-two species in 23 genera.
Distribution: all oceans.

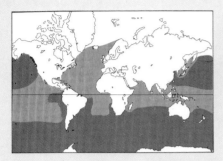

Albatrosses   **Storm petrels**

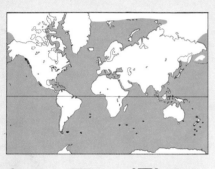

Shearwaters   **Diving petrels**

▶ **Preening** ABOVE is one of the means by
which pairs of albatrosses, such as these Laysan
albatrosses, maintain and reinforce their bond
during the mating season. All but a few birds
have a preen gland, which is normally situated
just in front of the tail base and secretes an oily
liquid. This is then spread with the bill over the
feathers. Preen oil improves the condition of the
feathers, but exactly how it works is not
known.

▶ **Nesting** in *Diomedea* species of albatross
often takes place in large colonies, sometimes of
thousands of birds. Several species, including
the Wandering albatross seen here, build
mound-size constructions of soil or vegetation
on which to form a nest cup lined with feathers
and grasses.

THE **albatross** was the bird of ill omen, the
repository of the souls of drowned
sailors, and consequently to kill one was to
court disaster. Yet paradoxically sailors
were happy to catch and eat albatrosses to
relieve the monotony of life and diet on long
voyages. They must also have spent many
hours admiring the effortless flight of the
albatrosses that followed their ships for
hours with barely a wing-beat. Adaptations
for long-distance flight allow the albatrosses
to exploit the vast spaces of the oceans from
their restricted breeding bases on oceanic
islands. The name albatross comes from the
Portuguese *alcatraz*, used originally for any
large seabird and apparently derived from
the Arabic *al-cadous*, used for the pelican.

Albatrosses are typically associated with
the belt of windswept ocean lying between
the Antarctic and the southern extremities
of America, Africa and Australasia. The
greatest number of individuals and species
occurs between 45 and 70 degrees south,
but they also breed in temperate waters of
the southern hemisphere and a few species
have spread into the North Pacific. The
Waved albatross of the Galapagos and Isla
de la Plata off Ecuador breeds on the equator, but where the climate is under the
influence of the cool Humboldt Current.
Steller's or the Short-tailed albatross (based
on islands off Japan), the Black-footed
albatross (of the northwest Pacific) and the
Laysan albatross (from the Hawaiian archipelago) all breed in the North Pacific. No
albatrosses breed in the North Atlantic.

Albatrosses are distinguished from others
of their order (Procellariiformes) by the position of their tubular external nostrils, which
lie at each side of the base of the bill rather
than being fused on the top of the bill. They
can be split into three convenient groups:
the "great" albatrosses (three species),
which have wingspans averaging 3m
(about 10ft); nine smaller species which are
often referred to as "mollymauks" from the
Dutch *mollemok* which was originally given
to the fulmar; and the all-dark Sooty and
Light-mantled sooty albatrosses, having
relatively long wings and tails and which
are sufficiently different to warrant a separate genus.

From their habit of following ships,
albatrosses are best known as scavengers of
offal thrown overboard. They have broad
diets, including oceanic water striders and
by-the-wind sailors (plankton) but detailed
analysis of diets shows that fish, squid and
crustaceans predominate. Prey is caught
mainly by seizing at the surface, but occasionally by plunging in the manner of gannets. They also feed during darkness, when
many marine organisms come to the surface. The proportions of prey types differ
between species and these profoundly affect
the breeding biology of the species.

Albatrosses are long-lived, with an
average life-span of 30 years, but slow
breeders. They are physiologically capable
of breeding at three or four years but they
do not usually start for several years after
this. Some may not breed until 15 years old.
When they first mature birds appear on the
breeding grounds for a short while towards
the end of the breeding season, and thereafter spend more time ashore courting prospective mates. When a pair has been
established they usually remain together
until the death of one, and "divorce" occurs
only after several breeding failures.

At the beginning of the breeding season the male arrives at the colony first and mating occurs on the female's reappearance. Most albatrosses nest in colonies, sometimes numbering thousands of pairs with close-packed nests, but Sooty and Long-mantled sooty albatrosses nest alone on cliff ledges. In several species the nest is a pile of soil and vegetation which may be so large that the adults find difficulty in climbing on. The tropical albatrosses make a scanty nest and the Waved albatross shuffles about with its egg on its feet.

The single egg is incubated in alternate shifts of several days by both parents, from about 65 days in the smaller species to 79 days in the Royal albatross. The newly hatched chick is brooded at first and later guarded. Throughout its life in the nest it receives regular feeds from the parents. Once brooding has finished the adults remain ashore only long enough to identify their chicks and transfer a meal of undigested marine animals and lipid-rich oil derived from the digestion of prey. Black-footed albatross chicks frequently wander up to 30m (about 100ft) from the nest and seek shade during the day, but they rush back when a parent arrives with food. Fledging takes from 120 days in Black-browed and Yellow-nosed albatrosses to 278 days in the Wandering albatross. The extremely long nesting period of the latter (356 days including incubation) means that it can attempt to breed only in alternate years

The 4 Families of the Order Procellariiformes   E Endangered.

Albatrosses
Family: Diomedeidae
Fourteen species in 2 genera.
Subantarctic, S America N to Galapagos Islands, S Africa, S Australia and New Zealand, Pacific N to Japan. Islands used for breeding and as bases. Size: ranges from bill–tail length 68–93cm (27–37in), wingspan 178–256cm (70–101in) in the mollymauks to bill–tail length 110–135cm (43–53in), wingspan 250–350cm (98–138in) in the great albatrosses. Plumage: white with dark wingtips; white with dark brow, back, upperwing and tail; uniform darkness. Eggs: 1; white. Incubation: 65–79 days. Diet: fish, crustacea.

Species include: **Amsterdam albatross** (*Diomedea amsterdamensis*), **Black-browed albatross** (*D. melanophris*), **Black-footed albatross** (*D. nigripes*), **Gray-headed albatross** (*D. chrysostoma*), **Laysan albatross** (*D. immutabilis*), **Light-mantled sooty albatross** (*Phoebetria palpebrata*), **Royal albatross** (*D. epomophora*), **Sooty albatross** (*Phoebetria fusca*), **Steller's albatross** or **Short-tailed albatross** E (*Diomedea albatrus*), **Wandering albatross** (*D. exulans*), **Waved albatross** (*D. irrorata*), **Yellow-nosed albatross** (*D. chlororhynchos*).

Shearwaters and petrels
Family: Procellariidae
Fifty-four species in 12 genera.
All oceans. Size: length 26–87cm (10–34in); wingspan maximum 2m (about 6ft); weight 130g–4kg (5oz–8.8lb). Plumage: most species black, brown or gray, and white; a few are all light or dark. Voice: unmusical; often nocturnal cacophony at colonies. Eggs: 1; white. Incubation: 43–60 days. Diet: fish, squid, crustacea, offal.

Species include: **Audubon's shearwater** (*Puffinus lherminieri*), **Blue petrel** (*Halobaena caerulea*), **cahow** or **Bermuda petrel** E (*Pterodroma cahow*), **Dark-rumped petrel** (*P. phaeopygia*), **Greater shearwater** (*Puffinus gravis*), **Manx shearwater** (*P. puffinus*), **Northern fulmar** (*Fulmarus glacialis*), **Short-tailed shearwater** (*Puffinus tenuirostris*), **Snow petrel** (*Pagodroma nivea*), **Southern fulmar** (*Fulmarus glacialis*), **Southern giant petrel** (*Macronectes giganteus*). Total threatened species: 8.

Storm petrels
Family: Hydrobatidae
Twenty species in 8 genera.
All oceans except Arctic seas. Size: length 14–26cm (5.5–10in); wingspan 32–56cm (12.6–22in); weight 25–68g (0.9–2.4oz). Plumage: chiefly dark brown, black or gray and white. Voice: some species "purr" and have chuckles at breeding colonies. Eggs: 1; white sometimes with speckles. Incubation: 40–50 days. Diet: small fish, squid, plankton, fish scraps.

Species include: **Hornby's storm petrel** (*Oceanodroma hornbyi*), **Leach's storm petrel** (*O. leucorhoa*), **Least storm petrel** (*Halocyptena microsoma*), **Madeiran storm petrel** (*O. castro*), **Wedge-rumped storm petrel** (*O. tethys*), **White-faced storm petrel** (*Pelagodroma marina*), **White-throated storm petrel** (*Nesofregetta albigularis*), **Wilson's storm petrel** (*Oceanites oceanicus*).

Diving petrels
Family: Pelecanoididae
Four species of the genus *Pelecanoides*.
Subantarctic, S America as far N as Peru, S Australia, New Zealand. Marine, breeding on islands and coasts. Size: bill to tail length 18–25cm (7–10in), wingspan 30–38cm (11.8–15in), weight 105–146g (3.4–4.7oz). Plumage: black above, white below. Eggs: 1; white. Incubation: 45–53 days. Diet: small marine organisms.

Species: **Common diving petrel** (*Pelecanoides urinatrix*), **Georgian diving petrel** (*P. georgicus*), **Magellan diving petrel** (*P. magellani*), **Peruvian diving petrel** (*P. garnotii*).

since, after breeding, it must have a "rest" period during which it molts. At least six species are known to breed biennially. These include all the "great" albatrosses, the two sooty albatrosses and the Gray-headed albatross along with the mollymauks (see box).

Breeding colonies of albatrosses are protected by their isolation on islands with no natural predators, but discovery by seafarers led to losses through egg-collecting and the killing of adults, followed by massive depredations for feathers which were used in clothing and bedding. Steller's albatrosses were almost wiped out by feather-collectors; huge numbers of birds were killed; and a tiny colony of 20 pairs on Toroshima, off Japan, contains the survivors. The Laysan albatross became a conservation problem when Midway Atoll was turned into a military airbase. The birds nested around the runways and installations and there were many deaths from collisions with aerial wires and aircraft.

Albatrosses face more insidious threats at sea. Contamination by oil spills and chemical pollution can occur, and albatrosses are known to suffer as "incidental catches" in fishing operations. As southern seas become exploited by the world's fishing fleets there is also the possibility that direct competition for krill or other marine species will affect the albatrosses, as well as other animals.

RWB/PAP

The **shearwater** family has one of the widest distributions of any bird family, ranging from the Snow petrels which nest 250km (about 150mi) inland in Antarctica to the Northern fulmar which breeds as far north as there is land in the Arctic. Although several species are localized and rare, others are abundant and undertake extensive migrations. Overall they are an extremely successful family. Some eat plankton, others dead whales, but the bulk catch small fish and squid at the sea surface or by underwater pursuit. Although there is a great variation between species in plumage and habits, the family divides neatly into four groups: fulmars, prions, gadfly petrels and true shearwaters.

The fulmars are a cold-water group, only venturing into the subtropics along cold-water currents. There are five species in the southern hemisphere, which is where the group probably evolved because the single northern species (the Northern fulmar) is closely related to the Southern fulmar. Most species are medium-sized, but the two sibling species of giant petrels (wingspan 2m, 6ft) are as large as some albatrosses.

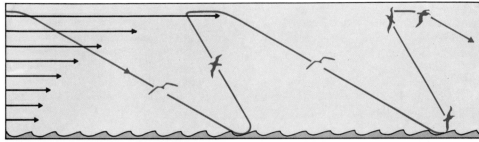

▲ **Riding the wind.** Albatrosses are adapted more for gliding than for flying, and have developed a gliding practice that makes best use of wind conditions in the southern seas. They take advantage of the phenomenon whereby wind near the sea surface moves at a slower speed than higher currents thanks to drag on the sea surface.

An albatross glides downwind from a height of about 15m (about 50ft), losing height. Just before it hits the water it turns into the wind and is blown back up to its original height by increasing wind speed.

▼ **Representative species of albatrosses and petrels.** (1) A Light-mantled sooty albatross (*Diomedea palpebrata*) with chick. (2) A Southern giant petrel (*Macronectes giganteus*) feeding on a dead seal. (3) A Cory's shearwater (*Puffinus diomedea*) with chick. (4) A Great shearwater (*Puffinus gravis*). (5) An immature Black-browed albatross (*Diomedea melanophris*).

There is speculation that the albatross shot in Coleridge's "Rime of the Ancient Mariner" (1798) was, in fact, a giant petrel. Fulmars' bills are large (enormously so in giant petrels) and broad. They once probably fed mainly on plankton, but some species now eat waste from fishing and whaling fleets; the exploitation of this new food resource has led to spectacular increases in numbers. Fulmars are fairly active on land and giant petrels can walk with upright shanks (tarsi); all other groups in this family shuffle with shanks flat on the ground. In flight they alternate flapping and gliding.

Prions (including the Blue petrel) are another southern group and breed mainly on subantarctic islands, but move into slightly warmer waters at other times. These small birds (length 26cm, 10in) all look very similar, blue-gray above, white below with a dark "W" across the wings. All eat small plankton which they filter out with plates (lamellae) on the bill, but the bill dimensions vary greatly suggesting subtle differences in diet. Some species pick fish from the surface while those with broader beaks hydroplane their way through the surface water.

Prions congregate in areas of high plankton density and vast flocks typically wheel low over the sea. They were once known as whale birds because they frequently occurred in the presence of whales.

Gadfly petrels are larger species (length 26–46cm, 10–18in) and are difficult to identify as some species have different color phases or variations. Most are black (or gray) and white above and white below with white faces; others are all dark. The short and stout bill with a powerful hook and sharp cutting edge is used for gripping and cutting up small squid and fish. They occur in the southern and tropical oceans. Some are restricted to single islands (eg the cahow) while other species roam far and wide. They are strong fliers and typically arc high above the sea. Their movements are imperfectly known but some Pacific species migrate across the equator from one hemisphere to another.

The true shearwaters and petrels are small to large birds (length 27–55cm, 10.6–21.6in); most are dark above and black or white underneath. Many species have a black cap and only one species has white on the head. Shearwaters are widespread and very mobile and pose considerable taxonomic problems; for example, should the similar, but not identical, black-and-white shearwaters breeding in the northeast Atlantic, Mediterranean, Hawaii, east Pacific and New Zealand be considered subspecies of the Manx shearwater or separate species? (A shearwater ringed in Britain was once recovered in Australia, and the whole of the British population migrates to South America each year: distance is thus

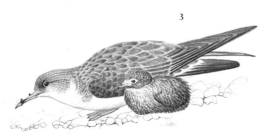

no barrier to dispersal. Indeed colonies are sometimes formed far outside the normal range, and during the last 20 years the Manx shearwater has started to breed off the coast of North America.)

Shearwater bills are proportionately longer and thinner than those of other groups but they still eat mainly fish and squid. Prey is caught either by the bird crashing down onto it or by swimming after it underwater.

All the species in the family are colonial to a greater or lesser extent. Sometimes this is due to limited suitable habitat; for example, Antarctic-nesting Southern giant petrels are forced to nest on the few patches of stones kept snow free by the wind, but it usually is by choice as birds enter and try to nest in seemingly overcrowded areas even with apparently suitable, but unused habitat nearby. Colony sites are as diverse as the species themselves, but safety from predators is a prerequisite.

Of the fulmars only the Snow petrel nests under cover; other species make a scrape on a cliff ledge or incubate the egg in the open. Birds discourage intruders by spitting or regurgitating foul-smelling oil, hence the old name of "stinker" for the giant petrel. Colonies tend to be small and nests dispersed. All the prions nest underground among boulders or in burrows they dig themselves; colonies may be very large. Except for a few surface-living species on Pacific islands, gadfly petrels and shearwaters nest in burrows or under rocks. Some line the nest chamber with vegetation; others make a mere token of a nest. Typically colonies are large and found on islands, less commonly among forests or high on mainland mountains. Whereas open nesters come and go from their nests by day, most burrow nesters are nocturnal at the colonies, so as to escape predators. It has recently been demonstrated that some species locate their burrows by smell.

Breeding is remarkably uniform throughout the family. Birds return to the colonies at least a few weeks prior to nesting and reclaim the nest sites used the previous season. Pairs usually remain together from one season to the next, and probably meet again at the nest sites. Adult survival is extremely high (at least 90 percent per annum) and pairs persist for many years. When "divorces" occur, they usually follow unsuccessful breeding. In the weeks prior to laying there are many noisy aerial displays and pairs spend days together at the nest. Many species have a "honeymoon" period, when the female leaves the colony for

about two weeks to feed so as to lay down reserves for the large egg. In some species the male is also away preparing himself for taking the first long incubation stint. However, in others he returns periodically to check the nest site.

In most species breeding is annual and synchronized. The most extreme case is the Short-tailed shearwater, whose colonies span 11 degrees latitude; all of its eggs are laid during a 12-day period with the peak always occurring between 24 and 26 November. In tropical species, which frequent the colonies throughout the year, eggs may be laid in all months. In a few species individuals breed at less than annual intervals but in most species pairs still breed annually. Even more rarely birds at adjacent colonies breed annually but are out of phase.

All species lay a single, very large white egg which varies from 6 percent (in the Giant petrel) to 20 percent (in prions) of the female's weight. Tropical species lay proportionately larger eggs than temperate or polar species, probably because food is often short so that the chick needs bigger food reserves at hatching to carry it over any shortage. Both sexes have a single large central brood patch (ie an area denuded of feathers and rich in blood vessels for transferring heat from parent to egg) and incubate in turn for spells of 1–20 days. Often the male takes the first and longest stint, presumably to let the female go back to sea to recover from laying. Lost eggs are very rarely, usually never, replaced. Eggs are tolerant of chilling, especially those safe in the uniform temperature of a burrow, but chilling can increase the incubation period by up to 25 percent.

The incubation period is long but the range (43–60 days) is less than expected given the great range of egg sizes (25–237g, 0.9–8.4oz). The chick is brooded for the first few days, but may then be left in the burrow to allow both adults to forage. It is fed on a soup of partly digested fish, crustacea, squid etc, and on stomach oil. Growth is rapid until the young may be much heavier than the adult. Burrow-living chicks are often deserted and complete their development on stored fat.

The young, eggs and adults of many species were once considered delicacies and were eaten in large numbers, and their fat was used extensively. Human predation has declined but not stopped. For instance, Great shearwaters are still killed at the colonies on Tristan da Cunha and in wintering grounds in the North Atlantic. Some shearwaters are

▲ Horny pincers. This Hall's giant petrel (*Macronectes halli*) feeds only at sea, including in its diet fish and squid. Not only is its bill powerful and tough but is also equipped with sharp hooks for holding prey.

◄ Screams, wails and choking sounds are among the vocalizations produced by members of the family of shearwaters and petrels. They enable individuals to recognize each other (especially at night), and perhaps also, as with these pairs of Northern fulmars, to assert the possession of territory.

known as muttonbirds and the young of one species, the Short-tailed shearwater are still harvested commercially for their meat; however, there is a strict quota and the harvest has no effect on the population. In contrast several gadfly petrels are seriously threatened by habitat destruction and introduced predators. The cahow or Bermuda petrel is a typical example. Occurring only in Bermuda it once lived inland where it was hunted for food and then killed by pigs, cats and rats. A few pairs survived on offshore rocks but their breeding success was very low because of competition with tropic birds for nest-sites. Management has prevented this and the species just hangs on. The Dark-rumped petrel is similarly threatened at both its nesting areas, in the Galapagos by rats and pigs, dogs and farming, in Hawaii by mongooses and rats. Several species of shearwaters and petrels will need help if they are to survive.   MPH

Storm petrels are the smallest and most delicate of seabirds. Their name may be derived from their habit of sheltering in the lee of a ship during severe storms and a corruption of St Peter since several common species appear to walk on the water while feeding.

Absent from brackish water and the Arctic, storm petrels can otherwise be found throughout the oceans. They are most abundant in the cold waters around Antarctica and in areas of marine upwelling, like the Humboldt Current off Peru. Some species occur only in the most desert-like areas of low biological productivity of the central tropical oceans, where there is apparently little food. A few species have very restricted distributions, others undertake long migrations. Wilson's storm petrel which breeds around Antarctica spends its non-breeding time throughout the Indian, central Pacific and Atlantic oceans north to Greenland. Storm petrels are not worried by man and many species feed in ships' wakes and a few come around fishing boats to pick up scraps.

Storm petrels are immediately recognizable by their fairly small but strongly hooked beak, pronounced tubular nostrils which are fused together, and a steep forehead. Despite the absence of color, many are striking birds with almost black plumage and white rump. Others are beautiful shades of brown and gray. The family is clearly divisible into two groups which presumably evolved in different hemispheres but which now overlap in the tropics. Species of the northern group, typified by Leach's storm petrel, are black and white and most have pointed wings, relatively short legs and feed by swooping down and picking food from the surface, rather like terns. Species in the southern group typified by the White-faced storm petrel, have more variable plumage (including species with several color forms), rounded wings and long legs which often are held down as the birds bounce or walk on the sea-surface as they feed.

All species are colonial and most breed on isolated islands lacking ground predators. However, Hornby's storm petrels breed well inland high in the Andes. Except for the Wedge-rumped storm petrel, all species visit colonies at night or, in high latitudes, when light density is lowest. Pairs defend a burrow among rocks, tree roots or (rarely) under a bush and remain together from one season to the next. In temperate regions breeding is fairly well synchronized and seasonal while in the tropics it often appears prolonged with birds present throughout the year. However, in the Galapagos Islands the Madeiran storm petrel has two breeding seasons a year due to two quite separate populations each of which breeds annually but at a different time.

The single white egg is laid on the ground and incubated for 1–6 days by each bird in turn for a total of 40–50 days. If lost the egg is only very rarely replaced that season, probably because the egg is so large (up to 25 percent of the female's weight) that it would take too long to produce another.

The young is fed a mixture of partly digested food and stomach oil. It fledges alone, and at night, after 59–73 days. Although fed less frequently near to fledging it is not, as is often said, deserted and the adults may visit the burrow after it has left.

Storm petrels eat mainly planktonic crustacea, squid and fish and oily scraps picked up in flight (indeed storm petrels rarely sit on the water).

In some species many immatures visit other colonies before they breed (usually 4–5 years) and these can even be attracted to other places by playing tape recordings of the purring calls. The potential conservation value of this has been demonstrated by the National Audubon Society of the USA who persuaded Leach's storm petrel to nest in artificial burrows on an island where they had never bred before.   MPH

One of the amazing sights in the southern seas is of a small flock of **diving petrels** flying through a steep wave, plunging in one side and coming out the other, or erupting from the depths of the sea without check. This is possible thanks to the adaptation of wings for swimming underwater. Diving petrels are a southern equivalent of the auk family, resembling the Little auk in particular; both have small wings for swimming underwater and a whirring "bumblebee" flight. There is even a remarkable similarity in the structure of wing bones.

Breeding is confined to cool waters north of 60 degrees south and up the Western side of South America, where the sea temperature is influenced by the cool Humboldt Current. Unlike many other petrels, diving petrels do not appear to make extensive movements, even outside the breeding season; they are usually seen in waters over the continental shelf near the breeding area.

The four species of diving petrels are very

▼ **Representative species of storm and diving petrels.** (1) A Gray-backed storm petrel (*Garrodia nereis*). (2) A Common diving petrel (*Pelecanoides urinatrix*). (3) A Wilson's storm petrel (*Oceanites oceanicus*). (4) Georgian diving petrels (*Pelecanoides georgicus*) flying into waves. (5) Head of a White-faced storm petrel (*Pelagodroma marina*).

similar in size and plumage, which makes identification difficult unless the bird is in the hand and the variable amounts of gray or white on the upper side can be seen. Only the Magellan diving petrel is distinctive with its white collar; it also has a distinguishable juvenile which lacks the white fringes on feathers on the back.

Diving petrels chase their prey by swimming underwater and feed mainly within the upper 10m (33ft). The diet consists of small marine organisms, but detailed analysis has been made only on Common and Georgian diving petrels at South Georgia. There Georgian diving petrels fed their chicks 76 percent krill (by volume) with lesser amounts of amphipod and copepod crustaceans, while Common diving petrels delivered 68 percent copepods and lesser amounts of amphipods and euphausids.

Breeding has similarly been described in detail at South Georgia for Georgian and Common diving petrels. Diving petrels nest in burrows, reexcavated each season. The birds fly in at night, presumably to avoid predation by skuas. The Georgian diving petrel tunnels into bare stony soil above the level of vegetation, whereas Common diving petrels nest in peaty, often waterlogged, soil beneath stands of tussock grass at lower levels. The birds are heard calling at night; the Georgian diving petrel makes a series of harsh "squeaks," the Common diving petrel utters a two-syllable phrase, rendered as *kuaka*, the Maori name of the species.

The Georgian diving petrel lays a single egg between 7 and 31 December which it hatches in late January. The Common diving petrel hatches on average 29 days earlier than the Georgian. Incubation spells last one to three days. After hatching, chicks of the Common diving petrel are brooded for at least 11 days, but Georgian chicks are covered for five days less. The chicks are fed on most nights by one or both parents. The feed contains very little stomach oil, unlike that of other members of the order, and is little digested, possibly because the feed is delivered so quickly after capture. Peruvian diving petrels nest under boulders, and have suffered as islands have been stripped of guano (excrement). The Magellan diving petrel appears to nest in peaty soil.

Colonies of diving petrels can be extensive; there are an estimated two million breeding pairs of Georgian diving petrels on South Georgia and the only current threat is that of predation by introduced rats. For the Peruvian diving petrel, however, the status is unclear. Only a few breeding sites are known; some have been destroyed by the clearance of guano and the future of the species is a cause for concern. RWB/PAP

PELICANS AND GANNETS

Order: Pelecaniformes
Families: Pelecanidae, Phaethontidae, Sulidae, Phalacrocoracidae, Anhingidae, Fregatidae.
Fifty-seven species in 7 genera.
Distribution: worldwide.

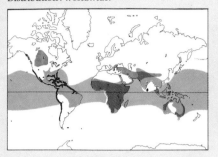

Pelicans   Tropicbirds   Darters

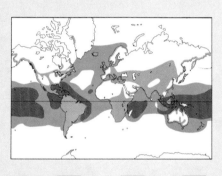

Gannets   Frigatebirds   Cormorants

▶ **Representative species of pelicans and gannets.** (1) A Brown pelican (*Pelecanus occidentalis*), the most colorful of pelicans. (2) A Reed cormorant (*Phalacrocorax africanus*), widespread in Africa. (3) A male Great frigatebird (*Fregata minor*) with his throat-pouch inflated. (4) A male Peruvian booby (*Sula variegata*) pointing to his mate in the sky. (5) Head of a Spotted shag (*Phalacrocorax punctatus*). (6) A Cape gannet (*Morus capensis*). (7) A White-tailed tropicbird (*Phaethon lepturus*). (8) An African darter (*Anhinga rufa*) swimming.

▶ **Pelicans afloat** OVERLEAF. A gathering of Australian pelicans.

With their long bill, saggy throat (gular) pouch, large size and lugubrious manner **pelicans** have attracted man's attention for centuries. The pelican has served as a symbol for Christian piety, based on a myth that the adult slits its own breast to feed its starving young with blood. The origins of this myth are obscure. Today the image of a pelican is one of the most widely used animal caricatures for commercial enterprises, such as hotels, restaurants, toys and books.

Pelicans are primarily birds of warm climates, although the desert regions where some species live become cold at night. Breeding occurs mainly in isolated areas away from mammalian (and especially human) predation and disturbance. Because pelicans eat fish exclusively they must breed near a ready and abundant fish supply. However, with their good flying ability and aptitude for using thermal updrafts they may commute hundreds of kilometers on a daily basis from their protected nesting areas to lakes with abundant fish. They eat fish ranging from a few grams to 0.5kg (1.1lb) which may be over 30cm (1ft) long.

The pelican family is divided into two groups, based on color of plumage and nesting habitats. The first group of basically all-white birds (Australian, Great white, Dalmatian and American white pelicans) nest on the ground in dense colonies. The second group (Brown, Pink-backed, and Spot-billed pelicans) have predominately gray or brown plumage and nest in trees. All species have distinct pouch and facial skin colors, which become intensely vivid prior to the breeding season and serve as both attractants and indicators of sexual readiness. Males are larger in all species, most noticeably in their weight and bill length. The young of all species are very noisy, yet adults are essentially silent. Young have either black or white down, according to species.

Courtship activities of all species are similar, with the male picking out the nest site and performing an "advertising" display which attracts a female and which is distinct in each species. Pelicans do not have a highly developed behavioral repertoire, probably because of the restrictions of having such a long bill. Once a pair bond is formed overt communication between members is minimal. Though pelicans are always colonial and often nest in clumped groups, there does not appear to be any established social hierarchy. Interactions

occur merely between individual birds. After the male has gathered the nesting material and the female built the nest, members of the pair cooperate in all nesting activities, including incubation and feeding of the growing chicks. Young are not fed once they fly away from the nesting colonies, although in the ground nesters individual young may receive food when they have wandered far from the actual nest site, but only from their own parents.

The marine Brown pelican feeds exclusively by diving for fish, sometimes from great heights. The other species either feed individually from the water's surface or "communally" by herding schools of fish and then synchronously scooping them up. Whole fish are fed to nestlings. Contrary to the famous lines about the pelican by Dixon Lanier Merritt ("it can keep in its beak enough food for a week") fish are not kept in the pouch for any length of time. The pouch is used as a dip net to catch fish, which are soon swallowed into the stomach, at the center of gravity, so that the birds can maintain their balance while flying.

Pelicans are long-lived, one living in a zoo for 54 years. It is known that in the wild many pelicans live 15–25 years. Most individuals probably begin to breed at three or four years of age. Food supply is the overwhelming factor involved in the onset and success of breeding. In tropical climes nesting can occur throughout the year. Temperate species nest in the "spring," when daylength increases. However, temperature is an important controlling factor; cold inhibits nesting.

The length of the pelican pair bond is unknown, but monogamy during the breeding season is essential because both members of a pair must meet the food requirements of the rapidly growing young. Occasionally two or three young can be raised. However, the more usual situation is the raising of only one young and some species virtually never raise more than one. Eggs are laid asynchronously with two or three days between eggs. Incubation begins with the laying of the first egg and lasts the same time for each egg. Thus the first sibling to hatch has advantages of age and size when feeding: these older chicks can take most of the food supply from the adults. If the parents cannot supply sufficient food for all the nestlings the smaller young starve. The adults must also bring enough food to enable the young to lay down stores of body fat for when they are first independent and developing the coordination of nerve and impulses and muscles necessary for feeding

▲ Diving for fish. All pelicans catch fish in their throat pouch but only the Brown pelican dives into water to take its prey. Each dive seems to be made to capture a particular fish. On sighting its prey (1), the pelican enters a dive, pulling back its wings to form the wings and back into the shape of a triangle (2 and 3). As the bill enters the water, legs and wings are thrust back, increasing speed (4).

As it comes into the water the pelican positions the mandibles of its beak above and below the fish whilst the throat pouch expands (5), trapping the fish. The bird then pulls its body and head above the water, enabling water to drain from the pouch. The bill is then lifted from the water and the fish swallowed. Since the water in the pouch can weigh more than the bird, it has to drain the pouch before it can move. It can take the pelican almost a minute to drain the water.

themselves. The vast majority of the young do not survive their first year out of the nest.

Two species of pelicans, the Dalmatian and the Spot-billed, are among the more endangered large birds of the world. Only 500–1,400 breeding pairs of Dalmatians still exist, in 19 colony sites between eastern Europe and China. Half the population breeds in the USSR. This species has been declining in both numbers and the extent of its range for the past century. Predation and human disturbance in colonies and flooding of nests appear to be the major factors causing the population decline.

The Spot-billed pelican is presently confined to four known colonies in India with fewer than 400 pairs and 23 colonies in Sri Lanka with 900 pairs. This species was once widespread in Asia with many nesting sites having thousands of pairs. Pesticides are implicated in the recent decline, but habitat destruction and disturbance in colonies by humans are also major problems. A decline in food availability is also a factor.

Little is known about either species and only concerted efforts at conservation and research will preserve these magnificent birds.   EAS/RWS

Gannets and **boobies** (or sulids)—large seabirds breeding from the Arctic circle through the tropics to the edge of sub-Antarctica—are notable for their dramatic plunge-diving, gaudy colors, teeming colonies and boldness (often to their undoing). All species share a basic body-plan, adapted for plunge-diving and for catching fish underwater: a tapered body, long wings and tail, a long bill with serrations on the cutting edges and a sharp point, occluded nostrils and shock-absorbing air sacs. Refining this uniform arrangement, however, there has been a wide range of further adaptations in response to different climates and habitats. Ecological adaptations are particularly visible in breeding arrangements. Where food supplies are abundant, reliable and easily exploited adults are able to feed larger broods. The Peruvian booby, which lives near the richest fishing area in the world, the Humboldt upwelling off Peru and northern Chile, usually raises three or four young. Blue-footed boobies, which live on the fringes of the upwelling areas, often have two or three young. All other members of the family usually raise just one young, though two of the tropical boobies (the Masked and Brown boobies) often lay two eggs, but within a few days of hatching one chick will always kill the other, regardless of the availability of food. This adaptation

seems to ensure that one stronger chick, rather than two weaker ones, has the opportunity to become independent. The laying of a second egg also ensures that a chick will survive should the first to hatch die from temporary famine or some other cause. (Famines are a recurring but unpredictable feature of tropical seas.) The other two tropical species of boobies (the Red-footed and Abbott's boobies) lay a single egg but provide for the survival of their offspring by producing large eggs with greater food reserves, so the chicks are more robust when they hatch. Also, the free-flying young continue to be fed for several weeks or months. The gannets also lay single eggs, but as they live where food is relatively abundant they feed their chicks well enough for them to become independent at an earlier stage than boobies, ie when they become free-flying. Until they become proficient at hunting for food the young of these species live partly off reserves of fat.

In temperate areas (eg where the Atlantic gannets live) breeding is a seasonal activity, but in the tropics, where climate and the availability of food do not occur in seasonal patterns, boobies may lay in any month.

The availability of food also influences the frequency with which sulids breed, which (for successful cycles) varies from once every nine or ten months in the Brown and Blue-footed boobies to once every two years in Abbott's booby.

▲ **Pelicans en masse.** These Great white pelicans live and breed in colonies that can vary in size from as few as 50 birds to as many as 40,000.

◄ **Pelicans in pod.** Three weeks after hatching pelican chicks become able to walk. There then follows a period of 8–10 weeks when they live in groups or "pods." Each chick, however, continues to be fed by its own parents, who provide regurgitated liquid matter in their bills. By this means chicks put on so much weight that they become heavier than an adult. At this point they are deserted and have to fly out into the world alone. These are Brown pelican chicks.

Sulids may expect to live about 20 years, though some individuals may last as long as 40 years. (The normal life span of most boobies is slightly less than that of gannets.)

After they have fledged (at about 90 days in the Atlantic gannet but about 150 days in Abbott's booby) all young sulids except gannets remain dependent on their parents for a further period of weeks or months. They then spend a period as nomads. Breeding normally begins within 2–5 years. Boobies generally breed at a younger age than gannets, and females at a younger age than males. Both gannets and boobies usually return to their natal colonies to breed, engaging in conspicuous displays when reestablishing their territories and forming pairs. After Atlantic gannets have begun to breed they normally attempt to breed every year, for as long as they retain their mate. Ninety-five percent of gannets remain faithful to their partner and to their nest-site. All species of booby except Abbott's booby,

however, change both partner and site from time to time, occasionally taking "rest" years. (It is not known whether partners remate after such a break.) Between breeding cycles all adult gannets and boobies disperse.

Today all species of gannets and boobies are having to cope with a number of difficulties, principally disturbance, pollution, introduced predators and the effects of man on their food supply, and are doing so with differing success. The Australasian and Atlantic gannets are increasing, the latter at about 3 percent per year, but the African gannet is probably declining. The Masked, Brown and Red-footed boobies have had to face extensive slaughter of adults and young, perhaps for tens of thousands of years. In this connection the tree-nesting Red-footed booby may have been at an advantage over the ground-nesting Masked and Brown boobies and is more numerous. The Peruvian booby is a classic case of a sea

The 6 Families of Pelicans and their Relatives

Pelicans

Family: Pelecanidae

Seven species of the genus *Pelecanus*.
East Europe, Africa, India, Sri Lanka, SE Asia, Australia, N America, northern S America, or on near coasts and inland waters. Size: length 1.27–1.7m (4.2–5.6ft); wingspan 2–2.8m (6.6–9.2ft); weight 2.5–15kg (5.5–33lb). Males slightly larger than females. Plumage: gray or white with black primary and flight feathers; washes of pink or orange on the body; Brown pelican is gray-black. Voice: hisses and grunts; nestlings are very noisy. Eggs: 1–4; chalky white. Incubation: 1 month. Diet: fish.

Species include: **American white pelican** (*Pelecanus erythrorhynchos*), **Australian pelican** (*P. conspicillatus*), **Brown pelican** (*P. occidentalis*), **Dalmatian pelican** V (*P. crispus*), **Great white** or **European white pelican** (*P. onocrotalus*), **Pink-backed pelican** (*P. rufescens*), **Spot-billed** or **Gray pelican** (*P. philippensis*).

Gannets and boobies

Family: Sulidae

Nine species in 2 genera.
Most pantropical oceans. Islands used for breeding. Size: length 60–85cm (23.6–33.5in); wingspan 1.41–1.74m (4.6–5.7ft); weight 0.9–3.6kg (2–8lb). In some species females are larger than males. Plumage: all species have white underparts with variable amount of black or gray above; some species have brightly colored bills, faces and feet. Voice: raucous or sonorous single or polysyllabic grunts or shouts and thin whistles. Eggs: according to species 1, 1 or 2, 2–4; plain, whitish with a limey coating that becomes stained. Incubation: 42–55 days. Diet: fish, squid, offal.

Species: **Abbott's booby** E (*Sula abbotti*), **Atlantic gannet** (*Morus bassana*), **Australasian gannet** (*M. serrator*), **Blue-footed booby** (*S. nebouxii*), **Brown booby** (*S. leucogaster*), **Cape** or **African gannet** (*M. capensis*), **Masked, Blue-faced** or **White booby** (*S. dactylatra*), **Peruvian booby** (*S. variegata*), **Red-footed booby** (*S. sula*).

Tropicbirds

Family: Phaethontidae

Three species of the genus *Phaethon*.
Tropical and subtropical oceans. Size: length 80–110cm (31–43in), including tail streamers; wingspan 90–110cm (35–43in). Plumage: white with black markings; some adults tinged rosy or gold. Sexes similar (but the greatly elongated two inner tail feathers are longer in the male, and absent in juveniles). Nest: on bare ground, or in holes in cliffs, trees. Voice: shrill screams. Eggs: 1; blotched red-brown. Incubation: 40–46 days. Diet: fish, squid.

Species: **Red-billed tropicbird** (*Phaethon aethereus*), **Red-tailed tropicbird** (*P. rubricauda*), **White-tailed tropicbird** (*P. lepturus*).

Cormorants

Family: Phalacrocoracidae

Twenty-nine species of the genus *Phalacrocorax*.
Worldwide; few at high latitudes; inhabiting inland waters and marine shorelines. Size: length 45–101cm (17.7–39.8in); wingspan 80–160cm (31–63in); weight 900–4,900g (2–11lb). Plumage: generally drab black, brown or blackish with a green sheen; some species have white breasts. Voice: grunts and croaks, but generally quiet. Eggs: 1–6; chalky blue, elongate ovoid. Incubation: 22–26 days. Diet: small fish and marine invertebrates.

Species include: **Brandt's cormorant** (*Phalacrocorax penicillatus*), **Cape cormorant** (*P. capensis*), **Double-crested cormorant** (*P. auritus*), **Galapagos flightless cormorant** R (*Nannopterum harrisi*), **Great cormorant** (*P. carbo*), **guanay** (*P. bougainvillii*), **Olivaceous cormorant** (*P. olivaceus*), **Pelagic cormorant** (*P. pelagicus*), **Pygmy cormorant** (*P. pygmaeus*), **Red-faced cormorant** (*P. urile*), **shag** (*P. aristotelis*), **Spotted shag** (*P. punctatus*).

Frigatebirds

Family: Fregatidae

Five species of the genus *Fregata*.
Pantropical oceans. Size: length 79–104cm (31–41in); wingspan 1.76–2.3m (5.8–7.5ft); weight 750–1,625g (26.4–57.3oz). Females 25–30 percent heavier than males. Plumage: males black with varying amounts of white beneath; females black in Ascension frigatebird, other species dark brown above and on head and belly with white breast. Voice: varied rattling, whistling, cackling and bill-rattling sounds; males give resonant drumming, hooting or whistling sounds. Eggs: 1; white, chalky. Incubation: 44–55 days. Diet: mainly flying fish and squid.

Species: **Ascension Island frigatebird** R (*Fregata aquila*), **Andrew's** or **Christmas Island frigatebird** V (*F. andrewsi*), **Great frigatebird** (*F. minor*), **Lesser frigatebird** (*F. ariel*), **Magnificent frigatebird** (*F. magnificens*).

Darters

Family: Anhingidae

Four species of the genus *Anhinga*.
America, Africa, Asia, Australasia inhabiting fresh waters (lakes, lagoons, rivers). Size: length 76–98cm (30–39in), wingspan 120–127cm (47–50in), weight 0.9–2.6kg (2–5.7lb). Plumage: mixture of black, brown, gray, silver and white; males darker than females. Voice: clicking, rattling, whistling and hissing calls. Eggs: 2–6 (average 4); elliptical, pale green with white chalky outer layer and some blood streaks. Incubation: 26–30 days. Diet: mainly fish.

Species: **African darter** (*Anhinga rufa*), **American anhinga** (*A. anhinga*), **Asian darter** (*A. melanogaster*), **Australian darter** (*A. novaehollandiae*).

▲ Bush booby. The Red-footed booby is unusual among sulids in nesting in bushes and trees. This has had some minor consequences in its behavior; its displays, for example, are slightly less elaborate than those of ground-nesting species. What has never been explained, however, is for what reason the bird has tomato-red feet.

◄ Cape gannets ABOVE. Living in the hot climes of Africa, this species has several minor adaptations to facilitate heat loss, including the enlarged strip of naked black skin on the throat.

▷ The packed multitude: African gannets OVERLEAF. All sulids breed in colonies, ranging from a few pairs to hundreds of thousands.

▼ Sulid displays. All species have highly developed territorial and pair displays. Each species has evolved variants on common forms, involving exaggerated postures and movements of head, wings, feet and tail, and in some species aerial displays. Display sequences may be long and protracted. Here a male Brown booby makes a territorial display (1), male and female Atlantic gannets greet each other (2), a pair of Cape gannets attain copulation (3).

bird whose numbers are controlled by its food supply, though not in relation to its own numbers. The area where it lives is normally rich in fish, but is periodically affected by incursions of warm water (El Ñino) which cause cold-loving anchovies to dive to depths where the boobies cannot reach them. The birds starve in their millions. In the past they have usually been able to restore their previous numbers quickly, but recently serious overfishing by man has prevented the birds from recovering from El Ñino. Numbers have remained at less than one-fifth of previous highest levels.

The enigma among boobies is the tree-nesting Abbott's booby. It once nested on islands in the western Indian Ocean, but has been driven from there by human destruction of its environment. But human activity does not apparently account for the small size of the sole remaining breeding population, about 1,000–1,500 pairs on jungle-clad Christmas Island in the Indian Ocean. It now faces a threat from the clearing of jungle for phosphate mining, but the Australian government has imposed conservation measures and research is in progress for devising a policy that will protect these birds.   JBN

Tropicbirds are among the most beautiful and widespread of tropical seabirds. Except when breeding they scorn land and are distributed, albeit sparsely, over vast areas of sea.

Sturdily built, tropicbirds appear larger than their body length of 45cm (18in). This is partly due to their brilliant white plumage, set off by black markings on the head, wings and upperparts, but also by the extremely thin central pair of white or red tail feathers which double the birds' length. The bill is either blood red or yellow, and stout and decurved with a vicious series of serrations on the cutting edge for holding prey. The legs are drab and very short, and webs join all four toes.

These birds forage well away from the col-onies. When hunting they fly high, hover when they see something interesting and then plunge into the sea. The basic foods are medium-sized fish, especially flying fish (up to 20cm, 8in long) and squid, but there are great seasonal and annual differences in the proportions of each that are eaten. After diving tropicbirds spend little time underwater which suggests that they do not go deep.

Tropicbirds are colonial, partly by choice and partly because suitable nesting sites are extremely limited on oceanic islands. The colonies are very obvious as the birds have noisy communal displays in which they glide close together with wings held high and tails flowing. Breeding seasons are complex (see p62), but pairs usually remain together and reuse the previous nest site, which is typically a hole in a cliff, under a boulder or bush; less commonly it is in a hole in a tree, a palm or even on the ground. The site must be safe from ground predators and be near a convenient takeoff point as tropicbirds have such short and backwardly placed legs that they only shuffle on land. There is much fighting for nest-sites which results in the loss of eggs and chicks.

The newly hatched young is covered with thick down. If conditions are good, it may be constantly protected until two-thirds grown. However, it is often soon left as it is necessary for both adults to be away foraging if the young is to be properly fed. It is given slightly digested fish or squid by direct regurgitation, sometimes every day, often only every two or three days. The young is normally fed until it flies off alone after some 60–90 days, again according to how well it has been fed. Its plumage is similar to that of an adult except that it is more heavily marked and lacks tail streamers and bright bill coloration. Young return to the colonies after three or four years and breed at about five years.

Adults were once killed for their feathers and young were considered delicacies. Rats and other introduced predators have reduced nesting success, but most populations

are now probably stable. On Bermuda, White-tailed tropicbirds are a threat to the endangered cahow, as they compete for nest-sites. Luckily this species of shearwater can use slightly smaller holes, so the conservation method of putting wooden baffles into the entrances to holes has proved successful.   MPH

Cormorants are common residents of seacoasts and inland water systems, accounting for over half the species of their order. They range from the duck-sized Pygmy cormorant of the Middle East to the Great cormorant of Europe and Asia, a bird about the size of a goose. They are the most aquatic of their order, being distributed worldwide and absent from only the uttermost polar regions, isolated oceanic islands and arid lands. Their commonness caused the naturalists of antiquity to give them the name *corvus marinus* ("sea raven") which passed to us through the early French *cor marin* to the present cormorant.

Cormorants feed in inshore waters, sharing fishing grounds with humans. Their voracious appetites and preference for breeding and feeding in large groups have left fishermen through the ages with the erroneous impression that they consume valuable fish. Periodic extermination campaigns have been waged, but later studies have shown such persecution to be unjustified. Cormorants are pursuit-divers; the Great cormorant and shag feed on midwater and bottom-schooling fish, such as mullet and sardines. Other species, for example the Pelagic and Brandt's cormorants, often prefer to take various invertebrates and rockfish that live on the bottom.

The cormorants share with the rest of the pelican-like birds webbing that connects all four toes (totipalmate feet) and a throat (gular) pouch. Loose folds of skin under the throat form a small pouch, but it is not as well developed here as in pelicans, probably because it is not used to capture fish. The expandable throat area helps to accommodate and position large fish for swallowing, but it serves mainly as a signaling device and as a means for cooling down the body. These primarily dark birds overheat quickly in direct sunlight. By panting and rapidly fluttering the gular pouch, blood passing through the rich concentration of capillaries is rapidly cooled. Like all other water birds cormorants have oil glands at the base of the tail for proper feather maintenance; however, their plumage is not waterproof. The special feather structure allows water to penetrate quickly and drive the air out, enabling them to sink and dive easily. After diving the wings are characteristically spread out, possibly to dry the feathers, but this action may also be a behavioral display or a means to warm up in the sun after a cold swim.

Cormorants are often seen swimming low in water, with only their long, sinuous necks exposed. To dive, the bird rises from the water in a graceful arc and then disappears often without a ripple, only to emerge minutes later some distance away. It used to be thought that cormorants swam underwater with their wings. Not only do they rely primarily on their superbly adapted totipalmate feet for swimming, but they press their wings tightly to the body, further reducing their underwater profile.

Cormorants' feet are placed close together and set far back on the body. Their propulsive thigh muscles are relatively large and strong for the size of the body. A unique bone at the base of the skull allows them to thrust at a fish and snap the bill shut independently. Even a fiercely struggling fish can be held by the serrated, strongly hooked bill.

Physiologically cormorants are more similar to diving birds such as penguins than to other seabirds. Their body and muscles are richly endowed with blood vessels and a relatively large blood volume, so that the oxygen supply is greatly enhanced. Cormorants can endure long periods of submersion and attain great depths; Brandt's cormorants have been caught in trawling nets set 50m (165ft) deep and deeper. Only a small amount of fat is stored in the body for insulation, and little is available for energy reserves. This restricts cormorants to the warmer, more productive waters. These adaptations, which improve the diving abilities of cormorants, also give the flesh a very strong flavor. North American natives would catch and hang cormorants in trees for a few weeks to improve the flavor; the Fuegian Indians of South America apparently caught and buried guanays in specially constructed pits.

Unusually for seabirds, cormorants have the ability to lay large clutches (up to 6 eggs and more), and to lay again late in the season should conditions require. The young are completely helpless at birth, being blind and naked, only able to move their necks and bills for feeding. Areas allowing protection from land predators and close enough to feeding grounds are uncommon, and may be the reason cormorants nest in large colonies. Even when only a few

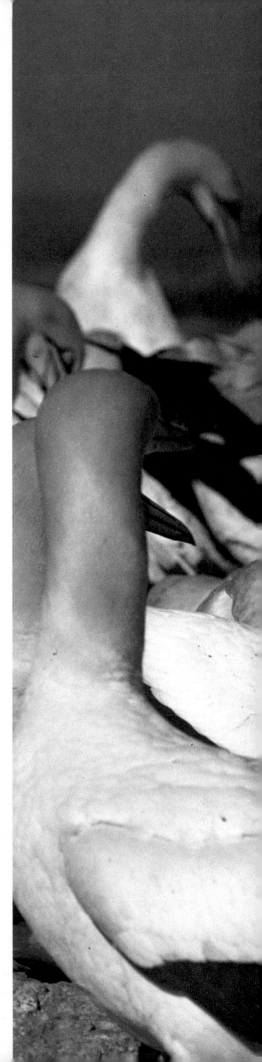

weeks into the breeding season these colonies become notoriously filthy with rotting fish and guano. In Chile, where the guanay breeds, and in South Africa with the Cape cormorant, rainfall is so rare that the guano accumulates to many meters thick and is mined as a rich source of nitrogen and phosphorus.

Although they are consummate aquatic birds, cormorants are nearly useless on land. They are able to waddle only with great effort and often trip over their own feet. The relatively small area of the wings, an advantage in moving between land and water, means that slight wind gusts while landing could cause them to overshoot and fall into a neighboring nest. Tree-nesting species like the Double-crested and Oliveaceous cormorants need also to avoid branches: nests are more landing pads than egg containers.

This unsteadiness on land and crowded colony conditions may be the reason that cormorant behaviors are more complex than those of any of the other members of their order. An adult preparing to leave the nest must signal its close neighbors that it is not moving to attack. The bill is opened, displaying the colored mouth and tongue, and a short hop is taken with the wings slightly outspread. The bill is then held down, often pointed at the feet; only then does the bird leap into takeoff. When landing, the neck is brought low and the hyoid bone in the throat is depressed to enlarge the throat pouch. Each cormorant species uses a distinct set of displays for takeoff, landing, courtship and other events, but the behaviors of the entire family are similar. The displays bring attention to the bright colors of the throat, gape, eyes, sometimes feet, which stand in contrast to their drab bodies. The range of coloration for these parts of the bodies is wide, from the jade-green eyes of the Pelagic cormorant, the iridescent blue throat pouch of Brandt's cormorant, the intense carmine of the Red-faced cormorant, to the blue pouch, white breast and varicolored eyes of the Spotted shag. Different colors, different displays and slight differences in food and feeding areas allow many cormorants to live together. In Australia and New Zealand some colonies may have four species breeding together; some islands in Tierra del Fuego have even more.

Since at least the 5th century in Japan and the early 17th century in Europe cormorants have been used for sport fishing. A ring is placed around the neck, preventing the bird from swallowing. When it comes to

the surface it is hauled to the boat on a special perch and the fish are removed. Later the ring is removed so the cormorant can feed itself, but experienced birds can be trained to fish without the ring. This type of fishing is still done in the Orient, but usually for the edification of tourists. DS-C

Frigatebirds are large seabirds, combining the soaring and gliding powers of vultures with the speed and agility of birds of prey. They nest in colonies on remote islands throughout the tropical oceans, where the males during courtship perform bizarre communal displays with huge inflated red throat-pouches. The name "frigatebird" and its alternative "man-of-war" refer to their robbing other birds of food or nest material. They are among the most oceanic of all birds, roaming far out to sea in search of food; yet their plumage is not waterproof and their legs are so tiny, and their feet so scantily webbed, that they cannot swim and have difficulty rising from the water.

Four of the five frigatebird species breed in the Atlantic; one of these now breeds only at Ascension Island and the only species not found in the Atlantic, Andrew's frigatebird, is confined to Christmas Island in the eastern Indian Ocean. Of the two most widespread species, the Great and Lesser frigatebirds, each shares about half its breeding stations with the other.

In general appearance frigates are one of the most distinctive of all seabird families. Soaring at sea, their long, angular, sharply pointed wings and long scissor-shaped tail give them an unmistakable outline. At shorter range their huge, sinuous, hook-tipped bill is equally distinctive, and the males' brilliant red throat-pouches, when inflated, adorn the trees of the breeding colony like ripe fruits.

▲ **Mother and chick:** Red-tailed tropicbirds. As inhabitants of the tropics, tropicbirds have had to establish breeding cycles in a part of the world where annual cycles are not well-established. Different situations have arisen. The Red-tailed tropicbirds on Aldabra on the western edge of the Indian Ocean breed throughout the year whereas on Christmas Island on a similar latitude in the eastern Indian Ocean there is a well-defined breeding cycle. On the Galapagos Islands there is an overcrowded colony of the same species where birds lay all year round within 20km (12.5mi) of an uncrowded colony where there is a regular breeding cycle. There are no obvious reasons for these different arrangements.

▶ **Adult and young** ABOVE. Blue-eyed cormorants (*Phalacrocorax atriceps*) on Bird Island, South Georgia.

▶ **Enjoying the sun,** a Galapagos flightless cormorant. Having loose-fitting feathers cormorants emerge from water, after fishing expeditions, thoroughly soaked. Before flying again they stand in the sun, to dry them off. The Galapagos cormorant (*Nannopterum harrisi*) does the same, even though it long ago lost the ability to fly and subsequently also lost the keel to which the flight muscles were attached.

All species breed in colonies on small or remote islands. The males choose possible nest sites; usually these are in trees—up to 30m (100ft) high or more in Andrew's frigate—but where there are none, they will use bare ground, as on Ascension Island. Males display in groups of up to 30, and when prospecting females fly overhead the males spread and vibrate their wings, throw back their heads and call or clack their bills above their distended scarlet throat-pouch. When a female lands by her chosen mate they snake their head and neck across each other, occasionally nibbling at the other's feathers. The male's courtship display, especially when given in concert with the others', is more noisy, vivid and spectacular than that of any other seabird; but the subsequent repertoire of displays between paired birds is primitive and desultory. Males collect most material for the nest, which the female builds while she guards it from theft by other males; so strong is the male's drive to gather twigs at this stage that if his mate is driven away a male will even "automatically" rob twigs from his own nest.

The female's single white egg weighs 5–14 percent of the female's weight, and is incubated by both birds for a total of 6–8 weeks in shifts of up to 12 days at a time. The young chick is born naked and grows a black cape of feathers on the back while white down begins to cover the rest of the body. It grows as slowly as any seabird, spending five to six months in the nest and remaining dependent on its parents for food for several months more—over a year in one case. Frigates first breed probably at about seven years, and their reproductive output is so low that adults must live 25 years on average.

A successful breeding attempt takes more than 12 months, so adults that rear young one year cannot breed the next; thus like some of the larger albatrosses most frigate-birds probably breed successfully only in alternate years. They cannot return to the same nest-site each year, reckoning to meet their mate there, because another pair will have taken it over; the pair-bond is accordingly weak and displays—apart from at the initial frenzied courtship stage—are vestigial.

One species, the Mangificent frigatebird, shows slight but illuminating differences from the family pattern. It feeds closer inshore than the other species and apparently has a more reliable food supply, for not only are incubation shifts shorter than in any other frigate (averaging 1 day or less),

but when the chick is about 100 days old the male deserts the colony leaving the female to raise their chick unaided. Probably he goes away to molt before returning for another breeding attempt with a different female, while his previous mate is still feeding their offspring, but this unique division of resources between the sexes remains to be proved with marked birds.

AWD

Darters are large slender waterbirds, somewhat like a cross between a heron and a cormorant. Head, neck and wings are heronlike, while plumage patterns, feather structure, rump and feet are cormorant-like. Darters differ from other water birds in having very long tails with corrugated outer tail feathers. They occur where there are quiet, waters in tropical, subtropical and warm temperate parts of America, Africa, Madagascar, Asia and Australasia.

The bill is dagger-shaped with each mandible having a cutting edge. The front end of this is serrated or saw-like as in gannets, boobies and tropicbirds. The bill does not have a terminal hook (unlike shags and cormorants). The head is very small, long and slender. The neck is thin and G-shaped. To reduce buoyancy the body plumage is permeable to water, as it is also in shags and cormorants. The legs are short and stout with long toes, all four of which are united in a web as in the other members of the order. Plumage patterns vary between species, sexes, ages and individuals. All are dark above. Long slender scapular and mantle covert feathers have silver, white, gray or light brown streaks, more marked in adults than in immatures. Males are blacker than females, and immatures paler than adults, mainly on the head, neck and underparts. All have dark tails. As in ducks and rails all flight feathers of the wings are shed at the same time and darters then are flightless. The tail feathers are shed gradually.

Darters are also adapted for soaring on thermal updrafts. Because of their long tails when gliding they look like flying crosses. They are further adapted for moving slowly underwater. They submerge slowly and often swim with only their head and neck out of the water, thus looking like a swimming snake, hence the popular name "snakebird." They stalk their prey underwater, often moving very slowly with spread wings and tail and coiled neck. Between the eighth and ninth neck vertebrae there is a special hinge mechanism which enables the neck to dart forward and snap up insects at the water surface, and to stab fish in the side

Piracy by Frigatebirds

Weak legs, tiny feet and non-waterproof plumage restrict frigatebirds to feeding at, or above, the surface of the sea. Their feeding technique is a spectacular swoop to just above the surface, the bill snapping down and back to pluck a flying fish or squid from the jaws of a pursuing tuna. They use the same method to pick up floating nest material, and can snatch a twig from glass-calm water without making a ripple. It takes years to perfect the technique sufficiently for a frigate to be able to take time off, as it were, to breed, and it is not surprising that some of them take the shortcut of waiting for other birds to catch the food and then robbing. This piratical behavior is so conspicuous around some colonies that frigates have the reputation of acquiring most of their food this way, but usually it is mostly young birds, or individual specialists, which force other birds to disgorge their prey. Adult males also chase birds—often of their own species—to rob them of nest material. As a feeding technique piracy is especially valuable to frigates because the depth at which they can feed for themselves is so limited; by robbing species which can dive below the surface, they effectively increase the depth of water they can exploit.   AWD

◄ **Different uses for the gular pouch.** In the order of Pelecaniformes the two families with the most developed throat pouches are the pelicans and frigatebirds. Whereas pelicans use their pouches for catching food, in male frigatebirds they are only inflated to attract a mate, in which this Great frigatebird has succeeded.

▼ **A passion for lakes.** For stalking prey underwater darters prefer quiet water. Though they can be found in a variety of aqueous habitats, lakes satisfy several important criteria to perfection: they provide a bounteous supply of prey, still water, vast areas free of underwater impediments and plenty of lakeside trees and islets on which to build nests. Large numbers of darters live on the natural lakes of several continents, and are quick to colonize man-made lakes. This colony of African darters lies on Lake Naivasha in Kenya.

with the bill slightly open. A stabbed fish is usually shaken loose, flipped into the air and swallowed head first. The same darting and stabbing mechanism is used in defense to stab at the eyes of predators and unwary human molesters.

The comfort movements of darters (ie movements designed to put the feathers in place) are like those of other birds and include also a spread-eagle extension of the wings, similar to that of cormorants and some species of shag.

Darters are more territorial than other kinds of pelecaniform birds, and may defend not only small resting and nesting sites but substantial feeding, resting and nesting areas. They do, however, intermingle with other kinds of water birds at roosts and nesting colonies. Long-distance flights are usually made by "spiraling up" on thermal updrafts and then gliding down to the next updraft. When taking off from water both feet kick together as in other pelican-like birds. Sometimes they climb up trees and bushes before takeoff.

Breeding starts with a male selecting a nest-site and claiming a territory round it, which may even include as much as a whole tree. He decorates his nest-site with a few fresh green leafy twigs, and displays to attract his mate and to ward off other darters from his territory, but not to repel other species of birds. Females select a displaying male and his nest-site including its approaches. The male's advertisements include wing-waving in which the partly closed wings are alternately raised, and twig-grasping, in which a nearby twig or stick is grabbed with the bill and shaken vigorously. After pair-formation the female builds the nest with material brought to it mainly by the male. Breeding may occur at any time during the year.

New nests consist of a base of mainly green twigs, a cup of about 150 dry sticks and a lining of leaves. Often an old nest is used as a base. The nest is usually built in the fork of a tree branch over water, but sometimes in bushes or reeds; it is always near water.

The first egg is laid 2 to 3 days after the start of a new nest by a pair, and subsequent eggs laid at intervals of 1 to 3 days. Incubation starts as soon as the first egg is laid and lasts for 26–30 days (average 28 days). Eggs in a clutch hatch at intervals of 1–4 days. The parents take turns in guarding the nest, from the start of building until the chicks are at least one week old. Relief takes place at least three times a day, usually at dawn, at noon and at dusk. At the nest-site the parents greet each other with several recognition displays by the bird on the nest and signals by the bird outside the nest before departure and before arrival. Some of these displays are very similar to those of other pelecaniform birds and herons. As long as the chicks are at the nest they are guarded, even during the night.

The chicks are fed a fluid of partly digested fish which flows down the inside of the upper bill. Larger chicks take food directly from the parent's throat. Small chicks are fed six to nine times a day. When they are two weeks old they are fed twice a day. When they are five weeks old they are fed only once a day.

Darters only incidentally come into conflict with man. None of the four species is in immediate danger of extinction. Locally darters depend on the availability of suitable waters to fish in. They readily colonize man-made lakes, and in New Guinea they increased in numbers following the introduction of the African fish *Tilapia* to the southern lowlands. Some darters become caught in nets set for fish. In Southeast Asia darters have been used for fishing in a manner similar to that practised by cormorants there and elsewhere.   GFvT

HERONS AND BITTERNS

Family: Ardeidae
Order: Ciconiiformes (suborder Ardeae).
Sixty species in 17 genera.
Distribution: worldwide but absent from high latitudes.

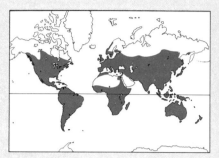

▶ **The Japanese night heron,** a relation of the cosmopolitan Black-crowned night heron. In the breeding season night herons feed during the day as well as at night.

IN Europe and North America herons steal fish from ornamental ponds in surburban back gardens and have learned to raid fish farms whenever they are left unprotected. In tropical rice growing countries they feed on insects and amphibians and greatly benefit the hard-pressed farmers. This highly diverse and adaptable family of birds can be either harmful or beneficial to man. Unfortunately, their fish-stealing habits have led to much persecution.

Herons are long-billed and long-legged wading birds, with short tails and long, broad wings. All are highly specialized predators adapted for the capture of live (usually aquatic) prey, which is often large compared with the heron. Prey are stalked with a variety of techniques, but always ending with a rapid stab to catch the animal. They preen themselves using special feathers that crumble to a powder which is rubbed into the other feathers. The claw of the third toe is flattened for combing out the powder.

The **day herons** show a tremendous range of form, coloration and behavior patterns, from the huge Goliath heron to the smaller egrets and the Squacco heron. Some are black, others white, while some, such as the Chestnut-bellied heron, are very brightly colored. Some breed singly, while many come together in huge colonies, and on the feeding grounds, some species are highly territorial, while others feed together in flocks.

The best-known and most widespread heron in the Old World is the Gray heron, most northerly populations of which migrate southward during the winter to find ice-free waters. Its equivalent in the New World is the Great blue heron, which breeds as far north in Canada as the Great Lakes and south to Honduras and the Caribbean. In Trinidad and South America, this

---

The Heron Family
[v] Vulnerable.

Day herons
Subfamily: Ardeinae (tribe Ardeini)
Thirty-four species in 8 genera.

Worldwide except at high altitudes. Temperate and tropical areas near fresh or salt waters. Size: 39–140cm (15–55in); males usually larger than females. Plumage: a wide variety, ranging from pure white in many egret species, to bright chestnut and green in the Chestnut-bellied heron. Geographical variations in some species are very marked. Voice: a loud croak, grunt or hiss. Many are silent outside the breeding season, but in colonies of breeding birds the general hubbub of sound is quite loud. Nests: mostly in trees (some on ground) and most species colonial nesters. Eggs: 2–7, usually pale blue, sometimes white; incubation period 18–30 days; nestling period 35–50 days. Diet: mainly fish, amphibians, small mammals, birds and insects. Species include: **Cattle egret** (Bubulcus ibis), **Chestnut-bellied heron** (Agamia agami), **Chinese** or **Swinhoe's egret** (Egretta eulophotes) [v], **Cocoi heron** (Ardea cocoi), **Goliath heron** (A. goliath), **Gray heron** (A. cinerea),

Great blue heron (A. herodius), **Green-backed heron** (Butorides striatus), **Squacco heron** (Ardeola ralloides).

Night herons
Subfamily: Ardeinae (tribe Nycticoracini)
Eight species in 3 genera.

N and S America, Europe, Africa, Asia. Wetlands, marshy areas, mangroves and woodlands near water. Size: 50–70cm (20–28in) long, weight 600–800g (21–28oz); sexes similar. Plumage: usually contrasting gray and black or brown and black; sexes similar; juveniles speckled brown. Nests: in trees, bushes or occasionally in reedbeds. Eggs: 2–5, white or bluish-white; incubation period 21–26 days; nestling period 6–8 weeks. Diet: omnivorous; mainly fish and small birds and mammals. Species include: **Black-crowned night heron** (Nycticorax nycticorax), **Boat-billed heron** (Cochlearius cochlearius), **Japanese night heron** (Gorsachius goisagi), **Nankeen** or **Rufous night heron** (Nycticorax caledonicus).

Tiger herons
Subfamily: Ardeinae (tribe Tigriornithini)
Six species in 4 genera.

New Guinea, W Africa, C and S America. Marshlands, wetland forests in the tropics. Size: mostly 60–80cm (24–32in) long; males generally larger than females; Zigzag heron only 30cm (12in). Plumage: brown, barred and striped in concealment patterns. Voice: a bittern-like "boom." Nests: usually in trees overhanging water. Eggs: usually 1 or 2, whitish, blotched red. Diet: fish, amphibians. Species include: **White-crested tiger heron** (Tigriornis leucolophus), **Zigzag heron** (Zebrilus undulatus).

Large bitterns
Subfamily: Botaurinae
Four species of the genus Botaurus.

One species each in Eurasia, Australia, N America, S America. Reedbeds. Size: 60–85cm (24–34in) long, weight 400–1,900g (14–67oz); males usually larger than females. Plumage: tawny brown, streaked

black; sexes similar. Eggs: usually 3–6, olive brown; incubation period 25 days; nestling period 40–55 days. Diet: fish, amphibians, small mammals, insects. Species: **American bittern** (B. lentiginosus), **Australian bittern** (B. poiciloptilus), **Eurasian bittern** (B. stellaris), **South American bittern** (B. pinnatus).

Small bitterns
Subfamily: Botaurinae
Eight species of the genus Ixobrychus.

Worldwide. Reedbeds, marshy grasslands. Size: 27–58cm (11–23in) long, weight 100–200g (3.5–7oz). Plumage: cream, tawny chestnut, brown and black; sexes markedly different, with males showing more contrast (black/brown and cream) than females (creamy-brown, streaked black). Eggs: usually 3–6, white or pale blue-green; weight 10–15g (0.35–0.5oz); incubation period 14–20 days; nestling period 28–30 days. Species include: **Black bittern** (I. flavicollis), **Least bittern** (I. exilis), **Little bittern** (I. minutus).

▲ **A pair of Purple herons** with young among the reeds. More slender than Gray herons, Purple herons (*Ardea purpurea*) forage in swamps and usually nest in reedbeds.

▷ **Poised to stab,** OVERLEAF a Gray heron waits at the water's edge, its neck held coiled into an S-shape, ready to shoot out when prey is spotted.

heron is replaced by the Cocoi heron, which, though widespread, is by no means as common as the other two species, nor has it developed distinct local races as have the Gray and Great blue herons.

These large herons have strong bills. When they fly they tuck in their long necks but let their long legs trail out behind them. Their wing beat is slow, but they are capable of flying very long distances.

All three species have blue, gray or blackish heads and bodies with some white and heavily marked white necks. The bills and legs vary in color according to the season, from yellow to dark brown, and during the brief period of courtship turn to deep pink

or red. Long plumes on the head, neck, breast and back develop well before the breeding season, assuming their most luxurious color, length and texture when courtship commences.

Just as the plumage varies from light gray basic plumes in the Gray Heron, to various shades of blue in the Great blue heron, so do the different races of these two species vary geographically in color and pattern of plumage. The most extreme form is the "Great white heron." Until recently, it was considered to be a separate species, but interbreeding with Great blue herons has now been proved. It is now accepted that birds living in an entirely marine tropical

habitat lost much of their darker markings with age until the final plumage becomes all white, or nearly so.

The day herons all nest colonially, mostly, but not always, in trees. Sometimes they join huge colonies of mixed species of egrets, storks, ibises, spoonbills, and other water birds. When nesting is complete the young of the year fly off in all directions, although northern birds do not remain long in their summer breeding areas before moving further south in search for their very varied diet of fish, amphibians, small mammals, crustaceans and insects, as well as snakes and sometimes small birds.

It is this ability to adapt to such a wide variety of diet, as well as to make use of reed-beds, sandy beaches and even stone walls for their nests, which has enabled them to survive in an increasingly hostile environment.

Tiger herons take their name from their strikingly barred or striped plumage. They have also been called tiger-bitterns as a result of their bittern-like postures and "booming" calls. Some live in dense tropical forests, where their solitary breeding habits and camouflaged plumage have kept many aspects of their biology a mystery. Few nests have been recorded of the six species in this group, but these have always been in trees, particularly by rivers. Dates of breeding strongly suggest that river height and rainfall may be important factors in determining the onset of breeding. All species are nocturnal feeders.

Night herons are very stocky birds with relatively short, thick bills and short legs. They are principally nocturnal feeders with large eyes but, particularly during the breeding season, they also feed by day.

The Black-crowned night heron is the most cosmopolitan of all herons, occurring in a wide range of non-arid habitats throughout the world (in Australasia it is replaced by the Nankeen night heron). It is the best-known of the night herons, being both gregarious on the feeding areas and a colonial breeder. Although an attractive bird to watch, it has the nasty habit of eating the eggs and young of other herons in the colony.

The Boat-billed heron, with its curious slipper-shaped bill, may be most closely related to the Black-crowned night heron, and occurs from Mexico south to Argentina. Recent evidence suggests that this largely nocturnal feeder captures its prey by touch rather than sight, the shrimps and small fish of its diet perhaps being sucked in by rapid bill movements.

Both groups of **bitterns** are solitary, mainly daytime feeders, stalking their prey with great stealth. Most have brown plumage, often very heavily streaked to camouflage them in their reedbed habitats. Their bills are yellowish and they have green feet. The largest are very stocky birds, while the Least bittern is the smallest heron. When disturbed, they freeze motionless, their bill pointed toward the sky.

The larger species can handle very large fish, while small fish, frogs and insects are taken by them all. The Eurasian bittern is famed for its "booming" call during the breeding season, which can be heard from distances up to 5km (3mi) away. The eggs are laid in a nest of reeds which is usually suspended over open water. The chicks leave the nest some time before fledging, and clamber out in the reeds.

Many different styles of breeding can be seen among the heron family. Most species are monogamous, the pair-bond being of at least seasonal duration. The Eurasian bittern male, however, may mate with up to five females during a single breeding season, and in such cases probably takes no part in incubation or raising the young. Most bitterns are solitary nesters, while egrets and some herons nest colonially, sometimes in huge numbers. On the feeding areas they also show a wide range of habits, some such as the bitterns being solitary, while many of the other species are highly gregarious, congregating in enormous numbers in good feeding places.

Breeding is often timed to coincide with peaks in food abundance. Nests are simply constructed of twigs or reeds, often being no more than a simple platform on which to lay eggs. Most species start incubation immediately after the first egg has been laid,

resulting in the eggs hatching over a period of time. This gives the first chick a great advantage over the others, and may be important in maximizing breeding success. The chicks are fed by their parents until they fledge, although many will leave their nests within a few days of hatching, to clamber around the vegetation near to the nest. All are fed by regurgitation.

Herons are very resilient—no family of birds has suffered predation on a greater scale. The ruthless slaughter of egrets at their breeding colonies to obtain the plumes for the adornment of ladies' hats caused the

▲ **Mantling.** A black heron (*Egretta ardesiaca*) creates a cowl over the water while hunting for fish. The shadow may attract fish, which may believe they are fleeing into cover, or enable the heron to see them better.

▶ **Frozen in the reeds,** a Eurasian bittern on its nest demonstrates its brilliantly effective camouflage. When the neck is held upright its markings blend perfectly with the reeds.

Herons and Fish Farming

Gone are the days when the wily wild trout was stalked by the fisherman along the streams of Britain and Ireland or in the Great Lakes and the rivers of North America. Today's sportsman fishes from a river stocked with fish specially reared on a farm and some species of trout, notably the North American Rainbow, are economically grown under captive conditions for the supermarket and restaurant trade. To meet this demand fish farms have sprung up quickly and often experimentally, in open ponds by the sides of rivers, or artificially created pools with no form of protection, both in Europe and America.

The highly adaptive heron was not slow to discover this rich new resource. In Britain the

Gray heron has become an expert at robbing unprotected fish farms, and defenses against it have proved extremely difficult. At most farms, predators include ospreys, cormorants, mink, gulls, kingfishers and above all human poachers, but herons as the most conspicuous visitors have taken most of the blame. Although the heron is a protected species in Britain, as elsewhere, it is nevertheless shot by fish farmers when they can prove its destructive effect.

In the late 1970s it was estimated that no fewer than 4,600 Gray herons were shot annually in England and Wales—when the adults were breeding birds, the young at the nest died of starvation. As the total breeding population of these two countries in 1979

was only 5,400 pairs, the level of the destruction clearly indicates that the species is in grave danger. When cold weather and other natural causes reduce breeding success, the additional loss due to shooting may make it impossible for the population to sustain itself as a breeding species in Britain.

Following a two year study by the Royal Society for the Protection of Birds, carried out with the full cooperation of the majority of the country's 250 fish farms, and continuing work by other conservation bodies, inexpensive deterrents such as steeper banks, lower water levels and, most effectively, cords and chains spread around the pools have proved very successful in discouraging the herons from fishing at the farms.

death of millions of adults and young and whole populations to be wiped out. The Royal Society for the Protection of Birds in Britain and the Audubon Society in America owe their existence to the outcry caused by this devastation.

In spite of this, herons have survived and in many areas even prospered. But the wetland habitats that they require have been destroyed at a greater rate than any natural habitat other than forests.

There are some herons, however, which have not been able to adapt. Highly specialized feeders needing, as all such species do, a very special set of circumstances, have reached dangerously low numbers, but the species involved are fortunately few, and are outnumbered by the species that have expanded.

The one most endangered, the Chinese or Swinhoe's egret, has been found nesting in pitifully small numbers in Hong Kong, and this is the only known colony in the whole of China, although recent reports from North Korea indicate increasing numbers nesting on islands there. The plume hunters obviously massacred most of the birds of this species and its remnant population found difficulty in recovering. They can only feed in salt water estuaries and virtually all of these have been utilized to grow rice right down to the water's edge. Mangroves and other vegetation have been eradicated to provide high intensity cultivated paddy fields.

This trend is noticeable in other parts of Asia, although the peoples of southern Asia and India do not cultivate as intensively as the Chinese. Small herons can live almost next door to man in villages and towns. Feeding at dusk and dawn and hiding in deep foliage, the small bitterns, the Greenbacked heron, and the often tamer, confiding pond herons (*Ardeola* species) have adapted easily to populated areas. Almost every zoo and park contains its resident, free-roaming population of these birds, and many cheekily steal the food from the troughs of captive animals.

As the forests of South America have been destroyed and cattle ranching expanded, so have the African emigrant Cattle egrets prospered. Originally arriving in South America probably in the first few years of this century, this species has spread rapidly. As their numbers have risen, they have moved northward into North America, and spread throughout the plains and ranches of the USA, which only 40 years ago had never seen this aggressive little heron.

JH

STORKS AND SPOONBILLS

Families: Ciconiidae, Threskiornithidae, Scopidae, Balaenicipitidae
Order: Ciconiiformes (suborders Ciconiae, Balaenicipites).
Fifty species in 25 genera.
Distribution: see maps and table.

Storks   Hammerhead stork

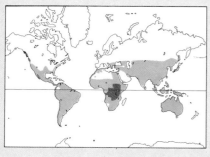

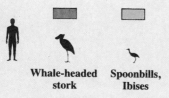

**Whale-headed   Spoonbills,
stork   Ibises**

▶ **Part of the furniture.** This church in Spain is festooned with nests of the White stork. Despite the ancient associations between storks and human habitations, many European villages have only a single pair of storks and even these are disappearing in many areas.

▶ **The gaping bill** of a Yellow-billed stork. Despite the scientific name (*Ibis ibis*), this is a stork not an ibis.

THE White stork has long been a symbol of pilgrimage and continuity in European and Islamic cultures. It nests happily close to people in villages, makes long migrations, but shows great fidelity to its nest-site. Such reliability has always appealed to human beings and perhaps led to the folk tale, which originated in Germany and Austria, that storks deliver babies. At any rate, storks are a reassuring presence.

Storks are large to very large wading birds having long legs, long bills, a stately upright stance and striding gait. They are birds of wetlands and water margins, as well as fields and savannas. They prefer warm continental climates and tend to avoid cool and damp regions. As a result, they are widespread in the tropics and subtropics, whereas few occur in temperate regions. The greatest numbers of stork species are found in tropical Africa (eight species) and tropical Asia (nine). White and Black storks are particularly widespread, nesting in Europe, East Asia, North Africa and southern Africa. Both species spend most of the year in Africa or India. The White stork inhabits cultivated countryside, whereas the Black stork tends to avoid areas of human activity.

Storks have long, broad wings and are strong fliers. They fly with their necks outstretched, except for the species of adjutants, which retract their head. Most storks alternate flapping flight with soaring in warm air-currents (thermals). Such currents are only found over land, which restricts the migration routes. Storks nonethe-less can engage in remarkable aerobatics, such as diving, plummeting from the sky, and flipping over in flight. The Black stork, having relatively narrow wings, relies more on flapping flight than on soaring.

The bills of storks are long and heavy. Most are straight but those of wood storks are downcurved, and that of the jabiru is slightly upcurved. Wood storks, adjutants, and the jabiru lack feathers on their heads. The sexes look similar, but males are noticeably larger than females. Dark irises distinguish male Black-necked and Saddle-bill storks from the yellow-eyed females. Air sacs lie under the neck skin, and the marabou and the Great adjutant have long, bare, pendent throat sacs. Juvenile plumage is dull, reaching full development over the first year. Nestlings of the otherwise white Maguari stork are black, probably as camouflage. The African open-bill stork is black, whereas the closely related Asian species is white.

The colors of the bill, together with the bare skin of the head and legs, are characteristic for each species, and they intensify during courtship. The breeding Maguari stork has a striking blue-gray bill, becoming maroon near its red face. The jabiru has a pink neck band that changes to deep scarlet when it is excited.

Most storks feed alone but also will form large flocks when food is abundant. They walk, wade, or run about, grabbing prey with thrusts of their bills. A typical stork will walk slowly across fields with its neck extended and head down looking for prey. The White stork's diet during nesting is varied, including aquatic vertebrates, insects and earthworms. On its African winter ground, this stork is known as the Grasshopper bird because it follows locust swarms. White storks also follow mowing machines. The Black stork is more closely associated with marshy margins of streams and pools where it feeds on fishes. The White-bellied stork often hunts in large flocks, especially near grass fires and locust swarms.

The adjutants are largely scavengers and carrion-eaters. They are well known for their attendance at carcasses, along with vultures and hyenas. Although not adept at tearing flesh, their size and large bills allows them to steal bits of meat from nearby vultures. Requiring over 700g (25oz) of food per day, marabou frequent predator kills, domestic stock yards, plowed fields and rubbish dumps, as well as drying pools that

Feeding by Touch

Most birds feed by sight, first observing a potential food item and then grabbing it with their bills. Storks, spoonbills and ibises also have an alternative foraging strategy, using the sense of touch rather than sight. Although all these birds can feed by sight, and some, such as the typical storks, do so customarily, spoonbills, wood and open-bill storks, the jabiru and most ibises usually feed by touch, and other species do so on occasions.

When a bird feeds by touch, it responds when an unseen prey animal encounters its open bill by immediately snapping it shut. In the American wood stork, this happens within 25 milliseconds, one of the fastest reflexes among vertebrates. Touch-feeding is probably facilitated in part by sensitive touch receptors under the horny covering of the bill. Or the bill snap may be stimulated by the jaw muscle being stretched by a prey item. Feeding by touch can be remarkably effective, and permits feeding in very turbid water, muddy pools, dense underwater vegetation or at night.

contain the natural prey necessary to raise young. Marabou are attracted from great distances to grass fires, where they march along the fire front. The size range of their prey varies greatly. Marabous stand at termite mounds eating swarming insects, but also take quite large prey, killing young crocodiles, young and adult flamingos, and small mammals. The Greater adjutant was formerly common in Indian cities, where it consumed refuse that included human corpses.

The four species of wood storks feed by touch, wading slowly with their partially opened bills inserted in shallow water (see box). The bill of the open-bill storks is used for dealing with mollusks, especially large water snails. The bill tip is inserted into the opening of the shell, cutting the snail's muscle, which permits extraction of the body. An open-bill may ride on a swimming hippopotamus to capture the snails it stirs up. The Black-necked stork sometimes feeds by running back and forth, jumping and wing-flashing. The largest New World stork, the jabiru, feeds by touch, wading slowly and periodically inserting its open bill into the water.

By soaring, storks can forage long distances from their colonies and roosts. The White stork, wood storks and adjutants are particularly adept at reaching high altitudes, and then gliding toward distant feeding sites. This behavior helps birds locate places of concentrated food, where many birds may forage together. In East Africa as many as seven species of storks may feed in the same location.

Most storks undertake seasonal population movement; several species (eg the White-bellied stork from North to South Africa) migrate across the equator. The migrations of the European storks have been known since biblical times. European White storks use two migratory routes, one down the Iberian Peninsula, the other across the Middle East through Egypt, both avoiding the long sea crossing of the Mediterranean. All storks, even those from Europe and Asia, therefore spend most of their year in the tropics; some yearling White storks remain in Africa throughout their first summer. The population movements of other species are less long distance migrations than population shifts in response to feeding conditions and rainfall patterns.

The nesting cycle of all storks is strongly seasonal, apparently determined by food supplies. Only the White and Black storks regularly leave the tropics to nest, during the temperate spring and summer. The American wood stork nests during the dry season when prey are concentrated in drying pools and are easily captured using touch to guide them (see box). Other species of wood storks nest during the wet season, when most food is available in their situation. The marabou nests in the dry season when carrion and drying pools become available, while the White-bellied stork is

▼ **Representative species of storks and spoonbills.** (**1**) Roseate spoonbill (*Platalea ajaja*), showing the broad, flattened bill characteristic of spoonbills. (**2**) Black stork (*Ciconia nigra*), a species similar in many ways to the White stork, but which lives in more wooded areas. (**3**) Whale-headed stork (*Balaeniceps rex*) in its freshwater swamp habitat. (**4**) Hammerhead (*Scopus umbretta*), showing the extreme wedge-shaped head that gives it its name. (**5**) Marabou (*Leptoptilos crumeniferus*) with its large throat pouch. (**6**) Glossy ibis (*Plegadis falcinellus*). (**7**) Sacred ibis (*Threskiornis aethiopica*), a species that was revered in Ancient Egypt. (**8**) White stork (*Ciconia ciconia*) performing the "Up-Down" display on the nest.

considered a "rain bringer:" in Ethiopia it nests during the first heavy rains, which produce a flush of its insect food.

Wood stork colonies may exceed tens of thousands of nests, whereas many European villages have only a single White stork family nesting there. Most storks nest in trees, but they may also use cliffs or nest on the ground. Non-colonial tropical species, such as Saddle-bill storks, may remain paired year-round, and White storks often re-pair because both birds are attracted to the nest of the previous year. Nests are situated near sites providing suitable food supplies; drying pools for American wood storks; carrion-producing rangeland for marabou; agricultural fields for White storks.

The nest site, selected by the male, is defended against all intruders. The male gives advertisement displays, and the attracted female responds with appeasement behavior (see pp82–83). Differing between the species, advertisements may consist of up-down movements, calls and bill-clattering. In its extreme form, a stork bends its neck backwards until its head touches its back. In some species, this posture forms a resonance chamber in the throat that amplifies the sound of snapping its two mandibles.

Even newly hatched young behave in this way. Both parents incubate and feed the relatively helpless young by regurgitating food onto the nest floor. Storks may also regurgitate water over their eggs and young, presumably to cool them.

Nesting success is determined by prey availability and weather conditions. Wood storks only fledge young when high densities of food remain available throughout the entire nesting season. White stork nesting success is poor in years or locations having very high rainfall.

Some populations of storks have undergone massive population decreases. As a harbinger of good fortune and many children, the White stork has been protected in Europe for centuries, and has been censused longer than any other bird. Nonetheless, between 1900 and 1958, western European populations decreased by 80 percent, and by 92 percent between 1900 and 1973. Storks no longer nest in Sweden or Switzerland, and occur only in small numbers in other countries. The reasons for the decrease are not certain, but the following factors have been suggested: cooler and wetter summers; loss of nest-sites; pesticide poisoning; hunting on the winter grounds; changing agricultural practices. The last hypothesis is of interest in that it is possible that storks had previously increased in Europe following deforestation; populations have decreased as modern agriculture has destroyed more and more foraging sites. Hunting pressure in wintering areas in Africa is also certainly an important cause of their decrease.

The Greater adjutant population has been critically reduced throughout its range. The Milky stork, confined to the mangrove forests of southeast Asia, is in jeopardy because of habitat destruction. Some species, such as the Black-necked stork, are rare over wide ranges, while others such as the Asian open-bill stork, are numerous, but only locally. Although remaining abundant in South and Central America, the American wood stork has decreased in southern Florida, because of ecological changes in the vast

▶ **The Saddle-bill stork,** a large species found from Ethiopia and Senegal to South Africa.

▶ **Unusually elegant** and serene for fledglings, BELOW three young White storks bask on their nest. They will almost certainly return close to this same nest-site after their first migration.

The 4 Families of Storks and Spoonbills   E Endangered.   V Vulnerable.   R Rare.

Storks
Family: Ciconiidae
Seventeen species in 9 genera.
Southern N America, S America, Africa, Eurasia, Australia, East Indies. Habitat: marshes, savannas and fields. Size: 75–150cm (30–60in) long; to 2–9kg (4–20lb); 145–320cm (57–126in) wingspan. Plumage: chiefly white, gray and black, some with pink tinge. Voice: bill-clatter; various species also hiss, moo, whistle, peep and grunt. Nests: platforms made of sticks in trees or on cliffs; one species nests on buildings. Eggs: usually 3–5 (the Saddle-bill stork lays one), white becoming stained with age; incubation period 30–50 days; nestling period 7–18 weeks. Diet: fish, insects, carrion, depending on species.

Species include: **African open-bill stork** (*Anastomus lamelligerus*), **American wood stork** (*Mycteria americana*), **Asian open-bill stork** (*Anastomus oscitans*), **Black-necked stork** (*Xenorhynchus asiaticus*), **Black stork** (*Ciconia nigra*), **Greater adjutant stork** (*Leptoptilos dubius*), **Jabiru stork** (*Jabiru mycteria*), **Lesser adjutant stork** (*Leptoptilos javanicus*), **Maguari stork** (*Euxenura maguari*), **marabou** (*Leptoptilos crumeniferus*), **Milky stork** V (*Ibis cinereus*), **Painted stork** (*Ibis leucocephalus*), **Saddle-bill stork** (*Ephippiorhynchus senegalensis*), **White-bellied stork** (*Ciconia abdimii*),

White-necked stork or **Woolly-necked stork** (*C. episcopus*), **White stork** (*C. ciconia*), **Yellow-billed stork** (*Ibis ibis*).

Spoonbills and ibises
Family: Threskiornithidae
Thirty-one species in 14 genera.
Southern N America, S America, southern Europe and Asia, Africa, Australia. Habitat: marshes, lake shores, plains, savannas. Size: 48–110cm (19–43in) long. Plumage: chiefly white, brown, or glossy black; the Scarlet ibis is red; the Roseate spoonbill is pink. Some, eg the Sacred ibis, the Straw-necked ibis, have modified display plumes on their neck, back or crest. Voice: honks, croaks; can bill clatter; one ibis yelps. Nests: platforms of sticks or reeds in trees, marsh plants, or on cliffs, often with an inner lining of leaves. Eggs: usually 2–5; white or blue, some with darker spots; incubation period about 21 days; nestling period 20–30 days. Diet: insects, crustaceans, carrion and other animal material.

Species include: **African spoonbill** (*Platalea alba*), **American white ibis** (*Eudocimus albus*), **Australian white ibis** (*Threskiornis molucca*), **Bald ibis** R (*Geronticus calvus*), **Black-faced spoonbill** (*Platalea minor*), **Black ibis** (*P. papillosa*), **Buff-necked ibis** (*Theristicus caudatus*), **Giant ibis** R (*Pseudibis gigantea*), **Glossy ibis** (*Plegadis falcinellus*), **Green ibis** (*Mesembrinibis cayennensis*), **hadada** (*Bostrychia hagedash*), **Hermit ibis** or **waldrapp** E (*Geronticus eremita*), **Japanese ibis** E (*Nipponia nippon*), **Oriental ibis** (*Threskiornis melanocephala*), **Puna ibis** (*Plegadis ridgway*), **Roseate spoonbill** (*Platalea ajaja*), **Royal spoonbill** (*Platalea regia*), **Sacred ibis** (*Threskiornis aethiopica*), **Scarlet ibis** (*Eudocimus ruber*), **Straw-necked ibis** (*Threskiornis spinicollis*), **Wattled ibis** (*Bostrychia carunculata*), **White-faced ibis** (*Plegadis chihi*), **White spoonbill** (*Platalea leucorodia*), **Yellow-billed spoonbill** (*P. flavipes*). Total threatened species: 6.

Hammerhead
Family: Scopidae
Sole species *Scopus umbretta*.
Hammerhead, hamerkop, or Hammerhead stork.

Africa south of the Sahara. Habitat: found near water; even small ponds are sufficient. Prefers open woodland to forest. During and after rains it may move seasonally to areas which are normally dry. Size: length about 50cm (20in). Plumage: dark brown; bill and legs black. Voice: usually silent, but utters wide range of high notes when flying or during courtship. Nests: an enormous domed structure built of sticks, weeds, grass, usually in a tree overhanging water at varying heights; the domed entrance is plastered with mud. Eggs: 3–7, white becoming mud-stained; average weight 27.6g (0.95oz); incubation period 30 days. Diet: amphibians, especially frogs, but also fish and invertebrates. Often scavenges near human habitation.

Whale-headed stork
Family: Balaenicipitidae
Sole species *Balaeniceps rex*.
Whale-headed stork or shoebill.

Swamplands of southern Sudan and western Ethiopia south through Uganda to southern Zaire and Zambia. Possibly to be seen in western Kenya (rarely) and more recently in Botswana. Habitat: fresh water swamps with tall vegetation of reeds, tall grass and papyrus. Feeds in pools and channels within the swamp. Size: length about 120cm (47in). Plumage: head gray with lighter crown. Slate gray wings with black tips. Belly nearly white. Adult bill color varies between pink and yellow, immature birds being darker. Legs black. Voice: usually silent. Frequent bill-clattering; at the nest, gives a high "gull-like" mew. Nests: on floating vegetation in deep water; sometimes on termite mounds which have become flooded. A large flat nest of reeds and other vegetation collected from nearby. Eggs: 1–3, usually 2, white. Diet: mainly fish, amphibians and reptiles, but also small birds and mammals.

Everglades marsh. The inability to obtain sufficient food to raise their young has caused continuous reproductive failure in this stork population. Thus protection of wetland habitat, and other feeding sites, is essential for conservation of storks. JAK

Ibises and spoonbills are medium-sized birds having distinctive down-curved or flattened bills. Most species are highly social, nesting, feeding, and flying in large groups. A formation of ibises gliding to their chosen night roost before a setting sun is a memorable sight. In most areas several species occur together: as many as seven in the Venezuelan *llanos*.

The most distinctive features of these birds are their bills. Ibises have long, thin, down-curved bills; spoonbills have long, broad bills, flattened at the tip. Both characteristically lack feathers on their faces; the Sacred ibis lacks feathers over its entire head and neck. Most are uniformly colored and have distinctive ornamentations, such as the elongated secondary feathers of the Sacred ibis, bright red skin color of the American white ibis, or the colored head tubercles of the Black ibis. Males are generally larger than females. The juveniles of White and Scarlet ibises have gray-brown backs for a year.

Ibises are an ancient group, the fossil record of which goes back 60 million years. The divergence of spoonbills from ibises represents the fundamental radiation within the group. Although fossils are few,

subfossils from Hawaii and Jamaica demonstrate the repeated evolution of flightlessness on islands. These island representatives may have become extinct in relatively recent times, because of man.

As birds of marshes, swamps, and savannas, both ibises and spoonbills feed on a variety of insects, frogs, crustaceans and fishes. Both feed primarily by touch rather than by sight (see p73). Ibises use their long bill for probing in soft mud, holes or under plants. Ibis species that are typically aquatic tend to have longer bills than terrestrial species. They catch slow moving or bottom-dwelling prey. The American White ibis specializes in eating crayfish and fiddler crabs; the Hermit ibis feeds on terrestrial insects and worms; the Sacred ibis often feeds on carrion scraps and associated insects. It also eats pelican and crocodile eggs broken by predators. Spoonbills usually swing their open bill from side to side in the water. The width of its bill is an aid for capturing prey, especially fish and aquatic insects.

Most species nest colonially, some at sites that can include tens of thousands of birds. Other species, such as the hadada, nest in isolation, but even this species is social when not breeding.

The nesting cycle is usually two to three months, with re-nesting sometimes occurring after a failure. Most species place their nests in bushes, but considerable variability occurs in placement. The American White

ibis nests on trees, bushes, reeds, or on the ground in marshes and swamps. Hermit and Bald ibises nest on cliffs; the hadada sometimes nests on telegraph poles. Black ibises take over raptor nests. The Buff-necked ibis nests in single pairs in palm trees in Venezuela, on cliffs in the puna and on the ground in colonies in Argentina. Isolated places, such as trees or islands surrounded by open water or marsh, are often chosen for nesting, as ground predators are less likely to occur there.

During pair formation, coloration and display accessories, such as the throat pouch of the American White ibis and black plumes of the Sacred ibis, are at their seasonal peak. In the few species studied, the male chooses a potential nest-site from which it advertises, using bill pointing and bowing displays. Females attempt to land near the male, who at first repulses them. When he accepts a female, the pair engages in mutual bowing and display preening. Solitary species use loud vocalizations to maintain contact, and may remain paired all year round. The common name of the hadada reflects its distinctive call.

The male usually gathers nest materials, which he ritually presents to the female, and both sexes defend the nest-site. Copulation takes place at the nest, and in some species "extra-marital" copulations are frequent. Both sexes incubate and feed the young regurgitated food, which the nestling

▲ **A flock of African spoonbills.** In flight, when the bill is seen side-on, spoonbills and ibises look similar. Both will travel long distances to find food when their swamps and marshes dry up.

◄ **As if dyed** from head to rump, a group of Scarlet ibises in their resplendent plumage, roosting in a tree. They are joined here by a few American white ibises, whose distribution extends north into the southern USA.

Nomadic Waders

Several species of ibises show remarkable nomadic tendencies. The Straw-necked ibis and White ibis of Australia depend on aquatic food made available by suitable water conditions. During droughts, both species disperse widely, but they concentrate to nest in intermittently flooded swamps after heavy rains bring forth an abundant supply of invertebrate food. Because such rains are unpredictable in their location, season and amount, nomadic migrations permit ibises to locate those water conditions suitable for breeding. As a result, except in areas of dependable food supplies, the size and location of ibis colonies vary.

The American white ibis undertakes similar population movements. Foraging flocks of White ibis wander over the vast inland marshes of southern Florida during the course of a year, remaining in areas where water is sufficiently shallow for foraging. As the flooded area contracts in the dry season, ibis follow the receding water, establishing a succession of night roosts near current feeding grounds. This population shift enables ibises to use most of the available habitat during the course of the year. If food supplies persist, such a roost may become a breeding colony.

Other characteristics also adapt ibises for nomadic life. They can rapidly begin nesting when conditions are suitable and can complete nesting within 2–3 months. Flock-feeding assists the birds in finding and using sites of short-lived food supplies. A variable nesting schedule and an ability to skip nesting completely are also adaptations of some ibises to make the best use of variable food supplies. As a result, some species are able to occupy highly changeable habitats and to maintain large populations.

obtains by inserting its bill down the parent's gullet. Young later leave the nest and, in colonial species, roost in groups. Fledging success depends on food supplies. Nesting failure at any stage is not uncommon when food supplies give out.

As a result of dependence on temporarily variable food supplies, local conditions determine breeding seasons. For example, the Sacred ibis has quite different breeding schedules in various parts of Africa, coinciding with local seasonal rainfall patterns. The nesting schedule in one area may vary from year to year. The Australian White ibis is particularly nomadic, nesting when and where water conditions become suitable (see box). In each case, water conditions determine food availability. Not all species in an area nest at the same time. In

▼ **The hammerhead's huge nest** attracts many other species. Verreaux's eagle owls have been known to take over the nest, and when completed Gray kestrels or Barn owls often evict the rightful owners. Smaller mammals such as genets sometimes take up residence. Monitor lizards will eat the eggs and snakes occupy the nests, making it dangerous to investigate too closely. Even during occupation by the hammerheads, small birds such as weaver birds, mynas and pigeons will attach their nests to the main nest. Old nests are quickly occupied by other hole-nesting birds such as the Egyptian goose, the Pygmy goose or the Knob-billed duck. Thus the presence of this species provides nesting sites for numerous species which otherwise would find no suitable place for breeding in the area.

Venezuela, the Green ibis nests in the wet season, but the Buff-necked ibis nests in the dry, presumably because of different choices of prey, although such dietary differences have not been established.

The migrations of ibises have figured prominently in the annual activities of various peoples. It is possible that the occurrence of Sacred ibis along the Nile was associated with the seasonal floods crucial to farming. Similarly, along the Euphrates, the Hermit ibis's return in spring was celebrated by a festival.

The high degree of sociability of most ibises and spoonbills is exposed in flocking and coloniality. Many species fly in compact flocks or in long undulating lines, alternating flapping and gliding flight. When feeding, most species form aggregations at suitable foraging sites, often with other wading bird species. In such situations, they tolerate other birds in close proximity and often move in unison. Communal roosts are located near feeding grounds, which may be shared with herons, storks and cormorants. Specific roost sites may be temporary, lasting only as long as nearby food supplies, or may persist for years.

The conservation of ibises and spoonbills depends on their protection and habitat preservation. The Sacred ibis, a seasonal resident along the Nile for millennia, has been absent from Egypt since the first half of the 19th century. The Hermit ibis had nested in the alpine area of central Europe from at least the Stone Age into the 17th century but is now confined to small areas of North Africa and the Middle East. Hunting, despite protective laws, led to its decline, hastened by habitat change. This ibis was lost from Europe very early, and it was not until the end of the 19th century that it was found to be extant in Asia Minor. These populations total less than a thousand birds. The most endangered ibis species is the Japanese crested ibis. Fewer than two dozen individuals are known to survive in China and Japan. The species was widely distributed in these two countries until the early 20th century, and in Korea until World War II. It is possible that loss of suitable habitat—pine forests surrounded by swamp land—may have contributed to its demise. The Giant ibis, only found in lowland Southeast Asia, is also nearing extinction, and Black-faced spoonbills are becoming very scarce.   JAK

The **hammerhead**, though often called "stork," is not a close relation of that family and is a distinctive species. Usually, it has been included in the heron family, but it is sometimes linked to the flamingos because it has a free hind toe; its true taxonomic position is as yet unclear.

Usually seen in pairs, this all-brown bird is common throughout the African savanna, even feeding at pools by the roadside. Its name derives from the crest extending behind the head. The toes are partly webbed. Its short tail and huge wings enable it to glide and soar easily, which it does with its head stretched forward. Usually when disturbed it will fly only a short distance. It is a sedentary species which remains in a well-defined territory, although some pairs will move to normally dry areas when the seasonal rains fill dry holes and ditches. Wherever man-made dams or canals are built, the hammerhead will quickly arrive and if trees are not available it will build its huge nest (often several in a season) on a wall, bank, cliff or sometimes even on the ground.

Hammerheads are also to be seen in group ceremonies, usually near a nest. They can involve a number of birds together and as many as ten birds may call loudly while running round each other in circles, a male

and the body plumage within a month. While both birds feed the young, they leave them for long periods, presumably being enabled to do so because of the thickness of the nest walls which protect them. When the young are fully fledged, they remain near the nest for another month, using it to roost in at night.

A disproportionately large bill and head give the **Whale-headed stork** both its name and an oddly unbalanced look. This large stork-like bird has some of the characteristics of herons, storks and pelicans, but has no direct affinity to any of these families, so is placed in a family of its own.

The Whale-headed stork is bulky and slow moving; when it feeds it stands with its bill, which is hooked at the end, pointed downwards. It then stretches its neck and hurls itself forward with wings outstretched and gulps its prey. The prey is ground apart by a scissoring action of the mandibles and accompanying vegetation is discarded. A large drink of water is taken after the meal is consumed.

The Whale-headed stork seldom travels far, preferring a favorite piece of marsh in which to fish, and not moving unless forced to do so by changing water conditions. It does, however, fly up on the thermals like a stork, though it tucks in its neck like a heron. It usually fishes alone, but will join with others of its own species, as well as herons and storks, in feeding in pools which are drying out, and where the large fish stocks can be easily harvested.

Both sexes incubate the eggs, often standing to turn them with bill or feet, and in hot weather pouring beakfuls of water over them to cool them. Greeting at the nest by a pair is done by bill clattering and bowing in a manner similar to that of storks. The young have silvery-gray down. Their heads are large, but the bill takes some time to develop its extraordinary shape. Early feeding of the chick is by regurgitating food onto the floor of the nest, but later whole prey are left and the chick swallows them whole. It is most unusual for more than one Whale-headed stork chick to be successfully reared each year.

Like many highly specialized large birds which require very special habitats, the Whale-headed stork is becoming dangerously low in numbers. While it is not persecuted by native populations, the drainage of wetlands, disturbance by cattle and the robbing of nests by zoos has reduced its numbers alarmingly and probably only 1,000–2,000 still remain over the vast area of its African habitat. JH

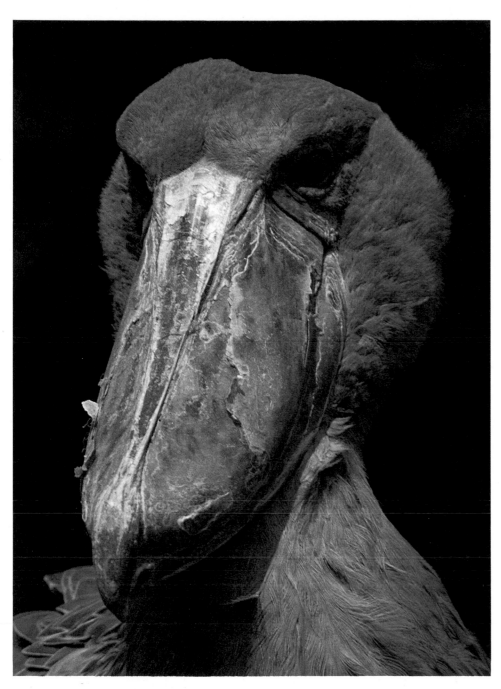

▲ **The flaking bill** of a Whale-headed stork. The huge bill is adapted for feeding on fish such as lungfish and gars and also frogs and perhaps young turtles, crocodiles and small mammals.

sometimes mounting a crouching female and sometimes pretending to copulate without actually doing so. Crests are raised, wings fluttered and a chorus of cries continues for several minutes.

True mating is usually done at a completed nest site, often on top of the nest, using displays similar to those used during the larger gathering of birds. When the eggs have been laid, both birds share incubation, although very frequently partly incubated clutches will be abandoned. When the young hatch they are covered with gray down, but quickly develop feathers, with the head and crest completed within 17 days

Up-down, Flying Around
Courtship and relationships among storks

"Advertising Sway," "Flap-Dash," "Flying Around," "Gaping," "Up-Down"—these are all names given to forms of courtship display found in storks. These gestures are as repeatable and consistent as bill-shape and plumage patterns, and can be used to assess evolutionary relationships, some gestures being considered more derived and others more primitive. The advertisement display of the White stork has been well known for centuries, and was illustrated in 13th century manuscripts.

The most typical, and in some storks the most remarkable, courtship behavior is the *Up-Down*. It is a greeting issued when one member of a pair returns to its nest. In giving the display a stork raises then lowers its head in a characteristic stylized manner. Although present in all storks, it differs importantly among species. The head movement is usually accompanied by a vocalization, such as the bill-clattering of the typical storks. The amount of bill-clattering differs among the species of this group. The White stork has a loud, resonant bill-clatter that may last ten seconds or more; yet the Black stork clatters only infrequently. Such a difference in the display suggests that within the group of typical storks these two species are not closely related. The White stork also differs from the other typical storks in that its *Up-Down* is not accompanied by whistling. The typical storks are distinguished from other groups of species by uniquely sharing a *Head-Shaking Crouch*, in which the male crouches on its nest and shakes its head from side to side as if saying "no," which is probably also the message of the display, since it is given as another bird approaches its nest.

The *Up-Down* behavior is simplest in the wood storks. It consists mainly of raising the head and gaping the bill, then emitting hissing screams as the head and bill are lowered. The display differs among the four species, forming an evolutionary sequence. The American wood stork does not snap its bill during the display; the Yellow-billed stork gives a single or double snap; the Painted stork gives double or triple snaps; the Milky stork gives multiple snaps. The wood storks share three displays that are unique among storks: *Flying Around*, in which a male that has just accepted a female leaves its nest and flies in a circle before returning; *Gaping*, in which a bird holds its parted mandibles open; and *Display Preening*, in which the male pretends to comb the feathers on its wing with its bill. The displays of the open-bill storks strongly resemble those of wood storks, especially their simple *Up-Down* and

also their copulation clattering, in which a male during copulation clatters his mandibles while knocking them against the bill of the female. Because of such resemblances, the wood storks and open-bill storks are thought to be more closely related to each other than they are to other storks. Open-bills also have a unique display, the *Advertising Sway*, in which a displaying male bends its head down between its legs and repeatedly shifts its weight from one foot to the next.

Differences in the details of the *Up-Down* display among closely related storks demonstrate important distinctions not otherwise obvious. The *Up-Down* of the adjutants includes moving the bill to vertical, accompanied by mooing and squealing. The marabou and Greater adjutant are similar-looking birds, which do not overlap in range. Their displays differ, however, in that marabous first throw their head upward and squeal with the bill near vertical, before pointing it downward and clattering loudly. The Greater adjutant clatters while the bill is pointed upward. The difference in this important pair-bonding display suggests that the birds would not interbreed should their ranges overlap, and so are best considered as separate species.

The Black-necked and Saddle-bill storks display infrequently because of their long-lasting pair bond. The *Up-Down* of the Black-necked stork is a spectacular greeting that includes rapid fluttering of fully extended wings and clattering of bills, but the head is not raised. These two species and the jabiru share a distinctive display given on the foraging grounds, the *Flap-Dash*, in which a bird dashes wildly through the water while vigorously flapping its wings.

Comparative behavioral observations have discovered distinctive traits from which relationships among the storks can be deduced. The distribution of these traits corresponds to other differences and similarities in morphology, plumage, and foraging habits, which support and confirm the relationships suggested by courtship displays.   JAK

▲ **Stork displays.** Storks have a wide range of aggressive and courtship displays. (**1**) The last stage of the 'Clattering Threat' in the Yellow-billed stork. (**2**) "Display Preening" in the Painted stork; in this courting pair the male in front is preening behind the wing. (**3**) A marabou showing the "Anxiety Stretch" in response to disturbance by people on the ground under the nest. (**4**) A male Yellow-billed stork giving an "Up-Down" display as his newly acquired mate approaches the nest-site. (**5**) A courting male Asian open-bill stork performing the "Advertising Sway" at a potential nest-site. (**6**) "Head-shaking Crouch" of a male White-bellied stork as a potential mate approaches. (**7**) "Full Back," a position in the "Up-Down" display of White storks.

◀ **"Up-Down" display** by a pair of Painted storks on the nest.

FLAMINGOS

Family: Phoenicopteridae
Order: Ciconiiformes (suborder Phoenicopteri).
Four species in 3 genera.
Distribution: around the world in a wide range of tropical and warm temperate sites, some at high altitude.

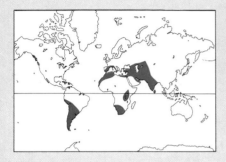

Habitat: shallow salt or soda lagoons and lakes.
Plumage: pink, sexes similar.

Size: 80–145cm (31–57in) long and 1.9–3kg (4.2–6.6lb), females smaller.

Nest: mud-built mounds.
Eggs: usually single, white, weight about 100g (3.5oz); incubation period 28 days, nestling period 75 days.
Diet: algae and diatoms, aquatic invertebrates, particularly crustaceans and mollusks.

Species: **James' flamingo** (*Phoenicoparrus jamesi*), **Lesser flamingo** (*Phoeniconaias minor*), **Andean flamingo** (*Phoenicoparrus andinus*). Subspecies: **Caribbean flamingo** (*Phoenicopterus ruber ruber*), **Chilean flamingo** (*P. r. chilensis*), **Greater flamingo** (*P. r. roseus*).

▶ **Bills tucked under** ABOVE in their characteristic style, these Caribbean flamingos are feeding by filtering food organisms from the water and mud taken in by their bills.

▶ **"Head Flagging"** in a group of Greater flamingos. This is the first stage in their ritualized group displays.

▶ **Flamingo twilight** OVERLEAF. A colony of Greater flamingos, picked out by the late sun. The dull brown plumage of the young birds in the foreground contrasts markedly with the pink-flecked white of the adults.

WHETHER flamingos are thought to be bizarre or beautiful depends on their numbers: individually they are rather grotesque, but two million pink birds massed around the edge of Lake Nakuru in Kenya's Rift Valley make a breathtaking spectacle.

Fossils suggest that flamingos once ranged through Europe, North America and Australia, as well as in areas where they are found today, but the group now occurs only in isolated pockets, mainly in the tropics and sometimes at high altitudes. They are unusual in feeding on the microscopic blue-green algae, diatoms and invertebrates that live in alkaline salt and soda lakes.

Flamingos have large bodies with long legs for wading, long necks and small heads. Their pink and crimson plumage, with black secondary and primary wing feathers, makes them conspicuous and unmistakable. The Caribbean flamingo is the brightest (as are the Caribbean ibis and spoonbill among their respective families) and there is a single molt of the feathers of wing and body per breeding cycle. Legs, bills and faces are brightly colored red, pink, orange or yellow. The rather small feet are webbed and the birds can use these webs to swim and to stir up debris from the mud by trampling. Males are larger than females, markedly so in some species, but this is the only obvious difference between the sexes. At hatching, the chick has gray down, a straight, pink bill and swollen pink legs, both of which turn black within a week. Juveniles in first plumage are gray, with brown and pink markings, and their legs and bills are black. When fully grown, bills are turned down in the middle, with the upper jaw small and lid-like and the lower one large and trough-like; both are fringed and lined with filtering comb-like structures called lamellae, and the tongue is thick and spiny.

The feeding method of flamingos is characteristic and peculiar. The bill is held upside-down in the water and the tongue acts as a piston so that water and mud are sucked in along the whole gape and expelled three or four times a second past the filtering lamellae. In the small Lesser, James' and Andean flamingos, which have deep-keeled bills, very fine particles, such as algae and diatoms are retained, and coarse particles are kept out by stiff excluder lamellae. The "shallow-keeled" Caribbean, Greater and Chilean flamingos are larger and feed mainly on invertebrates such as brine flies (*Ephydra*), shrimps (*Artemia*) and mollusks (*Cerithium*), which they obtain from the bottom mud, normally by wading in shallow water, more rarely while swimming, and sometimes by upending like ducks. The brilliant red color of flamingo plumage derives from the rich sources of carotenoid pigments (similar to the pigments of carrots) in the algae that the birds consume either directly or secondarily. Blue-green algae are also an extremely rich source of protein, and dense blooms of the planktonic algae *Spirulina platensis* are associated with the gathering of huge flocks of Lesser flamingos in East Africa; success in breeding probably depends on such blooms.

Flamingos are an ancient group, the fossil evidence for which goes back to at least the Miocene epoch (about 10 million years ago). Their classification is still controversial. Usually they have been considered a suborder of the storks (Ciconiiformes) and their egg-white proteins resemble those of

herons (Ardeidae). On the basis of behavior and feather lice they have seemed most like waterfowl (Anseriformes), but recently affinity with the waders (Charadriiformes) has been stressed because of supposed similarities between flamingos and the Australian banded stilt. The Caribbean flamingo seems to show more "primitive" displays than the other two subspecies of *Phoenicopterus ruber*, while the Chilean flamingo seems to be sufficiently different from the other two that it is treated, by some authorities, as a separate species. Andean and James' flamingos differ from the Lesser flamingo in having no hind toe, or "hallux", but all three have a more specialized feeding apparatus than the larger flamingos of *Phoenicopterus*.

Flamingos appear to be monogamous and can be very long-lived: 50-year-old birds are probably not unusual in the wild. The pair bond is strong and often sustained from one season to the next. They tend to be rather erratic in breeding, and whether they nest or not depends mainly upon rainfall and the effect it has on the food supply of the adult birds. The nest mound is made of mud and may be 30cm (12in) high, thus giving protection from flooding and from the often intense heat at ground level. Nests are built by male and female using a simple technique of drawing mud towards the feet with the bill. The single large chalky egg is incubated by both sexes in turn and, after hatching, the chick remains in the nest for some days. Here it is fed by its parents on a secretion from the glands of the upper digestive tract or crop (see box). The Caribbean flamingo chick can feed itself from 4–6 weeks of age but, in at least the Greater and Lesser flamingos, parental feeding continues until fledging, by which time the bill of the chick is hooked as in the adult and the youngster is capable of independent feeding. After they leave the nest, the young move into large creches which in the Lesser flamingo may contain as many as 30,000 birds; parents apparently find their own chick in the group and feed it alone, recognizing it by its calls. The young bird is fledged in about 11 weeks and gradually loses the gray juvenile color over two or three years but will not display and breed until it is fully pink. Flamingos did not nest successfully in zoos until the importance of good feather color of the adults was realized, and an effort made to increase the carotenoids in the diet. Carrots, peppers, dried shrimps and other such items were tried initially; today synthetic canthaxanthin is added to the food, and the large

Phoenicopterus flamingos are breeding more regularly in captivity.

The birds are highly gregarious at all stages of their life-history and the displaying and nesting colonies are noisy affairs. Breeding in small numbers is almost unknown; an exception is provided by the Caribbean flamingo, whose isolated population on the Galapagos islands occasionally nests in groups of only 3–5 pairs. Group display seems to bring all the birds of the colony to the same readiness to mate and thus ensures rapid and synchronized egg-laying in a potentially unstable breeding habitat.

It is interesting that the founder of systematic biology, Linnaeus, described the Caribbean flamingo as the typical flamingo

Flamingo's Milk

Two groups of birds, flamingos and pigeons, feed their young on "milk". Compared with pigeon milk, the secretion from the crop of the flamingo has somewhat less protein (8–9 percent versus 13.3–18.6 percent) and more fat (15 percent versus 6.9–12.7 percent). There is almost no carbohydrate in either case. About 1 percent of flamingo milk is made up of red blood cells whose origin is unknown. Thus bird milk is similar in nutritional value to that of mammals.

As with mammalian milk, secretion is controlled by a hormone called prolactin. In birds, the hormone causes a proliferation of the cells of the crop gland in males and females, so that both sexes feed their offspring, whereas in mammals "nursing" is only ever a female task. Flamingos have been studied extensively in captivity and it has been found that a few birds that are not parents produce milk, and even seven-week-old chicks can act as foster-feeders for smaller orphaned birds. The persistent begging calls of the youngster seem to stimulate hormone secretion. Milk is not produced until the crop is cleared of food, so that food items themselves are never regurgitated.

The crop milk of the flamingo contains initially large amounts of canthaxanthin (the pigment that colors the adult feathers), which gives the milk a bright red color. This pigment is stored in the young bird's liver and not in the down nor in the juvenile plumage, which is gray.

Parental feeding of this specialized kind seems to be an adaptation to ensure that the young obtain enough food, especially protein. The high alkalinity of the water in which the adults feed, their unusual feeding habits and bill structure, and the fact that they may nest some distance from their food source, probably encouraged the evolution of crop milk manufacture. The system is successful only because the clutch size of the flamingo is so small (usually a single egg), even smaller than in most pigeons.

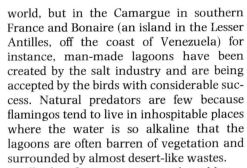

◀ **Flight of the flamingo.** Chilean flamingos at 4,000m (13,000ft) high in the Andes, near the limit of their range for height.

▶ **Flamingo displays** are similar to the preening and stretching movements that the birds adopt in everyday activity. The displays are only more stiffly performed, more contagious amongst members of the group, and given in predictable sequences. "Head Flagging" followed by "Wing Saluting," in which a bird spreads its wings to the sides and folds them again, is common. The general effect is a flash of black in a pink field. (1) "Wing Salute" in Chilean flamingo. (2) "Wing Salute" in Greater flamingo. A 'Twist-Preen' may then follow (3): a Caribbean flamingo twists its neck back, flashing a wing forward to expose the black primaries, and appears to preen behind the wing with its bill. In the "Inverted Wing Salute" (4), given here by a Greater flamingo, the bird bends foward and the wings are flashed partly open and held above the back. Mating displays between male and female are, on the other hand, almost non-existent and quite inconspicuous.

▼ **Inelegant feeders.** All flamingos feed with their bills upside-down. These are Lesser flamingos, the smallest species.

of the family Phoenicopteridae, and not the European Greater flamingo with which one might have thought he was more familiar. Early travelers to the West Indies must have produced the specimens that he described. They also returned with myths about the incubating postures of the birds: they were said to sit while dangling their legs in front of the mud nest mounds, whereas they fold them under in exactly the same way that other birds do. The color of flamingo feathers fades gradually in sunlight and this perhaps has been one reason why large numbers have not been taken in the past for the plumage trade, but their tongues were once pickled as a rare delicacy, and flamingo fat is still considered a cure for tuberculosis by some Andean miners. The development of salt and soda extraction works has been a particular threat in various parts of the world, but in the Camargue in southern France and Bonaire (an island in the Lesser Antilles, off the coast of Venezuela) for instance, man-made lagoons have been created by the salt industry and are being accepted by the birds with considerable success. Natural predators are few because flamingos tend to live in inhospitable places where the water is so alkaline that the lagoons are often barren of vegetation and surrounded by almost desert-like wastes.

All the flamingos are vulnerable to habitat change and exploitation. James' flamingo is rare, but the crimson Caribbean flamingo is perhaps more threatened because it breeds in only four main colonies around the Gulf of Mexico (Yucatan, Inagua, Cuba and Bonaire), and is in great demand by zoos. Many birds die when they are caught—they tend to travel badly and are susceptible to stress upon arrival. So far, the three smaller species have bred seldom or not at all in captivity, and birds are still taken from the wild for the zoo trade in regrettably large numbers. JK

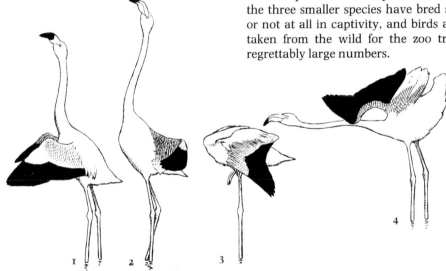

SWANS, GEESE, DUCKS – THE WATERFOWL

Order: Anseriformes
Families: Anatidae, Anhimidae.
One hundred and fifty-two species in 43 genera.
Distribution: worldwide except Antarctica.

Swans, Geese, Ducks   **Screamers**

Swans, geese and ducks

Family: Anatidae
One hundred and 49 species in 41 genera.
Total threatened species: 12.
Distribution: worldwide except Antarctica.
Habitat: chiefly coastal, freshwater wetlands.
Size: 30–150cm (12–59in) long, weight 250g
(8.8oz) to 15kg (33lb) or more.
Plumage: very variable, majority show some
white, combinations of black and white
frequent, some all white or all black; also grays,
browns and chestnut common; green or purple
gloss often on head or on wing-patch. In some
genera males bright, females dull camouflaged
brown, but sexes similar in others.
Voice: some genera very vocal (usually quack,
cackle, whistle or hiss), others mostly silent or
with soft calls connected with display.
Nests: majority a platform of vegetation,
occasionally on rocky ledge or tree crown;
some in already existing holes in trees.
Eggs: 4–14; white, creamy, pale green, blue,
unmarked; incubation 18–39 days; young
leave nest early, self-feeding except for Magpie
goose; fledging period 21–110 days.
Diet: wide variety of animals and plants,
including fish, mollusks, crustaceans, insects
and their larvae, and aquatic and terrestrial
vegetation—leaves, stems, roots and seeds.

Screamers

Family: Anhimidae
Three species in 2 genera.
Distribution: South America.
Habitat: open wet grasslands and marshes,
shallow lagoons.
Size: 70–95cm (28–37in) long, weight 2–5kg
(4.4–11lb).
Plumage: black, gray, brown; sexes similar.
Voice: loud screams.
Nests: large platform on ground near water.
Eggs: 2–6; whitish tinged buff or pale green;
incubation 40–45 days; young leave nest early,
self-feeding; fledging in 60–75 days.
Diet: vegetation.
Species: **Black-necked screamer** (*Chauna
chavaria*), **Crested screamer** (*C. torquata*),
Horned screamer (*Anhima cornuta*).

THE waterfowl (swans, geese and ducks)
have, for thousands of years, provided
man with eggs, meat and feathers. He has
hunted them, pursued them for sport, and
domesticated them. More recently, he has
become aware of the aesthetic pleasure
which they can give, and of the need to conserve both them and their habitats.

The waterfowl and the screamers are
birds of water and wetlands. Nearly all of
them nest on or beside fresh water, but
several species (eg Brant goose, steamer
ducks, scoters) live much of their lives in
estuaries and on shallow seas.

Unlike the screamers of South America,
waterfowl are found on every continent
except Antarctica, and on all larger, and
many very small, islands. A few species,
including the Hawaiian goose and some
subspecies, or races, of other species, are
numbered only in hundreds, and may be
confined to a single island. Others are
extremely numerous, perhaps occurring in
millions, and are distributed very widely.
Different distribution patterns may result
from great adaptability to a considerable
range of habitats and food, as in the case
of the mallard, or be linked to long-distance
migration, eg the White-fronted goose, or be
the consequence of some chance colonization of an oceanic island, followed by the loss
of any migratory instinct and gradual evolution to fit the conditions found there, as in
the Laysan teal in the Pacific, the Kerguelen
pintail in the Indian Ocean and the Falkland
Islands flightless steamer duck in the south
Atlantic. Two species of waterfowl are
restricted, apart from vagrants, to Europe,
12 to Asia, 18 to Africa, 10 to North

▲ **Male Black swan incubates the clutch,** taking turns with his mate. In nearly all other species of the family, incubation is largely by the female. Like other swans and geese, Black swans (*Cygnus atrata*) are often faithful to their mate for many years. Both build the bulky waterside nest, and share the care of the young, often through their first winter. Unlike other swans, the Australian Black swan usually nests in colonies.

◄ **Duckweed feast for mallard ducklings.** As well as "dabbling" just under water, they scoop up mouthfuls of surface water and then strain out the tiny leaves, seeds and insects that form their diet. The familiar mallard is widespread in the Northern Hemisphere, and is the ancestor of most domestic breeds of duck.

well back on the body, some very far back, and so progress on land can be slow and awkward. However, the many species which feed underwater (eg diving ducks, sea ducks, stifftails) are thereby able to move quickly and to maneuver well. A very few ducks (eg Red-breasted merganser) also use their wings underwater, but generally the wings are held tight to the body when diving. Geese and sheldgeese are generally more terrestrial, especially when feeding— their longer legs are placed more centrally beneath the body, they stand more upright and walk with ease.

Screamers are goose-like in overall shape, though they have a heavier body not unlike that of a turkey, and very broad wings. Their long, thick legs end in large feet with long toes which have only very slight webbing at the base. Their bill is quite different from any waterfowl species, being short, down-curved, ending in a distinct hook, and lacking any lamellae. Screamers rarely, if ever, swim, but use their long-toed feet to best advantage when walking over floating mats of vegetation. Their hooked bill is used for grasping and tearing off plant leaves and stems. The main plumage coloring is gray, black and white. Screamers are noisy birds, and their display appears to include a soaring flight on their broad wings, with frequent calling.

The **waterfowl** are divided here into eleven tribes based mainly on internal features, such as the skeleton, but also on external features—for example, the type and pattern of plumage both in adults and the downy (less than three-week-old) young—and, through fairly recent studies, on behavior, particularly the displays that accompany the formation and maintenance of pairs.

The **Magpie goose** of Australasia is the only member of the tribe Anseranatini. It shares features with the screamers, particularly the overall long-legged, long-necked shape and the reduced webbing between the toes. The bill is more typically waterfowl-shaped, though deep and broad at the base, and rising into a steep forehead ending in an enlarged dome to the head. The flight is steady and direct on broad, slow-flapping wings. The plumage of the Magpie goose is black and white, as it is in many waterfowl, but the wing feathers are not molted all at once as in nearly all other waterfowl, and so the birds do not become flightless during their wing molt. In contrast to all other waterfowl, Magpie goose parents feed their young, passing food items from bill to bill.

Whistling ducks (tribe Dendrocygnini)

America, 30 to Central and South America, and 25 to Australasia. The remaining 50 species of waterfowl occur more widely, in two or more continents. The Hawaiian goose is placed in a separate species, but all other forms on small oceanic islands are treated, in most classifications, as subspecies of mainland species.

Waterfowl are essentially aquatic birds, and so have a generally broad body, flattened underneath, a medium to long neck, and shortish legs with webbed feet. The bill is usually rather broad and flattened, with a horny "nail" towards the tip which in some species ends with a slight hook. The sides of the mandibles, in most species, have comb-like lamellae for straining food particles from the water, while the tongue is rather thick with short, spiny teeth along its edges, used in grasping and manipulating food items. Most ducks have their legs set have a wide distribution throughout the tropics and subtropics. Most are confined to rather small ranges, which do not overlap. The Fulvous whistling duck, however, has a most extraordinary distribution for a bird, occurring in the Americas, East Africa and Madagascar, and southern Asia; yet across all this enormous but discontinuous range there is no detectable variation of form.

Whistling ducks are mostly quite small, long-legged birds with an upright stance. They get their name from their high-pitched whistling calls. An alternative name for them is "tree ducks," from their fairly general habit of perching on branches. They have broad wings and are maneuverable fliers rather than fast ones. As well as walking well on land, they both swim and dive. The plumage is the same in both sexes, often highly patterned, particularly with brown, gray and fawn. The flank feathers of the Fulvous and three other species are enlarged in showy ornaments, and the downy young have a distinctive plumage quite unlike that of any other waterfowl except the Coscoroba swan. The unique feature is a pale yellow or white line running right round the head

under the eyes; the head is dark-capped. After copulation the whistling duck pair indulges in a mutual display, both sexes performing similar actions.

The **swans and "true" geese** (tribe Anserini) conduct a mutual display before copulation, and also a "triumph" ceremony after a rival male has been successfully driven off. The 15 species of geese are confined to the Northern Hemisphere, their place in the Southern Hemisphere being taken by the sheldgeese. Three of the six swan species are confined (apart from introductions) to the Northern Hemisphere, and three occur only south of the Equator. The swans include the largest of the waterfowl, over 2m (6.6ft) in wingspan, and weighing up to 15kg (33lb) or more. They are very long-necked but comparatively short in the leg, and not very mobile on land. In contrast, the geese are able to walk and run well; their moderately long legs being more centrally placed on their bodies. Their necks are medium to long. Both swans and geese are powerful fliers, and several undertake regular migrations covering thousands of kilometers.

The swans have either all-white plumage,

► **Representative species of swans and geese.** (1) Bar-headed goose (*Anser indicus*). (2) Red-breasted goose (*Branta ruficollis*) in aggressive threat posture. (3) Magpie goose (*Anseranas semipalmata*). (4) Crested screamer (*Chauna torquata*). (5) Hawaiian goose (*Branta sandvicensis*) male in triumph display after seeing off a rival. (6) Whooper swan (*Cygnus cygnus*) in similar situation. (7) Emperor goose (*Anser canagicus*) on nest in tundra region. (8) Pink-footed goose (*Anser fabalis brachyrhyncus*), most westerly of three subspecies of Bean goose. (9) Black-necked swan (*Cygnus melanchoryphus*) carrying cygnets on back.

The 11 Tribes of Swans, Geese and Ducks

<u>V</u> Vulnerable.   <u>Ex</u> Extinct.   <u>T</u> Threatened, status indeterminate.

Magpie goose
Tribe: Anseranatini
Sole species *Anseranas semipalmata*.

Whistling ducks
Tribe: Dendrocygnini
Nine species in 2 genera.
Species include: **Fulvous whistling duck** (*Dendrocygna bicolor*).

Swans and true geese
Tribe: Anserini
Twenty-one species in 4 genera.
Species include: **Barnacle goose** (*Branta leucopsis*), **Bewick's or Whistling swan** (*Cygnus columbianus*), **Brent goose** or **brant** (*Branta bernicla*), **Coscoroba swan** (*Coscoroba coscoroba*), **Hawaiian goose** <u>V</u> (*Branta sandvicensis*), **Mute swan** (*Cygnus olor*), **Snow goose** (*Anser caerulescens*), **White-fronted goose** (*A. albifrons*).

Freckled duck
Tribe: Stictonettini
Sole species *Stictonetta naevosa*.

Shelduck and sheldgeese
Tribe: Tadornini
Sixteen species in 7 genera.
Species include: **Egyptian goose** (*Alopochen aegyptiacus*), **Ruddy-headed goose** <u>V</u> (*Chloephaga rubidiceps*), **shelduck** (*Tadorna tadorna*).

Steamer ducks
Tribe: Tachyerini
Three species of the genus *Tachyeres*.
Species include: **Falkland Islands flightless steamer duck** (*Tachyeres brachyapterus*).

Perching ducks and geese
Tribe: Cairinini
Thirteen species in 8 genera.
Species include: **Comb** or **Knob-billed** goose (*Sarkidiornis melanotos*), **Hartlaub's duck** (*Pteronetta hartlaubii*), **Mandarin duck** (*Aix galericulata*), **Muscovy duck** (*Cairina moschata*), **Pygmy goose** (*Nettapus coromandelianus*), **Spur-winged goose** (*Plectropterus gambensis*).

Dabbling ducks
Tribe: Anatini
Forty species in 5 genera.
Species include: **Cinnamon teal** (*Anas cyanoptera*), **Eurasian widgeon** (*A. penelope*), **mallard** (*A. platyrhynchos*), **pintail** (*A. acuta*), **Pink-headed duck** (*Rhodonessa caryophyllacea*), **Torrent duck** (*Merganetta armata*).

Diving ducks
Tribe: Aythyini
Sixteen species in 3 genera.
Species include: **canvasback** (*Aythya valisineria*), **South American pochard** (*Netta erythrophthalma*), **Tufted duck** (*Aythya fuligula*).

Sea ducks and sawbills
Tribe: Mergini
Twenty species in 8 genera.
Species include: **Brazilian merganser** <u>T</u> (*Mergus octosetaceus*), **Common eider** (*Somateria mollissima*), **Common scoter** (*Melanitta nigra*), **Labrador duck** <u>Ex</u> (*Camptorhynchus labradorius*), **Long-tailed duck** or **oldsquaw** (*Clangula hyemalis*), **Red-breasted merganser** (*Mergus serrator*).

Stifftails
Tribe: Oxyurini
Eight species in 3 genera.
Species include: **Black-headed duck** (*Heteronetta atricapilla*), **Ruddy duck** (*Oxyura jamaicensis*).

---

or some combination of black and white, varying from white with black outer wings to black with white outer wings. The geese are more variable, with some species black and white, other predominantly gray or brown. The sexes are similar in all species.

The **Freckled duck**, only representative of the tribe Stictonettini, is rather duck-like in overall shape, and has comparatively short legs. Male and female are similar in plumage, being mottled gray-brown all over, though the male gets a reddish bill during the breeding season. There are sufficient structural and behavioral similarities to place this tribe next to the Anserini.

The **shelducks and sheldgeese** (tribe Tadornini) comprise one genus of shelducks (seven species, one probably extinct), four genera of sheldgeese (eight species), and two other single-species genera. Shelducks occur worldwide except for Central and North America, but the others are confined to the Southern Hemisphere, with the single exception of the Egyptian goose. They are medium-sized birds, the sheldgeese upright in stance, and all feed on land as well as in the water.

Plumage is very variable in this group, though the majority of species have a green speculum (patch on outer half of the secondaries) which is iridescent, and white wing coverts. Other common colors include some white, black, chestnut and gray. The sexes are similar in some species, but completely contrasting in others. The displays show some similarities with those of the geese. Some, if not all, sheldgeese molt their wing feathers sequentially (like the Magpie

goose, see above); furthermore, the wing molt may occur only every other year.

The **steamer ducks** (tribe Tachyerini) are often lumped together with the preceding tribe. They are confined to southern South America, where they lead a predominantly aquatic life, often round the coasts. Two species have such short wings that they are completely flightless, while the third flies infrequently and weakly. All are very sturdily built, with short necks and legs and powerful bills. Steamer ducks get their name from their habit of threshing over the water like a paddle-steamer's wheel, using wings and legs in order to move more quickly, when escaping from danger. Their plumage is predominantly gray and the sexes are alike.

The **perching ducks and geese** (tribe Cairinini) are a somewhat varied collection of small and medium-sized ducks, and some larger goose-like birds. They can perch on branches and other structures, an ability rare or absent in nearly all other waterfowl. Most are hole-nesters, and their young have sharp claws on their feet and rather stiff tails, both used in climbing out of the holes soon after hatching. Perching ducks and geese occur mainly in tropical and subtropical latitudes, extending into the temperate zone in a few cases (eg mandarins). The sexes are dissimilar among smaller species (eg pygmy geese), which show a wide variation in coloring, from dull brown to bright chestnut, green and white. Among larger species (eg Comb duck, Spur-winged goose) the sexes are alike in plumage, but the males are usually considerably larger than the

▶ **Seeing off a rival gander**, one male Canada goose intercepts and threatens another. There are 10 or more subspecies—the larger ones known as "honkers"—but all have a black head and neck and contrasting white cheek patches.

▼ ▶ **Representative species of ducks.**
(1) Mandarin duck (*Aix galericulata*).
(2) White-faced tree duck (*Dendrocygna viduata*).
(3) Red-breasted merganser (*Mergus serrator*).
(4) Ruddy duck (*Oxyura jamaicensis*)
CONTINUED OVERLEAF.

1

females. Black and white, the former often glossed with green, predominate.

The **dabbling ducks** (Anatini) are the largest tribe of waterfowl. The great majority are small, short-legged, aquatic birds, feeding on the surface of the water or, by up-ending (dabbling), just beneath it. One species, the Torrent duck, of which there are a number of well-marked geographic races, is highly adapted for living in the fast-flowing streams of the Andes in South America; it has a very streamlined shape, sharp claws for gripping slippery boulders, and a long stiff tail used for steering in the fast-rushing water. Dabbling ducks occur throughout the world, including remote oceanic islands, from where a number of non-migrating subspecies (eg Laysan teal, Andaman teal, and Rennell Island gray teals) have been described. Many other dabbling ducks (eg pintail, teal, widgeon) are highly migratory and fly long distances; the smaller species are also very maneuverable in the air, and take off from the water almost vertically.

In many species the male is brightly colored, generally with an iridescent speculum in the wing, while the female is a well-camouflaged brown. Brown, green, chestnut, white and pale blue all occur

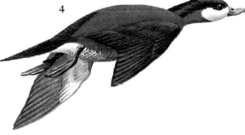

frequently. Displays involve complex movements by the male, which show off his plumage to best advantage. The female is much less demonstrative and mutual display movements are absent or rare.

The **diving ducks** (tribe Aythyini) have a worldwide distribution and are principally freshwater species, though some winter on the coasts, and obtain their food by diving. To facilitate this, their short legs are set well back on their generally plump bodies; they only rarely venture onto land. To become airborne usually involves a take-off run over the surface of the water, accompanied by rapid wing beats. Although males have different coloration from females, they are not especially brightly colored; gray, brown and black are the commonest colors. They lack the speculum of the shelducks and other members of the family, but often have a whitish wing stripe. Iridescence is quite frequent on the dark head and chest. Their displays are relatively simple.

The **sea ducks and sawbills** (tribe Mergini) here include the eiders, which are sometimes separated into their own tribe, the Somaterini. Most are principally saltwater species, diving for their animal food, though several breed beside fresh water. Most are restricted to the Northern Hemisphere, but the Brazilian merganser occurs in South America, and another species (now extinct)

5

6

once occurred on islands south of New Zealand. Many are rather bulky and heavily built, requiring a long take-off for their rather labored flight. Some of the small species are much more agile and fast moving. Almost all are sexually dimorphic, with the males mainly black or black and white, though often with iridescent green or blue heads, or with pastel coloring of green and blue. Displays by the males are often quite elaborate and vary greatly between species. The females are much less demonstrative.

The eleventh tribe, the **stifftails** (Oxyurini) are mostly found in the Southern Hemisphere, with just two occurring in the northern. They are small, dumpy birds, with tails of short, stiff feathers, used for steering underwater. Their legs are set very far back on their bodies and movement on land is limited. Males are mainly dark chestnut or brown, often with black or black and white heads, while many species have a bright

blue bill. The females are generally dull brown. Flight on their short stubby wings is rapid and direct, after a long take-off run. The displays by the males are relatively elaborate. Whereas most waterfowl molt their wing feathers (and become flightless) once a year, most if not all stifftails carry this out twice a year.

The closest relatives of the waterfowl and the screamers are the flamingos, and possibly the curassows, but the fossil record is not sufficient to reveal their precise origin. Between members of the waterfowl family (despite the division into tribes) relationships remain close; this is demonstrated by the very large number—over 400—of hybrids recorded between species, the majority of which have occurred in captivity, but some also in the wild. A number of inter-tribal hybrids have occurred.

Grazing on land and plucking vegetation from the water are the commonest feeding methods of geese, swans, sheldgeese and screamers. Some species also dig for roots of plants in soft mud and many geese and sheldgeese, and some swans, have adapted to feeding on agricultural land, at first by grazing grass and growing crops but more recently picking up waste grain, beans, maize and potato tubers. Some of the dabbling ducks, too, graze on land, while most take many seeds from the surface of the water as well as small insects. None of the vegetarian waterfowl or screamers have bacteria in the gut to help them digest cellulose. The nutrients they obtain from plant leaves and stems are restricted to the cell juices, obtained by breaking down the cell walls in their gizzards with the aid of small particles of grit, which they ingest for the purpose. These species have to feed long, often the majority of daylight hours in temperate winter latitudes, in order to obtain sufficient food. The plant remains pass through the gut in still recognizable form, and it is usually possible to identify the species of plants eaten.

While the grazers are known to select the most nutritious parts of the plant, such as the growing tips of grass leaves, dabbling ducks are much less selective, taking in relatively large quantities of surface water through the tip of their bills, and pumping it out of the sides through the comb-like lamellae with the aid of their tongues. The trapped particles, seeds and insects, are then swallowed at intervals.

Diving ducks feed on underwater plants and invertebrates of all kinds, generally in fairly shallow water a few meters deep. The sea ducks and sawbills may dive much deeper, the latter pursuing and catching fish and large free-swimming invertebrates, while the former prize mollusks from rocks, or catch crabs and other crustaceans in shallow water or soft mud. Their bills are large and powerful, well adapted for crushing the shells of such prey. Some of the shelducks also feed in a marine environment, sifting tiny mollusks and crustaceans from the mud in estuaries, while the steamer ducks use their strong bills to prize mussels from tideline rocks.

The stifftails feed exclusively underwater. They swim along the bottom, sifting through the silt with their lower mandible just entering it, and catching animal prey.

The lifespan of many waterfowl is greatly affected by man's hunting activities. While, if not hunted, the geese and swans are quite long-lived, with 20 years not uncommon, heavy shooting pressure can reduce life expectancy to no more than 5–10 years at most. The majority of dabbling ducks, diving ducks, small sea ducks and stifftails mature at one year old, and have a life expectancy thereafter of 4–10 years, this being greatly affected by whether or not they are quarry species of man. Most swans do not mature until they are 3–4 years old, and geese, sheldgeese and shelducks until they are 2–3. Similarly, the eiders and larger sawbills are commonly not mature until at least two years of age. Screamers probably also do not breed until they are 2–3.

The great majority of species breed annually, but some from the Southern Hemisphere may breed only every other year, or are adapted to await favorable conditions before attempting to breed, for example during the irregular rains in parts of Australia. In some years arctic-breeding species may, over wide areas, fail to breed (see p100).

The waterfowl show a wide range of variation in the maintenance of the pair bond and in parental care. Swans and geese mostly pair for life, and while only the female incubates the eggs, both parents look after the young, often throughout the first winter of their lives, the family only splitting up at the start of the following breeding season. This period may well include a long migration to winter quarters, the young birds thus being shown the route and resting areas by example, a pattern which often leads to highly traditional use being made of certain haunts over many years. Thus White-fronted geese have wintered in England on the Severn at Slimbridge since the 18th century, if not earlier.

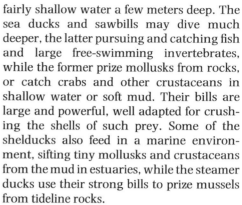

▷ **Stately thrash of the Eurasian Mute swan** OVERLEAF, bathing its plumage prior to preening.

◀ ▼ **Representative species of ducks** CONTINUED. (5) Shelduck (*Tadorna tadorna*). (6) Pintail (*Anas acuta*). (7) Common eider (*Somateria mollissima*). (8) Tufted duck (*Aythya fuligula*).

Almost all the ducks only pair for the breeding season, though pairing may take place during the previous fall, as in the case of many dabbling ducks, through to the spring, as in many diving and sea ducks. The pair bond usually breaks as soon as the female has begun incubation. She generally rears the young until they can fly, before deserting them, though some diving duck females may abandon their young when only half grown. "Creche care" of several broods by a few females takes place in some of the sea ducks, and in some shelducks.

The pair bond and parental care in stiff-tails are both very short lived, and most young fend for themselves almost from the day of hatching, as in the case of the off-spring of the Black-headed duck, which parasitizes other ducks' nests.

Screamers are closest to the swans and geese in their reproductive behavior, with a life-long pair bond and both parents looking after the young until well after they fledge.

The great majority of waterfowl are gregarious, some of them highly so. Swans, geese and sheldgeese are almost always found in flocks away from the breeding grounds, and some species even breed in colonies. A solitary individual can generally be assumed to be a lost straggler. Among these species, flock size is very variable, from a few tens to a hundred thousand or more.

Flocks of swans and geese comprise family units, pairs and immature non-breeding birds, while flocks of dabbling and diving ducks are frequently made up principally of males or of females, with considerable geographical separation between the sexes. In most species of the Northern Hemisphere, females winter further south than males, which leave the breeding grounds first.

The emphasis on conservation of water-fowl has moved in recent years from protection of individual species to a recognition of the vital importance of their wetland habitat. A few species, notably the Hawaiian goose, have been the subject of successful captive-rearing programs aimed at boosting small or declining wild populations.

While conservation measures are required for probably most species of water-fowl, there are circumstances in which they can be regarded by man as pests, particularly of agriculture, and to a lesser extent fisheries. While locally this can be important, worldwide it is not a major problem. The extinction in 1875 of the Labrador duck and the almost certain recent extinction of the Pink-headed duck of India and Nepal, are reminders that there is much to be done if no more species are to disappear.   MAO

A Race to Breed

Factors affecting breeding success in arctic-breeding geese

About 18 species or subspecies of geese breed in arctic regions, before migrating south to winter in more temperate latitudes in North America, Europe and Asia. The arctic summer is extremely short—there may be only eight weeks free of lying snow, the migrating geese may travel thousands of kilometers, and the food supplies they find on arrival at the breeding grounds can be scant or non-existent. In some years bad weather conditions may prevent successful breeding altogether.

Arctic-breeding geese have adapted to surmount these difficulties. Virtually all are smaller than close relatives that breed further south. Their own food requirement and that of their young is reduced, and they produce smaller eggs which require less time to incubate. Clutch sizes too, tend to be smaller, again shortening the time needed for laying. The goslings are able to feed throughout the long arctic day and so grow at a faster rate and can fly at a younger age than their southern relatives. Finally, geese are relatively long-lived birds, taking two or three years to reach maturity. Those years when no young are produced do not, therefore, seriously interfere with the overall population level, provided they do not occur too often.

It used to be thought that the weather conditions on the breeding grounds, particularly when the geese arrive and when the eggs are hatched, were the most important factors determining the success or other-wise of a season. For example, the geese may arrive to find the breeding grounds completely snow-covered. It has been found that, after waiting for a week to 10 days for the snow to clear, the geese give up all attempt at breeding; the egg follicles inside the females are reabsorbed without any eggs being laid. On other occasions severe storms of rain or snow at the time of hatching, or when the goslings are very small, are known to have caused numerous deaths.

Recent work, particularly on Snow geese in North America and, more recently still, on Barnacle geese in Europe, has shifted the focus of attention to the period immediately before the arrival at the breeding grounds, namely the spring. Migrant birds lay down fat deposits prior to their long flights as, during them, they will have less opportunity to feed. Geese are no exception, but it is now known that the arctic-breeding species lay down reserves not just for the migration itself but also, in the case of the female, for the production of eggs, and, for both parents, to tide them over until the vegetation on the breeding grounds has started to grow, often 2–3 weeks after their arrival.

A few species or populations remain on the southern wintering grounds through the spring before making a single long migration to the breeding grounds. Most geese, however, move at least some distance along their route, then stop for a few weeks, before undertaking the final stage of the migration. The advantage of finding a more

▲ **Within a flock of Snow geese,** family parties of pairs and immature non-breeding birds stay together as units. Groups of families tend to form larger groups within the flock.

◄ **Snow goose and goslings.** In arctic-breeding geese the birds arrive on the breeding grounds with sufficient resources (fat layers) to be able to lay eggs and incubate them before grass is available for them to feed. This enables them to raise young in the short, harsh arctic summer.

► **Migration route of Barnacle geese** in northern Europe, between their wintering grounds on the Scottish–English border and summer breeding grounds in the Norwegian island group of Svalbard (Spitsbergen), high in the Arctic (to 80°N). On their way north the geese stop off in Norway to feed up on succulent new growth of grasses, laying down food reserves that are vital for successful breeding. On the return journey, Bear Island is an important staging area.

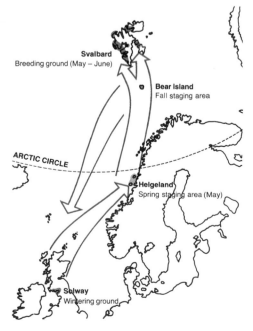

Svalbard
Breeding ground (May – June)

Bear Island
Fall staging area

ARCTIC CIRCLE

Helgeland
Spring staging area (May)

Solway
Wintering ground

northerly spring feeding place seems to stem from the fact that faster-growing vegetation is more nutritious. In temperate wintering latitudes the grass may be past its peak growth-rate well before the geese can move on to the breeding grounds. However, further north the grass will still be at its growing peak. Barnacle geese wintering on the Solway in Scotland leave in late April, then spend most of May at staging places in northern Norway, before reaching their breeding grounds in Svalbard as soon as conditions there become favorable, in late May and early June.

However, even with this timetable things can go wrong. A delayed spring on the wintering grounds and, particularly, the spring feeding areas, can so reduce the vital food intake that on arrival at the breeding site some birds lack sufficient reserves to lay any eggs, while others lay smaller clutches than usual. The layers may subsequently give up

if they cannot find enough food during the short breaks in incubation, which normally occur twice a day. Starving females have even died on the nest.

The conditions during the growing period of the goslings are still of great significance, whether the season has started well or poorly. Losses to bad weather or predation can be serious in many years. Finally, the fall migration must be undertaken when the young may have been on the wing for only a few weeks. Little is known about possible losses during their first long journey, but there is some evidence that they could be heavy when the migrating flocks meet strong headwinds or storms.

There is certainly no single most important factor governing breeding success of arctic-nesting geese. As more work is done, on both sides of the Atlantic, our understanding of the relative importance of the various hazards is becoming clearer. MAO

BIRDS OF PREY-THE RAPTORS

Order: Falconiformes
Families: Accipitridae, Cathartidae, Falconidae, Pandionidae, Sagitariidae.
About 286 species in 80 genera.
Distribution: worldwide except Antarctica and a few oceanic islands.

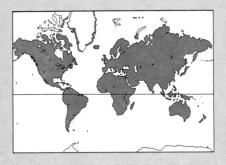

► **Proudly perched** on a rocky ledge, a Common buzzard, the most common European bird of prey, surveys his habitat.

▼ **Unprepossessing contrast** to the grandeur of most birds of prey is provided by the vultures. These are Lappet-faced vultures feeding on a zebra carcass in South Africa.

Falling like a dive-bomber, its wings folded back, an osprey dissolves into a cauldron of spray as it hits the surface of a lake. Moments later, it struggles from the water, shaking off the spray to reveal a fish firmly gripped in one of its talons. High drama like this is typical of birds of prey, one of the most exciting groups of birds, yet one which has suffered greatly at the hands of man.

The birds of prey or raptors (from the Latin, meaning plunderers) form a large and highly varied group of five families, but they all share the same specializations for finding food, and for holding and tearing apart the bodies of other animals: acute vision, strong legs and feet, mostly equipped with sharp, curved claws, and a hooked beak. There are two strategies for killing prey: most of the Accipitridae kill with their claws and use their beaks to tear up the prey; the true falcons grasp their prey with their claws and kill it with a blow from their beak. Most birds of prey sometimes take carrion, and for the vultures this is their main food. Although most have a varied diet, some are highly specialized, such as the Everglade kite, which feeds only on a single species of snail.

The condors are the most dramatic of the **New World vultures**—they are among the largest flying birds, with wingspans of up to 3m (10ft). New and Old World vultures are similar in appearance but are not closely related. Like the cranes, to which they may be related, New World vultures have perforated nostrils. The head and upper neck are bare of feathers, usually highly colored, and the larger species have a ruff of fluffy or lance-shaped feathers round the base of

the neck. The toes are long, and the claws are only slightly curved, not well adapted for grasping prey.

The Andean condor is still widespread, but the California condor is almost extinct, with fewer than 30 individuals left in the wild, all in one area of California. It is not clear what has caused the decline of the California condor, but persecution, including poisoning and shooting, have been major factors. Such a huge bird presents a tempting target for a trigger-happy hunter and, being carrion-feeders, the birds are easily killed by poisoned meat baits. Widespread poisoning campaigns to eliminate ground squirrels and jackals from certain areas have also taken their toll. Condors have a very low reproductive rate, producing at most only one chick every second year. Each young then develops for six or more years before it can itself breed. In an attempt to prevent extinction, four eggs were recently taken into captivity and hatched there. This did not affect the wild population, because the pairs concerned simply produced another egg for themselves some weeks later. Together with previous birds, there are now a total of nine California condors in captivity, in the San Diego and Los Angeles Zoos. The eventual aim is to breed the species in captivity for future release to the wild. The program will benefit from experience gained with the related Andean condor, which has already been bred very successfully in captivity.

The fossil record indicates that the New World vultures were formerly found in Europe too, and that species even larger than condors used to exist. One specimen, *Teratornis merriami*, from the Pleistocene (about 2 million years ago) of the southern United States, was truly massive. It weighed up to 15kg (33lb), had a large head and body, and a wingspan up to 7.5m (24.5ft). Some modern species inhabit mainly open habitats, while others are found in forest.

Some of the forest dwellers are unusual among birds in using smell, as well as sight, to locate their food. As well as carrion, most species eat eggs and some eat fruit and other vegetable matter. Certain species frequent rubbish dumps and abattoirs.

New World vultures nest in cliff-caves or tree-holes, and lay only one or two eggs, dependent on species; nestlings are fed by regurgitation. All species are long-lived.

Like a cross between a stork and a raptor, the **Secretary bird** is an oddity, having a whole family to itself. It has long stork-like legs—the bird is up to 1m (3.3ft) high, with a wingspan up to 2m (6.6ft)—and the long

THE 5 FAMILIES OF BIRDS OF PREY

E Endangered.   V Vulnerable.   R Rare.

New World vultures
Family: Cathartidae
Seven species in 4 genera.
S Canada to tip of S America. Mainly open habitats but some in forests. Size: length 60–120cm (23.5–47in); weight 0.9–14kg (2–31lb). Plumage: brownish black with paler patches on the underside of the wings, except King vulture which is mainly cream and white. Species include: **Andean condor** (Vultur gryphus), **California condor** E (V. californianus), **King vulture** (Sarcoramphus papa), **Turkey vulture** (Cathartes aura).

Secretary bird
Family: Sagittariidae
Sole species Sagittarius serpentarius.
Africa south of the Sahara. Savanna and other open habitats. Size: length 125–150cm (49–59in); weight 3.4–4kg (7.5–8.8lb). Plumage: pale gray with black wing quills, rump and thighs.

Osprey
Family: Pandionidae
Sole species Pandion haliaetus.
Osprey or Fish hawk
Worldwide. Primarily coastal; also lakes and rivers. Size: length up to 62cm (24.5in); weight 1.2–1.9kg (2.6–4.2lb). Plumage: dark brown above and white beneath.

Falcons, falconets and caracaras
Family: Falconidae
About 60 species in 10 genera.

Typical falcons
Thirty seven species of the genus Falco.
All continents except Antarctica. Size: length 25–60cm (10–24in); weight 110–2,000g (4–70oz). Plumage: enormously variable, but most species are darker above than below; reds, browns and blue-grays are frequent colors. Species include: **American kestrel** (Falco sparverius), **Common kestrel** (F. tinnunculus), **Eastern red-footed falcon** (F. amurensis), **Eleonora's falcon** (F. eleonorae), **Gray falcon** (F. ardosiaceus), **gyrfalcon** (F. rusticolus), **Laggar falcon** (F. jugger), **Lanner falcon** (F. biarmicus), **Lesser kestrel** (F. naumanni), **Mauritius kestrel** E (F. punctatus), **Peregrine falcon** V (F. peregrinus), **Prairie falcon** (F. mexicanus), **Red-footed falcon** (F. vespertinus), **Saker falcon** (F. cherrug), **Seychelles kestrel** (F. araea) R, **Sooty falcon** (F. concolor).
Total threatened species: 4.

Pygmy falcons and falconets
Genera: Spiziapteryx (1 species; Argentina), Polihierax (2 species, Africa), Microhierax (5 species, tropical Asia).
Size: length about 15cm (6in); weight 40–60g (1.4–2.1oz). Plumage: strongly contrasting dark above and whitish below, often with orange or reddish patch on upper or lower surface. Species include: **African pygmy falcon** (Polihierax semitorquatus), **Philippine falconet** (Microhierax erythrogonys).

Forest falcons
Five species of genus Micrastur.
New World tropics. Size: length 30–60cm (12–24in), including tail; weight 190–750g (6.7–26.5oz). Plumage: slate gray or dark brownish above, whitish or orange below; barred tail; some forms barred on the breast.

Laughing falcon
Sole species Herpetotheres cachinnans.
Tropical S America. Forest. Size: length 40cm (16in). Plumage: dark above; buff below.

Caracaras
About 9 species of genera Milvago, Phalcoboenus, Daptrius and Polyborus.
C and S America. Open country, forest or savanna. Size: length 35–60cm; weight 280–1,600g (10–56oz). Plumage: mainly dark; some species with pale below or on head; others finely barred, above and below.

Sparrowhawks to Old World vultures
Family: Accipitridae
Two hundred and seventeen species in 64 genera.
Total threatened species: 11.

Kites and honey buzzards
Thirty-one species in 17 genera.
Distribution: all continents except Antarctica. Size: length 30–70cm (12–27in). Plumage: enormously variable, but most species darker above than below. Species include: **Bat hawk** (Macheiramphus alcinus), **Black kite** (Milvus migrans), **Everglade kite** (Rostrhamus sociabilis), **Letter-winged kite** (Elanus scriptus), **Red kite** (Milvus milvus), **White-tailed kite** (Elanus leucurus).

Fish eagles
Eleven species in 3 genera.
Distribution: all continents except S America and Antarctica. Size: length 60–120cm (24–47in); weight 2–6.5kg (4.4–14.3lb). Plumage: most species have striking color patterns, with dark brown and white. Species include: **African fish eagle** (Haliaeetus vocifer), **Bald eagle** (H. leucocephalus), **Palm-nut vulture** (Gypohierax angolensis), **White-bellied sea eagle** (Haliaeetus leucogaster), **White-tailed eagle** V (H. albicilla).

Old World vultures
Fourteen species in 8 genera.
Europe, Asia and Africa. Size: length 60–140cm (24–55in). Plumage: mainly brown or dark with bare heads and necks. Species include: **African white-backed vulture** (Gyps africanus), **Asian white-backed vulture** (Gyps bengalensis), **Bearded vulture** (Gypaetus barbatus), **European black vulture** (Aegypius monachus), **Egyptian vulture** (Neophron percnopterus), **Griffon vulture** (Gyps fulvus), **Lappet-faced vulture** (Aegypius tracheliotus), **Rüppell's griffon** (Gyps rueppellii).

Snake eagles
Twelve species in 5 genera.
Africa, Europe, Asia. Size: length 40–60cm (16–24in); weight 1–2kg (2.2–4.4lb). Plumage: usually gray or brown. Species include: **bateleur** (Terathopius ecaudatus).

Harrier hawks and crane hawk
Three species in 2 genera.
Africa, S America. Size: 50–60cm (20–24in); weight 300–600g (11–21oz). Plumage: adults gray, young brown. Species include: **Crane hawk** (Geranospiza caerulescens).

Harriers
Ten species of the genus Circus.
All continents except Antarctica. Size: 45–55cm (18–22in); weight 290–600g (10–21oz). Plumage: males usually grayish or black-and-white; females and young brownish. Species include: **Australian spotted harrier** (Circus assimilis), **Hen harrier** or **Marsh hawk** (C. cyaneus), **Marsh harrier** (C. aeruginosus), **Montagu's harrier** (C. pygargus).

Goshawks and sparrowhawks
Fifty-three species in 5 genera.
All continents. Size: length 30–70cm; weight 100–2,000g (3.5–70oz). Plumage: generally gray or blackish above, white or reddish barred below. Species include **Cooper's hawk** (Accipiter cooperii), **Goshawk** (A. gentilis), **Lesser sparrowhawk** (A. gularis), **sparrowhawk** (A. nisus), **Sharp-shinned hawk** (A. striatus).

Buzzards, buteonines and harpies
Fifty-three species in 14 genera.
All continents. All habitats from tropical forest to arctic tundra. Size: length 45–100cm (18–39in); weight 0.5–4.6kg (1.1–10.1lb). Plumage: mainly brownish gray. Species include: **Broad-winged hawk** (Buteo platypterus), **Common** or **Steppe buzzard** (B. buteo), **Harpy eagle** R (Harpia harpyia), **Harris's hawk** (Parabuteo unicinctus), **Monkey-eating eagle** E (Pithecophaga jefferyi), **Red-tailed hawk** (Buteo jamaicensis), **Rough-legged buzzard** (B. lagopus), **Swainson's hawk** (B. swainsoni).

Booted eagles
Thirty species in 9 genera.
All continents except Antarctica. Size: 45–100cm (18–39in). Plumage: usually plain brown; specialized forest species often strongly barred with black and white. Species include: **Golden eagle** (Aquila chrysaetos), **Indian black eagle** (Ictinaetus malayensis), **Martial eagle** (Polemaetus bellicosus), **Tawny eagle** (Aquila rapax), **Verreaux's eagle** (A. verreauxii), **Wedge-tailed eagle** (A. audax).

▲ **Nest of Secretaries.** These Secretary birds are building their large nest on the top of an acacia, the flat crowns of which provide an ideal platform. Note the heavily feathered upper leg.

black-tipped plume-like feathers at the back of the head resemble pen quills, hence the name. It also has two very long central tail feathers, with black spots near the ends. The long legs have short stubby toes, which are adapted for walking, not for grasping prey.

The Secretary bird feeds by walking along the ground, in search of insects, small rodents and snakes. Small items are picked up in the bill and swallowed, but large ones, such as snakes, are first killed by stamping on them. Although the bird spends most of its time on the ground, it can fly well, and often soars like a stork. In fact, it has a spectacular aerial display, resembling that of some other raptors, involving a marked undulating flight, in which the bird swings upward, then tips gently forward into a steep dive, which is followed by another upward swing, and so on. In another display, on the ground, the pair run around with raised wings, and are sometimes joined by other individuals who perform similarly. Normally, however, a pair occupying a ter-

ritory will chase away other individuals. Territories may cover anything from 20sq km (7.7sq mi) to more than 200sq km (77sq mi), depending on region.

The nest is built on a flat-topped tree, often an acacia. Two or three greenish-white eggs are laid, and the incubation and nestling periods last 45 and 65–105 days respectively. Since the bird cannot carry prey in its feet, it brings food to the nest in its bill or crop, and either delivers it to or regurgitates it for the young.

One of the most distinctive birds of prey, the **osprey** is a large fish-eating bird. Its markings are unusual in being dark brown above and white beneath, a camouflage similar to that often used on warplanes. Its feet are very strong, since they take the first shock of the water as it dives for fish; the claws are long and sharp, and the toes have horny spines on their undersides to give a good grip on slippery fish. Furthermore, the outer toe is large and can be moved to face backwards, as in the owls. The toes' grip is so good that there are reports of osprey being dragged under by large fish.

Ospreys breed throughout the world except in South America, where they occur only in winter. They are highly migratory, and withdraw completely from boreal and temperate regions in winter. The European birds migrate to Africa, leaving a small resident population in the Mediterranean, and the North American birds migrate to Central and South America, leaving a resident population in Florida and the Caribbean region.

In some areas, ospreys are primarily coastal, while in others they also occur along lakes and rivers. They eat a variety of sizeable fish: whatever species are available locally. They sometimes commute more than 10km (6mi) between nesting and feeding areas. In parts of the range, particularly in eastern North America, their numbers were greatly reduced in the years around 1960 by DDT contamination. Following restrictions on DDT use, the species has begun to recover again.

Because it eats fish, the osprey has also been much persecuted, especially in Europe. It was exterminated completely in Britain, and after an absence of 50 years, began to nest again in Scotland around 1955. Since then, under careful protection, the species has increased to about 40 pairs.

The osprey hunts by cruising above the water surface and plunging in after fish. The talons are brought forward just as the bird hits the water to grab the prey. Only fish near the surface can be caught, but the bird

▼ ► Representative species of birds of prey.
(1) King vulture (*Sarcorhamphus papa*), a New World vulture which inhabits dense tropical forests. (2) Osprey (*Pandion haliaetus*), with a fish, almost its sole diet. (3) Laughing falcon (*Herpetotheres cachinnans*), a South American species with a striking black face mask. (4) A female Common kestrel (*Falco tinnunculus*) hovering. (5) A male Common kestrel (*Falco tinnunculus*). (6) Andean condor (*Vultur gryphus*), in soaring flight. (7) Head of a male Andean condor (*Vultur gryphus*) showing the fleshy wattle on top. (8) A female African pygmy falcon (*Polihierax semitorquatus*). (9) Aplomado falcon (*Falco femoralis*). (10) Secretary bird (*Sagittarius serpentarius*), a distinctive African species. (11) Crested caracara (*Polyborus plancus*). (12) Barred forest falcon (*Micrastur ruficollis*) eating a Black-spotted barbet.

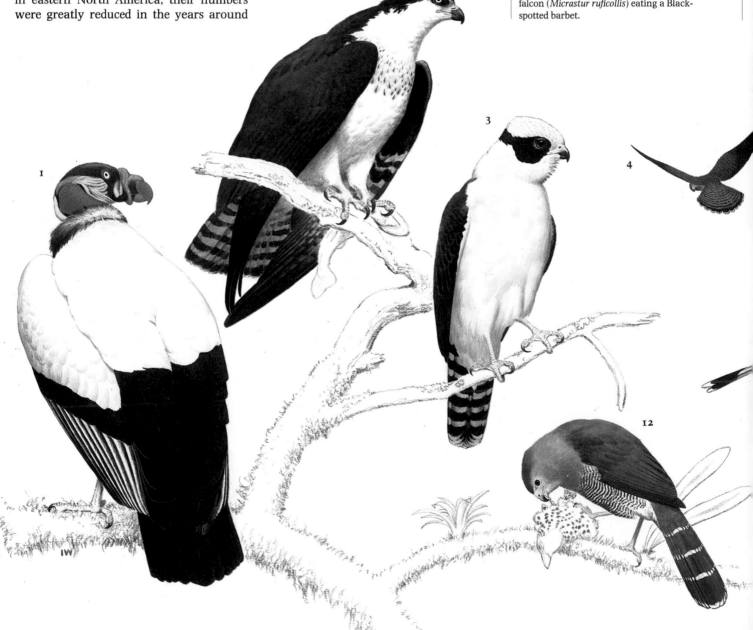

sometimes submerges completely. As it rises, with wings outspread on the surface, the bird shakes the water from its plumage, and carries the fish, head forward, to a suitable feeding perch.

The osprey has a spectacular aerial display which involves carrying a fish, and calling. Sometimes a bird may rise with rapid and pronounced wingbeats up to 300m (1,000ft) or more, then hover there for a moment with tail fanned and legs dangling, displaying the fish in its feet, before diving down on closed wings, only to rise again and repeat the performance. Such displays last for several minutes at a time, and serve to attract or retain a female.

Ospreys nest on the tops of trees or rock pinnacles, but on islands lacking mammalian predators they also nest on the ground. They build huge nests of sticks, which are normally used over long periods of years. Two to four eggs are laid, and the incubation and nestling periods span about 38 and 50 days respectively. The birds do not breed until their third or fourth year, and in extreme cases they may live for 15–20 years.

For most people, a kestrel hovering over the verge of a major road is probably the most familiar image of a bird of prey. Kestrels are **falcons** (family Falconidae), the second largest of the raptor families. Falcons are generally similar to the other great family of raptors, the Accipitridae, but differ in not building nests, in producing eggs with inside shells that appear buff against the light instead of pale green, in the sequence of molt in the primary feathers, and in some details of skeletal structure. There are four subfamilies of Falconidae: the large group of true falcons, forest falcons, the Laughing falcon, and caracaras.

The true falcons range from the tiny Philippine falcon, only 15cm (6in) long, to the spectacular gyrfalcon and Peregrine falcon, the falconer's choice *par excellence*. They can be considered as two main groups: the typical falcons of the genus *Falco* and the pygmy falcons.

The typical falcons have a wide range of types, and are found throughout the world, mainly in open or fairly open habitats. The largest of them are stocky, powerful birds of exceptionally swift flight, with pointed wings and relatively short tails. They are highly accomplished fliers, and habitually kill their prey, principally birds, in full flight, either striking them dead by a blow or seizing them with their talons and bringing them to ground. The largest species, the gyrfalcon, inhabits the Arctic tundra of North America and Eurasia and feeds largely on ptarmigan. It occurs in three main color phases, whitish, grayish and brown, depending on region.

The Peregrine falcon is one of the world's most spectacular birds. It is a perfect performer in the air, capable of feats of speed and precision flying scarcely equalled by any other bird. Maximum speed is achieved when the bird dives on prey, known as "stooping." Estimates vary from the conservative, which insist that the impression of great speed is illusory and that the bird hardly exceeds 160km/h (100mph), and the extravagant which claim that 400km/h

▶ **Stooping to conquer.** The Peregrine falcon lives mainly on birds, which it kills by diving ("stooping") at very high speed—there are controversial claims of 400km/h (250mph). The wings are folded back to increase speed, and the prey is killed by the sharp claw on the hind toe.

▼ **Kestrel in the straw.** A Common kestrel ferries its rodent prey back to the nest in a straw rick.

(250mph) is reached on occasion. Whatever the real figure, a stooping peregrine is a most impressive sight, and makes the species the falconer's first choice. In much of its range it was greatly reduced in numbers during the 1950s and 1960s by DDT and other organochlorine pesticides (see pp122–123), but is now recovering well.

Many raptors take quite small prey, and the hobbies, a group of small, long-winged, exceedingly fast falcons, live largely upon insects, although they can also take small birds, including swifts, in flight. They catch almost all their prey on the wing and hardly any on the ground. Two other species are

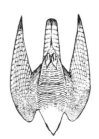

similar to hobbies, namely Eleonora's falcon, which breeds on certain Mediterranean and other islands, and the Sooty falcon, which inhabits the North African deserts. Both these species breed in late summer, so that they have young in the nest at a time when small birds, on which they prey, are migrating from Europe to Africa.

The kestrels are a large group of typical falcons, found on every continent, which hover in search of small mammals and insects on the ground. Typical representatives include the Common kestrel in Europe and Africa, and the American kestrel of the New World. There are several island forms, one of which, the Mauritius kestrel, is one of the rarest birds in the world, with fewer than five pairs left in the wild.

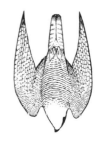

In their breeding habits, typical falcons are fairly uniform. Their displays, both aerial and perched, are often centered on nest-sites, and entail the male drawing the female's attention to potential sites. Thus the male kestrel has a special flight in which he glides down onto the site, with wings held up in a V, and many species have bowing displays at the site itself. They either breed on a scrape on a cliff ledge which may be resorted to year after year, or they appropriate the old stick nest of some other bird, such as a crow. Some use tree cavities. Their eggs are all very handsome, being generally buffish in ground color, thickly speckled with dark red-brown, sometimes obscuring the ground color completely. Clutches usually contain 2–3 eggs in hobbies, 3–6 in other small falcons and 3–5 in large species; the eggs are laid at 2–3 day intervals. Incubation periods range from 25–32 days in small species to 32–35 days in large ones; and nestling periods from 25–32 days in small species to 40–49 days in large ones. Vocalizations are heard mainly in the breeding season, and consist of chattering notes. Many species protest loudly when the nest is visited.

Pygmy falcons and falconets are the smallest of all birds of prey. The Philippine falconet, the smallest of all, hunts insects

▶ **Species of birds of prey** CONTINUED.
(**13**) Little eagle (*Hieraaetus morphnoides*) feeding young. (**14**) Gray chanting goshawk (*Melierax poliopterus*) calling on top of a termite mound. (**15**) Bald eagle (*Haliaeetus leucocephalus*). (**16**) Honey buzzard (*Pernis apivorus*) digging out a wasps' nest. (**17**) Red kite (*Milvus milvus*) with rabbit prey. (**18**) African harrier-hawk (*Polyboroides radiatus*) hunting for insects. (**19**) Black-breasted snake eagle (*Circaetus gallicus pectoralis*), a subspecies of the Short-toed eagle, with a snake. (**20**) Bearded vulture (*Gypaetus barbatus*). (**21**) Long-legged buzzard (*Buteo rufinus*). (**22**) Ornate hawk eagle (*Spizaetus ornatus*). (**23**) Black-mantled sparrowhawk (*Accipiter melanochlamys*) with newly captured prey. (**24**) Pied harrier (*Circus melanoleucus*).

from the tops of trees in the manner of a fly-catcher; it breeds in old holes of woodpeckers. The African pygmy falcon is likewise very small, but is capable of killing small birds as well as the large insects which form the major part of its food. In South Africa it breeds in the huge communal nests of Sociable weavers, and in East Africa it uses the thorny nests of Buffalo weavers.

Forest falcons are long-tailed, long-legged birds, with a partial face ruff, a feature which has sometimes led them to be classified with harriers. They are in fact primitive falcons, which have become adapted for life in dense forests. They have the short broad wings and longish tail typical of other forest-dwelling raptors, which gives them great maneuvrability in moving among the trees. They live largely on birds but are otherwise little known.

The Laughing falcon is a buzzard-sized bird, dark above and buff below, with a striking white crown set off by a black mask. It is found only in the forests of tropical South America, where it eats reptiles and other small animals. It nests in tree cavities, and produces only one young at a time, but again is very poorly known.

Caracaras are a group of large (buzzard-sized), long-legged birds that look quite unlike falcons. They inhabit open country, forest or savanna, and eat insects, and a range of food; they like carrion. Caracaras are very common in parts of Central and South America, and in general are rather sluggish birds, spending much of their time perched, or walking about on the ground; but they can run swiftly. They associate with New World vultures at carrion and sometimes force these and other caracaras to disgorge their food. Unlike the true falcons, caracaras build their own nests; they lay 2–3 eggs, and have incubation and nestling periods lasting about 32 and 42

days respectively. One species, the Guadaloupe caracara, has become extinct within historical times.

A snail-eating kite, carrion-devouring vultures, snake-eating eagles—these and many more belong to the family **Accipitridae**, the largest family of birds of prey. Because of these and other feeding specializations, their appearance is diverse.

Extreme specialization and versatility are both found in kites and honey buzzards. Honey buzzards eat wasp grubs; the Bat hawk eats bats caught at dusk as they emerge from caves or tree roosts; and snail kites eat aquatic snails. At the other extreme, the Black kite is one of the most noticeable and versatile raptors in warmer parts of the Old World, scavenging in hundreds in towns and villages.

Specializing mainly on fish, water-birds and carrion are the fish eagles, the most famous of which is the Bald eagle, the national emblem of the USA. This group also includes the remarkable Palm-nut vulture, which feeds mainly on the fruit of the Oil palm, with which it is always associated.

Although many birds of prey sometimes take carrion, the Old World vultures eat little else. Most are very large, with bare or down-covered heads and necks for "wallowing in putridity" as Darwin put it. The Egyptian vulture, which breeds in caves, is one of the few tool-using birds, breaking eggs by throwing stones onto them. The Bearded vulture has the curious habit of dropping bones onto rocks to gain access to the marrow. (See also pp124–125.)

Snake eagles are large birds, with large owl-like heads and yellow eyes, short toes adapted to killing snakes, which are carried in the crop and regurgitated to the single young. The unusual bateleur has very long wings and a very short tail; its name derives from the French for "juggler," a reference to its acrobatic courtship displays.

Harrier hawks and the Crane hawk are medium-sized woodland hawks. They have unique "double-jointed" legs which can bend either way at the middle joint; these are used, among other things, for reaching nestling birds and other small creatures in tree holes and crevices. Otherwise, the birds hunt by slow methodical searching of the ground for small animals.

Another group which hunts by slowly searching grassland and marshes are the harriers, a uniform group of medium-sized, slim-bodied, long-winged, long-tailed hawks. They feed mainly on small mammals and birds, and some reptiles and insects. They have owl-like faces, with ears spe-cialized to locate prey in thick vegetation. The males often maintain "harems" of females. Most nest amid tall herbs on the ground, laying 5–7 whitish eggs, but the Australian spotted harrier nests in trees.

The largest genus of raptors comprises the chanting goshawks, goshawks and sparrowhawks. They are small to medium-sized hawks, all with short rounded wings and long tails, adapted for woodland or forest; many feed largely or entirely on birds. The chanting goshawks eat various small animals caught on the ground.

Buzzard, buteonines and harpies are a large varied group feeding mainly on mammals and some birds. The largest and most powerful is the Harpy eagle, which inhabits tropical South American forests and eats monkeys, other mammals and large birds. The rare Monkey-eating eagle of the Philippines has a striking appearance, a spiky head plume giving it an oddly human face. The buteonines are particularly widespread, including the Common buzzard of Europe and the Red-tailed hawk of North America.

The true or booted eagles are distinguished from other eagles by having feathered legs. They feed mainly on live prey, but those of genus *Aquila* take some carrion and the Indian black eagle is specialized to feed on birds' eggs and nestlings. This group includes the Golden eagle.

All the Accipitridae build their own nests of sticks or similar material, usually on trees or cliffs, and lay whitish or pale-greenish eggs, often with brown marks. The small species lay 5–7 eggs and the largest species only one; incubation and nestling periods range from 32 days and 26 days respectively in small species to around 50 and 120 days respectively in large ones.

Like some other raptors, the Accipitridae are noted for their spectacular aerial displays. Some consist of little more than soaring over the nest-area, either single birds or the pair together, but others involve great flying skill. Some develop into "mock attacks," in which one bird may dive at the other, and even touch or grip feet, spinning down in cartwheeling fashion. Most species have a "sky-dance" display, which involves marked undulations, as a bird swings up on flapping wings and then down on closed wings, repeatedly. In some species the wing beats are slower and more exaggerated than normal. The harriers have a spectacular aerial food pass, in which the flying male drops food to the female, who flies up, turns over and catches it in mid air. In most other species, the food transfers usually take place in a perched position.

▲ **Aerial food pass.** In Marsh harriers, the male, when bringing food for the young, does not return to the nest. Instead, the female flies up to him, turns upside down and catches the prey dropped by the male.

▶ **Tail fanned** like the flaps of an airplane, an Augur buzzard (*Buteo rufofuscus*) swoops low. The pronounced aerofoil section of the wings is especially prominent here. The Augur buzzard is the most common buzzard of East and southern Africa.

▶ **Aerial courtship displays.** Not surprisingly, the birds of prey use their superb flying skills in courtship. BELOW LEFT "Whirling." A pair of African fish eagles grapple with each other's talons, tumbling together in cartwheels or swinging from side-to-side like falling leaves. (1) Undulating display. These undulations may be shallow or pronounced. In the Hen harrier the bird dives with wings partly closed, then regains height by flapping. (2) "Pot hooks." In this extreme form of undulating display, shown by Tawny eagles, the bird dives and swoops without wing flapping. (3) "Pendulum." In this display, shown by Verreaux's eagles, the bird describes a figure of eight over and over.

▶ **Landing the catch** OVERLEAF. An osprey brings a sizeable meal back to its mate and young nesting in mangrove vegetation in the Red Sea. Ospreys are found throughout most of Europe, Asia and North America.

Nearly every raptor species that has been studied performs some sort of migratory movement in at least part of its range. The longest journeys are made by those birds which fly regularly between eastern Siberia and southern Africa (eg Eastern red-footed falcons), or between northern North America and southern South America (eg tundra-breeding Peregrine falcons). This entails flying more than 30,000km (18,650ml) on migration each year.

Most raptors have only one mate in a year; some keep the same mate for several years. Some large eagles are generally thought to "pair for life," but as yet there is really little evidence for this. Polygyny, in which one male may have more than one female at a time, is frequent among harriers, and polyandry, in which one female may have more than one male, is frequent in the Harris hawk, a desert species of central America. Both mating systems have occasionally been recorded in other raptors too.

In most raptors there is a marked division

of labor during the breeding cycle. The male provides the food and hunts mainly away from the nest, while the female stays near the nest, and is responsible for incubating the eggs and for looking after the young. The difference between the parents persists at least until the young are about half-grown, after which the female may also begin to leave the nest area to hunt. The young themselves hatch with a full covering of down and with their eyes open, in contrast to most other nest-reared birds. In the majority of raptors the mother initially tears up small pieces of meat for the young, which they take from her bill, but before fledging they learn to tear up prey for themselves.

In vultures, the partners share parental duties more equally, as they take turns on the nest, and between times seek their own food, some of which they later regurgitate to the young.

As a group, raptors vary in the way they space themselves in their habitat, depending largely on how their food is distributed. Three main systems are found. In the first, pairs are spaced out in individual home ranges. This seems to be usual in about 75 percent of the 80 raptor genera, including some of the largest, such as *Accipiter*, *Buteo*, *Aquila* and *Falco*. Each pair defends the vicinity of the nest and a variable amount of surrounding terrain, so that home ranges may be exclusive or overlapping. Throughout suitable habitat, the nests of different pairs tend to be spaced fairly regularly, at distances from less than 200m (650ft) apart in some small raptors to more than 30km (18.5mi) apart in some large ones. Most species that space themselves in this way feed on live vertebrate prey and show considerable stability in numbers and distribution from year to year. Individuals usually hunt and roost alone.

In the second system, birds nest in loose colonies and hunt solitarily. This system is shown, among others, by the Black and Red kites and the Letter-winged kite, and by the Marsh harrier, the Hen harrier and Montagu's harrier. Groups of pairs nest close together in "neighborhoods" and range out to forage in the surrounding area. The different pairs may hunt in different directions from one another, or several may hunt the same area independently, from time to time shifting from one area to another. The breeding groups usually contain less than ten pairs, with nests spaced at 70–200m (230–650ft) apart. Larger groups have sometimes been found, including up to 30 pairs of Montagu's harriers and some 54 pairs of kites (49 Black kites and five Red

kites). In harriers, the tendency to coloniality is sometimes accentuated by polygyny, because each male may have two or more females nesting close together, and in both harriers and kites it is accentuated by the frequent need to concentrate in patches of restricted nesting habitat. Even where nesting cover is widespread, however, the colonial habit is still apparent. Such species often exploit sporadic food sources, such as local grasshopper or rodent plagues. They are nomadic to some extent, concentrating to breed wherever food is temporarily plentiful, so that local populations may fluctuate substantially from year to year. Not all pairs of such species nest in groups, however.

Outside the breeding season, kites and harriers tend to base themselves in communal roosts, from which they spread out to hunting areas during the day. Kites roost in trees and harriers in reeds or long grass, in which each bird tramples the vegetation to form a platform. The roosts usually contain up to 20 individuals, occasionally more, and up to 300 harriers of several species were counted at one place in Africa. The same roosts may be used year after year, but by greatly varying numbers of birds.

In the third system, pairs nest in dense colonies and forage gregariously. This system is shown by the small snail-eating Everglade kite, by the insect-eating kites of the genera *Elanoides, Gampsonyx, Elanus* and *Ictinia*; by the insect-eating Lesser kestrel, Red-footed falcon, Eastern red-footed falcon and Eleonora's falcon, and by the large Griffon vultures. In these species, the pairs typically nest closer together—often less than 70m (230ft) apart—and in larger aggregations than do those mentioned above. They also feed communally in scattered flocks or, in the case of the vultures, spread out in the air, but crowd together around carcasses. The feeding flocks are not stable, but change continually in size and composition, as birds join or leave. Colonies usually contain up to 20 or 30 pairs, but those of Everglade kites sometimes reach about 100 pairs and those of some Griffon vultures more than 250. The food sources of these various species are even more sporadic and fast-changing than those of the previous group. Food may be plentiful at one place on one day and at another place on the next. Such species roost communally at all times and, when not breeding, may gather in enormous numbers. The insect-eating falcons in their African winter quarters use the same roosts year after year, which often contain thousands of individuals of several species. One was found to hold 50,000–100,000

birds, mainly Eastern red-footed falcons. Such birds exploit local flushes of food, such as termites and locusts, and move around over long distances in response to changes in prey availability.

Whatever their dispersion, most raptors choose special places for their nests. Such places may be cliffs, isolated trees, groves of trees, or patches of forest or ground cover, depending on the species. Many such places are occupied over long periods of years. Particular cliffs are known to have been used by successive pairs of Golden eagles or of White-tailed eagles, Peregrine falcons or gyrfalcons for periods of 70–100 years. Among 49 British Peregrine cliffs known to falconers between the 16th and 19th centuries, at least 42 were still in use during 1930–39. In trees, too, certain eagle nests have been used for longer than a man's lifetime and, added to year after year, have often reached enormous size. One historic

▲ **Ugly ducklings** or rather Ferruginous hawk (*Buteo regalis*) chicks, a species of western North America.

▶ **A Booted eagle** (*Hieraaetus pennatus*) and its young, showing the immature plumage. Booted eagles are forest-steppe-dwelling species and they nest on wooded mountain slopes and in ravines.

Larger than the Male

One of the most interesting features of raptors is the marked difference in size between the sexes, with the female being larger than the male—up to twice as heavy in some species. This sexual dimorphism is evidently connected with the raptorial life-style, because the same occurs in other predatory birds, such as owls and skuas. In general, the difference in size increases with the speed and agility of the prey. At one extreme, those vultures that feed entirely on immobile carcasses show no consistent size difference between the sexes. In raptors which eat very slow moving prey, such as snails, the female is only slightly bigger than the male. The insect feeders and reptile feeders show a somewhat greater size difference, the mammal and fish feeders somewhat more, while the bird feeders have the largest difference of all. The greatest size difference is shown by the species that take the largest prey in relation to their own size. Thus the bird-feeding raptors often kill prey heavier than themselves. In such species, the size difference between the sexes is so marked that males and females eat mainly different sizes of prey. Despite this link with diet, it is not known why the female is the larger sex and not the male, but probably this is connected with the female's role in breeding.

Bald eagle nest in America spanned 8sq m (86sq ft) on top and contained "two wagon-loads" of material, while another was 3m (10ft) across and 5m (16.5ft) high. Such nests sometimes become so heavy from the continued addition of material over the years that the branch supporting them breaks off, and the birds are forced to start anew. Some osprey nests have been in continuous use for periods exceeding 40 years, and even patches of ground cover have been used by Hen harriers for several decades. In general, of course, sites on rock must be more permanent than those in trees, and sites in trees more permanent than those in herbaceous cover.

Colonial raptors also tend to nest in the same places year after year, and in southern Africa many cliffs whose names indicate that they were used by vultures in previous centuries are still used by these birds today. As in other colonial birds, the individuals defend only a small area around their nests, so that, given enough ledges, many pairs can crowd onto the same cliff, leaving other apparently suitable cliffs vacant.

Because of their special nesting requirements, raptors are among the few groups of birds whose numbers and nest success are in some regions clearly limited by numbers

of nest sites available. For example, the breeding density of cliff dwellers may be limited by the number of cliffs with suitable ledges, and their breeding success by the accessibility of these ledges to predators. Other raptors may be limited in open landscapes by shortage of trees. This is particularly true in the prairies, steppes and other grassland areas, which offer abundant food for raptors but also have huge areas without trees for nesting. Even in woodlands, nest sites may sometimes be fewer than they first appear. In a large area of mature forest in Finland, covering several hundred sq km, less than one in a thousand trees were judged by a biologist to be suitable for nests of White-tailed eagles, while in younger forests, suitable open-crowned trees were scarcer or non-existent. It has often proved

possible to increase the breeding density of birds of prey by providing nest sites artificially. Nest boxes for kestrels are an obvious example, but several species have taken readily to buildings and quarries where natural cliffs are lacking, and ospreys in North America nest freely on special platforms provided for the purpose.

Where nesting sites are surplus to needs, and where the birds are not reduced by human activities, their numbers seem to be limited by food supplies. Species with varied diets tend thereby to have fairly stable food supplies. Their breeding populations also remain stable, fluctuating in particular areas by no more than 10 percent of the mean over long periods of years. They provide extreme examples among birds of long-term stability in numbers. Examples include

HUNTING FOR FISH
—The White-bellied sea eagle

▲ **Feet first,** an eagle closes in for the kill.

▶ **Impact** BOTTOM. The force of the talons usually kills the fish outright. Here the impact has dragged the eagle's legs behind it as it begins to fly away with its catch.

▶ **The eagle's grasp** MIDDLE. The grip of one foot is sufficient to secure the prey as the eagle flies off to a safe perch to devour its catch.

▶ **Lost prey** TOP. An eagle is forced to drop its catch by harassment from two more eagles.

Peregrine falcons and Golden eagles in areas where they are free of adverse human influence. Such species may vary greatly in breeding numbers from one area to another, however, depending on local food supplies.

In contrast, raptors which have restricted diets, based on prey with seasonal population extremes, fluctuate in breeding density from year to year in any one area, in parallel with their prey. Examples include kestrels, Hen harriers and Rough-legged buzzards, which feed on rodents, and goshawks which in boreal regions feed on hares and grouse. The rodents and their various predators usually show intervals of 4 years between population peaks, and the hares, grouse and their predators more like 7–10 years. The goshawk is particularly instructive, because its breeding populations tend to remain stable in areas where prey-supplies are stable and fluctuate where prey supplies are unstable.

In general, small species of raptors, which feed on small and abundant prey, occur at higher densities than the larger raptors, which feed on larger, sparser prey. A small kestrel, for example, would normally have a hunting range of 1sq km (0.4sq mi) or less, a buzzard would have a range of 1–5sq km (0.4–2sq mi), whereas a large eagle would hunt over a much greater area. The African Martial eagle, which eats small antelopes and gamebirds, is extreme, as it occurs at one pair per 125–300sq km (48–116sq mi), with 30–40km (18.5–25mi) between pairs; it is thus one of the most thinly distributed birds in the world. Large colonial raptors, such as the Griffon vultures, occur in high numbers at their colonies, but when their extensive feeding areas are taken into account, their overall

densities are in fact extremely low. Feeding on other animals, it would of course be expected that raptors of whatever size would occur at low density compared with other birds feeding on small prey.

To counter the widespread population declines, many attempts have been made in recent years to increase raptor numbers, either by management of the birds themselves or of their habitat and food supplies. Management principles that have been applied for decades to game animals can be applied to the conservation of raptors, but conserving raptors is more difficult because of the greater land areas needed to sustain populations, and because their conflicts with other human activities create unsympathetic attitudes. For raptors in general, three main factors have been identified as causing declines (or limiting numbers): restriction and degradation of habitat, persecution by man and contamination by toxic chemicals.

On a world scale, habitat destruction has already accounted for bigger reductions in raptor and other wildlife populations than has any other factor; and with the continuing growth in human population and development, it is still the most serious threat in the long term. Irrespective of any other adverse influence, habitat sets the ultimate limit on the size and distribution of any wild population.

Since the carrying capacity of any area for raptors is usually set by nest-sites or food supplies, for some species a shortage of nest-sites can be rectified by adding sites artificially, as discussed above. Raising the carrying capacity of an area through increasing the food supply is much more difficult, because it usually entails changing the land-use to promote an increase in prey. Often the best that can be achieved is to preserve existing areas of good habitat, or prevent their further degradation. In North America and Africa, the larger national parks provide some excellent raptor habitat, capable of maintaining large populations; but in more heavily peopled countries, most areas that can be preserved in this way are too small

▲ **A secure future?** A Bald eagle chick in its nest high over the coniferous forest and lakeland habitat. The existence of suitable nest-sites is a prime factor in the conservation of birds of prey.

▶ **Feeding perch.** A Bald eagle has brought a Pink salmon to what is obviously a favorite feeding place on a jutting branch.

Preying on Game

The natural feeding habits of raptors inevitably lead some species to take gamebirds and domestic stock. This forms the major conflict between raptors and men, and is the main reason why raptors have been so heavily persecuted. In fact, the impact of raptors on game or domestic animals is usually negligible, though in a few cases it can be severe.

One serious problem in parts of Europe is predation by goshawks on intensively reared pheasants. The young pheasants are hatched in incubators, and when they are six weeks old are put out in woodland in open pens, from which they are gradually released to the woodland, and encouraged to stay by the regular provision of grain or other food. Goshawks often concentrate in pheasant rearing areas, and despite regular trapping programs, may take a substantial proportion of the stock. These pheasants would otherwise be available to the hunters, who have paid for their production. In Finland alone, some 4,000–8,000 goshawks are killed each year

by game hunters, yet here these hawks seem to maintain their numbers.

Other problems concern eagles. Wherever these birds live alongside sheep, they feed on dead sheep and lambs, and also kill some live lambs. This is true of the Golden eagle in parts of Europe and North America, the White-tailed eagle in Norway and Greenland, the Wedge-tailed eagle in Australia, and the Black and Martial eagles in southern Africa. In most areas, their impact on the lamb crop is generally negligible, but in some localities it can be serious. As a result, Golden eagles were killed on a considerable scale in western Texas and southeast New Mexico after the discovery that these birds could be shot down from airplanes. Over a period of 20 years, until it was banned in 1962, 1,000–2,000 birds were shot annually in sheep-ranching areas.

In most countries birds of prey are now protected by law, but some exceptions are made to deal with troublesome species in local areas. The law is hard to enforce, however, and illicit killing is common.

to support many birds. This is especially true of the large species that require huge areas to sustain them.

Human persecution is less serious now than in the past, at least in northern countries where bounty schemes have increasingly given way to protective legislation. At the time of writing, 14 European countries afford full protection to all raptors, 16 afford partial protection (certain species, certain regions or certain seasons), while one country (Malta) gives no protection. In North America, Japan and the Soviet Union, all species are fully protected. Such legislation has met with varying success in different countries, as attitudes towards it have ranged from respect to scorn, and bird protection is anyway difficult to enforce and to monitor.

The only long-term solution against the effects of pesticides is to reduce the use of the chemicals involved, so that their concentration in the environment falls. In northern countries this has been achieved by substituting other chemicals which are less toxic or less persistent than the offending ones.

At the same time, a number of different measures have been taken to counter the effects of organochlorine pesticides, until environmental levels fall sufficiently to enable the birds to survive on their own. These mostly entail the movement of eggs and young from one area to another or from captivity to the wild.

Several species have been propagated in captivity for release to the wild. The most notable is the Peregrine falcon, which has been recently re-established in the eastern United States from captive-bred stock. Similar schemes have involved the reintroduction of Griffon vultures in France, Bearded vultures in Switzerland, and Bald eagles in New York State. Other reintroduction schemes have entailed transplanting young birds from one region to another, as in the current program to re-establish the White-tailed eagle in Scotland. Wherever a species has been eliminated by human activities from otherwise suitable habitat, reintroduction is clearly worthwhile, for the long-term security of any species depends on its maintaining a diversified population. The distribution of many large raptors has been so fragmented by human activities that there is now little hope of such species recolonizing isolated patches of habitat naturally—at least not within the foreseeable future. For these, reintroduction schemes offer the best chance of success, wherever habitat is still good. IN

Shell-shock

Pesticides and birds of prey

Of all pesticides yet used widely, the so-called "organochlorines" have had the most harmful effects on wildlife populations, especially of predatory birds, some of which have been exterminated over areas up to half the size of the USA. Besides being toxic, these chemicals have three main properties which contribute to their devastating effects. Firstly, they are chemically extremely stable, so they persist more or less unchanged in the environment for many years. Secondly, they dissolve in fat, which means that they can accumulate in animals' bodies, and pass from prey to predator, concentrating at successive steps in a food chain. Raptors are at the top of their food chains, and are thus especially liable to accumulate large amounts. Thirdly, at sublethal levels of only a few parts per million in tissues, organochlorines can disrupt the breeding of certain birds, and reduce the number of young produced. Moreover, organochlorine pesticides can become dispersed over wide areas in the bodies of migrant animals, and in air and water currents, so can affect populations far removed from areas of usage. Some other pesticides may cause heavy mortality among wildlife locally, but because these pesticides break down more quickly they neither have lasting effects, nor do they affect organisms in areas remote from places of application.

All bird species that have been studied have been found to be susceptible to these pesticides. The most marked population declines have occurred in bird-feeding raptors, especially the Peregrine falcon, but also the sparrowhawk in Europe and the Sharp-shinned hawk and Cooper's hawk in North America. Certain fish-eaters have also declined greatly, including the osprey and the Bald eagle in parts of North America and the White-tailed eagle in northern Europe.

DDT, the first and commonest of the organochlorines, is not particularly toxic to birds, but its principal breakdown product, DDE, causes thinning of eggshells. Such shells often break during incubation, so that fewer young are produced. DDE and other breakdown products may also cause embryo deaths in intact eggs, thus further lowering the hatching success. If the birds

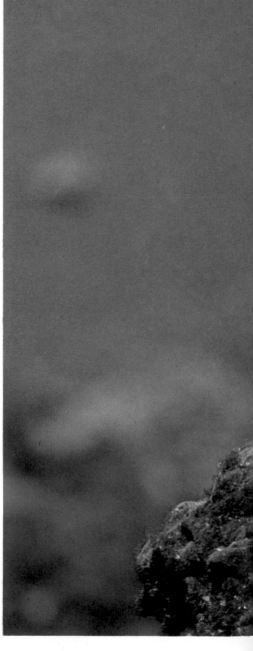

▲ **Fragile niche.** The Peregrine falcon was affected more severely than most birds of prey by the ravages of persistent pesticides. The peregrines are recovering but still need safe nest-sites and unspoiled habitat.

▶ **Toxic effect.** A peregrine egg, its shell thinned by the effects of DDT, has been crushed during incubation, resulting in the death of the young.

◀ **Fiercely maternal,** a sparrowhawk broods her young in the rain. In parts of the Northern Hemisphere, populations of birds of prey are slowly recovering from the damage inflicted by pesticides, but in developing countries many species are now threatened.

The more toxic organochlorines, such as aldrin and dieldrin, kill adult birds and in some cases have led to population decline. These chemicals were held responsible for the elimination of the Peregrine falcon and sparrowhawk from large parts of Britain in the period 1957–60. They were used as dressings on cereal grains to protect the grains against insect attack; some of the grains were eaten by seed-eating birds, and these birds were then in turn eaten by the raptors.

Death from organochlorine poisoning is often delayed. These chemicals are stored in body fat, and a bird may die when its fat is used to provide energy and the organochlorine is released to the other, more sensitive tissues. Thus birds may die during periods of food shortage or migration, from organochlorines accumulated in the body during the previous months.

Birds of prey which breed in areas free from pesticide use do not escape contamination if they, or their prey species, migrate to winter in areas where these chemicals are used. Peregrine falcons nesting in arctic North America have recently declined, as a result of increasing DDT usage in Latin America, where these Peregrines winter. Other migrant birds which breed in the Northern Hemisphere are also likely to decline, as a result of growing organochlorine use in tropical and subtropical countries.

In areas where organochlorine use has been curtailed, these birds have mostly begun to recover in numbers, and to recolonize areas from which they were eliminated. However, certain DDT residues—particularly DDE—are so persistent in soils that they could well remain a problem for birds of prey and other animals for several decades after use of DDT has ceased. There is as yet no sign that any bird species has developed any degree of resistance to organochlorine pesticides.

In Europe and North America, the use of organochlorines reached a peak in the 1960s, but since then it has declined, as one country after another has banned them. However, their use in the developing countries of the tropics and subtropics is increasing rapidly, under pressure from agriculturalists and from manufacturers, eager to exploit these new markets. Preliminary signs are that raptors and other wildlife are declining there as they did in the northern countries, twenty years earlier. Alternative pesticides are now available, which have less severe environmental effects, but many are more expensive than DDT. IN

do not produce enough young to offset the normal adult mortality, the population declines, eventually becoming extinct. Different groups of birds vary in their sensitivity to DDE residues. Birds of prey are particularly vulnerable, partly because a given level of DDE produces more shell thinning than in other birds, and also because, being predators, they accumulate larger amounts than most other birds. As assessed by shell-thinning, herons and pelicans are also relatively sensitive to DDE, whereas game-birds and songbirds are relatively insensitive.

Nature's Scavengers
Old and New World vultures

Vultures vary considerably in their nesting and foraging habits. The most strongly gregarious are the large griffons: the Griffon vulture (Eurasia), Rüppell's griffon (northern Africa) and Cape vulture (southern Africa), which nest on cliffs in big colonies numbering up to 100 pairs or more, with some nests only a few meters apart. One of the largest concentrations known is around the Gol escarpment in East Africa. It contains more than 1,000 pairs of Rüppell's vultures, distributed in several colonies, and supported largely by the big game populations of the Serengeti Plain. Such birds feed entirely from large carcasses and, being dependent on migrant animals, they often have to fly great distances for food, taking more than one day over each trip. They have been followed up to 150km (93mi) from the colony.

The food searching of Griffon vultures is extremely efficient. Following the Charge of the Light Brigade in the Crimean War (1854), so many birds gathered on the battlefields that shooting squads were posted to protect the injured. Abilities to find isolated carcasses and to gather quickly in large numbers in areas where they had apparently been scarce have caused some people to suspect a sensitivity to smell or telepathic ability, while some native Africans think that vultures dream the locations of food. In fact Griffons rely on vision, but

▶ **Plague of vultures.** Vultures are always on the look-out not only for carcasses but signs that other vultures have spotted a carcass. Hence the vast flocks that can gather very quickly. Their role as scavengers, although it might seem distasteful, is beneficial in speedily removing carcasses before putrescence has set in. These are Asian white-backed vultures.

◀ **Mobbing.** Birds of prey often suffer mobbing attacks by smaller birds. This Griffon vulture is being mobbed by ravens at 3,800m (12,500ft) in the Himalayas.

▼ **Stripped to the bone.** These Rüppell's griffons in Kenya will have devoured the wildebeest within half an hour. Contrary to popular belief, they normally eat only very fresh meat.

most find food indirectly by watching the activities of neighboring birds in the air.

If a bird spots a carcass, it begins to circle lower. Its neighbors notice this, and fly towards the scene. These birds are in turn noticed by their neighbors, so that, within minutes, birds are converging from all points of the compass. If trees are available, the birds sit for a while before descending, but once the first few individuals are down, there is a rush for a place at the carcass. A small animal, such as an antelope, can be stripped to the bone in 20 minutes. The birds themselves squabble and fight while feeding, and the more dominant individuals can cram so much food in their crops that they can hardly take wing again. With their efficient food-searching, Griffons are extremely effective scavengers. Their only drawbacks are that they cannot operate at night, nor can they compete with large mammalian carnivores, which can easily drive them from a carcass. Also, their gregarious habits make them extremely vulnerable where carcasses have been poisoned by man.

Other similar species, including the African and Asian white-backed vultures, also feed entirely on carcasses, but they depend more on resident and less on migrant game, and so travel less far than the cliff-nesting Griffons. They tend to nest in smaller, more scattered colonies, and occasionally as individual pairs, but on trees rather than cliffs. They weigh less, so can take wing earlier in the day. Like the large Griffons, they also gather in large numbers at carcasses.

Another group of Old World vultures, including the Lappet-faced vulture and the European black vulture, behave in some respects like eagles. Individual pairs nest far apart and hold large ranges around their nests. They feed partly from large carcasses, but also take smaller items, including living prey; they do not fly long distances to forage, so it is rare to find more than one or two pairs at the same corpse.

Although several species of vulture may assemble at the same carcass, they do not all feed in the same way, or take the same tissues. In southern Europe, the Griffon vulture eats mainly the softer meat, the large Black vulture more often tears meat and skin off bones, the small Egyptian vulture pecks off tiny scraps of meat remaining on the bones, while the Bearded vulture takes the bones themselves. Moreover, only the Griffon depends entirely on large carcasses, the rest have other foods as well.

The various New World vultures and condors are not closely related to the Old World ones, but have developed some similar habits. Individuals usually nest well apart from one another, but they roost communally and feed in groups, especially the nonbreeders. Pairs of Turkey vultures or Black vultures occasionally breed in loose aggregations where large cliffs hold several suitable caves, and the two species often roost together. Unlike the Old World vultures, at least some New World species which live in forest use smell to help locate carcasses. The Turkey vulture has this sense unusually well developed compared with other birds, and is capable of finding covered carcasses or those on the forest floor. Other New World vultures, such as the King vulture, have no great sense of smell, but reach food in the forest by following other species to it. A sense of smell has enabled New World vultures to occupy forests and woodland, habitats which are closed to the Old World species which depend on sight alone.   IN

GAME BIRDS

Order: Galliformes
Families: Phasianidae, Tetraonidae, Meleagrididae, Numididae, Megapodiidae, Cracidae.
Two-hundred and sixty-three species in 75 genera.
Distribution: worldwide except Antarctica and southern South America.

Turkeys   Guinea fowl

Grouse   Guans   Megapodes

Pheasants
and Quails

GROUND-DWELLING **pheasants and quails** make up the largest and most widespread family in the order Galliformes, which also contains the grouse, turkeys, guinea fowl, megapodes, guans and curassows.

The family includes some remarkable birds: the Domestic fowl, man's most useful bird; the Blue peacock, a byword for beauty and mythology; the Crested argus pheasant, which has the largest feathers of any wild species in its tail; the Tibetan snowcock, which lives at a higher altitude than any other bird. From the dense rain forests of Southeast Asia to the arid deserts of Arabia or the high rocks of the Himalayas, almost every habitat has its characteristic species of pheasants or quails. They are absent only from Antarctica, some oceanic islands, the southern half of South America (where they are replaced by tinamous) and the tundras and forests of the far north (where they are replaced by grouse).

Nearly all pheasants and quails are heavy, rotund birds with short legs and rounded wings. From the tiny Blue quail to the stately Blue peacock, they are strong runners and rarely fly except to escape from danger, when they burst from cover in an explosion of rapid wingbeats. Although some quails (*Coturnix* species) are migratory, for flying most members of the family rely only on glycogen-burning sprint muscles; they cannot remain airborne for long and are therefore sedentary, staying within a few kilometers of their birthplace. Except for some of the tree quails of Central America and the tragopans of eastern Asia which are partly arboreal in habits, they feed exclusively on the ground. Many species, however, roost in trees at night to avoid ground predators. Most are generalized herbivores, eating seeds or shoots, but some forest species search among leaf litter for insects or fallen fruit. All are day-active.

The family can be divided into four groups: New World quails, Old World quails, partridges and pheasants. The New World quails are most typically plump, little quails, boldly marked with black, white, buff and gray; some carry firm, forward pointing crests or "topknots." Perhaps the best known species is the Bobwhite quail which is often pursued by hunters in the USA.

Old World quails are found throughout the grasslands of Africa, Asia and Australia. The Common quail migrates from Africa to Europe and from India to Central Asia to breed. Two other species are nomadic, invading areas in large flocks following rain: the Harlequin quail in Africa and the

Blue quail in Asia, Africa and Australia.

The partridges are a diverse collection of stocky, medium-sized game birds found in a range of habitats throughout the Old World. They include the giant snowcocks which may weigh 3kg (6.6lb) and inhabit the alpine tundras of the mountains in Central Asia. In Southeast Asia, there are several poorly known species which inhabit tropical rain forests, including the splendid roulroul. Partridges are most commonly found, however, in open habitats such as semideserts, grassland and scrub. Many species adapt well to cultivation, notably the Gray or Hungarian partridge and the chukars, which are common in farmland throughout much of Europe and have been introduced to North America. In Europe, modern agricultural techniques, in particular the widespread use of pesticides and herbicides, have caused a steady decline in numbers in recent years. Africa has only two genera of partridges, the bantam-like

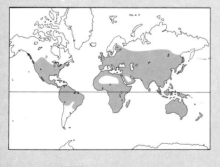

▲ **Iridescent plumage** of the Himalayan monal pheasant is rivaled by few birds. The metallic hues of the male pheasant contrast with the duller camouflage markings of females.

green, black and red. For a long time, European naturalists simply dismissed these birds as figments of the imagination of Chinese artists, so fantastic did they seem.

There is an interesting variation in social organization within the family. Most of the smaller quails and partridges are highly gregarious but monogamous. Some of the larger pheasants, such as peafowl, are also gregarious, but many are solitary, especially those that inhabit dense forest. These species are usually polygynous (one male mating with several females) or promiscuous, forming no pair bonds.

Among partridges and quails the basic social unit is the covey, one family party perhaps with a few other birds attached. In species which occupy open habitats (eg snowcocks, chukars or Bobwhite quail) coveys often fuse to form larger flocks. At the other extreme, in forest-dwelling partridges such as the Black wood partridge of Malaysia or some of the francolins, adults live singly or in pairs throughout the year.

Pair formation usually takes place before the covey breaks up, although males often join another covey to seek a mate. As recent experiments with Japanese quail have demonstrated, this is probably to avoid inbreeding, although the quail were found to prefer their first cousins to more distant relatives when choosing a mate.

Among the larger, polygynous pheasants, courtship involves long and spectacular rituals. An extraordinary but rarely seen sight is the display of the male Satyr tragopan from India and Nepal, which lowers a fleshy, electric-blue lappet from its throat and inflates two slender blue horns on its crown. In the Himalayan monal pheasant the iridescent males display in flight over the high cliffs and forests, calling wildly—a breathtaking sight. Perhaps the most exciting of all displays is the dance of the Great argus pheasant in the forests of Malaysia. Adult males have huge, broad, secondary wing feathers, each adorned with a series of circular, golden decorations shaded to appear three dimensional. An adult male prepares a special dance floor on the top of a hill in the middle of the forest. From this site he plucks leaves and stems and blows away leaf litter by clapping his enormous wings. Early each morning he gives loud, wailing cries to attract females. If a female arrives, he begins to dance about her and at the climax of his dance, throws up his wings into two enormous, semi-circular fans and makes hundreds of "eyes." In the gap between his wings, his real eye can be seen staring at the female.

Stone partridge and the diverse francolins of which there are more than 40 species, most of them confined to Africa. These partridge-like birds are sturdy, live in a variety of habitats, and tend to be rather noisy.

The term pheasant is usually reserved for the large, colorful, long-tailed members of the family. Of these 48 species in 16 genera, all but one are confined to Asia. The exception is the extraordinary and beautiful Congo peacock, the late discovery of which, by W. L. Chapin in 1936, was an ornithological sensation. Pheasants are forest birds; some live in the rain forests of Southeast Asia, others at various altitudes on the great mountains of Central Asia. Despite colorful male plumage and loud, raucous calls, most are shy and rarely seen. Extreme examples of this are the ruffed pheasants of western China—the Golden and Lady Amherst's (or Flower) pheasants. Males of both species are astonishingly gaudy, the Golden in red, yellow and orange, Lady Amherst's in white,

In the two species of argus pheasants, the display may end with mating, after which the female leaves to rear the brood unaided. However, in jungle fowl and Ring-necked pheasants the male forms bonds with a number of females and guards them as his "harem" until the eggs are laid. This mating system is almost unknown in other birds (though common in mammals).

With the exception of tragopans, all pheasants and quails nest on the ground, forming a single scrape, usually in dense, herbaceous vegetation. Clutch size varies from two in argus pheasants to nearly 20 in the Gray partridge (the largest clutch size of any bird). Predators often take a heavy toll of the eggs and female Ring-necked pheasants may make two or more nesting attempts each season. The female Red-legged partridge lays two clutches, one for the male to incubate, the second for herself. Apart from this species, males take little or no part in incubation. In captivity, female Golden pheasants have been found to incubate continuously without food, water, or even moving, for 22 days. In one case so still did the bird sit that a spider built its web across her back. Whether this happens in the wild, in China, has yet to be established.

The young are well developed—they leave the nest within a few hours, feed themselves from birth and can fly as young as one week old. Young Blue quail can and do breed when only two months old. Because they are so prolific, pheasants and quails can sustain heavy predation losses and man has learnt to exploit this by managing them for hunting. Many species are hunted, notably the Ring-necked pheasant.

The Red jungle fowl has an even more intimate relationship with man. Still a wild native of India and Southeast Asia, this species was domesticated at least 5,000 years ago. Since then it has been transformed into the many different forms of Domestic fowl used by man for purposes as diverse as egg production and cock fighting.

Unfortunately, the fact that pheasants and quails are good to eat has also led to excessive persecution. Not only have some species been hunted to the brink of extinction—over the brink in the case of the Indian mountain quail (although there are recent unconfirmed sightings) and the New Zealand quail, but many are vulnerable to destruction of habitat. This is because they are sedentary and, as ground feeders, are direct competitors with man's most effective ally in the destruction of natural ecosystems—the goat. The species in most serious trouble are the large, forest pheasants of the Himalayas and eastern Asia. More than one-third of pheasant species are threatened with extinction.

However, there is a glimmer of hope. Many pheasants can be bred in captivity with comparative ease. Breeding of the Cheer pheasant of India by aviculturalists, for instance, is so successful that a captive surplus population exists, and attempts have been made to return captive-bred birds of this (and other species) to the wild in areas of Pakistan in which they have become extinct. Such efforts have proved extremely difficult, but there are successes. The Masked race of the Bobwhite quail, for example, has been reintroduced successfully to Arizona. To educate the young quails about the real world it has proved necessary to scare them with simulated attacks from coyotes and men with guns. To teach them the arts of courtship and mating they were mixed with vasectomized quails of another wild subspecies.   MWR

The endless coniferous forests and tundra are home to most **grouse**. When the northern lands in winter are still and nearly empty of other birds, the grouse are there to be seen and heard. Their size and number make them important foods for many predators such as the Red fox and goshawk.

Many grouse inhabit coniferous or deciduous forest. They exploit the northern plant formations with roughly one species for each, eg the Spruce and Blue grouse in boreal forest. Others inhabit more open

▲ ▶ **Gaudy ruff or collar** of the male Golden pheasant ABOVE is spread forward, fanlike, and covers the beak during courtship. Both "collared pheasants" (the other is Lady Amherst's pheasant) are secretive inhabitants of the forests of central China. Competition for mates may flare, RIGHT, involving use of males' spurs, but confrontations rarely result in injury.

▼ **Popular game bird** in North America, the Bobwhite quail inhabits open country from Canada south to Guatemala. Males (distinguished by black-and-white head coloration from the female's buff-yellow) employ their "bob-white" call to attract a mate in spring. In winter, coveys may number up to about 30 birds.

areas, such as Red Grouse in moorland. Generally, grouse migrate short distances between a winter and a summer range within their local distribution.

In shape grouse resemble a plump chicken; in size they range from pigeon to goose; and they live mostly on the ground. They fly with a burst of wings and a long glide. All have camouflage markings but in display they startle with brilliant color, erect plumage, and arresting sounds. Many are well adapted to the winter cold and snow. Grouse have large flight muscles which also function in generation of heat, and storage of nutrients. The large crop and gizzard, and two very large ceca in the hindgut, permit the holding and digestion of large quantities of fibrous food.

The diet of most grouse is notable for its monotony and low quality. Throughout winter most species feed on one or two species of trees or shrubs. Moreover, these may contain oils that are distasteful or poisonous to other animals. The spring and summer provide a more varied diet of new growth and invertebrates. There is a steady ingestion of grit to the gizzard for the grinding of foods and perhaps supply of minerals.

In spring, usually at dawn and at dusk, males contend for mates by calling, wing fluttering, display of neck, tail and wing plumage and colors of the beaks, combs, and air sacs of the neck, and fighting. Females behave similarly but more subtly. Mating may be promiscuous, polygamous, or monogamous depending on species.

About half the species of grouse occupy a solitary territory; the others (eg Black, Sharp-tailed and Sage grouse, and Prairie chicken) form leks on traditional lekking grounds or arenas. A lek is a cluster of males gathered from often great distances and organized into a tight hierarchy of dominance. Hens visit the lek and usually mate with the central and most dominant males.

Some grouse present the puzzle of cyclic fluctuations in numbers. For example, Rock

ptarmigan are abundant or scarce at 9–
10 year intervals. While many believe that
food supply and predators control grouse
populations directly, grouse regulate their
density by their behavior to each other.
What drives this behavior and how it is
geared to the environment are unknown. In
Blue grouse it is almost certain that populations are regulated in spring by behavior
between members of the same species. The
nutrient quality of food may limit density by
affecting spacing behavior. Another view is
that interaction causes a rapid genetic
change in the frequency of aggressive or
more peaceful individuals in the population.
Aggressive individuals take large amounts
of space and cause populations to stop growing or decrease, peaceful animals tolerate
crowding and allow an increase of population. Such genetic selection may enable
grouse populations to adjust to change in
the amount of shelter, food and predators.

In the tundra, grouse are little affected by
man, while populations of forest and open
country species are decreased or increased
by logging, grazing or farming. Most
endangered is the Prairie chicken of North
America; some subspecies are near extinction. There is concern also over the magnificent Sage grouse. In parts of Europe, there
appears to be a new long-term decline in
numbers of Black grouse and capercaillie
that may be caused by acid rain.

Many millions of grouse are killed each
year for sport, food and trophies. Habitat
management helps preserve and even
increase populations of game birds such as
Ruffed grouse in North America and the
British Red grouse, a subspecies of Willow
ptarmigan that lacks white plumage in winter. The plumage of ptarmigan makes the
warmest and lightest clothing and bedding.
The feather adornments and foot-stamping
dance of the plains Indian are a derivative
of the plumage and courtship display of the
Prairie chicken. Tail feathers of the Black
grouse adorn the traditional Scotsman's
bonnet.   JFB

Spanish explorers of the 16th century
introduced the **turkey** to Europe and it is
thought that Mexican Indians first domesticated this valuable source of meat. Today's
Domestic turkey probably originated from a
Mexican race of the Common turkey.

Turkeys are large birds with strong legs,
which in the male have spurs. The two
members of the family differ in plumage,
especially the tail, and the spurs on the
males' legs. They generally walk or run, but
can fly strongly for short distances. Both

▲ **Puffed-up gobbler** appears twice its actual size, already up to double that of its potential mates. Among Common turkey males at the strutting ground, most mating is by the top males of the dominant groups, established by fighting prior to the breeding season.

◄ **Burrowing into snow** ABOVE, White-tailed ptarmigans (*Lagopus leucurus*) lie low to stay out of chilling winds and avoid predators. The downy-white plumage extending from nostrils to legs, and "snowshoe" scales on the toes, are adaptations to winter survival in these northerly grouse. The two hens in summer plumage BELOW display camouflage patterning typical of all grouse.

▶ **Courtship display of cock Sage grouse** OVERLEAF is one of the most spectacular seen in birds. As the long, pointed tail feathers are fanned upward, huge air sacs are inflated beneath the stiff white neck and breast feathers, which are rustled. At the same time, the male utters a deep, bubbling call. Bright yellow neck patches become visible at the peak of the display, then the air sacs are suddenly emptied with a whipcrack sound audible several hundred meters away.

species have similar plumages, but the much smaller Ocellated turkey lacks the "chest tuft" of bristles found on Common turkey males and some females. Both have naked heads (red in the Common and blue in the Ocellated), bearing wattles and other ornaments used in displays. The spurs are larger and more slender in the Ocellated turkey. The characteristic eyespots on the more rounded tail of the Ocellated turkey give the species its common name.

The Common turkey is the more widespread and at the time of European colonization was found as far south as Guatemala. A wide variety of food items has been recorded in the diet of both species. The bulk of the diet is made up of seeds and berries. Acorns are known to be an important part of the diet of the Common turkey in parts of the United States and the bird has a large muscular gizzard to cope with such food items. The male has a thick swelling on the chest during the breeding season, a store of fat and oil on which it draws during its extremely energetic courtship activities.

In the early 19th century turkeys were considered serious agricultural pests and

farmers often placed guards around their wheatfields to deter large groups of turkeys. Today grain is known *not* to be an important part of the diet. Small reptiles such as salamanders and lizards are also known to be taken by turkeys. Other rare food items include snakes. Many invertebrates, such as grasshoppers, make up the diet and must provide an important source of protein.

Common turkeys are polygynous (one male mating with several females). Females are thought to start breeding at one year old, whereas males usually have to wait until they are older, due to competition from older, more experienced birds. The male birds go through an elaborate display to acquire mates. Spreading their tail fans, drooping and rattling the main flight feathers, and swelling the head ornaments, they strut up and down on traditional "strutting grounds," gobbling as they do so.

After mating has taken place, the females go off by themselves and build the nest. The nests are usually not far from the strutting grounds and are no more than leaf-lined scrapes in the ground. Although the clutch size ranges from 8 to 15 eggs, one nest may have 20–30 eggs, as more than one female will often lay in a nest. The female alone incubates the eggs, and if she leaves the nest, even for a short period, will make sure the eggs are covered.

The well-developed (precocial) young are cared for by the female for their first two weeks and in the evening they are brooded. However, once the young have the basic use of their wings they spend the nights roosting in the trees. After a few weeks the brood is left to fend for itself.

The brood flock remains together until the young are around six months old, when the males will separate off to form all-male flocks. The males in such a sibling group are inseparable—even a solitary male will not try to join them. The juvenile sibling groups usually form flocks, as the older males can normally chase off the younger birds. This is a tough time for the young male, as he has to do a lot of fighting, both to determine his dominance among his siblings and to help determine his group's status within the flock. Fights can be very vicious and involve the use of wings and spurs. The contest can last for up to two hours and fights to the death have been recorded. However, once dominance has been established within a sibling group it is rarely challenged. Between groups, fights are usually won by the larger unit and, again, once dominance has been established there appears to be a fairly stable society.

Females, too, need to establish rank, but it does not appear to be anything like as overt as among the males. In general, older females are dominant to younger birds, and those females from sibling groups accustomed to winning contests also seem to win individual contests.

Towards the beginning of the breeding season the large male flocks break up, but the sibling groups remain tight. At the strutting grounds, it is males of the dominant groups that obtain most of the matings. Establishing dominance, even within a group, is vital as only the top birds mate. In one study it was shown that of 170 males present at the strutting ground, six carried out all the matings.

Very little is known of the social behavior of the Ocellated turkey. However, it is thought to be gregarious all the year round, and more readily flies, rather than runs, when disturbed.   MEB

The common name of **guinea fowl** derives from the Gulf of Guinea in West Africa, from which the common domesticated form originated. Guinea fowl are about two-thirds the

ate areas) gatherings of over 2,000 birds have been observed. These flocks are often extremely sedentary, rarely venturing more than 2km (1.2mi) from a central area which possesses a key resource, such as a drinking hole, a roost or an important foraging patch. Flocking seems to serve to detect patchily distributed, but locally very abundant, food (mainly dense concentrations of underground storage organs), and also to give protection against enemies. In the early morning the birds move in single file from their roost in a tree to a supply of water. The dominant males which usually take the lead are probably "scouts" since they spend a much higher proportion of their time than other flock members in alert postures. Later, the flock may advance in line abreast presumably in a "sweep" for food. In a third formation, the swarm, the birds are packed

flock containing very young birds. In such cases the more vulnerable young occupy a position in the center of the flock or on the side furthest from the threat.

The Helmeted guinea fowl has been domesticated and is found on farms (and dinner tables) the world over. The isolated Moroccan populations of this species are severely threatened if not already extinct due to hunting and habitat destruction. The only other guinea fowl requiring urgent

▼ **Representative species of game birds.** (1) Great curassow (*Crax rubra*). (2) Horned guan (*Oreophasis derbianus*). (3) Mallee fowl (*Leipoa ocellata*). (4) Greater prairie chicken (*Tympanuchus cupido*). (5) Bobwhite quail (*Colinus virginianus*). (6) Australian brush turkey (*Alectura lathami*). (7) Capercaillie (*Tetrao urogallus*). (8) Lady Amherst's pheasant (*Chrysolophos amherstiae*). (9) Vulturine guinea fowl (*Acryllium vulturinum*). (10) Chukar (*Alectoris chukar*). (11) Common turkey (*Meleagris gallopavo*).

conservation attention is the White-breasted guinea fowl, which is severely threatened by destruction of primary forest in West Africa.   TMC

The bizarre nesting habits of the robust, ground-dwelling **megapodes** set them well apart from the rest of the game birds. The eggs are laid in a variety of mounds and burrows where the heat for incubation comes from the sun, from fermenting plant matter, or even from volcanic activity. The young are well developed and independent (precocial); on hatching they burrow to the surface through the material of their "incubator," then run off into the bush. Another feature unique among birds is that the young can fly within hours.

The best studied species is the Mallee fowl of southern Australia which predominantly inhabits dry mallee scrub. The birds are strongly territorial and the males utter their calls (including a loud booming call) from anywhere in the territory during the breeding season. They probably pair for life but lead fairly solitary lives, usually roosting and feeding separately.

The mound is worked for up to 11 months of the year, but breeding is confined to spring and summer. About July, when the temperature inside the mound reaches about 30°C (86°F), the male removes the

covering sand and excavates holes in the fermenting organic matter. Eggs are laid from September to January at intervals of several days. The mound is then re-covered and its temperature regulated (mostly by the male) to a constant 33°C (91.4°F) by excavating and covering the mound as necessary. Heat comes from a combination of fermentation and solar energy.

The Australian brush turkey and the three New Guinean brush turkeys of the genus *Talegalla* also build large incubation mounds of leaf litter and soil.

The maleos of the Celebes leave their rain forest homes in the breeding season and walk up to 30km (18–19mi) to sandy beaches, by preference black volcanic sand, where the females excavate holes above high water and deposit one egg in each hole. The sand covering is presumably heated by the sun. The hatchling chicks make their way back to the far-off jungle.

The widespread Common scrub fowl may in fact consist of several distinct species. It lives in montane and lowland rain forest, monsoon forest, gallery forest, dune vegatation and scrubby "coral jungles," and has managed to reach many tiny isolated islands. It builds the largest mounds of all—up to 11m (36ft) in diameter and 5m (over 16ft) high—made of leaf litter and soil and, because of their size, usually encompassing

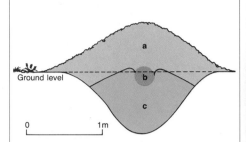

▲ **Bizarre nest-mounds of the megapodes** are unparalleled among birds. In southern Australia the Mallee fowl male works on the nest in most months of the year, digging out a hole, then scraping leaf litter into it and covering it with sandy soil (**a**); alternatively an already existing mound may be worked on. Mounds used year after year can reach 5m (over 16ft) in diameter. The female lays eggs in chambers (**b**) excavated by the male. Rotting vegetation (**c**) provides heat needed for incubation—once laid and covered, the eggs themselves are ignored by both parents, as are the chicks, which hatch in 50–90 days.

▶ **Portrait of a mound bird** ABOVE, the Brush turkey of eastern Australia.

▶ **Stylish elegance** of the African Crested guinea fowl BELOW: white "bead" patterning on black plumage, and a headdress of curly black feathers top a svelte silhouette.

Mock Fights and "Dating" in the Helmeted Guinea Fowl

The break-up of the Helmeted guinea fowl flocks at the onset of their breeding season results from an increase in aggression between the males—mainly ritualized chasing. In such interactions one male approaches another side-on in a characteristic hump-backed display posture (**1**). In this display (repeated by the males in courtship), the wings are compressed into the body and elevated, to give the impression, when viewed from the side, of a much larger bird. The approach elicits pursuit by the second male (who also assumes the hump-backed display), but the chaser rarely catches up with the initiator even if the latter slows down. Such chasing is a contagious activity, with sometimes as many as eight males running in single file. Females view these ritualized chases and presumably assess potential mates by determining the strongest male, ie the one who can sustain chasing the longest.

At the same time as this increase in chasing, males and females form short-term pairs. This "dating" probably allows females to compare potential mates more rigorously. After 2–3 weeks of such "dating" stable pairs form, and usually last until the female begins to incubate the eggs. Although male and female are closely similar, the male is easily

identified, since he spends most of his time sitting and resting, in alert postures (**2**), or in aggressive encounters with males who approach his hen. At this stage of the breeding season he is more aggressive, and chasing often leads to fighting (in captivity, sometimes culminating in the death of subordinate males with no escape route). The female of a stable pair does little more than feed and preen.

Once the hen begins incubating the eggs (she does all the incubation), the male deserts temporarily, since he can be sure of the paternity of the eggs and of his hen's commitment to hatching them. He then

associates with other females or may even "rape" (forced copulation without preliminary display) solitary hens. However, when the keets (chicks) are about to hatch, he returns to his original mate and helps to rear them, especially during their first two weeks. If the male is absent at this time the brood will almost certainly fail, since the hen cannot both care for the keets and find food to recoup the energy lost during incubation.   TMC

by leaves. Most remarkable of all are those Common scrub fowl that lay their eggs *en masse* in burrows in volcanically heated soil in New Britain, the Solomons and elsewhere. The burrows are often densely concentrated—up to one nest per 20sq m (215sq ft) on Simbo in the west Solomon Islands—and the underground hot streams and gases provide an incubation temperature of 34°C (93.2°F). Such concentrations of eggs are harvested regularly by local people, often according to strict rules. The committee at Gara village, New Britain, decrees that one man can only take 30 eggs a day and only harvest on two days, that no dogs may be used to find the nests and all eggs containing developing chicks are to be replaced. In the Celebes, rent is paid to the Government for permission to harvest at the breeding beaches of the maleo. Elsewhere, particularly on small islands in Micronesia, the gun and egg collectors are a significant threat to many island populations. FHJC

Unlike most game birds, **guans** are chiefly tree dwellers. They are big-bodied birds with smallish heads, thin necks, short, rounded wings and long, broad tails. This Central and South American family comprises three groups, the chachalacas, guans and curassows.

Chachalacas live fairly close to human settlements and are conspicuously gregarious, living in flocks of up to 100. The nine species of chachalacas (genus *Ortalis*) are the smallest and dullest, being generally plain brown with bare patches on the throat. They are predominantly ground feeders, their plumage providing excellent camouflage, but they readily take to the trees at the first sign of danger. They prefer low brush woodlands and wooded river banks, which has enabled one species, the Plain chachalaca, to survive in the remnant forests of the lower Rio Grande in southern Texas. Whole flocks usually call together, especially at dawn or dusk, and the rhythmic, repeated "cha-cha-lac-a" reverberates throughout the forest.

Guans are larger than the chachalacas and have a more colorful plumage, with some whitish edges to the body feathers, which range from deep green to black, often with a glossy sheen on the back and wings; most have long crown feathers which form a crest. The outer primaries are rather spine-like, strengthened and curved, and produce a peculiar drumming sound when the wings are vigorously shaken. These feathers are most developed in the two piping guans and

one or more tree bases. The temperature is regulated at 30–35°C (86–95°F)—depending upon the time after laying the egg—during the breeding season (August to January in north Queensland). The mounds attract predators, particularly the Komodo dragon and other monitors that excavate the mounds for eggs.

A large mound may be used by three or four pairs, but only one pair works at a time. Both male and female work the mound all year round. Their large strong feet sweep the ground clear around the mound. A 1kg (2.2lb) male was once seen to shift a stone which proved to weigh 6.9kg (15.2lb)! Mounds may be used for many years. Several in the Northern Territory have been used as "archaeological sites" to determine fire frequency (as indicated by charcoal layers) in the recent past.

Several species may lay eggs in the same mound. There is evidence that the Common scrub fowl parasitizes mounds of *Talegalla* and also other scrub fowls. Where sufficient natural heat is available, scrub fowls may not build a mound at all. On small islands and beaches they lay eggs in warm sand above high tide or even in rock clefts covered

N America, northern S America, Eurasia, Africa, Australia. Introduced to New Zealand (after extinction of native species), Hawaii and other islands. Some species widely introduced in Europe and America. Habitat: forest, woodland scrub, grassland, desert, farmland, alpine tundra; almost exclusively terrestrial. Size: length 14–122cm (5.5in–4ft) (excluding display trains) and weight 43g–5kg (1.5oz–11lb). Plumage: commonly brown, gray and heavily marked, but males often boldly patterned with blue, black, red, yellow, white or iridescent colors. Sexual dimorphism varies from almost none to extreme with males 30 percent larger than females and equipped with elaborate display structures and spurs. Voice: usually simple. brief but loud whistles, wails and raucous crows. Sociable species call often, solitary ones only at dawn or dusk in breeding season or when alarmed. Nests: chiefly simple ground scrapes, lined, if at all, with grass. Tragopans may nest in trees. Eggs: usually 2–20 whitish to dark olive, sometimes with markings; weight 4.8–112g (0.15oz–4oz); incubation 16–28 days; period in nest no more than a few hours or days. Diet: varied, chiefly seeds and shoots; also invertebrates, roots and fallen fruit. Chicks are mostly insectivorous.

New World quails

Thirty species in 10 genera, from Paraguay to S Canada.
Species include: **Bobwhite quail** (*Colinus virginianus*), **tree quails** or **wood partridges**, 3 species of *Dendrortyx*.

Old World quails

Eleven species in 3 genera, from Africa, Asia, Australia (Common quail migrates to Europe).
Species include: **Blue quail** (*Coturnix chinensis*), **Common quail** (*C. coturnix*), **Harlequin quail** (*C. delegorguei*), **Japanese quail** (*C. japonica*), and the extinct **New Zealand quail** Ex (*C. novaezelandiae*).

Partridges

Ninety-four species in 19 genera, from Africa, Europe, Asia, Australia.
Species include: **Black wood partridge** (*Melanoperdix nigra*), **chukar** (*Alectoris chukar*), the **francolins**, 41 species of *Francolinus*, **Gray partridge** (*Perdix perdix*), **Indian mountain quail** (*Ophrysia superciliosa*), **Red-legged partridge** (*Alectoris rufa*), **roulroul** or

Pheasants

Forty-eight species in 16 genera, from Asia; 1 species in Africa.
Species include: **Blue peacock** or **peafowl** (*Pavo cristatus*), **Cheer pheasant** E (*Catreus wallichii*), **Congo peacock** (*Afropavo congensis*), **Crested argus pheasant** R (*Rheinardia ocellata*), **Golden pheasant** (*Chrysolophus pictus*), **Great argus pheasant** (*Argusianus argus*), **Green peacock** V (*Pavo muticus*), **Himalayan monal pheasant** (*Lophophorus impejanus*), **Lady Amherst's** or **Flower pheasant** (*Chrysolophus amherstiae*), **Red jungle fowl** (*Gallus gallus*), **Ring-necked pheasant** (*Phasianus colchicus*), **Satyr tragopan** (*Tragopan satyra*), **Western tragopan** E (*T. melanocephalus*).

Grouse

Family: Tetraonidae
Sixteen species in 7 genera.

N America, N Asia, Europe. Habitat: forest, prairie, tundra. Size: 31–91cm (12–36in) long, and 0.3–6.4kg (10.5oz–14lb); in some species sexes very different in size (male capercaillie up to twice weight of female). Plumage: males black or brown, with white markings, and combs red to yellow; females brown and black flecked with white. Ptarmigan white in winter. Wings short, rounded, tail of various shapes, often large. Voice: hoots, hisses, cackles, clucks, clicks and whistles. Most drum wings. Nests: a simple depression in the ground. Eggs: usually 5–12, whitish to light brown and darkly blotched, weight 19–55g (0.7–1.9oz); incubation 21–27 days, by the female. Diet: adults eat leaves, needles, buds, twigs, flowers, fruits and seeds; chicks largely eat invertebrates.
Species include: **Black grouse** (*Lyrurus tetrix*), **Blue grouse** (*Dendragapus obscurus*), **capercaillie** (*Tetrao urogallus*), **Hazel grouse** (*Bonasa bonasia*), **Prairie chicken** (*Tympanuchus cupido*), **Red grouse** (*Lagopus lagopus scoticus*), **Rock ptarmigan** (*Lagopus mutus*), **Ruffed grouse** (*Bonasa umbellus*), **Sage grouse** (*Centrocercus urophasianus*), **Sharp-tailed grouse** (*Tympanuchus phasianellus*), **Spruce grouse** (*Dendragapus canadensis*), **Willow ptarmigan** (*Lagopus lagopus*).

(woodland and mixed open forest preferred) in regions with temperate winters. Size: both species 90–120cm (3–4ft) long; weight 3–9kg (6.5–20lb), to 18kg (40lb) in some domesticated form; males may be twice the weight of females. Plumage: generally dark, with brilliant metallic reflections of bronze and green especially in males; head and neck naked. Voice: a variety of gobbles and clucks. Nest: well concealed, on the ground; built by female. Eggs: 8–15, cream-colored, speckled with brown; incubation 28 days; young leave nest usually after one night. Diet: mainly vegetation, but also invertebrates and small vertebrates.
Species: **Common turkey** (*Meleagris gallopavo*) from E USA to Mexico. **Ocellated turkey** (*Agriocharis ocellata*), from Yucatan to Guatemala.

Guinea fowl

Family: Numididae
Six species in 4 genera.
Sub-Saharan Africa with isolated populations in Morocco; Helmeted guinea fowl introduced widely. Habitat: from subdesert steppe to tropical rain forest. Size: 39–56cm (15.5–22in) long and 1.1–1.6kg (2.4–3.5lb). Plumage: chiefly black spotted with white, two species unspotted. Males same size or slightly larger than females. Voice: usually harsh, loud cackling; two species with more musical piping notes. Nests: simple scrapes on ground, lined with leaves, grass or feathers. Eggs: usually 4–12, white to pale brown, pitted darker; weight 38–40g (1.4oz); incubation 23–28 days; young forage within 1–2 days of hatching and can fly short distances at 2–3 weeks. Diet: highly opportunistic; chiefly seeds, bulbs, tubers, roots and disused fallen grain in drier time of year; prefer insects and other invertebrates (often crop pests) in wetter months.
Species: **Black guinea fowl** (*Agelastes niger*), **Crested guinea fowl** (*Guttera pucherani*—including G. edouardi), **Helmeted guinea fowl** (*Numida meleagris*), **Plumed guinea fowl** (*Guttera plumifera*), **Vulturine guinea fowl** (*Acryllium vulturinum*), **White-breasted guinea fowl** (*Agelastes meleagrides*).

Megapodes

Family: Megapodiidae
Twelve species in 6 genera.
From Nicobar Islands, through Malaysia, Indonesia, Philippines,

and one (Mallee fowl) in semi-arid eucalypt woodland. Size: weight ranges between 0.9–8kg (2–17.6lb) and length 27–60cm (10.6–24in). Plumage: generally browns, grays and black, some species with colored facial skin, combs or wattles—red or yellow. Plumage differences between sexes slight. Voice: unmusical cackles and squawks. Nests: eggs laid in mounds of vegetation and holes in hot sand or volcanic areas. Eggs: white to brown with chalky covering; clutch size (5–33) known only for Mallee fowl. Diet: insects, seeds, fruits, roots, crabs, snails etc. Species include: **Australian brush turkey** (*Alectura lathami*), **Common scrub fowl** or **Jungle fowl** (*Megapodius freycinet*), **maleo** V (*Macrocephalon maleo*), **Mallee fowl** or **lowan** (*Leipoa ocellata*).

Guans and curassows

Family: Cracidae
Forty-four species in 8 genera.
Extreme south of N America, C and S America. Habitat: dense tropical forests, low riverside woods and thickets. Size: 52–96cm (20–38in) long and 470g–4.8kg (16.6oz–10.6lb). Males generally larger than females. Plumage: chiefly plain brown, deep green, blue or black with white patches. Many species crested, some with casques. Wings blunt; tail long and broad. Voice: a variety of raucous moans and calls, booming notes and whistles often repeated. Nests: usually of twigs and rotting vegetation, low down in trees or on ground. Eggs: 2–3, exceptionally 4, dull white or creamy; incubation 22–34 days, by female only; average weight 62g (2.2oz). Diet: chiefly fruits, berries, seeds; some take small animals or insects.
Species include: **Black-fronted piping guan** E (*Aburria jacutinga*), **Common piping guan** (*Aburria pipile*), **Crested guan** (*Penelope purpurascens*), **Helmeted curassow** (*Crax pauxi*), **Highland guan** or **chachalaca** (*Penelopina nigra*), **Horned curassow** (*Crax unicornis*), **Horned guan** E (*Oreophasis derbianus*), **Nocturnal curassow** (*Nothocrax urumutum*), **Plain chachalaca** (*Ortalis vetula*), **Red-billed curassow** E (*Crax blumenbachii*), **Sickle-winged guan** (*Chamaepetes goudotii*), **Wattled guan** (*Aburria aburri*), **White-winged guan** E (*Penelope albipennis*).
Total threatened species: 6.

▲ **Noisy "cha-cha-lac-a" call** and bare throat-patch give the Rufous-vented chachalaca of Venezuela its name. The Rufous-vented or Red-tailed chachalaca (*Ortalis ruficauda*) has the broad, long tail and plain brown plumage typical of the chachalacas of Central and South America, members of the guan family.

Curassows are the largest and heaviest members of the family and are poor fliers, spending most of their time at ground level. They range in plumage from deep blue to black, invariably with a purple gloss, and all have rather curly crests. The distinguishing feature, especially of the genus *Crax*, is the head or facial adornments of wattles and knobs which vary from yellow to bright crimson and blue; the Helmeted and Horned curassows have "horns" on the forehead which are used in elaborate courtship displays. The Nocturnal curassow, with its chestnut-colored plumage and red and blue bare face skin, is one of the most colorful of the whole family, yet this species is entirely nocturnal.

Like the chachalacas, the rest of the family are noisy, necessarily so, to maintain contact in the dense and often dark forests. The windpipe of some species, notably the guans, is adapted for amplifying calls which are some of the loudest and most far-reaching of all birds. Curassows utter one or two booming or whistling notes.

All members of the Cracidae are mainly vegetarian, chiefly fruit eaters but also eating leaves, buds and flowers; some also take small animals, large insects or frogs. The chachalacas and curassows, with their long legs, big feet and strong claws, scratch the litter on the forest floor in chicken-like fashion. Curassows are able to consume nuts and tough seeds by swallowing small stones which aid digestion.

Nests are either low down in a tree or on the ground under heavy cover. The usually fragile structure is quite small in relation to the adult bird. The eggs are rather large, and are smooth in some of the guans (genus *Penelope*), or rough and pitted in the chachalacas and most of the curassows. Females care for the young, which hatch with well-developed flight feathers and can leave the nest after only a few hours. The young of some species are able to fly within a few days.

Most species are relentlessly hunted for food and "sport," their tameness and inability to fly far or fast making them easy targets. The rapid destruction of tropical forest also threatens, in large areas, this little-known and strangely alluring family of birds. The White-winged guan was thought to have become extinct in 1870 but was rediscovered in 1977. Estimates of its population vary from 20 to 100 birds, all in an area scheduled for felling. The Red-billed curassow is also verging on extinction and is down to less than 100 individuals.

TWP

the Wattled and Sickle-winged guans. The spectacular drumming of their display flight through the treetops is augmented with deep raucous cackles.

Guans are the most widespread of the Cracidae. The 15 species of the genus *Penelope* are considered to be typical guans and, though tree-dwelling birds, also feed on the ground. More specialized and arboreal are the three species in the exclusively South American genus *Aburria*, which have shorter, less powerful legs and a well-developed wattle on the throat. The two species in the genus *Chamaepetes* are smaller and lack wattles. Of the remaining two species of guan, both restricted to Central America, the Highland guan is unique in that the female is larger than the male and differs in plumage. The Horned guan is the most distinctive, but also shows features of the curassows to which it is probably closely related. Its cylindrical, 5cm (2in) long horn rises from the center of its crown.

feathers, each adorned with a glowing "eye." Since ancient times, the peacock has had a close connection with man, and has been a graceful sight around many an Indian temple or European garden. Nevertheless, until recently, few of the details of the peacock's courtship dance were known, and even less, the purpose of that splendid fan was not understood. (It is not, incidentally, a tail, but consists of enlarged tail coverts.)

Peafowl live for most of the year in small groups or family parties. In the breeding season, however, the cocks become solitary and pugnacious. Each adult male returns to a place he occupied in previous years and establishes his territorial rights, threatening intruders and calling loudly to advertise his presence. Territories are small, from 0.05 to 0.5ha (0.02–0.2 acres) and center on clearings in forest or scrub. Occasionally a junior male will challenge a senior neighbor and a long and violent battle ensues. The combatants circle each other nervously, looking for an opening, then suddenly spring up in a kaleidoscope of tails and wings to slash out with their claws and spurs. Evenly balanced fights can last for a whole day or more and are as keenly watched by other peacocks as any boxing contest! Serious injury is rare and the winner is usually the bird with most stamina, who drives his opponent away.

Within his territory the peacock has 1–4 special display sites, where the famous dance takes place. These spots are carefully chosen; a typical one is an "alcove" no more than 3m (10ft) across, enclosed by bushes, trees or walls. In one English park, a male uses the stage of an open-air theater!

The cock waits near one of these sites until he sees a group of females approach. He then goes to the site and, turning modestly away from the females, spreads his

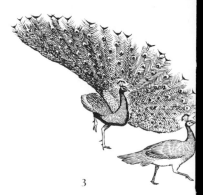

1

2

3

great fan with a long, loud shake, to bring each "eye" into place. He then begins to move his wings rhythmically up and down. As the females get nearer, he is careful to keep the unpatterned back of the fan towards them. Peahens have a reputation for being indifferent to the cocks' splendid shows, and it appears that at this stage they are drawn to the site more by chance than purpose.

As soon as a female enters the alcove, a transformation comes over the male. He backs towards her with rapidly fanning wings; she avoids him by stepping into the center of the display site. This is apparently what the cock has been waiting for. He swivels suddenly, so as to face her, ceases the movement of his wings and presses the fan forwards, almost engulfing the hen. Simultaneously, spasms of rapid shivering course through his fan causing the whole structure to rustle with a loud, silvery sound. The female normally responds by standing still for a few moments and the male then turns away and resumes his wing-fanning. Sometimes she then runs quickly round to the front of the male and, when he shivers the fan, runs excitedly behind him again. This may be repeated several times (see BELOW LEFT).

Charles Darwin recognized that the peacock's fan presents an evolutionary conundrum. Why should the females find this ornament attractive, when it is such an unnecessary encumbrance? An ingenious solution to this problem was proposed by the biologist Ronald Fisher and has been proved essentially correct.

Females choose ornamented males in order to have sons that will inherit their fathers' attractions; they merely follow the fashion. Any female with a different taste would have unattractive sons condemned by other females to evolutionary oblivion. So peahens use colorful rump feathers as a criterion of attractiveness in peacocks, and select the most adorned.

How, in practice, do females choose such a mate? The answer may lie in an extraordinary feature of the peacock's fan. The decorations on the fan are bright, bold concentric patterns with black centers—they are huge staring eyes. Peahens, like many animals, find eyes arresting, exciting, even hypnotic symbols. By suddenly exposing a peahen to this constellation of eyes, the peacock may be trying to transfix her, thus allowing him to mate. The better the performance and the brighter the eyes, the greater his chances of success. The "choice" is therefore made for her.   MWR

▲ ◄ **Huge, staring "eyes"** of the peacock's fan are arresting, even hypnotic, symbols for the peahen. During courtship, the peacock, after backing toward the female (1, LEFT), turns suddenly (2), exposing to her a shivering constellation of eyes. Sometimes, just as the male swivels toward the female, he suddenly launches himself forward with a strangled hoot and attempts to catch hold of her. The female usually dashes out of the way (3). However, on occasion she hesitates or crouches, and mating ensues (4).

4

One hundred and forty-three species in 47 genera.
Distribution: see maps and table.

Cranes   **Limpkin**

Trumpeters   **Rails**

Some fly over the Himalayas at more than 9,000m (30,000ft) above sea level and are among the highest-flying birds. Not only are cranes among the oldest groups of birds, dating back some 60 million years, but captive cranes have lived into their 70s and 80s. Their calls are among the loudest, and cranes' beauty and grace is difficult to surpass. Unfortunately the cranes are also among the most endangered families of birds. Mankind is entirely responsible for their decline.

Generally cranes are birds of the open marshlands, grasslands and agricultural fields. Most species usually nest in secluded areas of shallow wetlands, the exception being the two species of *Anthropoides*, which often nest in grasslands or semidesert areas.

Cranes have long, powerful, straight beaks and long necks and legs. They are heavy set and have loud, shrill calls that carry for several kilometers. The windpipe

Cranes fly with their neck extended forward. Usually the legs are stretched straight beyond the short stubby tail during flight, but in cold weather flying cranes fold their legs, so the feet are tucked under the breast feathers. Although they are predominantly aquatic birds, their feet are not webbed, and cranes are restricted to the shallows where they breed, search for food, and rest during the night. Only the two species of crowned cranes roost in trees.

The crowned cranes are also the "living fossils" among the cranes. In the remote Eocene (54–38 million years ago) these loose-plumed birds with enormous, gaudy crests, flourished in the northern continents for millions of years before the Earth cooled and the cold-adapted cranes evolved. The Ice Age restricted the range of the crowned cranes to the savannas of central Africa, where tropical conditions were maintained during the period when northern continents

The Crane Dance

Downy chicks, still wobbly on their legs, sometimes bow and run when excited by the close approach of their parents. Groups of subadult cranes engage in "social dancing" that helps redirect aggression and develop bonds between potential pair members. The newly paired cranes engage in intensive periods of vigorous dance, particularly immediately before mating. Established pairs copulate without prerequisite dancing, indicating that dancing is important in helping to stabilize and synchronize unstable relationships, much as it does in humans.

Cranes hesitating between escape and attack dance, for example when disturbed at their nest. Then, there are amusing times when cranes seem to dance for sheer pleasure. Sometimes within a flock of preening cranes, one will start to dance, and the contagious behavior will spread to the entire group. American Indians, Australian aborigines, the Ainu of north Japan and various African tribes all mimic the crane's dance.

The dance consists of head bobbing, deep bows (1), leaps, grasping with the bill and tossing up objects (feathers, stones, tussocks) (2), running with wings flapping, and short, low ritual flights. The bows and the leaps usually alternate between pair members, one bird bowed while the other leaps (3). The "unison call" (see text) on the other hand, is given simultaneously by the male and female. If the two cranes are upright at the same time and facing each other, they at once shift into stiff threat postures—exaggerated flapping, stamping and arching (4), before again flowing into other elements of the dance.

By dancing with a captive female Whooping crane that was imprinted on humans, and by remaining with this bird from dawn to dusk through the month of April, the author stimulated her to lay an egg. This genetically valuable bird was the *sole* descendent of a pair of Whooping cranes that were alive when the worldwide population had fallen below two score. By artificial insemination, her egg was fertilized; a male crane hatched and was reared to continue the line. So even a half-human hybrid of the dance served its breeding function.   GWA

▲ **Blue cranes in Etosha National Park, Namibia.** Like the closely related Demoiselle crane, the Blue or Stanley crane is short-billed and eats a wide range of food. Unlike northern cranes, it does not migrate.

were covered by miles of ice. Two species of crowned cranes still brighten the African grasslands, and of the cold-adapted species, 13 now stalk the wetlands of the Northern Hemisphere.

Today's successful crane species are omnivorous, opportunistic feeders that have adapted within the last few thousand years to benefit from man's agricultural fields. Several *Grus* species, both crowned cranes, and both species of *Anthropoides* have short beaks with which they can effectively grasp insects, pluck ripe seeds from grass stems, and graze on fresh green vegetation in a goose-like manner. In contrast, most of the endangered species have long, powerful mandibles, used in digging for plant roots and tubers in muddy soils or for grasping aquatic animals such as small fish, amphibians and crustaceans. The aquatic feeders include the larger cranes (eg Wattled and White-naped) and the white cranes

(Whooping, Siberian, Black-necked). Both species of *Bugeranus* and half of the *Grus* species fall within this category. If a wetland is drained, these specialized cranes must move to another wet area. Land drainage has been one cause of their decline. In addition, their size and their plumage render them conspicuous and easy prey for hunters and egg collectors. The Sandhill and Common cranes breed at 3–4 years old and often rear two chicks. The rare Siberian crane does not become sexually mature until six years old and never rears more than one chick per breeding attempt.

Cranes are monogamous, and with the onset of spring or the rainy season, mated pairs retreat to secluded grassland or wetland, where they establish and vigorously defend a breeding territory that may include several thousand hectares, depending on species or topography.

Mated pairs emit a loud "unison call"

duces several short, high-pitched calls. The display identifies the sex of each of the birds, a factor that assists in the development of the pair bond. However, after a stable relationship is established between two cranes, the unison call primarily functions as a threat. At dawn the crane pairs announce their territory with a unison call, and as the display is heard by neighboring pairs, the same is returned, so that for kilometers an extended chorus of crane calls announces occupancy of real estate.

The reproductive states of two members of a stable pair are synchronized by their bodily cycles, by the weather, length of daylight, and by elaborate displays such as nuptial dances (see box) and unison calls. Cranes begin copulating several weeks before eggs are laid. For fertility to be assured, a female crane must be inseminated two to six days before an egg is laid.

At a secluded spot within the wetland breeding territory, the pair constructs a platform nest. Crowned cranes often lay a three-egg clutch, while other cranes lay two eggs, with the exception of the Wattled crane that more frequently lays a single egg.

Male and female cranes share incubation

sometimes in a "neutral area" in company with other cranes. Within the 28–36 day range, the duration of incubation depends on the species and the parents' attentiveness at the nest. Crowned cranes do not initiate incubation until the clutch is complete, and their eggs hatch simultaneously. Other cranes begin incubation as soon as the first egg is laid, and successive chicks hatch at one- or two-day intervals.

Crane chicks are well-developed when they hatch (precocial) and follow their parents around the shallows and neighboring uplands until they develop flight feathers at 2–4 months of age. The larger and tropical species, such as the Wattled and Sarus cranes, have a longer pre-fledging period than do species such as the Siberian crane, in which the short arctic summer limits the period when food is available for the fast-growing chicks. Although all eggs usually hatch, many chicks die, and most of the endangered species usually only rear a single chick per breeding effort. Once fledged, the chicks remain with their parents until the onset of the next breeding season. Migratory cranes learn the migration path by accompanying their parents thousands

▼ **Representative species of cranes, rails and related families.** (1) Purple gallinule (*Porphyrula martinica*). (2) Limpkin (*Aramus guarauna*). (3) Demoiselle crane (*Anthropoides virgo*). (4) Crested coot (*Fulica cristata*). (5) Black crowned crane (*Balearica pavonina*). (6) Red-crowned cranes (*Grus japonensis*) dancing. (7) Siberian crane (*Bugeranus leucogeranus*). Heads only of: (8) Whooping crane (*Grus americana*), (9) Sarus crane (*G. antigone*), and (10) Sandhill crane (*G. canadensis*). (11) White-winged trumpeter (*Psophia leucoptera*) (12) Water rail (*Rallus aquaticus*).

3

2

1

4

of kilometers south to traditional wintering grounds. Foraging behavior is also learned, while the form of displays is generally predetermined.

In North America, the Whooping cranes have recovered from 14 birds in 1941 to approximately 75 birds in the "natural range" flock, and a total, including captive birds, of about 140 cranes. The Siberian crane is now reduced to fewer than 900 individuals, Black-necked cranes to fewer than 500, and Red-crowned cranes to fewer than 1,000 birds in the wild. Fortunately, cranes are appealing birds, and recent efforts in many Asian countries have resulted in the protection of wetlands critically needed by cranes. But crane hunting continues in Canada, Afghanistan, Pakistan and the United States of America, and the pressures on the wetlands for man's use increase as human numbers soar.

Although many cranes are severely endangered, they respond well to protection and management. In an effort to ensure their survival, captive flocks of the endangered species are now being established at several zoos and specialized crane research centers. Foremost in captive breeding has been the Patuxent Wildlife Research Center in Maryland, in the USA. A captive flock of Whooping cranes has been established at Patuxent by collecting one egg from each nest of the wild cranes containing two eggs. The eggs laid by the captive birds are now transferred from them and substituted for those in nests of Sandhill cranes in Idaho. The Whooping cranes reared by foster parents migrate south with them and learn to feed in the agricultural fields with the Sandhill cranes. The 30 or so birds constituting this new population show little interest in breeding with Sandhills, but pairing has not yet occurred between the Whoopers. GWA

The **limpkin** is the only member of the New World family Aramidae. It has anatomical features in common with the cranes and has a digestive system like that of the rails—in general appearance it is not unlike a very large rail.

In the swamps and shaded areas which are its principal home, the presence of the limpkin may be detected by the many conspicuous empty shells of large freshwater snails (*Pomacea caliginosa*) which it leaves on the muddy banks. To secure its food, the long-legged limpkin wades in shallow water, probing with its long, laterally compressed bill slightly downcurved at the tip. When it finds a snail, it carries it to the shore and sets it in the mud with the shell opening facing upwards, holding it there with its long toes tipped with long, sharp claws. With great dexterity the bird quickly removes the horny operculum that protects the snail, pulls out the mollusk and swallows it.

Limpkins walk rather slowly with a curious undulating tread that gives the impression of lameness or limping, from which the common name is derived. Although they lack webs on the feet, limpkins swim well. In flight the head and long slender neck are extended with the feet and legs projecting behind, in the manner of a crane. The wings are broad and rounded. On the ground as they move about, limpkins utter low clucking notes and then may burst into a loud "car-r-r-rao car-r-r-rao." Both parents incubate the eggs and tend the well-developed (precocial) young.

Although the limpkin also takes frogs, lizards and worms, the snail accounts for such a high proportion of its normal diet that it cannot exist without it. Where marshes have been drained, the snails have disappeared, and with them the limpkin. In the United States of America the bird is now well protected and, since the Everglades and Lake Okeechobee in Florida are too vast to drain, it is likely that the species will always survive there. PRC

Trumpeters are non-migratory, grounddwelling birds which live in small to sizeable flocks in the tropical rain forests of South America. The three closely related species are about the size of a domestic chicken. They may be distinguished by the color of their innermost flight feathers, inner wingcoverts and lower backs, which are gray in the Gray-winged trumpeter, white in the Pale-winged trumpeter, green in the Darkwinged trumpeter. The head in all three species appears small in relation to the body, and the large dark eyes give the head its "good-natured" expression. When it is standing, the trumpeter's very short tail is almost completely hidden by the outer webs of the secondaries. The typical hunch almost fur-like quality. The bill is short, stout and slightly curved.

Trumpeters have at least two different calls, a flock call and a threat call. The flock call is a booming "oh-oh-oh-oh . . . ooooo." The long drawn-out part of this call is delivered with the bill closed, which causes the sound to reverberate within its body. The threat call is a loud cackle, or trumpeting, from which the group takes its name. Trumpeters have the ability to run fast, but are rather poor fliers. At dusk they fly up rather laboriously, on deeply-rounded wings, some 6–9m (20–30ft) to roost in the forest trees, where they form noisy, quarrelsome groups.

Details of the trumpeters' breeding-cycle are still imperfectly known. At the beginning of the breeding season large flocks are reported to gather in clearings in the forest where the ground is smooth and free of

...ing and leaping and sometimes even somersaulting in their excitement. After mating, a pair of trumpeters will select a nest site which may consist of a hole in a tree, or on the ground. The average clutch size is about seven, and it is the female that incubates. When the young hatch they are covered with thick, black down with elaborate pinkish streaks. They do not stay long in the nest, and are soon running about after their parents.

Trumpeters are reported to make good eating. This, combined with the fact that they are unwary birds and poor fliers, has made them easy targets for hunters who, in some parts of their former range, have hunted them to extinction. PRC

Rails are a large but little-known family which might generously repay further efforts to tease apart the details of their lives. Most species inhabit remote areas; a few, especially the coots, are more common.

Families of Cranes, Limpkin, Trumpeters and Rails

E Endangered.　I Threatened, status indeterminate　V Vulnerable.　R Rare.

Cranes
Family: Gruidae
Fifteen species in 4 genera.
All continents except S America and Antarctica. Habitat: shallow wetlands in breeding season, grasslands and agricultural fields in non-breeding season. Size: height 0.9–1.8m (3–6ft), wingspan 1.5–2.7m (6–9ft), weight of smallest species 2.7–3.6kg (6–8lb), largest species (9–10.5kg (20–23lb). Males usually larger. Plumage: white or various shades of gray, with bright red bare skin or elaborate plumage on head. Long, elaborate secondaries, long, overhanging tail, or ruffled, curled and raised in display. Voice: shrill, carries long distances; in 11 species sex identifiable from unison call of adult pairs. Nest: a platform in shallow water or in short grass. Eggs: 1–3, white or heavily pigmented; 120–270g (4–10oz); incubation 28–36 days. Diet: insects, small fish and other small animals, tubers, seeds and agricultural gleanings.

Species include: **Black crowned crane** (*Balearica pavonina*), **Black-necked crane** I (*Grus nigricollis*), **Common crane** (*G. grus*), **Red-crowned crane** V (*G. japonensis*), **Sandhill crane** (*G. canadensis*), **Sarus crane** (*G. antigone*), **Siberian crane** E (*Bugeranus leucogeranus*), **Stanley** or **Blue crane** (*Anthropoides paradisea*), **Wattled crane** (*Bugeranus carunculatus*), **White-naped crane** V

(*Grus vipio*), **Whooping crane** E (*Grus americana*).
Total threatened species: 6.

Limpkin
Family: Aramidae
Sole species *Aramus guarauna*.
S Georgia, Florida, Cuba, S Mexico S to Argentina, chiefly E of Andes. Habitat: swamps (wooded or open) or arid brush (as in West Indies). Size: length 58–71cm (23–28in); weight 0.9–1.3kg (2–2.8lb). Plumage: dark olive-brown with greenish iridescence on upperparts, and broadly streaked with white; sexes alike. Voice: vociferous—loud wails, screams and assorted clucks, heard mostly at night. Nest: shallow, of rushes or sticks just above waterline in marshes, or in bushes or trees. Eggs: 4–8, pale buff blotched and speckled with light brown; average 5.6cm (2.2in) long, 4.4cm (1.7in) across; incubation about 20 days. Diet: almost exclusively large snails, some insects and seeds.

Trumpeters
Family: Psophiidae
Three species of genus *Psophia*.
SE Venezuela, Guianas and Amazon basin. Habitat: on ground of tropical rain forests. Size: length 43–53cm (17–21in); Gray-winged species weighs just over 1kg (2.2lb). Plumage: chiefly black, with purple, green or bronze reflections especially

on lower neck and wing coverts; soft, velvet-like on head and neck; outer webs of tertials and secondaries (white, gray or brown) form hair-like strands over lower back; sexes alike. Voice: loud trumpeting, loud deep-pitched cries, prolonged cackles. Nests: hole in tree or crown of palm. Eggs: 6–10, white or green, weight about 76g (2.7oz). Diet: vegetable matter and insects.
Species: **Dark-winged** or **Green-winged trumpeter** (*Psophia viridis*), **Gray-winged** or **Common trumpeter** (*P. crepitans*), **Pale-** or **White-winged trumpeter** (*P. leucoptera*).

Rails
Family: Rallidae
One hundred and twenty-four species in 41 genera.
Total threatened species: 8.
Europe, Asia, Australasia, N America, S America, and many oceanic islands and archipelagos. Habitat: generally damp forest, scrub, meadow and marshland. Size: length 10–60cm (4–24in); weight 30g (Baillon's crake) –3.3kg (takahe) (1oz–7.3lb). Males same size as or 5–10 percent heavier than females. Plumage: mostly drab brown, gray and rufous, sometimes with pale spots and flashes; a few species show bright and contrasting colors; differences in color between sexes in some species, but sexes similar in most. Voice: many whistles, squeaks and grunts, in combinations

from simple to complex. Many sound "unbirdlike." Nests: in wholly aquatic species (coots) conical nest emerges from shallow water on stick or pebble (Horned coot) foundation; others within clump of grass or reeds, sometimes roofed; a few species in bushes or low trees; always wholly of vegetation. Eggs: usually 2–12, but for many species poorly documented; color usually drab stone to rich brown, often spotted with darker shades; 10–80g (0.4–2.8oz); incubation 20–30 days. Diet: medium to large invertebrates, sometimes smaller vertebrates, some seeds, fruits etc; a few species largely herbivorous.

Groups:
Long-billed rails including the **Guam rail** V (*Rallus owstoni*), **Lord Howe rail** E (*Tricholimnas sylvestris*), **New Guinea flightless rail** (*Megacrex inepta*), **Virginia rail** (*Rallus limicola*), **Water rail** (*R. aquaticus*).

Crakes and gallinules including the **Asian water cock** (*Gallicrex cinerea*), **Baillon's crake** (*Porzana pusilla*), **corncrake** (*Crex crex*), **Gray moorhen** or **Common gallinule** (*Gallinula chloropus*), **Purple gallinule** (*Porphyrula martinica*), **Purple swamp hen** or **pukeko** (*Porphyrio porphyrio*), **takahe** E (*Notornis mantelli*).

Coots including the **American coot** (*Fulica americana*), **European coot** (*F. atra*), **Giant coot** (*F. gigantea*), **Horned coot** R (*F. cornuta*).

Without exception, they are birds of the ground or water level, running or swimming through a wide variety of habitats. Their distribution includes every major land mass (except Antarctica), and they are remarkable for colonizing even remote islands.

Rails are inhabitants of rather specialized, patchy habitats—such as river flood plains and forest clearings. Such habitats may be here one year and gone the next, and the life-histories of the rails are adapted to these circumstances. All rails are stout-legged and short-winged, adapted for traveling swiftly through dense, low vegetation.

Rails fall, with some degree of overlap, into three groups—the long-billed rails, the crakes and gallinules, and the coots.

The long-billed rails are characterized by a medium to long, often slightly down-curved bill. This is a general tool which can be pushed into mud, as the Water and Virginia rails will do when searching for worms, or used more powerfully in smashing eggshells, crushing horny grasshoppers, or even killing the occasional frog or duckling. In some of the larger rails the bill is even more of a hatchet. Larger vertebrates, even rats, may make a meal for the sturdy New Guinea flightless rail, one of few flightless birds to hold its own against man's introduced exterminators.

The social organization and behavior of most of the long-billed rails is a mystery. Most species, even the larger ones, seem to be able to breed in their first year—another adaptation to temporary habitats—and territoriality seems to be the rule. The rails are a vocal group, forced to defend their densely vegetated territories by voice, and many species seem to indulge in "duetting" in which the male and female of a pair each contribute to a coordinated song. This habit may inform potential intruders that there are indeed two adults in residence and that any incursions will be met by effective resistance.

The crakes and gallinules have shorter bills. Some species look rather like partridges, although they always have the slim body necessary for moving efficiently through dense vegetation. Their bills are not long enough to probe into mud and they depend more on surface foraging for smaller invertebrates and seeds. Some, like the endangered takahe of New Zealand, are almost entirely vegetarian. Consequently they have no great dependence on marshy and soft ground, although they may certainly be found in those places, sometimes even trotting about on lily-pads like the unrelated jacanas (Charadriiformes), and have therefore exploited a wide range of habitats. The corncrake, for instance, is a bird of coarse grasslands in the northern Palaearctic (Europe, North Africa, and northern Asia) and was formerly common all over Europe, occurring in many of the habitats where partridges are common today. Although very rarely seen, this shy bird could easily be detected by its distinctive call—sounding like a knife being scraped over the teeth of a comb. Changes in the timing of hay-mowing, and perhaps the introduction of pesticides, have eliminated this species over much of its former range, although it is still one of the more easily found crakes. However, we know almost nothing of its biology. Like many of its

◄ **Spectacular leap for food.** A Water rail shoots up a meter (3.3ft) from the water surface to seize a dragonfly.

▼ **Snails are not a delicacy,** but form the major part of a limpkin's diet. This bird holds a freshwater snail in its bill before taking it to the bank, holding it on the mud with one foot and extracting the animal from its shell with its bill. Drainage of marshes removes the snails, and also the limpkins which feed on them.

group, the corncrake is suspected to be monogamous, raising usually one brood per year, and being territorial.

Some crakes and gallinules may have quite complex, even fascinating breeding systems. In the moorhen the offspring of early broods sometimes remain with the parents through the raising of later broods in the same year, and even help to feed their younger siblings. This also happens in the Purple swamp hen or pukeko of New Zealand, although this species shows more complicated social behavior—several females may lay in a single nest, each female may copulate with many of the males in the breeding group; the whole group participates in parental care and territory defense.

Unlike the other rails, the coots are truly aquatic birds, able to swim and dive well using their generously lobed toes, and rarely found far from the water. They can thus colonize deep and desolate waters, such as the high altitude lakes of the Andes where the two largest and grandest species, the Horned and Giant coots, make their home. Because they gain their protection from open water rather than dense vegetation, they have less need of the slim profiles of their relatives, and are altogether stouter birds. They are omnivores, eating mainly plant material in winter but adding the seasonally abundant water insects to their

diet in spring and summer. The chicks are fed almost exclusively on insects for the first part of their lives, only gradually changing over to a diet of vegetation as their bodies, and intestines, grow larger and capable of coping with this relatively indigestible food.

Again unlike most rails, the coots can be gregarious, especially during winter when flocks of thousands of, for example, European coots may gather on large lakes and even the sea coast. The function of these gatherings is uncertain, but they do provide an excellent opportunity for some individuals to exploit their weaker subordinates. All coots return to the surface before eating their food haul, and this gives a chance for food stealing to occur—a bird may hardly break surface before its pondweed is snatched away by one of the pirates. During winter some individuals obtain most of their food in this way and thus avoid the costs and difficulties of deepwater diving.

All the rails have stout, well-muscled legs with three forward-facing toes and one hind toe, emerging from the leg slightly higher than the others and used as a brace during walking. The feet are important weapons in the struggle to gain a breeding territory. In the Asian water cock these male combats make spectacular sport and the birds are carefully cultivated, like champion fighting cocks. The legs and feet of newly hatched

▲ **Trotting on lily-pads** and other floating vegetation, the long-toed Black crake (*Limnocorax flavirostra*) of East Africa resembles the quite unrelated jacana of the wader family.

▶ **Coot hatchlings** BELOW bear a frontal shield that remains red in many species, but in the European coot becomes white in the adult.

▼ **Rasping call of the corncrake** was once common in coarse grasslands of Eurasia. Corncrakes of middle and northern Europe migrate to spend the winter in warmer climes of Africa or southern Asia.

Frontal Shields

A striking feature of some coots and gallinules is their frontal shield—a fleshy rearward extension of the upper bill which covers most of the forehead. In the European coot (1) it is a simple white lobe, about the size and texture of the ball of the human thumb, while in the closely related American coot (2) this is overlaid by a smaller, red callus. Easily the most complex such ornament is that possessed by the majestic Horned coot of the high Andes (3). In place of a flat shield this species, the largest of all coots, has a frilled proboscis or horn up to 5cm (2in) long!

Such forehead ornamentation is not peculiar to the family. The plantain-eaters (Musophagidae) and oropendolas (Icteridae) of the tropics have very similar shields to those of coots, while many waterfowl (Anatidae) have knobs or bulbs at the base of the bill. The puzzle is—why did they evolve?

One clue to their function is that the size of the shield in coots (and the knob in swans) is related to sex, the male's generally being larger. However there are enough exceptions to this rule to indicate that shield size is not primarily an indicator of the bird's sex.

Shields do however appear to signal status in winter flocks of coots in which food stealing is common. In food stealing incidents, the victim very rarely retaliates against the thief, but usually retreats and gives away its food as soon as the aggressor approaches. When the thief approaches a feeding individual which is facing away, and whose shield has not yet been seen, the "victim" will on occasion turn on the would-be thief and, with fierce fighting, drive it away. These are the only instances of

attempted food stealing when resistance is observed—presumably because most thieves make sure they have a good view of the victim before they attack. Shield size in winter may therefore signal differences in body size or fighting ability. Shields may signal something similar in the American coot, males of which show a rapid increase in shield size upon taking up a territory in the spring. Perhaps the shield is in effect saying "I now have a breeding territory, I have fought hard to get it, and will fight equally hard to keep it"?

JAH

tails grow faster than most other body parts, hence to become mobile is of the utmost urgency in these chicks. Rail chicks are very unusual among birds in being mobile and leaving the nest soon after hatching, but being fully dependent on parents for feeding for at least the first few days of life. Young coots may obtain at least some of their food from parents for up to 60 days after hatching, although in many rails and crakes this dependency is much briefer. But in all species chicks must accompany the parents around the territory in order to solicit food—thus the importance of early mobility.

In most rails the first laid egg hatches at least one day earlier than the last, a time-lapse that introduces differences between siblings within the brood. The eldest chick may already be sufficiently strong and agile to capture its insect food at a time when the youngest of the brood is still struggling from the egg. These differences persist throughout the dependent period, and the younger chicks often starve in the competition with larger siblings for food from the parents. This feature of breeding biology, which at first sight seems to diminish the reproductive success of the parents, may have evolved as a mechanism to match the size of the brood to an unpredictable and variable food supply. In part the greater success of some chicks in obtaining food is due to the inability of the younger chicks to follow parents as they swim around the territory. But, at least as important, parents tend to have preferences for particular chicks—for most of the time each parent is accompanied only by its "favorite" chick or chicks. The way in which parents maintain this division is astonishing. If a "wrong" chick approaches an adult, it is seized by the head and shaken about before being dropped back into the water. After this treatment the chick usually retreats, indeed the longer it is shaken the longer it stays away from that parent!

The rails interact with man very little indeed. Farmers have sometimes accused certain gallinules, such as the Gray moorhen, of eating spring crops, although the evidence points to these losses being very small. Some species are killed for food, especially the coot in eastern Europe, where each hunter takes an average of three or four per year. Rails pose severe problems for man only in their conservation. They tend to live in habitats which are vulnerable. Indeed, several species have become extinct within living memory and the prospects for a number of others do not look promising.

JAH

a ... to Sea of Japan, Indian subcontinent, Kampuchea, Australia and New Guinea.

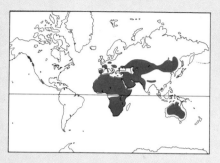

Habitat: grassland, arid plains, semidesert, light savanna.

Size: length 40–120cm (16in–4ft); wingspan 1–2.5m (3–8ft); weight 0.55–18kg (1.2–40lb). In some species males bigger than females. Plumage: mostly camouflage patterning on uppersides; head and neck with distinctive

patterns combining two or more of gray, chestnut, black, white and buff. Males of some species more brightly colored than females.

Voice: larger species generally silent, but smaller ones have distinctive, persistent, usually unmusical calls during breeding season.

Nest: a bare scrape on ground.

Eggs: mostly 1–2, but up to 6 in some small species; olive, olive-brown, reddish; incubation 20–25 days. From 41g in Little to 146g in Great bustard (1.4–5.2oz).

Diet: generally omnivorous—shoots, flowers, seeds, berries etc, and invertebrates (especially beetles, grasshoppers and crickets), but also small reptiles, amphibians, mammals, and eggs and young of ground-nesting birds.

Species include: the **Arabian bustard** (*Ardeotis arabs*); **Australian bustard** (*A. australis*); **Bengal florican** (*Houbaropsis bengalensis*); **Black-bellied bustard** (*Eupodotis melanogaster*); **Blue bustard** (*E. caerulescens*); **Denham's bustard** (*Neotis denhami*); **Great bustard** (*Otis tarda*); **Great Indian bustard** E (*Ardeotis nigriceps*); **houbara** (*Chlamydotis undulata*); **Kori bustard** (*Ardeotis kori*); **Lesser florican** (*Sypheotides indica*); **Little brown bustard** (*Eupodotis humilis*); **Little bustard** (*Tetrax tetrax*); **Nubian bustard** (*Neotis nuba*); **Red-crested bustard** (*Eupodotis ruficrista*); **White-bellied bustard** (*E. senegalensis*).

E Endangered.

... ...most typical member of the family, the Great bustard. The term is however appropriate for the whole family, for all bustards are strictly ground dwellers. The largest members are to the great open plains of Africa and Eurasia what cranes are to the world's big marshes: slow-breeding, long-lived birds of ancient lineage, reaching considerable size and weight whilst retaining the capacity to fly—among birds, the ultimate expression of adaptation to their stable habitats. Sadly, like cranes, they are among the first to suffer once those habitats start being exploited and disrupted by modern man.

Africa is the major home of the bustards and only four species do not breed there— the Australian bustard, Great Indian bustard, Lesser florican and Bengal florican. Great and Little bustards have only relict populations in North Africa; their patchy distribution extends across the plains of southern Europe into Russia, the Little bustard reaching as far as the northern Kazakh steppes, and the Great bustard ranging right through level uplands of northern China, Mongolia and the USSR, almost to the Sea of Japan. The houbara ranges through semideserts of North Africa, the Middle East, central Russia and Mongolia. These three northern species undertake migrations in the colder parts of their ranges. The Arabian bustard still occurs in the southern Arabian peninsula and in northwest Africa, but otherwise this and the remaining bustard species are found only in Africa, mostly in the tropics.

Within Africa there are two clear areas where different species have evolved: from the Zambezi southwest to the Cape and from the Nile to the Horn, with four species in the former and three in the latter. The kori occurs in both, as do the Red-crested and White-bellied bustards, although the latter two also have populations across the Saharo-Sahelian savanna belt in West Africa, and the White-bellied bustard has another scattered population in Central Africa. The Arabian and Nubian bustards occur in the Saharo-Sahelian zone, extending across to the Red Sea coast. Only two species, Denham's and the Black-bellied bustards, are widespread in Africa; the former has become very localized in many areas as a result of man's activities.

The bustards are a homogeneous family, although there are differences in structure, color, size and behavior which cloud the

relationships between species. All are rather long-necked and long-legged, with robust bodies and short bills, and have lost both the hind toe and the preen gland that most birds possess. These losses, together with the camouflage patterning (often exquisitely delicate) of black on buff, rufous or brown on the upperparts, are presumably adaptations to the dry, open landscapes they inhabit—hind claws are associated with birds that perch on trees or bushes and oil from preen (uropygial) glands is used by most birds for waterproofing. Two small species, Little and Red-crested bustards, have relatively short legs and necks. These and most other *Eupodotis* bustards fly with rapid wingbeats; the larger species use slow, deep, powerful wingbeats, but fly deceptively fast. On the ground bustards are strong but usually slow walkers, characteristically nervous and alert: they move into cover at the first sign of danger.

Bustards take their food in a slow, meandering walk through an area of grassland or scrub. Their diet is chiefly invertebrates, usually snapped up from the ground or off plants, but also sometimes dug up with the powerful bill. Small vertebrates may also be taken, often after a short pursuit and pounce. All species readily eat vegetable matter, especially plant shoots, certain flowers and fruit. Some larger species, notably *Ardeotis*, feed on gum that oozes from acacia trees. Concentrations of food may cause a bird to remain in one spot for some time. In Somalia birds have been observed leaping to snatch berries off the higher parts of a bush, and in Zimbabwe Denham's bustard has been seen to walk into water, apparently in quest of young frogs, and to defend a termites' nest, at which it was feeding, against other birds. Several species gather at bush fires to take fleeing and crippled insects. Bustards have no crop, but their powerful gizzard, long "blind gut" (cecum) and their habit of taking up quantities of grit assist the digestion of food.

No male bustard has been observed to incubate the eggs, an emancipation from parental duties that appears to have led to a variety of mating systems within the family, perhaps even within the same species. For example, it seems that Denham's bustard is monogamous in upland Malawi, whereas in South Africa males seem to mate with several females, the males keeping at least 700m (2,300ft) apart and displaying in response to each other and any passing female. Male Great bustards also operate such a dispersed lek system, but in this species many males appear not to be territorial, moving about instead, keeping their distance from each other, and displaying in various sites (see overleaf). In this and two other species which do not appear to form pair bonds, the houbara and Australian bustard, the display before copulation is very long and must often be impeded by rivals; territoriality is replaced by simple opportunism and/or a ranking system.

In southern Africa, birds in the genus *Eupodotis* with black underparts occur in quite dense grassland and savanna, give striking aerial displays, and apparently hold group territories within which one pair breeds. The newly hatched young of all species are well developed (precocial) and very soon leave the nest, but they are fed bill-to-bill by the mother initially and remain in her company for some months after hatching. Palaearctic species are notably sociable and sometimes occur in flocks; the remainder are more solitary, although some are commonly found in small groups.

◄ **Over two-thirds of bustards are African,** like this Black korhaan male in Namibia. The Black korhaan (*Eupodotis afra*) and other smaller bustards can fly strongly, but they depend more upon their strong legs and camouflage coloration to escape predators.

▼ **The Kori bustard is widespread in Africa** and is, together with the Great bustard of Eurasia, one of the largest of all flying birds.

This susceptibility to disturbance is a major cause of their decline, especially in northern parts of the family's distribution where grasslands are coming under ever more pressure from agriculture. Great bustards can tolerate a degree of disturbance—indeed they can only have colonized Europe thanks to man's felling of the forests—but the mechanization of agriculture and the reduction of croplands to monocultures by the use of herbicides and fertilizers have been disastrous for them. Farming of the steppes reduced the Russian population from 8,650 birds at the start of the 1970s to an estimated 2,980 by the end of the decade. Similarly, the Little bustard is now nearly extinct almost everywhere except the Iberian Peninsula, as a result of the disappearance of herb-rich grasslands.

endangered. The Bengal species survives only in a handful of protected areas in a widely fragmented chain along the foothills of the Himalayas (the Kampuchean population has not been seen since its discovery in 1928), while the Lesser florican appears to be restricted to tiny scattered patches of grassland ("vidis") in the far west of India, maintained as reserve grazing but in no other way protected. In the Himalayan foothills the grasslands have gone to tea estates, while in western India they are being converted to pasture; in neither case can the florican concerned survive the change.

Populations of the Great Indian bustard, though perhaps more tolerant of agriculture, have been steadily declining for decades. It now numbers less than 1,000 but, having recently been the subject of a

Courtship Displays of the Bustards

Male bustards are remarkable for their spectacular courtship displays. The Great bustard (1) inflates its neck like a balloon, cocks its tail forward onto its back, and stretches its wings back and down from shoulder to carpal. The primary feathers are kept folded so that their tips are held behind the bird's head, while the secondary feathers are lifted outwards to form huge white rosettes on either side of the body. Together with the billowing undertail coverts, this transforms a richly colored (if partly camouflaged) animal into a nearly all-white one. The posture may be held for minutes on end, and the bird is visible over great distances on spring mornings and evenings.

Male Australian (2) and Great Indian bustards cock the tail right forward and inflate the neck downwards so that it becomes a broad sack that swings around like a

punchbag, scraping the ground. The kori simply inflates its neck into a puffy white ball and trails its wings. The oddest of the ground displays is that of the houbara (3), which raises its white neck-ruff right over its head, and trots around in an irregular path with very little indication that it can see where it is going.

The small black-bellied species of Africa and India give impressive display-flights or display-leaps above the grass that otherwise conceals them. The most exciting aerial display is that of the Red-crested bustard, which flies vertically up to as much as 30m (100ft) above the ground, somersaults backwards, then drops like a stone, pulling out at the last moment and gliding nonchalantly away to land. On the ground, too, this bird has a beautiful display, fully erecting its crest and using stiff, clockwork-like movements as it approaches a female.

▲ **Female Little bustard** (male has black-and-white collar). Loss of grasslands has reduced the species' range in Europe to the Iberian Peninsula and part of southern France.

hunting controversy, commands a new popular interest in its survival and is currently showing signs of recovery in Rajasthan. The decline of its closest relative, the Australian bustard, is commonly attributed to continued remorseless, indiscriminate shooting from the earliest days of European settlement, but it seems certain that conversion of its habitat to farmland is the major factor in its disappearance.

The decline of the houbara is plainly the direct result of hunting. This is the one species of bustard that figures strongly in human culture, as the most prized quarry in the Arab tradition of falconry. In recent years, oil wealth and technology have vastly increased the scale and efficiency of such hunting, so it is feared that in many parts of its range the houbara is almost completely wiped out. Unfortunately, bustard hunting by Arabs appears to be growing in other parts of Africa, notably the Saharo-Sahelian zone, and certain other species—particularly the Nubian bustard—have suffered alarming declines as a result. No other purely African bustard is known to be seriously at risk, although the restricted ranges of the Blue and Little brown bustards must be cause for sustained vigilance. Moreover, throughout Africa the pressure to grow more food is unrelenting and it cannot be long before some of these peace-loving ground dwellers emerge as new candidates for extinction. NJC

Order: Gruiformes (part).
Twenty-seven species in 11 genera.
Distribution: see maps and table.

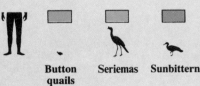

Button quails   **Seriemas**   **Sunbittern**

Plains wanderer   **Kagu**   **Finfoots**   **Mesites**

▶ **Belying its name,** the Sun bittern lives by shady riversides from Mexico to southeast Brazil. The "sun" refers to the markings displayed on the broad wings that are extended in a threat-defense posture.

sexual roles known in birds. Females are the more brightly colored sex, and are larger where the sexes differ in size; they defend territory, pugnaciously driving off other females, and initiate courtship of the males. Then, after the eggs have been laid, it is left to the male to incubate the clutch and tend the chicks. In some species, one female will mate with several males during a season.

Button quails inhabit warm, semi-arid regions of the Old World. They owe their alternative name, hemipode (half-foot), to the fact that the rear toe is missing. They are small, quail-like, essentially ground-dwelling birds, with a "crouching" posture. They are secretive and difficult to flush, even then flying only short distances. The one exception is the Lark quail of Africa, which has a strong lark-like flight, and flies some distance before alighting. Despite this general reluctance to fly in the face of disturbance, a few species are partially migratory, including the Yellow-legged button quail and the Little button quail. In regions lacking any marked seasonal variation in climate, button quails will breed opportunistically all year round and, as in the Old World quails, young can attain sexual maturity at 4–6 months old.

On the Melanesian island New Caledonia the now endangered **kagu** has become restricted, through persecution and habitat loss, to probably under 130sq km (60sq mi) in the valleys of the central mountain range. Formerly many kagu were trapped for keeping in aviaries and for decorative plumes for the millinery trade. This direct persecution has lessened (though some local people still

planted or nickel mining (the main island industry); wild populations of introduced mammals (pigs, cats and dogs) have spread to the remotest areas and constitute a threat to ground-nesting birds as well as being (in the case of pigs) possible competitors for food.

The kagu is a superficially heron-like bird of the forest floor, whose nearest (but not close) relative is probably the Sun bittern (see below). Both are plain-colored birds when seen at rest, but their broad wings, when opened in display, reveal striking patterns. The kagu is stocky but long-legged and stands relatively upright. It is almost flightless. The little we know of the kagu has been derived from observations of captive birds. The New Caledonian breeding season in the wild is believed to be August–January but it is April–November in captivity in, for example, Australia; the day-time activity of captive birds is at variance with suggestions from visitors to New Caledonia that the species is most active in the evening and at night—certainly the birds call a great deal at night. Most birds which lay single-egg clutches (as does the kagu) are long-lived, and captive kagus have lived for 20–30 years in warm climates.

The **Sun bittern**, like the finfoots, inhabits riversides in tropical and subtropical forests. It is not easy to locate or watch, and not particularly sociable, normally being encountered singly or in pairs along streams where the trees provide shade from the full heat of the sun. Sun bitterns seek cover within vegetation when disturbed and are easily overlooked by the would-be observer.

The Sun bittern is stout-bodied, with a

▲ **Cockatoo-like crest** of the kagu is made of feathers once prized in the milliner's trade. Today the kagu is restricted to the central forests of New Caledonia and is listed as endangered.

heron-like long neck and long legs. The impression of sombre, camouflage coloration in the feeding or skulking bird is belied in flight or display, when the spread wings reveal conspicuous patches of chestnut on the primary wing feathers, and bands of the same color across the tail. Adult males are no more brightly colored than females or even juveniles, and it now seems clear that the spectacular frontal display of the Sun bittern is for threat or defense rather than courtship. In this startling transformation from a skulking to a large and threatening

bird, the patches on the broad wings stand out as big, intimidating "eyes" (supposed also to look like a rising sun). In captivity, both parents share the tasks of incubation and chick care, and the chicks stay in the nest for 3–4 weeks.

The two **seriemas** are placed, on the basis of similarities in musculature and the skull, in the same order (Gruiformes) as the cranes and rails. However, they bear a superficial resemblance to the Secretary bird (order Falconiformes) of Africa, and are its ecological counterpart on the dry pampas and scrub-savanna of South America. They are ground dwellers, with a typically upright posture. Although their wings are developed, they seldom fly, preferring to run (with head lowered) when disturbed: their long neck and legs are well adapted for living in long grass, in much the same way as in the Secretary bird and, among much closer relatives, the Old World bustards (p152). Also like bustards, seriemas live in small groups, and their displays are said to be somewhat similar. One notable feature shared by the Secretary bird and the seriemas is that their diets include small snakes (seriemas are not, however, immune to snake poison). Often seriemas feed close to cattle and horses, presumably taking invertebrates disturbed by the grazing stock.

The Black-legged seriema has a more restricted range, prefers open woodland and scrub areas and is more arboreal (nesting above ground and roosting higher up) than the better-known Red-legged (or Crested) seriema of the grasslands. The young of both are often taken alive for taming, since they make efficient "watchdogs" against approaching predators when kept with domestic fowls. Though the newly hatched young are already well covered with down, they remain in the nest (under parental care) until well grown.

The **Plains wanderer** appears in the field to be a fairly typical button quail, with its broadly similar camouflage color patterning and habits. But, unlike button quails, it retains the hind toe, it lays pear-shaped (not oval) eggs, it tends to adopt a more upright (not crouching) posture, and the carotid arteries in the neck are paired.

The Plains wanderer was formerly widespread in eastern and southeastern Australia, but declined as agriculture became more intensive. It is now scarce or rare, its range is fragmented, and it is found chiefly on unimproved grasslands and on fields left fallow in alternate years; such conditions provide the mix of grass and weed seeds needed by the birds for food. There is no evidence except March and April; probably there is breeding year-round as the opportunity arises. As in the button quails, the more brightly colored female initiates courtship, then leaves the male to incubate the clutch and raise the young. In captivity, however, females sometimes help with incubation. Once the parent-young bond has broken, the birds become well separated in ones and twos. They seldom fly, instead running off or crouching for concealment when alarmed: and they have the habit of standing on tiptoe, neck outstretched, to gain a better view through or over the vegetation.

With the progressive destruction of the Madagascan forests (only 10 percent of the island remains forested) a disproportionate number of the island's species are now endangered, including all three **mesites**. The White-breasted mesite inhabits dry forest in western Madagascar; it is now extremely rare and localized, the last reported sighting being from Ankarafantsika (fortunately now a protected area) in 1971. The Brown mesite occurs in moist evergreen forest in the east, and has always been considered

Button Quails and Related Families

Button quails
Family: Turnicidae
Sixteen species in 2 genera.
Africa, S Spain, S Iran to E China and Australia. Open grassland, thin scrub, crop fields. Size: 11–20cm (4.5–8in) long. Plumage: buffy-brown with camouflage markings in browns, grays and cream; tail and wings short; females brighter and sometimes larger. Nests: in ground hollows lined with grass. Eggs: 3–7, oval, glossy, richly marked on pale background; incubation 12–14 days; chicks leave nest almost at once. Diet: small seeds and insects. Species include the **Lark quail** or **Quail plover** (*Ortyxelos meiffrenii*); **Little button quail** (*Turnix sylvatica*); **Yellow-legged button quail** (*T. tanki*).

Kagu E
Family: Rhynochetidae
Sole species *Rhynochetos jubatus*.
New Caledonia. Upland forest. Length: 60cm (24in). Plumage: drab gray, but spread wings show striking pattern of black, white and reddish; long, erectile crest. Bare parts red, bill downcurved. Nest: of sticks and leaves on ground (in captivity). Eggs:

1, light brown with dark brown blotches; incubation (probably by both parents) 35–40 days; young well developed, leave nest on hatching. Diet: snails, worms and insects from forest floor.

Sun bittern
Family: Eurypygidae
Sole species *Eurypyga helias*.
S Mexico to Bolivia and Brazil. Edges of streams and swamps in forests. Length: 46cm (18in). Plumage: camouflage patterns shown at rest, but chestnut marks on wings and tail conspicuous in display. Nest: of stems and leaves up to 6m (20ft) up in bush or tree. Eggs: 2, buff to off-white, with darker blotches; both parents incubate (27 days) and care for hatchlings. Diet: mollusks, crustaceans, aquatic insects.

Seriemas
Family: Cariamidae
Two species in 2 genera.
S America. Eggs: 2, off-white to buff with brown markings; both parents incubate (25–26 days) and tend young. Diet: omnivorous. Species: **Black-legged** or **Burmeister's seriema** (*Chunga burmeisteri*), dry open

woodland and scrub in W Paraguay, N Argentina; length 70cm (28in); black-tipped tail, negligible crest; black bill and legs; nest in bush or tree. **Red-legged** or **Crested seriema** (*Cariama cristata*), grasslands in Brazil to Uruguay and N Argentina; length 82cm (32in); white-tipped tail, large frontal crest; red bill and legs; nest of sticks on ground.

Plains wanderer
Family: Pedionomidae
Sole species *Pedionomus torquatus*.
SE and C Australia. Open grassland and stubble fields; avoids scrub areas. Length: 15–17cm (6–7in). Plumage: cryptic coloration of buff, brown and black, with collar of black spots on white; females larger and more brightly colored. Nest: a grass-lined ground hollow. Eggs: 2–5 (usually 4), gray and olive markings on yellowish; incubation 23 days; well-developed hatchlings leave nest at once. Diet: small seeds and insects.

Mesites
Family: Mesitornithidae
Three species in 2 genera.
Madagascar. Forest, marginal scrub (*Monias*). Length: 25–30cm (10–

12in). Plumage: brown to grayish above, paler below and (not Brown mesite) spotted. Bill straight or (monia) downcurved. Nests: a twig platform 1–2m (3–6ft) up in bush. Eggs: 1–3, off-white with brown spots; hatchlings leave nest at once. Diet: seeds and insects. Species: **Bensch's monia** R (*Monias benschi*); **Brown mesite** R (*Mesitornis unicolor*); **White-breasted mesite** R (*M. variegata*).

Finfoots
Family: Heliornithidae
Three species in 2 genera.
C and S America, Africa, SE Asia. Rivers and lakes in forest. Nests: on low branch or flood debris. Eggs: 2–4 (Masked finfoot 5–6?), reddish-brown or cream; incubation 11 days (Sun grebe). Diet: frogs, crustaceans, mollusks, aquatic insects. Species: **African finfoot** (*Podica senegalensis*), length 60cm (23in), white-spotted back, bill and legs orange-red; **Masked finfoot** (*Heliornis personata*), length 56cm (22in), back plain, face and throat black, yellow bill, green legs; **Sun grebe** (*Heliornis fulica*), length 30cm (12in), olive-brown, scarlet bill, black and yellow feet.

rare. Bensch's monia inhabit dry brush woodland in southwestern Madagascar; it may be less rare than the others, but is nevertheless probably declining and is designated rare by the ICBP.

Mesites are thrush-sized running birds of the forest floor. They have functional wings but rudimentary collar bones, and can probably fly weakly for short distances, despite seldom doing so. While they build nests above ground, these are invariably sited so that the birds can climb or scramble up to them. Breeding occurs in October–December. The mating system of the White-breasted and Brown mesites seems to be "normal," but it may be otherwise in Bensch's monia, in which the adult female is the more brightly colored. Some parties of Bensch's monia comprising males and one dominant female have been reported, but in a more recent study females have been observed sharing parental duties, with two of them (paired to one male) laying in one nest.

All three species of **finfoots** are shy and retiring, not easily observed in their tropical riverside settings. It is thought that the rails are their nearest relatives, though, seen on the water, finfoots look more like grebes. Finfoots combine characters of grebes and coots (lobed feet) and cormorants (long neck, stiffened tail). When taking flight they patter across the water before becoming air-borne, but their normal reaction to disturbance is to run ashore into dense undergrowth, or to swim away with body submerged and only head and neck visible. At least one species, the Masked finfoot, is partially migratory, reaching Malaya (probably from Thailand) in winter.

Sun grebe parents carry their young in flight as well as on the water. The adult has special folds of skin beneath each wing, forming cavities into which the chicks fit, muscular control probably helping to hold the chicks firmly against the parent's body. The naked, helpless hatchling chicks are carried from the nest before even their eyes have opened. It is not yet known whether this remarkable feature applies also to the two Old World finfoots. The African finfoot is known also to lay a clutch of two eggs, and so may have adopted such a strategy, but the Masked finfoot is said to lay a clutch of 5–6 eggs, though this is based on old information. In the American Sun grebe, both parents share the incubation, though as yet only the male is confirmed as carrying young; in the African finfoot, females have been seen accompanying well-feathered juveniles. **RH**

◄▲ **Button quails and related families.** (1) Brown mesite (*Mesitornis unicolor*). (2) Masked finfoot (*Heliornis personata*). (3) Crested seriema (*Cariama cristata*). (4) Plains wanderer (*Pedionomus torquatus*). (5) Little button quail (*Turnix sylvatica*).

ECKERS

One hundred and fifty-three species in 33 genera.
Distribution: see maps and table.

Plovers **Phalaropes**

Avocets **Sandpipers**

▶ **Defending its nest,** a south Australian Banded plover (*Vanellus tricolor*) challenges an intruder. Within the egg, the unhatched but noisy chicks fall silent when they hear their parents' alarm call.

America, to the sad "peewit" of its Eurasian counterpart, the lapwing. In southern Africa the Blacksmith plover breaks its silence with a loud, metallic "klink, klink" when disturbed.

The plovers are a large family of small to medium-sized plumpish shorebirds with rounded heads and large eyes. The "true plovers" (*Charadrius*) are at the lower end of the size range, the "lapwings" (*Vanellus*) in the middle and the *Pluvialis* species at the

to long legs and all are quick runners and strong fliers. The hind toe is small or absent, and most have three relatively short, unwebbed front toes. Leg colors may be black, flesh-colored, or striking reds and yellows.

Despite the bold color patterns of most species, the plumage is disruptive, and individuals blend easily into the background as soon as they stand still. The body feathers are molted twice, and the flight feathers at

▶ **Common on farm and marsh,** the Eurasian lapwing is immediately known by its tumbling flight, mournful call and, close up, its long wispy crest.

least once, a year during molts—the timings of which can be complex. There is usually a complete post-breeding molt. Juvenile plovers molt a few weeks after fledging.

The 22 species of *Vanellus* are mostly found inland. They are widespread in all tropical and temperate areas except North America, and are well represented in Africa. The breeding distribution ranges from the tideline to above the treeline—the Puna plover is found up to 4,500m (14,750ft) in the high Andes. The habitats include marshlands, lake edges, grasslands, steppes and sometimes arid areas well away from water. Among lapwing species, but not other members of the family, a crest, wattles and wing spurs are common.

The 30 species of true plovers or sand plovers (*Charadrius*) are found along sandy or muddy shores and along rivers and inland on fields. The Ringed plover is widespread along the coasts of the Old World and breeds up to the arctic tundra; the main wintering grounds are along the eastern Mediterranean and African coasts. Most true plovers show a black chest band, black forehead, and black line from eye to bill.

The largest plovers are the three species of *Pluvialis*, which breed at freshwater marshes and grasslands in the upland and tundra regions of the Northern Hemisphere. The Eurasian golden plover acquires a beautiful nuptial plumage in the spring which includes a coal black "face," breast and belly to accompany the golden spots on the upperparts. It breeds in northern Europe and is replaced in Siberia and North America by the American golden plover, which is a true long-distance migrant, journeying from the arctic tundra across the

Atlantic to Argentina and across the Pacific to Australia. One population flies directly from Alaska to Hawaii, a flight of some 4,500km (2,800mi). The Black-bellied plover (or Gray plover) breeds in the high Arctic of North America and Siberia, and although many individuals winter in temperate latitudes, some fly as far as Chile and Australia.

The wrybill from New Zealand has a bill that is bent laterally to the right at an angle of about 12°. This lateral asymmetry is unique among birds. So far there is no satisfactory explanation for this: there does not seem to be any benefit gained while feeding.

Most plovers do not wade in water in the same ways or to the same extent as other shorebirds. Typically they forage by walking in damp areas or at the water's edge and some species are adapted to feeding in arid zones well away from water. An exception is the White-tailed lapwing which, as well as feeding on land, wades in flooded areas taking prey from the surface or sometimes by submerging its head. Plovers have relatively large eyes which testify to the importance of sight during feeding. The range of food taken is broad, and includes adult and larval insects, beetles, crustaceans, mollusks, worms and sometimes berries. Typically they locate their prey by sight on the surface and quickly run forward a short distance to catch it. The Ringed plover, for example, largely feeds on crustaceans picked off mud or sand especially at the edge of the tide. It quickly runs in and out of the areas vacated by receding waves.

The diets of migratory species at their wintering grounds probably differ widely breeding grounds. On the lowland grasslands during the winter it feeds largely on earthworms and insect larvae. At this time the golden plovers are frequently found in fairly large flocks often mixed with lapwings. Black-headed gulls (see p30) may also station themselves among these flocks, and as soon as they see a bird capture an earthworm they fly over and try to steal it. This feeding off others by theft, or kleptoparasitism, seems to be more successful against lapwings because they are slower at taking and ingesting worms than are the golden plovers. The Eurasian lapwing is noted for its cold weather movements. Large flocks fly south and west ahead of cold weather fronts and quickly return to areas after a thaw.

Plovers may be paired on arrival at the breeding grounds or form pairs very shortly

The 4 Families of Plovers and Sandpipers ⬚ Endangered. ⬚ Rare.

Plovers
Family: Charadriidae
Sixty-two species in 10 genera.
Worldwide except for permanently frozen areas. Most species migratory. Coastal, marshland, inland water, rivers, grassland to mountains and tundra regions. Size: length 14–41cm (5.5–16in); weight 34–296g (1.2–10.5oz). Males usually slightly larger than females. Plumage: usually light-colored below, often marked features on head and neck. Voice: a variety of mono- to tri-syllabic calls often repeated. Nests: simple scrape on bare or open ground. Eggs: typically 4 (range 2–6); variable backgrounds, small flecks to large dark blotches; 5.3–33g (0.2–1.2oz); incubation 18–38 days; young precocial, fledging at 21–42 days. Diet: wide range of terrestrial and aquatic invertebrates, sometimes berries.

Species include: the **American golden plover** (*Pluvialis dominica*), **Black-bellied** or **Gray plover** (*P. squatarola*), **Blacksmith plover** (*Vanellus armatus*), **Eurasian golden plover** (*Pluvialis apricaria*), **Greater sand plover** (*Charadrius leschenaultii*), **killdeer** (*C. vociferus*), **Kittlitz's plover** (*C. pecuarius*), **lapwing** or **peewit** (*Vanellus vanellus*), **Masked plover** (*V. miles*), **New Zealand shore plover** ⬚ (*Charadrius novaeseelandiae*), **Puna plover** (*C. alticola*), **Red-wattled lapwing** (*Vanellus indicus*), **Ringed plover** (*Charadrius hiaticula*), **Wattled plover** (*Vanellus senegallus*), **White-tailed lapwing** (*V. leucurus*), **wrybill**

(*Anarhynchus frontalis*). Total threatened species: 2.

Sandpipers
Family: Scolopacidae
Eighty-one species in 18 genera.
Most species breed in N Hemisphere, a few in tropics, Africa and S America. Most species migratory. Breed in wetlands and grasslands, mainly in tundra, boreal and temperate zones. Winter along coasts, estuaries and other wetlands. Size: length 13–66cm (5–26in); weight 18–1,040g (0.6–37oz). Plumage: upperparts mottled browns and grays; underparts light; markings cryptic. Voice: variety of twitterings, rattles, shrill calls and whistles. Nests: made in tussocks or on dry ground, exceptionally in trees or holes. Eggs: typically 4 (range 2–4, rarely more), buff or greenish backgrounds with variable markings, pear-shaped, 5.8–80g (0.2–2.8oz); incubation 18–30 days; young precocial, fledging at 16–50 days. Diet: mollusks, crustaceans, aquatic worms and flies, some plant material at times.

Species include: **Black-tailed godwit** (*Limosa limosa*), **Bristle-thighed curlew** (*Numenius tahitiensis*), **Broad-billed sandpiper** (*Limicola falcinellus*), **Common sandpiper** (*Tringa hypoleucos*), **Common snipe** (*Gallinago gallinago*), **Curlew sandpiper** (*Calidris ferruginea*), **dunlin** (*C. alpina*), **Eskimo curlew** ⬚ (*Numenius borealis*), **Eurasian curlew** (*N. arquata*), **Eurasian woodcock** (*Scolopax*

rusticola), **Green sandpiper** (*Tringa ochropus*), **Little stint** (*Calidris minuta*), **Long-billed curlew** (*Numenius americanus*), **Long-billed dowitcher** (*Limnodromus scolopaceus*), **Pectoral sandpiper** (*Calidris melanotos*), **Red knot** or **knot** (*C. canutus*), **redshank** (*Tringa totanus*), **Ruddy turnstone** (*Arenaria interpres*), **ruff** (*Philomachus pugnax*), **sanderling** (*Calidris alba*), **Sharp-tailed sandpiper** (*C. acuminata*), **Solitary sandpiper** (*Tringa solitaria*), **Spoon-billed sandpiper** (*Eurynorhynchus pygmeus*), **Sub-antarctic snipe** ⬚ (*Coenocorypha aucklandica*), **Upland sandpiper** (*Bartramia longicauda*), **Western sandpiper** (*Calidris mauri*), **Wood sandpiper** (*Tringa glareola*). Total threatened species: 5.

Avocets and stilts
Family: Recurvirostridae
Seven species in 4 genera.
Europe, Asia, Australasia, Africa, N and S America. Fresh, brackish and saline waters. Size: 30–46cm (12–18in) long and 140–435g (4.9–15.3oz). Females usually slightly smaller. Plumage: basically brown or black and white on body and wings. Sexes similar. Voice: mostly mono- or di-syllabic yelping calls. Nests: scrapes, sometimes lined, on bare ground or short vegetation near water. Eggs: usually 4 (range 2–5), light background with dark markings: 22–44g (0.8–1.6oz); incubation 22–28 days; young precocial, fledging at 28–35 days.

Diet: wide range of aquatic invertebrates or small vertebrates.

Species: the **American avocet** (*Recurvirostra americana*), **Andean avocet** (*R. andina*), **Banded stilt** (*Cladorhynchus leucocephalus*), **Eurasian avocet** (*Recurvirostra avosetta*), **Ibisbill** (*Ibidorhyncha struthersii*), **Red-necked avocet** (*Recurvirostra novaehollandiae*), **stilt** or **Black-winged** or **Black-necked stilt** (*Himantopus himantopus*). Total threatened species: 1.

Phalaropes
Family: Phalaropodidae
Three species of the genus *Phalaropus*.
Breed in N Hemisphere, winter in tropics or S Hemisphere. Breed beside shallow water bodies; in winter 2 species oceanic, 1 in inland waters. Size: 16.5–19cm (6.5–7.5in) long and 29–85g (1–3oz) weight. Females larger than males. Plumage: breeding—reds, white, buff, gray and black, males considerably duller; non-breeding—dark above and light underparts. Voice: some short calls, noisy at times. Nests: in tussocks near water. Eggs: usually 4, oval to pear-shaped, olive-buff with irregular black or brown spots and blotches; 6–9.4g (0.2–0.3oz); incubation 16–24 days; young precocial, fledging at 18–21 days. Diet: chiefly insects and plankton in oceans.

Species: **Gray** or **Red phalarope** (*Phalaropus fulicarius*), **Red-necked** or **Northern phalarope** (*P. lobatus*), **Wilson's phalarope** (*P. tricolor*).

◄ **A simple scrape on bare ground** is the nest of the Black-fronted plover (*Charadrius melanops*) of Australia. The disruptive plumage of the adult makes an incubating bird hard for a predator to spot. Even harder to detect may be the eggs. Plovers that nest on sand or gravel produce eggs covered with small dark flecks or spots. Other species nesting on bare earth or among sparse vegetation lay eggs that are mottled, while eggs of moorland and tundra species have large spots and blotches. These inherited egg color characters may even vary within a species according to the terrain of different populations.

Faced with danger, the young can run within an hour or so of hatching, or they may crouch close to the ground, their first plumage rendering them practically invisible.

► **Displays of breeding plovers** include sometimes spectacular aerial advertisement of the territory, as (1) in the tumbling flight of the lapwing. On the ground, when warning off rivals from the mate or territory, the effect of the display may be enhanced by vocalizations and the display of plumage, including crests, colored wattles, and wing spurs. (2) "Song duel" between Eurasian golden plovers. (3) Spur-winged plover (*Vanellus spinosus*) in challenge or threat posture, and (4) running at opponent.

after arrival They have some very aggressive and highly vocal displays. Aerial displays often contain spectacular twisting, plunging, diving and hovering movements. On the ground there may be displays involving quick running, wing-dropping, tail-fanning and much bowing and curtseying, especially by the males during scrape making. The importance of displays in this family is emphasized by the presence of a crest in some species, such as the Eurasian lapwing, of prominent red and yellow facial wattles in species such as the Wattled plover of southern Africa and, in several species, well-developed wing spurs growing at the bend of the wing (carpal joint). These are particularly long in the Masked plover of Australia.

The males create many scrapes on open, bare or slightly vegetated ground and the female appears to choose one in which to lay her eggs. The four eggs of the usual-sized clutch are commonly produced at intervals of $1\frac{1}{2}$–4 days. Among the few exceptions, Kittlitz's plover and the wrybill lay only two eggs. The eggs and young are highly camouflaged and are well defended by their parents. Nests may be flooded out if they are made near water and they are often subject to heavy predation. A completed clutch of the large, pear-shaped eggs represents some 50–70 percent of the female's body weight. Incubation, typically by both sexes, begins after the last egg is laid and lasts for some 18–22 days in the smaller species and 28–38 days in the larger species.

Most species are noticeably gregarious. Migrating flocks can number thousands. Within a species some populations, especially northern ones, can be highly migratory while other southern ones can be virtually sedentary, eg redshank and golden plovers. Prior to migration birds put on a lot of subcutaneous body fat. Breeding densities vary between species. Some nest in colonies of several hundred pairs, others nest in small groups and defend fairly large territories.

The family contains one of the rarest members of the order Charadriiformes, and certainly the most restricted wader or shorebird in the world—the New Zealand shore plover. Formerly found along New Zealand's many coasts, it is now an endangered species limited to one small island of 220ha (about 0.9sq mi) in the Chatham Islands some 800km (500mi) to the east. It was probably never very numerous but was seriously affected by commercial collectors at the turn of this century. By 1937 the population was down to about 70 pairs and today there may be slightly fewer than 100 birds. They are sedentary, docile and highly vulnerable to mammalian predators. The removal of sheep from the coastal areas of the island has allowed the vegetation to grow unchecked which has probably reduced the amount of appropriate habitat. In the early 1970s the introduction of adults and juveniles (some partially wing-clipped) onto a nearby predator-free island failed, because of the strong homing abilities of the birds. Further research into its ecological requirements may make it possible to devise a successful management plan for this plover, whose plight is so typical of many other birds found on remote islands.

Plovers' eggs used to be collected in large

extensively trapped after the breeding season and sold at many markets. Areas of grassland would be temporarily flooded to provide food, and the arriving birds, mostly lapwings, then caught in large clap nets. Live decoys were used by the trappers to lure the birds to the precise area as efficiently as possible.

In the northern winter, the estuaries of \tlantic Europe hold over 2 million waders, mostly members of the **sandpiper** family. Nearly half the wintering birds are to be found in Britain, with concentrations of 100,000 in larger estuaries, such as the Wash in the east and Morecambe Bay in the west, which are of immense importance as feeding and roosting sites. Flocks, sometimes of tens of thousands, of dunlin and Red knot, together with smaller numbers of other species, are marveled at by birdwatchers. At low tides all are widely dispersed over the sands and muds and are busy feeding. As the tide comes in and the feeding grounds become covered, the waders are concentrated into tighter and larger groups. They are forced into the high salt marshes or arable farmland to roost or rest during the high tide period. Before settling, the large flocks wheel and turn in the sky like billowing plumes of smoke. The roosting flocks break up when the tide recedes and the birds then stream back to the shore to start another feeding cycle.

The sandpiper family (Scolopacidae) comprises the largest family of shorebirds. Most species breed in the Northern Hemisphere, especially in the arctic and subarctic regions. The breeding range of many species encircles the Pole, and only a few sandpiper

types of wetlands and grasslands, ranging from coastal salt marshes to mountainous moorland. Temporary pools and areas of tundra freed from winter snows are favored by many species. Some nest on prairies and along rivers. Wintering areas are mainly sand and mudflats in estuaries, although some species use inland freshwaters, pastures, or rocky shores.

All sandpipers have relatively long wings and a short tail. Their legs and neck are often long. All have three fairly long front toes and, except for the sanderling, a short hind toe. There is a great variety of bill shapes and sizes (see p169). The bill is at least the length of the head in all species, but is usually much longer. Plumage patterns are generally cryptic—mottled browns

▶▼ **Representative species of plovers, sandpipers and phalaropes.** (1) Golden plover (*Pluvialis apricaria*) on nest. (2) Killdeer (*Charadrius vociferus*) in "broken wing" distraction display. (3) Wattled plover (*Vanellus senegallus*) in alert posture, showing spurs on carpel joint of wing. (4) Common snipe (*Gallinago gallinago*) in "drumming" display flight. (5) Redshank (*Tringa totanus*) in courtship display. (6) Eurasian curlew (*Numenius arquata*) feeding. (7) Sanderling (*Calidris alba*) foraging along waterline. (8) Red-necked or Northern phalarope (*Phalaropus lobatus*) "spinning" on water while feeding.

and grays above, with paler underparts sometimes with streaks and spots. The sexes look alike but in some species there may be some sexual differences in breeding plumage. All are quick runners, can wade in water and swim if necessary.

The main foods of most species during the breeding season are two-winged (dipterous) flies, especially crane flies and midges. Sometimes plant foods are taken before the insects emerge. The main foods of the shore feeders in winter are mollusks such as tellins and spire snails, crustaceans such as *Corophium*, and marine worms such as ragworms and lugworms. Snipes and woodcocks mostly take oligochaete worms from damp soils, the snipes from marshy ground, the woodcocks often in damp woodland. Surface foods may be located by sight and picked up, but those beneath the surface are probed for and located by touch. The Bristle-thighed curlew is, somewhat unusually, fond of eating the eggs of other birds, particularly seabirds. The eyes are so placed in the head to give feeding waders a wide field of view; this adaptation is so complete in the woodcock that it has a 360° field of view.

Temperate-nesting species have a more protracted breeding season and individuals may spend several weeks at the breeding grounds before nesting. All species have elaborate display flights or song flights and there are ground displays involving wing-lifting prior to copulation. Sandpiper calls may be mono- to tri-syllabic and range from the noisy piping calls made by the redshank to twittering calls made by the true sandpipers. Most species nest in tussocks on dry ground or amid ground vegetation, where they are well concealed. The Black-tailed godwit often fashions the vegetation into a cupola over its nest to give increased cover. The Sub-antarctic snipe nests in burrows made by other birds. Green sandpipers, Solitary sandpipers and occasionally Wood sandpipers lay their eggs in abandoned songbird nests in trees and bushes. Green sandpipers seek out well-wooded areas in which to breed. Most species are highly territorial, at least in the early part of the breeding season, and nesting densities range from 1 pair per sq km (2.6/sq mi) in the Long-billed curlew to 5–10 pairs per ha (12–25/acre) in Sharp-toed sandpipers and Western sandpipers.

Eggs are laid at 1–2 day intervals; incubation begins after the last egg is laid, and for most species lasts for 21–24 days. The markedly pear-shaped eggs are relatively large and neatly "fit together" in the nest bowl. The eggs are proportionally very large in the stints and a clutch represents some 90 percent of the female's body weight. Typically, both male and female incubate, but the division of labor varies between species. However, in the ruff and Pectoral sandpiper only the females incubate. The female of the Arctic-nesting sanderling lays two clutches, one of which she incubates herself, the other incubated by her mate.

The chicks hatch out within 24 hours of each other. They are well camouflaged and are able to fend for themselves. Once dry, they are typically tended by both parents and are led to suitable feeding grounds. However, only the female Pectoral and Curlew sandpipers tend their young. The dowitchers are most unusual, if not unique, in that only the females incubate the eggs and only the males tend to the young. Female dunlins may leave the males to tend the chicks with the assistance of non- or failed breeding birds. Male and female Common snipes may split up the newly hatched

brood between them. Woodcocks and red shanks are known to transport their young, in flight, holding the chicks between their thighs. The fledging period varies from about 16 days in the smaller species to some 35–50 days in the curlews.

Male ruffs take part in complex communal displays or "tournaments" prior to mating. At this time they acquire elaborately colored "collar" feathers and also long ear-tufts of various colors. This color range between individual males is perhaps the most extreme case of sexual polymorphism in plumage. The males gather at a display ground, or lek, which is usually an open, slightly raised spot. Some of the dark-colored ruffs are known as independent males and defend small patches of ground at the lek. Other dark-colored males are kept at the edge of the lek and do not defend any ground. White-collared males do not defend any ground but, unlike marginal dark birds, are allowed to wander among the territories of the independent males. These "satellite" white males may serve to attract females for the independent males. There are short periods of frenzied activity at the lek, as the males spar, posture, leap and flap, followed by periods of calm. Females ("reeves") are allowed to walk through the lek. The successful males copulate with several females

in a short space of time. No true pairs are formed and subsequently the females undertake all the incubation of the eggs and tending the chicks.

Displaying Common snipes are vociferous (notably, "chipping" noises) but are best known for their aerial "drumming" display. They dive at an angle of about 45° with the tail fanned out. The two outer tail feathers have highly asymmetrical vanes, the leading edges comprising very narrow strips. When the diving speed reaches about 65km/h (40mph) the air passing over these feathers causes them to vibrate and give off the resonating bleat or drumming sound which can be heard some distance away. Most drumming is done by the males, although the females may drum early in the

▶ **Skulking through damp undergrowth** OVERLEAF in search of worms, its main food, the Jack snipe (*Lymnocryptes minimus*) is distinguished from other snipes by its small size (length 19cm/7.5in), shorter bill, and more pointed tail lacking white feathers.

◄ **Marbled godwit** (*Limosa fedoa*) ABOVE of North America probing for marine worms along the tide edge.

◄ **The Sharp-tailed sandpiper** BELOW breeds in Siberia. Among sandpipers the longest migrations are often undertaken by the most northerly breeding species. Thus, Sharp-tailed sandpipers winter in tidal estuaries and natural harbors in Australasia.

Fitting the Bill

Sandpipers' bills show a great variety of forms, which is related to variation in feeding behavior between species. They range from the short, straight bill (1.7cm/0.7in) of the Little stint (1) to the outsized down-curved bill of the Long-billed curlew (2) (20cm/8in in females). The short, thin bills of the stints allow them to pick at surface prey, such as crustaceans, which they detect by sight. The Curlew sandpiper's (3) is the largest and most decurved bill of the small true sandpipers and is used to probe for a variety of marine animals including small mollusks.

The Broad-billed sandpiper has a heavy bill (4) which allows it to feed on relatively large prey which includes mollusks. The Spoon-billed sandpiper has a broad and flattened tip to both mandibles (5) but the function of this design is not properly understood. The head and bill are sometimes moved from side to side when the bird feeds (eg on insects and other larvae)—sometimes in quite deep water. The two turnstones have short, thickset bills (6)

which they use adeptly to turn over stones and seaweed to expose such foods as sandhoppers and crabs.

The curlews probe with their long, decurved bills for such animals as the deeper-burrowing shellfish and marine worms which are out of reach of most other shore feeders. Godwits, with their long straight bills (7), also probe, often rapidly, deep into wet substrates for prey such as aquatic worms. The dowitches (8), woodcocks (9) and snipes (10) have long, straight bills which are proportionately longer than in all other waders. In these, and other deep-probing species, the parts of the bill towards the tip are well endowed with Herbst's corpuscles. These touch-sensitive organs are essential in helping to locate the buried prey. Another adaptation in some of the long-billed waders is the ability to move the portion of the bill near the tip independently of the rest. This is very useful when manipulating prey, either on the surface or while probing underground.

small groups (eg Common sandpipers), but most species are gregarious and travel in flocks of several hundred. On the wintering grounds some species, eg Red knot and dunlin, are highly gregarious and are found in mixed-species flocks numbering tens of thousands. Species which nest in the high Arctic, such as the Ruddy turnstone and sanderling, migrate south over most of the coasts of the world as far south as Australia, Chile and southern Africa. Ruffs breeding in Siberia fly westward to northwest Europe and then continue on a remarkable journey over the Mediterranean and Sahara deserts. Up to one million have been recorded in the Senegal delta in West Africa.

Several species have been extensively taken by hunters in both the Old and New worlds and some have never recovered their former numbers. Upland sandpipers, now scarce in their prairie breeding grounds, were extensively shot in North America in the 1880s–90s and large numbers used to be packed in barrels and shipped to the cities for sale as food. (In part, this hunting pressure was brought about by the failing supply of Passenger pigeons, which were being hunted to extinction.) Vast numbers of Eskimo curlews were shot in the 1870s–80s, particularly when they made their northward journey from the Argentine pampas to the tundra breeding grounds. Today no wintering or breeding sites are known for this near-extinct species, but there have been a few recent sightings of individuals on passage and on former breeding grounds.

The most striking physical feature of the **avocets and stilts** is the proportions of their bills and legs. The long, slender bills may either be straight or curve upward. Their legs, too, are long, and in the case of stilts extremely long. Avocets and stilts are thus adapted for feeding in deep water; the three species of stilts usually feed in slightly deeper water than the avocets.

The ibisbill is found only in mountainous river valleys between 1,600 and 4,400m (5,250–14,450ft) above sea level in parts of Asia, while the Andean avocet is restricted to lakes and marshes above 3,600m (11,800ft) in the Andes. The five other species are largely found in a variety of lowland wetlands which include freshwater marshes, brackish and coastal salt marshes and coastal and inland salt lakes. The stilt is the most widespread, with six subspecies found

over six continents. Some populations of the most widespread species migrate over considerable distances. Up to 30,000 Eurasian avocets have been counted wintering in the Great Rift Valley of East Africa.

Stilts have characteristic black bills and bright pink legs and feet, while avocets have black bills and blue-gray legs and feet. The ibisbill, however, has a red bill and legs. The front toes are well webbed in avocets and the South Australian Banded stilt, but only partly so in the other species.

The variation in the amount of webbing on the feet is related to the importance of the swimming habit in each species. Avocets and stilts fly with quick wingbeats and the legs trail behind the body.

All species take a wide range of aquatic invertebrates and small vertebrates in relatively deep water. Important prey include mollusks, crustaceans including brine shrimps, insect larvae, annelid worms, tadpoles and small fish. Stilts seize their prey from above or below the water surface with their long needle-like beaks. Avocets either seize their prey directly in the water or with a scything motion of the bill. With this last method the curved part of the submerged bill locates the prey by touch as it moves from side to side in the water or soft mud. Ibisbills wade breast deep in the mountain rivers and can probe for prey under stones and boulders.

Avocets appear to prefer nesting on islands, where predation may be reduced. In all species incubation is done by both sexes. Most birds first breed when they are two years old. The Banded stilt is highly colonial: colonies of up to 27,000 pairs have been recorded, with the nests only about 2m

◄ **Stilts and Eurasian avocet** ABOVE at Masai Mara nature reserve, Kenya. The avocet is an immature, tinged with brown.

◄ **A female stilt tends her nest** BELOW atop a tussock by the water's edge.

▼ **Mating ceremony of the stilt.** The female solicits the male by adopting, usually in shallow water, the rigid posture (1) which she maintains for most of the ceremony. The male responds by dipping his bill in the water (1), shaking it, and preening himself, a procedure repeated several times (2,3). Then the male mounts the female (4). The male mates (5) and dismounts almost in one movement, the two birds crossing bills, and the male's wing across the female's back breaking the descent (6). After mating, in the "leaning" ceremony (7), the two may stand apart then lean toward one another several times.

(6.6ft) apart. Stilts usually nest in loose colonies of 10–40 pairs, American avocets in loose colonies of 15–20 pairs and Eurasian avocets in colonies of 10–70 pairs. Ibisbills defend linear territories of about 1km (0.6mi) along rivers. All species seem highly territorial, have fairly aggressive displays, defend nesting territories and noisily mob intruders and potential predators. The young leave the nest within 24 hours of hatching and the brood-rearing areas, which may change during the one-month fledging period, may be vigorously defended by the adults.

The habitats of most species, although sometimes specialized, do not appear to be universally threatened. In 1969 there were about 10,000 pairs of Eurasian avocets in northwest Europe. Breeding numbers had increased in a few countries, including Britain, Denmark and Sweden, but had decreased in a few countries in southeast Europe, probably due to changes in land use. The Hawaian race of the stilt may be endangered: in 1944 there were only about 200, but these had increased to 1,500 in 1969 as a result of protection measures.

Small and graceful, the **phalaropes** are the most specialized swimmers among the shorebirds. The three species have lobed, partially webbed toes, laterally flattened tarsi (lower legs) that reduce underwater drag and plumage like that of a duck on their underparts. This provides a layer of trapped air on which they float—as lightly as corks. Indeed, phalaropes are so buoyant that they cannot remain waterborne in strong gales. Outside the breeding season vagrant individuals may appear almost anywhere in the world, as they get blown

ing distribution of the other two species is circumpolar, the Gray (or Red) phalarope in the high arctic tundra and boreal zone and the Red-necked phalarope in the subarctic tundra. All three species select shallow waters, ponds and lakes near to marshy and grassy areas. The Red-necked phalarope favors permanent bodies of fresh water, Wilson's phalarope fresh to salt semi-permanent waters, and the Gray (Red) phalarope temporary ponds of the tundra. Wilson's phalarope winters at inland and coastal waters in South America, while the other two species winter in the open oceans.

Phalaropes have relatively long necks and beautiful breeding (nuptial) plumages, acquired in late spring but quickly lost. All have some white parts on the head, and red and black markings. The amount of red is variable. The "Gray phalarope" is actually the reddest: the description "gray" refers to the predominant color of the upperparts of the winter plumage; in the United States, "Red" phalarope is the more usual name for this species. The female birds are markedly different from the males, both larger (10 percent in the Red-necked, 20 percent in the Gray or Red, and 35 percent in Wilson's phalarope) and gaudier in their breeding

necked and Wilson's phalaropes, thicker in the Gray (Red) species. All are active feeders, scarcely stopping as they peck at their prey. All can feed while spinning—swimming in tight circles. This may be a technique for stirring up invertebrate foods, making them more obvious and causing them to rise to the water surface, where they can be picked off. All phalaropes forage in shallow water, along the shoreline or among wracks of seaweed. The fine bills and large eyes help in catching the prey, which is chiefly insects (all lifestages), especially midges and gnats. The range of prey taken is large, and includes water snails, water beetles, caddis flies and large plankton. Phalaropes are highly opportunistic feeders at their breeding grounds—Red-necked phalaropes will quickly change from swimming and pecking at newly emerged midges to walking along the shoreline and pecking at emerging caddis flies as they dry off on partly submerged stones. The oceanic plankton taken includes tiny fishes, crustaceans and small jellyfish. Gray (Red) phalaropes sometimes pick parasites off the backs of whales.

Adult females are known to live at least five years, and probably breed first when they are one year old. The breeding season

▲ **Long legs trailing,** and upcurved bills to the fore, a group of American avocets takes flight.

▶ **Male Northern or Red-necked phalarope on nest.** The larger and more brightly colored females choose the nest site, secure mates by display flights, then after mating and egg-laying may mate with other males. The males do all the incubation of the eggs and care for the chicks.

The Fall and Rise of Avocets in Britain

Avocets bred regularly in eastern England until the early 19th century, before they were wiped out by wetland reclamation followed by persistent egg collecting and shooting. For over a hundred years there was no regular breeding, until in 1947 Havergate Island and Minsmere in Suffolk were colonized. During the 1939–45 World War, the cattle-grazed fields of the Minsmere level had been deliberately flooded as a defense measure, and, as a result of damage to a main sluice caused by a stray shell from a nearby firing range, the pastures on Havergate became inundated.

Breeding numbers at Havergate steadily increased to almost 100 pairs over the next 10 years, with an average 1.5 chicks successfully fledging for each pair of breeding adults. This success coincided with a steady increase in numbers of breeding Black-headed gulls in the same area to about 6,000 pairs. There was intense competition for nest sites. Gulls took over avocet nests within hours of their completion, and also killed newly hatched avocets as they were being led through the densely packed gulleries. Over a period of eight years from 1957, the fledging success of avocets averaged about 0.5 per breeding pair, and breeding numbers dropped

to 48 pairs. Constant removal of Black-headed gulls' nests and eggs by conservationists caused the larger birds' breeding numbers to drop to 1,000–1,500 pairs by 1965—a level at which they have since been maintained. The effect on avocets was marked. Over the next five years from 1965 to 1969, their breeding population recovered (118 pairs in 1969), fledged chicks averaging 1.7 per pair.

By the late 1970s breeding success at Havergate had again dropped, this time to 0.1 per breeding pair. This decline was a result of a fall in numbers of prey species, which were adversely affected by hyper-salinity in the lagoons caused by a shortage of fresh water from the island's artesian wells. New sluices were built, and the island's ditches cleared, so that a regular flow of tidal brackish water could circulate throughout the lagoons. A new range of invertebrate food species is now developing, and the breeding performance of the 100 pairs of avocets is again improving.

At Minsmere the 1947 breeding attempt was not repeated until 1963. Since then avocets have built up to over 50 pairs.

Havergate and Minsmere are now nature reserves. The avocet is now the emblem of the Royal Society for the Protection of Birds.

is very short. Generally females arrive at the breeding grounds in June ahead of the males, but the sexes sometimes arrive together, apparently paired. Otherwise pairing takes place in a few days. The females may participate in nest-site searches and both sexes make nest scrapes. It appears that the female selects the chosen site and the male prepares the final nest, hidden in a dry grass or a sedge tussock near to water. Some roles are sex-reversed. The female takes the initiative in courtship and with display flights. She pays the male constant attention until a pair bond is formed. Incubation of the eggs and care of the young are exclusively carried out by the male.

The two birds are seldom far apart for the duration (often brief) of the pair bond, and keep in touch with repeated short calls. Nesting can be solitary or loosely colonial. The two arctic-nesting species often nest in or near colonies of Arctic terns, which may help in providing an increase in vigilance against predators. Gray (Red) phalaropes copulate on land, Red-necked while swimming, and Wilson's phalaropes while either standing in water or swimming.

Normally one egg is laid each day for four days. The male begins to incubate some time between the production of the first and third eggs. After the initial egg laying, female Red-necked and Gray (Red) phalaropes may mate with other males if there are enough males around. A female will start to lay a clutch of eggs for a new male some 7–10 days after completing her first. She will remain at the breeding ground and provide second clutches for the original or second male should the first ones be destroyed.

The incubating male rarely leaves the nest. The small eggs, the brief courtships and polyandrous habit (one female mating with several males) all seem to be adaptations for the short breeding season. The chicks of one clutch hatch more or less at the same time. The hatchlings are well developed and leave the nest when some 3–6 hours old. They are cared for by the male only. He broods them frequently in the day and night during the first few days, and also at times of bad weather. They swim and feed like ducklings under his supervision, before he abandons them at 11–14 days.

All three phalaropes are relatively common throughout most of their breeding range which, in the case of the Red-necked and Gray (Red) phalaropes, is usually well beyond any damaging human activities. However, in the case of the Wilson's phalarope some of its prairie marsh habitat is being drained.   GJT

wilderness areas such as coastlands and arctic tundra.

But the highly migratory nature of shorebirds (waders) poses its own problems for their survival. A single population of a species may depend, for example, on summer breeding areas in the Soviet Union, sites for feeding to deposit fat as fuel for migration in, say, Sweden or Poland, a molting area on the German or Dutch coast, and several sites used at different stages of the winter, in Britain and France. Arctic-breeding populations tend to suffer naturally from very variable breeding success, and it can therefore be difficult to estimate the quality of habitat they require in the non-breeding areas. The concentration of shorebirds from their widespread breeding areas to relatively small coastal and wetland sites at other times of the year makes them particularly vulnerable.

Drainage of wetlands and reclamation of coastal salt marshes has been a traditional activity around the coasts of Europe probably for 2,000 years, but modern technology has caused a drastic increase in the rate and nature of this change. Today reductions in intertidal habitat result from the increasing need for deepwater ports, and land for related industry, especially the development of North Sea oil, areas for waste disposal, tidal power projects, and water storage. Such developments, of course, occur throughout the world.

Paradoxically, the international scale of the problem has its advantages, in that international conventions encourage national governments to conserve sites. By 1983, for example, 34 countries had complied with the 1971 "Ramsar" Convention on Wetlands of International Importance especially as Waterfowl Habitat, which requires governments to conserve at least one designated site of international importance. The European Economic Community Directive on Conservation of Birds (1979) requires the designation of areas of habitat, especially wetlands, and recognizes the need for both further research and for updating, in the light of the findings, of its own provisions.

International protection measures came earlier in North America, and from different causes. The Treaty on Migratory Birds in 1916, between the USA and Canada (extended in 1936 to Mexico), was a response to excessive commercial hunting—some

vary between (and even within) countries. The pattern is similarly mixed in the areas of Africa used by some of these same populations: in parts of West Africa, important for waders, there is no local tradition of killing birds, while elsewhere in Africa, birds have long been an important food source. In the Far East, there are bilateral agreements on bird protection between two or more of the USA, the USSR, Japan and Australia, but uncontrolled hunting occurs in other areas.

When all the appropriate habitat at a site disappears then so do all the waders. However, sometimes only part of the habitat is lost to the birds (or "reclaimed" by man for industry, etc). When 60 percent of intertidal land was lost at Seal Sands, in the Tees estuary, northeast England, the resulting decreases in numbers of different shorebird species varied between 0 and 95 percent. This variation is related to the resulting changes in duration of tidal exposure and the differing feeding times required by various species, the adaptability of different species to using alternative feeding areas, especially at high water, the effects of the changes on numbers and sites of prey species, and alterations to the competitive balance between different bird species.

What happens to birds that are displaced—do they survive elsewhere, or die? In recent decades, snipe populations have been displaced by extensive drainage of the wet agricultural "polder" land in the Netherlands. Information on the numbers of snipes ringed and recovered reveals a shift of a main fall molting area from the Netherlands to Britain between the 1950s and the 1970s. However, corresponding numbers of birds may have been displaced from the new winter grounds, and it is possible that any reprieve was relatively short lived—a 1982–83 survey revealed a major and continuing loss of wet meadowland in Britain, again due to drainage.

The loss of wet meadowland and other pasture, often to the plow, is encouraged by agricultural policies in Europe, even where it is not by itself economically viable. This change is serious also for some breeding populations. For example, snipe, which were formerly widespread and common in the English and Welsh lowlands, were restricted by 1982–83 to about 2,000 pairs, half of them on only five sites. Similarly, afforestation of moorland areas is becoming a threat for upland-breeding shorebirds in

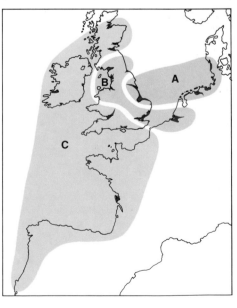

▲ **A flock of Marbled godwits** on their coastal wintering ground. Marbled godwits breed in west central Canada and winter along coasts south to Peru. Birds with white wing-bars and tails are willets (*Catoptrophorus semipalmatus*).

◄ **Uses and abuses of intertidal areas.** Coastal sites in northwestern Europe marked in red have been subject to major losses of the shorebirds' intertidal habitat induced by the activities of man, or are currently under threat.

Areas within broken lines illustrate the way in which one shorebird species, the dunlin, uses northwestern Europe as its major non-breeding area. Sites in area (**A**) are used in the fall, while the birds replace their summer plumage, before moving further east for the winter. The birds may return to use these sites in spring before moving on to their more northerly, or arctic, breeding areas. Sites in area (**C**) are mainly used in winter. Sites in area (**B**) are used extensively in both fall and winter, often by different birds. Individual birds depend on a sequence of sites. Loss of one site may affect populations at others.

some areas, including Britain. Recreational use of beaches, another principal breeding habitat in temperate regions, causes problems for species in Europe, North America and for some Southern Hemisphere species.

In arctic breeding areas, waders tend to be dispersed thinly over wide areas and damage from localized development is less likely. However, protected sites, where required, have to be extensive. Few major threats are known to breeding areas in the Arctic of the Old World or Greenland, though little information is available from the USSR. However, as oil-related developments increase in coastal areas of Alaska and arctic Canada, waders may face problems, as the tundra breeding habitat is very sensitive to any disturbance.

One recent conservation success has been in the Netherlands, where the delta of the Rhine, Meuse and Scheldt rivers has been progressively closed by barrages since the disastrous floods of 1953. Because of pressure from environmentalists and fisheries groups, the final closure was changed from a permanent dam to a closable tidal-surge barrier, allowing the Oosterscheldt estuary to remain tidal, albeit with a reduced tidal range and area.

On estuaries, at least, public demand can help mitigate adverse effects, and even enhance the areas for shorebirds. However, this requires the involvement of shorebird biologists early in the feasibility and planning stages of such projects—which is all too rare. Biologists can also assess, using counts and studies of shorebird movements, the areas where such developments can cause least damage to shorebird populations. MWP

Order: Charadriiformes (suborder: Charadrii, part).
Forty-eight species in 19 genera.
Distribution: see maps and table.

Jacanas   **Crab plover**   **Oyster-catchers**

Seed snipes   **Sheathbills**   **Pratincoles**

Stone curlews   **Painted snipes**

than duck- or tern-like, yet sufficiently different to be put in families separate from the sandpipers and plovers. Some, like the oystercatchers and painted snipes, are obviously shorebirds, with their long legs and long slender bills. But others, such as the seed snipes and sheathbills, are so different in appearance that their inclusion in the order (mainly on the basis of skull characters) comes at first as a surprise.

Jacanas are a small group of waterbirds characterized by their striking plumage and extremely long toes and claws, which enable them to walk with ease on floating vegetation and on the leaves of waterlilies (they are sometimes called "lily-trotters"). The seven species occur widely throughout the marshlands, rice fields and freshwater margins of the tropics. Though often quite abundant, they are often inconspicuous in the reedy vegetation despite their generally

the Bronze-winged jacana and lobed red or yellow in the American jacana; on the Comb-crested jacana it is yellow or red and developed into a vertical comb. All have short tails except for the Pheasant-tailed jacana, which in breeding plumage sports long central tail feathers which add 25cm (10in) to its normal 30cm (12in) length. All have a short spur, sharp or blunt, on the carpal joint of the wing.

All records indicate that jacanas have a mixed diet of predominantly aquatic insects, mollusks, and the occasional small fish and the seeds of aquatic plants. These are found as the birds stalk nimbly from leaf to leaf, occasionally jumping a patch of open water with the help of a flick of the wings.

In most species the breeding season is protracted and coincides with the local wet season, when insect food is more abundant. In all but the Smaller jacana the female is

◄▼► **Representative species of jacanas and other waders.** (1) Territorial "piping" display of Black oystercatchers (*Haematopus bachmani*). (2) Territorial display of female Painted snipe (*Rostratula benghalensis*). (3) Greeting posture of Stone curlew or thick-knee (*Burhinus oedicnemus*) in courtship. (4) An American jacana (*Jacana spinosa*) or "lily-trotter." (5) A Crab plover (*Dromas ardeola*) teaches its single young to hunt crabs; IN BACKGROUND, ABOVE Crab plovers return along an Indian Ocean coastline to their communal roosting site.

in the African and American jacanas the type of habitat seems to influence whether mating is monogamous or polyandrous. For example, American jacanas breeding in uniform marshy habitats are monogamous, each pair inhabiting a relatively large territory. In areas containing scattered ponds in Mexico and Puerto Rico, females have 1–4 mates and while they take no part in incubating or rearing young they help defend the males' territories against intruders.

Even in the monogamous species the male performs all the duties of nest building, incubation and the care of the chicks. The exceptions are the Smaller jacana, in which both male and female bear brood patches, and the Comb-crested jacana in which both sexes tend the young.

Adaptations to a life in watery places include the Pheasant-tailed jacana's reported habit of incubating the eggs two under each wing, away from the water, and the ability of both adults and chicks of the African jacana to hide from predators by submerging, leaving only the bill and nostrils above water. Several species have been observed, when disturbed, to carry small young to safety under their wings or attempting to lure predators away with a "broken wing" display.

The intricate plumage of **painted snipes** is both extremely beautiful and a wonderful disruptive camouflage. The plumage of the South American bird is basically alike in the two sexes, while in the Old World species the slightly larger female is the gaudier. Both have broad, round wings, a characteristic rail-like flight and long bills, down-curved at the tip, with the nostrils set in deep narrow grooves that extend over half the bill's length.

Both species feed in typical wader fashion, probing soft soils and mud for insects and seeds, and they forage mostly at dawn and dusk, when they may leave the thicker vegetation to exploit open grassland and pasture.

So far as is known, the South American painted snipe is monogamous and territorial in its breeding habits. The better-studied Eurasian species is, however, generally polyandrous. Toward the beginning of the breeding season, females start their evening displays, calling from the ground or from a low display flight. The display call is a succession of low hooting notes which, thanks

◀▲ **Eurasian oystercatcher on its nest** LEFT and probing in sand for food ABOVE. Pied or black plumage and a blunt-ended, straight red bill are characteristic of all oystercatchers.

◀ **Long toes take the weight** of the African jacana, enabling it to "lily-trot" on floating vegetation.

to the birds' long, convoluted, resonating trachea, are audible from well over a kilometer (0.6mi) away. In this way the female claims a territory for herself and attracts male birds. Intruding females are repelled with a display in which the wings are outstretched and turned forward to show the spotted flight feathers. Later on, when competition for males intensifies, females may actually fight to defend their mates from the advances of rivals. Females take the initiative in courting, circling the male in the spread-wing posture and giving a melodious "boo" call, reminiscent of the sound made by blowing across the neck of a bottle. After mating, the male builds a nest into which the female lays her eggs before leaving to court other males. Her progress is rapid and the next clutch is usually laid before the first hatches.

The males are not territorial and those mated to a single female usually nest quite close together. The chicks can run as soon as they are dry and are fed and brooded solely by the male, who may give the spread-wing threat display to distract or deter predators or human intruders. After breeding, small flocks comprising two or more males and their broods may form before the birds finally disperse.

The **oystercatchers** are a very uniform family characterized by their long, straight, blunt-ended red bills, pied or black plumage and relatively short legs. Their taxonomy is rather confused and up to 11 species and 21 subspecies are recognized by some authorities. All are coastal, though the wholly black species (Sooty, Black and Blackish) generally prefer rocky shorelines to the sandy or muddy ones favored by the others. Though not at all well studied, they all appear similar in their habits. The following details, based mainly on the Eurasian species, are probably typical.

Oystercatchers are gregarious and flock throughout the year, except while breeding, when pairs take up territories on beaches, on fields near the coast or occasionally inland by lakes and rivers. They do not breed until between three and five years of age but usually form pairs earlier than this, non-breeding birds roosting in flocks during the breeding season. Territories are proclaimed and boundaries contested by means of a ritualized "piping display" in which a bird stands at its territory boundary, neck arched and bill pointed downward, and gives a succession of piping notes. The display normally attracts the owners of adjacent territories and up to 10 pairs may gather and display either standing or rushing up and down. A version of this display may also be given on the wing and is perhaps the most familiar sight for a casual intruder in oystercatcher territory.

Usually, three eggs are laid in a scrape and are brooded by both parents. Predation rates are often high and several replacement clutches in a season are common. The chicks can run within a short while of hatching, but due to the oystercatcher's specialized diet they are unable to feed themselves and must follow the parents who forage for them. The first chick to hatch is fed first and soon a size hierarchy develops in which the largest chick has first refusal of any food the parents offer.

Adult oystercatchers feed mainly on various types of bivalve mollusks, both surface-dwelling species such as mussels and those, such as cockles, which live buried in the sand. Two main methods of opening these prey are used. Should the bird be able to surprise an open shell, either by stalking it on the surface or probing in the sand, the bill is driven in between the shell halves. The adductor muscle which holds together the shell halves is cut with a scissor-like bill action and the flesh is chiselled or shaken out of the defenseless mollusk. If the shell halves are closed, one side may be broken into by hammering with the bill, and the flesh removed. Individual birds tend to specialize on one particular type of prey and develop their own technique for consuming

Female Cassanovas—Polyandry in Waders

In several of the shorebird and wader families, notably among the jacanas, painted snipes, and phalaropes, the roles of male and female are reversed. One female takes a number of mates and leaves them to incubate the eggs and rear the young. This breeding system, called polyandry, is very rare in birds and has been reported regularly or occasionally in only thirteen families comprising less than one percent of all bird species. The rarity of polyandry attests to the rarity of the pressures required for its evolution, and much about it remains a mystery.

The young of many bird species stay in the nest and require the efforts of both parents to feed them. However, in more primitive species, whose precocious young leave the nest and feed themselves, it is possible for just one parent to guard them. One parent may thus have the opportunity to desert its mate and breed again without fear of its first brood dying. The deserted partner must of course remain with its young or lose all of its offspring. Since natural selection tends to favor individuals with the ability to produce large numbers of offspring that survive to

breeding age, desertion will be beneficial only if the deserter gets more matings and if its original mate assumes entire responsibility for the young it is left with. Since the female lays the eggs and in most birds is the partner required for most of the incubation, most species show little possibility for the development of polyandry. What factors might act to result in the female playing the Cassanova?

One factor that facilitates polyandry is that the male should spend more time incubating than the female. It may be that poor food supply obliges the female to continue feeding in order to recoup the reserves of energy lost in egg laying, or heavy predation on eggs and chicks may force females to feed to gather reserves for repeat clutches. A further requirement is a surplus of males in the population for females to mate with. Certainly among shorebirds and waders, whose eggs are laid in the open, predation pressures are often very high. Once the polyandrous system starts, females may evolve conventional "male" characters, such as gaudy plumage and large size in order to compete better with other females for males.

and prey preferences. It may be as long as two years after independence before they are sufficiently skilled to survive on mussels alone and during this period they feed extensively on ragworms and other invertebrates found on mudflats and fields by the coast.

The sole representative of its family, the **Crab plover** is instantly recognizable by its massive bill and pied plumage. Like a cross between an avocet and an oversized plover, this curious, little-studied bird inhabits sandy beaches and mudflats of the African and Asian coasts of the Indian Ocean. When walking, the long neck is often carried hunched between the shoulders, giving a silhouette that is somewhat gull-like but made distinctive by the long wader legs with their short toes and partial webs.

Crab plovers are highly gregarious at all seasons and usually feed in flocks of 20 or more searching the intertidal zone for the crabs which are their staple food. Once captured, a crab is easily broken by the powerful bill and swallowed. Crab plovers tend to be nocturnal, as they feed on tropical fiddler crabs which emerge in numbers at dusk to feed and find mates.

Crab plovers breed colonially and thousands may congregate in an area of just a few thousand square meters (up to about feet, and enlarge a chamber at the end in which the single egg is laid. This feature is surprising in a long-legged bird, and unique among shorebirds. Unusually for a shorebird, the chicks remain in the nest until well after they are full grown, possibly as a precaution against predation by the crabs that will later be their prey. Food is brought to them by both parents. After leaving the nest, young birds apparently take some time to acquire the skills necessary to successfully tackle an angry crab. They accompany their parents, begging for food and often standing by, watching them capture a crab, as though unsure of which is the predator and which the prey.

Outside the breeding season the gregarious habit persists, large flocks forming to fly to and from the traditional roosting sites. On several occasions flocks have been observed to gather to mob a human hunter who has shot one of their number.

Stone curlews' alternative name of thick-knees derives from their especially knobbly leg joints, but the most striking feature about their appearance is their large, piercing yellow, hawkish eyes which stare out from under pronounced eyebrows and fit them well for evening and night-time activity.

RG

Stone curlews are a fairly uniform family, all having cryptic brown plumage heavily streaked with brown and black above, pale underparts and pronounced white wing-bars shown in flight. The two *Esacus* species are plainer above and pale below and have prominent black markings about the eye and crown. All have stout to massive bills, well able to cope with their varied diet of insects, crustaceans, mollusks and small vertebrates. They are terrestrial birds and run swiftly, flying low only when necessary, with their long legs trailing behind. Typically they inhabit dry open country and semi-desert, though the Water thick-knee and Senegal thick-knee favor lake and river margins, and the Great and Beach stone curlews frequent coasts. Out of the breeding season they often gather in small groups.

When breeding, pairs of most species take up territories in open areas that are free of vegetation and afford a good view in all directions. The European species defends its territory with an aggressive display in which the bird draws itself into as upright a position as possible, body almost vertical, fanned tail pointing downwards and folded wings held away from the body. Pairs collaborate in territorial defense and the period

during which a territory is established may be prolonged. The courtship posture is quite the opposite, the pair standing together with necks arched and bills pointed downward.

The eggs are laid in a scrape in the ground and incubated by both birds in turn, the off-duty parent usually standing guard nearby, watching out behind its sitting partner. The chicks can stand and walk by the second day and disperse from the nest soon thereafter. The parents feed them for the first few days and they gradually learn to feed themselves. If danger threatens, the parents may pick up small chicks in their bill and carry them to a hiding place. Distraction displays are not common but when they are given are very strenuous, the bird jumping and falling fluttering to the ground to roll with extended wings and hissing cries.

In Europe, the Stone curlew is now much reduced in numbers due to loss of suitable habitat and increasing disturbance. Stone curlews require open ground and absolute freedom from human activity, and such places are becoming increasingly rare.

The **pratincoles and coursers** are distinct groups within the family Glareolidae, which also contains the rather anomalous Egyptian plover and Australian dotterel. The Egyptian plover is usually considered to be a closer relative of the coursers, while some include the Australian dotterel with the pratincoles and others place it in another family altogether, the true plovers (Charadriidae).

Pratincoles are wonderful flyers, their long pointed wings, forked tails and agile flight in pursuit of winged insects being reminiscent of swifts. However, they also feed on insects on the ground and are fast runners. The Long-legged pratincole is the odd one out and is mainly terrestrial in its habits. Pratincoles favor flat open country, both near water and in more arid areas,

The chicks stay in or near the nest for 2–3 days, fed by both parents, after which they gradually learn to feed themselves. As in other waders, elaborate "broken wing" displays are commonly given by the parent to lure predators from their chicks.

The coursers, with their longer legs, short tails and characteristic upright stance, are running birds which take flight only if forced. Their cryptic sandy plumage is plainer than the pratincoles', though many sport conspicuous black-and-white eye stripes. They favor arid and desert areas and are also gregarious, gathering in flocks and family parties after breeding. Poorly known, they appear to be monogamous and territorial, both parents tending the young which stay with them until well after fledging.

The Egyptian plover is a beautiful and striking bird with blue-gray wings, orange belly and bold black-and-white marking on the head. It prefers the margins of inland lakes and rivers and neighboring fields and grasslands, feeding on insects and invertebrates taken on the ground, particularly at the water's edge. They are extremely tame and often frequent the vicinity of human habitations. Old stories that they feed on the scraps left between the teeth of basking crocodiles make good telling, but have never been properly authenticated! Though they may flock outside the breeding season they are basically solitary, nesting in pairs in territories. Members of a pair greet each other on landing with an elaborate wing-raising display in which the beautiful wing markings are shown to advantage. When leaving the nest, the incubating bird buries its eggs in the sand, smoothing over the side so that the nest is completely invisible. This is still done if the bird is surprised, though haste makes for a less than perfect job. Newly hatched chicks receive the same treatment and are covered totally with sand. Should the eggs become too hot, they are cooled with water gathered in the adult's belly feathers. Very young chicks are cooled in the same way and may also drink from the soaked feathers. Distraction displays are not common but adults may feign a broken wing on occasion. The chicks feed themselves from the outset but must be shown food to start with.

The squat, short-legged, short-billed **seed snipes** are, with the sheathbills, perhaps the

Least seed snipe prefers the arid coastal and dune areas and inland dry plains of lower altitudes. The White-bellied and Gray-breasted seed snipes range further into the higher, dry slopes of the Andes, and the Rufous-bellied species favors wetter moorland in the high mountain pastures. They are all fast-running, ground-dwelling birds, and tend to be gregarious, often gathering in coveys like partridges. Their short, stout bills are an adaptation to their mainly seed diet, though cactus buds and the succulent parts of growing plants are also eaten. Their plumage is generally cryptic, with brown feathers edged with black and buff above, but the Gray-breasted and Least seed snipes have a gray forehead and black and buff markings on the sides of the head and neck which are more pronounced in the male than the female.

Males of the two *Thinocorus* species take up territories and perform a display flight reminiscent of a lark, flying up then gliding down on stiff wings giving a rapid staccato song. The ascent of the Least seed snipe is higher than that of the Gray-breasted and the display lasts rather longer. Both species may also sing from a perch and the Least seed snipe has been observed performing a "butterfly" flight, beating its wings in a stiff, exaggerated manner.

In all but one species the buff or cream eggs with darker markings blend with the dry stony soil by the scrape. The dark olive

▲ **A Water thick-knee** (or dikkop) confronts a monitor lizard.

◄ **A Long-legged or Australian pratincole** broods its young on the simple scrape that is its nest.

larger Black-faced sheathbill is resident on some of the remotest subantarctic islands, while the Snowy sheathbill breeds in the Antarctic but migrates, in rather random fashion, to the Falklands and coasts of Argentina during the southern winter.

These are indeed peculiar birds, forming a possible evolutionary link between the shorebirds and the gulls. They share certain anatomical features with both groups and have a rudimentary spur on the carpal joint of the wing—a typical plover feature. They have a bald patch around the eye and naked carbuncled skin above the pale yellow (Snowy sheathbill) or black (Black-faced species) bill. The bill is broad and strong with a horny sheath which partially covers the nostrils. The plumage is white, the flight pigeon-like, the gait like that of a rail and the general behavior like a crow or gull. They are terrestrial by preference but will fly if forced or when on migration.

Sheathbills are opportunistic feeders and their diet is very varied. In winter they boldly frequent the rubbish heaps of whaling stations and antarctic survey bases, scavenging offal and household scraps as well as feeding among seaweed for intertidal invertebrates. When the seals come to breed, like crows at lambing they grow fat on stillborn pups and the afterbirths. In their own breeding season they turn for food to the large colonies of breeding penguins. Pairs of sheathbills take up territories, containing a number of penguins, which they defend vigorously from other sheathbills, and harass the penguins in order to steal the krill they bring for their chicks. Pairs often join forces to surprise the adult penguin, drive off the chick and scoop up the krill as it is regurgitated. This rich food is ideally suited for the rapidly growing sheathbill chicks, which wait at the nest to be fed. Penguin eggs are also stolen, and adult sheathbills feed extensively on penguin droppings. The penguins clearly resent these depredations and may lunge out with their bills. However, they generally make little impression on the bold and agile sheathbills.

After fledging, the young disperse to the shoreline to scavenge for scraps of fish, limpets and kelp. Because of their messy feeding habits, sheathbills take great pains to keep clean, and they spend a considerable proportion of their time in bathing and preening. They have no obvious predators, except for the odd egg lost to other sheathbills, and share with skuas the easy life afforded to scavengers in an area so rich in food resources.   ASR

and black eggs of the White-bellied seed snipe are better camouflaged for the mossy soils of its heathland habitat. In the *Thinocorus* species, and probably the others also, the female alone incubates, kicking loose material over the eggs to hide them if she wants to leave the nest or is disturbed. In the latter case she may use a distraction display, fluttering low over the ground or trailing a wing. The young are very precocious and feed themselves soon after hatching. Both parents guard them and the male, too, may use distraction displays, running to and fro with hunched back and drooping wings to lure intruders away.

For some European people, the first time they heard of the strange Antarctic **sheathbills** was the discovery of a lone stowaway on a British troopship returning from the Falkland Islands in 1982. The two species are closely similar in appearance and habits but geographically separated. The slightly

New Guinea, N Australia, C and S America. Marshes, still and slow-moving water covered in floating vegetation. Size: length 15–30cm (6–12in), except Pheasant-tailed jacana (see text); weight 40–230g (1.4–8.1oz); female larger than male in most species. Plumage: striking; mostly black and white on head and neck; upperparts various chestnut browns, often darker below and with white on flight feathers; sexes similar. Voice: generally noisy, with variety of high, staccato, squawking calls. Nests: simple, of aquatic leaves, usually on floating vegetation or raised platforms; occasionally, partially submerged. Eggs: normally 3–4, highly polished with dark spots, streaks and lines; incubation about 21–26 days; fledging period several weeks at least. Diet: insects and seeds of aquatic plants.

Species: **African jacana or lily-trotter** (*Actophilornis africana*), **American jacana** (*Jacana spinosa*), **Bronze-winged jacana** (*Metopidius indicus*), **Comb-crested jacana** (*Irediparra gallinacea*), **Madagascar jacana** (*Actophilornis albinucha*), **Pheasant-tailed jacana** (*Hydrophasianus chirurgus*), **Smaller jacana** (*Microparra capensis*).

Painted snipes

Family: Rostratulidae
Two species in 2 genera.
Africa, India, SE Asia, Australia, southern S America. Swamps, marshes, rice paddies. Size: length 20–26cm (8–10in), weight 76–165g (2.7–5.8oz), females slightly larger than males. Plumage: brown and chestnut, marked with black and buff above and white or cream below. Prominent buff stripes on head and across shoulders. Striking round yellow spots on wing feathers. Voice: soft booming notes, growls and hisses. Nest: simple cup of stems and leaves hidden on ground in tall vegetation. Eggs: 2–4, cream to yellow-buff, heavily spotted with black and brown; 13g (0.5oz); incubation 19 days. Young are nidifugous. Diet: insects, earthworms, snails and seeds.

Species: **Painted snipe** (*Rostratula benghalensis*), **South American painted snipe** (*Nycticryphes semicollaris*).

S America except in high latitudes. All types of coast and fresh and brackish waters and marshlands. Size: length 37–45cm (14.6–17.7in), weight 425–770g (15–27.2oz). Plumage: pied or uniform black; sexes alike. Voice: wide variety of simple and complex piping calls. Nest: shallow scrape in sand or shingle, generally unlined. Eggs: 2–3 (range 1–5), brown or gray with black, gray and brown spots and streaks; generally 40–50g (1.4–1.8oz); incubation 24–27 days; fledging period 28–32 days (Eurasian oystercatcher). Diet: chiefly bivalve mollusks; also limpets, crabs, worms, echinoderms (starfishes, sea urchins).

Species: **American oystercatcher** (*Haematopus palliatus*), **Blackish oystercatcher** (*H. ater*), **Black oystercatcher** (*H. bachmani*), **Eurasian oystercatcher** (*H. ostralegus*), **Magellanic oystercatcher** (*H. leucopodus*), **Sooty oystercatcher** (*H. fuliginosus*). Total threatened species: 1.

Crab plover

Family: Dromadidae
Sole species *Dromas ardeola*.
Africa, Madagascar, Middle East, India, Sri Lanka. Tropical coastlines of sand dunes, mudflats, coral reefs and estuaries. Size: length 33–36cm (13–14in); weight about 250–325g (8.8–11.5oz). Plumage: white with black back and primary feathers; sexes alike. Voice: noisy with variety of harsh, barking calls and sharp whistles. Nest: unlined hollow at end of tunnel in the sand. Eggs: 1, occasionally 2, white; about 45g (1.6oz); incubation and fledging periods not known. Diet: chiefly crabs, also mollusks, worms and other invertebrates.

Stone curlews

Family: Burhinidae
Nine species in 2 genera.
Stone curlews, thick-knees, stone plovers or dikkops

Europe, Africa, Asia, Australasia, S America. Sparsely vegetated open country, near water or in more arid regions, steppe, deserts, mudflats, savanna and open coastlines and estuaries. Size: length 32–55cm (12.6–21.7in); weight up to 1kg (2.2lb). Plumage: pale sandy browns above, streaked black; pale streaked breast and whitish underparts; sexes alike. Voice: wailing bi-syllabic whistles given communally at dusk, and variety of other hoarse, rasping

gray marked with brown, black and purplish-gray spots and blotches; in Stone curlew, average 38g (1.3oz), incubation 24–27 days, fledging 36–42 days. Diet: terrestrial invertebrates, small vertebrates (frogs, rodents), crabs and mollusks in coastal species.

Species: **Beach stone curlew** (*Esacus magnirostris*), **Double-striped thick-knee** (*Burhinus bistriatus*), **Great stone curlew** (*E. recurvirostris*), **Peruvian thick-knee** (*B. superciliaris*), **Senegal thick-knee** (*B. senegalensis*), **Southern stone curlew** (*B. magnirostris*), **Spotted thick-knee or Cape dikkop** (*B. capensis*), **Stone curlew** (*B. oedicnemus*), **Water thick-knee or dikkop** (*B. vermiculatus*).

Pratincoles and coursers

Family: Glareolidae
Seventeen species in 4 genera.
Europe, Asia, Africa, Australasia. Open or scrub country, generally in arid regions. Plumage: pratincoles generally brown above with white rump and belly; many have colored throats bordered with black. Coursers generally cryptic buffs and sandy browns; many have bold black markings on head and breast; sexes alike. Nest: unlined or sparsely lined scrape in sand or gravel. Eggs: 2–3 (occasionally 1, 4 or 5), yellow-brown, cream or buff, speckled with black, brown and gray; generally about 15g (0.5oz) where known; incubation 17–31 days; fledging period 25–35 days where known. Diet: chiefly insects, occasionally other invertebrates.

Species: **Australian dotterel** (*Peltohyas australis*), **Black-winged pratincole** (*Glareola nordmanni*), **Collared pratincole** (*G. pratincola*), **Cream-colored courser** (*Cursorius cursor*), **Eastern collared pratincole** (*Glareola maldivarum*), **Egyptian plover** (*Pluvianus aegyptius*), **Gray pratincole** (*Glareola cinerea*), **Heuglin's courser** (*Cursorius cinctus*), **Indian courser** (*C. coromandelicus*), **Jerdon's courser** (*C. bitorquatus*, possibly extinct); **Little pratincole** (*Glareola lactea*), **Long-legged pratincole** (*G. isabella*), **Madagascar pratincole** (*G. ocularis*), **Temminck's courser** (*Cursorius temminkii*), **Two-banded courser** (*C. africanus*), **Violet-tipped courser** (*C. chalcopterus*), **White-collared pratincole** (*Glareola nuchalis*).

Size: length 19–30cm (7.5–12in); weight 60–250g (2.1–8.8oz). Plumage: generally various browns above, marked with black, gray and cinnamon; females like males but less strongly marked. Voice: song a series of rapid tri-syllabic notes, also short, rasping and peeping alarm calls. Nests: scrape in the ground lined with any available loose material. Eggs: 4, buff or cream, speckled dark brown and lilac or olive, blotched with black; incubation about 25 days; young nidifugous; fledging 49–55 days (in Least seed snipe). Diet: seeds and succulent vegetation.

Species: **Gray-breasted seed snipe** (*Thinocorus orbignyianus*), and **Least seed snipe** (*T. rumicivorus*); **Rufous-bellied seed snipe** (*Attagis gayi*), **White-bellied seed snipe** (*A. malouinus*).

Sheathbills

Family: Chionididae
Two species of the genus *Chionis*.
Antarctic and sub-Antarctic islands. Coasts. Size: length 38–41cm (15–16in); weight 290–550g (10.3–19.4oz). Plumage: entirely white; sexes alike. Voice: harsh crow-like calls and guttural, rattling croaks. Nests: in crevice in rocks or in former petrel burrow; may be lined with stones, debris, seaweed or lichen. Eggs: 2, sometimes 3 or 4, white or grayish with dark brown blotches; incubation 28–32 days, fledging 50–60 days. Diet: omnivorous, opportunist feeders and scavengers.

Species: **Black-faced sheathbill** (*Chionis minor*), **Snowy sheathbill** (*C. alba*).

▶ **Wet and bedraggled,** a recently hatched American jacana chick drying out on leaves of waterlilies in a Brazilian rain forest.

Ninety-five species in 15 genera.
Distribution: see maps and table.

Gulls   **Skimmers**

Terns   **Skuas**

breeding sites. As a group they are outstanding opportunists, which partly distinguishes them from their close but more specialized relatives, the terns (p196) and skuas (p199).

In adapting to a wide variety of life-styles, gulls range enormously in size, from the dainty and diminutive Little gull to the heavily built piratical Great black-backed gull. The larger species have robust, slightly hooked bills, while the smaller species have slender, forceps-like ones. In most species the underside is white, with gray or darker coloring on the back and uppersides of the wings. The generally pale coloring below is thought to make the flying bird less conspicuous to its fish prey below in the surface waters of the sea. A minority, notably the aptly named Lava gull and the Sooty gull, are much darker all over.

The bill and legs of gulls are usually yellow or bright red, but there is much variation, both between species and at different times of year in the same species. However stoutly built, gulls are always graceful in flight, switching easily from powerful forward flight to gliding and soaring, their maneuverability serving them well on updraughts near cliff nesting sites. They are equally at home on the water surface, where their webbed feet provide ample propulsion.

Most gulls fall into one of two major subgroups, distinguished by summer plumage pattern. The "white-headed" group contains the largest species, including the well-known and highly successful Herring gull of Europe and North America, and its close relative, the more strictly marine Lesser black-backed gull (see box, p190). Further north, various species, including the Glaucous gull, form a circumpolar distribution. The second major group, the "hooded" or "masked" gulls, are mostly of slighter build, and characterized in breeding plumage by a bold chocolate-brown or sooty-black head; in winter this hood is molted, and the birds then have a predominantly white head with a residual dark patch or collar behind the eye. In Europe, the best-known representative is the ubiquitous Black-headed gull. American allies include the Laughing gull, Franklin's gull and Bonaparte's gull. Less closely related, and sometimes placed in a separate genus *Xema*, are Sabine's gull and the tern-like Little gull. Two other gulls, strikingly different in appearance from these, are placed in separate genera: Ross's gull breeds almost

exclusively in northeast Siberia and is unique in having rosy-pink plumage on the hood and underparts, as well as a black collar instead of a complete hood; also confined to the high Arctic is the Ivory gull, resplendent in its all-over pure white plumage.

Although the gulls enjoy a worldwide distribution, the largest concentrations occur in the Northern Hemisphere, where they have succeeded in colonizing the harshest of marine environments. The Ivory gull, for example, breeds in the presence of pack ice and snow where none but the hardiest vegetation survives. Although gulls are well represented in temperate and subtemperate latitudes, they are more sparsely distributed in the tropics; this has been attributed to a relative lack of shore food. Although most gulls live on or near the coast throughout much of the year, others live deep in the heart of the continents. The Great black-headed gull and the rare Relict gull thus breed on islands in the inland seas and lakes of the central Asian steppes, many hundreds of kilometers from the nearest ocean.

At the end of the breeding season, when adherence to a colony on land is no longer required, many gulls disperse into offshore waters and some, like the kittiwake, then lead a truly open-sea (pelagic) existence, British-bred birds journeying as far as the coasts of Canada. While there may be a strong random element in such dispersal, birds often congregate at food-rich cold-water upwellings at the edge of continental shelves. Compared with the terns and skuas, however, rather few gull species are true migrants. A notable exception is Sabine's gull, which has a circumpolar breeding distribution but at the end of summer migrates

◄▲► **Representative species of gulls.**
(1) Great black-backed gull (*Larus marinus*), largest of all gulls, in first-winter plumage, scavenging on a dead razorbill. (2) Kittiwake or Black-legged kittiwake juvenile (*Rissa tridactyla*). (3) Ivory gull (*Pagophila eburnea*) in first-winter plumage. (4) Little gull (*Larus minutus*) juvenile, world's smallest gull. (5) Sabine's gull (*L. sabini*) on nest. (6) Ross's gull (*Rhodostethia rosea*). (7) Swallow-tailed gull (*Creagrus furcatus*) of the Galapagos and La Plata Islands (Ecuador), said by some to be world's most beautiful gull.

Current off Namibia and South Africa. Gales in the fall not uncommonly blow Sabine's gulls towards the British coast, where enthusiastic bird-watchers delight in identifying these rare and elegant visitors. Some species regularly migrate overland, like Franklin's gull, which passes in the spring and fall over the Great Plains of North America.

Outside the breeding season, gulls typically continue to be highly gregarious, often assembling in massive flocks for feeding, roosting and bathing. The favored roosting sites are extensive open areas that offer a good all-round view for early detection of ground predators. Gulls often loaf on the flat expanses of airfields, where they can present a serious obstacle to low-flying aircraft.

All gulls can store substantial quantities of food in their crops, from which they regurgitate when feeding mates or young. Birds usually settle at their night roosts with full crops, and leisurely digestion follows. Indigestible parts of the meal are periodically disgorged in the form of pellets. Analysis of these gives a good idea of the diet.

Gulls have a range of feeding habits unparalleled in almost any other group of birds. In the Arctic, for example, where there is a limited variety of prey, Glaucous and Ivory gulls regularly eat the feces of marine mammals, and also associate with whales to exploit the invertebrates they force to the surface. Swallow-tailed gulls are exceptional among gulls in feeding entirely at night, their large eyes apparently helping them to detect and capture fish or squid. In temperate latitudes, the flexibility and ingenuity of foraging habits is just as striking. Herring gulls and their kin smash open shellfish by carrying them to a height and dropping them onto the rocks below.

Many Herring gulls have, during the course of this century, cashed in on the abundance of food offal on garbage dumps, and in consequence have increased remarkably in numbers during recent years. Gulls which breed inland also enjoy a wide variety of natural foodstuffs, the smaller species such as Little and Franklin's gulls dipping tern-like to pluck insects as small as midges from the water or land. Many species follow the plow for earthworms and other soil creatures. The Lesser black-backed gull, which is essentially a fish-eating species, in some places includes large numbers of mammals that share their breeding stations. The Glaucous gull is an important predator of Little auks, while the Great black-backed gull plunders a wide variety of seabirds, notably puffins, and can dispatch a good-sized rabbit. Gulls have also learned, skua-like, to harry other seabirds, forcing them to disgorge their food; terns which share colony space with, for example, Black-headed or Silver gulls, regularly suffer from such piracy. Sometimes gulls shadow foraging ducks, cormorants or pelicans, and rob them as soon as they surface with prey. In the same way, Black-headed and Common gulls are frequently found in fields among flocks of lapwings, which are greatly superior in the art of locating and extracting earthworms; the gulls are quick to pounce on a successful lapwing to relieve it of its worm. In Australia, the Silver gull has begun to forage on plowed fields far inland, repeating a pattern found in other parts of the world where man has developed arable farming on a significant scale.

In most regions, gulls breed once a year during a well-defined season that corresponds with the summer flush of food in the environment. In the tropics, where the food supply is less seasonal, more complex patterns may occur. The Swallow-tailed gull, for example, is known to breed in every month of the year; pairs that raise young successfully will mount another breeding attempt 9–10 months later, unsuccessful

▲ **A Dolphin gull** (*Larus scoresbii*) feeds on mussels on the shores of the Falkland Islands.

▶ **Loud and clear,** the call of the abundant Herring gull can be heard along the coasts, in the harbors, and on the garbage dumps, lakes and rivers of North America and Eurasia and into North Africa and Arabia. Its large gape enables it to swallow surprisingly large prey such as mackerel and herring.

"Nature" *and* "Nurture" Set Species Apart

The Herring gull and the Lesser black-backed gull are two distinct species: they are dissimilar and they do not normally interbreed when they occur together. However, the two do illustrate how closely related species may be induced to interbreed if the recogniton barriers which separate them are broken down.

During the ice ages of the Pleistocene epoch, 2 million to 10,000 years ago, the ancestors of today's Herring gull diversified, as a result of being isolated into a number of refuges separated by extensive ice sheets. A yellow-legged form confined to Central Asia later gave rise to the Lesser black-backed gull, while a pink-legged form spread from northwest Asia via North America to Europe, where it came into contact with Lesser black-backed gulls. By this time, however, the Herring gull had diverged in ecology and behavior to such an extent that the two did not readily interbreed.

Today, Lesser black-backed gulls differ from Herring gulls in Britain not only in appearance but also in being more migratory, and, to a lesser extent, in diet. How influential is nature as opposed to nurture in maintaining these differences and keeping the species distinct? In an experiment designed to explore this question, eggs in a mixed colony were interchanged between nests of the two species. On hatching, the resulting Herring gull chicks were raised by Lesser black-backed parents, and vice versa. There was not much change in the migratory tendencies of the cross-fostered gulls. However, their breeding habits were markedly affected. On reaching adulthood, many of the fostered young, especially females, mated up with a member of the "wrong" species, and successfully raised hybrid young. Thus the isolating mechanisms between the two species may fail if the young of each are brought up to "think" that they belong to the other species.   EKD

Gulls are generally monogamous and usually pair for as long as both members survive. However, in species such as the kittiwake, divorce is not uncommon, especially among inexperienced birds, and individuals will seek a new mate if the existing pair-bond proves unfruitful. As the breeding season approaches, gulls typically assemble in large, dense colonies, frequently reclaiming their nest site of the previous year. Many species breed on cliff ledges or atop coastal islands, while inland species often seek the safety of a marsh. Common gulls may build their nests on the stump or fork of a tree up to 10m (33ft) above the ground, also not uncommonly on stone walls and buildings. In keeping with their growing use of man's domain, Herring gulls are also favoring rooftops, chimney stacks, etc. The kittiwake, a gull of the open seas for much of the year, also sometimes adopts a window ledge as a substitute for its usual cliff-nesting habitat. The Gray gull breeds in one of the most inhospitable habitats chosen by any bird—the hot, arid deserts of Peru and Chile, while Ivory gulls sometimes nest on stony patches on ice floes.

The density of nesting depends partly on the local food supply. In temperate regions, where fish stocks are high in summer, many gull species breed in huge colonies, siting their nests only a meter or so from one another, and defending a territory little larger than the nest itself. Such gulls are notably successful in ousting smaller competitors from their nesting space, and populations on the increase often completely expel less competitive seabirds from

abandon the island as a breeding site. Where the food supply is less plentiful, gulls may nest much more sparsely. In an extreme case, Lava gulls, which number about 300–400 pairs and occur only on the Galapagos Islands, typically nest over 3km (1.9mi) from each other.

In species which nest densely, there is much rivalry as the pairs stake out territories at the start of the breeding season; males are the main aggressors, but the females also join in. Gulls command an impressive repertoire of aggressive and appeasement displays and calls during these contests. Although prolonged fights sometimes take place, most of this behavior is ritualized and injuries are avoided. Black-headed gulls, for example, regularly avert their heads ("head-flagging") when squaring up to one another, so hiding the provocative black mask and bill. Rival Herring gull males may symbolically tug and tear at the vegetation along a contested territorial boundary, then each may claim victory by throwing their heads back and "long-calling" vociferously, before resuming hostilities. Such shows of strength also attract females, which typically approach bachelor males tentatively in a submissive cowed posture. Once accepted by the male, the female is fed by the male as a prelude to egg-laying.

The clutch is typically 2–3; the tropical Swallow-tailed gull is unique in laying only one egg. Both sexes share incubation, changing over several times each day until the eggs hatch, usually after about four weeks. The emerging young are mobile as

soon as their down dries, but remain in or near the nest for a week or so where their parents can brood and tend them closely. When small, they seek for food by pecking at the parent's bill; in some species a brightly colored spot near the parent's bill-tip serves as a target and stimulus for this begging action. Once liberated from the need for brooding, the young may seek refuge in vegetation, etc near the nest. If they trespass onto neighboring territories they are often fiercely attacked by the owners. Injury and even death may result.

In the larger gulls, some adults specialize in killing the young of other broods and feeding them to their own offspring. At one Herring gull colony it was observed that almost a quarter of all hatchlings were cannibalized in this way and many eggs were also pirated. In species which lay three eggs, the last laid egg is typically the smallest. Gull clutches hatch over a few days, so that the last chick has to compete with larger siblings. This third "runt" chick is therefore prone to succumb if food is short, and more likely to fall victim to adult cannibals. Occasionally, a cannibal Herring gull has difficulty in distinguishing the instinct to nurture its own offspring from the urge to kill and eat the young of other pairs. One such adult ate over 40 chicks while sharing incubation of its own clutch. When its own brood hatched, it continued to bring live chicks to its nest site, but failed to kill them. Over a week, it added eight live healthy young to its own brood. The task of raising this extended family proved insurmountable in the end, but one of the adopted young was successfully raised to fledging.

By the time the young leave the nest at 3–7 weeks (depending on species), they are fully feathered, but in a mottled brown garb quite different from their parents. This dress is lost by degrees, until breeding age is reached. The parents usually continue to feed their offspring for some time after fledging, up until $1\frac{1}{2}$ months afterwards in some of the larger gulls.

Like other seabirds, gulls that survive the rigors of juvenile life can, on average, look forward to a relatively long life. Ringing studies show that Black-headed gulls and Herring gulls can live over 30 years. Presumably because breeding is a hazardous venture, requiring considerable experience, gulls generally do not breed until they are several years old—two years in Little and Black-headed gulls, usually five in Herring and Lesser black-backed gulls. When they approach breeding age, some birds may return to the colony where they coastal waters. Size: 25–78cm (10–30in) long and 90g–2kg (3oz–4.4lb); males somewhat larger than females. Plumage: chiefly white, gray and black in adult, streaked or mottled brown when immature. Sexes similar. Voice: wide repertoire includes ringing, laughing sounds, yelping, mewing, and whining notes. Nests: typically a cup of vegetation, seaweed, etc, sometimes substantial, often on a cliff ledge or on the ground, some on marshes, bushes or trees. Eggs: usually 2–3, olive, brownish or greenish, heavily mottled; weight ranges from 19g (0.7oz) in the Little gull to 117g (4.1oz) in the Great black-backed gull; incubation 3–5 weeks; young fledge after 3–7 weeks. Diet: fish, crustaceans, mollusks, worms and, in smaller species, insects; also vegetable food, refuse and carrion, some preying on birds and mammals.

Species include, in arctic latitudes: **Glaucous gull** (*Larus hyperboreus*), **Iceland gull** (*L. glaucoides*), **Ivory gull** (*Pagophila eburnea*), **Ross's gull** (*Rhodostethia rosea*), **Sabine's gull** (*L. sabini*); in temperate latitudes: **Black-headed gull** (*L. ridibundus*), **Bonaparte's gull** (*L. philadelphia*), **Common** or **Mew gull** (*L. canus*), **Franklin's gull** (*L. pipixcan*), **Great black-backed gull** (*L. marinus*), **Great black-headed gull** (*L. ichthyaetus*), **Herring gull** (*L. argentatus*), **kittiwake** or **Black-legged kittiwake** (*Rissa tridactyla*), **Laughing gull** (*L. atricilla*), **Lesser black-backed gull** (*L. fuscus*), **Little gull** (*L. minutus*), **Relict gull** R (*L. relictus*), **Ring-billed gull** (*L. delawarensis*), **Western gull** (*L. occidentalis*); in Mediterranean latitudes: **Audouin's gull** R (*L. audouinii*), **Mediterranean gull** (*L. melanocephalus*), **Slender-billed gull** (*L. genei*); in comparable, or warmer, climate, S Hemisphere: **Gray gull** (*L. modestus*), **Silver** or **Hartlaub's gull** (*L. novaehollandiae*); in the tropics: **Gray-headed gull** (*L. cirrocephalus*), **Lava gull** (*L. fuliginosus*), **Sooty gull** (*L. hemprichii*), **Swallow-tailed gull** (*Creagrus furcatus*), **White-eyed gull** (*L. leucophthalmus*).

Terns

Family: Sternidae
Forty-one species in 7 genera.

Worldwide. Chiefly coastal and offshore waters, some up rivers and in marshes. Size: 20–56cm (8–22in) long and 50–700g (1.8oz–1.5lb), males somewhat larger than females. Plumage: chiefly white, gray and black. Voice: most varied repertoire from shrill to hoarse, penetrating calls

to soft crooning notes. Nests: usually a simple scrape, occasionally well lined; some make floating rafts (marsh terns); others in trees and on cliff ledges (White tern and noddies), in holes in cliffs (Inca tern), sometimes under boulders or down burrows. Eggs: 1–3, pale cream to brown or greenish, with darker blotches; most weigh about 20g (0.7oz), but range 10g (Little tern) to 65g (Caspian tern) (0.4–2.3oz); incubation 18–30 days; fledging mostly at 1–2 months. Diet: chiefly fish, squid and crustaceans; in marsh terns insects, amphibians and leeches.

Species include, in temperate latitudes: **Aleutian tern** (*Sterna aleutica*), **Arctic tern** (*S. paradisaea*), **Black tern** (*Chlidonias nigra*), **Caspian tern** (*Sterna caspia*), **Common tern** (*S. hirundo*), **Gull-billed tern** (*S. nilotica*), **Little** or **Least tern** (*S. albifrons*), **Roseate tern** (*S. dougallii*), **Sandwich tern** (*S. sandvicensis*), **Whiskered tern** (*Chlidonias hybrida*), **White-winged black tern** (*C. leucoptera*); in the tropics: **Black noddy** (*Anous tenuirostris*), **Bridled tern** (*Sterna anaethetus*), **Brown noddy** (*Anous stolidus*), **Damara tern** R (*Sterna balaenarum*), **Inca tern** (*Larosterna inca*), **Sooty tern** (*Sterna fuscata*), **White tern** (*Gygis alba*). Total threatened species: 2.

Skuas or jaegers

Family: Stercorariidae
Six species in 2 genera.

Large skuas
Three species of the genus *Catharacta*. Antarctic, sub-Antarctic, southern S

America, Iceland, Faroes, N Britain. Coastal heaths. Size: 1.1–1.9kg (2.4–4.2lb); females slightly larger than males. Plumage: brown, with white wing flashes. Elongated central tail feathers in adults. Voice: limited range of yelps. Nests: scraped depression on ground. Eggs: normally 2; olive with brown blotches; weight 70–110g (2.5–3.9oz); incubation 30 days; nestling period 45–55 days. Diet: catholic, particularly fish, krill, seabird eggs and chicks, adult seabirds.

Species: **Great skua** (*Catharacta skua*), **South polar skua** (*C. maccormicki*), **Chilean skua** (*C. chilensis*).

Small skuas or jaegers
Three species of the genus *Stercorarius*. Arctic and boreal regions. Tundra and coastal heaths. Size: 250–800g (8.8oz–1.8lb); females slightly larger than males. Plumage: dimorphic; all brown, or brown above and creamy white below. Voice: mewing cries. Nests: scrape on ground. Eggs: normally 2; olive with brown blotches; incubation 23–27 days; nestling period 24–32 days. Diet: small mammals, insects, berries, birds, eggs, fish (often stolen from other seabirds).

Species: **Parasitic jaeger** or **Arctic skua** (*Stercorarius parasiticus*), **Long-tailed jaeger** or **skua** (*S. longicaudus*), **Pomarine jaeger** or **skua** (*S. pomarinus*).

◀▶ **Terns.** (1) Blue-gray noddy (*Procelsterna cerulea*). (2) Lesser noddy (*Anous tenuirostris*). (3) White tern (*Gygis alba*). (4) Inca tern (*Larosterna inca*). (5) Arctic tern (*Sterna paradisaea*). (6) Large-billed tern (*Phaetusa simplex*). (7) Black tern (*Chlidonias nigra*) juvenile. (8) Sooty tern (*Sterna fuscata*). (9) Caspian terns (*S. caspia*) adult and RIGHT first-winter plumage.

Skimmers

Family: Rynchopidae
Three species of the genus *Rynchops*.

Tropical Africa, S Asia, southeastern N, C, and S America. Major river systems and ocean coasts. Size: length 35–45cm (14–18in); to 400g (14.1oz) (males), about 300g (10.6oz) (females); Plumage: chiefly black or dark brown above, white or light gray below; sexes similar. Voice: simple barks (Black skimmer) or shrill, chattering calls (others). Nests: simple scrape in sand or on shell bank. Eggs: usually 3–4 (range 2–5), whitish or beige with dark brown or black blotches and irregular spots; about 4 × 3cm (1.6 × 1.2in); incubation 22–24 days; nestling period 25–30 days. Diet: primarily small fish, also small invertebrates such as shrimps, prawns, and other small crustaceans.

Species: **African skimmer** (*Rynchops flavirostris*), **Black skimmer** (*R. niger*), **Indian skimmer** (*R. albicollis*).

other colonies, a dispersal that probably helps to mitigate the possible adverse effects of inbreeding.

Many, but not all, gull species have probably never been as numerous as they are now, given the new food supplies made available by man. Foremost among scarce gulls is the Relict gull, of which no more than 1,500–1,800 pairs are known from Lake Alakul and Lake Barun-Torey deep in the interior of the USSR.   EKD

Terns are among the most graceful and appealing inhabitants of shorelines and marshes. Many are familiar summer visitors to north temperate coasts, catching the eye with their winnowing flight and spectacular plunge-diving for fish. Some, like the massive Caspian tern, show the close kinship of terns with the gulls (p188), while the resemblance of other members to the skimmers (p202) is also evident.

Most terns (22 species) belong to the "black-capped" group of species of *Sterna*. These sea terns or "sea swallows" have a slender form, long tapering wings, a deeply forked tail, and are agile in flight. The typical plumage pattern is white below and gray above, with a black crown which in some species is crested. Juveniles are often mottled brown, especially on the back, and may take 2–3 years to assume adult appearance. In the marsh terns (three species of *Chlidonias*) and noddies (three species of *Anous*), the plumage is generally darker or even black. Conspicuously different is the slate-blue Inca tern, with its yellow gape wattles and white moustache. Among the terns, the bill—often bright yellow, red, or black—varies in shape from pincer- to dagger-like, depending partly on the size of the prey taken. The flight, though buoyant, is strong, often allowing a sustained hover. Although the feet are webbed, most terns seldom settle on water for long.

The terns are to be found worldwide, extending to all but the highest, ice-fast latitudes. Habitat preference divides the species broadly into two groups, sea terns and marsh terns. Some sea terns, such as the Roseate tern and Caspian tern, are among the most cosmopolitan of all birds. While the majority prefer warm tropical and subtropical waters, others favor colder latitudes for breeding, and the sea terns thus range from the Arctic to the Antarctic. By contrast, the marsh terns have adopted a largely inland

rich waters of higher latitudes to breed, and resorting to tropical climes for the winter. The Arctic tern undertakes possibly the longest migration of any bird species. Many breed north of the Arctic Circle and move south to the Antarctic for the northern winter, an each-way journey of some 15,000km (9,300mi) "as the crow flies." By doing so, they exploit the long daylight for prolonged feeding time in both hemispheres. The ringing of terns and plotting their movements has done much to unravel the routes taken; many Canadian Arctic terns, for instance, cross the Atlantic on westerlies to the European coast on their way south. While most travel by sea, feeding as they go, overland routes are not uncommon, and many marsh terns, for example, cross the Sahara *en route* from their breeding grounds to their African winter quarters.

The sea terns are primarily fish-eaters, though squid and crustaceans are also relished. The black-capped terns are bold plungers, spotting their prey as they hover into the wind, before diving headlong (see box). In general, the bigger the tern, the higher and deeper it dives; the Caspian tern may plunge from 15m (50ft). Unlike gannets (p38), terns do not swim underwater, and prey is seized near the surface. Noddies typically dip to the surface and may use their feet for pattering like storm petrels (p33). They often catch flying fish in mid-air. Noddies and some other tropical terns range far

▲ The only tern with all-white plumage, the White tern ranges widely throughout the tropical and subtropical oceans. It lays its single egg directly on a tree branch.

◄ Elaborate courtship of terns. (1) Female Arctic tern pursues male upward in "high flight." (2) Male Sandwich tern feeding his mate. (3) Common terns mating. (4) Erect or "pole" stance of Sandwich tern pair, seen after copulation and also after high-flight.

Apprentice Plunge-divers

Plunge-diving for fish is the hallmark of many terns. A typical plunge-diver in European waters is the Sandwich tern. The bird flies upwind, usually 5–6m (16–20ft) above the surface, and, on spying its prey just below the surface, hovers briefly before diving headlong into the water. The prey is seized in the vice-like grip of the bill, just behind the gills, and quickly eaten. When young are being fed, the fish is held cross-wise in the bill and carried back to the colony.

As a technique for obtaining food, plunge-diving is remarkably successful. An adult tern often secures a fish in one dive out of three. But it is a difficult technique and many factors can make the task more so. Fishing success is greatly reduced in strong winds, partly because the shoaling prey, often sprats or sand eels, sink deeper to avoid the turbulent wave action. Very calm seas also appear to pose problems, possibly because the fish can see the tern overhead and take evasive action.

It is also possible that in calm conditions the fish can sense the tern's splash on entry just soon enough to veer off.

The young Sandwich tern not only has to learn the best places to fish, but also needs to develop skills over time. Its first efforts are often shallow, unrewarded belly flops, but it gains practice by picking up bits of seaweed and other flotsam. Faced with the additional hazards of migrating south, the young bird continues to be fed by its parents for perhaps 3–4 months after fledging. Meanwhile, it gradually learns to dive from greater heights, and gains access to prey at greater depths, down to a maximum of about 1m (3.3ft) below the surface. However, even at 7–9 months old, in their West African winter quarters, some juveniles are still noticeably less adept than their parents at catching fish.

This long apprenticeship probably helps to explain why most young Sandwich terns stay in the winter quarters for two years.   EKD

at night. The dainty marsh terns are well adapted for hawking insects or hovering to pluck them off vegetation. They also make shallow plunges for frogs and other aquatic animals. The Gull-billed tern is the most terrestrial of all, and swoops to seize large insects, lizards, and even small rodents from the ground. The rate of feeding visits to the young varies according to the distance the parents must travel to hunt. While a marsh tern may feed its young every few minutes, the Sooty tern, which ranges hundreds of kilometers to forage, may only deliver a meal once a day.

In common with many other seabirds, most terns are long-lived, if they survive to adulthood. Arctic terns have been shown by ringing to live 33 years or more, and a life span of 20 years is probably not unusual. Breeding may begin as early as two years, but more often at three or four in temperate breeding species, generally later in tropical species. Most Sooty terns, for example, do not reach sexual maturity until at least six years old.

In higher latitudes, terns usually have a well-defined breeding season once a year, in Europe from about May to July. In the tropics, breeding is generally not synchronized to a particular time of year. In a few populations, however, terns breed both at intervals of less than a year and synchronously. On Cousin Island in the Indian Ocean, Bridled terns breed every $7\frac{1}{2}$ months, while the highly adaptable Sooty tern breeds, depending on location, at intervals varying from six to 12 months; in some cases it seems likely that food is more or less equally abundant at all times of year.

Terns generally pair for life. Even though the pair bond breaks down outside the breeding season, there is a strong tendency to return to a previously successful breeding site, which enables former mates to rendezvous at the start of each new breeding season. Courtship is an elaborate ritual, especially in birds seeking a mate for the first time. In many terns, the first stage of pairing is the "high flight," in which the male ascends at speed, as if to demonstrate his prowess, to often several hundred meters, while the female pursues him. At the end of the climb the prospective pair glide and zigzag earthwards. With growing familiarity, the male increasingly courtship-feeds his mate; this has more than just symbolic value—it helps the female to form eggs

etting with raised tail and drooped wings. This is usually the prelude to copulation.

Most terns breed in bustling colonies, often at high density. They also roost *en masse* and may join together to mob predators at the colony. The colony site is usually on flat open ground, often on an island or reef. Noddies, however, crowd on trees, bushes and cliff ledges, while Inca terns seek crevices in rock. The White tern is celebrated for building no nest, opting to lay its single egg directly on to, usually, the branch of a tree. Most ground nesters are scarcely more constructive, merely fashioning a shallow scrape, at the best thinly lined. Noddies and marsh terns, however, build a more substantial platform of vegetation, the latter anchoring a raft of reeds, etc to submerged plants. Both sexes defend the nest territory, often only a square meter or so in extent, while the "crested" terns, which nest most densely of all, may be within jabbing distance of neighbors.

▷ **Pirates' shoreline squabble** OVERLEAF. The Great skua will harass other birds, forcing them to disgorge their food, which it eats, or occasionally killing and eating them. These birds, photographed on the Auckland Islands south of New Zealand, belong to the sub-Antarctic population.

▼▶ **Skuas and jaegers.** (1) Great skua (*Catharacta skua*) long-calling. (2) Pomarine skua or jaeger (*Stercorarius pomarinus*) in adult breeding (pale) plumage. (3) Arctic skua (*S. parasiticus*) in adult breeding (pale) plumage, harrying Atlantic puffins.

The normal clutch varies from one egg in tropical species to 2–3 in higher latitudes; incubation, shared by the sexes, lasts 3–4 weeks. On hatching, the downy chicks are soon actively exploring their surroundings, but seldom stray far unless disturbed. Then they take refuge in vegetation, or under stones, driftwood and the like, while the well-grown young of "crested" terns may seek safety in numbers, forming a mobile crèche. Parents returning with food recognize their own young in the crèche by voice, and feed only them. After the young fledge, they have much to learn about catching prey for themselves (see p 197) and are fed by their parents for some time, before gradually being weaned off.

The isolation sought by terns for breeding purposes is an increasingly scarce resource as man turns more to the coast and sea for leisure, commercial fishing, and other activities. Pressure on land use in South Africa has reduced the Damara tern to a precarious 1,500 pairs, while snaring for food and sport in its West African winter quarters is believed to have contributed to the decline of the European Roseate tern to around 1,000 pairs. By contrast, many populations continue to flourish in remoter regions, and on Pacific Christmas Island alone, the Sooty tern is numbered in millions.   EKD

During their breeding season, **skuas and jaegers** are the pirates and predators of the skies in high latitudes. They have been seen closer to the South Pole than any other vertebrate apart from man. One individual ringed as a chick at Anvers Island, Antarctica, was shot five months later in Godthabsfjord, Greenland—the longest journey of any bird ever recorded by ringing. Skuas will harry other seabirds until they disgorge their last meal, which they then catch in mid air. In North America and elsewhere the small skuas are called "jaegers," after the German word meaning hunter. The Great skua has been seen to kill prey many times heavier than itself, such as the Gray heron, Graylag goose, shelduck and Mountain hare.

Outside the breeding season, skuas migrate over all the world's oceans, the jaegers also traveling in some numbers directly overland. Records of Arctic skuas in Austria and Switzerland in the fall are not uncommon. The large species, on the other hand, tend to remain some distance offshore, but a few storm-tossed young Great skuas have been picked up, exhausted, in central Europe. One, ringed as a chick in Shetland, was rescued from the central reservation of ably evolved from, the gulls, which clearly originated in the Northern Hemisphere. However, early in the evolution of the skuas, one form must have colonized the Antarctic, where it has given rise to the three very similar large skua species. The small populations of the Great skua in the North Atlantic are almost certainly recently derived from birds blown north from the South Atlantic, as measurement and plumage of the two subspecies are very similar. The Great skua is thus unique among seabirds in that it breeds in both the sub-Antarctic and the Northern Hemisphere.

The three species of large skua are generally brown. The Chilean skua has conspicuous rufous underwing feathers, while the South polar skua has both dark and light phases (dimorphic plumage)—light-phase birds increase in frequency towards the Pole. It is not known why skuas should benefit from having plumage that is paler on the upperparts in regions with more snow and ice.

All three jaegers display two color phases. The dark phase is extremely rare in the Long-tailed jaeger. In the Arctic and Pomarine jaegers the proportions of birds of each phase within the population vary geographically. In Shetland less than 25 percent of Arctic jaegers are light; the proportion tends to increase northwards, with nearly 100 percent light in Spitzbergen and arctic Canada. The elongation of the two central tail feathers, characteristic of adult skuas, is prominent in the Arctic jaeger and extreme in the Long-tailed jaeger. The Pomarine jaeger has twisted club-shaped central tail feathers. All juvenile jaegers are barred below.

The skuas have feet that are gull-like, but with prominent sharp claws. The bill is hard and strongly hooked at the tip, adapted for tearing flesh. In gulls, as in many other bird families, males are slightly larger than females, but the opposite is true for skuas, as for birds of prey. In both these groups the male does most of the hunting and the female remains in the territory to guard the nest or young.

Skuas take many types of food. Pomarine jaegers feed largely on lemmings in summer and on small seabirds in winter, less regularly by fishing or by harassing other birds (piracy). Long-tailed jaegers feed on lemmings, insects, berries, small birds and eggs in summer and by piracy, chiefly by

coastal areas they feed almost exclusively by piracy of terns, kittiwakes and auks.

Skuas are normally monogamous and pair for life. In New Zealand and on Marion Island, Great skua trios comprising one female and two males occur regularly, a social system not yet found in any other skua. Distances between skua nests vary enormously, from often 2km (1.2mi) apart on arctic tundra, down to just 5–10m (16–33ft) within the largest Great skua colonies in Shetland. On Foula, Shetland, 306 pairs of Arctic jaegers breed in a colony occupying 1.7sq km (0.7sq mi), approximately the area defended by a single pair breeding on arctic tundra. Part of the explanation for this difference is that skuas nesting in Shetland do not obtain food within their territory, but feed at sea. Skuas defend their nests by dive-bombing intruders, including humans. Jaegers have a "broken wing" distraction display.

Skuas have only two brood patches, and birds with three eggs usually fail to hatch any. Most pairs with two eggs manage to hatch both, but if food is short, the older chick, which hatches 1–3 days before the second, will attack and kill its smaller sibling. In Shetland, Arctic jaegers begin breeding when 3–6 years old, while Great skuas first breed when between five and 10 years old. Presumably this long period of immaturity helps the skua to learn the many skills needed to be an effective hunter and parasite of other seabirds.   RWF

Skimmers are among our better-named birds, for they skim the surface of lakes, rivers and lagoons, deftly snapping up fish with their uniquely adapted bills. They crowd by the hundreds into nesting colonies on sand bars, where the contrast between their brilliant bills and legs, and their stark plumage, make them a prized "target" of wildlife photographers and artists.

Even though the skimmer family is represented by only three species in the world, it is widely distributed. Three subspecies (or races) of the Black skimmer are found in the New World: the North American subspecies inhabits the ocean coasts and the Salton Sea in the western USA. The two South American subspecies are almost exclusively riverine, using coastal areas out of the breeding season. African skimmers are most abundant in East and Central Africa on the larger river systems. Indian skimmers range from Pakistan across India to the Malay

black toward the tip) and vermilion legs and feet in the breeding season (duller at other times), while the African skimmer has yellow legs and feet and a yellow-orange bill. The young of all species are lighter brown above and less white below, and the tail is mottled, unlike the mostly white tail of the adults. The wings are very long, with a span $2\frac{1}{2}$ times the length of the bird.

But the most striking feature in all species is the large, scissor-like bill with its flattened "blades," the upper mandible fitting into a notch between the edges of the lower mandible, which is $\frac{1}{4}-\frac{1}{3}$ as long again as the upper. It was once thought that the lower mandible had great touch sensitivity, but recently this has been found not to be the case. When feeding, skimmers hold the bill open in such a position that the tip of the lower mandible slices the water. When the lower mandible touches a prey item, usually a small fish, the head flexes downward rapidly, trapping the prey sideways between the "scissors" (hence the popular name "scissorbill"). The musculature of the head and neck is well developed and acts as a shock absorber. Skimmers often feed at dusk and throughout the night, especially in the non-breeding season. The skimmer eye has a vertical pupil, much like that of a cat, which may enhance its light-gathering properties. Skimmers prefer to feed in waters with little surface turbulence, such as lakes, pools, marsh and river edges. After "cutting a trail" in the water, birds often double back and retrace their course. snapping up prey

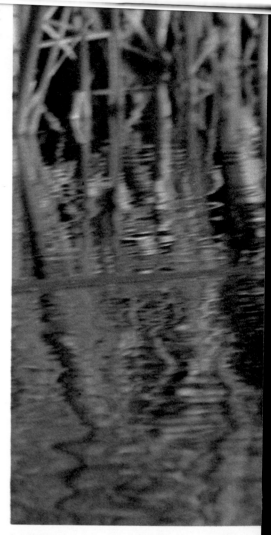

▲ **"Cutting a trail"** a Black skimmer slices the surface with its long lower mandible as it skims shallow water foraging for fish.

◄ **The bill of a skimmer** (again the Black species of the New World). The lower part may be one-third as long again as the upper. Bill and strengthened neck muscles are adaptations for a method of fishing that is without parallel among birds. This is a young bird.

families, only skimmers have a shorebird-like "broken wing" distraction display.

Skimmers are highly social birds in all seasons of the year. When they reach breeding age (probably at 3–4 years), they gather on open, sandy bars and small islands where courtship begins. Vertical flights and aerial chases by courting birds are common at this time. The breeding colonies, established on these sites after a few weeks, range in size from a few pairs up to 1,000 or more. Skimmers often form mixed colonies with terns and they probably benefit from some terns' greater display of aggression in driving off predators.

Skimmers have small nesting territories, with nests spaced 1–4m (3.3–13ft) apart, depending on vegetation and terrain. The degree to which birds nest at the same time (synchrony) can be very high in certain areas in the colony. Aggression is high during the period of territory establishment and egg-laying, and both sexes engage in disputes over space and mates. The males are more aggressive toward other skimmers, while females more frequently interact with other species nesting nearby. Males incubate and brood more than females, at least during the day. Males and females switch incubation duties frequently, especially in the hottest part of the day. Foot and belly-wetting by adults helps to regulate the temperature of the incubated egg. After the young hatch, the females feed the young more than the males do. Parents feed the young beyond the four-week nestling period, and the fledged young accompany adults on feeding forays, perhaps learning where and how to fish.

The nesting period at a skimmer colony is often considerably longer than that of most of their gull and tern relatives—along the eastern USA the Black skimmer may nest from May to October. After the nesting season, skimmers gather in loose flocks at certain "staging areas." They follow major river systems and coastal routes when migrating to distant wintering areas. Some populations of skimmers are non-migratory.

Skimmers are not presently considered threatened. However, damming of rivers in India, Africa and South America continues to reduce the nesting habitat. This, coupled with destruction of tropical forest, diminishes water quality and productivity which, in turn, affects skimmers' diet. In North America, many coastal habitats have been disturbed, forcing Black skimmers (and other species) to nest on small saltmarsh islands and even roofs of buildings in some areas. **RME**

in their wake. They usually feed alone or in pairs, but on occasion groups of 10–15 birds may engage in brief bouts of intense feeding in a particular spot. In coastal areas, feeding increases at low or ebbing tides.

Male Black skimmers are much larger than females. Measurements of wing-span, bill, tail, and weight show males ranging from about 10 percent (wing, tail) to 25 percent (weight, bill length) larger than females. Such dimorphism is not confirmed for African and Indian skimmers.

Skimmers used to be considered more closely related to terns than gulls—unlike gulls, neither skimmers nor terns use their wings during aggressive encounters. However, further analysis of breeding behavior suggests that the skimmers split from the ancestral stock before the divergence between terns and gulls. Of the three

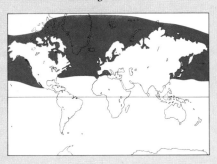

Distribution: N Pacific, N Atlantic and Arctic oceans and coastal regions.

Habitat: breeding, mainly along coasts on islands and headlands; non-breeding, mainly in coastal waters.

Size: from 16cm (6.5in) long and 90g (3.2oz) in the Least auklet to 45cm (18in) long and 1kg (2.2lb) in the Common guillemot (extinct Great auk up to 5–8kg/11–17.6lb); males of most species only slightly larger than females.

Plumage: most species dark above, pale below; some have colored (red, yellow) bill or feet.

Voice: growls and yelps; some species almost silent.

Nests: breed on open ledges (no nest), in crevices or burrows, with very simple nest; Marbled murrelet on large branches of conifers.

Eggs: 1–2; 16–110g (0.7–3.9oz); pear-shaped and variable in color and markings (razorbills and guillemots) to ovoid and plain; incubation 29–42 days; chick stays at nest site for very variable period, 2–50 days.

Diet: fish or crustaceans caught by diving from the surface.

Species include: **Ancient murrelet** (*Synthliboramphus antiquus*), **Atlantic** or **common puffin** or **puffin** (*Fratercula arctica*), **Black guillemot** or **tystie** (*Cepphus grylle*), **Cassin's auklet** (*Ptychoramphus aleuticus*), **Common murre** or **guillemot** (*Uria aalge*), **Craveri's murrelet** (*Brachyramphus craveri*), **Great auk** Ex (*Pinguinus impennis*), **Japanese murrelet** (*Synthliboramphus wumizusume*), **Kittlitz's murrelet** (*Brachyramphus brevirostris*), **Least auklet** (*Aethia pusilla*), **Little auk** or **dovekie** (*Plautus alle*), **Marbled murrelet** (*Brachyramphus marmoratus*), **Parakeet auklet** (*Cyclorrhynchus psittacula*), **Pigeon guillemot** (*Cepphus columba*), **razorbill** (*Alca torda*), **Thick-billed murre** or **Brünnich's guillemot** (*Uria lomvia*), **Whiskered auklet** (*Aethia pygmaea*), **Xantus's murrelet** (*Brachyramphus hypoleuca*).

Ex Extinct.

and their eggs for thousands of years, yet it is only in the last 10 years or so that many features of auks' bizarre and varied biology have been discovered. For example, most auks breed in colonies on rocky coasts, but the nest of one species, the Marbled murrelet, occurs up to 30m (100ft) above ground level in the branches of coniferous trees in remote areas up to 10km (6mi) or more inland. Fewer than five nests of this common seabird have been found.

In many respects, the auks are the ecological counterparts of the Southern Hemisphere's penguins—both groups have much

waters. Outside the breeding season, auks may move further south. Some British puffins and razorbills winter as far south as the Mediterranean, and in the Pacific several auks which breed in Alaska winter as far south as California. Auks spend most of their lives at sea, coming ashore only to breed. Eighteen of the 22 species breed in the Pacific, and six in the North Atlantic—the Common and Thick-billed murres are common to both oceans. The large number of species in the Pacific, particularly the Bering Sea, suggests that the family might have originally evolved there.

When Young Auks Leave Home

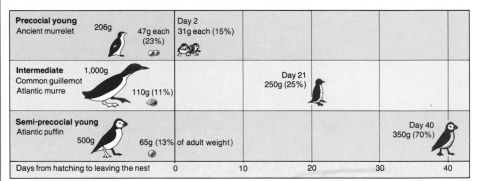

In most bird families, the newly hatched young are either naked and helpless, remaining in the nest for days (nidicolous), as in blackbirds and sparrows, or they may be covered with down, with their eyes open and able to feed themselves (precocial), as in chickens and ducks. The auks are unique in the range of precocity and developmental patterns shown by the young.

Most auks (eg puffins, auklets and Black guillemots) hatch semi-precocial young (down-covered with open eyes, but dependent upon their parents for food), which remain at the nest site for 27–50 days until they have grown to almost full size. They then leave the nest site independently of their parents. (The Little auk may be exceptional among the semi-precocial species, as the chick may be accompanied by its father in the same way as in the murres—see below.)

At the other extreme are four Pacific murrelets (Xantus's, Craveri's, Ancient and Japanese murrelets). They all produce a clutch of two eggs and hatch precocial young which leave the nest site when only two days old and are accompanied by their parents. The eggs of these species are large—even for auks—and the chicks are well-developed on hatching, with feet almost adult size!

The third pattern, shown only by Common murres, Thick-billed murres and the razorbill, is intermediate. Young birds leave the colony after 18–23 days, one-quarter grown and still

flightless. They are cared for by their father, at sea, for several weeks.

The early life-histories have evolved in relation to the amount of food the parents can bring to their chicks. In the species which hatch semi-precocial young, parents can find sufficient food to rear the chick to full size at the breeding site. For the species with precocial young, their plankton food supplies are either difficult for the parents to locate, or a long way from the colony. By taking their young to sea soon after hatching, the parents avoid the energetic expense of commuting between feeding and breeding areas. This also allows them to rear two chicks, rather than one as in most other auks. The intermediate pattern is a compromise between the other two.

It may be that the evolution of truly precocial young has not been possible in murres and the razorbill because of the size of the eggs of these species. Relative egg size in auks (as in other birds) is inversely proportional to body size: large auks produce relatively smaller eggs than small auks. The precocial murrelets are among the smallest auks and produce relatively enormous eggs, from which it is possible for the young to hatch at a sufficiently advanced stage of development to become independent early on. The guillemots and razorbill are the largest auks, and therefore unlikely to lay an egg large enough to produce a precocial chick.

▲ **Bill-full of fish** for the Atlantic puffin's single chick. Specialized spines on the tongue and upper mandible of the bill make it possible to carry up to 50 or more larval fish back cross-wise in the bill to the nest burrow.

The auks feed in both inshore and offshore waters. They are not, however, such lovers of the open oceans as some other seabirds, including shearwaters and petrels. Auks feed by diving and pursuing prey under-water, and all species feed on fish or plank-ton (invertebrates and larval fish). Some species, like the auklets of the Pacific, and the Atlantic Little auk (or dovekie), feed almost entirely on plankton; others, like the Common murre, eat mainly fish.

Auks are small to medium-sized birds with short tails and small wings. Unlike penguins, all auks can fly (though the much larger Great auk couldn't). In fact the size of their wings is a compromise: large enough for flying but small enough to use in the denser medium of water—hence their rapid wingbeats and whirring flight.

The legs of most auks are positioned toward the rear of the body, which accounts for their upright posture. Some species, including the puffins, walk on their toes, as do most birds, but the murres and razorbill walk on their tarsal bones. The legs of auks are slightly compressed laterally, an adap-tation for swimming, although less so than in grebes and shearwaters. The three toes are connected by webs, and in species such as the Atlantic puffin and Black guillemot the legs and feet are bright orange or red. The mouth is also brightly colored in some species, red in the Black guillemot, yellow in the razorbill. The shape of the bill varies

markedly between species, partly reflecting differences in diet and feeding methods. In all auks the bill is relatively short, and in the razorbill and puffins it is laterally compressed. The large, colorful bill of the Atlantic puffin plays an important role in pair formation and courtship. The bill comprises nine distinct plates which are shed each year during the molt. Outside the breeding season, the puffin's bill is much reduced in size and is less brightly colored.

All auks have distinct winter plumages, and in some species the change in appearance between summer and winter can be quite dramatic. The Black and Pigeon guillemots are black with a white wing patch in the summer, but during the winter they are mainly white and gray. The Marbled murrelet and Kittlitz's murrelet have cryptic brown summer plumage, but outside the breeding season are mainly black or gray above and white below. In some of the auklets, such as the Whiskered auklet, long head plumes and "whiskers" are lost during the winter. During the molt, which in most species occurs soon after breeding is over,

Close Neighbors in the Colony

Common murres characteristically breed in bodily contact with their neighbors, at densities greater than any other bird species— up to 70 pairs per sq m (7.5/sq ft) have been recorded! Like several other auks, murres make no nest, but lay their single egg directly onto bare rock. The eggs or chicks of solitary pairs, or of pairs in low-density groups, often fall prey to marauding gulls or crows. The high-density groups present an impenetrable barrier to such predators, and in these colonies most pairs successfully rear young.

However, breeding in large, dense colonies is not without its own problems. Despite such high-density breeding, each pair vigorously defends a tiny territory: the close proximity of neighbors results in almost continuous social interaction.

Common murres have evolved a large repertoire of calls and displays that enable them to live together with some degree of harmony. Sometimes a threat (**1**) is employed to warn off an intruder. Fights, although common, are usually very brief, because they are cut short by one of several appeasement displays. These include: (**2**) side-preening; (**3**)

stretching away or turning away; and (**4**) a ritualized walk when passing other birds in the colony.

With breeding so close together, and in the absence of distinct nests, the chances of the eggs and chicks of different broods becoming mixed up are fairly high. Since it would not be to any bird's advantage to rear an unrelated chick, Common (and Thick-billed) murres have evolved to a marked extent the ability to pick out and retrieve both their egg and their chick. Egg color and markings are extraordinarily variable between individuals

▲ **Common murre (guillemot) with its single egg.** Color and patterning of the eggs are more varied than within perhaps any other bird species, the different base colors (turquoise to white) and markings (red, brown, or black) helping the parent to recognize its own egg.

▷ **Densely packed nests** OVERLEAF of the Common murre or guillemot give protection against gull and crow raiders. Guillemots nest closer to one another than almost any other bird.

◀ **Atlantic or Common puffins** leave their summer nesting colonies to spend the winter on the open seas.

the larger auks are flightless, probably for some 45 days, as the flight feathers are dropped simultaneously. The wing-loadings (ratio of body weight to wing size) of the murres, razorbill and other large species are so high that the sequential loss of feathers (one after another at intervals, as in most birds) would merely preserve a reduced ability to fly that was grossly expensive in terms of energy required. The wing-loading of the smallest species is lower; they can molt their flight feathers one at a time and still retain the ability to fly. The flightless Great auk also molted in this way.

Auks obtain all their food from the sea, by diving from the surface and pursuing prey underwater. Most of what we know about auk diets has been learned from what the chicks are fed while at the colony. It is interesting that in the North Atlantic only one species, the Little auk, feeds almost exclusively on plankton, whereas in the North Pacific there are at least six plankton-feeding auk species, among them the Least auklet, Cassin's auklet and Parakeet auklet. This difference may be due to a greater total biomass and diversity of plankton in the North Pacific. Certainly there are also more individuals and species of plankton-feeding whales in the North Pacific than in the North Atlantic.

Auks are long-lived birds and there are several records of Common murres and Thick-billed murres that were ringed as

adults and found still breeding 20 years later! Like many other seabirds, auks show a number of features associated with great longevity. They characteristically have a low reproductive rate, laying only one or, in some species, two eggs each year. Young birds disperse away from the breeding colony and may spend two or three years at sea before they start breeding activities. The young of most auks do not breed until they are at least three years old. The Atlantic puffin provides a typical example of the sequence of events after the chick leaves the colony. It remains at sea away from the breeding area until its second summer, when it may visit its natal colony for a few weeks. Usually such two-year-old birds spend very little time on land. In its third summer the young puffin will return a little earlier and attempt (probably unsuccessfully) to find a mate and a suitable burrow to breed in. Egg-laying may occur for the first time in the fourth or fifth summer. Although auks generally breed with the same partner each year, the pair does not remain together over the winter. In all auk species, individual pairs use the same site year after year, whether it is a tiny rock ledge (eg Thick-billed murre) or an earth burrow (eg puffins and auklets). One advantage of such nest-site fidelity is that it enables pair members to meet up again each spring.

In ice-free areas, auks may return to their breeding colonies several weeks or months before breeding. This is particularly true of Common murres – at some British colonies, the birds may be present for four or five months before any eggs are laid. Even in more northerly regions, auks may spend several weeks at the colony prior to breeding. This time is spent re-establishing pair bonds, mating and, for puffins and auklets, cleaning out the nesting burrow. Copulation takes place at, or near, the breeding site (razorbills) or, in a few species (puffins), on the sea. Mating is frequent and, in some species, a noisy affair. In Common murres mating may occur 3–4 times a day in the 2–3 weeks prior to egg-laying, and each copulation lasts 20 seconds on average. In most songbirds, by comparison, copulation lasts only 1–2 seconds. Monogamy is the rule in all species, the male and female cooperating to rear the chick(s). Despite the monogamous mating system, male Common murres also attempt to mate with any unattended female in the colony. The arrival of a female can result in a frenzy of mating activity, with up to 10 males simultaneously trying to mount the female. These attempts may sometimes succeed, since the female is

of the same species. If the egg rolls away, as frequently occurs, the adult will retrieve it, ignoring the eggs of its neighbors.

It is just as important for chicks not to get mixed up, and chicks are also individually recognizable—by their voice. Common murre chicks take between one and five days to hatch after making the first hole in the eggshell. During this time the chick and parents call to each other, learning each other's voice. Once hatched, adults and chick can recognize one other; the parents care for and feed only their own chick.

The eggs of auks are relatively large, and constitute between 10 and 23 percent of the female's body weight. Among burrow-nesting auks, the eggs are mainly white with a few darker markings. The eggs of Kittlitz's murrelet and the Marbled murrelet are cryptically colored olive green with dark blotches. These two species nest alone and in the open—Kittlitz's murrelet on the ground in the tundra vegetation or on rocky mountain slopes, and the Marbled murrelet on the ground or, probably more often, on the moss- and lichen-covered branches of large coniferous trees. The eggs of the Common murre and Thick-billed murre are among the most striking of any bird species, being very pointed and ranging in color from bright blue or green to white (see box, pp206–207).

Most auk species, in common with most other seabirds, breed a considerable distance from their food supply, and can only provide enough food for a single chick. However, two-egg clutches do occur, typically in species which either feed close inshore (Black and Pigeon guillemots) or have chicks that are well developed on hatching (see p204). These two eggs are laid several days apart—three days in the Black guillemot and seven days in the Ancient murrelet. Incubation starts when the second egg is laid, so the chicks hatch at about the same time.

The male and female change places on the nest at intervals varying from just a few hours in the Black and Pigeon murres, to 12–24 hours in Common and Thick-billed murres, up to 72 hours in the Ancient murrelet. The duration of these incubation shifts also reflects the time required by the off-duty birds to find food.

In most species which have been studied, breeding success is generally high, with 50–80 percent of pairs successfully rearing young. Failures usually occur because of predation and infertility or, in cliff-nesting species, by eggs rolling off the breeding ledges. The pointed (pyriform) shape of guillemot eggs is commonly thought to prevent eggs from rolling off the breeding ledges. However, experiments have indicated that the shape is more likely to be an adaptation to the semi-upright posture of guillemots as they incubate. The shape maximizes the area of the egg touching the adult's brood patch.

The young of most species are fed by their parents at the colony. Among those species which breed on open ledges, such as the chick at a time. The other parent must remain to brood the chick and protect it from predators such as gulls.

The Little auk feeds its young on crustaceans, such as shrimps, which range in size from 2 to 16mm (0.08–0.6in) in length. As in other plankton-feeding auks, food is carried back to the chick in a throat pouch, as a "plankton soup." Little auks feed their young 5–8 times a day and each meal contains on average 600 items, with a total weight of 3.5g (0.1oz). In contrast, the Common murre feeds its young mainly on fish that school at medium depths, such as capelin, sand eels or sprats. A single fish, weighing 10–15g (0.4–0.5oz) is carried back lengthwise in the bill; the chick is fed 2–5 times a day. The Black and Pigeon guillemots specialize in bottom-dwelling fish of similar size, such as blennies and sculpins. A single fish is carried crosswise in the bill to the chicks about nine times a day. Puffins usually carry several larval fish (up to 60 have been recorded) cross-wise in their bill.

The process of young auks leaving the colony, conveniently but inaccurately referred to as "fledging," varies between species. Until relatively recently the details were poorly known, and obscured by strange myths and legends. For several species the truth is indeed quite remarkable, and seeing young auks leave the colony can be an unforgettable experience.

It was previously thought that young Atlantic puffins were deserted by their parents and starved into leaving the colony. In fact the parents continue to feed the chick up until the day it leaves the colony. Young puffins, Black guillemots and auklets fledge alone, at night, unaccompanied by their parents. They probably fly several hundred meters before alighting on the sea and dispersing away from the colony. By contrast, the young of the two other murres and the razorbill are still flightless when they leave the colony, accompanied by their father. Where they breed on 300m (1,000ft) cliffs, fledging can be spectacular. For several hours before leaving, the chicks become more and more excited, jumping up and down as they exercise their tiny wings, and uttering shrill "weeloo, weeloo" cries. Chicks may deliberate for several minutes before launching themselves into the air, and fluttering down onto the sea, closely followed by the father. In some areas, razorbills and murres do not have direct access to the sea; the chick may land on another ledge during its descent and may have to scramble

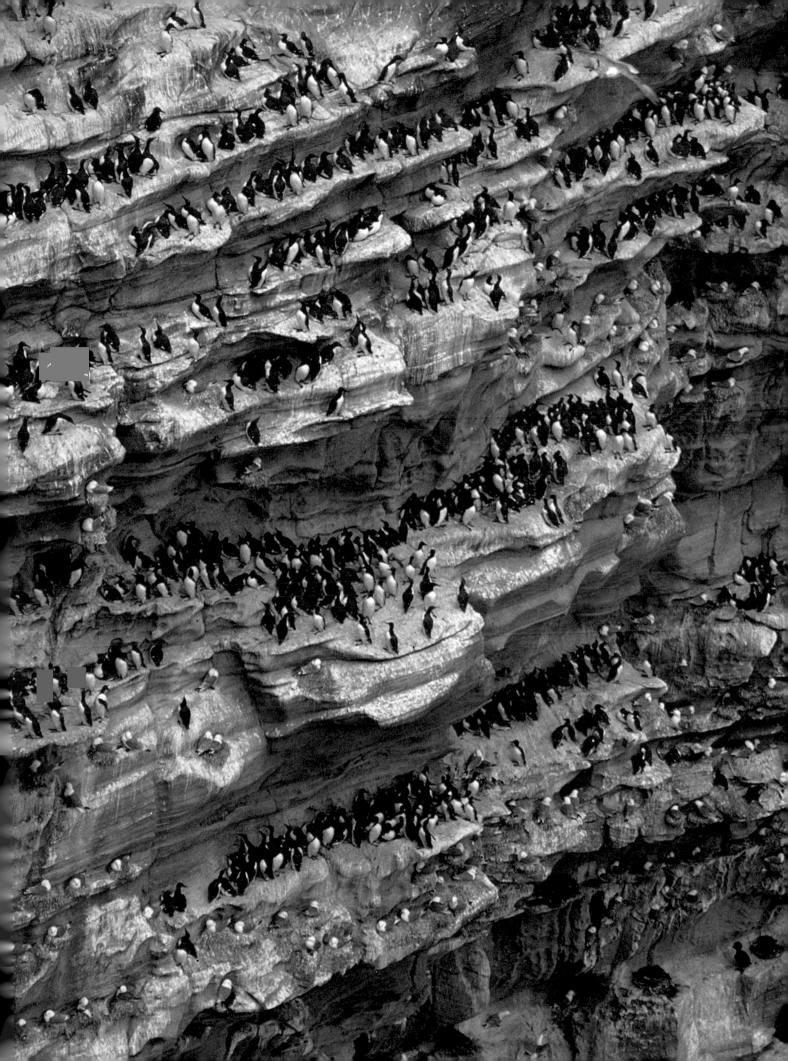

over boulders to reach the sea. Father and chick recognize each other's calls and the adult may find the chick and guide it to the sea. In a third variation on the fledging theme the young leave the nest when only about two days old. Among the four species of precocial murrelets (Ancient, Craveri's Japanese and Xantus's), both parents accompany the two tiny young to the sea. It is not known how long these auk chicks are cared for at sea by their parents.

Some colonies, like those of the Little auk, may be enormous and contain over a million birds. Only two species breed in solitary pairs, Kittlitz's murrelet and the Marbled murrelet. The Black and Pigeon guillemots breed in small, loose colonies. Solitary or loosely colonial species feed inshore on a predictable food supply. In contrast, colonial species typically feed further offshore and exploit patchily distributed, unpredictable prey, such as shoaling fish or plankton. The mobility of such prey makes it difficult to locate. It may be advantageous to be part of a colony so that information on the whereabouts of food can be obtained from other colony members. At large colonies the "traffic" between feeding areas and the colony may be sufficiently dense to enable birds to locate feeding areas simply by following the flight line of incoming birds.

Auks are especially vulnerable to any factor which reduces their numbers, because of their slow reproductive rate. Whereas a small songbird species might recover from

▲ **Razorbills,** stouter in build than murres (guillemots), and with a heavier bill bearing a white stripe. All auks use their wings to "fly" underwater in pursuit of their prey—fish or, in smaller species, plankton and crustaceans such as shrimps.

▲ **Black guillemot with sand eel prey** ABOVE RIGHT. Guillemots take fish from medium depths.

◄ **Whiskered and "horned,"** a Rhinoceros auklet (*Cerorhinca monocerata*) of the North Pacific.

► **The Least auklet,** smallest of the North Pacific plankton feeders, is half the size of the Rhinoceros auklet.

► **The Tufted puffin** FAR RIGHT (*Lunda cirrhata*) like other auks has a summer plumage with more white feathers; many auks also have heavier and more brightly colored bills, and some have whiskers or tufts, in the breeding season.

a 50 percent population reduction in one or two years, most auks might take 20 years to recoup such losses. In most parts of their range auks are thought to be much lower in numbers than they were previously.

Auks themselves, and their eggs, are highly palatable. Traditional hunting, using nets, snares etc on a local scale, probably had little effect on auk numbers, but the use of firearms and commercial egg-collecting have caused the extinction of many colonies and one entire species. Excessive egg-collecting of Common murre eggs at the Farallon Islands off California caused the murre population to fall from about 400,000 birds in 1850 to just a few hundred in the 1920s. The Thick-billed murre has suffered a similar fate in Novaya Zemlya, USSR, where both adults and eggs have been overexploited. Large numbers of the Great auk once bred on Funk Island, Newfoundland, but in the 17th century this

became a regular stopping-off place for sailors and fishermen, who took many adult birds for food. Towards the end of the 17th century, the Greak auks were systematically killed for their feathers and, by 1800, the colony was extinct. The last Great auks were killed in 1844 on Eldey, a small island off Iceland.

Auks are particularly vulnerable to oiling, because they spend so much of their time on the sea. Fuel oil released onto the sea, either deliberately when cleaning tanks or as a result of accident, coats the birds' plumage and destroys their waterproofing. In some cases, oil is ingested as the birds attempt to clean themselves, and this may be toxic. During the past 40 years oil pollution has been a major cause of deaths in most auk populations.

Commercial fishing activities have also taken their toll. The Danish salmon gill-net fishery, for example, destroyed one half to three quarters of a million Thick-billed murres each year between 1968 and 1973. In recent years the number of auks drowned in gill nets may have fallen somewhat. A more widespread phenomenon is competition for the same species of fish. Up until the last 10 years or so, fish such as capelin, sand eel and sprat were important to the birds but of no commercial significance to man. However, now that the stocks of larger commercial fish, like cod, have been fished-out, man has turned his attention to those small fish upon which many species of auks depend for their food. If such fisheries are allowed to develop extensively in an unrestricted way, the consequences for the auks may be very grave.   TRB

SANDGROUSE

Order: Pteroclidiformes
Family: Pteroclididae.
Sixteen species in 2 genera.
Distribution: Africa, S Iberia and France,
Middle East to India and China.

Habitat: desert, semi-desert, dry grasslands,
arid savanna and bushveld.

Size: 27–48cm (10·6–19in) long, weighing
150–400g (5.3–14.1oz).

Plumage: mainly dull tones of buff, ocher,
rufous, olive, brown, black and white. Males
usually spotted or barred; most have black,
white or chestnut chest bands. Females usually
ocher or buff with black streaking and barring.
This sexual dimorphism is marked and
invariable. Central tail feathers very long in
several species.

Eggs: almost always 3, sometimes 2; elongated,
equally rounded at each end; light cream,
grayish, greenish or pink, blotched, smeared
and spotted with brown, red-brown, olive-
brown and gray; incubation 21–31 days;
fledging period about 4 weeks.

Diet: almost exclusively small dry seeds; some
other plant material, insects, small mollusks
and grit.

Voice: mellow whistled or chuckling calls in set
phrases of 2 or more syllables, usually given in
flight, and highly characteristic for each
species.

Nest: simple scrape in open or by a bush, stone
or grass tuft; sometimes scantily lined with dry
plant fragments or small stones.

Species: **Black-bellied sandgrouse** (*Pterocles
orientalis*), **Black-faced sandgrouse**
(*P. decoratus*), **Burchell's** or **Variegated
sandgrouse** (*P. burchelli*), **Chestnut-bellied
sandgrouse** (*P. exustus*), **Crowned** or **Coroneted
sandgrouse** (*P. coronatus*), **Double-
banded sandgrouse** (*P. bicinctus*), **Four-
banded sandgrouse** (*P. quadricinctus*),
Lichtenstein's sandgrouse (*P. lichtensteinii*),
Madagascar sandgrouse (*P. personatus*),
Namaqua sandgrouse (*P. namaqua*), **Painted
sandgrouse** (*P. indicus*), **Pallas's sandgrouse**
(*Syrrhaptes paradoxus*), **Pin-tailed sandgrouse**
(*Pterocles alchata*), **Spotted sandgrouse**
(*P. senegallus*), **Tibetan sandgrouse** (*Syrrhaptes
tibetanus*), **Yellow-throated sandgrouse** (*Pterocles
gutturalis*).

WITH their robust bodies, small heads and short legs, sandgrouse can be mistaken for pigeons in silhouette, but their markings are very different—beautifully colored and patterned for camouflage in their open, usually arid, habitat.

Most sandgrouse species are cryptically spotted, barred or streaked; they crouch on the ground to avoid detection, but their long, pointed wings also enable them to make a quick getaway in swift, direct flight, rather like that of a plover. Their plumage is dense; the entire body is covered with a thick undercoat of dark down, and even the base of the bill and the legs are feathered (only in front in *Pterocles*, all round and down to the toes in *Syrrhaptes*). This insulates the bird against the temperature extremes of night and midday, winter and summer, and protects the nostrils against windblown sand and dust. The hind toe is lost (*Syrrhaptes*) or reduced (*Pterocles*) and the three short front toes are stout and fairly broad for walking on loose sand.

To judge from their feather structure, general biology, behavior and chick plumage patterns, the sandgrouse appear to have arisen from a wader (shorebird) ancestor, probably from the coursers (p183). By contrast, the skeleton resembles very closely that of the doves to which they are undoubtedly related, but which arose earlier from the same evolutionary line.

Sandgrouse eat mainly small seeds with a relatively high protein content (in particular those of legumes) and a low water content (less than 10 percent water as a rule). These they pick up by walking with small steps, pecking frequently with their short bills. The crop of an adult Black-bellied sandgrouse was found to contain about 8,700 indigo plant seeds, while that of a Namaqua sandgrouse chick just a few days old contained 1,400 tiny seeds. Sandgrouse take up

▶ **Water hole gathering** OVERLEAF of Namaqua sandgrouse in southwestern Africa. Large flocks of hundreds or thousands of birds gather daily at set times to drink at water holes. Males also soak their belly feathers in the water which they then take back to feed the chicks.

◀ **Chicks drink** from the belly feathers of a male Namaqua sandgrouse on his return from the water hole.

◀ **The Pin-tailed sandgrouse,** BELOW from southwestern Europe and North Africa to Central Asia and India.

grit to help break down the seeds in the gizzard. They feed for most of the daylight hours, resting only in the extreme heat of midday in summer, usually in the shade of a bush.

Sandgrouse need to drink every 2–3 days, possibly every day in hot weather. Large flocks of hundreds or thousands of birds gather daily at set times (depending on the species) at water holes. Most species drink in the morning only, but four are exclusively night-time drinkers (Painted, Lichtenstein's, Four-banded and Double-banded sandgrouse) and form a subgenus *Nyctiperdix*, characterized also by barred plumage in both sexes, and bold black-and-white frontal patches in the males.

Sandgrouse may fly up to 80km (50mi) one way to water, though seldom more than 20–30km (12–20mi). They assemble in ever-increasing numbers near the water, then fly or run to drink quickly, taking about 10 gulps of water, raising the head to swallow between each gulp. Some species, like Burchell's sandgrouse of the Kalahari, land

Flying Water Carriers

Young sandgrouse have a diet of dry seeds and are unable to fly or walk to the nearest isolated water hole. They must have water, however, and it is the male parent that is uniquely adapted to provide it. From the day they hatch, until at least two months later, young sandgrouse are brought drinking water in the soaked belly feathers of the adult male.

When the chicks are very small, the female flies off first to drink. On her return the male takes his turn while she takes over brooding. Before walking into the water, he rubs his belly in dry sand or soil to remove waterproofing preen oil; then he wades in belly-deep, keeping wings and tail well clear of the water, intermittently rocking his body up and down to work the water deeply into the belly feathers; this may take a few seconds or as much as 20 minutes. The returning male stands erect and the chicks run to drink from the central groove in his belly plumage. The chicks having drunk their fill, the male walks away, rubs his belly on a patch of sand to dry the feathers, and the family moves off to feed for the rest of the day.

The male's belly feathers have a unique structure which allows them to hold relatively large amounts of water on their inner surfaces, where evaporation is kept to a minimum. The barbules of the central portion of each belly feather are spirally coiled when dry, and they lie flat on the feather vane, tightly coiled together to give the feather structural cohesion. When wet, the barbules uncoil and stand at right angles to the feather vane, forming a dense bed of hairs about 1mm deep, which holds water like a sponge.

With one exception, all sandgrouse species so far studied employ this water-carrying mechanism. (The Tibetan sandgrouse does not need to, as snow melt is always close by in the Central Asian mountains that are its home.) It certainly prevents the male parent from depleting his own internal water supply, as would happen if he were to regurgitate water from his crop in the same way as the doves. Furthermore, although the parents start with three young, usually only one survives to fly, so the demand for water transport by the male is limited.

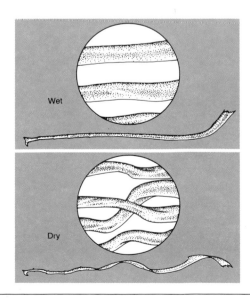

Wet

Dry

right at the water or even on the surface, floating like ducks while drinking, and taking off without effort. Sandgrouse will not normally drink water with a salt content higher than about 40 percent of that of sea water, since their kidneys are poorly adapted to excreting high salt concentrations. Furthermore they lack a salt gland, unlike most shorebirds, with which to excrete excess salt. In high temperatures (above about 37°C/99°F) sandgrouse tend to become inactive, seek shade and cease feeding, drooping their wings and holding their wrists well away from the body to increase heat loss.

Courtship involves head-down, tail-up chasing displays, similar to some threat displays. All species so far studied are monogamous, but are not very territorial. Northern Hemisphere species breed in spring and summer, Southern Hemisphere species mainly in winter; but in the Namib and Kalahari deserts of southern Africa times may vary depending at least partly on rainfall. The female usually incubates by day and the male at night, though this pattern may be somewhat different in the four members of the subgenus *Nyctiperdix* .

The chicks begin to feed on small seeds within a few hours of hatching. Seeds are shown to them by the pecking movements of the female parent. The young can fly a little at about four weeks, but are provided with water by the male (see box, p213) for at least another month, when they can fly well enough to accompany the parents to the water hole. They attain sexual maturity at about a year.

Non-breeding flocks of thousands of birds are known (such as in Namaqua sandgrouse), but these are exceptional other than at water holes. Flocks usually number 10–100 birds on their feeding grounds.

Sandgrouse are among the favorite prey of raptors, especially the Lanner falcon which hunts mainly at the water holes, as well as of such carnivores as foxes, jackals and mongooses, to which they are particularly vulnerable when nesting.

Sandgrouse are no longer in great demand for the pot and for sport, as they once were (attempts to introduce them from India and Pakistan into arid regions of the USA for sporting purposes have failed). Poor agricultural practices, exacerbated by drought, may be increasing the extent of suitable habitat. Combined with the provision of watering places fed by bore holes, conditions for most sandgrouse species have undoubtedly been improved by man's activities.   GLM

PIGEONS

Order: Columbiformes
Family: Columbidae.
About 300 species in 42 genera.
Distribution: widespread except Antarctica and high northern latitudes; members of the family have reached many isolated islands.

Habitat: most in woodland or forest; some in open country or on cliffs.

Size: 15–82cm (6–33in) long, weight 30–2,400g (1–85oz).

Plumage: the majority of species quietly colored in grays and browns; some more brightly colored; birds of the large tropical genus *Treron* mainly bright green. Some with crests. Sexes usually similar.

Voice: a wide range of soft calls and coos; song usually simple, consisting of only a few notes.

Nests: the large majority build simple twig nests on the branches of trees, a few nest in holes or on the ground.

Eggs: almost always either one or two, white; weight 2.5–50g (0.1–1.8oz). Many species have several broods. Incubation period 13–18 days in most species but 28 days in the largest; nestling period not well known for many species, but up to 35 days, possibly longer in some. However, in many species the young leave the nest before they are fully grown and complete their growth later.

Diet: primarily vegetable matter: fresh green leaves, fruit or seeds; several are serious pests of crops as a result.

Species include: **Collared dove** (*Streptopelia decaocto*), **Diamond dove** (*Geopelia cuneata*), **Eared dove** (*Zenaida auriculata*), **imperial pigeons** (*Ducula* species), **Mauritius pink pigeon** E (*Columba mayeri*), **Orange dove** (*Ptilinopus victor*), **Passenger pigeon** Ex (*Ectopistes migratorius*), **Plain-breasted ground dove** (*Columbina minuta*), **Purple-crowned pigeon** (*Ptilinopus superbus*), **Rock dove, Feral pigeon** or **Racing pigeon** (*Columba livia*), **Scaly-breasted ground dove** (*Columbina passerina*), **Stock dove** (*Columba oenas*), **Turtle dove** (*Streptopelia turtur*), **Victoria crowned pigeon** (*Goura victoria*). Threatened species: 16.

E Endangered. Ex Extinct.

THAT pigeons are successful is evident to anyone who has seen the huge populations of feral birds (all descended from domesticated Rock doves) dwelling in the cities of Europe, Asia and America. These pigeons have benefited from the decline of their predators, the birds of prey, the presence of suitable nest-sites on buildings, and the human habit of feeding them. Pigeons, being mainly seed-eaters, have also benefited from the spread of agriculture. In both city and country, this success has brought them into conflict with people.

The family is found almost worldwide, with members in all regions except Antarctica. Some species, such as the Rock dove and Collared dove are even found north of the Arctic Circle. Pigeons are good dispersers, judging from their wide distribution on islands of the Indian and South Pacific Oceans, although they failed to reach a few isolated groups, such as the Hawaiian archipelago. Throughout their range, pigeons occur in a wide variety of terrestrial habitats, from tropical rain forests to deserts, and from above the snowline in the Himalayas to the centers of the largest cities.

Pigeons generally have plump stocky bodies with a small head and bill, and short legs. The plumage is soft and dense, and some tropical species are brilliantly colored or have ornamental crests, but most pigeons are dressed in neutral browns, grays and pinks, although often with small bright, or iridescent, patches on the wings or neck. In most species the sexes look similar, with the female slightly duller, but in some, for example the Orange dove, the sexes are very different in color. Juvenile plumage generally differs from that of adults, but molt into adult plumage occurs within months of leaving the nest.

Pigeons are typically tree-dwelling, but some cliff-dwelling and ground-dwelling species occur too. Tropical fruit-pigeons spend the most time in trees, feeding, roosting and nesting there, whereas many other species nest in trees but feed on the ground. Pigeons and doves feed on a wide variety of vegetable matter, with seeds, fruits, leaves, buds and flowers forming most of the diet, but many species take a limited amount of small snails and other invertebrates, particularly during the breeding season. Most species have a strong muscular gizzard and a long narrow intestine. Grit is often taken to help break down hard seeds in the gizzard. Some fruit-eating species, such as the imperial pigeons, have a strong stomach and a short wide gut. They digest only the pulp of the fruit they eat, voiding the stones

▲ **The Spotted dove** (*Streptopelia chinensis*), one of the turtle doves, and a species that has been successfully introduced to Mauritius, Hawaii, Reunion, Celebes, Moluccas and islands of the Flores Sea in Indonesia.

▶ **Peacock of the pigeon family** is the Victoria crowned pigeon. It is the largest pigeon, and the male uses the crest in a bowing display during courtship.

▼ **A flurry of white** from doves outside a mosque in Afghanistan. These are feral birds derived from white breeds of the Rock dove.

intact. Because the seeds are undamaged, pigeons can be important in the dispersal of fruiting plants, and many examples of the coevolution of fruiting plants and pigeons are known.

Unlike most birds, pigeons drink actively by immersing their bill in water up to their nostrils and sucking without raising their heads. Some species may fly considerable distances to water, where they gather in large flocks at dawn and dusk.

As a family, pigeons have a very limited range of vocalizations, most of which are recognizable as modifications of a "cooing" call. Some species additionally utter muted cries in certain circumstances. Normal flight is often noisy and in some situations this may be used as a social signal; during display and escape flights a wide range of species apparently attract attention by the loud noise made by clapping their wings together.

Pigeons are strong fliers and some migrate thousands of kilometers, for example the Turtle dove. Wing muscles make up as much as 32 percent of the body-weight of Rock doves which have been specially bred for their speed and homing abilities. Good "racing pigeons" can achieve mean flight speeds of around 70km/h (44mph).

Pigeons are often gregarious, gathering in large flocks at good feeding or roosting sites, and some species, such as the Eared dove, even breed colonially. The extinct Passenger pigeon of North America nested in enormous colonies: in the late 18th century there were thought to be as many as 3,000 million of them. Some of the colonies occupied several square kilometers and it was so easy to shoot them in large numbers that the bird was hunted commercially even

Pigeon Milk

Pigeons are very unusual among birds in that they produce a milk which has a chemical composition similar to that produced by mammals; flamingos are the only other birds to share this feature.

Pigeon or crop milk is a secretion of the adult crop which forms the complete diet of nestlings for the first few days of life. Thereafter, nestlings are fed an increasing percentage of food items obtained by the parents, but the actual quantity of milk in the mixture remains fairly constant until the young are well grown.

Crop milk is produced by both sexes in response to secretion of the pituitary hormone, prolactin (the same hormone is responsible for milk production in mammals). From about the midpoint of incubation the tissue of part of the crop begins to thicken and blood vessels grow into this region. Growth of the crop wall can more than triple the weight of the crop over the last half of incubation, and so by the time the young hatch, reddish folds with a honeycomb texture are visible in the crop. From this region, cells containing the "milk" are successively detached into the crop, and these are then regurgitated to the young. Milk cells are initially sloughed off only when the crop is empty, thus ensuring that it is not contaminated by other foods. Later, crop milk production is confined to periods when adults tend the young, but the milk is mixed with other foods.

Crop milk is a thick solution (19–35 percent dry matter) with a consistency and appearance of cottage cheese. It contains 65–81 percent water, 13–19 percent protein, 7–13 percent fat, 1–2 percent mineral matter and vitamins A, B and B_2, but no carbohydrates. The dry matter is mostly protein, which is composed of a large variety of amino acids. Crop milk compares well with mammalian milks as a source of essential fatty acids: it is low in calcium and phosphorus, but is high in sodium. Because of the high water content, milk production puts a relatively heavy drain on the adult body water reserves.

Milk production seems to be an adaptation to ensure that nestlings receive the adequate and predictable supply of energy and nutrients that are required for the high growth-rates that are characteristic of pigeons.

when it was greatly reduced in numbers. The species was exterminated in the wild in about 1900 and the last specimen died in Cincinnati Zoo in 1914.

Most pigeons and doves build a fragile-looking nest of interwoven twigs, usually in the branches of a tree, but sometimes on man-made structures. Some species nest in open situations on the ground, but others such as the Rock dove naturally nest in crevices or caves and, exceptionally, a few species such as the Stock dove nest in a true hole in a tree or in a burrow. The female

On the other hand, breeding seasons are often very long and many species have multiple broods, with up to eight in a year in some cases. This is helped by having short incubation and fledging periods compared with other birds of similar size, and by having successive clutches overlapped; that is, a new clutch is laid (sometimes in the same nest) while the parents are still tending young from the previous brood. Both sexes share in incubation and the care of young, and both produce pigeon milk (see box), which is rich in energy and nutrients and helps the nestlings to grow exceptionally rapidly. Chicks of all open-nesting pigeons studied to date fledge when still not adult size, and when still well below adult weight (usually about 65 percent, but as little as 26 percent in the case of the Purple-crowned pigeon). However, chicks of hole-nesting Stock doves fledge at about adult size and weight.

Some pigeons can breed at an exceptionally early age—five months in the case of Scaly-breasted ground doves—and many species are relatively long-lived, especially when kept in captivity.

The creation of large areas of agricultural land has greatly benefited a number of species. Many species were adapted to feed on grains and fruits before these were developed for human use, and in certain areas they have become a serious agricultural pest, for example the Eared dove in South America. Pigeons have the ability to fly into an area, quickly fill their crop with food, and return to the safety of woodland to digest their meal. Some species are potential carriers of agricultural diseases and even pose a health hazard to humans, especially the feral pigeons found in towns.

In recent years, the Collared dove has shown a dramatic spread. Originally it bred in Europe only in the extreme southwest. About the turn of the century, it started to spread slowly through the Balkans. From about 1930 it spread very rapidly north-westwards through Europe. It first bred in England in 1955 and within 15 years it has spread to almost all of the British Isles. Since then it has continued to increase very rapidly and is now virtually uncountable.

At the other end of the spectrum, many pigeons have very limited distributions, especially some of the island species, and many are seriously threatened by habitat destruction. Attempts are being made to increase the numbers of the Mauritius pink pigeon by re-introducing into the wild birds that have been raised in captivity.

generally builds the nest, but the male brings most of the material. All species lay only one or two white, or near-white eggs. The majority of species lay two eggs, but tropical, fruit-eating, or large species generally lay one-egg clutches. Pigeon eggs are exceptionally small in relation to adult body-size when compared with those of other birds and this, combined with the small clutch size, means that the pigeons have the smallest total clutch weights in relation to adult weight (about 9 percent) of all the families of nest-reared land birds.

▲ **Protected by prickles** of a cactus, a Mourning dove (*Zenaida macroura*) on its nest. This is the common dove of North America.

◄ **Young Turtle doves** begging food from parent. Even when nearly fledged, the regurgitated food will contain some milk secreted from the crop.

HR

PARROTS, LORIES AND COCKATOOS

Order: Psittaciformes
Family: Psittacidae.
Three hundred and twenty-eight species in 77 genera.
Distribution: S and C America, Africa and Madagascar, southern and SE Asia, Australasia and Polynesia.

▶ **The strikingly demarcated** colors of the male Australian king parrot, one of the most vivid of all parrots, seen here in heavily wooded country in eastern Australia.

▼ **Green-rumped parrotlets** (*Forpus passerinus*). Despite their reputation for gaudy coloring, most parrots are predominantly green.

PARROTS have been valued as cage-birds and pets since ancient times. Our earliest written account of a pet parrot is a Greek description of a Plum-headed parakeet dating from about 400BC. The author, a physician, was clearly captivated by the bird's ability to speak the language of its homeland, India, and also observed that it could be taught to speak Greek. From then on, it seems, exotically colored talking parrots became favorite status symbols among the ruling classes of Greece, Rome and Europe. Later, 15th and 16th century explorations in the New World brought to light many new parrot species, and these and subsequent discoveries in the East Indies and Australia helped to fuel the interest of European collectors.

Nowadays, a huge range of species is kept in captivity and, unfortunately, the aviculturist's obsession with novel or exotic forms is undoubtedly accelerating the extinction of some species. The budgerigar of Australia is the only species of parrot which has been truly domesticated. After the dog and cat it is probably the most common household pet in western countries.

The parrots form a distinctive and fairly uniform order of birds comprising the single family Psittacidae. Because of their many unique and specialized features it is difficult to determine the relationship between parrots and other groups of birds. They are usually, however, classified somewhere between pigeons and cuckoos, although their affinity with either of these orders is, at best, tenuous and indistinct. This suggests that parrots diverged from other lineages at a comparatively early stage in bird evolution. The earliest known fossil remains of a parrot is a single leg bone from *Achaeopsittacus verreauxi*, a lower Miocene species, some 30 million years old.

Parrots are widely distributed within the tropics and the Southern Hemisphere. The Carolina parakeet of North America was at one time the most northerly representative of the family. However, the species was wiped out in the early 20th century, and this title now belongs to the Slatey-headed parakeet of eastern Afghanistan although there are more northerly populations of introduced species such as the Monk parakeet in the eastern USA. Tierra del Fuego, the home of the Austral conure, marks the southern limit of parrot distribution. The Rose-ringed parakeet has the widest geographical distribution of any parrot. Its range extends from North Africa to the Far East and, recently, it has been introduced accidentally to parts of Europe. The parrot with the most restricted world distribution is probably Stephen's lory, a small species confined to the 35sq km (13.5sq mi) Henderson Island in the South Pacific. By far the largest number of different species of parrot is found in South America and Australasia, whereas relatively few species occur in Africa and Asia.

All parrots share a number of distinctive features in common. The most obvious of these is the characteristic parrot bill which consists of a downward-curving and somewhat hooked upper mandible which fits neatly over a smaller, upward-curving lower mandible. The upper half of the bill is attached to the skull by a special kind of hinge and this gives it greater mobility and leverage. The parrot bill is a highly adaptable structure. It can be used to perform delicate tasks such as preening, but at the same time is powerful enough to crush the hardest nuts and seeds. The bill also serves as a third "foot"—a kind of grappling-hook which the bird uses in conjunction with its feet when clambering about among the treetops. In the Great-billed parrot of Indonesia, the bill is abnormally large and bright red in color. This conspicuous structure presumably serves as some kind of visual display.

The feet of parrots are also unusual: the two outer toes of the foot point backwards and grip in opposition to the two forward-pointing inner toes. This arrangement

The Parrot Family (Psittacidae)

Ex Extinct.   E Endangered.   R Rare.   V Vulnerable.   I Threatened, but status indeterminate.

Three hundred and twenty-eight species in 77 genera.
S and C America, southern N America, Africa and Madagascar, southern and SE Asia, Australasia and Polynesia. Principally lowland tropical and subtropical forest and woodland; occasionally in mountain forest and open grassland. Size: length from 9–100cm (3.5–39in). Plumage: exceptionally variable: many species brilliantly colored, others predominantly greenish or brownish. Males and females usually similar or identical in appearance and coloration, with some notable exceptions. Voice: typically noisy and unmusical, involving enormous variety of calls. In captivity, some species become accomplished vocal mimics. Nests: usually in holes in trees; rarely in burrows in cliffs, soil or termitaria. A few species nest communally in large grass or twig nests. Eggs: generally 2–8, depending on species; invariably white and relatively small; length from 16–54mm; incubation period 17–35 days; nestling period 21–70 days. Diet: chiefly vegetable material: fruit, seeds, buds, nectar and pollen. Small insects occasionally ingested.

Species include: **African gray parrot** (*Psittacus erithacus*), **Austral conure** (*Enicognathus ferrugineus*), **Australian king parrot** (*Alisterus scapularis*), **Black lory** (*Chalcopsitta atra*), **Blue-crowned hanging parrot** (*Loriculus galgulus*), **Blue-and-yellow macaw** (*Ara ararauna*), **Blue-winged parrot** (*Neophema chrysostoma*), **Brown-throated conure** (*Aratinga pertinax*), **budgerigar** (*Melopsittacus undulatus*), **Buff-faced pygmy parrot** (*Micropsitta pusio*), **Carolina parakeet** Ex (*Conuropsis carolinensis*), **Crimson rosella** (*Platycercus elegans*), **Derbyan parakeet** (*Psittacula derbiana*), **Eclectus parrot** (*Eclectus roratus*), **galah** (*Cacatua roseicapilla*), **Glaucous macaw** E (*Anodorhynchus glaucus*), **Golden-shouldered parrot** R (*Psephotus chrysopterygius*), **Great-billed parrot** (*Tanygnathus megalorhynchus*), **Ground parrot** V (*Pezoporus wallicus*), **Hispaniolan parrot** (*Amazona ventralis*), **Hyacinth macaw** (*Anodorhynchus hyacinthus*), **Imperial parrot** E (*Amazona imperialis*), **kakapo** E (*Strigops habroptilus*), **kea** (*Nestor notabilis*), **Monk parakeet** (*Myihopsitta monachus*), **Night parrot** I (*Geopsittacus occidentalis*), **Papuan lory** (*Charmosyna papou*), **Patagonian conure** (*Cyanoliseus patagonus*), **Peach-faced lovebird** (*Agapornis roseicollis*), **Plum-headed parakeet** (*Psittacula cyanocephala*), **Puerto Rican parrot** E (*Amazona vittata*), **Purple-crowned lorikeet** (*Glossopsitta porphyrocephala*), **Rainbow lorikeet** (*Trichoglossus haematodus*), **Red-capped parrot** (*Purpureicephalus spurius*), **Red-rumped parrot** (*Psephotus haematonotus*), **Red-tailed amazon** E (*Amazona brasiliensis*), **Rock parrot** (*Neophema petrophila*), **Rose-ringed parakeet** (*Psittacula krameri*), **Scaly-breasted lorikeet** (*Trichoglossus chlorolepidotus*), **Sierra parakeet** (*Bolborhynchus aymara*), **Slatey-headed parakeet** (*Psittacula himalayana*), **Stephen's lory** (*Vini stepheni*), **Sulfur-crested cockatoo** (*Cacatua galerita*), **Swift parrot** (*Lathamus discolor*), **Varied lorikeet** (*Trichoglossus versicolor*), **Wilhelmina's lorikeet** (*Charmosyna wilhelminae*), **Yellow-faced parrot** (*Poicephalus flavifrons*). Total threatened species: 30.

(zygodactyly) not only provides parrots with an extremely powerful grasp, but also enables them to use their feet like hands for holding and manipulating objects close to the bill. In terms of manual dexterity, parrots are unsurpassed by any other group of birds. However, this ability is absent in species which feed habitually on the ground. Like humans, parrots also display both right- and left-handedness, or rather, footedness. In one study it was found that out of a flock of 56 Brown-throated conures, 28 consistently used the right foot to hold food while the other 28 used the left. When walking along a perch or on the ground, most parrots are noticeably pigeon-toed, and have a characteristic and somewhat comical swaggering gait.

Parrots are variable in their powers of flight. In general, flight is swift and direct in small species and relatively slow and laborious in larger ones. There are, however, some notable exceptions. The South American macaws, for instance, are fast fliers despite their size. Species such as the budgerigar and many of the lories are highly nomadic and are capable of flying considerable distances in search of food. The Swift parrot and Blue-winged parrot, both from southeastern Australia, are migratory and every year fly across Bass Strait—a distance of 200km (124mi)—in order to breed in Tasmania. As its name implies, the Swift

parrot flies with exceptional speed and directness.

Differences in flying ability in parrots are linked with differences in wing structure. Generally speaking, species which fly rapidly have comparatively narrow, tapering wings, while the wings of slow-flying forms are correspondingly broad and blunt. The kakapo of New Zealand has very short wings and is the only parrot which is entirely flightless. The structure of the tail in parrots is highly variable. In macaws and in the Papuan lory, tails are especially long and elegant and may comprise almost two-thirds of the bird's total length. Long tails like this probably serve an important signalling function. At the other extreme, the tail of the Blue-crowned hanging parrot is so short and blunt that it is almost concealed by the tail coverts. The racket-tailed parrots of Indonesia and the Philippines have distinctive elongated central tail feathers which consist of long, bare shafts with flattened spoon-shaped tips. The function of these unusual tail structures is unknown. The tail feathers of the New Guinea pygmy parrots also terminate in short bare shafts. These are stiffened and help to support these tiny birds when they are climbing about and feeding on tree-trunks.

Parrots are renowned for their gaudy plumage, and some of the larger, tropical species such as the South American macaws

◀▲ **Representative species of parrots.** (1) Hyacinth macaw (*Anodorhynchus hyacinthinus*) using zygodactylous claws to grip Brazil nut. (2) Rainbow lorikeet (*Trichoglossus haematodus*). (3) Fischer's lovebird (*Agapornis fischeri*). (4) Female Eclectus parrot (*Eclectus roratus*). (5) Sulfur-crested cockatoo (*Cacatua galerita*). (6) Black-capped lory (*Lorius lory*) showing the adaptation of the tongue for feeding on nectar. (7) Crimson rosella (*Platycercus elegans*). (8) Red-capped parrot (*Purpureicephalus spurius*). (9) Blue-crowned hanging parrot (*Loriculus galgulus*). (10) Kea (*Nestor notabilis*).

are undoubtedly among the most brilliantly colored of all birds. Despite this, the majority of species are predominantly green and are well camouflaged among the foliage in which they live. The large cockatoos of Australia are highly conspicuous. Most of them have prominent erectile crests on their heads, and they are generally either white, salmon-pink or black in color. Males and females in the majority of parrots are either very similar or identical in appearance. However, there are some notable exceptions to this rule. For example, males of the Australian king parrot have brilliant scarlet plumage, whereas females and juveniles are almost entirely green. In the Eclectus parrot of New Guinea and Australia, males and females are so different in coloration that for many years they were thought to belong to different species. Males are bright emerald green with scarlet underwings and flanks, while the female is a rich crimson red with a violet-blue belly and lower breast. This species is also unique among parrots in that the female is gaudier and more conspicuous than the male.

The vast majority of parrots are very much tree-dwellers, and they tend to be most plentiful in and around lowland tropical forests. A number, such as the budgerigar of Australia and Fischer's lovebird of East Africa, inhabit more open, grassy habitats, but even these species are generally never seen very far from the cover of trees. Two exceptions are the completely terrestrial Ground and Night parrots of Australia. The former inhabits coastal heaths and sand dunes; and the latter, which until very recently was thought to be extinct, is confined to arid desert grassland. Although parrots are generally less common at high altitudes, several distinctive species are restricted to mountains. These include the Papuan lory from New Guinea, the Derbyan parakeet from the Himalayas, the Yellow-faced parrot from Ethiopia, and the Sierra parakeet from the South American Andes.

The kea of the Southern Alps of New Zealand is perhaps the most unusual of all highland forms. These large bronze birds live among snow-covered mountains between 600 and 2,000m (2,000–6,500ft), and appear to enjoy rolling and frollicking in the snow. Around ski resorts and human habitations they are bold and inquisitive and have been known to enter buildings through chimneys in order to steal food. In addition to their normal vegetarian diet, keas have also taken to feeding on rubbish tips and carrion, and they have even

acquired a widespread though exaggerated reputation for killing sheep.

Seeds and fruits of various kinds make up the diet of the majority of parrots, although the lories and lorikeets of Australasia specialize in feeding on tree pollen and nectar (see pp228–229). Most parrots procure their food in the treetops, where their zygodactylous feet and hooked bills enable them to climb about with extraordinary skill and agility. However, some of the smaller parakeets, parrotlets and lovebirds feed extensively on grass seeds on or near the ground.

Parrots have a reputation for extreme longevity. In captivity, some of the larger species live from 30–50 years, and 80 years has even been reported in some cases. Generally speaking, the smaller species have much shorter life spans. Most parrots attain sexual maturity between their second and fourth years.

The timing and duration of the breeding season in parrots depends very much on their geographic location and on the principal types of food on which they depend. In general, species living outside the tropics, where food availability tends to be

► **Yellow blaze in the sky** of a Blue-and-yellow macaw, a large species often kept in captivity. Distribution of macaws, largest of all parrots, is centered on the Amazon Basin. Like all macaws, collectings birds in the wild is threatening populations. However, captive breeding is successful and may stop this drain.

▼ **A flock of galahs.** These elegant pink and gray birds are the commonest parrots in Australia. They feed in large numbers on crops, often causing considerable damage.

seasonal, have more regular and better defined breeding seasons than those in tropical regions. For instance, the Purple-crowned lorikeet of southern Australia breeds from August to December, whereas the Varied lorikeet from Australia's northern tropics will breed at any time of the year. Most parrots are monogamous, and males and females often pair for life. Pairs remain together constantly and the bond between them is reinforced by mutual feeding and preening. The details of courtship have only been described for a few species. Prior to copulation, the males of most species display to the females with a variety of relatively simple movements and postures, including bowing, hopping, wing-flicking and flapping, tail-wagging and strutting. Areas of conspicuous plumage are often incorporated in these movements and, in many species, the brightly colored irises of the eye are expanded—a phenomenon known appropriately as "eye-blazing." When the female is ready to mate she adopts a characteristic crouching position and allows the male to mount. The male's attempts at copulation are often interspersed with curious treading movements performed on the female's back. The function of these movements is unknown.

The two New Zealand species, the kea and the kakapo or Owl parrot, are both polygamous. In the former, males sometimes mate and share parental duties with several different females at the same time. The mating system of the nocturnal kakapo is highly unusual. The males congregate at night in specific areas, known as leks, and advertise their location with loud booming calls. Females then visit these sites and mate with the male of their choice. As far as is known, male kakapos play no part in parental care. Because it is flightless and therefore highly vulnerable to introduced domestic cats, the kakapo has vanished from the North Island of New Zealand and is almost extinct on the South Island, where a few individuals are known to survive still in Fjordland. A small population of kakapos still exists on Stewart Island, and some of these have recently been transferred to Little Barrier Island.

The majority of parrots—large and small—nest in holes in the limbs or trunks of trees, often at a considerable height above the ground. These they either excavate themselves or steal from other hole-nesting species such as woodpeckers. The nest cavity is generally lined with a layer of decayed wood-dust, although the African lovebirds and the hanging parrots of Asia line their nests with grasses, leaves and strips of bark which the female collects and carries to the nest tucked under the feathers of her rump. Termite colonies are also exploited as nest-sites by a number of parrot species. The Golden-shouldered parrot of Australia excavates its nest burrow in terrestrial termite mounds, while the Buff-faced pygmy parrot of New Guinea makes its nest in tree-borne termitaria. The termites presumably provide a certain amount of protection from predators.

Talking Parrots

The talking abilities of captive parrots have attracted human interest since ancient times. Most people assume that parrots merely mimic sounds at random and are incapable of using speech in appropriate contexts—hence the phrase: to learn something "parrot-fashion," meaning to memorize things without understanding them. Recent research in the USA, however, suggests that some parrots can be trained to use human language as a means of communicating intelligently with people.

After months of careful instruction, researchers at Purdue University have succeeded in training Alex—a young male African gray parrot—to learn verbal labels for 23 different objects or materials such as paper, cork, nut, rock and water. He also knows five different colors, four different shapes, numbers up to five, and commands such as "want," "come here" and "you tickle me." More to the point, Alex is able to combine these vocalizations to identify, request or refuse more than 50 different items, even items which were not included as part of his original training schedule. During his second year of training, and without any formal instruction, Alex also began using the word "no" when he didn't want to be handled. This was a particularly interesting development, since linguists regard negation as a relatively advanced conceptual achievement. Alex is a long way from being able to hold a conversation with his trainers, but he is less than three years old and his verbal abilities already far exceed any previous expectations.

Unlike many other avian mimics, parrots have never been observed to imitate calls of other species in the wild. It is therefore something of a mystery why this ability appears so well developed in captive birds. The calls of wild parrots are often enormously diverse and variable, and it has been suggested that parrots need their extraordinary imitative powers in order to learn to communicate effectively with each other. However, in the abnormal social conditons of captivity this desire to imitate members of the same species is transferred to humans and human vocalizations.

The Rock parrot nests only under rocks just above the high-tide mark on the coast of southern Australia, while the Patagonian conure excavates nesting burrows up to 3m (10ft) long in the cliffs and river banks of Patagonia. The Ground parrot of Australia makes its nest in a shallow depression under a bush or grass tussock. Several species of parrot nest colonially. The Peach-faced lovebird either constructs its own nesting colonies from grasses and leaves or, more often, invades and takes over the existing colonies of weaver-finches. Perhaps the most advanced nesting behavior among parrots is found in the South American Monk parakeet. This species nests communally in immense structures which they build from twigs in the tops of trees. Within the main structure, each pair has its own separate nest-chamber.

In all but a few species of parrot, the eggs are incubated exclusively by the female. The male, however, keeps her supplied with food during this critical period. The young are blind and helpless when they hatch, and develop rather slowly. In small species such as the budgerigar they leave the nest 3–4 weeks after hatching, but in the much larger Blue-and-yellow macaw the nestling period may be as long as 3½ months. As a rule, both parents play an equal role in feeding the young. Juvenile parrots are generally noticeably smaller than the adults of either sex and they also tend to have duller plumage colors.

Although a few atypical species, such as the Australian Ground parrot, seem to be largely solitary, the vast majority of parrots are sociable and gregarious birds which are usually observed in pairs, family parties or small flocks. Occasionally, when conditions are appropriate, some of the smaller species aggregate in very large numbers. Observers in Australia, for example, sometimes report flocks of wild budgerigars so vast that they darken the sky. When wild populations of parrots reach these proportions they sometimes cause serious damage to crops. Fortunately, population explosions of this kind are comparatively rare, and are usually brought under control by natural mortality due to starvation and diseases such as ornithosis (psittacosis), to which parrots are particularly susceptible.

Apart from man, the most important predators of parrots are various hawks and falcons, although monkeys and other tree-dwelling mammals are also responsible for taking a significant number of eggs and nestlings. When feeding in flocks, parrots are often noisy and quarrelsome and appear to be oblivious to potential predators. However, when danger threatens, these flocks fall perfectly silent before exploding suddenly from the treetops accompanied by harsh screams. Most predators find the ensuing chaos and confusion disconcerting.

On the principle that there is safety in numbers, many species of parrot also roost communally at night. Communal roosts are often in traditional locations and tend to be used year after year. Favored sites often consist of exceptionally tall or isolated trees where the birds can get a good view of approaching predators. Asian hanging parrots have the distinction of roosting suspended upside-down like bats. At a distance, it is difficult to distinguish a dead tree full of roosting hanging parrots from a tree with normal foliage.

Parrots are among the noisiest of all birds and, in general, their voices are harsh and unmelodic. Calls include a range of chatters, squeaks, shrieks, clicks, squawks and screams, many of them loud, discordant and thoroughly disagreeable. The Crimson rosella of Australia has a pleasant whistle-like call and another Australian species, the Red-rumped parrot, produces a melodious trilled whistle which is about the nearest any parrot has come to a song. In some species, pair-mates perform vocal duets—rapidly alternating sequences of calls which are exchanged between partners. Parrots are notorious vocal mimics, although this ability is only apparent in captive birds (see box). Parrots, particularly the larger species, are playful and inquisitive and are thought to be relatively intelligent. Like primates, they are easily bored by captivity and may become destructive and belligerent as a result.

Although as a group parrots are comparatively successful, many species have become extinct within the last few centuries and many more are seriously endangered. One of the most mysterious disappearances was that of the Carolina parakeet of the southeastern USA. During the early part of the 19th century this species was common throughout its range, but by 1831 it was already on the decline and the last known specimen died in Cincinnati Zoo on the 21st February 1918. It is not known what caused the extinction of the Carolina parakeet. However, the species was regarded as an agricultural pest and there is little doubt that human persecution played a major part in its initial decline.

Nowadays, the most serious threat to parrots is the continued uncontrolled destruction of the world's tropical and subtropical

▲ **Rainbow rockface.** The Green-winged (or Red-and-green) macaw (*Ara chloroptera*) and the Scarlet (or Red-and-yellow) macaw (*A. macao*) belie their names in having most of the other colors of the rainbow as well.

▶ **A budgerigar** leaving its nest-hole in a tree. In the Australian outback all but a very few (yellow) budgerigars are green. Budgerigars have been bred in captivity for 100 years for their colorful plumage, lively disposition and ability to mimic or "talk." Captive breeds may have blue, gray, violet, red-eyed, clearwing or pied plumage.

forests, since these are the preferred habitat for the majority of parrot species. In southeastern Brazil, for example, forest cover has been so reduced by felling that species such as the Glaucous macaw and the Red-tailed amazon are now seriously threatened and, in the case of the macaw, may already be extinct. The other major threat to rare parrots is the voracious demand of the pet-trade.

Island species of parrot are especially vulnerable to human activities. Most have small populations and relatively slow breeding rates and, because they have evolved in isolation, they tend to be more sensitive to habitat destruction and less able to cope with introduced competitors, predators and diseases. In 1975 there were only 13 Puerto Rican parrots left in the wild and it looked as though the species was doomed. However, an emergency conservation program involving strict control of hunting and trapping, artificially increasing the number of suitable nest-sites, and cross-fostering of eggs and nestlings between the Puerto Rican parrot and the closely related and non-endangered Hispaniolan parrot, has had dramatic success. In October 1982 the wild population had more than doubled and there were also 15 birds carefully maintained in captivity. This recovery clearly shows what can be done when sufficient manpower and resources are available.

JAS

Lotus-eaters

Nectar-feeding lories and lorikeets

Lories and lorikeets are flamboyant, almost theatrical birds. The Rainbow lorikeet possesses up to 30 different ritualized gestures, including a variety of stylized hopping, walking, flying and preening movements, which it incorporates into elaborate "dances." Most of these performances are aggressive and are used to intimidate rivals of the same species, but males also use similar displays to impress females during courtship.

The lories and lorikeets form a distinct subgroup within the parrot family. They occur throughout much of Indonesia, New Guinea, Australia and the Pacific, and they differ from other parrots in their habit of feeding mainly on pollen and nectar from flowering trees and shrubs.

Typically, lories and lorikeets have sleek, glossy plumage, and the group includes some of the most brilliantly colored of all parrots. In the wild, they are mostly gregarious and their behavior is generally noisy and conspicuous. The most widespread of the lories is the Rainbow lorikeet which is distributed throughout eastern Indonesia, New Guinea, northern and eastern Australia, and the western Pacific islands. The species is divided up into 22 distinct island races or subspecies. The mountainous island of New Guinea has by far the highest diversity of different species and is also close to the geographic center of their distribution.

In order to cope with their specialized diet, these birds have evolved structural modifications of the bill, tongue and alimentary canal. The bills of lories are narrower, more elongate and less powerful than those of other parrots, and the gizzard—the muscular organ used by most other species to pulverize hard or fibrous foods—is relatively thin-walled and weak. Their most striking adaptation is the tongue, which is rather long for a parrot and equipped with a tuft of thread-like papillae at its tip. These papillae are normally enclosed within a protective cup-like sheath when the bird is at rest or feeding on fairly substantial foods such as fruit or seeds, but they can be expanded like the tentacles of a sea-anemone when the tongue is extended to feed on flowers. In this state, the tongue is an effective instrument for mopping up pollen and nectar. Fringe- or brush-tipped tongues are also found in several other families of nectar-feeding birds (the same adaptations are found in some species of nectar-feeding bats).

Few of the tree and shrub species exploited by lories for food have distinct flowering seasons. Individual flowering trees of the same species are often highly dispersed, and pollen and nectar production can vary considerably from year to year, as can the length of the flowering period. The locally abundant but highly erratic nature of this food resource has a number of important consequences for the birds. For example, most species of lory and lorikeet are highly nomadic and cover considerable distances in search of food. In the Pacific region, Rainbow lorikeets have been observed flying up to 80km (50mi) between neighboring islands. Lories also tend to be opportunist breeders. In other words, instead of confining themselves to a fixed breeding season, pairs generally start to breed whenever sufficient pollen and nectar is available. In practice, breeding tends to peak during the rainiest part of the year, since this also corresponds to the period when most trees come into flower. Lories are monogamous and, as far as is known, males and females pair for life. As in many other parrots, enduring pair-bonds have probably evolved in response to ecological factors. The absence of a well-defined breeding season favors a continuous, year-round association between pair-mates so that their reproductive cycles are always synchronized, as they

▲ **Pugnacious lorikeets** have a large repertoire of displays which they incorporate into "dances" performed in the face of rivals and, by males, in courtship. Among the gestures employed are: (1) the "hiss-up," (2) "strong fluttering," (3) "ritualized scratching," (4) "bobbing," (5) "bouncing."

▶ **A Rainbow lorikeet** feeding on a silk oak, *Grevillea dryandrii*. The tongues of lorikeets have a tuft of thread-like papillae at the tip which they use to mop up pollen and nectar from flowers.

▼ **Lorikeets all in a row.** The four birds lower down the branch are Rainbow lorikeets; that at the top of the branch is a Scaly-breasted lorikeet.

5

can commence breeding whenever conditions are suitable.

Lories are exceptionally pugnacious birds and many have evolved unusually elaborate threat displays. This behavior may also be an adaptation to feeding on flowers. When trees come into flower within the tropics they tend to attract considerable numbers of birds of different species, all eager to exploit the temporary abundance of pollen and nectar. Within this highly competitive environment, the more aggressive species such as lories seem to be at an advantage. In Australia, lories have also become exceptionally bold and opportunistic in their rela-

tionships with people. Rainbow and Scaly-breasted lorikeets inhabit city suburbs and are easily persuaded to visit bird-tables. In parts of Queensland, huge flocks of these two species are fed publicly for the entertainment of tourists.

The group includes a number of very rare and endangered species. Stephen's lory, the most easterly representative of the group, is confined to Henderson Island in the Pitcairn Archipelago. Several members of the eastern Polynesian genus *Vini* are currently threatened by habitat destruction, illegal trapping and the effects of introduced avian malaria.   JAS

CUCKOOS, TURACOS AND HOATZIN

Order: Cuculiformes
Families: Cuculidae, Musophagidae, Opisthocomidae.
One hundred and fifty species in 34 genera.
Distribution: see map and table.

Turacos   Hoatzin   Cuckoos

► **The Great spotted cuckoo** ABOVE, an African and southern European species, and one of the most elegant cuckoos. Its main hosts are small crows such as magpies.

► **The Blue-headed coucal** BELOW (*Centropus monachus*) of Africa builds its own, domed nest and cares for its young.

IN ENGLAND, spring begins in a curious way: buyers of the London *Times* eagerly turn to the letters page, hoping that nature's own confirmation of springtime—the cuckoo's *cuck-coo, cuck-coo* call—has been duly reported. The irony is that many of these keen correspondents and readers will never have laid eyes on a cuckoo, having detected its presence only by the call. The European cuckoo thus has the distinction—to add to its notorious parasitism—that its annual cycle impinges on human habits in this peculiar way.

The **cuckoos** are a very diverse family: the sturdy roadrunner of arid North American deserts bears precious little resemblance to the delicate Klaas's cuckoo of the African bush. Details of internal anatomy, as well as the possession of a foot having two toes pointing forwards and two back (zygodactyly), distinguish cuckoos from the superficially similar songbirds and relate them to the parrots and nightjars. This unusual foot structure gives the cuckoos the ability to climb stealthily among slender reed stems or run swiftly over the ground with almost equal poise.

Many species are reminiscent of small hawks, having a distinctly downcurved bill and long tail, and share with these birds the discomfort of "mobbing" attacks by small songbirds. The reason for these unwelcome attentions is, of course, that many cuckoos reproductively parasitize the smaller birds.

The 3 Families of Cuckoos, Turacos and Hoatzin

Cuckoos
Family: Cuculidae
One hundred and twenty-seven species in 28 genera.
Europe, Africa, Asia, Australasia, N America, S America. Most species sedentary, tropical or subtropical, though a number of migratory species extend to temperate latitudes. Arid desert to humid forest and even moorlands (European cuckoo), but most species typical of light to heavy scrub and woodland, often with an affinity for watercourses. Size: 17–65cm (7–26in) long and 30–700g (1–25oz). Sexes usually similar in size, males sometimes slightly larger. A family characteristic is that sizes and weights are unusually variable within each sex. Plumage: generally subdued grays and browns, underparts often barred and/or streaked, tail sometimes conspicuous with spots or flashes when opened. Voice: generally simple flutes, whistles and hiccups exemplified by the disyllabic note which gives the

group its name. Also many harsh notes, especially by fledglings. In at least some species, voice differs between the sexes. Eggs: parasitic species may lay 10–15 per season, although more may be stimulated by unusually high losses; nonparasitic species 2–5; weights from 8–70g (0.3–2.5oz). The eggs of nonparasitic species are very heavy relative to female body-weight. Incubation period 11–16 days; nestling period 16–24 days. Egg color variable due to mimicry of host eggs in parasitic species. Diet: almost completely insectivorous, with most species taking noxious prey (eg hairy caterpillars) unavailable to other groups of birds. Larger forms take some smaller vertebrates; one genus (*Eudynamys*) largely vegetarian.

Species include: **Black-billed cuckoo** (*Coccyzus erythropthalmus*), **European cuckoo** (*Cuculus canorus*), **Great spotted cuckoo** (*Clamator glandarius*), **Groove-billed ani** (*Crotophaga sulcirostris*), **Klaas's cuckoo**

(*Chrysococcyx klaas*), **koel** (*Eudynamys scolopacea*), **Pheasant coucal** (*Centropus phasianinus*), **roadrunner** (*Geococcyx californianus*).

Turacos
Family: Musophagidae
Twenty-two species in 5 genera.
Central and southern Africa. Evergreen forest, wooded valleys. More rarely savanna. Size: 35–75cm (14–30in) long, weight 230–950g (8–34oz). Plumage: either dark glossy green with red patches on wings and head crest, or duller gray or blue-gray; sexes similar. Voice: one- or two-syllable barks with some longer wailing notes. Eggs: 2–3, usually glossy white or pale blue/green; weight 20–45g (0.7–1.6oz); incubation period 21–24 days; nestling period 10–12 days. Diet: fruit, some invertebrates.

Species include: **Great blue turaco** (*Corythaeola cristata*), **Guinea turaco** (*Tauraco macrorhynchus*), **Violet**

plantain-eater (*Musophaga violacea*), **White-bellied go-away bird** (*Corythaixoides leucogaster*).

Hoatzin
Family: Opisthocomidae
Sole species *Opisthocomus hoazin*.
Northern S America. Rain forest. Size: 60cm (24in), weight 800g (28oz). Plumage: dark brown on back, buff below, shading to chestnut on abdomen and sides; facial skin electric blue; head quills chestnut with dark tips; tail with a broad buff tip. Voice: various calls, including a clucking courtship call, a mewing feeding call, a wheezing alarm call, and a sharp screech like a guinea fowl. Nests: twigs and sticks, in trees or large bushes, usually over water. Eggs: 2–3 (occasionally 4 or 5), buff, dappled with brown or blue spots; weight 30g (1oz); incubation period 28 days; chicks start to feed themselves at 10–14 days. Diet: leaves, flowers and fruits of marsh plants.

The cuckoo egg develops very rapidly and, even if some host eggs were already incubated when parasitism occurred, is generally the first in the nest to hatch. At this point the cuckoo nestling displays an adaptation at least as remarkable as those of its mother. The tiny pink body thrashes about in the nest until a hollow in its back comes into contact with another object, either another egg or another small chick. The cuckoo then begins to climb the inside of the nest, using surprisingly powerful legs, until it reaches the rim and ejects its little load into oblivion. Within a short time it begins again, repeating the task until all other objects have been ejected from the nest. What the cuckoo has done, of course, is to eliminate any possible competition and ensure that its innocent foster parents concentrate their reproductive efforts on one thing—the raising of the voracious cuckoo!

This pattern is not invariant among the cuckoos. Many species, for instance the Great spotted cuckoo and the koel, do not show ejection behavior and share the nest with offspring of the host species, in these species usually crows. However, the aim is the same and only the methods are different. The rapidly growing and more active cuckoo nestling either tramples the crow chicks to death underfoot or, more subtly, monopolizes the food brought to the nest by its foster parents.

In an evolutionary sense it is surprising that cuckoo nestlings succeed in obtaining parental care from foster parents, when selection against this behavior must be very strong indeed (see pp236–237). Mimicry of egg color and size may increase the chances of host acceptance, and appear to be very finely tuned to the resident host population. For example, the Brown babbler is a central African host species which lays clear blue eggs over most of its range, but in one part of northern Nigeria lays pink or mauve eggs. Incredibly, its cuckoo parasite has evolved to faithfully mimic these changes in coloration. The accuracy of this kind of local mimicry is presumably dependent upon the high degree of breeding site tenacity in both migratory and nonmigratory cuckoos: a female which tried to breed other than close to where she was hatched might find her eggs a discordant mismatch to those of the resident hosts!

Even after hatching, the cuckoo nestling must continue the deception to be able to obtain food from its foster parents. This trickery seems to be achieved by the cuckoo exploiting the signals that usually pass between parent and offspring in the nest.

About 45 species have no other habit of reproduction than to place their eggs in the nests of another species of bird. The European cuckoo female defends a territory within which she keeps a close eye on the comings and goings of the resident songbirds. In fact she is concerned only with one of her resident species, for her eggs are characteristic in color and will closely match the eggs of only one potential host species. Some of these territorial females also allow a second, subordinate female to use the territory, but perhaps only if these are dependent upon an entirely different host species, thereby avoiding competition for host nests. When a suitable nest becomes available, usually one in which laying has just begun, the cuckoo flies warily down, takes one host egg in its bill, and quickly deposits a single egg in the nest. The stolen host egg, and the mimicry of the egg color, ensure that the clutch appears untouched when the rightful owner returns. This delicate operation successfully completed, the cuckoo eats the stolen egg as reward for its stealth!

◄ ▲ ▼ Representative species of cuckoos, turacos and hoatzin. (1) European cuckoo (*Cuculus canorus*). (2) Koel (*Eudynamys scolopacea*). (3) Violet plantain eater (*Musophaga violacea*). (4) Yellow-billed cuckoo (*Coccyzus americanus*). (5) Hoatzin (*Opisthocomus hoazin*). (6) White-bellied go-away bird (*Corythaixoides leucogaster*). (7) Roadrunner (*Geococcyx californianus*). (8) Groove-billed ani (*Crotophaga sulcirostris*). (9) Pheasant coucal (*Centropus phasianinus*).

The Great spotted cuckoo produces a passable imitation of the begging calls of nestling magpies and its wide open gape is even more vivid than those of the host nestlings. The motivation to respond to these stimuli is so strong in small songbirds that, once it has left the nest, the fledgling European cuckoo may be fed by passing birds that are neither true nor foster parents! This huge adoptee could in fact be quite a hazard to foster parents or others which attempt to feed it. A cuckoo's bill is powerful compared with that of a dunnock or Reed warbler host and capable of causing injury if the nestling is too eager to seize offered food. For this reason, the acceptance of food in the cuckoo is quite unlike that in other nestlings which close the bill rapidly over that of the parent as the food is transferred. The parasite, in deference to its tiny guardians, keeps its huge gape open until well after the parents have safely departed!

The remarkable behavior of such cuckoos tends to obscure the fact that about two-thirds of the species appear to be nonparasitic in breeding habits, mating monogamously and remaining together while the offspring are reared. The Pheasant coucal is one such species—producing one or two grotesque black nestlings which, in common with many cuckoos, excrete a foul liquid when they suspect the presence of a predator. However, our knowledge of most species is extremely poor, and some of these may turn out to be parasitic at least in certain circumstances.

One of the most remarkable things about the cuckoos is that even the nonparasitic members turn out to be unusual in other ways, and the roadrunner is just such a bird. This "outlier" of the cuckoo family, living in the desert chapparal of southwestern North America, was once heavily persecuted in the belief that it was harmful to populations of gamebirds. In fact it eats an assortment of large invertebrates and is also a voracious predator on small lizards. Travelers' tales have embellished the reputation of the roadrunner: in one popular story the bird delicately wields a cactus leaf, teasing an angry rattlesnake until it strikes and becomes impaled on one of the bird's thorny weapons.

Rather more firmly established is the fact that this species displays a physiology which is most unusual among birds—it is to some extent cold-blooded! When air temperatures become very low, as in deserts during the night, most birds need to increase metabolism to maintain their internal body temperature at a constant, high level. This of course means burning internal food reserves at an increasing rate. The roadrunner takes a more economical course—it simply allows its body temperature to fall slightly, turning down the "central heating" with no ill effects, and a saving in energy costs. The bird does in fact go into a slight torpor and may not be able to respond as quickly to sudden danger, but for a bird which has few predators this slight disadvantage may be relatively unimportant.

When the first rays of light break the cool of the desert night, the roadrunner displays a neat trick for warming up. Areas of skin on the back, just between the wings, are darkly pigmented and absorb the energy of sunlight, warming the skin and underlying blood vessels. To hasten this process, the bird fluffs the feathers covering the patches so that the light penetrates more effectively, and with this mechanism the bird can save up to about 50 percent of the energy it would otherwise use to warm up to a working temperature.

Thankfully, and unlike many other groups of fascinating and understudied birds, the cuckoos do not seem at great risk from man's activities. Many species are characteristic of scrub, secondary forest,

and other types of disturbed ground which, if anything, increase under human interference.   JAH

For all its weird and wonderful animal species Africa contains only one large family of birds totally restricted to that continent—the **turacos**. This group is so poorly known that for years it labored under the name of "Plantain-eaters," until reports filtered through that they rarely or never ate plantains or bananas. Subsistence through the aeons of time would, in any case, have been difficult for plantain-eaters because it was man, comparatively recently, who introduced these fruits to Africa!

The turacos are, to be sure, committed frugivores, taking a wide variety of fruits, including certain berries highly poisonous to man, as they forage through the dense foliage in parties of up to a dozen birds. The few reports that there are describe the nestlings also as being fed largely on a fruit diet supplemented by the occasional invertebrate, especially snails. This is unusual among young birds, most of which are fed on a high protein diet of invertebrates during their growth spurt between hatching and independence. The turaco life-style is a half-way house towards that of an even more specialized vegetarian, the hoatzin, and this fact, along with a general resemblance in form, has prompted some students to suggest a common ancestry. In fact, there are almost as many ideas about the evolutionary origins of the turacos as there are species within the family. Evidence from their feather parasites suggests an affinity with the fowls (Galliformes), while eye-lens proteins appear similar to those of songbirds (Passeriformes), and the structure of the foot places them close to the cuckoos (Cuculiformes).

One characteristic which the turacos seem to share with no other living birds is the possession of two vivid feather pigments—a green turacoverdin and a red turacin. The latter is known to be a copper compound and colors the crimson wing flashes and head ornamentations found in most turaco species. The turacoverdin has not been fully investigated, but may also be a copper compound and produces the rich green body feathers of 14 species. Most birds' feathers produce their colors by refracting light with specialized feather structures (iridescence) and turacoverdin is the only green pigment found in birds. The lengthy period of about a year taken by a young turaco to develop full adult coloration may perhaps be related to the difficulty of acquiring the relatively scarce copper for the pigment.

The common observation that turacos forage in groups might suggest that these birds, like some others in the tropics, are social breeders, organizing themselves so that individuals other than the parents contribute to the nesting chores of incubation, brooding, and feeding the hungry young. Our knowledge of their breeding habits is, however, so poor that this mode of reproduction has been confirmed in only a single species. In captivity, turacos will nest in simple pairs, although their success rate is low, perhaps due to unknown dietary deficiencies. Monogamy seems to be the rule, and the close similarity between the sexes is typical of other monogamous bird species—the only sexual difference seems to be one of bill color.

For several weeks before egg-laying, the male regurgitates gifts of fruit pulp for his female. Once reproduction proper has begun, both birds contribute equally to incubation, brooding, and feeding of the two or three chicks. These nestlings are covered in a fine down, of varying color and thickness, and they advertise their hunger with a large orange-red gape. Parents respond by regurgitating the fruit/insect mixture directly into the throat and, unlike some birds, this operation takes place in silence, perhaps because of the high density of predators in the forest habitat. Yet another affinity with the peculiar hoatzin emerges once the young have recovered from hatching and increased their strength with a few

▲ **Eclipsed by acacia blossom,** the Go-away bird (*Corythaixoides concolor*) is uniformly gray. The tall crest is the most distinctive feature of these African birds.

▶ **Elegant coiffure** of the Angola red-crested turaco (*Tauraco erythrolophus*). The green coloration is due not to iridescence, as in most birds, but to a green pigment peculiar to turacos—turacoverdin.

The Remarkable Hoatzin Chick

High above the shallow, muddy waters of a South American river, a newly-hatched hoatzin chick weakly lifts its head above the nest rim while its parents are away foraging. The hoatzin chick is naked and ugly and, like many other young birds, it appears to be virtually helpless. The latter could hardly be further from the truth. Upon the noisy return of its clumsy parents, the dark-skinned nestling leaves the nest, climbing gingerly among the thin branches, to intercept any tender young leaves which the parent may be carrying back to its hungry brood.

Two unique events are occurring here! The hoatzin is the only tree-living bird species which feeds its young on foliage to any great extent. Indeed, the adult hoatzin is one of the strictest vegetarians of the bird world, and its plant-crushing crop has evolved to be extremely large—about one-third of body-weight! The hoatzin is also the only tree-living bird in which the chicks habitually leave the nest very soon after hatching. Such a lightly muscled body hardly has the strength to balance on the swaying twigs, but the task is eased by the use of tiny claws emerging from the "elbow" bends of the unfeathered wings.

These appendages are not at all unique among birds—very young European coots bear single claws to aid their frequent climbs back into nests that may tower high above the water surface, and some species of geese carry sharp spurs on the wing-edge even as adults. Many species of animal in South America show similar adaptations to a precarious life over water: the American monkeys and anteaters possess gripping tails as an added insurance against a hazardous fall. The hoatzin chick has an additional safety net. Even if it should fall into the brown waters several meters below, all is not lost—the leathery bundle simply swims to the nearest branch and begins a slow deliberate climb back up to parental care!

meals. The silky nestlings are endowed with tiny claws on their wing-joints and can use these, and their adaptable foot structure, to leave the nest and sit on the periphery or even on adjoining twigs. In fact the young leave the nest for good, at an age of about four weeks, several days before they can fly. Independence from parental feeding seems to be gained at about six weeks, although the offspring continue to beg long after this age. If social breeding does occur in turacos it might even be expected that, as in other co-operative breeders, some offspring remain within the parental home range for much of the early part of their lives.

JAM

The strange unbirdlike **hoatzin** has defied conventional methods of classification for generations, and has traditionally been aligned with the Galliformes— an assemblage of "fowl-like" birds whose relationships to each other are not fully understood.

With its stout legs, coarse plumage, and weak flight, it certainly resembles a domestic hen rather more closely than a typical cuckoo. It has long been put in its own, single-species family, and, in the past, because of its superficial resemblance to reconstructions of the extinct bird *Archaeopteryx*, the hoatzin was often labelled as a "living fossil." In fact, probably nothing could be further from the truth.

Early birds, in common with many of their reptilian ancestors, were probably insect eaters, whereas the hoatzin is one of the most refined and specialized herbage eaters in the whole bird class. Many features of its appearance and biology seem to be consequences of its highly specialized way of life, rather than any evolutionary "hangover" from the distant past. Recent investigations of its biochemistry suggest that the hoatzin has closer affinities with the cuckoos than with any other group of birds.

JAH

Cuckoo in the Nest

The evolution of parasitism in birds

Although about two-thirds of the family are nonparasitic, cuckoos are infamous for their ability to divert the normal parental energies of a host species to their own ends. The mechanisms by which they accomplish this trickery may be fascinating but the selection pressures causing the evolution of the habit itself are equally intriguing.

There are two sides to this evolution, that of the cuckoo and that of its host, and of the two the former is the easier to visualize. Many bird species seem to be limited, in their reproductive capacity, not by the number of eggs they can lay but by the number of chicks they can successfully feed through to independence—increasing the number of eggs laid would not increase the number of chicks eventually reared. Imagine, however, that in a population of birds a parasitic mutant arises which can somehow foist its offspring successfully onto others. The major limitation of reproductive capacity is at a stroke removed and this mutant female is limited only by the number of eggs she can lay. If she is thus able to increase her fecundity, this mutant will increase in frequency in the population through time and the population will evolve towards a parasitic habit.

This scenario need not apply only to cuckoos. Females of such diverse species as House sparrow, starling, Redhead duck, and moorhen have been shown to deposit eggs in nests which are not their own, although these are usually nests of their own, more rarely of other, species. Parasitic females may lay in territories very close to their own and also complete a "legitimate" clutch of their own which they care for in the normal way. The adaptations of these part-time parasites are unlikely to be as perfect or extreme as those of the specialist cuckoos, but in one study of magpies in Spain it was unexpectedly found that an introduced swallow nestling repeatedly tried to eject the host eggs from the nestcup, exactly in the manner of a European cuckoo!

One evolutionary "half-way house" between these habits and full-scale cuckoo parasitism is the Black-billed cuckoo. In most years, pairs of this species build a nest and raise a brood of 2–4 nestlings exactly in the manner of any "ordinary" bird. When food is unusually abundant, however, each female also attempts to parasitize the nests of others in addition to raising a brood via her own parental care. Many of these parasitic eggs are foisted upon other Black-billed cuckoos but some are deposited in the nests of other species. What ecological factors have caused the evolution of this mixed policy? The interesting features of these cuckoos is that they have very large eggs, relative to body size, and that these large eggs have an extraordinarily fast development time, hatching in only 11 days—the shortest incubation period of any bird! Rapidly hatching eggs are of course essential for successful parasitism because the host's nest will already contain developing eggs when discovered by the cuckoo. If the cuckoo's eggs hatch much later than those of the host their chance of success will be very small. In comparison with other bird species showing longer incubation periods, the Black-billed cuckoo's efforts at parasitism are more likely to succeed, and the habit will become fixed in the population.

The more difficult evolutionary problem is understanding just how the host species continues to be fooled by the cuckoo's tactics. Any female songbird, a dunnock or Meadow pipit for example, which accepts a cuckoo's egg into her nest will leave no offspring that year. Other females, which may be able to discriminate and throw out cuckoo eggs or nestlings, will of course leave a reduced but significant number of offspring and so it is precisely these types which we should see in the population. Intensive study of several cuckoo species has shown that, within many species of host, there are discriminating and nondiscriminating females. How then do nondiscriminating females remain in the population in the face of their inability to reproduce themselves? One possible explanation has been proposed, which does however require that the cuckoo be even more cunning than we imagined. She must ensure that the discriminating birds leave no more offspring than the gullible hosts, and one way in which she could do this is to visit each nest she laid in and destroy the contents of any that had rejected her offspring.

Cuckoos are very difficult to watch, especially after egg-laying, but there is some evidence to support the foregoing. In an observation on Klaas's cuckoo, one host nest which rejected the cuckoo egg was quickly destroyed, probably by the cuckoo: the host birds (obviously discriminators) set about building a new nest and laying a fresh clutch nearby. This nest was also found and destroyed, although this time no cuckoo eggs were laid. Other observations on several species of cuckoo show that it is only the females which commonly eat eggs, as one would predict if they do so only to regulate the evolution of host discrimination.

JAH

▲▶ **The exploited Reed warbler.** TOP The imperfect mimicry of this cuckoo's egg, being pinkish when the Reed warbler's are green, does not prevent incubation and hatching. ABOVE The cuckoo hatches first and, naked though it is, maneuvers the other eggs until they fall out of the nest—it even has a hollow in its back into which the egg fits snugly. RIGHT The dainty Reed warbler then begins to bring food to the voracious maw of the cuckoo. The cuckoo's bill is so large relative to the Reed warbler that the cuckoo leaves the bill open till well after the "mother" has departed to avoid the risk of serious injury to the Reed warbler.

▼ **Half-way house.** These young Black-billed cuckoos are actually being reared by their true mother. This species though, does sometimes resort to parasitism.

OWLS

Order: Strigiformes
Families: Strigidae, Tytonidae.
One hundred and thirty-three species in 24
genera.
Distribution: worldwide except Antarctica and
some remote islands.

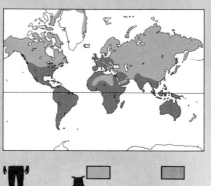

Typical owls   **Barn owls**

► **Full frontal.** All of the owls' characteristic
features are evident here as a Great horned owl
flies towards the camera. Superb nocturnal
predator though it obviously is, this specimen
is in fact a juvenile.

▼ **Diminutive predator.** A Saw-whet owl, one
of the smaller owls, with a short-tailed shrew.
Note the typically large head in relation to the
size of the body.

L ESS than three percent of all bird species
are active at night and over half of these
are owls—they are the nocturnal counterparts of the day-hunting hawks and falcons.
Although the largest species is one hundred
times the weight of the smallest, all owls are
instantly recognizable as such—a uniformity which stems from their unique adaptations for their role as nocturnal predators.
New species are still being discovered at the
rate of one every decade.

Owls occur wherever there are animals
on which they can prey. Most are associated
with trees, but others are adapted to living
in grasslands, deserts, marshes or even arctic tundra. The diets, biology and behavior
of many tropical owls are unknown, but
about 80 of the 133 species of all owls are
thought to be primarily night-hunting and
most of the rest can hunt at any time but
do so especially at dusk and dawn.

All owls are easily recognized by their
shape: an upright stance, short tail, large
head and dense covering of feathers giving
them a neckless, rounded outline. Equally
characteristic are the huge frontally placed,
often orange or yellow eyes, which stare out
from saucer-shaped disks of radiating
feathers. Daytime-hunting species have
smaller eyes and ill-defined facial disks.
Many owls have flexible tufts of feathers
above the eyes used in visual communication; these "ear tufts" have no connection
with hearing. All owls have powerful, usually feathered legs with sharp curved talons
for gripping prey. The short hooked beak is
curved downwards and may be hard to see
among the feathers.

Birds active only in darkness do not
require striking plumage; owls mostly spend
the day roosting in quiet places, often pres-
sed tight against a tree-trunk, and so both
sexes are usually similarly patterned with
various somber shades of brown to aid concealment. If discovered by small birds, owls
are mobbed to advertise their presence and
to persuade them to move on.

Owls which live in open habitats are paler
than those from woodland: desert forms are
often sandy-colored and the Snowy owl is
mainly white to match its arctic surroundings. Some woodland owls have two distinct
color-phases—gray in northern coniferous
forests, brown in deciduous woods further
south. With few exceptions, juveniles look
similar to adults. In most owls the female
is larger than the male, although the difference is not usually as marked as in some
of the day-hunting birds of prey.

Most owls are "typical" owls of the family
Strigidae. The largest genus (*Otus*) contains

33 screech or scops owls—a far-flung group,
though absent from Australia; all are small
to medium-sized, unspecialized "eared"
owls of tropical woodland or scrub. Most are
nocturnal and feed on insects, but the few
temperate species switch to rodents in winter. The 12 eagle owls are the nocturnal
equivalents of the large day-hunting eagles
and buzzards. They are absent from Australia and the Pacific Islands. Between them
they occupy most habitats apart from arctic
tundra, where they are replaced by the
equally large and powerful Snowy owl, a
species which often hunts by day.

The seven large fishing owls of Asia
(*Ketupa*) and Africa (*Scotopelia*) are the only
food specialists among the owls—the nocturnal counterparts of the osprey and fish
eagles and equivalent to the fish-eating bats
of tropical America. They occur from cold
northern forests to equatorial jungles. The
twelve pygmy owls (*Glaucidium*) are shared
equally between Eurasia, Africa and the

The 2 Families of Owls

Rare.　 Endangered.

Typical owls

Family: Strigidae
One hundred and twenty-three species in 22 genera.

Almost cosmopolitan, except Antarctica. Chiefly woodlands and forests; some grasslands, deserts and tundra. Size: 12–71cm (4.7–28in) long and weight 40–4,000g (1.4–141oz). Sexual dimorphism slight but females usually larger. Plumage: patterned brown or gray; one white, several black and white. Voice: a wide range of shrieks, hoots and caterwauls. Nests: chiefly holes, or abandoned nests of other species; a few on the ground and in burrows. Eggs: 1–14 depending on food supply, usually 2–7, white and rounded; weight 7–80g (0.2–3oz); incubation period 15–35 days; nestling period 24–52 days, but young may leave nest before able to fly (15–35 days after hatching). Diet: mostly small ground-living rodents, also birds, reptiles, frogs, fish and crabs (fishing owls), earthworms and large insects (especially small owls).

Species include: **African wood owl** (*Ciccaba woodfordii*), **Barking owl** (*Ninox connivens*), **Barred owl** (*Strix varia*), **Black and white owl** (*Ciccaba nigrolineata*), **Blakiston's fish owl** (*Ketupa blakistoni*), **Boobook owl** (*Ninox novaeseelandiae*), **Brown fish owl** (*Ketupa zeylonensis*), **Burrowing owl** (*Athene cunicularia*), **Eagle owl** (*Bubo bubo*), **Elf owl** (*Micrathene whitneyi*), **Giant scops owl** (*Otus gurneyi*), **Great gray owl** (*Strix nebulosa*), **Great horned owl** (*Bubo virginianus*), **Hawk owl** (*Surnia ulula*), **Laughing owl** (*Sceloglaux albifacies*) (possibly extinct), **Least pygmy owl** (*Glaucidium minutissimum*), **Little owl** (*Athene noctua*), **Long-eared owl** (*Asio otus*), **Long-whiskered owlet** (*Xenoglaux loweryi*), **Madagascan scops owl** (*Otus rutilus*), **Oriental hawk owl** (*Ninox scutulata*), **Oriental scops owl** (*Otus sunia*), **Pearl-spotted owlet** (*Glaucidium perlatum*), **Pel's fishing owl** (*Scotopelia peli*), **Powerful owl** (*Ninox strenua*), **Pygmy owl** (*Glaucidium passerinum*), **Saw-whet owl** (*Aegolius acadicus*), **Scops owl** (*Otus scops*), **Screech owl** (*Otus asio*), **Short-eared owl** (*Asio flammeus*), **Snowy owl** (*Nyctea scandiaca*), **Sokoke scops owl** [R] (*Otus ireneae*), **Spectacled owl** (*Pulsatrix perspicillata*), **Spotted eagle owl** (*Bubo africanus*), **Tawny owl** (*Strix aluco*), **Tengmalm's owl** (*Aegolius funereus*), **Ural owl** (*Strix uralensis*). Threatened species: 3.

Barn and bay owls

Family: Tytonidae
Ten species in 2 genera.

Europe except far north, SE Asia, Africa, N America to Canadian border, S America, Australia. Open areas, including farmland, scattered woodland, and forests. Size: 23–53cm (9–21in) long, weight 180–1,280g (6.3–45.5oz). Females usually slightly bigger than males. Plumage: orange-buff to blackish brown above, white, rufous or blackish-brown below; a striking facial "disk." Voice: shrill hissing, screeching or whistling. Nests: in barns, holes in rocks or trees, or on the ground (grass owls). Eggs: usually 2–6, sometimes up to 11, white, elliptical; most weigh 17–42.5g (0.65–1.5oz); incubation 27–34 days; nestling period 49–56 days. Diet: small mammals and birds, fish, frogs, lizards and large insects.

Species include: **African bay owl** (*Phodilus prigoginei*), **Barn owl** (*Tyto alba*), **Common bay owl** (*Phodilus badius*), **Grass owl** (*Tyto capensis*), **Madagascar grass owl** [E] (*T. soumagnei*), **Masked owl** (*T. novaehollandiae*), **Sooty owl** (*T. tenebricosa*).

Americas. They include the sparrow-sized Least pygmy owl of tropical South American forests, which shares with the Elf owl of the American West the distinction of being the smallest owl. Both are closely related to the Long-whiskered owlet of the Peruvian Andes, not discovered until 1976. Most medium-sized owls of Indonesia and Australasia are hawk owls (*Ninox*). Of these only the Oriental hawk owl of the Asian mainland has a wide distribution; most of the other 15 species are confined to single islands and their ranges do not overlap. In Australia, where most owl genera are absent (eg *Bubo, Otus, Strix* and *Glaucidium*), three *Ninox* species do exist side by side, including the small Boobook owl which also occurs in New Zealand and New Guinea. The five *Ciccaba* owls are rarely-seen medium-sized owls of the tropical forests of Africa and the Americas. In temperate woodlands they are replaced by the 11 *Strix* species, including the extensively studied Tawny owl, whose range extends from Britain across Europe and northwest Africa to the mountains of Burma and China. The five *Asio* species fall into two ecologically distinct groups: "long-eared," found in broad-leaved or coniferous woodland, and "short-eared" which frequent open country.

The genus *Athene* contains four species and takes its name from the Greek goddess of wisdom Pallas Athene. The Little owl, which sometimes hunts by day, is a familiar sight in open habitats from western Europe and North Africa across to China. In the late 1800s it was introduced into Britain and New Zealand. The only New World representative is the Burrowing owl, a long-legged, daytime-hunting, terrestrial species of open treeless grasslands. The genus *Aegolius* is a basically New World family of four geographically-separated, small, nocturnal, forest owls. The most widespread is the Boreal or Tengmalm's owl. Like several other owls of northern coniferous forests (eg the Great gray and the Hawk owl) its range extends in a belt right across the Old World.

The **barn** and **bay owls** form the other family (Tytonidae). They are distinguished from the typical owls by their heart-shaped rather than round faces, middle and inner toes of equal length (the inner is shorter in strigids), serrated middle claws and wishbones fused to the breastbone. The rodent-hunting Barn owl of open country is one of the most widely distributed of all birds (see box), found on every inhabited continent. The other seven barn owls occur in Africa, islands in the Indian Ocean and Southeast

▶ **Representative species of owl.** (1) Elf owl (*Micrathene whitneyi*) in the roosting posture. (2) Barking owl (*Ninox connivens*) with nestlings at the nest-hole. (3) White-faced scops owl (*Otus leucotis*) listening for prey. (4) Tengmalm's owl (*Aegolius funereus*) about to catch a vole. (5) Common bay owl (*Phodilus badius*). (6) Spectacled owl (*Pulsatrix perspicillata*). (7) Malaysian eagle owl (*Bubo sumatranus*). (8) Spotted wood owl (*Strix seloputo*) being mobbed by passerines. (9) Pel's fishing owl (*Scotopelia peli*) with fish.

Asia, and in Australasia. The little-known Common Bay owl is found in Asian forests from India to Java and Borneo; the African Bay owl is known only from a single specimen collected in the Congo in 1951.

In spite of their general resemblance, owls are not closely related to the hawks and falcons; both groups evolved to exploit similar food supplies and so possess the same basic anatomical features for a predatory way of life. Study of egg-white proteins suggests that the nearest relatives of owls are another nocturnal order—the nightjars and allies (see pp248–53). Nightjars use their huge mouths to snap up insects in flight, oilbirds find ripe fruit by smell, but owls are unique among nocturnal birds in using vision and/or hearing to locate their food.

The adaptations needed for hunting at night limit the kinds of food that owls can exploit efficiently. There are no carrion-feeding owls equivalent to vultures and kites (although some do take carrion occasionally), no soaring forms, and owls seldom pursue and capture birds in flight—a common specialization among day-hunting birds of prey.

Owls catch most of their prey on the ground in the open. Woodland owls have short, rounded wings and when hunting sit quietly on a low perch watching and listening for small mammals. On hearing a likely noise they rapidly rotate their head until the sound registers equally in both ears; they are then directly facing it. When the source of the sound is pin-pointed, the owl glides silently down towards it; at the last second it swings its feet forwards to hit the prey, often killing it outright. Many owls of open country hunt mainly in flight. They have long wings which enable them slowly to quarter the ground like the day-hunting harriers, with little expenditure of energy. Long-eared owls spend about 20 percent of the night hunting. Once prey is located, it is pounced on from a low height in the manner of perch-hunting owls; about one in five attempts is successful. Owls are opportunistic hunters and will often try to catch prey any way they can: insects (and sometimes birds) may be chased in flight, birds are grabbed while roosting, several species (eg Little and Burrowing owls) bound across the ground in search of invertebrates, and Tawny owls will plunge into water to catch frogs. The specialist fishing owls swoop down to pluck fish from the water surface. Roadsides also provide good hunting areas for owls and in developed countries many are killed by traffic.

Unlike hawks and falcons, owls carry all but the largest prey in their bill and swallow it whole, head first. Sorting out what is nutritious takes place internally and any indigestible remains such as bones and fur are regurgitated as pellets, which provide a good record of what owls eat (see box). Owls have no crop in which to store food but sometimes cache prey.

Owls feed on a wide variety of animal prey; what they eat depends mainly on their size and the habitat they occupy. Tawny owls living in woodland feed mainly on mice and voles, but in the towns they feed on birds, especially house sparrows. Small owls are mostly insectivorous; medium-sized ones feed mainly on small rodents or birds; the largest species take mammals (up to the size of hares or even small deer) and medium-sized birds—including other owls and birds of prey!

Owls are well insulated by their dense covering of feathers and get by on about 30 percent less food than most other birds of equivalent size. They can have a substantial impact on prey populations: in one study, a pair of Tawny owls, consuming a maximum of seven 20g (0.7oz) rodents per day, removed 18–46 percent of the Bank voles and 28–70 percent of the Wood mice

Man's Friend—The Barn Owl

The Barn owl's nocturnal life-style, ghostly white appearance and association with ruins or churches where it likes to nest, have earned it a place in the folklore of many cultures but, as its name suggests, it is best known for its association with farmers. Wherever crops are grown, large populations of rats and mice build up and these attract the rodent-hunting Barn owl. It is found almost everywhere between latitudes 40°N and 40°S, and its range also extends into northwestern Europe and to the tip of South America.

In the Netherlands, farmers actively encourage owls by installing special "owl doors" to allow them easy access to their buildings, and by providing food in hard weather, which otherwise causes heavy losses. Unfortunately, this close association with agriculture was almost the Barn owl's undoing in western Europe, and they suffered more from poisoning by agricultural chemicals than other owls. In Malaysia, Barn owls and chemicals are actually used together to control the plagues of rats which cause severe damage in oil-palm plantations. Formerly rare, Barn owls have invaded the plantations since nest-boxes were erected for them to breed in. The owls can now raise several families per year and often congregate in flocks of up to 40 birds. Each owl family eats about 1,300 rats per year, which can slow the recovery of rodent populations that

have first been reduced by poisoning.

Not every pest-control scheme involving Barn owls has had such a happy outcome. In the 1950s they were introduced into the Seychelles, again to control rats. Unfortunately, the owls found the native birds easier to catch and in 12 years they exterminated the White tern from two islands, reduced the numbers of the rare Blue pigeon, and competed for nest sites with the endangered Seychelles kestrel. They now have a bounty on their heads and are killed at every opportunity.

▲ **Nocturnal killer.** The Barn owl's oval facial disk is characteristic of many owls, and is thought to aid in the fine location of sound.

The Barn owl's range extends from northwestern Europe to the tip of South America, and throughout the world this species is an important predator of agricultural pests.

present in their hunting range in each two-month period.

Periodic fluctuations in the numbers of rodents have striking effects on the owls themselves. In years when they are scarce, many owls either do not breed or lay reduced numbers of eggs; Snowy owls and Short-eared owls lay 2–14 eggs, depending on prey availability. Generally, breeding is timed so that food is most plentiful when the young are learning to hunt for themselves and the adults are undergoing their annual molt (which reduces their hunting effi-

ciency). Extra food is also needed to grow the new feathers and to compensate for the reduced insulation properties of their plumage. In tropical regions, breeding is geared to rainfall—small species have young in the nest when the onset of the rainy season produces a flush of insects. Many owls have only a single brood per year, but some open-country species can breed whenever rodents are abundant, and may raise several broods in a year. Most owls can breed in their first year if conditions are suitable.

Many owls adopt another family-planning measure. Single eggs are laid at intervals of two or more days but incubation begins with the first, so that the earliest chick to hatch may be up to three weeks older than the last. If food is plentiful, all the chicks survive, if not, the youngest die and are eaten by the rest. In this way, brood size is adjusted to the food available.

Owls are not great nest-builders: most breed in holes in trees, rocks or the ground, but some open-country owls line depressions in the ground and Burrowing owls can dig their own underground nest chambers (although they usually take over prairie dog lairs). Small species appropriate old woodpecker holes. Large owls unable to find appropriate old woodpecker holes, and most woodland owls, readily occupy nest-boxes provided for them. Large owls unable to find appropriately sized natural fissures take over abandoned tree-nests of crows or birds of prey.

Incubation tends to be by the female alone, with the smaller male providing all the food from before egg-laying until the young—initially born blind, helpless and covered in sparse grayish-white down—no longer need brooding or their prey torn up for them. This division of labor allows the inert female to accumulate fat reserves and remain on the nest even when the male finds hunting difficult as, for example, in wet weather. In many species, the larger female vigorously defends the young against intruders, including humans (some people have even lost eyes to them). Other species have threat displays in which the female tries to make herself look larger and even more fearsome. To further reduce the chances of predation, the young of open-nesting owls grow faster than those which are reared in holes and leave the nest before they are fully feathered.

Fledged young beg loudly for food and are often dependent upon their parents for several months before they disperse. Newly independent owls suffer a high mortality:

over half the young Tawny owls die in their first year, many of starvation, but once settled they can expect to live for at least four or five years and some have survived for more than 15. Larger species probably live even longer—a captive Eagle owl survived 68 years.

Most owls are territorial and non-migratory, especially those living in the tropics or woodland. Here pairs often spend all their lives in strictly defended territories, switching to alternative prey if one kind becomes unavailable; the populations of such species remain stable over long periods. Northern owls and those of open country which feed mainly on rodents have a narrower range of quarry available to them. They usually defend territories in the breeding season but their populations tend to fluctuate in parallel with those of their prey. Some are found far outside their normal ranges if food supplies fail. Large numbers of Snowy owls sometimes appear in the USA when lemming or hare populations have crashed in the Arctic. The birds are often very tame when in unfamiliar surroundings: North American bird-banders catch the impressive looking Great gray owl by casting out a dead mouse attached to a fishing line (without a hook)—a hungry owl will pounce on it and can be reeled in! A few owls undertake regular north–south migrations, like the Scops owl, which exploits the summer flush of insects in southern Europe; the Short-eared owl is nomadic, settling wherever prey is temporarily abundant.

Owls which are territorial throughout the year live in pairs but forage alone so as not to interfere with each other's hunting. The rest usually live alone outside the breeding season, except some owls of open country which congregate in areas where prey is plentiful; these often roost communally but disperse at dusk to hunt alone. Only the Burrowing owl is colonial.

Breeding territories tend to be smaller where more prey is available. In Britain, Tawny owls defend 12–20ha (30–50 acres) in open deciduous woodland where small rodents are abundant but over 40ha (100 acres) in more sterile conifer plantations. The huge Eagle owl takes bigger, less common prey and needs a correspondingly larger territory: their nests are usually spaced 4–5km (2.5–3mi) apart. To communicate over such long distances at night, owls have well-developed vocabularies and they are much more vocal than day-hunting birds of prey. The familiar territorial hooting of many owls is equivalent to the song of other birds serving to warn off rival males and to attract a mate. The hoots of male Eagle owls can be heard 4km (2.5mi) away and like many other owls the pair frequently answer one another in a duet, probably to

▲ **Owls' eyes.** The large wide-set eyes of these young Tengmalm's owls help them to see in poor light. Tengmalm's owls are found in North America, Europe and Asia.

◄ **Owl pellets:** the content of a pellet from a Long-eared owl.

► **The gape, stare and ear tufts** of a Malaysian fishing owl (*Ketupa ketupa*) give it an eagle-like appearance. Fish owls of Africa and Asia feed mainly on fish which they strike with their talons on the surface of the water. They also hunt crabs and crayfish in the shallows, and may take small mammals and insects.

Owl Pellets

Owls usually bolt their prey whole and much of what is indigestible, such as fur, bones, teeth, claws, beaks or the head capsules and wing-cases of insects, are compressed into a sausage-shaped pellet which is cast back out through the mouth. To ease the pellet's passage the hard parts are enclosed by the softer fur or feathers. Pellets can be collected, teased apart and their contents identified, to provide a record of what the owl has been eating. Mammals can usually be identified and counted from their skulls, jaws or teeth; birds from their beaks, feet or certain bones. Even the hard remains of earthworms and other invertebrates can often be recognized.

The ease with which pellets can be collected and analyzed depends on the species. Barn owls roost in the same place day after day and it is an easy job to collect the accumulation of pellets at regular intervals. Other species, like the Tawny owl, deposit their pellets at widely scattered nocturnal roosting or feeding sites, making them difficult to find; they also seem better at digesting bones than other owls and sometimes decapitate their prey.

Most owls of temperate regions produce one or two pellets per 24 hours, depending on season. In summer, when nights are short,

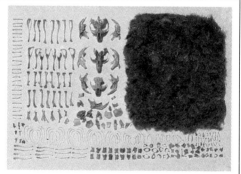

they produce one large pellet at their day-time roosts. In winter they often cast a second, smaller pellet (about 7 hours after the first) while hunting at night.

The size and appearance of pellets is often characteristic of a particular species. In general the largest owls produce the largest pellets. Those of the Eagle owl average 77 × 31 × 28mm, those of the Pygmy owl only 27 × 11 × 9mm. Barn owl pellets are black, shiny and hard, those of the Tawny owl gray and crumbly.

Although the analysis of remains in pellets has drawbacks, it provides the best clue to the diets of owls, allowing comparisons to be drawn between different seasons and species.

maintain the pair bond between them. Day-hunting owls are generally less vocal and the Barn owl does not hoot, perhaps because its light color makes it easily visible, removing the need for long-distance vocal communication. All owls can produce loud tongue-clicking sounds when they are frightened or angry.

Many owls will answer imitations of their hoots, and territories can be mapped in this way. Local names for owls often reflect their distinctive calls: the names boobook, and saw-whet are respectively phonetic rendering and description.

Owls sometimes share their habitat with day-hunting birds of prey; on the Galapagos Islands, Short-eared owls hunt both by day and night where the Galapagos hawk is absent, but only at night where hawks are present. Where several owls co-exist they are usually of different sizes and feed on different prey—in Australia three hawk owls occur together: the small Boobook owl feeds on insects and small birds, the medium-sized Barking owl takes small marsupials and birds up to crow-size, and the large Powerful owl catches medium-sized arboreal marsupials. Where owls feed on similar prey in the same habitat, for example Great-horned and Barred owls in parts of North America, they avoid competition for food by defending territories against rival species. Modern forestry reduces the number of nest-sites for owls and in Scandinavia many nest-boxes have been erected for Ural and Tawny owls—these species have increased but they prey upon Pygmy owls, which have consequently become rare.

Like most predators, owls are persecuted by man wherever their presence might conflict with his interests, particularly game preservation. In Europe, Eagle owls have been exterminated in densely populated regions. Ironically, in other areas these owls are used to lure other birds of prey (which mob them) within gunshot range.

Owls did not suffer as much as some birds of prey when toxic chemicals were introduced as pesticides in agriculture. A greater threat is the destruction of their habitats. The Madagascar grass owl, the Sokoke scops owl (discovered in 1965 in coastal rain forest in Kenya), the races of the Madagascan scops owls on the Seychelles and the Comoros, and the Giant scops owl of the Philippines are all endangered for this reason. The Laughing owl of New Zealand may already be extinct. Its decline followed the introduction from Europe of stoats and weasels which destroyed its nests and competed with it for food.   GH

A Face for the Night
Why an owl looks like an owl

Owls are generalized predators—their specialization lies not in feeding on a particular type of prey but in catching it in darkness. The modifications which enable owls to do this create their distinctive appearance.

Owls have particularly highly developed hearing and vision, and need oversized skulls to accommodate ear openings and eyes much bigger than those of other birds—the largest owls have eyes comparable in size to those of humans. What, therefore, is the advantage of these large frontally placed eyes?

Large eyes can have large pupils to allow more light to fall on the retina (the light-sensitive layer at the back of the eye). A Tawny owl's eye has 100 times the light-gathering power of a pigeon's and produces a large retinal image to provide the visual acuity necessary to discriminate potential prey. Owls have tubular (rather than spherical) eyes, placed frontally in order to accommodate the huge lens and cornea. Unfortunately, tubular eyes have a reduced field of view and are virtually immobile, giving owls a visual field of only 110° compared with a man's 180° and a pigeon's 340°. To overcome this, owls have remarkably flexible necks, enabling them to invert their heads as well as to look directly behind! Frontally-placed eyes can also provide binocular vision, in which both eyes view the same area from different aspects. This allows better judgement of distance.

Although owls see much better at night than birds active during the day, the popular belief that their eyes are vastly superior to man's in the dark but function poorly in bright light is not correct. The Tawny owl has color vision, sees in daylight as well as a pigeon, and has eyes only some two to three times more sensitive than man's in the dark. Owls can only hunt successfully at night because their visual sensitivity is allied to exceptional hearing. Owls are especially sensitive to sounds with a high frequency component, such as the rustling of dry leaves—some species can even locate and capture small rodents in total darkness just from the noise they make in moving across the woodland floor.

The characteristic facial disks of owls are part of this specialized hearing apparatus. The tightly-packed rows of stiff feathers which make up the rim of this disk reflect high-frequency sounds which are channeled by the mobile facial disks into the ears behind, in the same way that mammals use their large, fleshy external ears. The ear openings themselves are enormous—vertical slits running almost the whole

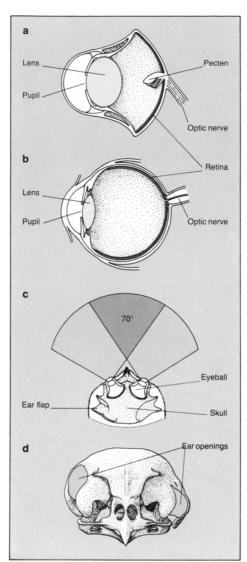

▲ **Owl senses.** The eyes and ears of owls are extremely sensitive. The eye (**a**) differs from the mammalian eye (**b**) in having the retina close to and equidistantly spaced from the lens. The retina is packed with rods (which only detect black and white) and can function at very low light intensities. The pecten is a structure thought to provide nutrients to the eyeball. The owl's field of vision (**c**) is not large, but provides good stereoscopic vision over an angle of 70°. This intense tunnel vision is an adaptation to homing in on its prey. The ears of owls (**d**) are asymmetrically placed to aid in the location of sounds.

▶ **The face mask** of this Short-eared owl shows the barbless feathers characteristic of the area surrounding the ears.

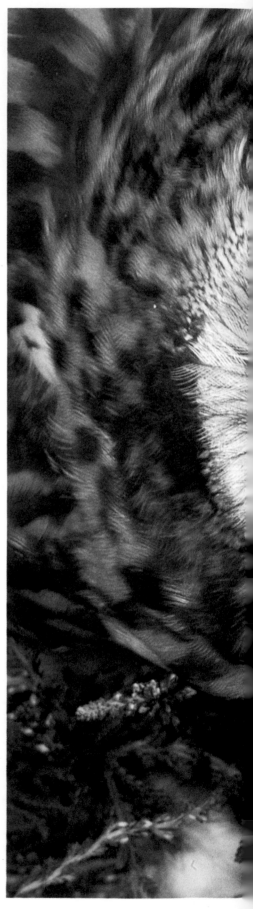

depth of the skull and hidden beneath feathered flaps of skin.

The broad skull helps in sound location— a noise from one side will be louder and perceived fractionally sooner in the ear nearest to it. Owls can locate sounds in the horizontal direction four times better than a cat, but an owl hunting from above needs to pin-point sound in the vertical direction as well as to fix the prey's position exactly. Barn owls can do this with an accuracy of one or two degrees in both horizontal and vertical directions—one degree is about the width of a little finger at arm's length! Owls achieve this by moving their ear flaps to alter the size and shape of the ear openings to make reception different for the two ears. In some highly nocturnal owls (eg Tengmalm's) the ear openings themselves are placed asymmetrically on the skull.

To be able to hear their prey and not frighten it off, owls are equipped to fly silently. From head to toe they are covered with an enormous number of soft, downy feathers. This gives them their characteristic rounded outline and makes them appear much larger than they really are. Long-eared owls are known to have over 10,000 feathers.

The wing feathers of owls lack the hard sheen of other birds and have soft fringes with fluted leading edges to ease the flow of air over them. These adaptations, coupled with extreme lightness in relation to their wing area, enable owls to fly very efficiently and silently over the countryside while hunting. Fishing owls lack these adaptations as their prey cannot hear the owl approaching.

The other prominent characteristics of owls, such as talons, are common to most predatory birds, although in owls the hooked beak is deflected downwards so as not to interfere with the already limited field of view. To grasp and kill prey, the legs and feet are immensely strong and armed with needle-sharp claws. One peculiarity of owls is the reversible outer toe which can point either forwards or backwards to increase the "catching area" of the feet and improve gripping ability. Like mammal-hunting hawks, owls have relatively short legs; these are feathered to the toes, probably to aid thermoregulation, but possibly also to protect against bites from prey. Exceptions are the fishing owls which specialize in catching prey in water and have bare legs and osprey-like feet equipped with spiny soles to grasp slippery fish, and terrestrial species like the Burrowing owl, which have noticeably longer legs.   GH

NIGHTJARS AND FROGMOUTHS

Order: Caprimulgiformes
Families: Caprimulgidae, Podargidae,
Aegothelidae, Nyctibiidae, Steatornithidae.
Ninety-eight species in 21 genera.
Distribution: worldwide except for the far
North.

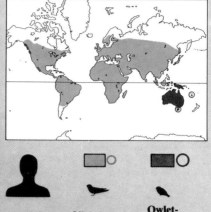

Nightjars   **Owlet-frogmouths**

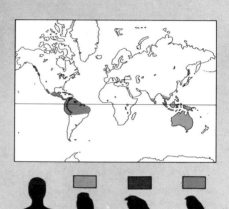

Frogmouths   **Oilbird**   **Potoos**

► **Representative species of the order
Caprimulgiformes.** (1) Tawny frogmouth
(*Podargus strigoides*) on nest showing its large
gape. (2) Standard-winged nightjar
(*Semiophorus longipennis*). (3) Whip-poor-will
(*Caprimulgus vociferus*). (4) Oilbird (*Steatornis
caripensis*) in a cave. (5) Common potoo
(*Nyctibius griseus*) characteristically perched on
a stump. (6) Owlet-nightjar (*Aegotheles
cristatus*). (7) Philippine frogmouth
(*Batrachostomus septimus*) eating a caterpillar.

GOAT herdsmen, flushing the big-mouthed, moth-like nightjars from pastures or hearing their "night-jarring" voices through the wee hours just when the goats were failing to give milk, decided that these strange birds were the culprits, hence the alternative name of "goatsucker." Other species also have mysterious names.

Most **nightjars** look like big soft moths, dressed as they are in variegated patterns of brown, gray, black, and white. Even their comparatively silent and often dancingly graceful flight suggests moths. Their overall appearance is sleek, with the limpid, generally dark eyes and large heads with tiny bills giving them a "baby-faced" charm that big-headed, small-billed birds always seem to possess. Their wings are usually long and tapered, the tail typically long and wide. Males of tropical savanna and desert include several audaciously ornamented forms. These ornaments, elongated wing or tail feathers, are employed in courtship displays, and are molted or broken off after the breeding season. Nightjars have astonishingly large gapes. When one opens its mouth, the whole front of the head becomes a giant glistening cavern fringed with bristles that form an effective insect trap.

The nightjar family is usually subdivided into two subfamilies, the Chordeilinae or nighthawks and the Caprimulginae or nightjars. The former is restricted to the New World while the nightjars, although having a number of New World representatives, are also widespread in Europe, Asia and Africa; the genus *Caprimulgus* itself contains some 45 species.

Being largely insectivorous, nightjars live mainly in tropical climates or migrate to temperate ones only in warm seasons. Nocturnal counterparts of swallows and swifts, they forage mainly in sustained flight. Woodland dwellers, such as the Dusky nightjar, hawk single insects from a perch, returning to it after each sally.

Nightjars are superbly equipped to capture insects on the wing at night. A nightjar can engulf large numbers of mosquitoes in a single snap or wheel about and sweep up a Luna moth having a 10cm (4in) wingspread. Small birds are also sometimes taken by larger species such as the chuck-wills-widow, and probably *not* by accident! There is some indication that these birds can echolocate, thus avoiding collisions with trees while foraging at night. In an experiment, captured Common nighthawks flying in a darkened underground tunnel hung with a complex pattern of wooden and rope obstacles, negotiated the maze without mishap, uttering their "beans" call notes as they flew. However, when temporarily deafened, they struck objects of the maze, and this suggests their difficulties arose from not being able to hear high frequency sounds reflected from those objects.

There is little information on life span in nightjars. A whip-poor-will ringed as an adult was recovered dead four years later. Since it is a migratory species, it may be safely assumed that many tropical forms live longer. Breeding is generally timed to coincide with surges in insect populations that occur at the beginning of warm or wet seasons. Tropical species may have two broods. Courtship is sometimes elaborate. In the Standard-winged nightjar, the observed clustering of a few nests and the highly ornamented male plumage suggest that the males may have several mates simultaneously. Highly elaborate plumages are useful in mate attraction but impractical in parental care. Clustering of nests of a harem of females permits the male to oversee his mates easily and keep out other males. A male keeps a harem by constant vigil, displaying himself from a prominent perch or in flight. As in birds-of-paradise, the male's role is limited to the mating act.

Nightjars are generally non-social, but

1

nighthawks often feed and migrate in large loose aggregations. A few other species may forage in groups, but perhaps due only to swarming of insects.

The poorwill is the *only* species of bird known to become torpid for long periods in winter. A Hopi Indian folk tale was recently confirmed when a hibernating poorwill was discovered three winters in succession in a rock crevice in southern California. Its body temperature was about 18°C (64.5°F). The Hopi Indians called the poorwill *Holchko*— "the sleeping one."

Nightjars are not so much threatened by the advance of civilization as are many other groups of birds. Most thrive in open, often disturbed habitats, but the whip-poor-will, a true forest dweller once common throughout the eastern USA, has completely disappeared from many now heavily disturbed parts of its range. Conservation and management of nightjars requires preservation of habitat and low use of insecticides.

JWH

The **frogmouths** closely resemble true nightjars. They sometimes hunt, adopting a sim-

The 5 Families of Nightjars and Frogmouths   ℝ Rare.

Nightjars or goatsuckers
Family: Caprimulgidae
Seventy-two species in 16 genera.

Throughout the tropical and temperate world, except New Zealand, southern S America, and most oceanic islands. Mostly forest edge to savanna and desert, a few woodland dwellers; mostly crepuscular and nocturnal. Size: 19–29cm (8–11in) long, weight 40–120g (1.4–4oz). Plumage: concealment patterns of browns, grays and black with patches of white on tail, wings and head; females often differ from males in having less white on the wings, tail or on the head. Some tropical forms with elongate wing or tail feathers. Voice: loud, repetitive trilling or whistled male song; other calls and sounds made with wings. Eggs: 1–2, white or buff-colored, usually with blotches; incubation period 16–19 days; nestling period 16–20 days. Diet: insects.

Species include: **chuck-will's-widow** (*Caprimulgus carolinensis*), **Common nighthawk** (*Chordeiles minor*), **Dusky nightjar** (*Caprimulgus pectoralis*), **European nightjar** (*C. europaeus*), **Little nightjar** (*C. parvulus*), **Pennant-winged nightjar** (*Semiophorus vexillarius*), **poorwill** (*Phalaenoptilus nuttallii*), **Puerto Rican nightjar** ℝ (*C. noctitherus*), **Rufous nightjar**

(*C. rufus*), **Sooty nightjar** (*C. saturatus*), **Standard-winged nightjar** (*Semiophorus longipennis*), **whip-poor-will** (*C. vociferus*).

Frogmouths
Family: Podargidae
Twelve species in 2 genera.

SE Asia, Australia, Indonesia, Sri Lanka. Mostly confined to tropical rain forest. Size: 23–54cm (9–32in) long. Plumage: brown to gray; most species have at least 2 color phases. Voice: usually a low repetitive booming; Marbled frogmouth has an "ooo" call; young Gould's frogmouths have a soft, kitten-like mew. Nests: twigs in trees. Eggs: 1–3, according to species, white; size 40 × 29mm; incubation period about 30 days; nestling period about 30 days. Diet: mainly insects but Marbled frogmouth known to take a wide range of small animals, including even small vertebrates such as mice.

Species include: **Gould's frogmouth** (*Batrachostomus stellatus*), **Large frogmouth** (*B. auritus*), **Marbled frogmouth** (*Podargus ocellatus*), **Papuan frogmouth** (*P. papuensis*), **Tawny frogmouth** (*P. strigoides*).

Owlet-nightjars
Family: Aegothelidae
Eight species of the genus *Aegotheles*.
Australia and New Guinea. Tropical

rain forest in New Guinea, open country in Australia. Size: 20–30cm (8–12in) long, weight 45–115g (1.6–4.1oz). Plumage: from ash-gray to black, sometimes with considerable variation within species. Voice: a variety of shrills and churring sounds. Nests: tree hollows lined with leaves and fur, or holes in a cliff face. Eggs: 2–5, white. Diet: mostly insects.

Species: **Archbold's owlet-nightjar** (*Aegotheles archboldi*), **Barred owlet-nightjar** (*A. bennettii*), **Large owlet-nightjar** (*A. insignis*), **Mountain owlet-nightjar** (*A. albertisi*), **New Caledonian owlet-nightjar** (*A. savesi*), **owlet-nightjar** (*A. cristatus*), **Sunda** or **Halmahera owlet-nightjar** (*A. crinifrons*), **Wallace's owlet-nightjar** (*A. wallacii*).

Potoos
Family: Nyctibiidae
Five species of the genus *Nyctibius*.
S and C America, southern N America. Forest. Size: 23–50cm (9–20in) long. Plumage: concealment coloration of barred and mottled gray and browns; soft and fluffy; young mostly white with a few speckled dark patches. Voice: whistles and barking wows; described as "kwak," "kaw," "graw-ar;" the Giant potoo has a loud "baw-woo." Nests: no nest is constructed but egg is laid on broken tree branches, stumps etc. Eggs: usually one,

sometimes two, spotted, size 36 × 29 to 52 × 38mm. Diet: insects.

Species: **Common potoo** (*Nyctibius griseus*), **Giant potoo** (*N. grandis*), **Long-tailed potoo** (*N. aethereus*), **Rufous potoo** (*N. bracteatus*), **White-winged potoo** (*N. leucopterus*).

Oilbird
Family: Steatornithidae
Sole species *Steatornis caripensis*.

S America from Guyana and Venezuela along the Andes to Bolivia; Trinidad. Forested country with caves. Size: about 45cm (18in) long and 400–430g (14–15oz); nestlings up to 50 percent heavier. Plumage: mainly rich brown with a scattering of white spots which are especially large and conspicuous on wing-coverts and outer secondaries; males somewhat grayer and darker than females. Voice: a variety of harsh screams, squawks and clucking calls; also series of short staccato clicks, used for echolocation in darkness. Nests: on ledges in caves from half-light to pitch darkness. Eggs: 2–4, white, 17–22.5g (0.6–7.9oz); incubation period 32–35 days; nestling period 88–125, usually 100–115 days. Diet: exclusively the flesh of fruits from forest trees (the seeds being regurgitated), especially of the palm (Palmae), laurel (Lauraceae) and incense (Burseraceae) families.

▲ Nightjar courtship. Some nightjars have dramatic courtship displays. (1) The male Common nighthawk dives from a great height, then swoops upward near the female, making a booming sound by the rush of air over the soft inner vanes of certain wing feathers. (2) The male Standard-winged nightjar circles his mate in fluttering flight, which causes an updraft that elevates the extended inner primaries into fluttering pennants.

◄ A European nightjar ABOVE shows its marbled markings while displaying aggressively on its nest.

ilar manner to nightjars, by hawking after insects, but they are also known to chase insects on branches of trees.

Frogmouths are nocturnal birds similar in color to other Caprimulgiformes. The immature birds tend to have plumages either similar to the adult birds or much paler, with a lot of white specks. They have a very large, sharply hooked beak much bigger than other Caprimulgiformes, with a large gape. However, they have very weak legs and feet. In general, they are considered to be lethargic birds and perhaps the weakest fliers in the order. Their wings are rounded—rather owl-like—and their flight is neither direct nor powerful. They have a distinguishing tuft of bristle-like feathers around the nostrils at the base of the beak, which seem partly to conceal the beak and nostrils. Eye color is brown, red or yellow.

Their hunting method has been described as owl-like, shrike-like or roller-like. It seems that they pounce on their terrestrial prey items from a regular perch. In addition, some species are thought actually to scour the branches of trees for food. Although the majority of frogmouths appear to be catholic in their choice of woodland, the Tawny frogmouth has a distinct preference for eucalypts.

As well as the geographical variation between the two genera, there are also behavioral and physiological differences: *Podargus* has no oil gland while *Batrachostomus* does have one. Some species may be migratory: the Papuan frogmouth has been observed on passage from Cape York in northern Australia to New Guinea.

MB

The **owlet-nightjars** or moth owls are shy dumpy little birds which look like a cross between an owl and a nightjar. They are typically nocturnal, tree-dwelling birds, usually feeding on flying insects; in Australia they are often found in open country. Owlet-nightjars are closely related to frogmouths.

Owlet-nightjars have relatively large beaks and more forward-facing eyes than the rest of the Caprimulgiformes, which tends to make them seem owl-like, as does their habit of sitting across branches rather than along them. However, they do have typical nightjar features in that they possess long "bristles" around the beak and a wide gape. They fly less erratically than their close relatives.

Males and females are similar. Within a number of species there is considerable variation in plumage, and some color variations are recognized as separate species by some authorities. The Large owlet-nightjar usually occurs as a light reddish brown phase or in a variegated dark brown and black phase.

Very little is known about the behavior of owlet-nightjars. There is some confusion as to how they catch their prey. Some species are credited with hawking rather like true nightjars, while others are thought to catch their prey on the ground. Analysis of stomach contents has shown that the diet can consist of non-flying prey such as millipedes, ants and also spiders. The fact that they have long, strong legs tends to support the idea that they spend at least some time on the ground chasing insects as well as hawking.

The owlet-nightjar is known to breed from September to December. Some pairs have been known to rear two broods in one season. The nestlings have whitish down which is soon replaced. When they leave the nest they are almost identical to their parents except for a tinge of buff color around the neck. Little is known about the parental care of the young. MB

Potoo is a Creole name and refers to the call of the Giant potoo, one of the five species closely related to nightjars. They have concealment coloration, and roost during the day, resting bolt upright on a tree stump or fence post. They feed at night by dashing off from a regular perch to catch flying insects such as moths, beetles, crickets and termites.

Potoos differ from nightjars in not having facial bristles or the usual comb on the middle claw. However, they do have modified cheek feathers on either side of a very large gape. They have long pointed wings and a shortish tail and legs. The bill is small with a downcurved tip. They have a very large gape partly because the upper mandible can be turned up and the lower mandible turned down.

As potoos are nocturnal, one would predict they should have loud distinctive calls which in fact they do. In general, their calls consist of a series of whistles and barking wows. The very loud "baw-woo" of the Giant potoo is often credited to something much larger than a bird, often a cat. During the pre-mating period, quacking sounds are repeated every 10 or 20 seconds.

Potoos do not build nests but lay their solitary egg on a tree stump or even in a crevice in the bark. The egg is oval and spotted. Both sexes appear to take it in turns to incubate and the adults rely on camouflage to avoid detection from natural predators but can often be approached and even touched at this time. Nothing is known about the parental care of the young.   MB

Discovered in 1799 by Alexander von Humboldt in a cave near Caripe, northern Venezuela, the **oilbird** became famous for its nestlings which, being fed on the oily fruits of palms and other trees, can weigh up to half as much again as the adults. They were regularly collected by the people of the Mission at which Humboldt was staying, and boiled down to give oil for their cooking and lighting. Exploitation by man still continues locally, although in most areas the bird is given legal protection. The English and scientific names (*Steatornis caripensis*—the "fat bird of Caripe") derive from this peculiarity of the nestlings.

The oilbird is related to the large, worldwide group of nightjars and related birds, but it is so specialized, and peculiar in so many ways—in its anatomy, behavior and ecology—that it is placed in a family of its own. Oilbirds are large birds, with long wings, ample tail, very short legs, a strong hawk-like bill surrounded by long whiskers, and large eyes. They are the only nocturnal fruit-eating birds in the world. They spend all day, even during nesting, deep within caves, coming out at nightfall to forage and returning to their caves before daylight. They are highly social, and large caves may contain thousands of birds. The essential requirement of large caves, with ledges on which they can roost and nest, restricts them to mountainous areas, especially limestone formations. In Trinidad, however, they also occupy a few of the large sea caves on the island's north coast.

The most immediate impression made on an intruder into an oilbird cave comes from the unearthly snarling screams uttered by the birds as they mill around in the darkness overhead, a noise that can be almost deafening in a large colony. Not surprisingly, they have been thought of by native peoples liv-

---

Whip-poor-will—Nightjar Music

The whip-poor-will is a widespread species from southern Canada to Central America. The whip-poor-will of the eastern USA has a clear, slightly warbled song, that of the geographically separated whip-poor-wills of the southwestern USA and Mexico have a guttural quality, yet both species clearly say "whip-poor-will."

In many birds with stereotyped vocalizations song is an inherited trait. It may offer clues to relationships. Nightjars communicate mostly by voice, and males of a given population all sing basically the same songs.

A little known species, the Sooty nightjar of mountainous Costa Rica and Panama, has only recently been tape-recorded. Its voice is strikingly similar to that of the western whip-poor-wills, being higher-pitched but containing the same syllables. Based on this close resemblance and its general physical

similarity to the whip-poor-will, the Sooty nightjar perhaps should be regarded as merely a Central American subspecies of the whip-poor-will. The Puerto Rican nightjar was originally described as a separate species, but is currently regarded as a form of the whip-poor-will. However, its "will-will-will-will" song does not support that merger!

The Little nightjar is widespread in tropical South America. Birds from eastern Peru sing a charmingly guttural song (rather froglike), while birds in Venezuela sing a complex series of clear resonant "tick-tock" notes—possibly more than one species is "hidden" under the name Little nightjar.

Based on physical appearances, the chuck-wills-widow of the southern USA and the Rufous nightjar of northern South America are each other's closest relative; voice evidence strongly supports this.   JWH

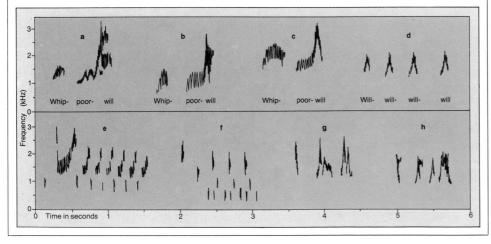

▲ **A Tawny frogmouth** and young, showing the way in which the markings of the bird mimic closely the texture of bark. Adults typically roost in this stiff, upright posture with the beak and forehead bristles pointing obliquely up.

▶ **A plump owlet-nightjar** at the entrance to its nesting hollow in a tree. As with the nightjars, the color is a remarkable match for its surroundings. Owlet-nightjars roost during the day in hollow trees and tree-holes. At dusk they become active, leaving the roost to forage in forest and woodland.

◀ **Sonograms** or voice prints of the songs of nightjars. (**a**) Eastern whip-poor-will (*Caprimulgus vociferus vociferus*). (**b**) Western whip-poor-will (*C.v. arizonae*). (**c**) Sooty nightjar. (**d**) Puerto Rican nightjar. (**e**) Little nightjar. (**f**) Venezuelan little nightjar. (**g**) Chuck-will's-widow. (**h**) Rufous nightjar.

clicking as they emerge into the open air and, while outside the cave, use what is evidently very sensitive night vision to find their way about. There is some evidence that, in locating some of their food trees, they also use the sense of smell. Many of the fruits of the trees at which they feed are aromatic, and oilbirds have an unusually large and sensitive organ of smell.

Adult oilbirds occupy their nests continuously, returning to them to roost even when they are not breeding. The nests are built of regurgitated fruit matter and grow year by year, in the form of a truncated cone with a saucer-shaped depression in the top. The nesting cycle is extremely long. It is usual for the eggs to be laid at intervals of three days or more, an extreme of nine days being recorded. Incubation starts with the first egg, so that they hatch, after the long incubation period of about 33 days, in the sequence in which they were laid. At hatching, the young are sparsely down-covered, but in their second week a second and much thicker generation of down feathers grows. This is succeeded by plumage of adult type, which begins to appear at the age of about five weeks. There is no distinct juvenile plumage, nor any other visual character obviously distinguishing a recently fledged young bird from an adult, doubtless because such a distinction would be without function in a dark cave. By about the 70th day, the nestling reaches its maximum weight, and for the remaining 30 or so days it loses weight as the plumage finishes its growth, until both wing-length and weight reach the adult condition and the young bird is able to fly. During the nestling period, both parents feed the young, on the same fruits that they themselves eat.

In Trinidad, where oilbirds have been most thoroughly studied, the breeding season is long, lasting for most of the year. It is just possible for a pair of birds to fit two breeding cycles into a year and some do so, but most pairs nest only once per year. In other areas, especially the Andes of Ecuador and Peru, there is evidence that the birds leave their caves for part of the year, perhaps in consequence of seasonal changes in the availability of fruit; but it is not known where they go. Possibly, colonies alternate between two caves some distance apart, where seasonal fruit regimes are complementary. What is certain is that some oilbirds, probably young birds, at times wander far from their caves. Stragglers have reached Panama, and even the island of Aruba off the coast of Venezuela.

DWS

ing near the caves as devils or lost spirits rather than birds. Among the Spanish-speaking people of South America they are generally known as *guácharo* ("the one who cries"), and in Trinidad as *diablotin* ("little devil"). These loud cries are calls of alarm and of communication with each other, probably also serving to indicate the position of the calling bird to others flying near it. Its other main call—a staccato click which can always be heard when the birds are flying round and undisturbed in the darkness of their caves—is used for echolocation; by picking up echoes from the cave walls and other surrounding objects the oilbird is able to avoid obstacles in pitch darkness. Their echolocation is, however, much less highly developed than that of bats; the clicks are not supersonic, and echoes are not reflected from very small objects. When oilbirds leave their caves at night they stop

SWIFTS

Families: Apodidae, Hemiprocnidae
Order: Apodiformes (suborder: Apodi).
Seventy-four species in 10 genera.
Distribution: see map and table.

Swifts   Crested swifts

Swifts
Family: Apodidae
Seventy-one species in 9 genera.
Distribution: worldwide except high latitudes
and some islands.
Habitat: aerial feeders rarely coming to rest.
Size: 10–30cm (4–12in), weight 9–150g
(0.3–5oz).
Plumage: most species dull black or brown,
many with conspicuous white or pale
markings.
Voice: shrill piercing screams.
Nests: in rocks, crevices or caves; a variety of
materials cemented with saliva.
Eggs: 1–6, white, weight 1–10g (0.04–
0.35oz); incubation period 17–28 days;
nestling period 34–72 days.
Diet: flying insects, other airborne arthropods.
Species and genera include: **Alpine swift** (*Apus
melba*), **Black swift** (*Cypseloides niger*), **Chimney
swift** (*Chaetura pelagica*), **Common swift** (*Apus
apus*), **Edible-nest swiftlet** (*Collocalia
inexpectata*), **Palm swift** (*Cypsiurus parvus*),
swallow-tailed swifts (*Panyptila*), **White-throated
spinetail swift** (*Hirundapus caudacutus*), **White-
throated swift** (*Aeronautes saxatilis*).

Crested swifts
Family: Hemiprocnidae
Three species of the genus *Hemiprocne*.
Distribution: SE Asia.
Habitat: woodland.
Size: 17–33cm (6.5–13in), weight 70–120g
(2.5–4oz).
Plumage: mainly soft gray or brown, with
white stripes on sides of head and crest on front
of crown.
Nest: tree bark and feathers glued to a branch.
Eggs: 1, white, weight 6–10g (0.2–0.35oz).
Diet: flying insects.
Species: **Crested tree swift** (*Hemiprocne
longipennis*), **Lesser tree swift** (*H. comata*),
Whiskered tree swift (*H. mystacea*).

▲▶ **Precarious perches.** Swifts are only agile
in the air; grounded, they are extremely
ungainly birds. ABOVE A Northern white-
rumped swift (*Apus pacificus*) perched on a rock.
RIGHT A Common swift clinging to a house
wall.

S WIFTS are a symbol of summer over
much of the world, wheeling and darting
through the air, never alighting on the
ground or on vegetation. Several species,
such as the Common swift of Europe,
regularly breed in or on buildings even
within large cities; indeed, hardly any
breeding records exist of this common species in "natural" sites in Britain. In the
primeval forests of Europe, such as those
remnants still to be found in Poland, nests
have been found in high, broken-off hollow
branches and down the trunks of ancient
hollow trees.

Swifts rely on catching insect prey on the
wing, which restricts their winter range to
areas where the temperature allows insects
to keep on flying in some numbers (see box).
At such times most species have to retreat
far from the temperate parts of their range.
Common swifts from Britain winter in East
Africa, Chimney swifts from Canada in the
upper Amazon Basin and White-throated
spinetail swifts from China and Japan in
Australia. Such long-range migrations are
easily within their flying capability for, of all
groups of land birds, they seem to be most
at ease in the air and would, in any case,
fly hundreds of kilometers every day while
feeding, even if they were not migrating. In
experiments, nesting Alpine swifts have successfully returned home from 1,620km
(about 1,000mi) in three days and a ringing
record from Britain has shown a newly
fledged young Common swift reaching
Madrid from Oxford in only three days.

Most swifts seem ungainly and primitive
in the hand or when inadvertently brought
down to earth—none will willingly settle on

the ground. They have short, weak beaks
which open very wide to reveal a huge gape.
This allows them more easily to catch
insects in flight. Most species have rather
dull plumage, although several have this
shot through with blue, green or purple
gloss. Many have forked tails, although the
spine-tailed swifts have the shafts of their
tail feathers extending beyond the vane to
form a row of spines. These help the birds
when they are clinging to vertical surfaces,
by giving them support. All species have
very short legs (Apodidae means "lacking
legs") but very strong feet for grasping vertical surfaces when breeding or roosting. For
instance, Chimney swifts are so named for
their habit of breeding and roosting inside
tall chimneys, which must be a recent
adaptation.

Swifts are almost always seen in flight and
appear to fly very fast indeed. Their
silhouette, with the wings making a thin
crescent and their bodies a small cigar
through it, would seem to be built for speed,
but this is not the case. The long, thin wing
is an adaptation for efficient gliding flight—
like a sailplane—and most of the time swifts
are not flying particularly fast. Indeed, while
they are feeding this would be very inefficient for they must see and snatch their prey
on the wing and too fast a speed would make
this much more difficult. However, during
displays they can fly very fast and are often
able to take advantage of the wind to cover
the ground very rapidly even when their air-
speed is not exceptional.

The temperate, migratory species that
have been studied in detail are long-lived
and faithful both to their breeding site and

to their mate. They have to undertake their breeding attempt quickly as there may only be sufficient aerial food for them for 12–14 weeks, even in areas where they commonly breed. For instance, Common swifts arrive in Britain to breed in early May and leave at the end of July. The males generally arrive first and take possession of the breeding site. This is nowadays almost always in a roof and the birds will make a small ring of material, taken in flight and glued down with saliva, at the place where the eggs will be laid. The chicks are brooded by one or other of the parents for the first few days after hatching and food is brought to them as "boluses"—gobs of insects stored in the parent's throat. These can weigh up to 1.7g (0.06oz) and may contain over 1,000 tiny insects and spiders. In fine weather, feeds may be brought in every 30 minutes or so and thus the parents may provide 30–40g (1–1.4oz) of food in a single day. In such circumstances, the minimum nestling period is roughly five weeks but, should the weather be bad, it may reach eight weeks.

Individual Common swifts undoubtedly recognize each other by voice—their shrill piercing screams—but apparently not by sight. Colonial breeding can lead to several dozen pairs breeding in a single roof-space or, more often, in adjacent buildings. In this species the first year birds seldom return to the breeding grounds and many do not breed until their third or fourth year. The pre-breeding birds form the large screaming parties which display in mid-summer and often fly up to occupied nesting sites in a very excited state—much to the annoyance of the resident birds.

It has been proved that the Common swift regularly spends the night on the wing. Birds have been watched rising in the evening long past the time when they are capable of finding their way into a nest. They have been seen from planes and gliders and regularly tracked by radar. They may well never come to land at all except when breeding and so complete a nonstop flight of 500,000km (312,500mi) between fledging late one summer and their first landing at a potential nesting site two summers later!

The other 70 or so species of swift include some swiftlet species (*Collocalia*) whose colonies in vast Asian caves may contain several hundred thousand individuals. These birds include species that make their nests entirely from dried saliva and stick it to the roof and walls of the caverns. They are of economic importance, for the nest is the source of "Bird's nest soup." The collection of the nests is a very hazardous under-

taking, involving ropeways and ladders up to 100m (330ft) high. The crop of nests taken may be very valuable and very considerable—more than 3.5 million nests were exported in one year from Borneo to China. These Edible-nest swiftlets use echolocation to find their way round the interior of their nesting caves—it is much too dark for them to be able to see. With such vast colonies, the droppings (guano) also accumulate in the caves and are mined from the floor for use as a fertilizer.

In order to provide the material for the nest, even those species that only use the saliva as cement to glue together other nesting material have much enlarged salivary glands during the nest-building phase of the breeding season. The glands of the Chimney swift, which glues its nest of twiglets to a vertical wall, undergo a 12-fold enlargement. This swift, and the other species which use twigs for nest-building, break them from trees in flight. Other materials are gathered while they are being blown about—feathers, seeds, grasses, straw—during World War II, even the tinsel strips used to confuse enemy radar were incorporated into swift nests.

The varied shapes of, and construction methods used for, nests are often particular to individual species. For instance the Palm swift of the Old World is only found where the Fan palm grows. Its nest is made along the vertical channel on the inside of one of the palm's leaves, from feathers and fibers, and has a small lower rim. This is for the bird to perch on, as it incubates while clinging vertically to the nest into which its two eggs are firmly cemented.

In the New World, the palm swifts belong to a different genus (*Tachornis*) and build their nest inside the vegetation hanging from the crown of the palm trees. In this case, the bag-shaped nest is glued to the leaf and the bird enters along the leaf side and lays its eggs in a cup formed inside the lower, outer edge. Very complex nests are also built by two more New World species, the swallow-tailed swifts, which may form a tube 70cm (28in) long hanging vertically from a rock face. The birds have a nest at the top of the tube, close to the point of attachment. These nests may be very durable and used year after year.

The setting of the Chimney swift's nest, down a vertical chimney, is obviously the equivalent of nesting in a hollow tree and the species still does this too. Several other species will fly down to nest underground in potholes—even 70m (230ft) below ground—and the Black swift has been described as nesting in sea-caves whose entrances are covered by each successive wave. At least three different species habitually nest in the vertical faces of cliffs behind waterfalls and have to fly in and out through the falling water.

These varied nesting sites and structures are a particularly interesting illustration of how a group of aerial birds, without the opportunity for collecting much nesting material, has managed to make use of safe

▲ **Representative species of swifts and some typical nests.** (1) Seychelles cave swiftlet (*Collocalia elaphra*), a colonial cave-nester. (2) Common swifts (*Apus apus*) mating on the wing. (3) Palm swift (*Cypsiurus parvus*) in flight. (4) Alpine swift (*Apus melba*) chasing an insect. (5) Crested tree swift (*Hemiprocne longipennis*) perching on a branch while incubating its egg. (6–9) Nests. (6) Lesser swallow-tailed swift (*Panyptila cayennensis*) builds a tubular nest attached to a tree trunk or rock. (7) Fork-tailed palm swift (*Tachornis squamata*) builds a bag-shaped nest hanging from a fan frond of a palm. (8) Edible-nest swiftlet (*Collocalia inexpectata*) builds cup-shaped nests largely of saliva. (9) Palm swift (*Cypsiurus parvus*) glues its nest to the underside of a palm leaf; the eggs also may need to be glued to the nest.

Survival in Cold Weather

Birds, like the Common swift, that feed on flying insects, may have a considerable problem in the northern part of their range: when the weather turns cold, wet and windy their food may become very scarce—even nonexistent. Outside the breeding season, the birds may make good their escape by flying south to warmer areas but this is not possible while they are nesting.

Detailed studies have shown a range of adaptations to overcome this problem. The adult birds are able to store a considerable amount of subcutaneous fat which they can utilize while food is scarce. They can roost at the nesting site for several days on end with a very slow metabolism and a depressed temperature. Swift eggs are capable of withstanding chilling much more than those of most species; the parents may even practice a rather crude form of birth control, for many observers have reported eggs being removed from the nest-cup in times of cold weather.

Much the most interesting adaptation is the ability of the young to withstand long periods of starvation and cold. Young which have not been fed for a week or more at some stage of the nestling period may still fledge successfully if conditions improve and their parents start to feed them again. Indeed, fasts of up to 10 days have been reported with weight losses of more than 50 percent. The young may be so cold and torpid that they seem dead even to the experienced observer. In such circumstances, the fledging period will approach 60 days instead of the five weeks to be expected in summers with consistently good weather.

Torpidity has been recorded for several other species of swift and also for nightjars and hummingbirds. In Europe, swallows have also been found in a similar state and it is suspected that this may have given rise to theories of hibernation in birds. A record of eight White-throated swifts in a torpid condition during January in California was probably an immediate response to poor weather locally and not an example of true hibernation—so far the only bird which seems to approach true hibernation is the poorwill (see p250).

nesting sites. Most of them are very inaccessible to mammalian or reptilian predators: this safeguards not only the egg and young but also the vulnerable parents. None of the adult swifts are at all maneuverable when on the ground or perched.

The nest of the **crested swifts** is a tiny structure with paper-thin walls stuck on the side of a thin branch. The nest is only about 2.5cm (1in) across and just big enough to take a single egg, glued in with saliva for safety. It is not strong enough to take the weight of the incubating adult or of the developing youngster, so the perched adults incubate sitting along the branch, and the nestling, quite soon after hatching, takes to perching on the branch also. Food is brought to the nestling in boluses and the construction of the nest and the wing structure of the bird point to a fairly close relationship with the true swifts. However, the feeding behavior recalls a shrike or flycatcher, since a perched bird flies out to catch a particular insect and then returns to the perch.

CJM

HUMMINGBIRDS

Family: Trochilidae

Order: Apodiformes (suborder: Trochili).
Three hundred and fifteen species in 112 genera.
Distribution: throughout Americas from Strait of Magellan to Alaska. Also W Indies, Bahamas, Juan Fernandez islands. Many species migratory.

Habitat: wherever nectar-producing flowers blossom, from sea level to 4,500m (15,000ft).

Size: 5.8–21.7cm (2.3–8.5in) long and 2–20g (0.07–0.7oz).

Plumage: most have glittering blue or green plumage often with brilliant iridescent areas in other colors mostly on head, throat or breast; males often more brilliant, some with crests or elongated tails.

Voice: most calls high pitched, brief. Flight calls characteristic of each species, uttered by both sexes. Male advertising song, a brief warble or one or two notes frequently repeated.

Nest: in most species, a small cup nest astride a horizontal twig or stalk. In hermit hummingbirds and cave-nesting species, a hanging nest attached by cobweb beneath a large leaf or to a rock surface.

Eggs: 2 (occasionally 1) elongated white eggs, 8 × 12mm to 12 × 20mm, weight about 13 percent of female's; incubation period 14–23 days, nestling period 18–38 days.

Diet: mostly nectar and small insects.

Species and genera include: **Andean hillstar** (*Oreotrochilus estella*), **Anna's hummingbird** (*Calypte anna*), **barbthroats** (*Threnetes*), **Bearded helmetcrest** (*Oxypogon guerinii*), **Black-throated mango** (*Anthracothorax nigricollis*), **Blue-chested hummingbird** (*Amazilia amabilis*), **Blue-throated hummingbird** (*Lampornis clemenciae*), **Costa's hummingbird** (*Calypte costae*), **emeralds** (*Amazilia*), **fairies** (*Heliothryx*), **Fiery-tailed awlbill** (*Avocettula recurvirostris*), **Giant hummingbird** (*Patagona gigas*), **Green-backed firecrown** (*Sephanoides sephanoides*), **hermits** (*Phaethornis*), **incas/starfrontlets** (*Coeligena*), **lancebills** (*Doryfera*), **Marvelous spatuletail** (*Loddigesia mirabilis*), **metaltails** (*Metallura*), **Mountain avocetbill** (*Opisthoprora euryptera*), **pufflegs** (*Eriocnemis*), **Purple-throated carib** (*Eulampis jugularis*), **Purple-throated mountain gem** (*Lampornis calolaema*), **Rufous-breasted hermit** (*Glaucis hirsuta*), **saberwings** (*Campylopterus*), **sicklebills** (*Eutoxeres*), **sunangels** (*Heliangelus*), **sunbeams** (*Aglaeactis*), **Sword-billed hummingbird** (*Ensifera ensifera*), **thornbills** (*Chalcostigma*), **violetears** (*Colibri*). Threatened species: 6.

Hummingbirds are unique for their agility in flight, extremely brilliant iridescent plumage, long bills and generally small size. To many Europeans they first became known as decorative objects on the ornate hats worn by women in the 19th century, when many thousands were imported for this purpose. This unhappy relationship between humans and hummingbirds has long since ceased.

Most hummingbirds are immediately recognizable by their small size, long thin bills, brilliant plumage and ability to hover. Nearly all these characteristics are adaptations for securing their main nourishment: nectar.

The hummingbirds' long bill enables them to reach nectar inside flowers; in addition they have long extendable tube-like tongues up which the nectar is drawn. Nectar is usually extracted while the hummingbird hovers in front of the flower; it hovers forward while inserting its bill and backwards when removing it. This ability to hover forwards and backwards is unique among birds and the structure of the hummingbird's wings differs from that of all other birds except their closest relatives, the swifts. The hummingbirds' wing consists mainly of elongated "hand" bones to which the flight feathers are attached, and the whole wing can rotate as a wrist does. In flight, a hummingbird's wing is only visible as a blur, because of the speed of its wing beat, between 22 and 78 beats per second, with the highest rate in the smaller species.

Hummingbirds' feet and legs are peculiarly small because in most species they are used only for perching. The exceptional species are a few that live in the high Andes, the Bearded helmetcrest, the thornbills and the Andean hillstar, all of which occasionally walk about, gleaning insects off bare ground and rock, and have relatively larger legs and feet.

The bills of hummingbirds vary greatly in length and shape, according to the flowers at which they feed. The hermits, which inhabit tropical and subtropical forest, all have long, slightly curved bills (except for two species with long straight bills), the degree of curvature matching the shape of the flowers at which they feed. The mostly smaller emeralds have straight bills varying between 1.8–2.5cm (0.7–1in). The thornbills, living in the temperate Andes, have short bills of 0.8cm (0.3in) and take many insects. The sharp, strong, medium-length bills of the two fairy hummingbirds are used to pierce the corollas of flowers and so steal the nectar. The Fiery-tailed awlbill and the Mountain avocetbill have bills that curve upwards, presumably to match some flower corolla, but this has not yet been investigated.

Hummingbird plumage is extremely varied, but in general green, usually a glittering green, is a common color for the upperparts, while the underparts are often paler, particularly in females.

In about a third of the family the sexes are alike; these include most of the larger duller hummingbirds such as hermits, saberwings and incas, but also the brilliant violetears, emeralds and others. In the remainder of the family the sexes are different, as males have many adornments which females lack, such as ear tufts, crests and greatly elongated tails. Many males have patches of brilliant iridescent feathers, usually on the crown, throat or upper breast; these are most often green, blue or purple, but also red or yellow.

The majority of hummingbird species occur in Central and South America with the greatest diversity within the latitudes 10°N to 10°S of the equator. In this broad latitudinal belt, as one passes from near sea level in the tropical Amazon forests up the slopes of the Andes through subtropical and temperate zones to the open bush and grasslands of the paramo, a different assemblage of up to 20 hummingbird species is found in each altitudinal belt until the paramo, which supports around five species. In the temperate latitudes of Chile and Argentina there is only one species of hummingbird to

▲ **Hummingbird nests** are small delicate cups fixed by cobwebs to a twig, often in a fork, as here. A female Anna's hummingbird is feeding her young. Note the lichen-encrusted bark on the outside of the nest.

◄ **Gleaming like pyrites,** the yellow-green iridescence of a male Allen's hummingbird (*Selasphorus sasin*). This species nests up the west coast of Mexico into California. The male has a dramatic display flight involving a dive from about 30m (100ft) above the female.

be found, the Green-backed firecrown.

North of Mexico, 13 species of hummingbirds breed, the number decreasing from the southwest to the northwest of the subcontinent. All these hummingbirds migrate south to winter in Mexico or Central America, except for Anna's, Costa's and the Blue-throated hummingbirds, some individuals of which remain in the southern USA while others migrate.

Some hummingbirds have an extremely wide distribution, such as the tropical Black-throated mango, found from Panama to Paraguay; others have a very restricted range, such as the Marvelous spatuletail— known only from one valley in the Andes of Peru. Two new species of hummingbird, with very restricted ranges, have been discovered in Peru in the 1970s, a sunangel at subtropical levels and a metaltail at temperate levels.

Hummingbirds feed mainly on nectar taken directly from flowers, but all species that have been studied also take small insects.

Within the hummingbird family two major strategies for nectar-feeding are employed. A large number of species with medium-length bills defend from other hummingbirds a dense patch of flowers capable of supplying most of an individual's nectar needs. The defended flowers may or may not be exploitable by insects, and are usually produced by trees or shrubs and herbaceous plants growing in the open and receiving full sunlight. These plants typically have relatively brief but intense flowering periods, so the territory holder must periodically abandon one nectar territory and take up a new one. Emeralds, pufflegs, sunangels and sunbeams are some of the many territorial hummingbirds.

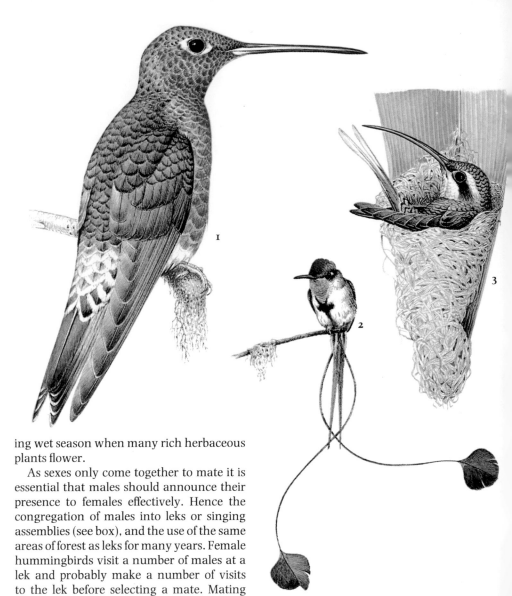

The other main nectar-feeding strategy is non-territorial and has been termed "trap-lining." This term is borrowed from the human trapper who sets traps over a wide area which are then periodically visited. Trap-lining hummingbirds have long bills and the flowers they visit have evolved characteristics that make their nectar available only to long-billed hummingbirds and not to insects or short-billed hummingbirds. This type of flower is usually produced by vines, epiphytes (ie plants that grow on other plants), understory trees and herbaceous plants of forest and shady areas. Typically, these plants have a long flowering season and produce a few flowers at a time, so providing a long-term food source for their hummingbirds. Typical trap-lining hummingbirds are the hermits, the swordbills, and some incas.

In addition to these two major feeding strategies there are also small trap-lining hummingbirds with shorter bills, which feed at small dispersed patches of unspecialized flowers.

Hummingbirds catch their animal food by either hawking for flying insects or by gleaning resting insects or small spiders from the vegetation or spiders' webs. Most straight-billed hummingbirds use both methods, but the curve-billed hermits catch most of their insects and spiders by picking them off the tips, edges and undersides of leaves.

Because hummingbirds are so small they need a high intake of food to maintain their body temperature, particularly at night. Food intake varies with temperature and activity but typically a hummingbird takes over half its body-weight in food a day. If a hummingbird needs to conserve its energy it becomes torpid at night, its body temperature, normally about 41°C (105°F) falling to near air temperature. Nightly torpidity is usually a response to low night temperatures but it can also be a response to insufficient food reserves.

The breeding seasons of hummingbirds are closely tied to the flowering seasons of their major nectar sources. In temperate latitudes this corresponds to the northern and southern springs; in arid areas, rain which stimulates plant growth may be more important than length of day. Thus in California, Anna's hummingbird breeds from November to March, the main rainy season. In high rainfall areas of the tropics and subtropics such as Trinidad and Costa Rica, hummingbirds start nesting at the end of the wet season and beginning of the dry season when many trees and shrubs flower; but they also continue breeding into the follow-

ing wet season when many rich herbaceous plants flower.

As sexes only come together to mate it is essential that males should announce their presence to females effectively. Hence the congregation of males into leks or singing assemblies (see box), and the use of the same areas of forest as leks for many years. Female hummingbirds visit a number of males at a lek and probably make a number of visits to the lek before selecting a mate. Mating

Hummingbirds and Their Flowers

When a hummingbird inserts its bill into the corolla of a flower, its forehead, beak and chin may become well dusted with pollen, some of which will be transferred to neighboring flowers of the same species, so achieving cross-pollination.

From the plant's point of view, hummingbirds are very desirable pollinators because they are long lived and can fly long distances in all weather conditions. For this reason, many plant families of the Americas have evolved flower characteristics which make their nectar available only to hummingbirds and not to insects. Such characters are long tube-like corollas with narrow openings and the absence of landing platforms which insects require. These flowers are oriented well away from leaves and entangling vegetation so that the feeding hummingbird can hover in front of or below them. They are usually colored red or orange, because hummingbirds, but not insects, can distinguish these colors. The nectar in hummingbird flowers is abundant but not very concentrated compared with that of bee-pollinated flowers, as bees are more efficient at collecting small quantities of concentrated nectar.

It is generally the larger hummingbirds with longer bills, such as the hermit hummingbirds, that get most of their nectar from hummingbird flowers at which insects cannot feed. The smaller, shorter-billed hummingbirds, such as emeralds, do much of their feeding at less specialized flowers which they may share with insects.

Two hummingbirds with highly specialized bills—the swordbill with a bill up to 10.5cm (4in) long, twice as long as that of any other hummingbird, and the sicklebill with a deeply curved sickle-shaped bill—have a particularly high degree of co-evolution with certain plants. Bird and plant are interdependent: the swordbill with a climbing Passion flower, which has a corolla tube of 11.4cm (4.5in) and produces up to 500ml of nectar a day, and the sicklebill with certain heliconias whose sickle-shaped corollas fit its bill exactly. The larger sicklebills, which weigh about 12g (0.4oz), prefer to perch while feeding, and the flowers of the heliconias at which they feed are arranged to make this possible.

▲ Representative species of hummingbirds showing the variety of bill shapes. (1) Giant hummingbird (*Patagona gigas*). (2) Spatuletail (*Loddigesia mirabilis*). (3) Long-tailed hermit (*Phaethornis superciliosus*) in its nest attached to a drooping leaf. (4) Bee hummingbird (*Mellisuga helenae*). (5) Amethyst woodstar (*Calliphlox amethystina*). (6) Frilled coquette (*Lophornis magnifica*). (7) Ruby-topaz hummingbird (*Chrysolampis mosquitus*). (8) Bearded helmetcrest (*Oxypogon guerinii*). (9) White-tipped sicklebill (*Eutoxeres aquila*). (10) Sword-billed hummingbird (*Ensifera ensifera*).

▶ In-flight refueling. OVERLEAF With perfect control, a male Broad-billed hummingbird (*Cynanthus latirostris*) approaches a flower. The bird sucks-up nectar provided by the flower, while in return it transfers pollen dusted onto its bills to other flowers, so achieving cross pollination for the plant—nature in harmony.

takes place on the lek perch and also occasionally nearby.

Although mating has been observed infrequently, the males of the four species of hermit frequently "false mate" with leaves near their lek perches, performing the same display to the selected leaf before mounting it, as they perform to females.

Most hummingbird songs are very simple, high-pitched and unmelodious to our ears. The more elaborate and attractive songs, such as that of the barbthroats, are warbles lasting 4–5 seconds. Many songs are just repeated single notes, each lasting only a quarter of a second.

In spite of the simplicity of the song, careful analysis has shown that it varies between leks or singing assemblies, and even between groups of males within a lek. Young males joining a lek copy the song-type of the males near whom they settle.

Only the female hummingbird builds the nest, incubates the eggs and feeds the young. In all but three or four species, male hummingbirds do not even know the whereabouts of nests. Most hummingbird nests are small open cups fixed by cobwebs astride a twig. Although small, the cups are deep and have relatively thick walls of moss lined with vegetable down to assist the female in keeping the eggs and small young warm. Hermit hummingbirds build hanging nests attached by cobwebs to the underside of large leaves such as palms and ferns. Some hillstars, metaltails and lancebills build hanging nests attached by cobwebs to the ceilings of caves, shafts or rocky overhangs.

Occasionally, two females lay in the same nest. This has been recorded among barbthroats and Rufous-breasted hermits, but there are no records of more than two young surviving from these double clutches. The nestlings are fed by regurgitation, usually while hovering. The mother inserts her bill into the nestling's throat and pumps in nectar and insects.

After leaving the nest the fledgling hummingbird is fed by its mother for as long as 20–40 days. A second nesting attempt is usual and a third is not uncommon in the long tropical breeding season. A nest that has been successful may be used again when refurbished or a new one built nearby.

Where the sexes are different, most young hummingbirds fledge into the female plumage, but in a few, such as the Mountain gem, males fledge directly into male plumage. Males which fledge into female plumage acquire their adult plumage at 2–10 months after fledging. Young male hummingbirds start to sing, either alone or at the edge of singing assemblies, a few months after independence. Females probably make their first attempt to nest when about one year old. In captivity, hummingbirds live for about 10 years. In the wild, a Blue-chested hummingbird (identified by its unique song) lived for 7 years.

Most hummingbirds inhabiting humid tropical and subtropical areas, where there are no seasonal extremes, are resident all the year round, making only short local movements when foraging. But in areas where latitude, altitude or drought cause a dearth of flowers at certain times of year seasonal migrations are undertaken. Thus in the highlands of Costa Rica at 3,000m (almost 10,000ft) four species breed but only one is present throughout the year. Anna's hummingbird, which breeds in winter and early spring in California and adjacent areas, moves in midsummer high into the mountains, away from the heat and the drought of the lower country.

The first human threat to the survival of hummingbirds came in the 19th century, when stuffed hummingbirds became a desirable decoration on women's hats. During this period, as many as 400,000 skins were being imported in a single year by one London dealer, and the dealers in Paris and New York were equally active. Although most of these skins were destined for a short life on a hat, others were bought by naturalist collectors and museums. There are six species of hummingbird now in museums that are known only from these trade skins: three from Colombia, two from Brazil and one from Bolivia. Whether they are extinct or not remains to be seen; some are believed to be hybrids and not true species. The fact that new species of hummingbird have been discovered within the last 10 years suggests that some of these six "extinct" species may yet be found. The main threat to the survival of hummingbirds now comes from the destruction of forest and the replacement of other natural vegetation by crops.

The species of hummingbirds most threatened are the larger hummingbirds with long specialized bills who need the flowers with which they have coevolved to survive (see box). The smaller hummingbirds, which are mainly territorial and less specialized, can adapt to feed on many garden and wayside flowers or second-growth shrubs. These are the species that learn to come to feeders put out by people. These feeders, containing a sugary solution accessible only through a narrow tube, are put out by many people in North America and by a few in Central and South America. Originally, the feeder tube was surrounded with an artificial flower, but soon such enticement proved unnecessary and hummingbirds came to undecorated feeders, and the territorial species even set up feeding territories based on them.

The provision of suitable nest-sites and nest materials are also crucial if hummingbirds are to continue to live in man's altered environment. For the hanging nest of the hermit hummingbirds, a suitable tapering leaf, such as the tip of a palm leaf, is essential, and the nest-site must be low off the ground (0.5–3m; 2–10ft), as nests in higher sites are liable to be overturned by the wind.

Of the nest materials, the soft down from seeds or furry leaves is essential for most species, but may be missing from some man-made habitats. Building hummingbirds very often reuse such downy material from old nests, which suggests that it is relatively rare and could be a limiting factor. Finally, hummingbirds must have a plentiful supply of cobwebs, which are used in the nests of all species.   BKS

TROGONS AND MOUSEBIRDS

Orders: Trogoniformes, Coliiformes
Families: Trogonidae, Coliidae.
Forty-three species in 8 genera.
Distribution: see map and table.

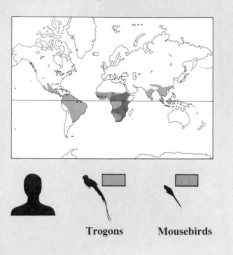

Trogons   **Mousebirds**

▶ **Clinging Speckled mousebirds** showing the versatile use of their claws—the outer toes are reversible, enabling them to grip like parrots.

▼ **Jewel of a bird.** Many birds have bright iridescent patches of color but the Resplendent quetzal glows from head to foot. Its tail can be as long as 60cm (24in). The Guatemalan currency is named for this dramatic bird.

TROGONS are some of the most brilliantly colored birds in the world. According to Guatemalan Indian legend, the male Resplendent quetzal, most brilliant of all, with glittering metallic green above and crimson below, received its stunning plumage during the Spanish conquest of South America. After a particularly gruesome battle, huge flocks of quetzals (which were then only green) flew down to keep a watch over the dead Mayas, thus staining their breasts red.

The feathers of the Resplendent quetzal's head are bristly and upstanding, forming a narrow ridged crest. The bright green middle wing-coverts are very long, overlapping onto the flanks, while the green uppertail coverts are so elongated that they extend far beyond the normal tail length, forming a graceful curving train which hangs below the bird when perched. Climax cloud forests appear to be essential for the existence of the Resplendent quetzal which ranges along a 1,600km (about 1,000mi) stretch from southern Mexico to western Panama. Unfortunately, the species has much decreased as a consequence of habitat destruction, and there are few areas where it can now be claimed to be abundant. Especially important to the quetzal are the trees of the laurel family, and it is particularly fond of the *Ocotea* fruit.

Unlike other species of trogon, the Resplendent quetzal has a well-marked display flight in which the male flies high above the forest canopy, circling around before dropping back into the foliage, giving distinctive "wac-wac" call notes. The nest chamber is a roughout in a rotting tree trunk, often at some considerable height. Both sexes incubate and tend the young. Outside the breeding season, Resplendent quetzals are mainly found singly, although small flocks are occasionally reported.

The rare Eared trogon is found in western Mexico in mountain pine or pine-oak forest. It normally perches in the middle and upper branches of a tall tree, or flies with a fluttering undulating flight, high up. The small brush-like ear tufts of this trogon are unique, but not easily seen and it differs from other similarly plumaged trogons by having a black rather than a yellow bill. The head and upper parts are glossy green and it is scarlet below, showing a good deal of white on the underside of the square-ended black tail.

The 15 species of the genus *Trogon* range from southern Mexico to northern Argentina. They are birds of similar appearance, glossy green or greenish-blue above, and

either scarlet, pink or yellow below. The Collared trogon has the largest range of all New World trogons, also occurring in the tropical forest zones of Trinidád and Tobago as well as on the subtropical slopes of the Andes up to 2,500m (about 8,000ft).

There are three species of trogon found in Africa, of which the Narina trogon is the commonest and most widespread, being found from lowland forest up to 3,300m (almost 11,000ft) in montane forest. The male is bright glossy green above and on the throat and breast, with a scarlet belly. The Bar-tailed trogon has a darker head and a narrowly barred whitish underside to the tail. The Yellow-cheeked trogon is a larger bird with brighter red underparts and is a little known species of primary evergreen forest.

The 11 species of Asian trogons belonging to the genus *Harpactes* range from western India to southeast China, Indo-China, Malaya and Indonesia. Like the New World and African trogons they have colorful plumages, short rounded wings, a long square-tipped tail and very short, weak legs. The bill is short and broad, and is cobalt blue in most species, as is the bare patch of skin around the eye. Unlike the New World trogons, which include a very high proportion of fruit in their diet, the oriental trogons feed mainly on large insects and small vertebrates, which they snatch from leaves as they swoop past. Several species are widely distributed, such as the Orange-breasted trogon, which lives in evergreen forest from Burma to Malaya, from Thailand and southwest China to Java.

The Malaysian region is by far the richest in trogon species, with eight present in Sumatra and six in Borneo. The largest species, Ward's trogon, is found in forest above 1,800m (5,900ft) in northeast Burma and northwest Tonkin, also in Bhutan and Assam.   PRC

Mousebirds are so called because of their curious way of moving through the thick foliage of their African forest environment— they crawl around the branches, sometimes resting on the leg rather than the foot, as well as pulling themselves up by their bill, parrot-fashion. These habits are reflected in the anatomy of the foot: normally the bird holds the center two toes forwards and the other two splayed out partly sideways, but the latter are very mobile and can be held forwards or backwards.

All species are rather loosely feathered in gray or brown, though several have a single distinctive marking such as a chestnut rump

(Red-backed mousebird), a blue back to the head (Blue-naped mousebird), or a red mask (Red-faced mousebird).

Mousebirds are common—sometimes very common—and widespread over the African continent. They live in small flocks from about 6–20 birds. They tend to clamber about in dense bushes and then fly to the next, only a very short distance away. They have short rounded wings and are not strong fliers; flight is usually a series of rapid, whirring wing beats followed by a longish glide. Members of the flock keep in contact with a series of short whistles or twitters.

Mousebirds not only live in flocks by day, but they roost together at night, often tightly packed. They have also been reported as sleeping hanging head downward in a tight cluster. At least some species appear to allow their body temperature to fall at night, warming themselves up again in the morning; presumably by doing this they help to conserve energy by reducing overnight heat loss. This habit might point to a relationship with the nightjars, swifts and hummingbirds, some of which have the same ability.

Mousebirds have short, stubby, finch-like beaks and feed mainly on berries and fruits, though they sometimes also take animal matter; they use their feet to help hold food items. They are considered serious pests in gardens and orchards.

Their breeding biology is not particularly well-known. In at least some species, both sexes incubate the eggs, though in the Speckled mousebird the female seems to do most of the brooding of the young. The young are naked in the early stages; although they remain in or near the nest until they are able to fly, the larger young may clamber around in the branches close to the nest.

CMP

The Trogon and Mousebird Families   v Vulnerable.

Trogons

Family: Trogonidae
Thirty-seven species in 7 genera.
Southern half of Africa, India and SE Asia; Malaysia, Philippines, Arizona, southern Texas, Mexico, C and S America, W Indies. Forest, woodland and second growth, also montane forests to 3,000m (9,850ft). Size: 23–38cm (9–15in) long. Plumage: soft and dense, with adult males having the breast and abdomen bright pink, red, orange, or yellow and the head and upper parts often brilliant metallic green. Females duller. Voice: a variety of simple calls,

including hollow whistles, hoots, coos, churring and squeaky notes. Eggs: 2 to 4, white or buff to greenish blue; incubation period 17–19 days; nestling period 17–18 days. Diet: insects, spiders, small frogs, lizards, snails, also berries and small fruits.

Species include: **Bar-tailed trogon** (*Apaloderma vittatum*), **Collared trogon** (*Trogon collaris*), **Cuban trogon** (*Priotelus temnurus*), **Eared trogon** (*Euptilotis neoxenus*), **Hispaniolan trogon** (*Temnotrogon roseigaster*), **Narina trogon** (*Apaloderma narina*), **Orange-breasted trogon** (*Harpactes oreskios*), **Resplendent quetzal** v

(*Pharomachrus mocino*), **Whitehead's trogon** (*Harpactes whiteheadi*), **Yellow-cheeked trogon** (*Apaloderma aequatoriale*).

Mousebirds

Family: Coliidae
Six species of the genus *Colius*.
Africa south of the Sahara (not in Madagascar). Open woodland and bushy country; avoids dense forest. Size: 30–35cm (12–14in), but much of this is due to long tail which may be 20–25cm (8–10in); weight about 45–55g (1.6–1.9oz). Plumage: light brown or gray, lighter below; loose

crests; some have bright face or neck marks (red or blue); tail strongly graduated. Sexes similar. Voice: a single whistle-like note or a series of more twittering notes. Nests: in an open cup, sometimes bulky and untidy, usually in a thick thorny bush. Eggs: usually 2–4, whitish with blackish or brownish streaks; size usually in range 20–22 × 15–17mm.

Species include: **Blue-naped mousebird** (*Colius macrourus*), **Red-backed mousebird** (*C. castanotus*), **Red-faced mousebird** (*C. indicus*), **Speckled mousebird** (*C. striatus*).

KINGFISHERS

Family: Alcedinidae
Order: Coraciiformes (suborder: Alcedines, part).
Eighty-six species in 14 genera.
Distribution: cosmopolitan except very high latitudes.

Habitat: interior of rain forests, woodlands far from water, desert steppe, grassy savannas, streams, lakeshores, mangrove, seashores, gardens, mountain forest, oceanic islands.

Size: 10–45cm (4–18in) long (excluding any tail streamers) and weight 8–500g (0.3–18oz); in many species females slightly larger than males.

Plumage: azure blue above and reddish below; also light and dark blue, green, brown, white and black; bill and legs vermilion, brown or black. Males and females similar in most species, pronounced differences in a few others.

Voice: loud song of ringing notes in slowing tempo and falling cadence, or single loud coarse cry, or occasional weak, quiet notes.

Nests: in earthen holes excavated by the birds, including termitaria on ground or in trees, and tree holes.

Eggs: clutches vary from 2–3 in tropics up to 10 at high latitudes; white; weight 2–12g (0.07–0.4oz). incubation period 18–22 days; nestling period 20–30 days.

Diet: terrestrial arthropods and small vertebrates, aquatic insects and fish.

Species and genera include: **African dwarf kingfisher** (*Ceyx lecontei*), **African pygmy kingfisher** (*C. pictus*), **Amazon kingfisher** (*Chloroceryle amazona*), **Beach kingfisher** (*Halcyon saurophaga*), **Belted kingfisher** (*Megaceryle alcyon*), **Black-capped kingfisher** (*Halcyon pileata*), **Blue-breasted kingfisher** (*Halcyon malimbica*), **Common paradise kingfisher** (*Tanysiptera galatea*), **Crested kingfisher** (*Ceryle lugubris*), **Eurasian kingfisher** (*Alcedo atthis*), **Giant kingfisher** (*Megaceryle maxima*), **Gray-headed kingfisher** (*Halcyon leucocephala*), **Green kingfisher** (*Chloroceryle americana*), **Green-and-rufous kingfisher** (*C. inda*), **Laughing kookaburra** (*Dacelo gigas*), **Mangrove kingfisher** (*Halcyon chloris*), **Oriental dwarf kingfisher** (*Ceyx erithacus*), **paradise kingfishers** (*Tanysiptera*), **Pied kingfisher** (*Ceryle rudis*), **Pygmy kingfisher** (*Chloroceryle aenea*), **Ringed kingfisher** (*Megaceryle torquata*), **Ruddy kingfisher** (*Halcyon coromanda*), **Shovel-billed kingfisher** (*Clytoceyx rex*), **Stork-billed kingfisher** (*Halcyon capensis*), **Tuamotu kingfisher** (*Halcyon gambieri*), **Variable dwarf kingfisher** (*Ceyx lepidus*), **woodland kingfishers** (*Halcyon*).

THE Eurasian kingfisher is a vibrant bird, both in looks and behavior. A stab of electric blue contrasted with the warm chestnut orange of the underparts, is the usual image that it presents. And then it is gone, leaving behind the impression of a living cobalt and azure jewel.

Kingfishers are small-to-large, monogamous, more-or-less solitary, bright-plumaged birds of forests, savannas and waterside situations. The great majority of species are tropical, but one or two species from each subfamily have extended as migrant breeders into temperate latitudes.

Primitive species are forest-dwelling predators feeding mainly on forest-floor insects; more specialized types plunge into shallow water for small animals, flycatch for airborne insects, forage in leaf-litter for earthworms, prey on birds and reptiles, and deep-dive for fish from a perch or (particularly the Pied kingfisher) from hovering flight.

Like other birds of their order, kingfishers are large-headed, short-necked, stout-bodied and short-legged, with weak, fleshy feet having the second and third toes partly joined. The bill is straight, strong and long, flattened from top to bottom in insectivorous species and from side to side in fish-eating species. The extraordinary Shovel-billed or Earthworm-eating kingfisher has a short, wide, conical bill. Other forms have the bill sharp-pointed and dagger-like, but in the adult African dwarf kingfisher it is blunt-tipped (sharp in the juvenile). For no obvious reason, several not-closely related lineages of kingfishers are three-toed, having lost the fourth toe. Plumage and other characters show that three-toed species are very closely allied with some four-toed species in the genera *Ceyx* and *Alcedo*, and that the three-toed kingfishers do not comprise a single natural assemblage as they were

formerly held to do. Although colorful, the colors are in general muted, with shades of blue and red predominating. Shoulders and rump are usually shining azure blue, and a dark cap and back are commonly separated by a white or pale collar. Juveniles of paradise kingfishers are dusky, differing markedly from their adults, but in other species juveniles are bright in plumage, though duller than adults. There is little geographic variation within a species, and color conservatism has led to allied species looking much alike. Notable exceptions are the Variable dwarf kingfisher, whose subspecies on islands from the Philippines to the Solomons vary from red to blue or yellow, Africa's Gray-headed kingfisher and the much larger Black-capped kingfisher of China. Although the last two differ in appearance, biochemical and biological characteristics, as well as the geographical relationship of their ranges, suggest very strongly that they are of immediate descent from a common ancestor.

The evolutionary history of other groups of kingfisher species is better understood than for most groups of birds. The family almost certainly arose in tropical rain forest, partly in the northern Australasian region (insectivorous woodland kingfishers, subfamily Daceloninae), and partly in adjacent Indonesia, Borneo and Southeast Asia (forest insectivores, evolving into waterside fishers, subfamily Alcedininae). Both subfamilies extended into Asia and repeatedly invaded Africa, on as many as 12 separate occasions; the Alcedininae invaded the New World to give rise to the Green and Giant kingfishers there (exclusive fishers, subfamily Cerylinae). The several Pacific archipelago species of woodland (*Halcyon*) kingfishers have clearly evolved from the wide-ranging complex formed by the

Mangrove and Beach kingfishers and the more southerly Sacred kingfisher. African mangrove, Woodland and Blue-breasted kingfishers are similarly of recent descent from a single ancestor; their habitats keep them apart, though they are acquiring sufficient ecological differences to permit some degree of geographical overlap. Belted, Ringed, Giant and Crested kingfishers respectively in North America, tropical America, Africa, and southern Asia, are all very closely allied and it is thought that the Giant and Crested descended from small populations of the first two which crossed the Atlantic (Belted kingfishers occasionally still arrive in Europe as vagrants). Species multiplication is also demonstrated by the four green kingfishers of the neotropics. Long ago, their common ancestor there separated into two geographically distinct populations which duly happened to evolve differences of size, enabling them to overlap as distinct species. Later, each of the two species repeated the separating process, and the

► ▼ **Representative species of kingfishers.**
(1) Pied kingfisher (*Ceryle rudis*) hovering.
(2) Blue-breasted kingfisher (*Halcyon malimbica*).
(3) Belted kingfisher (*Megaceryle alcyon*).
(4) Amazon kingfisher (*Chloroceryle amazona*).
(5–7) Kingfisher bill-types. (5) Shovel-billed kingfisher (*Clytoceyx rex*). (6) Laughing kookaburra (*Dacelo gigas*) with a long bill flattened top to bottom. (7) African mangrove kingfisher (*Ceyx pusillus*) with a long bill flattened side to side.

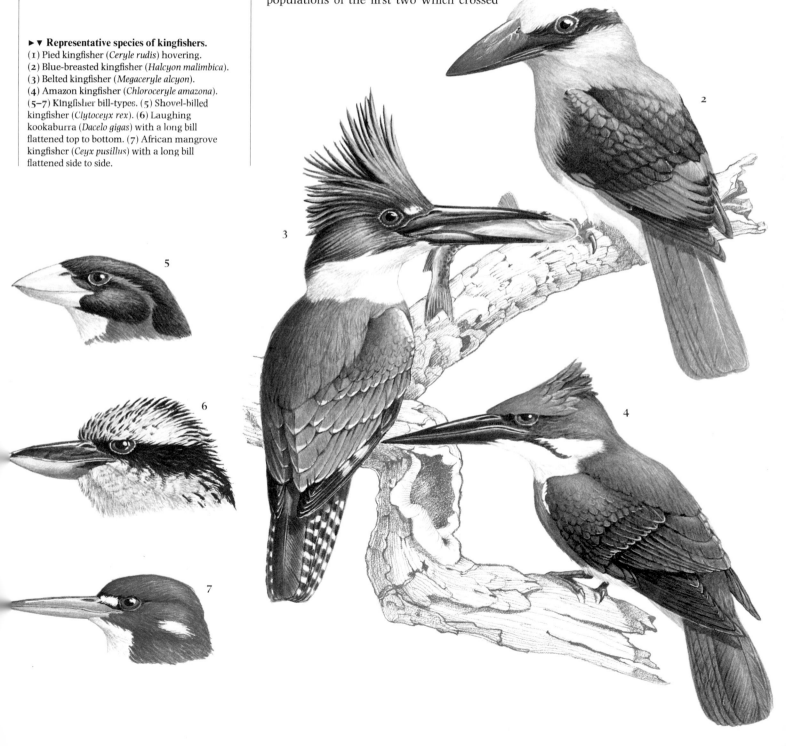

result today is four species all occupying much the same range, having body-weights close to the proportions 1:2:4:8, with the smallest and second-largest (American Pygmy and Green-and-rufous kingfishers) being almost alike in appearance and the largest and second-smallest (Amazon and Green kingfishers) also being remarkably similar.

All fishing kingfishers take a certain amount of invertebrate prey in addition to fish; Eurasian kingfishers, for instance, have about 21 percent of insects in their diet, mainly aquatic but some caught on dry land. Pied kingfishers, fishing from hovering flight more than from a perch, are in that sense at the pinnacle of evolution of the family; in Africa they live entirely upon fish (but in India take insects and crabs too, and can even "hawk" for flying termites). Not having to rely on a perch means that they can fish far from shore: on Lake Kariba they fish up to 3km (1.9mi) offshore at dawn and dusk, catching sardines, a deep-sea fish which rises to the surface at those times. In Natal, 80 percent of their fish food consists of *Sarotherodon mossambicus*, mainly in the 1–2g (0.035–0.070oz) weight class, and on

▲ **The Laughing kookaburra** is obviously a kingfisher, although it lives in wooded country and eats insects and some reptiles.

◄ **The kingfisher's dive.** (1) The kingfisher has spotted a fish and tenses for the dive. (2) A 45° plunge with powerful wingbeats takes him to the water. (3) The kingfisher enters the water, having made last-second adjustments to its aim by fanning the tail feathers. (4) With eyes closed, the fish is seized. (5) The kingfisher, its eyes still closed, emerges from the water with the fish. (6) The kingfisher returns to its perch and swallows the fish head-first after beating it against the branch.

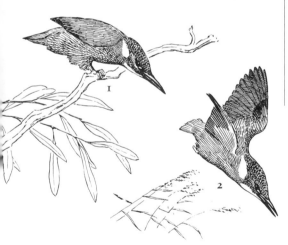

Lake Victoria they prey almost exclusively on fish from the genera *Haplochromis* and *Engraulicypris*. When they forage close to the shore, they dive from hovering flight in windy conditions when ruffled water seems to make fishing from a perch unrewarding. Only when the surface is calm do they fish from perches to a greater extent than from hovering. A Pied kingfisher flies low over the water to a desired hunting station, then rises up to 10m (33ft) and hovers on rapidly beating wings with the trunk held almost vertically and the bill pointing acutely down, keeping station for 5–10 seconds, then diving steeply to

ritorial advertising display, singing loudly and repeatedly from a conspicuous treetop perch, spreading the wings widely, with the patterned undersides facing forwards, and rotating the body about the vertical axis. Other species have little by way of any courtship display. Both sexes dig the nest tunnel and the male takes a minor role in incubation. The eggs hatch at about daily intervals, in the sequence of laying, so nestlings vary considerably in size. They are fed by both parents equally.

Laughing kookaburras in Australia and Pied kingfishers in Africa have a more complex social system than solitary monogamy. Each has adult helpers at the nest, and in Pied kingfishers there are two kinds of helpers: primary helpers (those helping their own parents) and secondary helpers (those helping an unrelated pair). "Helping" includes defense of territory and feeding the young in the nest and after fledging. This species breeds in loose colonies, the only kingfisher to do so.

Kingfishers have not, in general, come into direct conflict with man. As fish-eaters a few species have occasionally been viewed as pests on fishing streams and dealt with accordingly; but usually they are treated with respect—and often with admiration. Formerly, great numbers of Eurasian kingfishers were shot or netted to make fishing "flies" from their feathers, and in earlier times (in Britain at least) superstition caused the destruction of many, for a dried kingfisher corpse in the house was supposed to avert thunderstorms and keep out moths! Today, man's harmful effects upon kingfishers are more accidental than deliberate, in the pollution of fresh waters and the modification of habitats, especially rain forest. Bird-catchers destroy many; at Jatinga in Assam great numbers of migrating Eurasian, Stork-billed, Ruddy, and Oriental dwarf kingfishers are killed (and presumably eaten) when they are attracted to light beacons around the village at night. In some Mediterranean countries, many kingfishers are killed by netting, shooting and liming, although they are not target species.

Few populations are at great risk. So many species are confined to tropical rain forests, however, or to small Pacific islands or archipelagos, that their fate depends entirely on the preservation of their habitats. Almost certainly extinct is the distinctive race of the Tuamotu kingfisher, which lived until about 1922 on the island of Mangareva, 1,250km (about 800mi) from Tuamotu in the central Pacific.   CHF

▲ **Bringing it back home.** A Eurasian kingfisher returns with a fish in its beak to its nest in a bank. There may be as many as 6–7 young, each of which will eat 15 or more fish a day. Thus each parent may need to catch 50 fish each day for the young—as well as those they need for themselves.

penetrate possibly 2m (6.5ft) underwater, occasionally catching more than one fish at a time. Similar behavior is exhibited by the Belted kingfisher of North America.

Most kingfishers are monogamous and territorial, a pair defending an area of woodland on a stretch of river against incursion by other birds of the same species. Several species are migratory, both in the temperate zone and within the tropics; others are sedentary. What little is known suggests that most species breed at the end of their first year, and are quite long-lived. Woodland kingfishers (*Halcyon* species) have a ter-

MOTMOTS AND TODIES

Families: Motmotidae, Todidae
Order: Coraciiformes (suborder: Alcedines, part).
Thirteen species in 7 genera.
Distribution: see map.

Motmots   Todies

Motmots
Family: Motmotidae
Eight species in 6 genera.
Distribution: C and S America.
Habitat: forests below the canopy.
Size: most 28–45cm (11–18in), but Tody
motmot only 17cm (6.5in); this length includes
long tails in all species except Tody motmot.
Plumage: all species bright green above (some
with blue in wings and tail), several with green
or brown crowns; a mixture of browns and
greens below depending on species; several
have a black spot on the breast and most have
a black mark through the eye; all with very
long, graduated tails with (except for Blue-
throated and Tody motmots) bare shafts just
before the end of the longest (central) tail
feathers, so that the tips appear like "rackets".
Sexes similar.
Voice: a wide range of hoots and squawk-like
notes, many far-carrying.
Nests: sometimes in crevices in rocks, but
mostly in burrows in banks excavated by the
birds themselves.
Eggs: 3–4, white, incubated by both sexes.

Species include: **Blue-crowned motmot**
(*Momotus momota*), **Blue-throated motmot**
(*Aspatha gularis*), **Keel-billed motmot** (*Electron
carinatum*), **Tody motmot** (*Hylomanes momotula*).

Todies
Family: Todidae
Five species of the genus *Todus*.
Distribution: confined to the larger islands of
the Caribbean.
Habitat: forest and woodland, often along
streams.
Size: 11–12cm (4.3–4.7in).
Plumage: all species iridescent green above,
with red throats; underparts vary with species.
Sexes similar.
Voice: a harsh chatter, often a disyllabic *cherek*.
Nest: a burrow in a bank.
Eggs: 2–5, white, roundish.

Species: **Broad-billed tody** (*Todus subulatus*),
Cuban tody (*T. multicolor*), **Jamaican tody**
(*T. todus*), **Narrow-billed tody** (*T. angustirostris*),
Puerto Rican tody (*T. mexicanus*).

A COLORFUL bird sitting on a branch in a
South American forest, swinging from
side-to-side a long tail, shaped at the end like
the flights of a pair of darts, is almost
certainly a **motmot**—a close relative of the
kingfishers. Motmots are medium-sized
insectivorous birds that are usually found in
pairs, well separated from their neighbors.

All species are bright green or turquoise
green on the back and tail, several are also
green beneath; others have brown underparts. Some have brown heads, but the
crowns of most species are turquoise, blue
or black. All have black marks through or
near the eye and in many this mark is
highlighted by thin turquoise stripes above
and below. Several have a black spot on the
breast.

The most distinctive feature of most motmots is their long, highly graduated tail. In
all species except the Blue-throated and Tody
motmots the vanes of the two longest (central) tail feathers are missing for 3cm (1in)
or more a short way from the tip, leaving
the bird with "racket" tips to the feathers.
Some reports describe the birds as stripping
the barbs off the feathers themselves, but it
seems as if the barbs are anyway weakly
attached to the quill at this point and that
they work loose shortly after the feather is
fully grown; doubtless they are more likely
to break loose while the bird is preening,
which probably explains the different
accounts. It is not known why the feathers
should be like this except that they are
extensively used in display.

Motmots have longish, powerful bills

which are slightly downcurved and which
have sharp serrations along the edges; the
bill of the Keel-billed motmot is strongly
keeled. The birds feed on large insects and
lizards and use their powerful bills for crushing their prey; they also sometimes feed on
berries. They sit around on perches beneath
the forest canopy and sally forth, flycatcher-
like, to catch flying insects or to pounce on
small animals on the ground.

All motmots nest in holes, usually in a
bank or sometimes in a burrow dug in the
ground; they dig the burrows themselves.
At the end of the burrow they excavate a
largish chamber in which the female lays
the eggs. Both sexes incubate the eggs and
feed the young. The young do not leave the
nest until they are fully able to fly, but their
elongated tail feathers have not developed
at this time.   CMP

Todies are close relatives of the motmots of
Central and South America: both groups
have many characteristics in common, but
todies are considerably smaller.

Todies are confined to the larger islands
of the Caribbean, where each species has a
limited distribution. The Cuban tody lives on
Cuba and the Isle of Pines, the Puerto Rican
tody on Puerto Rico, the Jamaican tody on
Jamaica; Hispaniola has two species, the
Narrow-billed tody at low altitudes and the
Broad-billed tody in the mountains. The
Narrow-billed tody is also found on Gonave,
off Hispaniola.

All are a brilliant, iridescent green above,
with a bright red throat. The color of their

◄ **Tody on a twig.** A diminutive Jamaican tody devouring an insect on its perch. The bird will beat the butterfly against the branch to knock the wings off and then either swallow the body or take it back for the young.

▼ **Attentive motmot.** A Blue-crowned motmot in characteristic pose, waiting for prey to appear. The powerful beak has sharp serrations along the edges, enabling it to grip prey firmly.

underparts varies from species to species; they may be pale—whitish or grayish—and some have a pink or yellow wash on their flanks. Unlike the motmots, todies have short tails. All have long, straight bills which vary somewhat in width; they are usually black above and red or orange-red below. In flight, both sexes may make a whirring noise. This is apparently made by the wings and may be associated with courtship display.

The todies are also like miniature versions of their mainland motmot cousins in their ecology. They live in wooded country, usually in forests and frequently along the edges

of streams or rivers. They spend much of the day, either alone or in pairs, sitting still, perched on small twigs from which they sally out to catch small passing insects; occasionally they may pounce on tiny lizards or other small animals, and they also hover briefly to pluck prey from leaves. They are extremely tame and approachable.

During the breeding season they use their beaks to excavate tiny burrows in a bank of a stream or road. They lay their eggs in a chamber at the end. Both parents incubate and care for the young. When the young hatch they are naked, and remain in the nest until they can fly.   CMP

BEE-EATERS

Family: Meropidae
Order: Coraciiformes (suborder: Meropes).
Twenty-four species in 3 genera.
Distribution: Eurasia, Africa, Madagascar, New Guinea, Australia.

Habitat: mostly open country: woodlands, savannas, steppe; 6 species in rain forest.

Size: 17–35cm (6.5–13.5in) long (including tail streamers), weight 15–85g (0.5–3.0oz).

Plumage: mostly green above, buff below; some species black or blue or carmine with black eye mask, black gorget, and colored throat. Males and females very similar; some males brighter than females, with longer tail streamers.

Voice: rolled liquid syllables, melodious *en masse* or hoarse cawing.

Nests: unlined chamber at end of a tunnel 5–7cm (2–3in) in diameter and up to 3m (10ft) long, dug in cliff or flat ground.

Eggs: 2–4 in tropics, up to 7 in Eurasia; white; weight 3.5–4.5g (0.12–0.16oz); incubation period 18–23 days; nestling period 27–32 days.

Diet: airborne insects, mainly wasps and bees.

Species include: **Black bee-eater** (*Merops gularis*), **Blue-bearded bee-eater** (*Nyctyornis athertoni*), **Blue-cheeked bee-eater** (*Merops persicus*), **Carmine bee-eater** (*M. nubicus*), **Celebes bee-eater** (*Meropogon forsteni*), **European bee-eater** (*Merops apiaster*), **Little bee-eater** (*M. pusillus*), **Little green bee-eater** (*M. orientalis*), **rainbowbird** (*M. ornatus*), **Red-bearded bee-eater** (*Nyctyornis amicta*), **Red-throated bee-eater** (*Merops bullocki*), **Swallow-tailed bee-eater** (*M. hirundineus*), **White-fronted bee-eater** (*M. bullockoides*).

▶ **Adorning a bank,** a colony of Carmine bee-eaters. Some of the nest-holes are visible here. This is the southern race (*Merops nubicus nubicoides*) which lacks the greenish blue throat of the northern race.

Bee-eaters do indeed eat bees, and this has brought them into conflict with bee-keepers. The bees are caught usually on the wing, and are taken to a perch to be relieved of their venom and sting before being swallowed—this involves beating the bee against a hard object.

Bee-eaters are highly colored birds: most are green above and green, buff or chestnut below, but one is predominantly black, one blue, one pink and gray, and one carmine. All have a black eye mask, most have a black band on the upper breast, and the intervening chin and throat are strikingly bright yellow, red, reddish, blue or snowy, often with a cheek stripe of contrasting color. Wings are rounded (in forest dwelling bee-eaters) or long and pointed (in open country species, particularly those that hunt or migrate long distances). In most species the wings are green with a broad black trailing edge. The tail is quite long, not much patterned, but often with slightly or greatly elongated central feathers, or elongated outer feathers in the Swallow-tailed bee-eater. In other respects, all species are physically much alike: large-headed, short-necked birds with a long, slender, downcurved bill, very short legs and weak feet. When perched, all move the tail backwards and forwards through a small arc—these are balancing movements which have come to have a social function. All sunbathe using a number of postures, the commonest being to sit back-to-the-sun with mantle feathers acutely raised.

The bee-eater family is essentially tropical, and its more primitive members inhabit Southeast Asian rain forests: this and other clues suggest that bee-eaters arose there, and spread to Africa, where they proliferated. Repeated intervention of rain forest between northern and southern tropical savanna isolated ancestral populations and

allowed them to differentiate. Northern and southern Carmine bee-eaters are thought to have diverged from a common ancestor only about 13,000 years ago, and the northern tropical Red-throated bee-eater and southern tropical White-fronted bee-eater diverged about 75,000 years ago.

The commonest prey of most bee-eaters are honeybees. When readily available—near their hives or around flowering trees and herbs—they seem to be taken in preference to other equally abundant flying insects. All four species of honeybee are eaten, and the geographical ranges of honeybees and bee-eaters coincide so closely as to suggest that honeybees have always

▷ **Poised with prey,** OVERLEAF a European bee-eater prepares to swallow a cicada. Note the subtle color scheme: lilac-blue breast, russet back of the head, yellow throat patch.

◀ **The rainbowbird,** a bee-eater that lives in Australia and migrates to Indonesia. This species nests in very loose colonies. Sometimes the nests are so far apart that they seem to be solitary.

▼ **Bee-eater at work.** (1) Bee-eaters often perch on bustards to spot their prey, as with this Carmine bee-eater on an Arabian bustard. (2) The pursuit of a bee is usually short and direct but sometimes involves twisting and turning; shown here is a European bee-eater. (3) The bee is caught by an upward movement of the head, as with this Blue-cheeked bee-eater. (4) The bee-eater (as with this Swallow-tailed bee-eater) glides to a perch and rubs the bee on the perch to procure venom discharge and to tear away the poison sacs and sting before (5) swallowing it whole; shown here is a Rainbow bee-eater.

been the birds' staple food. Other insects taken by some species include wasps, hornets, dragonflies and damselflies. The great majority of bees caught are venomous workers. The few non-stinging drones (male bees) taken probably reflects their scarcity outside of the hive. A European bee-eater requires about 225 bee-sized insects to sustain it and its young every day.

Bee-eaters hunt mainly by keeping watch for flying insects from a perch. They sit alertly on a vantage point such as a treetop twig, fence or telegraph wire, turning the head to scan on all sides, then fly out quickly to intercept a passing insect. The prey is seized adroitly in the bill, taken sometimes from below and at other times after a short twisting and turning pursuit; in a graceful glide the bird returns to its perch where it tosses the prey until held in the tip of the bill, and strikes it several times against the perch to left and right. A stinging insect is then held near the tip of its tail, which is rubbed against the perch with the motion of someone using an india-rubber. A bee's bowel fluid is squeezed out, wetting the perch, and its sting and poison sacs are torn away. Several beating and rubbing bouts alternate, and the immobilized insect is swallowed entire.

Like their close allies the kingfishers, bee-eaters excavate nest burrows in soil. Most species dig both in perpendicular banks and in flat ground; but Red-throated and White-fronted bee-eaters nest only in banks. Tunnels decline in flat ground, are horizontal or inclining in cliffs, and end in a broad oval egg-chamber. Red-throated bee-eaters' tunnels have a hump separating entrance tunnel from egg chamber, which helps to prevent eggs from accidentally rolling out. There is no nest lining, but a blackish carpet of trodden-down regurgitated pellets soon accumulates and can almost bury the clutch. Later, nests become fouled with feces, the debris full of scavenging beetle larvae, and a large colony has an ammoniacal stench.

At the end of its first year a bee-eater either breeds or, like many other tropical birds, attaches itself as a helper to a breeding pair. In most species there is little by way of courtship display, although chasing away rival males and adjacent-nesting pairs, and "courtship"-feeding, are commonplace. White-throated bee-eaters, however, have a courtship "butterfly-flight," with raised wings, slow beats and deep-chested appearance. In many bee-eaters, a perched bird also greets its incoming mate by raising its wings, fanning and vibrating the tail, and

calling vociferously. Both sexes—and any helpers—excavate the nest, but the female does most of the incubating. Eggs are laid at 1-day intervals (or up to 2-day intervals in larger species) and incubation begins sporadically with the first egg and fully with the second or third egg. Hence the eggs hatch at about daily intervals, in the laying sequence, and the brood of young are graded in age and size, with the oldest often 2–3 times the weight of the youngest.

Both parents, and any helper(s), feed the young equally, with single insects generally larger than those that the adults themselves eat. The newly hatched young are blind, naked and pink. Their skin soon turns gray, eyes open and spiny, rudimentary feathers appear at about a week; growth is then rapid and the youngsters fledge at a weight up to 20 percent greater than the mean adult weight. After fledging, they and their parents and helpers may all continue to roost in the nest-hole for a few days, but usually start roosting in distant vegetation.

The family group—4 in Black, about 6 in Little, 4–9 in European, or up to 12 in White-throated bee-eaters—stay together in some instances until next year's nesting. After fledging, the young accompany the adults particularly closely for some six weeks, depending on them for food.

Red-throated and White-fronted bee-eaters in Africa have some of the most complex bird societies in the world. The White-throated bee-eater, a Saharan species, has up to six helpers at the nest. Red-throated bee-eaters are densely colonial, with up to 150 birds occupying nest holes in 1–2sq m (11–22sq ft) of cliff face. About two-thirds of nests are attended by a pair only, and pairs at the remaining third have 1–3 helpers which are generally their own progeny from a previous year. White-fronted bee-eaters are similarly colonial, but have 1–5 helpers at a majority of nests, and an individual bird alternates between breeding and helping breeders in successive nestings. Certain pairs and their helpers within a colony form a clan, and a colony may comprise 3–6 clans.

No bee-eater species is greatly threatened, but some may be depleted if commercial bee-keeping is developed in Africa. Bee-eaters were known to the ancient Egyptians as pests at apiaries, and many thousands are killed every year in Mediterranean countries. Since we now know that they consume vast amounts of hornets, bee-wolves and other honeybee-eating insects, it might well benefit bee-keepers in the long run *not* to molest the birds.   CHF

ROLLERS AND HOOPOES

Families: Coraciidae, Leptosomatidae, Phoeniculidae, Upupidae
Order: Coraciiformes (suborder: Coracii).
Twenty-five species in 8 genera.
Distribution: see maps and table.

Hoopoe   Wood-hoopoes

Rollers   Cuckoo roller

▶ **The silky plumage** TOP RIGHT of the Lilac-breasted roller, a species of tropical Africa.

▶ **A hoopoe** bringing prey to its young at the nest in a tree-hole. The young hatch at intervals and are at first brooded by the female and fed by the male. Later both sexes take part in feeding.

▶ **A Rufous-crowned roller** (*Coracias naevia*) BOTTOM RIGHT on an acacia tree in Etosha National Park, Namibia. Confined to the southern half of Africa, this species is less noisy and aggressive than other rollers. It occurs singly or in pairs in open woodland.

COLORFUL, numerous and attractive birds, rollers and hoopoes have attracted much attention, principally because of the recently discovered mass-emigration of hundreds of thousands of European rollers from East Africa. Cinnamon rollers, whose diet consists of swarming termites, and Green wood-hoopoes, who have "helpers" at the nest, have also attracted attention.

Rollers are not particularly closely allied with hoopoes. Appearances and ways of life are very different, yet there are underlying affinities of breeding and biology and structure: 22 of the 25 species belonging to these four families breed in the Afro-tropical region and the two most northerly breeding species, European roller and hoopoe, are of immediate descent from relatives in the tropics.

Rollers are so-called because of the spectacular tumbling courtship flight of "true" rollers (*Coracias*) and of broad-billed rollers (*Eurystomus*). The former spend much time aloft, defending their territory with raucous calls and rolling flight; but they feed mainly on the ground, dropping onto small animals from a perch. Broad-billed rollers, by contrast, feed on the wing. For most of the day a pair sits on treetops, eating little, and aggressively chasing other birds away; but in the late afternoon up to 200 gather, dramatically losing their aggressiveness to feed on winged termites. With pointed, quite long wings, large head, short neck and thickset body, they have a fast, wheeling and swooping flight and resemble falcons or huge swifts. One bird can eat up to 800 termites (half the weight of the bird itself) in the 90 minutes before dusk. One African species is resident in rain forests; another is a migrant within the tropical savannas and between Africa and Madagascar. The Oriental species is called dollar-bird because of the coin-sized white "windows" in its wing tips, and migrates between Australia and New Guinea.

All *Coracias* rollers are also strongly migratory. European rollers enter Africa in September, when the closely allied and very similar Abyssinian rollers are also migrating up to 1,000km (600mi) southwards within the northern tropics. But European rollers travel ten times as far, and winter mainly in arid country in Kenya, Tanzania and Namibia. In the first few days of April, huge numbers concentrate in eastern Tanzania, and fly together in a narrow coastal corridor through Kenya and Somalia, where thousands can be seen together, evenly dispersed in the sky from horizon to horizon.

All rollers appear to be monogamous, highly territorial, hole-nesters. Apart from the spectacular rolling flight, the breeding biology of European and Indian rollers is not unusual. Most African species are curiously ill-known, considering how common and eminently studiable the birds are. Madagascan ground rollers are even less well known; they seem to be mainly active at twilight, feeding entirely on the ground, and nesting in holes in open ground (Long-tailed ground roller), around forest tree roots (Pitta-like and Crossley's ground rollers), or in trees (Short-legged ground roller). There is a strong native tradition that these birds hibernate in the dry season.

The **Cuckoo-roller** is restricted to Madagascar and the Comoro islands, and may well be more closely related to "true" rollers than are the ground rollers. Cuckoo-rollers have the proportions and flight characteristics of "true" rollers but they seek their food neither in the air nor on the ground, but in the upper story of large forest trees. Chameleons appear to be a staple food item and it is likely that Cuckoo-rollers specialize on them.

Wood-hoopoes comprise one of the very few bird families confined to Africa. Smaller species are rather solitary, but larger ones are gregarious, in parties of 5–12, and make themselves highly conspicuous by periodically interrupting foraging to indulge in noisy mutual displays. Each bird cackles vociferously (they are called *kakelaars* in Africaans, or cacklers), and with each call the head is exaggeratedly bowed and the tail raised high. After a few seconds, they all fly from the nest tree and quietly resume foraging, probing into bark crevices with their long slender bills and often clinging below a horizontal limb or crosswise on a trunk. The bill is straight in some species, down-curved in others, and in the scimitar-bills greatly downcurved, bending through 90 degrees. "Cackling" functions to maintain the identity and cohesion of the group, which is more or less an extended family of parents, helpers and young. Studies in Kenya show that one advantage to the helper, which foregoes breeding in order to help at another adult's nest, is that the helper forms bonds with the young it helps to raise and in a subsequent nesting season those young will assist the former helper, improving its breeding success.

Best known of all these birds is the **hoopoe**, with a vast breeding range in three continents. Being conspicuous and common in gardens and cultivated land, it has a special place in folklore and people's affections.

Hoopoes are small-headed, short-legged perching and ground birds. They forage by walking over turf, probing with their long slender bill for grubs and, like wood hoopoes, taking insects from fissured bark in trees. They fly readily, with irregular, butterfly-like beats of rounded black wings with white bars across the flight feathers, and on perching often momentarily fan the crest. Races vary in the amount of white in the wing, and the depth of body color. Southern African hoopoes are reddish, with little white in the wing, and being readily distinguished in the field from wintering Eurasian migrants, they were formerly held to be a distinct species. Nests are scantily-lined cavities in termite-mounds, old wood-pecker holes, rough stone walls, drainpipes or clefts in trees; the entrance is narrow, so that the bird has to squeeze in, and the hole itself fetid. Young are downy. They have five methods of defense: by spraying excreta; hissing; poking upward with the bill; striking with one wing; and a stinking excretion of the preen gland. Adult hoopoes react to overhead birds of prey by flattening themselves against the ground, with wings and tail spread conspicuously and bill pointing straight up. CHF

The 4 Families of Rollers and Hoopoes Ⓥ Vulnerable. Ⓡ Rare.

Rollers
Family: Coraciidae
Sixteen species in 5 genera.
Africa, Madagascar, Eurasia, Australia. Forests, woodlands, savannas. Size: 25–45cm (10–18in). Plumage: muted pink-browns, cinnamon, dark and light blue; sexes alike. Voice: repeated short gruff caws. Nests: in cavities in trees and masonry, or (ground rollers) in tunnel in ground. Eggs: 2–3 near Equator, 3–6 in high latitudes; white; weight 10–17g (0.35–0.6oz); incubation period about 18 days; nestling period 25–30 days. Diet: mainly insects; some small vertebrates.

Species include: **Abyssinian roller** (*Coracias abyssinica*), **Cinnamon roller** (*Eurystomus glaucurus*), **Crossley's ground roller** Ⓡ (*Atelornis crossleyi*), **dollar-bird** or **Broad-billed roller** (*Eurystomus orientalis*), **European roller** (*Coracias garrulus*), **Indian roller** (*C. benghalensis*), **Lilac-breasted roller** (*C. caudata*), **Long-tailed ground roller** Ⓥ (*Uratelornis chimaera*), **Pitta-like ground roller** Ⓡ (*Atelornis pittoides*), **Purple roller** (*Coracias naevia*), **Racket-tailed roller** (*C. spatulata*), **Scaly ground roller** Ⓡ (*Brachypteracias squamigera*), **Short-legged ground roller** Ⓡ (*Brachyptera leptosomus*).

Cuckoo-roller
Leptosomus discolor.
Family: Leptosomatidae
Sole species
Cuckoo-roller or gourol
Madagascar, Comoro Islands. Forests, scrub. Size: 42cm (17in). Plumage: male, iridescent green back, gray head, white underparts; female, greenish back, brown head, spotted underparts. Voice: loud "qui-yu," repeated. Nests: in tree cavity. Eggs: 2, cream-buff, rounded ovals. Diet: insects; chameleons and other small vertebrates.

Wood-hoopoes
Family: Phoeniculidae
Seven species of genus *Phoeniculus*.
Subsaharan Africa. Forests, wooded savannas. Size: 23–46cm (9–18in). Plumage: black with green or violet gloss, conspicuous white marks on wing and in long tail, some species with buff or brown head; bill and legs scarlet or black. Voice: repeated fluty notes, or cackling by flock in unison. Nests: in tree cavities, unlined. Eggs: 2–4, blue, spotted; incubation period 17–18 days; nestling period 30 days. Diet: insects.

Species include: **Buff-headed wood-hoopoe** (*Phoeniculus bollei*), **Green wood-hoopoe** (*P. purpureus*), **scimitarbill** (*P. cyanomelas*).

Hoopoe
Upupa epops.
Family: Upupidae
Sole species.
Europe, Africa, Madagascar, southern Asia. Wooded farmlands, orchards, savannas. Size: 27–29cm (11–11.5in) long, weight 50–80g. (1.8–2.8oz). Plumage: pink-brown, with black-and-white banded crest, wings and tail. Voice: "hoo-poo." Nest: unlined or simply-lined cavity in tree, masonry or ground. Eggs: 2–5 in tropics, 7–9 in high latitudes; color very variable–yellowish, greenish, brownish; weight 4.5g; incubation period 15–16 days; nestling period 28 days. Diet: insects, small vertebrates.

◀ ▼ **Representative species of rollers and hoopoes.** (1) Hoopoe (*Upupa epops*) in defensive posture. (2) Cuckoo roller (*Leptosomus discolor*). (3) Green wood-hoopoes (*Phoeniculus purpurens*) with two performing the calling display. (4) Racquet-tailed roller (*Coracias spatulata*). (5) European roller (*Coracias garrulus*).

HORNBILLS

Family: Bucerotidae
Order: Coraciiformes (suborder: Bucerotes).
Forty-five species in 14 genera.
Distribution: Africa, and S Asia and islands east to New Guinea.

► **Triple-decker bill.** The huge bill of the Northern pied hornbill (*Anthracoceros albirostris*), with its casque above the upper mandible.

▼ **The White-crested hornbill** of Asia. This species lacks a casque but does have a crest growing forwards over the bill.

HORNBILLS are celebrated for their large bill, often surmounted by a large casque. They are conspicuous with their bold colors, varied calls and rushing wing-beats. Their biology is also remarkable, especially the unique breeding habits—the female seals herself into a nest hole for the entire nesting cycle.

Hornbills are an Old World group—unrelated to the toucans of the New World—with about half the species in Africa south of the Sahara (not Madagascar), half in southern Asia, and a single species extending to New Guinea. The larger forest species, most of which occur in Asia, are usually the largest avian fruit-eaters in their habitat and are probably important dispersers of the seeds of many forest tree species. More than half the African species inhabit savanna and woodland, especially the 15 small *Tockus* species, which are mainly insectivorous, but also the two ground hornbills, which are among the larger avian predators.

The large bill characteristic of the family may be why hornbills are the only birds with the first two neck vertebrae (axis and atlas) fused together. The bill is long and down-curved, often with only the tips of the mandibles meeting properly, to form dextrous forceps. The cutting edges are often serrated for breaking up food. The casque surmounting the bill is in its simplest form a narrow ridge that may reinforce the upper mandible. However, in many species the casque is elaborated into a structure that is cylindrical, upcurved, folded or inflated and sometimes exceeds the size of the bill itself.

The casque is invariably poorly developed in young birds. In the adults of most species it is much larger and more elaborate in males. In all but one species the structure is a light skin of keratin overlying a bony support; it is probably used in recognizing the age, sex and species of an individual, as well as for amplifying calls in a few cases. However, in the largest Asian species, such as the Great and Rhinoceros hornbills, it may be used in fighting or to knock down fruit. Most remarkable is the Helmeted hornbill, with its straight, short bill supporting a casque containing a block of solid keratin and together with the skull forming 10 percent of its body weight—possibly a weighted digging tool.

The wings are broad and, in the larger species, produce a whooshing noise in flight as air rushes through the base of the flight feathers (which lack underwing coverts). The tail is long in most species, especially in the Long-tailed hornbill or the White-

crested hornbill, while in the Helmeted hornbill the central pair of tail feathers is up to a meter (3.3ft) in length. In most species of the genus *Rhyticeros* the tail is short and pure white, and the ground hornbills also have short tails.

Notable colors and structures are found on the head and neck. The eye color may differ between species, or between sexes as in the genus *Buceros*. Coloration of the bare skin around the eyes and on the throat may distinguish the species, sex or age of a hornbill and in some species the throat skin is inflated (ground hornbills, *Rhyticeros*, *Aceros*) or hangs as wattles (*Ceratogymna*). Hornbills are also notable for their long eyelashes, and for the rather stubby legs and toes, with broad soles and the bases of the three front toes partly fused.

There is considerable evidence that hornbills are closely related to hoopoes and wood hoopoes (p278) in both their anatomy and their behavior. Hoopoes and the small *Tockus* hornbills that they most resemble are both primarily African groups, which suggests the source and basic form of their common ancestor.

Hornbills in Africa, except ground hornbills, seem more closely related to each other than to those in the Oriental region. The large African species of *Bycanistes* (which have white rumps) and *Ceratogymna* are unusual in that the head and neck of young birds and females are colored brown in contrast to the black of males. In otherwise similar Oriental forms, such as *Anthracoceros*, the young birds resemble males, as in most other hornbills, with brown heads being confined to females in such genera as *Rhyticeros*, *Aceros* and *Penelopides*. The smallest hornbills, in the genus *Tockus*, have diversified into 13 species in Africa, with a further two similar but probably unrelated

species in India and Sri Lanka, and the Long-tailed hornbill of Africa is very similar to them.

Among African hornbills only the ground hornbills are apparently allied to Oriental species, although this is far from obvious at first sight. The largest Oriental forest hornbills in the genus *Buceros*, together with the specialized Helmeted hornbill, are derived from smaller *Rhyticeros* species. Some of these share with them the use of preen gland oils to color cosmetically the bill, casque and white areas of plumage with red, orange or yellow. However, only in *Buceros* species and the Helmeted hornbill is the preen gland clothed in a special dense tuft of feathers to improve the application, and this same special feature is found in the ground hornbills of Africa. The ground

▲ **A Southern ground hornbill** and young in Kruger National Park, South Africa.

▶ **A snake-eating Yellow-billed hornbill,** an African species found from Somalia to Kenya and South Africa.

▼ **Displaying ground.** Southern ground hornbills live in cooperative groups of up to eight birds. Social communication is rich. (1) A female soliciting attention from a male. (2) A female bringing insects to a male. (3) A female beating her bill on the ground and flashing the wing feathers.

hornbills are so different from other hornbills in many aspects of their design and biology that this difference may be discounted were it not that they also share a special genus of feather lice with their Oriental relatives.

The larger forest hornbills are mainly fruit-eaters and most travel widely in search of fruiting trees. The irregular fruiting and dispersal of the food source also mean that these species are not territorial and tend to gather in large flocks in search of fruiting trees. The birds use the long bill to reach out to fruits and toss each fruit back into the gullet, where the stubby tongue can assist the swallowing. Undigested remains, such as pips, are regurgitated or defecated, facilitating seed dispersal.

Breeding hornbills have been observed to swallow as many as 69 small fruits and carry them to the nest to be regurgitated for the young. At one nest of a Silvery-cheeked hornbill it was estimated that the male delivered 24,000 fruits, in the course of 1,600 nest visits spanning the 120-day breeding cycle. Any small items of animal food are snapped up if encountered and in several species it appears that animal food is specially sought during breeding, probably as a source of extra protein for the growing young.

Most of the smaller hornbills are primarily insectivorous, taking other small animals and some fruit when available, and most are also sedentary and defend a permanent territory. However, some of the African species which occupy seasonally dry savanna are forced to range widely once the rainy season has passed. Exceptions to these two main feeding strategies are suspected for some large Oriental forest species, such as the White-crested and Helmeted hornbills, which are known to be sedentary—the

The Hornbill Family (Bucerotidae)

☐ Threatened, status indeterminate.

Forty-five species in 14 genera. Africa S of Sahara, S Asia and islands east to New Guinea.
Most species in forest but some, mainly in Africa, occupy savanna. Size: length 38–160cm (15–63in), with elongated tail of Helmeted hornbill up to 55cm (20in) longer; weight 85g–4kg (3oz–8.8lb), and wingspan up to 180cm (6ft). Males usually 10 percent larger than females, with bill 15–20 percent longer. Plumage: mainly areas of black and white, but in some species gray and brown predominate— apparently no plumage pigments other than melanin. Bill, casque, bare facial and throat skin, eyes or feet

often brilliantly colored in black, red, blue, yellow or combinations of these. Juveniles and sex of adults evident from plumage, facial skin, eye, bill or casque color, structure or a combination of these. Voice: considerable range from basic clucks and whistles to soft hooting, deep booming, raucous cackling or high squealing. Eggs: 1–2 in larger species, up to 7 in smaller ones, oval, white with finely pitted shells. Incubation 25–40 days, depending on size. Nestling period 45–86 days, depending on size. Diet: omnivorous; some species largely insectivorous, others largely frugivorous and two predominantly carnivorous.

Species include: in Africa, **Abyssinian ground hornbill** (*Bucorvus abyssinicus*), **Black-casqued hornbill** (*Ceratogymna atrata*), **Dwarf red-billed hornbill** (*Tockus camurus*), **Jackson's hornbill** (*T. jacksoni*), **Long-tailed hornbill** (*Tropicranus albocristatus*), **Red-billed hornbill** (*Tockus erythrorhynchus*), **Silvery-cheeked hornbill** (*Bycanistes brevis*), **Southern ground hornbill** (*Bucorvus cafer*), **Von der Decken's hornbill** (*Tockus deckeni*), **Yellow-billed hornbill** (*T. flavirostris*); in Asia, **Brown-backed hornbill** (*Ptilolaemus tickelli*), **Bushy-crested hornbill** (*Anorrhinus galeritus*), **Celebes tarictic hornbill** (*Penelopides exarhatus*), **Great hornbill** (*Buceros*

bicornis), **Helmeted hornbill** ☐ (*Rhinoplax vigil*), **Indian gray hornbill** (*Tockus birostris*), **Malabar pied hornbill** (*Anthracoceros coronatus*), **Narcondam hornbill** (*Rhyticeros narcondami*), **New Guinea hornbill** (*R. plicatus*), **Philippine brown hornbill** (*Buceros hydrocorax*), **Rhinoceros hornbill** (*B. rhinoceros*), **Rufous-necked hornbill** (*Aceros nipalensis*), **Sri Lankan gray hornbill** (*Tockus griseus*), **White-crested hornbill** (*Berenicornis comatus*), **Wreathed hornbill** (*Rhyticeros undulatus*).

◄ **Sealed inside her nest-hole** until the chicks are half-grown, the female Red-billed hornbill relies on the male to provide food. Here, a male is about to pass fruit through the nest-hole.

▼ **The curious reptilian chick** of a Southern ground hornbill. This large species does not wall itself into a hole but nests in a very large cavity, such as the top of a broken-off tree. Commonly only a single chick is raised and it may remain with its parents for several years.

former probably carefully searching the foliage and forest floor for prey, and the latter possibly excavating prey from rotten wood and loose bark. Only the very large ground hornbills are almost entirely carnivorous, using their pickax-like bills to subdue prey as large as hares, tortoises, snakes and squirrels, together with smaller fare found as they stride over the African veld.

Hornbills reach sexual maturity at between one (*Tockus*) and six (*Bucorvus*) years, depending on their size, but how long they live in the wild is unknown. Breeding seasons depend mainly on the birds' choice of food, with forest fruit-eaters showing little seasonality compared with savanna insectivores, which breed during the warm wet season.

Courtship feeding of females, mutual preening and copulation is all the activity reported to precede breeding in larger forest species. In many species the loud calls function to proclaim defended territories, and in some the calls accompany conspicuous displays. Territory size, in those non-fruit-eaters that do not just defend an area immediately around the nest, ranges from 10ha (25 acres) for the Red-billed hornbill to 100sq km (39sq mi) for the Southern ground hornbill.

Hornbills nest in natural cavities, usually in trees but also in rock faces and earth banks. In all species but the two ground hornbills, the female seals the nest entrance— apart from a narrow vertical slit—using mud initially (while working from outside) but later her own droppings, mixed with food remains. In some species the male

assists, by bringing lumps of mud or sticky foods, and in a few, such as *Byncanistes* and *Ceratogymna*, the male forms special pellets of mud and saliva in his gullet and helps to apply these to the entrance. In some genera the male continues to feed the female and their offspring for the rest of the nesting cycle, while in others (*Tockus, Buceros, Rhinoplax, Bycanistes, Ceratogymna, Rhyticeros, Aceros, Penelopides, Anthracoceros*) the female breaks out of the nest when the chicks are about half grown and helps to feed them. In the latter cases the chicks reseal the nest unaided and only break their way out when ready to fly. The vertical slit, with the nest floor sited below it, provides good air circulation through convection and the small opening and wooden walls provide good insulation. The sealed nest, and the long escape tunnel usually present above it, also provide protection from predators.

Food is brought to the nest either as single items held in the bill tip (eg *Tockus, Tropicranus*) or as a gullet-full of fruits which are regurgitated one at a time and passed to the nestlings. Food remains and droppings are passed out of the nest slit, the latter being forcibly expelled. In most species the female undergoes a simultaneous molt of all her flight and tail feathers, which are dropped at the time of egg laying and regrown by the time she emerges. The ground hornbills are an exception to the basic hornbill pattern; the female does not seal the nest (although sitting throughout incubation and the early nestling period, and being fed in the nest), droppings and food remains are not expelled and no unusual feather molt occurs.

Most hornbills are monogamous, with each member sharing all aspects of the nesting cycle. However, in some species, scattered through several genera, cooperative breeding has developed in which some individuals, usually males, although sexually mature, do not breed but help a dominant pair to rear their young. This habit is recognizable by the birds living in groups (of up to 25 in some species) and by the immatures being colored very differently from the adults. It is found in species as diverse in form and size as the Southern ground hornbill, the White-crested hornbill, Bushy-crested hornbill, the Brown-backed hornbill and Philippine brown hornbill.

Several hornbill species have suffered severe reductions in their ranges, especially in Southeast Asia and West Africa. Others, such as the Narcondam hornbill, are endemic to small islands and hence also vulnerable to alteration of habitat. AK

Hornbills in Human Cultures

The conspicuous hornbills have been incorporated into the cultures of many peoples. Many Africans regard hornbills as sacred birds and some species, especially the large ground hornbills, thrive unmolested even in areas of quite high human population density. Members of some West African ethnic groups, such as the Hausa, use stuffed heads of ground hornbills as camouflage when stalking game. Breeding individuals of some smaller species are taken for food or for preparation of medicines.

Hornbills are especially important in certain Southeast Asian societies, notably the Dayaks of Borneo. The great and raucous Rhinoceros hornbill was recognized as the god of war: *Singalang Burong*. Elaborate effigies, which exaggerated the recurved casque into dramatic spirals, used to be carved in wood and hoisted above longhouses. Today this hornbill is the emblem of the Malaysian state

of Sarawak, and the country is advertised to tourists as the "Land of Hornbills." Its white tail feathers with a single black band once featured prominently in dancing cloaks and head-dresses, as did the similarly colored, greatly elongated central pair of tail feathers of the Helmeted hornbill.

The solid block of "hornbill ivory" forming the front part of the casque of the Helmeted hornbill is unique. It is carved by the indigenous Kenyah and Kelabit people of Borneo into ear ornaments or belt toggles, but in the past was an important item of trade with Chinese visiting Brunei. The Chinese executed exquisite three-dimensional carvings on the casque and worked the ivory (named *ho-ting*) into thin sheets. They also fixed the golden-red pigment derived from the preen gland oil. These sheets were cut into belt buckles that were worn by high officials of the 14th- to 17th-century Ming dynasty in China.

TOUCANS, HONEYGUIDES AND BARBETS

Families: Ramphastidae, Indicatoridae, Capitonidae
Order: Piciformes (suborder: Galbulae, part). One hundred and thirty-one species in 20 genera.
Distribution: see maps and table.

Honeyguides   Toucans

Barbets

▶ **Representative species of toucans.** (1) An Emerald toucanet (*Aulacorhynchus prasinus*) calling. (2) A Black-billed mountain toucan (*Andigena nigrirostris*) revealing a flash of yellow on its rump as it clambers around in tree branches. (3) A Chestnut-mandibled toucan (*Ramphastos swainsonii*) tossing its head, enabling food held at the tip of the bill to be transferred to the throat. (4) A Toco toucan (*Ramphastos toco*) at full stretch searching for berries. (5) A Guianan toucanet (*Selenidera culik*) examining a possible nest cavity. (6) A Saffron toucanet (*Andigena bailloni*) flying from tree to tree. (7) A Collared aracari (*Pteroglossus torquatus*) preparing to leave its nest-hole.

1

Toco toucans are so often depicted by artists and designers that they have become a symbol of the warm forests of tropical America. Of all the rich bird life of the Neotropics, probably only hummingbirds are more often illustrated.

The most prominent feature of **toucans** are their bills, often vividly colored, which are much lighter in weight than they appear. A thin horny outer sheath encloses a hollow which is crisscrossed by many thin, bony, supporting rods. Despite this internal strengthening, toucans' bills are fragile and sometimes break. Nevertheless, some manage to survive a long time with part of their bills conspicuously missing. The biggest bill of any toucan is that of the male Toco toucan which accounts for 20cm of the bird's total length of 66cm (8 of 26in).

Naturalists have speculated for centuries about the uses of the toucan's exaggerated beak. It enables these heavy, rather clumsy birds to perch inside the crown of a tree, where branches are thicker, and reach far outwards to pluck berries or seeds from twigs too thin to bear their weight. Seized in the tip of the bill, food is thrown back into the throat by an upward toss of the head. This behavior explains the bill's length but not its thickness or bright coloration. The diet of toucans consists mainly of fruit but includes insects, an occasional lizard and eggs and nestlings of smaller birds. The huge, vivid beak so intimidates distressed parents that not even the boldest of them dares to attack the plunderer perching beside its nest. After the toucan flies and is unable to defend its back in the air, an enraged parent may pounce upon it, to withdraw prudently before the larger bird alights. The varied patterns of toucans' bills may help these birds to recognize each other. In Central American forests Chestnut-mandibled and Keel-billed toucans have such similar plumage that they are only readily distinguished by their bills—and voices. The Keel-billed's beak is delicately tinted with all but one of the colors of the rainbow, whereas that of its relative is largely chestnut, with much yellow on the upper mandible. Possibly the bills also play a role in courtship.

Toucans are moderately gregarious and fly in straggling flocks, one after another, rather than in compact bands, like parrots. In flight, the big *Ramphastos* toucans beat their wings a number of times, then close them, whereupon they lose altitude, as though borne downward by their great, forwardly directed beaks. Immediately the black wings are widely spread, the fall is converted into a short glide, followed by more wing beats that recover the lost altitude. Thus the toucan traces an undulatory course from one treetop to another that is rarely far distant. Toucans prefer to remain high in trees, where they hop from branch to branch. They bathe in pools of rain water in hollows high in trunks and limbs—never, apparently, at ground level. They offer food to their companions and, perching well apart, preen them with the tips of long bills.

Toucans are playful birds and often engage in various games. After striking their bills together, two clasp each other's bills and push until one is forced backward from the perch and retreats. Another individual may then cross bills with the winner, and

5

▲ Channel-billed toucan. The ten large toucans of the genus *Ramphastos* all have black or blackish plumage. Other features are more variable. Throats and breasts are yellow or white, upper tail coverts red, white or yellow. But *Ramphastos* toucans are most easily distinguished by their bill colors. This species (*R. vitellinus*) is a medium-sized *Ramphastos* toucan widespread in South America, from the north to southern Brazil.

the victor in this bout may be challenged again. Participants in such a wrestling match reveal no sign of aggression. In another form of play, one toucan tosses a fruit which another catches in the air, then throws it in similar fashion to a third, who may pitch it to a fourth member of the flock.

Toucans are often reported to sleep in holes, but this is only known to occur in the medium-sized aracaris and the Guianan toucanet (see box).

The big *Ramphastos* toucans appear to nest regularly in holes resulting from the decay of tree trunks, the availability of which may limit the number of breeding pairs. A favorable hole, in sound wood with an orifice just wide enough for the adults to squeeze through, may be used year after year. The hole may be only a few cm or 2m (6.5ft) deep. A suitable cavity near the base of a trunk may tempt toucans closer to the ground than is normal. Smaller toucans often occupy woodpeckers' holes, sometimes evicting the owners. They may clean out and enlarge existing cavities, and sometimes try to carve their own holes in soft, decaying wood, but apparently rarely with success. The nest chamber is never lined, but the 2–4 white eggs rest upon a few chips at the bottom, or upon a pebbly bed of regurgitated seeds of various sizes, shapes and colors, which grows thicker as incubation proceeds.

Parents share incubation and are, for birds of their size, impatient sitters, rarely remaining at their task for more than an hour and often leaving their eggs uncovered. Far from trying to repel intruders with their great bills, the least threat causes them to slip out and fly away.

After about 16 days of incubation the nestlings hatch blind and naked, with no trace of down on their pink skins. Like newborn woodpeckers, which they closely resemble, they have short bills with the lower mandible slightly longer than the upper. Around each ankle joint is a pad of spike-like projections, which protects it from abrasion as the nestlings stand on their rough floor, supporting themselves on heels and swollen abdomen. Nestlings are fed by both parents, with increasing quantities of fruit as they grow older, but they develop surprisingly slowly. The feathers of the small toucanets do not begin to expand until they are nearly four weeks old, and month-old *Ramphastos* nestlings are still largely naked. Both parents brood the nestlings, sometimes the male by night, as in woodpeckers. They carry large billfuls of waste from the nest, some, including Emerald toucanets, keeping the nest perfectly clean, whereas Keel-billed toucans permit decaying seeds to remain.

When finally fully feathered, young toucans resemble their parents, but their bills are smaller and less highly colored. Small toucanets may fly from the nest when 43 days old, but the larger *Ramphastos* toucans remain for about 50 days. Aracaris are led back to the nest to sleep with their parents but, as far as is known, other fledglings roost amid foliage.

The biggest toucans, 10 species of the genus *Ramphastos*, are chiefly inhabitants of lowland rain forests, from which they make excursions into neighboring clearings with scattered trees. They are rarely seen at altitudes of 1,500m (5,000ft) above sea level. Their plumage is chiefly black or blackish and their calls are largely croaks and yelps, but the vesper song of the Chestnut-mandibled toucan (*dios te dé*), is almost melodious when heard in the distance.

The 11 species of aracaris are smaller and more slender than the other toucans. They too are inhabitants of warm forests, but rarely venture as high as 1,500m (4,900ft). They have black or dusky green backs, crimson rumps and are usually black on head and neck. Their largely yellow underparts are crossed by one or two bands of black or red. Their long bills are black and ivory white, wholly ivory white or mainly fiery red. Exceptional for this group, the Curl-crested aracari has its crown covered with broad, shiny feathers that resemble curled horny shavings. The calls of the better-known species are sharp and high-pitched for such large birds. They are the only toucans which, as far as is known, regularly

Cooperative Breeding in Aracaris

Aracaris are slender, middle-sized toucans, which inhabit woods amid farmlands. Calling sharply *pitit pitit*, they fly swiftly and directly in small, straggling flocks. At nightfall they retire into old woodpecker holes or other cavities, turning their heads over their backs and their tails forward to cover them, to fit into a narrow space.

In a Panamanian forest six Collared aracaris were once observed to squeeze with difficulty through a narrow orifice in the underside of a thick horizontal branch, 30m (100ft) up in a great tree. As weeks passed the number of birds using this hole for sleeping decreased until only one remained, apparently incubating a clutch of eggs. After the eggs hatched five of the original six birds again slept in this hole, and all brought food to the nestlings, at first chiefly insects grasped in the tips of their great beaks. As the nestlings grew

older the five attendants brought increasing quantities of fruits, some of which they regurgitated.

At about 43 days the first young aracari flew from its high nursery. At nightfall its attendants led it back to sleep with them. While the fledgling tried inexpertly to enter the narrow, downward-facing doorway, a White hawk swooped down, seized the piteously crying young bird in its talons, and carried it off, followed by all the adults.

Three of the attendants at this nest were probably nonbreeding helpers, possibly older offspring of the parents. In the half century since these observations were made no other nest of the Collared aracari has been available for study, and we still do not know whether cooperative breeding, widespread in other families of tropical birds, is usual in any species of toucans.   AFS

▲ **Largest and most familiar** of the *Ramphastos* toucans is the Toco toucan of Brazil. It has the largest bill of any toucan, in both absolute and relative terms. In trees it is agile, but slightly awkward in flight, taking an undulating line. Here the use of the bill for holding fruit is clearly shown, as is the slightly serrated edge.

lodge in holes throughout the year.

Toucanets of the genus *Aulacorhynchus* (7 species) are small to large with mainly green plumage. Their calls are unmelodious croaks, barks and dry rattles. They chiefly inhabit cool mountain forests, between 1,000 and 3,000m (3,300–10,000ft), and rarely descend into warm lowlands.

The five species of toucanets belonging to the genus *Selenidera* dwell in rain forests at low altitudes from Honduras to northeast Argentina. Their plumage is more variable than that of the foregoing species, and they are the only toucans of which the sexes differ conspicuously in color. The reddish brown

bill of the Tawny-tufted toucanet is prominently striped with black. Little is known of the habits of these small toucans.

Least known of all are the four species of mountain toucans which, as their generic name *Andigena* implies, inhabit the Andes from northwest Venezuela to Bolivia. From the subtropical zone they extend far upward into the altitudinal temperate zone. One of the more colorful is the Black-billed mountain-toucan, whose light blue underparts are exceptional in the toucan family. Its crown and nape are black, its back and wings olive brown, rump yellow, throat white, undertail coverts crimson and thighs chestnut. Although these and many other toucans are becoming rarer as their habitats are destroyed, many remain to be studied by naturalists hardy enough to pass long months in remote forests.   AFS

The dull plumage, remote habitat and retiring disposition of **honeyguides** disguise a family whose behavior is among the most extraordinary—and least known—of any birds. They are named for the habit, of one species in particular (the Greater honeyguide), of guiding people and other large mammals to bees' nests. Experiments have in fact shown that the birds prefer the bees' larvae and even their waxy comb to honey. Honeyguides combine two specializations: the unique one of eating wax and the less unusual one of laying their eggs in other birds' nests.

Honeyguides are probably most closely related to woodpeckers and barbets. They occur only in the Old World tropics, most in Africa but two species in Asia. Their main habitat is broadleaved forest, though in two genera (*Prodotiscus* and *Indicator*) some inhabit more open woodland. Most of the African species form several groups of closely related species which are so similar to each other that even specialists find them very hard to identify, especially in the field.

The 3 Families of Toucans and Their Allies.   ⓥ Vulnerable.

Toucans
Family: Ramphastidae
Thirty-eight species in 5 genera.

Tropical America, from S Mexico to Bolivia and N Argentina, excluding Antilles. Rain forests and more open woodlands. Size: 33–66cm (13–26in) long (including bill). Males' bills slightly longer than females'. Plumage: several varieties, black with red, yellow and white; olive brown and blue; chiefly green. Sexes similar in color except in *Selenidera* species. Voice: usually unmusical, often croaks, barks, rattles or high, sharp notes. Nests: in natural cavities in trees; smaller species may occupy woodpeckers' holes, sometimes enlarging them. Eggs: 2–4, white, unmarked; incubation: 15–16 days; nestling period: 43–51 days. Diet: chiefly fruits supplemented by insects and other invertebrates, small lizards, snakes, birds' eggs and nestlings.

Species and genera include: **aracaris** (genus *Pteroglossus*), **Black-billed mountain toucan** (*Andigena nigrirostris*), **Chestnut-mandibled toucan** (*Ramphastos swainsonii*), **Collared aracari** (*Pteroglossus torquatus*), **Curl-crested aracari**

(*P. beauharnaesii*), **Emerald toucanet** (*Aulacorhynchus prasinus*), **Guianan toucanet** (*Selenidera culik*), **Keel-billed toucan** (*Ramphastos sulfuratus*), **Orange-billed toucan** (*R. aurantiirostris*), **Tawny-tufted toucanet** (*Selenidera nattereri*), **Toco toucan** (*Ramphastos toco*).

Honeyguides
Family: Indicatoridae
Fifteen species in 4 genera.

Africa, Asia. Evergreen forest, open woodland. Size: 10–20cm (4–8in) long, weight 10–55g (0.35–1.9oz). Plumage: somber olive, gray or brownish, paler below, often with white sides to the tail; two species have yellow wing patches; one has orange on head and rump; difference between sexes is slight except for one species. Voice: poorly known; males of several species give a simple monotonous song from a high post; one species gives a distinctive chatter when guiding people to bees' nests. Nests: none; in all species whose breeding habits are known the egg is laid in the nest of a hole-nesting bird. Eggs: normally one per nest; white (blue in one species), thick-shelled; incubation: 12–13 days; nestling

period: 38–40 days. Diet: chiefly insects, but all species include some form of wax.

Species include: **Eisentraut's honeyguide** (*Melignomon eisentrauti*), **Greater** or **Black-throated honeyguide** (*Indicator indicator*), **Indian honeyguide** (*I. xanthonotus*), **Lesser honeyguide** (*I. minor*), **Lyre-tailed honeyguide** (*Melichneutes robustus*), **Scaly-throated honeyguide** (*I. variegatus*).

Barbets
Family: Capitonidae
Seventy-eight species in 11 genera.

Africa S of the Sahara, India, Sri Lanka, SE Asia, Philippines, Java, Bali, Borneo, NW S America, Panama, Costa Rica. Primary and secondary tropical forest, plantations, savanna woodland and (in Africa) arid habitats. Size: ranges from 9cm (3.5in) in the tinkerbirds to 33cm (13in) long in the Great barbet. Plumage: Asian and American species are predominantly green with red, blue and yellow markings about the head; some African species are mainly black, red and yellow, heavily spotted or streaked. There are well-

developed differences between sexes only in the S American species. Voice: rapid repetition of a single or series of notes resembling honks, chirps, or the tapping of a hammer; duetting is well developed in the family. Nests: most species excavate holes in decayed trees; others use termite mounds, sand or earth banks, or burrows; no nest lining. Eggs: 2–5, white; incubation: varies, 12–14 days in some species, 18–19 in others; nestling period: 20–21 days, 24–26 days or 33–35 days. Diet: fruit, buds, flowers, nectar, insects; larger species also eat tree frogs and small birds.

Species and genera include: **Black-backed barbet** (*Lybius minor*), **Black-spotted barbet** (*Capito niger*), **D'Arnaud's barbet** (*Trachyphonus darnaudii*), **Great barbet** (*Megalaima virens*), **ground barbets** (genus *Trachyphonus*), **Lineated barbet** (*M. lineata*), **Pied barbet** (*Lybius leucomelas*), **Prong-billed barbet** (*Semnornis frantzii*), **Red-headed barbet** (*Ebucco bourcierii*), **tinkerbirds** (genus *Pogoniulus*), **Toucan barbet** ⓥ (*Semnornis ramphastinus*), **White-mantled barbet** (*Capito hypoleucus*), **Yellow-fronted tinkerbird** (*Pogoniulus chrysoconus*).

▲ **Ambidextrous bill**—Cuvier's toucan (*Ramphastos tucanus*). Although often largely fruit-eaters toucans frequently eat other birds' eggs and nestlings, which can be firmly grasped in the bill.

Within each group darker-colored species tend to live in broadleaved forest, paler ones in drier woodland. So cryptic and inconspicuous can they be that a totally new species was described from West Africa as recently as 1981 (Eisentraut's honeyguide). In most species the somber camouflage is relieved only by light sides to the tail which are conspicuous in flight and possibly help to lure potential hosts away from their nests. Only three species depart from this drab uniformity: the Lyre-tailed honeyguide of West Africa, in which the tail of both sexes is curved outwards and the two pin-like outermost feathers make (like those of snipes) a loud tooting noise in diving flight; the Indian honeyguide of the Himalayas, which has orange on the head and rump; and the Greater or Black-throated honeyguide in which the male has a black throat, white cheeks, yellow shoulder-flashes and a pink bill, and which is the only species in which the sexes have a different appearance. All species have zygodactyl feet (ie feet in which the second and third toes of each foot point forward and the first and fourth backward), like woodpeckers, and many also have curiously prominent nostrils, edged with a raised ridge; several species seem to be attracted to wood-smoke, perhaps especially to burning wax, and may have a keen sense of smell connected with locating bees' nests, though this intriguing possibility has not been investigated.

All species, so far as is known, include wax of some kind in their diet, though most eat mainly insects. Birds cannot digest wax without the aid of bacteria in their gut; the existence of these has been reported in Lesser honeyguides but not confirmed in this or any other species. Experiments have shown that both Lesser and Greater honeyguides can certainly digest wax somehow, since they can survive on a diet of pure wax for about 30 days. The small species in the genus *Prodotiscus* eat mainly scale insects, which are thickly coated in wax.

Male Indian honeyguides defend bees' nests, at which they feed, and to which females are admitted if they will mate. This species lacks white in the tail and may not be parasitic, since females bring young to bees' nests and their eggs have never been found despite searches of nests of likely hosts. In several other species males give simple monotonous calls from perches to which females come to mate; some species seem to defend possible hosts against other honeyguides. Honeyguide eggs are laid in holes in trees or banks, in the nests of other species, almost always singly. Young of at least two species hatch with sharp hooks on the tip of the bill, with which they puncture hosts' eggs or kill their chicks. They have an insistent begging call which sounds like several of the host young calling together.

Honeyguides are birds of forest and woodland, and their future is as threatened as that of their habitat. The Greater honeyguide, with its unique mutually beneficial relationship with man (see box), must adapt to changing human behavior as well as to shrinking habitats if it is to survive.   AWD

Any visitor to Africa is certain of hearing the monotonous repetitive calls of **barbets** as

---

Man and the Behavior of the Greater honeyguide

Two species of honeyguide are known to guide people and other large mammals to bees' nests. One, the Greater honeyguide, does this so often that it has been well studied but the other, the Scaly-throated honeyguide, is much less well known. Many African tribes use Greater honeyguides to show them bees' nests, whose honey they relish and which was once their only source of sugar. Greater honeyguides give a distinctive chattering call to attract attention, and then fly towards a bees' nest in short stages, stopping frequently to call and, apparently, to check the progress of the followers. Usually the bird falls silent when it reaches the nest, which is then opened by the men with an ax after stupefying the bees with wood-smoke. Most tribes leave some honeycomb for the birds, believing that if they do not the bird will lead them to a dangerous animal next time; but other tribes say honeycomb spoils the bird and leave it to find its own.

Such bizarre behavior is especially surprising in a nest-parasite, whose opportunities for learning such guiding behavior from adults are at first sight more limited than in most birds. Hand-reared Greater honeyguide chicks eat both the larvae and the wax in the first honeycomb they are given, and develop the guiding call without ever hearing it, directly from the begging call. They do not need wax or grubs in their diet, but some constituent of the honeycomb may play a role, as yet unrecognized, in attaining breeding condition. Wild honeyguides can open bees' nests for themselves (since many species eat beeswax but do not guide), so it is not clear to what extent Greater honeyguides depend on human help for obtaining their honeycomb.

The tradition of using honeyguides is dying out in many parts of Africa as the old life-styles crumble and refined sugar becomes easily available.   AWD

they occur in all the major vegetation zones; 5 African genera (39 species) are recognized and within these there is a greater divergence in size, bill shape and color pattern than is found in Asian and American genera. Adaptation to more arid habitats within Africa is thought to have given rise to the tinkerbirds and ground barbets. Species equivalent to these ecologically do not occur in Asia or tropical America. In these continents the barbets are larger and in the main arboreal, 3 genera (13 species) being recognized in South America and 3 genera (26 species) in Asia (where 2 genera contain only one species each). There are some notable instances of convergence in the family. The Black-backed barbet of Central Africa is similar to the White-mantled barbet of South America, and each continent has a medium-sized brown plumaged species which is highly social.

Barbets are compact, thickset birds with rather large heads. The bill is stout, conical and sharply tipped, being more formidable in the larger species. The *Lybius* species have notched bills that assist in gripping food and in the Prong-billed barbet the tip of the upper mandible fits into a deep cleft in the lower mandible. Many have bristles around the gape and chin and tufts over the nostrils. The legs are short and strong, the feet zygodactylic (ie on each foot the second and third toes point forward, the first and fourth backward). They climb like woodpeckers and their short tail is often used as a support. The large barbets appear heavy and cumbersome in their movements but others (eg the Red-headed barbet and the tinkerbirds) are agile and probe and search much like tits. The wings are short and rounded, and unsuitable for sustained flight. Ground barbets move by inelegant hops.

The *Eubucco* species of South America have green wings, back and tail, and underparts of yellow streaked with green. They differ from each other in the color pattern of their head, throat and breast; the sexes have different appearances. The male Red-headed barbet has the whole head and throat scarlet shading to orange on the breast, and a blue collar on the nape. The female has blue on the side of the head, a gray throat and yellow orange on the upper breast. The sexes of the *Capito* species are also different. Both sexes of the Black-spotted barbet have scarlet on head and throat, black upperparts streaked with greenish yellow and creamy yellow underparts. The female differs from the male in having black spots on the throat and being more heavily spotted black on the under-

parts. Most Asian barbets are predominantly green and differences between species lie in the head colors (brown, red, yellow, orange) and their pattern; the sexes are identical in the field. The Great barbet has a yellow bill, maroon-brown upperparts, a violet blue-black head, multicolored underparts (olive brown, blue, yellow) and red under-tail coverts. In contrast, there is very little green in African barbets, and the majority are patterned black, yellow and red and their plumage is heavily spotted and barred, much more so than in Asian and South American species. Some are a very drab brown (*Gymnobucco* species) and have a tuft of rictal bristles and a head more or less bare of feathers. The sexes are alike in the majority of species.

Most species feed on fruit, much of which is lost when plucked from the tree, but some are more efficient and hold the fruit with a foot when eating. Petals, flower heads and nectar are eaten by some species (for example, the Great barbet, Prong-billed barbet). Most, if not all, species feed insects to newly hatched young and some take insects regularly, particularly termites which may be caught either on the wing or on the ground. Ants and grasshoppers are taken and the larger species (for example, the Lineated barbet) occasionally take lizards, tree frogs and small birds. The Red-headed barbet is mainly insectivorous and feeds in the ground litter. Insect remains are regurgitated as pellets. Fruit-eating barbets often feed in mixed flocks of other species. There are no seasonal migrations; local

▲ **A tight squeeze.** A Yellow-fronted tinkerbird emerges from its nest-hole, which it probably gouged out in a rotten section of the branch.

▶ **Groundhunter.** This Red-and-yellow barbet (*Trachyphonus erythrocephalus*) is one of the three species of ground barbets. Unlike other barbets, which live in tree tops, ground barbets forage on the ground. This species is particularly attracted to stream beds, termite mounds and areas with irregular topography. It excavates nests and roosting sites in the earth walls of ravines.

▼ **Iridescent barbet.** The Golden-throated barbet (*Megalaima franklinii*), a member of the main Asian genus of barbets, is found across a large area of Southeast Asia, from Nepal to Laos and Vietnam. It has well-developed rictal bristles.

movements are governed by the availability of food sources.

The breeding behavior of barbets is varied but little studied. The Prong-billed barbet in Costa Rica lays only one clutch of eggs and has a restricted breeding season beginning in March. Other species are paired throughout the year and have a prolonged breeding season covering both dry and wet seasons in which three or four broods may be raised (for example, the Yellow-fronted tinkerbird) or else breed only in the wet season (for example, ground barbets). The same hole is often used for successive broods and is deepened after each brood. D'Arnaud's barbet, one of the ground barbets, bores a tunnel vertically downwards into level ground and then bores horizontally before forming the nest chamber. The Pied barbet has been known to use deserted nests of swallows and martins when nest-sites are scarce. Both sexes excavate the nest-hole, share in incubation and feeding nestlings, and in nest sanitation. Feces are sometimes swallowed or else pounded with sawdust in the nest-hole into small balls which are then removed. In several of the African species extra helpers, often young of a previous brood, have been recorded feeding nestlings but little detail is known of the cooperative breeding. The African *Gymnobucco* species breed colonially and with other African species are often parasitized by honeyguides.

Because of the difficulty of observing barbets, particularly the forest species, little is known of their courtship behavior, only that the male frequently pursues the female. In ground barbets the male postures with raised crown feathers and struts around the female. Duetting is a common feature of barbets from all three continents. Its exact function is not certain. It occurs throughout the year and there is an immediate response by birds to the play-back of a duet sequence. It probably helps to maintain both territories and family bonds. Barbets are highly territorial and aggressive to other birds (eg woodpeckers, honeyguides) and may then be defending a food source (fruit) or a roosting or nest site. Communal roosting of family parties is frequent, even in aggressive species.

The metallic quality of the voices of several African and Oriental species has earned them names such as stinkerbird, blacksmith and coppersmith.

The young hatch blind and naked and have heel pads. These may be used to enlarge the cramped nest-hole; the honeyguides that are parasitic on barbets also have the pads.   LGG

JACAMARS AND PUFFBIRDS

Families: Galbulidae, Bucconidae
Order: Piciformes (suborder: Galbulae, part).
Forty-seven species in 15 genera.

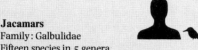

Jacamars
Family: Galbulidae
Fifteen species in 5 genera.
Distribution: Mexico to S Brazil.
Habitat: forest, thickets, savanna.
Size: 13–31cm (5–12in) long.
Plumage: shining iridescent green above,
mostly rufous below, or dull brown or blackish;
white below. Slight differences between sexes.
Voice: often prolonged and complex song with
whistles, squeals and trills.
Nests: in short burrows in ground or termite
mounds.
Eggs: 2–4, white, unmarked; incubation
period: 20–22 days; nestling period: 19–26
days (in Rufous-tailed jacamar).
Diet: insects caught in the air, including many
butterflies, beetles and wasps.

Species include: **Chestnut jacamar**
(*Galbalcyrhynchus leucotis*), **Great jacamar**
(*Jacamerops aurea*), **Pale-headed jacamar**
(*Brachygalba goeringi*), **Paradise jacamar**
(*Galbula dea*), **Rufous-tailed jacamar** (*Galbula
ruficauda*), **Three-toed jacamar** (*Jacamaralcyon
tridactyla*).

Puffbirds
Family: Bucconidae
Thirty-two species in 10 genera.
Distribution: Mexico to S Brazil.
Habitat: rain forest, dry open woodland,
shrubbery, savanna.
Size: 14–29cm (5.5–11in) long.
Plumage: black, white, brown, rufous, buff,
often barred, streaked or spotted (never
brilliant); slight differences between sexes.
Voice: thin and weak to loud and ringing;
rarely melodious.
Nests: burrows in ground or cavities carved in
termite mounds; occasionally abandoned nests
of other birds, sometimes lined (leaves or grass).
Eggs: 2 or 3, occasionally 4; unmarked; white;
incubation period: unknown; nestling period:
20 days (White-faced puffbird) or about 30
days (White-fronted nunbird).
Diet: chiefly insects, occasionally small frogs or
lizards; rarely fruits.

Species include: **nunbirds** (genera *Hapaloptila*,
Monasa), **nunlets** (genus *Nonnula*), **swallow-wing**
(*Chelidoptera tenebrosa*), **White-fronted nunbird**
(*Monasa morphoeus*), **White-whiskered puffbird**
(*Malacoptila panamensis*).

A DAINTY, glittering green, iridescent,
straight-billed hummingbird the size
of a thrush or mockingbird — such would be
an apt description of one of the more brilliant **jacamars**. These, however, are more
closely related to woodpeckers, toucans, barbets, and puffbirds than to hummingbirds.

The jacamar's long, slender, sharp bill
seems poorly fitted for its aerial insect-
catching niche and for excavating its nest
chamber — a broad, flat bill would seem
more efficient. However, the long bill can
reach across the wings of a butterfly or
dragonfly (which if seized might break and
release the insect) to grasp the body firmly.
Moreover, it keeps the flailing wings away
from the jacamar's face while it knocks its
victim against a branch until the wings flutter earthward; it also holds stinging wasps
at a safe distance.

Jacamars appear to be charged with irre-
pressible vitality. While perching on an
exposed twig above a stream, path or open
space in woods or thicket, they constantly
turn their bright-eyed heads from side to
side, looking for flying insects which they
dart out to seize. The high, thin notes of their
calls convey a sense of urgency. For birds
that are not true songbirds, their vocal performances are surprisingly complex.

Jacamars nest in tunnels which they dig
in vertical banks or sloping ground or in
hard, black termite mounds. The Rufous-
tailed jacamar, the best-known species, may
use both sites in the same locality. The male
not only helps his mate to excavate but
frequently feeds her, to the accompaniment
of much singing. The horizontal burrow,
29–79cm (11–31in) long, according to the
species, ends in a chamber where 2–4 white
eggs lie on the bare floor, which is soon
covered by a growing accumulation of
regurgitated beetles' shards and other indigestible parts of insects. By day the sexes
incubate alternately, often for an hour or
two at a time. The female occupies the nest
by night. Unlike most birds of their order
(Piciformes), the nestlings hatch with a thin
coat of long white down. They are nour-
ished wholly with insects by both parents,
and soon become loquacious, practicing
songs of the adults while they await their
meals. Fledgling Rufous-tailed jacamars do
not return to sleep in the burrow, but four
young Pale-headed jacamars in Venezuela
continued for several months to lodge with
their parents in their longer tunnel.

The eight species of *Galbula* are a glittering
golden green or purple glossed with green,
with chestnut or white underparts. Exceptional in the family is the long-tailed

▶ **Waiting for a butterfly?** Jacamars use their
long tapered bills to catch butterflies and insects
of similar size. The Rufous-tailed jacamar
(*Galbula ruficauda*) is widespread from South
Mexico to Brazil.

▼ **Surveying its territory.** A White-eared
puffbird (*Nystalus chacuru*) sits ready to leap out
after passing prey.

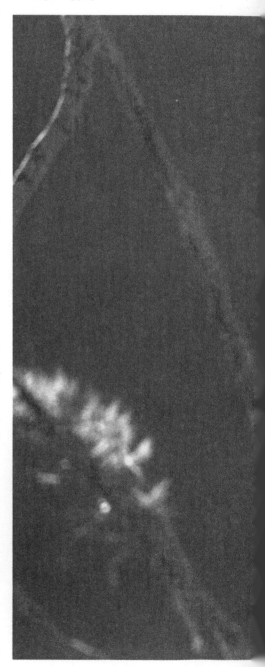

Paradise jacamar of Amazonia and the Guianas with bronzy black plumage.

The Chestnut jacamar has a pink, kingfisher-like bill and the Three-toed jacamar of Brazil is a small bird with a chestnut head and blackish and grayish body. (Other jacamars have four toes, two directed forward and two backward.) The Great jacamar is a stout bird with heavier bill, golden green and rufous, like some of its smaller relatives.

Puffbirds are so named because their large heads, short tails and often loose plumage give them a stocky aspect. Their bills are usually stout and hooked at the end, less often tapering and pointed. Their habit of resting motionless and often permitting a close approach by humans causes the unperceptive to call them stupid. Actually, they are wisely conserving energy, while with keen eyes they scrutinize surrounding vegetation. Suddenly they fly out, perhaps to snatch a green insect from green foliage 20m (65ft) away.

Exceptional in the family are the swallow-wings, which are short-tailed, long-winged, blue-black birds with white rumps and cinnamon chestnut abdomens.

White-whiskered puffbirds are among the few species with sexual differences in plumage, the males being largely chestnut-brown and cinnamon, the females more olive and grayish. Although they live chiefly at mid heights of the rain forest, they nest in short, descending tunnels in the forest floor. On a bed of dead leaves they lay two or three white eggs, which the female incubates through a long morning, the male for the remainder of the time. The blind, wholly naked nestlings are at first brooded by their father and fed by their mother. After daytime brooding ceases, the father helps to feed the nestlings for the remainder of their 20 days underground.

Most social of the puffbirds are the four species of nunbirds. Their pointed, bright red or yellow bills contrast with their somber, black or dark gray plumage. The calls of the White-fronted nunbird are extremely varied, ranging from wooden rattles to notes soft and deep. Up to 10 perch in a row on a high horizontal branch or vine and lift up their heads to shout all together, for 15 or 20 minutes, in loud, ringing voices. Their long burrows in sloping or nearly level ground are lined with dead leaves and have a collar of leaves and sticks around the entrance. Three or four adults, probably parents with older, nonbreeding offspring, feed three nestlings. Blind and naked, the nestlings toddle up the long entrance tunnel to receive their meals at the mouth. When about 30 days old they fly up into the trees.

The four species of *Notharchus*, boldly patterned in black and white, use stout black bills to carve nest chambers deep into hard, black termite mounds. Male and female share this task, and later take turns incubating two or three white eggs on the unlined floor. Their notes are mostly weak and low. Species of *Bucco* and *Hypnelus* also breed in termite nests.

The five species of nunlets are small nunbirds that range from Panama to N Argentina. Unobtrusive forest-dwellers colored gray, brown, cinnamon and white, their habits are little known.   AFS

WOODPECKERS

Family: Picidae
Order: Piciformes (suborder: Pici).
Two hundred species in 28 genera belonging to 3 subfamilies.
Distribution: America, Africa, Eurasia.

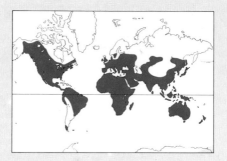

Habitat: tropical, subtropical and deciduous forest; orchards, parks, grasslands.

Size: ranges from height 8cm (3in), weight 8g (0.3oz), in the Scaled piculet to height 55cm (22in), weight 563g (19.9oz) in the Imperial woodpecker.

▶ **Representative species of woodpeckers.**
(1) A Three-toed woodpecker (*Picoides tridactylus*). (2) A Common flicker (*Colaptes auratus*) in a dance posture. (3) A Green woodpecker (*Picus viridis*). (4) An Olive-backed three-toed woodpecker (*Dinopium rafflesi*) foraging. (5) A Northern wryneck (*Jynx torquilla*). (6) A Great spotted woodpecker (*Picoides major*). (7) A Red-headed woodpecker (*Melanerpes erythrocephalus*) at a nest-hole feeding young. (8) A Yellow-bellied sapsucker (*Sphyrapicus varius*). (9) A Pileated woodpecker (*Dryocopus pileatus*).

WOODPECKERS are unmistakable, thanks to their climbing and pecking habits. Especially impressive however—indeed unique—are their tapping and drumming communication signals, which can be heard in many of the world's woods during the breeding season. With their specialized climbing and pecking methods, woodpeckers are unrivaled as predators on insects that lie hidden under bark, within wood, or, like ants and termites, live in nests with tunnels far below the surface. Woodpeckers also create permanent dwellings for rearing their young and for daily roosting; excavated holes last for years.

Woodpeckers play an important role in the earth's forest eco-systems. They help to control numbers of bark- and wood-boring insects, thereby contributing to the health of the tree trunk and its bark covering. Where woodpeckers have pecked, other smaller birds (tits, nuthatches, treecreepers) can forage successfully for any remaining insects and spiders, and woodpecker holes are used for nesting or roosting by many other hole-nesting insectivores. Owls, martens and other mammals also benefit from using woodpecker holes. Woodpeckers thus help indirectly to exert pressure on the huge populations of insects and mice or voles. They also play an important part in the cycle of decay and regeneration of matter in so far as they peck at huge amounts of dead wood, making it accessible to other decomposing organisms.

True woodpeckers (subfamily Picinae) are small- to medium-sized birds of powerful and stocky build. Their bill is adapted for hacking and chiseling. Their tongue, capable of extreme protrusion (up to 10cm, 4in, in the Green woodpecker), is a highly efficient catching device which enables the bird to extract insects from deep cracks and crevices and from the tunnels bored by insect larvae and made by ants and termites. Woodpecker feet are especially adapted for climbing, with two toes pointed forward and two back. The fourth toe can be bent sideways so that the crampon-shaped claws can always be positioned so as best to suit the curve of trunk or branch. Climbing movements and pecking postures are facilitated by the wedge-shaped supporting tail feathers, the shafts of which have additional strengthening. Such a tail allows the woodpecker's body to be cushioned and permits a good, relaxed posture for pecking or for pauses between bouts of climbing. Special adaptations for pecking, tapping and drumming protect internal organs, particularly the brain, against impact damage. This is absolutely necessary considering the number of pecking blows executed daily (in the Black woodpecker 8,000 to 12,000).

True woodpeckers eat mainly arthropods, particularly insects and spiders, but also take plant food (fruits, seeds, berries) and nestling birds from holes in trees. The Acorn woodpecker eats acorns, storing these for the winter in specially excavated holes. Sapsuckers drill holes in horizontal rows (so-called "ringing" behavior) and then lick up the exuding droplets of sap with the tongue, the tip of which is frayed and brush-like. Great spotted woodpeckers make so-called "anvils" into which they wedge cones in

The 3 Subfamilies of Woodpeckers

True woodpeckers

Subfamily: Picinae
One hundred and sixty-nine species in 23 genera.

America, Africa, Eurasia. Forests; orchards, parks, grasslands, areas of cultivation with hills or earthen banks; up to 5,000m (16,400ft). Size: length 16–55cm (6–22in), weight 17–563g (0.6–19.9oz). Plumage: upperparts usually appropriate to habitat (blackish, brownish, grayish or greenish); head and neck mostly bright colors: red, yellow, white or black patches and stripes; bills are black, gray, brown or bright white. Sexes differ in plumage (sometimes slightly), size, weight. Voice: loud, high-pitched calls; series of calls. Nests: excavated holes. Eggs: 3–11, white. Incubation period: 9–20 days. Diet: insects, spiders, berries, fruits; acorns, seeds; sap, honey.

Species and genera include: **Acorn woodpecker** (*Melanerpes formicivorus*), **Black-backed three-toed woodpecker** (*Picoides arcticus*), **Black woodpecker** (*Dryocopus martius*), **Common flicker** (*Colaptes auratus*), **Gray-headed woodpecker** (*Picus canus*), **Great spotted woodpecker** (*Picoides major*), **Green woodpecker** (*Picus viridis*), **Imperial woodpecker** (*Campephilus imperialis*), **Lewis's woodpecker** (*Melanerpes lewis*), **Olive-backed woodpecker** (*Dinopium rafflesi*), **Pileated woodpecker** (*Dryocopus pileatus*), **Red-bellied woodpecker** (*Melanerpes carolinus*), **Red-headed woodpecker** (*Melanerpes erythrocephalus*), **sapsuckers** (genus *Sphyrapicus*), **Three-toed woodpecker** (*Picoides tridactylus*), **Yellow-bellied sapsucker** (*Sphyrapicus varius*), **Yellow-tufted woodpecker** (*Melanerpes cruentatus*). Total threatened species: 5.

Piculets

Subfamily: Picumninae
Twenty-nine species in 4 genera.

America, Africa, Eurasia. Tropical and subtropical forests, secondary forests, woods; coffee plantations; up to 2,100m (6,890ft). Size: length 8–15cm (3–6in), weight 8–16g (0.28–0.56oz) (28g, 0.98oz, in the Antillean piculet). Plumage: brownish with red, orange, yellow marks; three white stripes on the tail; females have white spots on a black crown. Voice: sharp calls and series of calls. Nests: holes (usually enlargements of existing ones) in rotted tree trunks and soft wood. Eggs: 2–4, white; incubation: 11–14 days. Diet: insects, larvae, ants, termites, wood-boring beetles.

Species include: **Antillean piculet** (*Nesoctites micromegas*), **Scaled piculet** (*Picumnus squamulatus*).

Wrynecks

Subfamily: Jynginae
Two species of the genus *Jynx*.

Africa, Eurasia. Open deciduous forests, grassy clearings, copses, gardens; in Africa up to 3,000m (10,000ft). Size: length 16–17cm (6.3–6.7in), weight 30–39g (1.05–1.38oz). Plumage: chiefly brown, nightjar-like pattern of peppered and blotched markings; dark line through eye; no difference between sexes. Voice: series of calls, up to 18 *kwee* calls. Nests: natural cavities; holes excavated by woodpeckers; nest boxes; no nest material. Eggs: 5–14, white; incubation: 12–13 days; nestling period: 21 days. Diet: ants.

Species: **Northern wryneck** (*Jynx torquilla*), Eurasia migrating to C Africa, SE Asia, Japan; **Rufous-necked wryneck** (*J. ruficollis*), SC and S Africa.

holes to peck out the fat-rich seeds. Up to 5,000 cones may be found under a "primary anvil" of which there will be three or four in a territory. The ability to deal with fruits and seeds in "anvils" or to store them in holes is a great aid to survival for woodpeckers in areas of winter cold and consequent seasonal insect shortages.

Woodpeckers catch their prey with a great variety of different techniques, the simplest of which is the gleaning of items from leaf, branch or trunk. Slightly more complicated is probing into bark crevices combined with the scaling of bark. Both sapsuckers and the Three-toed woodpecker obtain insects that lie hidden under bark or within wood by drilling round holes, inserting the tongue and harpooning the item. Other "pecking woodpeckers" and also the large species chisel and lever off large pieces of bark and carve out deep holes in their quest for insects. A Black woodpecker may consume up to 900 bark beetle larvae or 1,000 ants at a single meal. "Ground" woodpeckers mostly peck only funnel-shaped holes in ants' nests, then extend their long "lime-twig" tongue along tunnels and into chambers to spoon up adult ants and pupae. A Green woodpecker needs to eat about 2,000 ants daily, mostly lawn and meadow ants. When this is not possible, in extreme winters such as that of 1962–63, a large part of the population will perish. Some species, for example the Yellow-tufted woodpecker and Lewis's woodpecker and related species of the genera *Melanerpes* and *Centurus*, are able (like flycatchers and tyrants) to take some insects in flight.

▲ **Woodpecker foraging methods:**
(1) gleaning; (2) shooting out the tongue after pecking.

▶ **Takeoff!** OVERLEAF A male Great spotted woodpecker launches itself from its nest while a red-crowned juvenile watches from the hole.

◀ **The naked condition.** Woodpecker young hatch small and naked and require almost four weeks to become ready for flight. For the first few days they huddle like this in a pyramid to share body heat. When an adult brings food—in this case a Common flicker—it wakes the young by touching the swollen white pads to the side of the mouth.

▼ **Not obviously a woodpecker,** the Northern wryneck. The two species of wrynecks belong to a separate subfamily. Although they possess some adaptations of woodpeckers they look more like perching birds and also perch and forage in bushes.

Most woodpeckers are sedentary and may remain in the same territory for a long time. Only a few species, including the Yellow-bellied sapsucker and the Red-headed woodpecker in North America, are migratory. Northern races of the Great spotted woodpecker and the Three-toed woodpeckers undertake far-reaching eruptive movements at intervals of several years, when their main seed-crop diets fail. The Great spotted woodpecker penetrates into central and southern Europe in years of cone shortage; Three-toed woodpeckers invade areas of North America and Europe where the forests periodically suffer from infestations of insect pests.

The great majority of woodpeckers are territorial, living in individual, pair or family territories, in some cases for several years. A ringed Great spotted woodpecker showed fidelity to its 25ha (62 acre) territory for a period of 6 years; in most other species studied most individuals remained in or close to their territory for the whole of their lives. Defending a territory helps to ensure not only breeding success but also adequate food supplies and, above all—especially important for woodpeckers—roosting possibilities in holes affording shelter from the weather. As a rule woodpeckers react aggressively towards intruders of their own kind.

Genuine family territories are found in the Acorn woodpecker. Up to 15 individuals of different generations live in the territory, providing an effective defense of their acorn stores against any competitors.

Woodpecker courtship generally begins with drumming, display ("excitement") flights and prominent calls. These signals are used by both sexes to advertise territory limits and trees with holes, to attract prospective partners to suitable nest-sites (nest-showing), to stimulate the partner sexually and to intimidate rivals. A new nest-hole is not excavated every year and an old one can certainly be used for several years. Black woodpeckers may use the same hole for up to 6 years, Green woodpeckers for up to 10 years or more. However, even these species are forced to excavate new holes when they are evicted by jackdaws or starlings.

Excavation of a hole takes 10–28 days, according to species and method. Both sexes participate. About 10,000 wood chips have been found under a Black woodpecker's hole. When the hole is completed the birds chip off small pieces from the inner wall to serve as a cushion in the nest-scrape for eggs and young.

Copulation usually takes place without any special ceremony. The female assumes a precopulatory posture—crossways on a branch—and the male simply flies onto her back. Lengthy physical contact is avoided. Mutual courtship feeding has been recorded in only a few species, for example the Olive-backed woodpecker of Asia. The glossy white eggs are laid in the early morning, one per day until the clutch is complete. Constant guarding of the nest-hole is typical once the first egg has been laid. In all species of woodpeckers the male spends the night in the nest-hole during both incubation and nestling periods; in the *Melanerpes* woodpeckers, male and female roost there together.

During incubation and brooding, birds of a pair change over at intervals of 30 to 150 minutes. The nest-relief ceremony resembles that of nest-showing: calling, demonstrative tapping, also drumming. The "pecking woodpeckers" collect food in the bill, the "ground woodpeckers" and all large species feed their young by regurgitation. Nestlings give almost ceaseless whirring or rattling food-calls.

The nestling period is 18–35 days. When they leave the nest, young woodpeckers can climb and fly. Soon afterwards they follow the adults through the territory, contact being maintained with calls which in Black, Pileated, Green and Gray-headed woodpeckers are the same as those given to attract a partner or to guide another bird to a hole. In some species both adults tend the young after fledging, in others (eg Great spotted woodpecker and others of the genus *Picoides*, and also Green and Gray-headed woodpeckers) the brood is split, each adult caring for one to three young. The family

breaks up within 1–8 weeks of leaving the nest, adults increasingly using various forms of threat to drive away their offspring (ruffling of crown feathers, wing-spreading, threat calls) which finally move off, eventually to establish their own territories.

The tiny piculets (subfamily Picumninae) climb about tree branches in the manner of woodpeckers or, at times, like titmice and nuthatches. Their flight is undulating. Foraging piculets peck at bark and soft wood to get at ants, termites and wood-boring insects. Their tail, which does not serve as a support when climbing and does not have the stiffened quills of the larger woodpeckers, shows three conspicuous white longitudinal stripes in almost all species. Piculets excavate a nest-hole in tree trunk or branch, or enlarge available holes. During courtship they call and drum. The clutch consists of 2–4 eggs and incubation takes 11–14 days. The young fledge after 21–24 days. Disjunct distribution in Asia, Africa and America indicates the piculets to be of very ancient origin.

Wrynecks (subfamily Jynginae) live in open woods, orchards, parks and meadows with copses. Like woodpeckers they obtain their main food (various kinds of ants) with the help of the tongue. The name wryneck derives from their defense behavior in the nest: when threatened by a predator they perform snake-like twisting and swaying motions of the neck and simultaneously hiss. Filmed sequences show that such behavior is effective in intimidating small predators. A prominent feature in spring is the rather nasal *kwee* call which rises slightly in pitch and which is given by both sexes to attract a partner to prospective nest-holes. The 7 or 8 eggs are usually laid on the bare floor of the nest chamber (after throwing out any nest that may have already been started). Incubation takes 12–14 days and the young spend a further 21 days in the nest, the parents feeding them with adult and pupal ants (about 8,000 individuals daily for all the nestlings); post-fledging care lasts 2 weeks.

From July onwards Northern wrynecks begin their migration south from breeding grounds in Europe and Asia to wintering areas in Africa and Southeast Asia. Populations of the Northern wryneck are threatened and the species has almost completely disappeared from England in recent years. The Rufous-necked wryneck is found in southern Africa, including mountainous regions up to 3,000m (10,000ft). Brown cocktail ants *Crematogaster* make up 80 percent of its diet.　　　　DB

Woodland Drumbeats and Dances
The communication system of woodpeckers

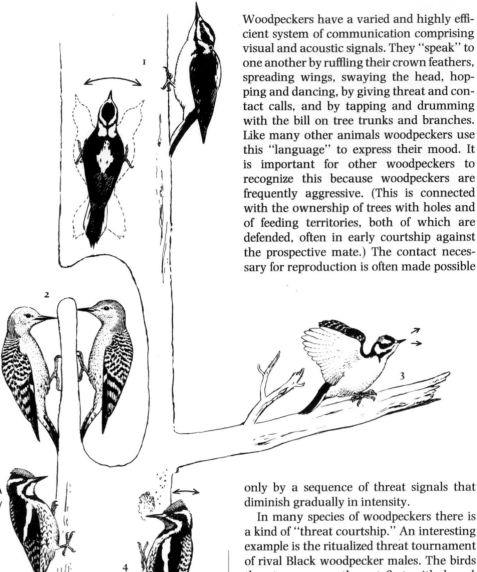

Woodpeckers have a varied and highly efficient system of communication comprising visual and acoustic signals. They "speak" to one another by ruffling their crown feathers, spreading wings, swaying the head, hopping and dancing, by giving threat and contact calls, and by tapping and drumming with the bill on tree trunks and branches. Like many other animals woodpeckers use this "language" to express their mood. It is important for other woodpeckers to recognize this because woodpeckers are frequently aggressive. (This is connected with the ownership of trees with holes and of feeding territories, both of which are defended, often in early courtship against the prospective mate.) The contact necessary for reproduction is often made possible only by a sequence of threat signals that diminish gradually in intensity.

In many species of woodpeckers there is a kind of "threat courtship." An interesting example is the ritualized threat tournament of rival Black woodpecker males. The birds threaten one another at first with *keeyak* calls, then fly to the base of a tree and attempt to drive one another upwards. From time to time they thrust their bills into the air, as if on a command, and wave them about. In these movements the red crown is prominently displayed. The birds then sink into a waiting posture, only to repeat the maneuver after a few minutes. Such a tournament may last for over an hour, until one of the birds gives up. If a male and female meet they threaten one another in similar fashion, but the male's aggression then gradually wanes. This is presumably because the smaller area of red on the female's head and her lower-intensity swaying movements inhibit the male's aggression. Characteristic of this threat ceremony is a very quiet *ryrr* call.

Head-swaying with presentation of the head pattern is found in many species, for example the genera *Colaptes* and *Picus*, many of the sapsuckers and the Pileated woodpecker. The behavior is especially pronounced in the Common flicker which dances about with wings spread and tail fanned and shows off part of the head which, in the male, bears a moustache-like stripe. If such a stripe is artificially painted on a female she will be treated like a male, ie she will provoke intense aggression.

Multiunit calls, reaching long distances, often combined with demonstrative flights at tree-top height, serve as signals to attract a partner and to advertise trees with holes. In many species drumming and tapping sequences fulfil this function. Some species combine vocal and instrumental (drumming) signals. Each species has its own specific pattern of drumming. In the Black woodpecker long series (43 strikes in 2.5 seconds) function as long-range signals with a great power of attraction while quiet and shorter series are used at close range to advertise the entrance to a hole. When a female has followed a male as far as the hole, or conversely, a male has approached a female showing a nest, the active partner marks the hole entrance with long tapping sequences. Eventually the other bird is attracted nearer and gives threat calls to drive the exhibitor away so that the nest is free for inspection. Woodpeckers sometimes advertise what prove to be unsuitable holes; in such cases the inspecting bird will leave the site, look for another tree, and attempt to lure its future mate to this new site, but success may come only after several days.

The basic scheme of the language of courtship, in a sense its grammar, is found in the majority of woodpecker species: *drumming*—guiding with calls and special flights—*drumming, tap-drumming, tapping*—hole inspection—agreement over choice of hole.

The Red-bellied woodpecker shows a high degree of ceremony in this sequence. Male and female perform a tapping duet in precise harmony. Where a hole has only been started, they then sit close together on the trunk; if there is a completed hole one bird taps inside, the other outside. Later, there also has to be some understanding between the birds for changeovers during incubation and brooding. Nest-relief has a ceremonial character: the incoming bird gives particular calls, mostly quiet and muttering, or soft and long-drawn. The bird in the hole confirms its readiness for a changeover by tapping on the wall of the nest-chamber and then leaves to allow its mate to take over. In this nest-relief ceremony there is a remnant of antagonistic behavior: when, for example, the bird in the hole is reluctant

▲ **Woodpecker interactions.** (1) Conflict behavior of two female Hairy woodpeckers (*Picoides villosus*) along the boundary of a territory. The owner threatens by jerking her body; the intruder freezes. (2) Red-bellied woodpeckers (*Melanerpes carolinus*) synchronizing behavior: the male taps on the inside, his mate on the outside. (3) An aggressive Downy woodpecker (*Picoides pubescens*) displaying its wings. (4) Male and female Yellow-bellied sapsuckers change place while excavating a hole. The male (right) taps as his mate alights and does a bobbing dance accompanied with "Quirk" notes. This is part of the highly developed ritualized behavior centered on nest-holes or prospective nest-holes.

▲ **Conflict in the desert.** A Gila woodpecker (*Melanerpes uropygialis*) in Arizona invades the territory of another member of the same species sitting on a cactus. This species commonly nests in large cacti.

to leave, its mate uses threat calls and postures to force the other's departure.

If a female dies after the young have hatched the male is able to rear the brood alone, although initially in addition to the feeding of the young his normal response is intense drumming. Such behavior has been observed in the Great spotted woodpecker. After a short time, however, this renewed courtship behavior wanes and the feeding adult becomes noticeably quiet in its territory.

Woodpeckers that have failed to acquire a mate in the breeding season, or have lost one early on, mainly of course males, may drum and call persistently up until the end of the season. Sometimes this enables them to attract another bird, pair up and rear a family in the late spring.

DB

PART III - THE PASSERINES

BROADBILLS

Family: Eurylaimidae
Order: Passeriformes (suborder Eurylaimi).
Fourteen species in 8 genera.
Distribution: Sino-Himalaya to SE Asia; Africa
S of the Sahara.

Habitat: tropical forests and thickets.

Size: length 12.5–28cm
(5–11in), weight 20.5–160g
(0.7–5.6oz). Little difference
between sexes.

Plumage: browns with gray to black; or green,
red, black or silvery gray with areas of bright
color contrast, often including the bill. Little or
no difference between sexes. Juveniles resemble
adults except that colors are duller.

Voice: screaming whistles, explosive trills,
cooing rattles, croaks.

Nest: large, domed, suspended.

Eggs: 2–3, more in Sino-Himalayan
populations; white to pinkish, unmarked or
speckled purple or reddish.

Diet: chiefly arthropods or fruit.

Species: **African green broadbill**
(*Pseudocalyptomena graueri*), **Banded broadbill**
(*Eurylaimus javanicus*), **Black-and-red broadbill**
(*Cymbirhynchus macrorhynchus*), **Black-and-
yellow broadbill** (*Eurylaimus ochromalus*),
Black-capped broadbill (*Smithornis capensis*),
Dusky broadbill (*Corydon sumatranus*), **Gray-
headed broadbill** (*Smithornis sharpei*), **Green
broadbill** (*Calyptomena viridis*), **Hose's broadbill**
(*C. hosei*), **Long-tailed broadbill** (*Psarisomus
dalhousiae*), **Philippine broadbill** (*Eurylaimus
steerii*), **Rufous-sided broadbill** (*Smithornis
rufolateralis*), **Silver-breasted broadbill**
(*Serilophus lunatus*), **Whitehead's broadbill**
(*Calyptomena whiteheadi*).

BROADBILLS are sturdy birds whose squat appearance is accentuated by a rather short, square tail, except in the Long-tailed broadbill which has a fine-pointed tail. The family is named for the great width of the mouth, which reaches a grotesque extreme among passerines in the outsize pink bill of the Dusky broadbill. Broadbills inhabit chiefly the interior of evergreen or semiever-green broad-leaved lowland forest. Only two species are exclusive mountain dwellers although Long-tailed and Silver-breasted broadbills are restricted to mountainsides in inner tropical Southeast Asia.

No genus is common to both areas of the broadbills' distribution and the diminutive, mainly brown, ventrally streaked Black-capped, Rufous-sided and Gray-headed broadbills look so different from their gaudy Asian relatives that they were long classified as flycatchers—shape of bill not withstanding. Anatomical studies exposed this apparent error, adding broadbills to the African bird stock in 1914 though 19 more years elapsed before the discovery of the African green broadbill. Three genera are green with black, blue or yellow on the head, wings, belly or tail. Long-tailed, Hose's and occasional male Green broadbills have all of these colors. The Banded broadbill is wine-red with a blue bill, and other species are black with areas of red, lilac, yellow and/or white. Black is replaced by rich chestnut in the Philippine broadbill.

For all their color, however, bright plumages are not especially conspicuous in forest and the most prominent feature of, for example, the Black-and-red broadbill, sitting in the shade of a waterside thicket, is its almost luminous pale blue and yellow bill (which fades after death and cannot be appreciated in museum specimens). Several species, including those of the genus *Smithornis*, also have on their backs one or more white, yellow or orange flashes on a dark background, exposed during flight, and Silver-breasted broadbills have a bright chestnut rump, often fluffed out when they perch.

In most species the bill is both wide and rounded along its sides, perhaps to aid the aerial capture of large arthropods by rather slow-moving birds. It is also variously hooked, almost hawklike in the Dusky broadbill which has been seen snatching big orthopterans in an upward leap from the perch. This bill-form is otherwise found only in trogons and frogmouths, which share the broadbill habitat and feed similarly. Other foraging modes include "flutter-snatching" from foliage and bark, and a Banded broadbill is recorded capturing a lizard. Most species forage at mid levels of the forest but the Dusky broadbill is a high canopy bird. Two others, the Black-capped in Africa and Black-and-red in Asia, inhabit forest edge and thickets, and will go to the ground to feed. Besides taking insects in their water-side habitat, Black-and-red broadbills sometimes also capture aquatic organisms.

The African green broadbill and *Calyptomena* species alone have bills that are straight-sided but still very wide at the base. The latter feed largely on fruit and while

▲ **The considerable nests** of broadbills are usually constructed so that they hang over rivers or streams. They are made of fibrous material, drawn down underneath to provide disguise. This is the Black-capped broadbill.

◀ **Plumage gives disguise** in the case of Green broadbills. It is difficult to see them in the dense foliage of forests in Thailand and peninsular Malaysia.

(4,000ft) in montane forest where fruit supplies may be more stable.

Insect-eating broadbills are more sedentary. Banded and Black-and-yellow broadbills space themselves through the forest. Their presence is advertised with loud, explosive trilling calls, invariably answered by neighbors. Most others are less vociferous. *Smithornis* species are peculiar in producing a nonvocal croaking noise, apparently during short, circular flights. This sound is produced by vibrating wings. These flights are thought to have a courtship function but the noise produced by the Black-capped broadbill carries up to 60m (about 200ft) and could also be a territorial signal. Most species give a clear two-syllable whistle, most often when foraging groups assemble after breeding. These groups are usually small but as many as 20 Silverbreasted broadbills may gather and up to 26 Long-tailed broadbills have been counted progressing together through mountain forest in North Sumatra. Only the Dusky broadbill is permanently gregarious, and occurs in noisy parties of up to 10 strong.

Broadbill nests are large, pear-shaped bags with a crudely overhung side entrance, slung by a long woven cord of nest material from an isolated branch, creeper or frondtip. They are roughly made, of all kinds of vegetation, drawn out below into a wispy beard. Leafy creeper, lichen and moss and leafy liverworts are often included and it is common for the nest chamber to be lined with fresh green leaves. Usual nest-sites are well off the ground but the Green broadbill, whose nest is broadly strapped over its support, invariably builds low, as do *Smithornis* species. Black-and-red broadbills often use a dead stump or snag in a stream, and will sometimes take advantage of a service wire over a stream or road. There are no records of helpers attending broadbill nestlings, but the Dusky broadbill flock cooperates in nest construction. In Malaya Black-and-yellow broadbills have been seen feeding fledglings of the Indian cuckoo (*Cuculus micropterus*) and are presumed to be a brood host of this cuckoo. The one definitely identified egg of the local subspecies of the Indian cuckoo is a fairly close match for the broadbill egg in color and size.

Though only casually studied, most broadbills are frequently seen and even the least known, the Philippine and African green, are unlikely to prove rare once their habitats have been explored. With the rest of their communities, most nevertheless face the threat of habitat destruction.

these two genera are not necessarily closely related there is evidence that the African green broadbill also takes much plant material.

Green broadbills often advertise their presence by cooing rattles, and pairs will drive members of the same species off small, defendable fruit sources. At larger sources several may gather, as will Hose's broadbills. These two live mainly in lowland forests where fruit is scattered and like other fruit-eating birds they must wander over a sizable area if they are to find sufficient food. Green broadbills even disperse at night. Their much larger relative, Whitehead's broadbill, lives exclusively above 1,200m

DRW

LYREBIRDS AND SCRUB-BIRDS

Families: Menuridae, Atrichornithidae
Order: Passeriformes (suborder Menurae).
Four species in 2 genera.
Distribution: see map and table.

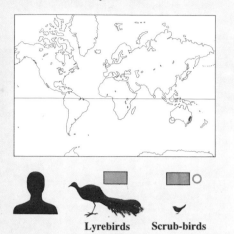

Lyrebirds   Scrub-birds

▶ **Front view of a glittering cascade,** a male
Superb lyrebird in full courtship display.

▼ **The side view** of the same species reveals the
contrast between the fowl-size body and the
enormous tail. Male Superb lyrebirds occupy
territories of 0.8–4ha (2–10 acres) in which
they construct the mounds on which they sing
and display. Each territory can contain up to six
mounds.

THE existence of **lyrebirds** became known
to Europeans in Australia in 1797
through the reports of an ex-convict who
had lived for some years with, and fomented
trouble among, aborigines in the bush. Sur-
rendering to the authorities clad only in a
kangaroo-skin apron, he told suspicious officials of the existence of "pheasants" near
the Hawkesbury River. He was pardoned
and the following year his bush-craft put to
practical use on two arduous official expeditions on foot into the hinterland west of Sydney, on the first of which the first Superb
lyrebird specimen was collected.

The affinities of the bird were controversial from the outset. It was variously claimed
in early accounts to be a pheasant, a close
relative of the domestic fowl, a bird of
paradise and even a thrush. It was not until
1875 that a relationship with the scrub-
birds was recognized, but even now the affinities of these two families with other groups
are controversial.

The Superb lyrebird occurs from south
Victoria to extreme southeast Queensland
from sea level to above the snow line in
dense temperate and subtropical rainforest
and also in drier, open woodland in
southern Queensland. It was introduced to
temperate rainforest in Tasmania in 1934.
The Albert lyrebird is restricted to subtropical and temperate rain forest in a narrow
belt of northeast New South Wales and
south Queensland (in some instances co-
occurring with the Superb lyrebird).

The Superb lyrebird is a pheasant-sized
bird, dark brown above, gray-brown below,
with long legs and powerful feet, both dark
gray. The Albert lyrebird is smaller, more
rufous above and buff below and the male's
tail resembles the Superb's, but lacks the
lyre-shaped outer tail feathers.

Lyrebirds are mainly adapted for running
and fly weakly, mostly by gliding. Nevertheless they roost high in the forest canopy, and
are "shy" and hard to observe. They feed
principally on soil invertebrates which they
expose by digging with their powerful, long-
clawed feet. Superb lyrebirds catch about
13–17 prey per minute spent foraging, dig
to about 12cm (5in) deep and walk or run
a few to several paces between excavations
during steady foraging. They also obtain
invertebrates living under the bark of rotting logs by ripping it away with their claws.
Prey seem to be taken unselectively, the
main ones in the nestling diet and probably

also in the adult diet being earthworms, amphipods, beetles and their larvae, spiders, millipedes, centipedes, slaters (sow bugs), fly larvae, ants, hemipterans and scorpions.

In both species females undertake all parental duties unaided. Female Superb lyrebirds spend about 160 hours on average collecting material for and building nests in fall and early winter. The female incubates the single egg for only 45 percent of daylight hours and the egg is deserted for 3–6 hours continuously each morning, during which embryonic temperature falls to ambient levels of less than 10°C (50°F) and development is interrupted. Consequently the incubation period is exceptionally long for a passerine bird.

The chick is brooded until it is able to maintain its own temperature at about ten days old. Thereafter it is fed on average every 23 minutes during daylight and its fecal sacs are deposited away from the nest by its mother. At fledging in October or November it weighs about 63 percent of its mother's weight and is accompanied and partly fed by her for up to eight months. Eighty percent of nest failures are attributable to predation by mammals and birds. The breeding biology of the Albert lyrebird is broadly similar.

Male Superb lyrebirds live up to 15 years and acquire the typical adult tail over the first 5–7 years. In early life they range widely in small groups, but at maturity they establish large, partly overlapping territories averaging 2.5–3.5 ha (6–8.6 acres) which they defend especially strongly in winter by singing, displaying and chasing intruders. They are therefore fairly even spaced throughout suitable habitat, although some local clustering results from neighbors often having adjacent preferred display areas within their territories. Males scratch up many earth mounds 1–1.5m (3–5ft) across, up to 20 of which they use extensively for display and copulation in a season. In the peak mating season up to 50 percent of daylight hours are spent singing.

Males are polygamous. They exhibit no parental behavior and associate with females only briefly for courtship and mating. Although some female nesting territories lie entirely within a male territory, many overlap more than one and some females visit at least two males immediately prior to mating. While some females do mate with the same male in successive seasons, there is little sign of pair-bonding and males appear to be promiscuous.

Females probably breed at an earlier age than males. The evolution of single-parent

The Song of the Superb Lyrebird

Standing in full courtship display on his mound, the male Superb lyrebird presents a beautiful and bizarre spectacle. His specialized tail feathers are held horizontally over his back and droop forward over his head, forming a silvery-white fan. Periodically they are relaxed and then thrust forward once again.

The bird emits a continuous stream of loud, melodious song and turns slowly. When a female visits the mound, the tail feathers are held forwards but unfanned and are quivered rapidly as the male utters a curious clicking call. At the climax of his display, he prescribes several semicircles around the female with such rapid, short paces that he seems to glide and then leaps forward and back repeatedly in time with a rhythmical call ending in two, far-carrying, bell-like notes.

The song contains a component typical of the species lasting 5–6 seconds, audible from 1km (0.6mi) away when there is little wind and exhibiting marked local dialects. To this is added a stream of accurately mimicked calls of cohabiting bird species, including such subtle imitations as the precisely timed duetting of whipbirds (*Psophodes olivaceus*) and kookaburras (*Dacelo gigas*) and the multiple wingbeats and calls of flying parrot flocks. Males also mimic the barking of dogs and, reputedly, occasionally even sounds made by inanimate objects such as car horns, although some of these latter claims are probably exaggerations. Up to 16 bird species may be mimicked in a local population, the particular models and their relative importance in the repertoire varying according to locality. Young males may partly learn their repertoires from older males rather than entirely acquiring them directly from the mimicked species.

Singing seems to be important in repelling rival males and attracting prospective mates, but why mimicry should be particularly effective in doing so is puzzling and controversial.   AL brood-care, a crucial step in the evolution of bird promiscuity, was probably facilitated particularly by the small clutch size and hence low costs of egg production and feeding young; the embryo's ability to withstand cooling when it has to be deserted daily by its mother when she goes foraging, and the roofed nest which prevents wetting and probable death of eggs and nestlings at low temperatures.

Emancipated from parental duties, males can increase their reproductive success by copulating with several mates because females commence breeding at different times over a seven-week period. The regular, territorial spacing of males is probably the best way for them to meet and court several potential mates given that females and their territories are also evenly dispersed.

Although lyrebirds were slaughtered indiscriminately for their tail plumage in the 19th century, they are now fully protected and common in suitable habitat. The main threat to both species is further extensive habitat alteration and destruction.   AL

Scrub-birds are small, solidly built birds with strong pointed bills, long powerful legs, long tapered tails, short rounded wings and brown plumage: ideal attributes for birds that live close to the ground in dense vegetation. They are fast and alert, but have limited powers of flight. The Noisy scrub-bird is Australia's rarest passerine and the Rufous scrub-bird, although more numerous, is also rare. The Noisy scrub-bird is only found at Two Peoples Bay, 40km (25mi) east of Albany in Western Australia,

while the Rufous scrub-bird occurs in a number of isolated mountain localities in northern New South Wales and southern Queensland. Both species are terrestrial, eat insects and mainly occupy forest edges where the light and moisture allow the growth of a dense ground layer of shrubs and rushes. In their dense habitat the most conspicuous character of scrub-birds is the loud territorial song of the male.

Scrub-birds are closely related to lyre-

birds, but their relationship with other passerine groups is uncertain. Arguments have been put forward suggesting relationships with bowerbirds and birds of paradise and with the tapaculos of South America. Their disjunct distribution suggests that they were once distributed across Australia; their present relict status is the result of climatic and vegetation changes since the Miocene era (26–7 million years ago) and in particular the severe climatic oscillations in the

---

The 2 Families of Lyrebirds and Scrub-birds   E Endangered.   R Rare

Lyrebirds
Family: Menuridae.
Two species of the genus *Menura*.
E Australia. Temperate and subtropical rain forest. Size: males 89–100cm (35–39in) long, up to 1.15kg (2.5lb); females 76–86cm (30–34in), up to 950g (2lb). Plumage: brown above, buff to gray-brown below. The male's tail is very long, train-like and comprised of highly modified feathers; the female's is shorter and simpler. Voice: loud carrying song; much mimicry of other birds and mammals; also high-pitched alarm whistles, display calls. Nests: bulky, domed chambers of twigs, bark, moss and fern fronds, lined with rootlets and body feathers, having a side entrance. Located on the ground, earth banks, rock faces,

boulders, tree buttresses and exposed roots, logs, wire-grass clumps and in dead and living trees to a height of about 22m (72ft). Eggs: usually 1, light gray to deep khaki or purplish brown with blackish brown or deep gray spots and streaks; weight: 49–72g (1.7–2.5oz). Incubation period: about 50 days. Nestling period: about 47 days; from fledging to independence maximum 8 months. Diet: invertebrates in soil and rotting wood.

Species: **Albert's lyrebird** (*Menura alberti*), **Superb lyrebird** (*M. novaehollandiae*).

Scrub-birds
Family: Atrichornithidae.
Two species of the genus *Atrichornis*.

Noisy scrub-bird E (*Atrichornis clamosus*): Australia at Two Peoples Bay near Albany in Western Australia. Forest edges. Size: 16–21cm (6–8.5in) long, weight 30–50g (1–1.8oz); females smaller than males. Plumage: upper parts brown with darker fine cross bars; underparts range from white on throat to rufous around the anus; male has black bar on the upper breast. Voice: two alarm notes and a three-note call; loud variable song of 10–20 notes; another shorter and variable song that uses modified songs of other birds. Nest: domed with small side entrance. Eggs: 1, buff with irregular patches of brown, mainly at

the larger end; 2.9 × 2cm (1.1 × 0.8in). Incubation period: 36–38 days; nestling period: 21–28 days. Diet: invertebrates with occasional small lizard, gecko or frog.

Rufous scrub-bird R (*A. rufescens*): Australia in New South Wales and southern Queensland. Forest edges. Length 16–18cm (6–7in); females smaller than males. Plumage: upper parts rufous brown with fine black cross bars; underparts white on throat, remainder rufous brown; male has black bar across the upper breast which extends down the breast and belly. Voice: loud repeated chip; two alarm notes; also mimics other birds. Eggs: 2, pink buff with blotches of brown, mainly at larger end. Incubation and nestling periods: unknown. Diet: invertebrates.

▲ **Longsome maternal care** is a feature of the lyrebird social cycle. The female feeds her single offspring for up to 8 months. Here a female Superb lyrebird feeds a young male.

▼ **One of the world's rarest birds,** a male Rufous scrub-bird. In 1949, several decades after it had last been seen, a memorial to the species was erected near where it had originally been discovered.

Pleistocene era (2 million–10,000 years ago).

The diet of scrub-birds consists of a wide variety of invertebrates with the occasional small lizard, gecko or frog. Nestling Noisy scrub-birds eat species from at least 18 orders of invertebrates, the most common being spiders, grasshoppers, cockroaches and various larvae. Adults forage mainly in leaf litter, rushes and small shrubs where they move slowly while looking and listening and occasionally turning over leaves with a quick flick of the head. The smaller Rufous scrub-bird may even move under the litter layer while foraging. Prey may also be flushed out when the bird stands still and rapidly drums one foot on the litter.

Male Noisy scrub-birds occupy well-dispersed territories of 6–9ha (15–22 acres) within which they spend at least 80 percent of their time in a core area of 1–2ha (2.5–5 acres) which is usually centered on the best feeding area. The males roost in tall shrubs or trees away from the core area. There is normally one female within the male's territory who occupies a nesting area of 1–2ha (2.5–5 acres) outside the core area or on the periphery of the territory. There is little contact between the sexes, and as well as mating with the female in his territory a male may mate with females in adjacent areas not occupied by males or with young females on the periphery of his territory.

Male Noisy scrub-birds defend their territories throughout the year, with song. During the breeding season they sing throughout the day. Their singing begins in the breeding season of their second year and they develop their territorial song during the year. In addition the male Noisy scrub-bird has a short, more variable song, incorporating modified elements from the songs of other species, which it uses when interacting with other males or with females. The male Rufous scrub-bird sings only during the mating season. It is an excellent mimic.

Rufous scrub-birds breed in spring and summer while Noisy scrub-birds breed in winter. Female Noisy scrub-birds breed in their first year, males from the age of three onwards, perhaps living until they are nine years old. The female Noisy scrub-bird builds a domed nest with a small side entrance and lines the bottom of the cavity with decayed nest material or decayed wood which dries to a hard papier-mâché-like material. (Female Rufous scrub-birds line the nest cavity completely.) The nest takes up to three weeks to build and the single egg is laid a week later. Eggs are laid from May to October with the main peak in June (mid winter). The female incubates the egg, which hatches after 36–38 days, an exceptionally long period but, as in the lyrebird, the egg is usually left unincubated for part of the day. As well as feeding the chick, she maintains hygiene in the nest by removing fecal sacs and placing them in a creek or under a bush away from the nest. After the chick leaves the nest it stays with its mother, probably until after it has finished its first molt when two to three months old. If the egg is lost the female may build another nest and lay again, but if the chick dies a second clutch is not attempted.

The Noisy scrub-bird was originally found in six isolated coastal localities between Perth and Albany between 1842 and 1889. Then nothing more was heard until 1961 when a small population was discovered. A battle by conservationists resulted in the bird's locality being set aside as a reserve for the species. The near extinction of the Noisy scrub-bird was caused by the changed fire regime initiated by Europeans and by destruction of habitat. The conservation area has been managed so as to prevent outbreaks of wildfires, and the population has grown, the number of singing males (the only measure of population) rising from 45 in 1970 to 138 in 1983. A second population has been established to the northeast of the original one, and the species could now be bred in captivity if necessary.

The distribution and abundance of the Rufous scrub-bird have also been affected by habitat destruction and fire and the species is now confined to a small number of National Parks. Although rare it is not considered endangered.   GTS

OVENBIRDS AND THEIR ALLIES

Families: Furnariidae, Dendrocolaptidae, Formicariidae
Order: Passeriformes (suborder Tyranni, part).
Four hundred and ninety-seven species in 121 genera.
Distribution: see maps and table.

Ovenbirds

Woodcreepers

Antbirds

THE **ovenbirds** take their name from the remarkable nest of the Rufous hornero. Made of mud, strengthened with hair or fiber, it has the shape of an old-fashioned baker's oven, rounded with a dome-shaped top. A narrow entrance leads to a chamber about 20cm (8in) wide which is lined with soft grass. One penalty of building this curious cave is that the ovenbird has become host to a bed-bug (family Cimiccidae). Only a few of these blood-feeders occur on birds, most of them on swifts and swallows.

Based on the number of species ovenbirds form the fourth largest, the most diverse and yet the most drab of South American bird families. They are found in a variety of habitats, some occupying niches that elsewhere would belong to such groups as larks, wheatears, dippers and nuthatches. On the basis of ecology and behavior three subfamilies have been recognized: Furnariinae, Synallaxinae, Phylidorinae.

The subfamily Furnariinae includes terrestrial birds of open land of mainly South America. Miners occupy arid land, where they walk or run but rarely fly. They resemble drab wheatears. Earthcreepers are similar but have longer tails, longer more downcurved bills and are even duller in color. Unlike the miners they may be closely associated with water. Dipper-like cinclodes are much more strictly associated with water; a few are even partly marine: Surf cinclodes rarely leave the water's edge where they feed. All these species nest in holes in the ground, either digging their own burrow or using the holes of other birds or rodents, or nesting between rocks. Nests can be as much as 1.2m (4ft) from the entrance.

The true ovenbirds are also birds of the open land but penetrate further into the tropical belt, even close to forest, although in general they keep to open valleys and floodplains. At least the best-known species, the Rufous hornero, has adapted well to humans and is welcomed around settlements.

The subfamily Synallaxinae includes the spinetails, canasteros and thornbirds. They are usually rather small with longish, more or less graduated and often forked tails. The tails show great variation. The remarkable Des Murs's wiretail has only six main feathers in the tail, the short outer pair hidden in the tail coverts, the middle and inner pair very long but reduced to little more than the central shaft.

Members of the Synallaxinae mostly inhabit dense vegetation in or on the edge of forest, in reed beds, scrubland, grassland or even mangrove, while a few species are found in barren areas and a few others live in trees. The ovenbird family in particular is famous for its unusual nests and it is in this subfamily that they show the greatest diversity.

The Wren-like rushbird weaves a sphere of clay-daubed grass around growing reeds. An entrance near the top is protected by a woven awning and sometimes even by a hinged woven trapdoor. Often a depressed clay platform on top acts as a singing perch. Other ball-like nests of grass, etc, are built near or on the ground. The nest of Red-faced spinetails is also globular, but hung from the tip of a slender hanging branch. Some species nest on a branch and enter from below onto a platform lined with feathers; others build a nest 30cm (12in) in diameter with a side entrance into a small chamber leading by a tortuous tunnel to near the top of the nest where the tunnel opens directly into a nest chamber.

There are also various forms of nests of thorns with tunnels to the nest-chamber. That of Rufous-breasted spinetails is roughly oblong or retort-shaped and as much as 75cm long by 50cm high (30 × 20in). A large dorsal platform leads via a tunnel through a tangle of thorns to a thatched nest-chamber lined with downy leaves. Cordilleran canasteros build large exposed vertical cylindrical baskets of thorny twigs; where there are no thorns available the nest is built into cactus plants. Rufous-throated thornbirds build a large unkempt-looking double-chambered nest of thorny twigs. In subsequent seasons other chambers are added to produce an apparently colonial nest. It is unlikely that more than one pair occupy a nest at any one time, but surplus chambers may be used by non-breeding members of a previous brood, other ovenbirds or even birds of other families. The Firewood gatherer also builds a voluminous thorny nest and often incorporates oddments of debris, eg bones, metal, colored rag. The lining of the neatly arched tunnel may include bits of bark, snake skin, snails and crab shell.

Members of the subfamily Phylidorinae generally live in trees and make simpler nests. (Cachalotes are the only members that build huge thorny nests, that of the White-throated cachalote being up to 1.5m (5ft) in diameter.) Many nest in banks at the end of tunnels up to 1.8m (6ft) long which are quite tortuous. Nest-chambers contain well-woven nests or small collections of loose leaves or rootlets. The bird may dig its own tunnel or improve an already existing one. Many use rock or tree fissures or holes, usually with a simple nest or using only wood chips.

Perhaps the only standard feature of ovenbirds is that their nests are always well enclosed—well, nearly always! Bay-capped wren-spinetails usually build flat open nests of grass lined with feathers a few centimeters above the water in a reed bed. Sometimes a rim is built and occasionally the rim is so well developed that there is only a small hole at the top. Some canasteros lay in what is virtually a well-concealed scrape on the ground, sometimes lined with a few bits of bone and fur from owl pellets. Rusty-backed spinetails make a crude chamber in a tangle of drift vegetation trapped by a branch during flood levels, or use the abandoned nest of another ovenbird. Tit-spinetails will also take over abandoned nests, but will use a variety of other sites, including holes in cacti.   AMH

The **woodcreepers**, sometimes known as woodhewers, are tree-climbing birds of Central and South America. Most are medium-sized, slender birds, brown to rufous with a variety of spots or streaks on the head, mantle and underparts. The tail is rufous with very stiff-tipped woodpecker- or treecreeper-like feathers. The main variation is in the bill which ranges from short, thick and slightly upturned to very long, thin and strongly downcurved. For a long time woodcreepers were considered a part of the ovenbird family, but while a few spe-

cies have characters intermediate between the typical woodcreepers and the ovenbirds, they are now regarded as sufficiently distinct to warrant inclusion in a separate family.

They are usually found alone or in pairs but occasionally in small groups that are often family parties. Some species will join flocks of mixed-species. Most spend much time in trees, using their tail as well as their strong legs and feet to work their way spirally up trees and out onto branches, then flying in the fashion of a treecreeper down to the base of another tree and starting their way upwards again. Some species spend a considerable amount of time feeding on or very close to the ground.

The Spot-crowned woodcreeper is a fairly typical species with a slightly downcurved bill of medium length, 2.5cm out of a total length of 20cm (1in of 8in). It occurs on wooded slopes to an altitude of 3,000m (10,000ft), ie higher than most of its relatives. Solitarily or in pairs woodcreepers hunt around the forest, poking among epiphytes, such as ferns and bromeliads, and under bark which may be levered off with the bill; it takes mainly small prey. This is one of the first species active in the morning and last to roost. Hence their roosts are difficult to find; but they roost alone in a crevice or hole in a tree. The eggs are laid in a concealed hole or crevice that is often enlarged. The nest hole is lined with wood chippings collected by both parents and added to throughout the nesting period. Both parents attend the eggs and young. The young hatch blind and almost naked; they tend to be rather noisy.

The Buff-throated woodcreeper has a fairly heavy and straight bill, enabling it to take quite large prey, including small

▲ **Work in progress.** Two partly built Rufous horneros' nests. Each completed nest will consist of between 1,500 and 2,500 lumps of clay.

▼ **Holding tight to branch and prey** a Gray-throated leafscraper (*Sclerurus albigularis*), a species of ovenbird from northern South America.

lizards. Although generally birds of thick forest, they will frequent clearings and open woodland and will often feed on the ground or on fallen logs. More solitary than the Spot-crowned woodcreeper, they rarely join flocks of mixed species and are rarely to be seen in pairs. Their clear melodious notes can be heard at all times of day, but unlike the Spot-crowned and other members of its genus, which form lasting pair-bonds, no such pair-bonds exist in this genus. In this genus the female takes entire responsibility for the nest and will frequently attack an intruding male. She may spend up to 80 percent of the daylight hours incubating and will return with extra bits of bark for the nest after her periods off the nest. Similarly she rears the young alone, bringing single food items at intervals of about half an hour. A further contrast to the Spot-crowned group is that the young of these single-parent families remain silent until they leave the nest. Having once left the nest they do not return, even to roost. Both groups lay the same number of eggs, and in spite of their different social organization incubation and fledging periods are the same.

The Plain-brown woodcreeper and its relatives lack the spots and streaks but are otherwise typical woodcreepers. They tend to spend much more time close to the ground and are common ant-followers.

They will often feed around the periphery of ant-swarms or in the absence of larger antbirds can be the dominant bird, feeding on vertical trunks with occasional sorties to pick insects off vegetation or from the air. Members of this genus and the Olivaceous woodcreeper are also one-parent families.

The Wedge-billed woodcreeper is by far the smallest member of the family and its short stout upturned bill is unlike that of any other woodcreeper. It lives mostly in trees and feeds actively on small invertebrates. Its nest is usually in a crevice or rot-hole close to the ground, but occasionally as high as 6m (about 20ft) above. This is another species in which both parents care for the nest and young. The young are fed with insects which are carried one at a time in the adult's bill.

The largest woodcreepers have the largest bills: the Great rufous woodcreeper, the size of a small crow, has a particularly heavy bill, the Long-billed woodcreeper has a long straight bill about one fifth of its total length, while the curved bill of scythebills can be a quarter of the total length. With this bill the scythebills probe around trunks and logs and investigate cracks and crevices that are beyond the reach of other woodcreepers. They also take small vertebrates. Although it might seem essential that such a bill should be in good condition. a Black-billed scythebill trapped in southeast Brazil had

The 3 Families of Ovenbirds, Woodcreepers and Antbirds

Ovenbirds
Family: Furnariidae
Two hundred and seventeen species in 56 genera.
C Mexico, C America, S America, Trinidad and Tobago, Falkland and Juan Fernandez Islands. Deep forest to open arid land; sea level to snow line. Size: 10–26cm (4–10in) long, weight 9–46g (0.3–1.6oz). Plumage: generally somber browns, often rufous on head, wings or tail; underside streaked, spotted or plain, sometimes very pale. Voice: very varied, generally resonant; harsh rattles and creaks, screams, clear harmonious notes, whistling trills, etc. Nests: vary from mud chambers to huge bundles of twigs; burrows also used. Eggs: white, occasionally off-white or blue; incubation: about 15 days. Diet: mainly insects and other invertebrates.

Species and genera include: **Bay-capped wren-spinetail** (*Spartanoica maluroides*), **cachalotes** (genus *Pseudoseisura*), **canasteros** (genus *Asthenes*), **cinclodes** (genus *Cinclodes*), **Cordilleran canasteros** (*Asthenes modesta*), **Des Murs's wiretail** (*Sylviorthorhynchus desmursii*), **earthcreepers** (genus *Upucerthia*), **Firewood gatherer** (*Anumbius annumbi*), **miners** (genera *Geobates, Geositta*), **Red-faced spinetail** (*Cranioleuca erythrops*), **Rufous-breasted spinetail** (*Synallaxis erythrothorax*), **Rufous hornero** or **Rufous ovenbird** (*Furnarius rufus*), **Rusty-backed spinetail** (*Cranioleuca vulpina*), **Surf cinclodes** (*Cinclodes taczanowskii*), **thornbirds** (genus *Phacellodomus*), **tit-spinetails** (genus *Leptasthenura*), **White-chinned thistletail** (*Schizoeaca fuliginosa*), **White-throated cachalote** (*Pseudoseisura gutturalis*), **Wren-like rushbird** (*Phleocryptes melanops*).

Woodcreepers
Family: Dendrocolaptidae
Fifty species in 13 genera.
N Mexico S to C Argentina. Forest, forest edge, open woodland. Size: 13.5–35cm long (5.5–14in), weight 12–120g (0.4–4.2oz). Plumage: brown to rufous, often streaked or spotted; stiff spiny tails. Voice: trills and repetitive notes, often loud but generally not unmusical. Nest: tree holes or hollows, sometimes behind loose bark. Eggs: 2–3; plain white to greenish white. Incubation: 15–20 days. Diet: insects, other invertebrates, small vertebrates.

Species and genera include: **Black-billed scythebill** (*Campylorhamphus falcularius*), **Buff-throated woodcreeper** (*Xiphorhynchus guttatus*), **Great rufous woodcreeper** (*Xiphocolaptes major*), **Long-billed woodcreeper** (*Nasica longirostris*), **Olivaceous woodcreeper** (*Sittasomus griseicapillus*), **Plain brown woodcreeper** (*Dendrocincla fuliginosa*), **scythebills** (genus *Campylorhamphus*), **Spot-crowned woodcreeper** (*Lepidocolaptes affinis*), **Wedge-billed woodcreeper** (*Glyphorynchus spirurus*).

Antbirds
Family: Formicariidae
Two hundred and thirty species in 52 genera.
C Mexico S to C Argentina. Forest; sometimes open woodland or brushland. Size: 8–35cm (3–14in) long, weight 9–75g (0.3–2.6oz). Plumage: males usually gray to black with varying amounts of white spots or bars, sometimes with rufous; females usually duller or browner. Voice: most species unmusical; many produce harsh churring alarm or contact calls; some species have attractive songs and melodious calls. Nests: open cup in forks; occasionally tree cavity or on ground. Eggs: usually 2; white, usually with dark spots. Incubation: about 14 days. Diet: mainly insects, some small fruit, vertebrates.

Species include: **Bicolored antbird** (*Gymnopithys leucaspis*), **Black-crowned antpitta** (*Pittasoma michleri*), **Bluish-slate antshrike** (*Thamnomanes schistogynus*), **Ocellated antbird** (*Phaenostictus mcleannani*), **Spotted antbird** (*Hylophylax naevioides*), **White-plumed antbird** (*Pithys albifrons*). Total threatened species: 6

the front third of the upper mandible broken off; its weight was normal, but its plumage was in poor condition and it seemed inefficient at controlling the level of parasites on its body.   AMH

Antbirds comprise a very large family restricted to the forested areas of Central and South America. Most species occur in the lower levels of forest or on the ground and prefer fairly close undergrowth, but a few occur in quite open areas or in the forest canopy. They are usually smallish birds.

The antbirds form a very diverse family, this diversity being reflected (not always accurately) in their names: antshrike, antvireo, antwren, antthrush and antpitta. In most species there is a strong difference between sexes: males are mainly dark gray to black with various amounts of white spots or bars; females tend to have more rufous or olive plumage. Some of the ground-dwelling species are more distinctively patterned and the sexes look alike in some of the most striking species, such as the White-plumed antbird. Many species have a concealed white patch on the back.

Antwrens and antthrushes are not especially wren- or thrush-like, but the former are small active birds of forest undergrowth, the latter are ground-dwellers, some with boldly streaked underparts (although mostly with very short upturned tails). Antpittas bear a strong resemblance to the Old World pittas, but are by no means so colorful. One group of large antpittas hops on the ground in dense cover, while the other group of small species lives in the undergrowth just above ground. The antvireos do not look especially like their northern counterparts, but resemble them in color, behavior and, to some extent, in breeding habits and song. Antshrikes have the robust, predaceous appearance of Old World shrikes, but little other similarity. The species of these groups make up a little more than half the family, most of the rest being simply called "antbirds."

Antbirds feed on insects and other invertebrates and some species take small vertebrates or fruit. Many species associate with or lead the mixed-species flocks that roam the forests (see box).

The feature of antbirds that is presumably responsible for their name is the habit of some species of following swarming army ants. Ants of the subfamily Dorylinae are well known for their frequent swarming through forests, either to move their colony or in raids for feeding. In Central and South America grossly exaggerated tales are told

of the ants' activities, but certainly several army ants (eg *Eciton burchelli*) swarm very frequently and a variety of birds takes advantage of the mass movement of the ants to feed on the other insects, etc, that are disturbed by the passage of the column of ants. So do a number of predatory and parasitic insects, and reptiles. The main bird families involved are cuckoos, woodcreepers, antbirds and tanagers. About 50 species are regular ant-followers, but many other birds will occasionally join in. Large colonies of regularly nomadic ants can attract at a time up to 25 birds of one or two species plus scattered individuals of up to 30 other species. Many "professional" ant-followers obtain up to 50 percent of their food from antswarms, keeping a regular eye on the colonies to take advantage the moment the swarm starts to move. There is often a strict

▲ **Courtship feeding** is an important stage in the formation of the monogamous pair-bond in antbirds. In the Ocellated antbird much singing is involved. (**1**) A female (left) screams at her mate who bobs his head ritually. Having brought food the male sings faintly while holding the item in his mouth (**2**). The male then feeds the female (**3**), who takes a low posture while eating the food (**4**). When the feeding session is over the female pecks at the male's bill while he bobs his head (**5**).

Feeding Flocks in Tropical Forests

Although European observers will be used to seeing mixed flocks of birds (eg tits, kinglets, nuthatches, creepers, finches) moving through woodland it is in the tropical forests that this activity is most manifest. In such forests it is often difficult to see birds at all, but a mixed-species flock gives the opportunity to study a number of species and compare their differing feeding behavior.

The function of such flocks is not fully understood, but the various suggestions fall into two categories: either to enhance feeding or to reduce the risk of predation by being with other birds, as in this case each individual is less likely to be caught unawares by a predator.

Whatever the reason, a mixed flock of insectivorous and omnivorous species in the tropics works through the forest at about a third of a kilometer (0.2mi) per hour occupying feeding levels from the ground to close to the canopy. The path followed may be very erratic and frequently crosses itself.

There is usually one bird or species that

maintains the cohesion and impetus of the flock. In Central America this is often one of the parulid warblers, eg the Three-striped warbler (*Basileuterus tristriatus*); in South America it is more frequently an antbird, eg the Bluish-slate antshrike. As these core birds move through changing forest habitats, calling frequently, other birds are attracted to the flock while it is within their home range. Thus there may be only one pair (perhaps together with its fledged young) of each highly territorial species involved in the flock at any one time. In this way a single ant-bird has been seen to involve about 80 species in two days and, of course, a large but unquantifiable number of individuals.

Nevertheless birds do not always join a flock that moves through their territory; they are more likely to do so if a trespassing member of their own species is present and are less likely to do so during the breeding season, during the early morning or late afternoon and during inclement weather.

AMH

▲ **The Barred antshrike** (*Thamnophilus doliatus*), from central and northern South America. This female shows well the hooked tip of the bill typical of antthrushes.

▼ **This stout bird of warm colors** is a Rufous-crowned antpitta (*Pittasoma rufopileatum*) of northwest South America.

hierarchy in the attendant birds, with the larger antbirds, such as the Ocellated antbird, holding a central "territory" just ahead of the ant column while smaller species, such as the Bicolored antbird and the Spotted antbird, hold increasingly peripheral territories. Some small species, such as the White-plumed antbird, are able to utilize the whole area by making raids from the periphery, at the expense of being frequently attacked. Large and potentially dominant ground birds, such as Black-crowned antpittas, have to occupy peripheral zones. Territories exist vertically as well as horizontally and many of the non-professional ant-followers feed in the outer or upper reaches or even between the territories of the professionals. Many of the less regular drop out as the ant-swarm moves out of their territory, while the professionals are prepared to share the resource to some extent, although individuals of a species only remain dominant over others of their own species while they are in their own ter-

ritory. These antbirds have learnt to utilize the movements of the ant-swarms.

Antbirds pair for life and the parents share nest building, incubation and care of the young. Nests are usually fairly frail, deep structures of loosely interwoven plant strands slung between the fork of a twig near the ground. Usually the nest is lined with leaves and sometimes with finer material. A few species nest on the ground and others in tree fissures, among epiphytes such as ferns well above the ground or in the crown of low tree ferns. The eggs are incubated by the female during the night and part of the middle of the day, with the male brooding for the morning and late afternoon. Young are fed on insects brought singly, but they fledge quickly, and sometimes before they are able to fly strongly, in about two weeks. The young birds often stay with the parents for a long time and young males may even bring a female into the family group prior to establishing their own breeding territory.   AMH

TYRANT FLYCATCHERS AND PITTAS

Families: Tyrannidae, Pittidae
Order: Passeriformes (suborder Tyranni—part).
Four hundred and two species in 89 genera.
Distribution: see map and table.

Tyrant flycatchers   **Pittas**

► **The nest of the Dusky flycatcher**
(*Empidonax oberholseri*) is made of grasses and
fibers and lined with grass and feathers. The
young fledge 18 days after hatching. This
species breeds in western North America.

► **The Pied water tyrant** BELOW (*Fluvicola pica*)
loves water. Its range is Central America and
the West Indies.

▼ **Open country near water appeals** to the
Boat-billed flycatcher (*Megarhynchus pitangua*),
which is found from Panama south to Uruguay.
It occupies a variety of habitats, from sea level
to 1,900m (6,200ft), where it is an active
forager. Access to water, however, enables it to
dine on frogs.

THE **tyrant flycatchers** comprise the largest and most diverse family of birds in
the New World. No other bird family contains species that breed from the spruce forests of northern Canada to the rugged,
treeless hillsides of Tierra del Fuego. Flycatchers occupy every habitat in between,
from tropical forests and seacoasts up to the
snow line on the highest mountains. In
South America, the center of diversity of the
family, more than one tenth of all land bird
species are tyrant flycatchers.

By no means do all flycatchers make their
living "catching flies." Rather, the widespread diversity of the flycatchers in the New
World results largely from a tremendous
diversity of ecological roles and associated
body forms found within the family. True
"fly-catchers," ie species that perch motionless and make aerial sallies after passing
insects, are actually in the minority within
the family. In South America flycatcher
equivalents exist for numerous other types
of birds found on other continents.

The largest flycatchers are the drab,
grayish or brownish shrike-tyrants of the
high-altitude grasslands in the Andes. These
jay-sized birds search for prey by scanning
the ground from elevated perches, and they
tear apart large insects and small lizards
with their strong, hooked bills. The related
ground-tyrants, mostly grayish, run along
the rocky slopes of the high mountaintops
on long legs, looking very much like pipits.
They pick insects from the ground, and on
long, pointed wings they can rapidly dart
after any escaping prey. Among the larger
flycatchers is a large group of species that
shares a similar, conspicuous plumage pattern of bright yellow underparts and black-
and-white striped crowns. Best known of
these is the Great kiskadee, widespread from
North America south to central Argentina.
This species eats almost anything, but is
especially fond of catching small fish or tadpoles from shallow lakeshores. At the
opposite size extreme are the tiny, greenish
tody-tyrants and pygmy-tyrants, which live
in dense foliage in the moist, tropical lowlands. Some of these species are smaller than
most hummingbirds, and the Short-tailed
pygmy-tyrant (Costa Rica through to
Amazonian South America) is the smallest
species in this enormous order.

Many pygmy-tyrants have wide, spoon-
shaped bills with which they scoop insects
from the undersides of leaves during rapid
darts through the vegetation. Related to
these are the spadebills, named for their
weird, oversized bills that are shaped like
wide shovels or spoons.

The most common type of flycatcher is of
medium size, dull olive in color, and lives in
the treetops or scrubby forest edges. Many
of these species have relatively wide bills
bordered with well-developed rictal bristles.
These apparently aid in snagging insects
that are captured on the wing, although
some evidence now indicates that bristles
also serve to protect the eyes from damage
during active foraging through dense vegetation; they probably also have a sensory
function. A few flycatchers, such as the
Scissor-tailed flycatcher, possess extraordinarily long, forked tails. Typically these
belong to species that sally out into mid-air
to capture flying insects. The long outer tail-
feathers aid in the rapid aerial maneuvering
required to capture wary insects in the open.

Only a few flycatchers are brightly colored. The male Vermilion flycatcher is entirely scarlet on the crown and underparts. He displays these colors to other males and the drab brown females, during a conspicuous aerial flight display over open meadows, accompanied by a melodious, warbled song. The Many-colored rush tyrant, perhaps the strangest flycatcher, is a wren-like inhabitant of tall, dense reed beds in the high Andes and in Argentina. This species is a patchwork pattern of blue, green, black, white, yellow and red. The Royal flycatcher occasionally displays its wide, vivid red crest by holding it erect across its crown while it opens its bill to display a bright orange mouth.

The size and colors of males and females are usually similar but there are a few exceptions. The female Strange-tailed tyrant is straw-brown above and whitish below, with slightly elongated tail feathers. The male, however, is boldly marked with black and white, with a huge, streamer-like tail and a bright yellow, bare throat patch during the breeding season. This species belongs to a group of closely related forms, nearly all of which have black or black and white males and drab-colored females. These species inhabit open country, especially grasslands and marshes. The conspicuous, flashy patterns of the males are associated with aerial displays that are visible over great distances across these habitats. The females perform most nesting duties, and their brownish color serves to camouflage their activity around the nest.

Most flycatchers eat insects, captured after brief, almost motionless searches from exposed perches near vegetation or above the ground. Many of the variations in size and body shape found within the family are associated with slight differences in the exact manner of searching or prey capture. For example, those that frequently sally to or along the ground have long legs, for strength and stability on the ground. Those that sally into the air have long, forked tails, relatively long wings and short legs. Species that pick their insect prey from tiny crevices in leaves and twigs have narrow, tweezer-like bills, usually with few or no rictal bristles. Those that snatch prey from leaf surfaces during a quick flight off the perch have rather broad bills and long bristles. Nearly all flycatchers eat some fruit, usually small berries found while foraging for insects. A few species actually specialize on fruit taken from large trees.

Virtually all flycatchers are monogamous. Some species, especially migratory ones, pair anew each year as the breeding season begins. Many nonmigratory tropical species remain paired the year round, dwelling on permanent territories. In many smaller species only the female constructs the nest, usually with the male close by. With few exceptions only the female incubates eggs and broods young. The male defends the territory and the nest-site, frequently perching within a few meters of the nest for hours on end while the female incubates. Typically both sexes feed the young, but again females of some smaller species perform this role exclusively. In a few small, fruit-eating species, such as the Ochre-bellied flycatcher, the male has no role in the nesting process whatsoever. In these species males display in traditional arenas or "leks," separate from the nest sites, and females visit these sites to mate.

In most species the young reach independence within a few months of leaving the nest, and are breeding on their own territories the following year. In many tropical species the young remain with their parents during this intervening year, the family foraging together as a group. The White-bearded flycatcher carries this association one step further: the young remain with their parents for up to several years and help raise subsequent broods of siblings.

Virtually all flycatchers live on defended territories. Those breeding in North America abandon the territory in late summer and migrate to Central or South America. In some cases migration is accompanied by dramatic shifts in habits. The pugnacious Eastern kingbird is a monogamous breeder on vigorously defended territories in open country throughout much of North America. However, while wintering in the Amazon basin it travels in huge, nomadic flocks, prefers forest habitats, eats mostly fruit instead of insects, and is subordinate to resident birds in the region. Other migratory flycatchers, including some that move northwards out of Patagonia during the southern winter, join mixed species flocks in the treetops. These flocks usually contain various species of resident flycatchers as well, and can include up to 30 species or more when swelled with migrants. Such flocks of mixed species jointly defend their giant territories against other flocks, just as pairs defend smaller territories against other pairs in nonflocking species. JWF

The brightly colored **pittas** form a compact and remarkable family of primarily terrestrial forest birds centered in the Southeast Asian tropics. Like precious jewels, their brilliant hues, combined with their rarity and mysterious origins, have given them a popularity amongst songbirds that may only be surpassed by the birds of paradise.

All pittas are stocky, long-legged, short-tailed birds with strong bills, well adapted to life on or near the forest floor, where most of their time is spent. Their bright plumage is often intensely vivid scarlet, turquoise blue, rich and delicate greens, velvety black or porcelain white. As the brightest colors are usually found on the undersides of pittas they can be very difficult to see in the dense understory of the forest, particularly with their characteristic habit of standing motionless with their backs toward any

◄▲ **Representative species of tyrant flycatchers and pittas.** (1) An Indian pitta (*Pitta brachyura*). (2) A Gurney's pitta (*P. gurneyi*). (3) A Short-tailed pygmy flycatcher (*Myiornis ecaudata*). (4) A Great kiskadee (*Pitangus sulphuratus*) holding an insect. (5) A Scissor-tailed flycatcher (*Tyrannus muscivora*) chasing an insect. (6) A Vermilion flycatcher (*Pyrocephalus rubinus*). (7) A Royal flycatcher (*Onychorynchus coronatus*).

source of alarm; otherwise they flee by rapid, bounding hops or short flights close to the ground. Larger species, such as the Rusty-naped pitta, possess disproportionately large eyes, an adaptation to their preference for gloomy forest areas that seldom receive any sunlight, even at midday; they are also known to forage at night. Evolution has provided some pittas with white wing patches (specula) and iridescent patches of light blue on the shoulders and primaries to facilitate visual contact in dim light.

Pittas range widely throughout tropical Asia, extending to Japan (Fairy pitta), Australia and the Solomon Islands (six species), and tropical Africa (African pitta), occurring from sea level up to 2,500m (8,200ft). All species are found in forested regions, especially the remaining tracts of extensive lowland to mid-montane evergreen rain forest. These forests are inhabited by the rarest and least known species (including the very distinctive Eared pitta, Blue pitta, Giant pitta), and confined to a few Philippine islands are the red-bellied Koch's pitta and the black and sky-blue Steere's pitta. The striking blue, yellow and black Gurney's pitta is unique in having a limited

Elusive Flycatchers

In the humid forests of the eastern Andes and the Amazon basin up to 70 flycatcher species may occur together at a single locality. The distributions of many of these species are very restricted. With so many flycatcher species occupying small ranges, scientists still occasionally discover new ones, but the process is not easy. Some recently discovered species, which have escaped detection through 200 years of scientific exploration, had special reasons for being so elusive.

In 1976 a team of ornithologists became the first scientists to explore the cloud-enshrouded summit of a mountain ridge in extreme northern Peru. Here they discovered a tiny flycatcher new to science, later described as the Cinnamon-breasted tody-tyrant. This species is restricted to the mossy, stunted cloud-forests atop a few isolated peaks

in this region. Because it evolved on these high, remote mountain "islands" it remained undiscovered until scientists were able to work their way up to those peaks.

In 1981 another new flycatcher was discovered in the rainy tropical forests at the base of the eastern Andes in southern Peru. This new "bristle-tyrant" (still unnamed) lives high in the treetops, where it joins flocks of tanagers and other flycatchers. It is in its locality quite common, but escaped detection because of its tiny size (weighing just 7g, 0.24oz), its treetop habits and its restriction to remote foothills of the Andes.

Many scientists suspect that more of these startling new flycatchers remain hidden and unknown, awaiting future generations of explorers of the remote tropical corners of South America. JWF

distribution in continental Asia between two faunal zones (about 500km (310mi) of peninsular Thailand and adjacent Burma). The shy and secretive habits of many pittas have also been a source of anomalies in distribution and this is illustrated by an example from the Malay Peninsula. For 30 years sightings were reported of an unknown and elusive large pitta from Fraser's Hill in the highlands of Central Malaysia. The mystery was solved in 1977 when one was caught and identified as a new form of the Rusty-naped pitta.

Apart from some minor dispersion according to season and altitude only eight pittas (including the Indian pitta and Blue-winged pitta) are known to undertake regular migration. These pittas are nocturnal migrants and many unusual records have resulted from their attraction to lights. The African pitta was thought to be sedentary until 50 years ago when an ornithologist living in Tanzania found that over several years records of birds flying into lighted houses at night developed a seasonal pattern. Further study has shown that regular migration occurs in East Africa where a long-winged form is found, but records of night movements from West and Central Africa suggest that the picture is still incomplete. A survey of nocturnal migration in Malaysia has not only established the dates of movements, but revealed that pittas are unusual among song birds in that the peaks of migration are during the new moon, not the full moon as with other song birds.

Pittas spend much of their time searching for their food, particularly worms, snails and insects, in the leaf litter and humus soil of the forest floor. Leaves and other debris are flicked over with their strong bills, or small openings are made in the litter in the manner of a chicken. Occasionally prey is located by sound with the pitta's head turned sideways, or flushed by wing-flicking movements. Some pittas are attracted to sites favored for snails, eg Banded pittas at limestone cliffs, and will readily use a rock or log as an anvil when breaking open the shells. Pittas also have the most highly developed sense of smell among song birds, a useful adaptation in dimly lit habitats or at night. A study of the food habits of a captive Hooded pitta revealed a strong preference for earthworms: it would dig for them with its bill completely immersed in the damp soil, where a sense of smell would enable it to locate the prey more easily. This bird ate approximately its own weight in food each day.

Pittas' large bulky nests may be found up to 8m (26ft) above ground (but usually less than 3m, 10ft) or on the ground, in stumps, root buttresses, fallen trees, tangled clumps of vegetation, in banks or rock clefts. If disturbed at the nest the entrance may be concealed with a leafy twig, and the parent bird may attempt to draw the intruder away from the nest by calling.

▲ **Cleaning up,** a Hooded pitta in New Guinea removes a fecal sac. Such sacs are produced by the nestlings of many passerines and a few close relatives. It is an adaptation that enables nests made of delicate materials to be kept clean. Sacs and such nests must have evolved in parallel.

▶ **From Thailand to Bali** lives the Banded pitta. The word "pitta" comes from the Madras area of south India where it merely signifies "bird."

The 2 Families of Tyrant Flycatchers and Pittas

1 Threatened, but status indeterminate.

Tyrant flycatchers
Family: Tyrannidae
Three hundred and seventy-six species in 88 genera.

N (except extreme N), C and S America, West Indies, Galapagos Islands. Forest, woodland, savanna, temperate grassland, alpine zones, cultivated land. Size: 6–50cm (2.5–19.7in) long, weight 4.5–80g (0.16–2.8oz). Plumage: dull olive-green above, pale yellowish below; also black, brown, rusty or white; one species is bright scarlet; many have brightly colored crown patches. Voice: generally weak, whistled or warbled notes, sometimes in simple phrases or trills. Nests: highly variable, including woven cups, globular nests with side holes, pendant- and purse-shaped nests, simple cups on the ground or in natural or excavated cavities. Eggs. 2–8, usually 3 or 4; white or whitish, sometimes lightly to heavily mottled with reddish brown. Incubation: 14–20 days. Nestling period: 14–23 days. Diet: chiefly insects; fruits of tropical trees and vines; occasionally small fish, lizards, snakes and tadpoles.

Species and genera include: **Cinnamon-breasted tody-tyrant** (*Hemitriccus cinnamomeipectus*), **Eastern kingbird** (*Tyrannus tyrannus*), **Great kiskadee** (*Pitangus sulphuratus*), **ground-tyrants** (genus *Muscisaxicola*), **Many-colored rush tyrant** (*Tachuris rubigastra*), **Ochre-bellied flycatcher** (*Mionectes oleagineus*), **Piratic flycatcher** (*Legatus leucophaius*), **pygmy-tyrants** (genera *Atalotriccus, Colopteryx, Hemitriccus, Lophotriccus, Myiornis, Pseudotriccus*), **Royal flycatcher** (*Onychorhynchus coronatus*), **Scissor-tailed flycatcher** (*Tyrannus muscivora*), **Short-tailed pygmy-flycatcher** (*Myiornis ecaudatus*), **shrike-tyrants** (genus *Agriornis*), **spadebills** (genus *Platyrinchus*), **Strange-tailed tyrant** (*Yetapa risora*), **Vermilion flycatcher** (*Pyrocephalus rubinus*), **White-bearded flycatcher** (*Conopias inornatus*), **White-**cheeked tody flycatcher (*Poecilotriccus albifacies*).

Pittas
Family: Pittidae
Twenty-six species of the genus *Pitta*.
Africa, E and S Asia to New Guinea, the Solomon Islands and Australia. Evergreen and deciduous forest, bamboo jungle, mangroves, wooded ravines; secondary forest, plantations, overgrown gardens. Size: 15–28cm (5.9–11in) long, weight 42–218g (1.5–7.7oz) (some heavier weights known). Plumage: very colorful with brightly contrasting blues, greens, reds, yellows and intermediate shades with the brightest parts on the head and underparts; little or no difference between sexes (four species have drab females). Young birds are more brownish and mottled or spotted. Voice: short series of variably pitched whistles, often of two syllables; range of trilling, rolling sounds and loud barking notes when alarmed. Nests: huge, untidy globular or elliptical structures, built of twigs and rootlets, often decorated with moss and lined with finer materials; all have low side entrance, also a small platform in front. Eggs: 1–7, usually 3–5; varying from broad blunt oval to spheroidal in shape, some with much gloss; white or buffish with reddish or purplish spots or speckles and fine gray or lilac undermarkings; weight about 5–10g (0.18–0.35oz). Incubation: 15–17 days. Nestling period: 2–3 weeks.

Species include: **African pitta** (*Pitta angolensis*), **Banded pitta** (*P. guajana*), **Blue-banded pitta** (*P. arcuata*), **Blue Pitta** (*P. cyanea*), **Blue-rumped pitta** (*P. soror*), **Blue-winged pitta** (*P. moluccensis*), **Eared pitta** (*P. phayrei*), **Fairy pitta** (*P. nympha*), **Giant pitta** (*P. caerulea*), **Gurney's pitta** 1 (*P. gurneyi*), **Hooded pitta** (*P. sordida*), **Indian pitta** (*P. brachyura*), **Koch's pitta** (*P. kochi*), **Noisy pitta** (*P. versicolor*), **Rusty-napped pitta** (*P. oatesi*), **Steere's pitta** (*P. steerii*).

The breeding season in the summer at higher latitudes may cover most months near the equator, except at the height of the monsoon period. The male initiates courtship by confronting the female with erect posturing, vertical movements of the body, and wing spreading, accompanied by loud calls. If the female responds in kind, mating takes place and the male starts nest-building with some assistance from the female. Both sexes share incubation and the care and feeding of the young, but they may drive away the young shortly after they have fledged. Pittas may be long-lived birds as a pair of Giant pittas first bred after 10 years in captivity.

When calling pittas will perch in trees up to 10m (33ft) above ground, and may throw back their heads when repeating their loud, penetrating whistles, usually at dawn and dusk, before rainstorms and on moonlit nights, and often in chorus with one or several others. They readily respond to imitations of their calls. Outside the breeding season pittas are usually solitary and occupy foraging territories. They quickly respond to intruders and a threat display recorded for some species, such as the Noisy pitta, involves a crouching posture with feathers fluffed, the wings outspread and the bill pointing upward. The Blue-rumped pitta has a similar display, but the head is bent low over the back to expose a triangular, white-spotted patch below the throat.

In 1979–81 the World Wildlife Fund supported a fauna survey of Sabah, North Borneo. It found pittas, regarded as strictly forest-dwelling birds, to be one of only a few families (and the only one of the song birds) of special value in studying the dynamics of change in bird communities after the effects of logging. It was found that pittas are adversely affected, but will return to lightly disturbed or partially regenerated forest. So far only Gurney's pitta is considered threatened by habitat destruction and this survey provides the first evidence of the adaptability of pittas to habitat changes.

The word "pitta" comes from the Madras area of South India where it merely signifies "bird" and was first applied to the Indian pitta in 1713. In parts of Indonesia the local names, based on the call, are likened to variations of the Malay word for "grandfather" and have given rise to a favorite story of a child walking with its grandfather in the forest but who loses its way only to be transformed into a bird that must now always call for its grandfather. In Borneo some inland tribes dry the skins of pittas for use as children's toys.   MDB

MANAKINS AND COTINGAS

Families: Pipridae, Cotingidae
Order: Passeriformes (suborder Tyranni, part)
One hundred and eighteen species in 42 genera
Distribution: see map and table.

Manakins   Cotingas

T HE manakins and cotingas are closely related to each other and quite closely related to the huge American family of tyrant flycatchers (Tyrannidae). They are distinguished from the tyrant flycatchers by some anatomical characters and, more obviously, by the fact that they are mainly fruit-eaters rather than insect-eaters, and in most species there are considerable differences between the sexes with males brilliantly colored. Courtship behavior is very elaborate.

Typical **manakins** (*Pipra, Manacus, Chiroxiphia* and some smaller genera) are small, compact, highly active birds with short bills and large heads. They live in the understory of forest, feeding on small fruits and insects which they take in rapid flight sallies. Although semisocial in feeding and other routine activities they do not form pairs. The males spend a great deal of their time at traditional display sites, some species at "leks" or communal display areas, others singly but usually within ear-shot of other males. A large lek of the White-bearded manakin, one of the best known species, is an extraordinary sight when in full activity. Each male clears a small "court" on the ground, within a few meters of its neighbors, and on and round it performs an astonishing range of rapid maneuvers accompanied by sharp calls and loud snaps made by the modified wing-feathers (see box). The females visit the leks solely for the purpose of mating, carrying out all nesting duties single-handed, as is the rule in all manakins studied. They sling their delicate cup nests between two parallel or diverging twigs of some low plant, often beside a forest stream, and after an unusually long incubation period for a small bird (about 19 days) feed the young by regurgitation on a mixed diet of insects and fruits.

Manakins of the largest genus, *Pipra*, display on higher perches, usually 3–10m (10–33ft) above ground, on which they perform rapid slides, "about-faces," "twists" and other maneuvers. The details vary according to species, but a swift flight to the display perch, ending in a conspicuous landing, is a feature of all of them. A unique feature of the display of the Wire-tailed manakin brings into play the elongated wire-like filaments which project from the tips of its tail-feathers. Backing towards the female, the male raises its posterior and rapidly twists its tail from side to side, so that the filaments brush the female's chin. The third main genus, *Chiroxiphia*, is supreme in the complexity of its displays. In the initial stages two or more males perform a vocal duet followed by a synchronized joint dance before the female, while the final phase of the courtship, leading to mating, is carried out by the dominant male of the group alone (see box).

The **cotingas** are such a diverse family that practically no generalization applies to all species. At one extreme of size is the Kinglet calyptura, about 8cm (3in) long, and at the other the huge umbrellabirds, the size of a crow. In proportion they range from short-winged heavily built birds, for example the Guianan red cotinga, to the long-winged, almost swallow-like purpletufts. In color form they range from the most highly dimorphic species, with brilliantly ornamented males, to species in which both sexes are uniform gray or brown. In behavior they are equally varied, with social systems ranging from conventional monogamy to extreme polygamy. It is by no means certain that they are monophyletic,

---

The Catherine Wheel Courtship of the Blue-backed Manakin

Probably no other birds have courtship displays as complex as those of some manakins. The Blue-backed manakin's is among the most spectacular. Males display in pairs, and the whole courtship sequence is in three distinct phases.

Phase one, two males perch side by side in a tree, facing the same way and almost in contact, and utter long series of almost perfectly synchronized calls. Although the calls are so well synchronized that they seem to come from a single bird, in fact one bird, the dominant member of the pair, begins each note about one twentieth of a second before the other. The function of this duet is to attract a female.

hovering, to land behind the second male, who hitches forward and in turn jumps up and moves back in hovering flight. The two males thus form a revolving Catherine wheel in front of the female. As it proceeds, the Catherine wheel dance becomes more and more rapid and the twanging calls more frenzied, until the dance is brought to a sudden end by the dominant male, who utters one or two very sharp calls, whereupon the subordinate male leaves the perch.

Phase two, when a female approaches, the two males fly down to a special display perch near the forest floor. Perching side by side they begin to jump up alternately, rising a few centimeters in the air and accompanying each jump with a nasal twanging call. The female may then come to the display perch, in which case the two males turn to face her and continue their coordinated dance in a different form. The male nearer the female jumps up, facing her, and then moves back in the air,

Phase three, the dominant male performs an aerial display around the female, criss-crossing the display perch, every now and then perching, crouching to present his red head-shield, then flying on to continue his butterfly flights. Occasionally he flies to an outlying perch, crouches and with a snap of his wings flies back towards the display perch. If the female remains on the display perch, showing that she is ready to mate, the male eventually lands beside her and mounts.

▷ **Jungle jewels,** OVERLEAF a pair of Peruvian cock-of-the-rock (*Rupicola peruviana*). The male is on the right. The two species of cocks-of-the-rock live on rock cliffs and rocky outcrops in South American forests.

◁ **A bird of striking contrast,** the Red-capped manakin (*Pipra mentalis*).

▽ **The call of the male bellbird** may be the loudest of any bird. This is the Three-wattled bellbird (*Procnias tricarunculata*).

The 2 Families of Manakins and Cotingas

ⓘ Threatened, but status indeterminate.

Manakins

Family: Pipridae
Fifty-three species in 17 genera.
C and S America. Forest at tropical levels. Size: 9–19cm (3.5–7.5in) long, weight 10–25g (0.35–0.88oz). Plumage: males of most species brightly colored, black with patches of red, orange, yellow, blue or white; females olive-green. (A few species are mainly olive-green or brown with no difference between sexes.) Voice: variety of sharp whistles, trills, buzzing notes; no true songs; some species also make loud mechanical sounds with modified wing feathers. Nests: open cups, usually in low vegetation. Eggs: almost always 2;

dull white or buff with brown markings (blackish markings in the Thrush-like manakin). Incubation: 17–21 days. Nestling period: almost always 13–15 days.

Species include: **Blue-backed manakin** (*Chiroxiphia pareola*), **Thrush-like manakin** (*Schiffornis turdinus*), **White-bearded manakin** (*Manacus manacus*), **Wire-tailed manakin** (*Pipra filicauda*).

Cotingas

Cotingidae
Sixty-five species in 25 genera.
Mexico, C and S America. Forest, at all levels from tropical to temperate montane. Size: 8–50cm (3–20in)

long, weight 6–400g (0.21–14oz). Plumage: extremely varied; males of many species brilliantly colored with reds, purples, blues, etc, and unusually modified display plumage; females usually duller without ornamentation. Voice: very varied, ranging from sharp whistles and rapid trills to booming sounds and hammer- or bell-like clangs; some species make mechanical sounds with modified wing-feathers. Nests: mainly open cup- or saucer-shaped nests, in some cases very small and frail for the size of the bird. (Cocks-of-the-rock are exceptional in building bracket-shaped nests attached to rock faces.) Eggs: 1–3, usually buff or olive in ground color with spots and blotches

of darker browns and grays. Incubation: 19–28 days. Nestling period: 21–44 days. Diet: fruits and insects.

Species and genera include: **bellbirds** (genus *Procnias*), **blue cotingas** (genus *Cotinga*), **calfbird** (*Perissocephalus tricolor*), **cock-of-the-rock** (genus *Rupicola*), **Guianan cock-of-the-rock** (*Rupicola rupicola*), **Guianan red cotinga** ⓘ (*Phoenicircus carnifex*), **Kinglet calyptura** (*Calyptura cristata*), **purpletufts** (genus *Iodopleura*), **umbrellabirds** (genus *Cephalopterus*), **White-cheeked cotinga** (*Ampelion stresemanni*), **White-winged cotinga** (*Xipholena atropurpurea*), white-winged cotingas (genus *Xipholena*). Total threatened species: 4.

that is, more closely related to one another than any of them are to other groups of birds, and it may be that they are descended from a number of different lines that evolved from primitive tyrant flycatchers and became specialized for fruit-eating. Only a few of the diverse types can be mentioned.

One group, the "typical" cotingas, includes the blue cotingas, the white-winged cotingas and some other genera of medium-sized, sexually highly dimorphic birds with short wide bills. They are preeminently birds of the forest treetops and for this reason the details of their behavior are not well known, but in some species, and perhaps in all, the conspicuously colored males—clad in blue, purple or white—display aerially above the forest canopy, while the cryptically colored females (to judge from the few species whose nests are known) build tiny nests which they tend single-handed, laying a single egg.

Yet more highly dimorphic and with even wider, shorter bills that give the head an almost frog-like appearance are the four species of bellbirds. They are among the most specialized of fruit-eaters, their very wide gape enabling them to swallow comparatively huge fruits for their size. Bellbirds are notable for the males' extraordinarily loud calls, perhaps the loudest made by any bird, the main element of which is an explosive clang or "bock," reminiscent of a hammer striking an anvil. The call advertises the male on his display perch and is audible for a kilometer (0.6mi) or more. When a female ready for mating visits a male, a complex courtship ritual follows, which varies according to the species and culminates in a leap by the male, accompanied by a deafening "bock," onto the female's back. Male bellbirds display in loose groups, occupying perches within earshot but not very close to each other.

The same type of display organization is found in some other cotingas, for instance the umbrellabirds, in which each male occupies a separate display tree and attracts females by uttering deep booming calls accompanied by visual displays. In a few species the males display at much closer quarters. Thus in the calfbird the males display in groups, occupying adjacent perches in the same tree. This species acquired its name from the strange lowing or "mooing" calls that accompany the males' grotesque display movements.

The cocks-of-the-rock have developed communal display to an extreme degree. In the Guianan cock-of-the-rock the males display in groups, each bird maintaining a cleared "court" on the forest floor, a system similar to that of the White-bearded manakin. The main display is static: the male crouches in the middle of his court with the brilliant plumage spread and the head turned sideways so that the semicircular topknot is fully displayed to the females who come into the trees above. As in so many of the manakins and cotingas, the details of the different phases of the courtship display are so complex that no brief description is adequate. The two cocks-of-the-rock are unique in their nesting habits: the female fixes her bracket-shaped nest of mud and rootlets, hardened with saliva, to a vertical rock face. Since suitable nest-sites are limited, several females may nest in close proximity. Unlike the other large cotingas, whose relatively tiny nests can hold only one egg and nestling, the cock-of-the-rock lays a two-egg clutch.

The brilliantly colored cotingas are mainly birds of tropical and subtropical forest. At temperate levels in the Andes are found a number of species with sober plumage, similar in both sexes, which live conventionally in pairs. These too are primarily fruit-eaters, feeding on the berries of montane shrubs and epiphytes. Some are highly specialized for particular fruits. Thus the White-cheeked cotinga of the Peruvian Andes is reported to feed solely on the fruits of two kinds of mistletoes, and it undoubtedly serves as their main dispersal agent because it wipes regurgitated seeds onto suitable tree branches and no other fruit-eating birds occur in its bleak montane habitat. These high-altitude cotingas build substantial cup nests, doubtless as an adaptation to the cold climate, and lay two or three eggs, with both parents attending the nest.

Among the more aberrant cotingas the four species of purpletufts are outstanding. These very small cotingas are long-winged and superficially martin-like. They take mistletoe fruits, but also hawk for flying insects from treetop perches above the forest canopy. The only purpletuft nest ever found is of a type unique in the cotingas, a tiny cup reminiscent of a hummingbird's nest. The Kinglet calyptura is also very different from other cotingas. A tiny, very short-tailed bird about the size of a goldcrest and much like a goldcrest in color, it is known from a handful of specimens collected in the mountains of southeastern Brazil and ranks as one of the least known of birds, unrecorded in this century although there is no obvious reason why it should have become extinct.   DWS

GNATEATERS AND OTHER NOISEMAKERS

Families: Conopophagidae, Rhinocryptidae, Oxyruncidae, Phytotomidae, Xenicidae, Philepittidae
Order Passeriformes (suborder Tyranni, part).
Forty-eight species in 19 genera.
Distribution: see maps and table.

Gnateaters   Tapaculos   Sunbird-asitys

Sharpbill   Plantcutters   New Zealand wrens

▶ **Representative species of gnateaters and other noisemakers.** (1) A Crested gallito (a tapaculo; *Rhinocrypta lanceolata*). (2) A Rufous gnateater (*Conopophaga lineata*). (3) A False sunbird (a sunbird-asity; *Neodrepanis coruscans*). (4) Two riflemen (New Zealand wrens; *Acanthisitta chloris*), male above, female below. (5) A Rufous-tailed plantcutter (*Phytotoma rara*). (6) A sharpbill (*Oxyruncus cristatus*).

WITH their long legs, very short neck and tail and short rounded wings, **gnateaters** have the appearance of a dumpy, tailless robin. The males of most species have a distinctive tuft of often very long white or silvery-white feathers behind their eyes; the females sometimes have a similar but less conspicuous tuft.

The eight species of gnateaters are distributed across most of Brazil and adjacent countries, but few species overlap. Even where the ranges of two species do overlap, they often occupy different habitats. They are mainly ground-dwelling forest birds and although it is relatively easy to call them into view, they normally skulk in dense undergrowth.

When approached Rufous gnateaters give sharp alarm calls very different from their melodious, if simple, song: a series of short whistles gradually increasing in pitch and volume. Other species have similar vocalizations and males of some species can produce a harsh sound with their wings.

Alone or in pairs they work through leaf litter or low vegetation feeding on relatively small insects. The nest is placed close to the ground and made mainly of large leaves and lined with softer plant fibers. Both sexes incubate and will feign injury if disturbed at the nest.

The two species of antpipit (*Corythopis*) used to be included in the gnateater family, but they have little general resemblance to the gnateaters and are now placed with the tyrant flycatchers.   AMH

The **tapaculos** occur mainly in the cooler humid parts of South America at altitudes above 1,000m (3,300ft). Only in the south do they occupy lowland habitats. Although seven genera are restricted to the tropical belt, the greater number of species are in the temperate southern Andes. Only *Scytalopus*, by far the largest genus with 11 species, spans almost the entire range of the family.

Perhaps the most distinctive feature of tapaculos is a large movable flap covering the nostrils. They are rather compact with short rounded wings and large strong feet and legs. The most distinctive species is the Ocellated tapaculo of the northern Andes; it is strikingly patterned, has a very heavy bill, which is markedly flattened on top, and a very long straight hind claw. Most other

species are rather drab and wren-like, particularly in that the tail is usually raised, often lying almost along the bird's back. The tail is usually short, but is long in genera such as the bristlefronts of eastern Brazil.

Tapaculos skulk in thick vegetation. Rarely leaving the ground, they walk (or run rapidly) scratching among ground litter in search of invertebrates and occasional plant material. The difficulty of seeing them is compensated for by their loud and often weird songs. Some species (eg the two bristlefronts and the two huet-huets) are quite musical, but others (especially many of the *Scytalopus* species) produce characteristic monotonous repetitions of one or two unmusical notes.

Nests are usually on or close to the ground, sometimes several meters up in the undergrowth or in tree-hollows, while some (eg the two *Scelorchilus* species) dig nest burrows. Most nests are domes with a small side entrance, although some of the hidden nests are cup-shaped. Eggs are relatively large and round and are incubated by both parents. AMH

The **sharpbill** has a wide but curiously discontinuous distribution from southern Brazil to Costa Rica, with some variation in plumage and voice. Despite being widely distributed and reasonably common in some areas, its tendency to be a solitary bird of rain and cloud forest (from 400–1,800m, 1,300–6,000ft) keeps it poorly known. Even its status as a one-species family is uncertain.

It is a strong direct flier. The male has a serrated edge on his outer primary feathers which may be used to produce sound, but no sound has been associated with the bird's curious display flight. In parts of south Brazil its long thin whistle, smoothly descending from a very high pitch, can be frequently heard in good, usually montane forest, but it generally stays high in the canopy. It will move around in a tit-like fashion in the outermost leaves of the canopy, often hanging upside-down to pick invertebrates from leaf clusters or rolled leaves. It will also hang on bunches of small fruits to feed, rejecting many of the hard stones. Its peculiar sharp bill and short strong legs are well-adapted to these feeding techniques.

So far only one nest has been described. It was saddled onto a small horizontal branch near the top of the canopy of one of the tallest trees (30m, 100ft) in the area. It was a shallow cup of roughly interwoven leaf stalks with a few leaves. The outer surface had a thin coat of mosses, liverworts and spiders' webs secured with a dried saliva-like substance. Young were fed by regurgitation of small fruit and invertebrates. Only one parent was ever in attendance and was thought to be female; certainly birds singing in the breeding season show no interest in nesting activities. AMH

Plantcutters are a small group of South American species of uncertain affinities. Their bill, which earns them their name, has finely serrated edges and is used to pluck and cut buds and tender leaves as well as fruits and seeds. With short rounded wings and relatively long tail they have a heavy undulating flight, usually keeping close to the ground. Although usually occurring singly or in pairs, numbers may accumulate in orchards and small parties of up to six or more occur in winter.

Away from any conflict with man, they live in wooded mountain valleys to an altitude of 3,000m (10,000ft) and on prairie interspersed with bush (especially thorns) and trees. The southern populations of the White-tipped plantcutter, the smallest and brightest species, migrate to winter in bushy pastures of northeast Argentina and Uruguay. The Peruvian plantcutter, the dullest and most tropical species, is more sedentary.

From high in bushes and trees, the males

sing an unmusical song, that of the White-tipped being likened to tree branches rubbing together, to sheep bleating, or to frogs croaking, with other discordant squeaks. Sometimes they make a slow display flight with very rapid wing beats. The Rufous-tailed plantcutter produces a rasping trill. The White-tipped nests inside thick, thorny bushes, or even cacti, but the Rufous-tailed normally nests in tree-forks (often in fruit trees). At least in the White-tipped plantcutter most of the care of the nest and the young is performed by the female, who may raise two broods. Plantcutters have been recorded as hosts to the parasitic Shiny cowbird.   AMH

New Zealand wrens are a small, obscure family of three species with no known affinity to other groups of birds. There was once a fourth species, the Stephen Island wren, which may have been flightless. It was discovered in 1894 when a lighthouse keeper's cat carried in 15 specimens. The cat is assumed to have destroyed the entire remaining population.

The three living species are the Rock wren, the Bush wren and the rifleman; none is a strong flier. Having lived for so long in

The 6 Families of Gnateaters and Other Noisemakers   <small>[E] Endangered.   [I] Threatened, but status indeterminate.</small>

Gnateaters
Family: Conopophagidae
Eight species of the genus *Conopophaga*.
S America. Forest undergrowth. Size: 11–14cm (4.5–6in) long, weight 20–23g (0.7–0.8oz). Plumage: pale brown above, very pale below, head variously patterned (usually including a tuft of long white plumes behind the eye in the male). Voice: simple, melodious whistling. Nest: bowl-shaped near ground. Eggs: 2; yellowish with spots or smudges. Diet: insects.

Tapaculos
Family: Rhinocryptidae
Twenty-nine species in 12 genera.
S and C America. Dense forest, brushland undergrowth. Length: 11–25cm (4.5–10in). Plumage: mostly dark gray or brown with rufous or black and white bars on underparts. Voice: usually loud and repetitive. Nests: grass, twigs, moss, etc, in burrows, tree hollows, thickets. Eggs: 2–4; white. Diet: insects, spiders, some vegetable matter.

Species include: **Black-throated huet-huet** (*Pteroptochos tarnii*), **Brasilia tapaculo** [I] (*Scytalopus novacapitalis*), **Chestnut-throated huet-huet**

(*Pteroptochos castaneus*), **Ocellated tapaculo** (*Acropternis orthonyx*), **Slaty bristle-front** (*Merulaxis ater*), **Stresemann's bristle-front** [I] (*M. stresemanni*).

Sharpbill
Family: Oxyruncidae
Oxyruncus cristatus
C and northern S America. Forest canopy. Length: 17cm (7in). Plumage: green above, heavily blotched white below; yellow to scarlet crest bordered with black; cheeks and throat narrowly barred. Voice: long, smoothly descending whistle. Nest: cup straddling branch. Eggs: 2? Diet: small fruits and invertebrates.

Plantcutters
Family: Phytotomidae
Three species of the genus *Phytotoma*.
W and southern S America. Bushland, low woodland, open cultivation. Length: 17–20cm (7–8in). Plumage: upper parts gray-brown, streaked in male; forehead and underparts rufous (male) or light ocher (female). Nest: shallow untidy structure of twigs in horizontal fork, lined with fine roots, etc. Eggs: 2–4; greenish blue with sparse dark

spotting. Diet: fruit, buds, tender leaves, seeds.

Species include: **Peruvian plantcutter** (*Phytotoma raimondii*), **White-tipped plantcutter** (*P. rutila*).

New Zealand wrens
Family: Xenicidae (or Acanthisittidae)
Three species in 2 genera.
New Zealand. Forest or woodland. Size: 8–10cm (3–4in), weight 6.3–9g (0.2–0.3oz). Plumage: upperparts greenish, underparts whitish with yellow wash on the sides; females are generally duller and are striped brown (blackish above in the rifleman). Voice: Bush wren produces a succession of merging cheeps or subued trill; Rock wren produces a whirring call of three notes and piping sound; rifleman produces a rapidly repeated *zsit–zsit* sound. Nests: built in holes in tree trunks, banks, walls, and posts, of roots, leaves, moss and ferns; lined with feathers. Eggs: 2–5; white; incubation period 19–21 days in the rifleman; nestling period 23–25 days in the rifleman. Diet: arthropods.

Species: **Bush wren** [E] (*Xenicus longipes*), **rifleman** (*Acanthisitta chloris*), **Rock wren** (*X. gilviventris*). Now extinct: **Stephen Island wren** (*Xenicus lyalli*).

Sunbird asitys
Family: Philepittidae
Four species in 2 genera.
Madagascar. Forest. Diet: insects, fruit.

Asitys (genus *Philepitta*), two species. Length: about 15cm (6in). Plumage: male is dark black with yellow fringes on feathers after molting; yellow fringes wear off and greenish wattle develops over the eye; Schlegel's asity has larger extent of yellow with black head and wattle surrounding the eye; females have greenish plumage; bill is black, short and broad. Voice: thrush-like whistle. Eggs: white. Other breeding characteristics unknown. Species: **Schlegel's asity** (*Philepitta schlegeli*), **Velvet asity** (*P. castanea*).

False sunbirds (genus *Neodrepanis*), two species. Length: about 10cm (4in). Plumage: males have metallic blue plumage above, canary yellow below; in the Small-billed wattle sunbird the undersides of both sexes are yellower; females are dark green above, yellowish below; bill is brown, long, tapering and curved. Voice and breeding characteristics unknown. Species: **False sunbird** (*Neodrepanis coruscans*), **Small-billed wattle sunbird** [I] (*N. hypoxantha*).

◀▲ **The rifleman lives on insects and spiders,** spending much of its time foraging for them on large branches and trunks. It is often to be seen working its way up and around tree trunks, taking a spiral route to a height of 6–9m (20–30ft). Having mounted one tree it flies off to the foot of another.

The Rifleman's Assistants at the Nest

Riflemen occasionally have one to three "extra" adult or juvenile birds (ie not parents) to help feed nestlings and fledged offspring. When this occurs in first clutches nestlings are about eight days old. These extras are adults and may be males or females. It appears that they are not necessarily related to the parent birds. The extras' activity at the nest involves feeding offspring, defending them against predators and cleaning the nest.

Two types of extras occur at first-clutch nests: those that help to feed regularly and frequently at only one nest and those that feed sporadically at more than one nest. In one intensively studied population most adult extras were unpaired males who were later in the season seen paired with female offspring from the brood they had earlier been feeding. Though data are inconclusive the increased likelihood of acquiring a mate could be seen as one reason for extras' involvement at the nest.

When young fed by extras left the nest they did not weigh significantly more than those at other nests. However, the benefits of extras may be experienced by parents because the parents might carry less responsibility than they otherwise would for feeding the young and defending the nest.   GHS

the absence of predators they have been ill able to cope with new predators introduced by man and with modification of their habitat. They have a stocky appearance, with large shanks and toes, and almost no tail. Their bill is slender, about the same length as the head; in the rifleman it is slightly upturned. They have soft plumage and short, rounded wings.

The Bush wren and the Rock wren are thought to be examples of an indigenous genus that developed two forms, the former inhabiting vegetation at low altitudes, the latter living in alpine vegetation.

The Rock wren occurs on the mountainous divide of South Island at altitudes between 900 and 2,500m (3,000–8,000ft), preferring sparsely vegetated rock and bolder screes and moraines. It eats mainly insects, foraging for them in cracks and crevices, under bolders and in short, tight plant swards, even when these are covered with snow (in which case the bird moves through air spaces between the snow and the ground surface). It also uses crevices and holes for nest-sites and for caching food. Rock wrens occupy well-defined territories, using three-note calls to advertise the location of their boundaries.

The Bush wren, of which there are three subspecies, could now be extinct in the North and South Islands. As a weak flier, nesting in holes near the ground, it was particularly vulnerable to habitat changes wrought by man and mammal predators introduced by man.

Under modern conditions it is the rifleman that has fared best of all the New Zealand wrens. One of its main habitats, beech forest, remains abundant on both main islands and it has begun to enter cultivated areas. It is slightly more secure than the Bush wren because it nests in holes with tiny openings high in tree trunks.

The rifleman is one of the smallest birds in New Zealand. But a female's egg weighs about 20 percent of her body weight, and since she lays every other day and a complete clutch is five eggs a female produces, in nine days, her own body weight in eggs. This combination probably explains some of the factors influencing the rifleman's breeding characteristics.

Most of the nest building is undertaken by the male rifleman who also increases his mate's intake of food during the 10 days before and during egg-laying by bringing her up to nine food items an hour. Between the laying of each egg there is an interval of two days. The young hatch in an undeveloped condition and then take longer than usual to develop: the breeding cycle for one clutch may take up to 60 days. After the clutch has been laid the male undertakes most of the daytime incubation and is also more active than the female in feeding the young, though this may be done with the assistance of other adults (see box). The young birds put on a lot of weight; prior to fledging they may be considerably heavier than their parents.

Before the young of the first clutch have left the nest their parents have usually started building a nest for a second clutch. This time the breeding pattern differs slightly from the first one, due to the continuing demands of the first brood on the parents. The nest is smaller, loosely built, often unlined. In the period of egg production and during incubation the male does not bring extra food to the female. The size of the second clutch is on average one egg smaller than the first. After all eggs have been laid there is sometimes a pause of several days before incubation begins, probably because the parents are still feeding dependent young from the first clutch.   GHS

Sunbird asitys have two well-known features: differences between the two genera and similarities of False sunbirds with true sunbirds. Their ecology and behavior however are little known. The asitys have been described as "quiet" and "sluggish" with an apparently limited vocal repertoire. They are thought to eat fruit but probably take insects as well. It has been suggested that the False sunbirds' conspicuous long, curved and tapered bill is an adaptation for feeding on nectar and has evolved in the virtual absence of competitors that exploit flowers for nectar and possibly pollen. False sunbirds have a specialized tongue similar to that of other nectar feeders which supports this view. However, few field data exist indicating the feeding preferences of False sunbirds.

The radically different bills and dissimilar plumage of the sunbird asity genera illustrate the wide radiation that has occurred in the family and suggest that intermediate genera may have existed in the past. Indeed Madagascar is well known for the relatively recent extinction of both birds and other animals. The development of obvious differences between false sunbirds and asitys has been paralleled with the evolution of striking similarities with the true sunbirds. These similarities include their tubular tongue, bill shape and biannual molt.

GHS

SWALLOWS

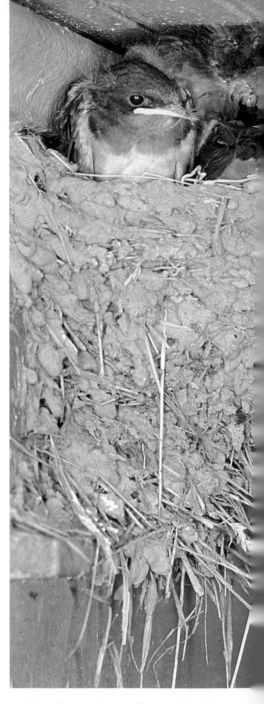

Family: Hirundinidae
Order: Passeriformes (suborder Oscines, part).
Seventy-four species in 17 genera.
Distribution: worldwide except Arctic,
Antarctic and some remote islands.

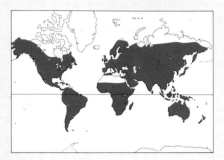

Habitat: open areas along rivers, above forests, etc.

Size: 11.5–21.5cm (4.5–8.5in)
long, weight 10–55g
(0.4–1.9oz).

Plumage: upperparts chiefly metallic blue-
black, green-black or brown; underparts often
white, buff or chestnut; some species have
white or buff rumps. Little or no difference
between sexes (males are sometimes brighter
with longer tails than females). Juveniles are
often duller and have shorter tails than adults.

Voice: simple rapid twittering or buzzing song.

Nests: hole, burrow or open or enclosed mud
nest.

Eggs: usually 3–8 (Southern martin 1 or 2);
white or white with red-brown spots;
incubation: 13–16 days; nestling period:
16–24 days (New World martins 24–28 days).

Diet: chiefly insects.

Species and genera include: **African river
martin** (*Pseudochelidon eurystomina*), **American
rough-winged swallow** (*Stelgidopteryx ruficollis*),
Barn swallow or **swallow** (*Hirundo rustica*), **Blue
swallow** (*H. atrocaerulea*), **Brown-chested martin**
(*Progne tapera*), **Cliff swallow** (*Petrochelidon
pyrrhonota*), **House martin** (*Delichon urbica*),
New World martins (genus *Progne*), **Purple
martin** (*Progne subis*), **Rough-winged swallows**
(genus *Psalidoprocne*), **Sand martin** or **Bank
swallow** (*Riparia riparia*), **Southern martin**
(*Progne modesta*), **Tree swallow** (*Tachycineta
bicolor*), **White-eyed river martin** ⅰ
(*Pseudochelidon sirintarae*).

ⅰ Threatened, but status indeterminate.

▶ **A multitude of hungry birds,** ABOVE the first
annual brood of a Barn swallow. While young
are in the nest each parent will make between
11 and 50 visits per hour to the nest, the exact
number depending on the size of the nestlings
and the weather.

▶ **Drinking in flight,** BELOW a fast-moving
Barn swallow.

S WALLOWS have for long enjoyed a
harmonious association with man, often
nesting in and on his homes and other buildings, whether they be mud huts or concrete
skyscrapers. Because swallows eat insects
they are usually popular birds. In temperate
lands, returning swallows are welcomed as
the symbolic ending to the long, cold winter.

The family is almost cosmopolitan, occurring in open habitats from sea level to high
mountains, from small forest clearings to
extensive grasslands. Twenty-nine species,
including 19 members of the largest genus
Hirundo, are confined to Africa south of the
Sahara; it is likely that the family originated
here. Twenty-five species are found only in
the New World, 5 in Australasia and 4 in
Asia. The rest are widespread in the Old
World. Sand martins and Barn swallows
(the latter known in Europe as the swallow)
have the most extensive ranges, breeding in
both North America and Eurasia.

There are no taxonomic differences
between "swallows" and "martins," the
names being interchangeable. European
Sand martins, for example, are known as
Bank swallows in North America. Although
superficially similar to swifts, swallows and
martins form a distinct family. They are
streamlined in appearance with a short
neck; long, pointed wings with nine primary feathers; a short, broad, flat bill with
wide gape; small, weak feet; and, usually,
a forked tail which makes them very
maneuverable in flight. African and White-
eyed river martins, however, have large,
robust bills and feet and are placed in a
separate subfamily (Pseudochelidoninae)
from other swallows (Hirundininae). The
distribution of the river martins is unusual,
since the ranges of the two species lie
10,000km (6,000mi) apart. African and
American rough-winged swallows are also
distinctive; they have a hook-like thicken-
ing on the outer margin of the first primary
feather, the function of which is unknown.

All swallows are insect-eaters, feeding
almost exclusively while in flight. Tree swallows, however, also eat some seeds and berries (in particular the bayberry), especially
in cold weather when insects are scarce.
Swallows eat a wide variety of insects but
some specialize on a particular size or type.
The largest of the swallows, the New World
martins, for example, consume moths, butterflies and dragonflies. Different species of
swallows living in the same area often have
different diets so competition between them
is avoided. Thus in Britain Barn swallows
eat mainly very large flies such as blue-
bottles and hoverflies; Sand martins eat
smaller flies and mayflies; while House
martins feed on small flies and greenfly.
Swallows in the tropics differ from their
temperate counterparts in eating more flying ants and parasitic wasps but fewer flies
and aphids. Similarly, when in their winter
quarters Barn swallows also feed on ants
rather than flies.

The feeding behavior of swallows changes
with the weather. In cold, wet weather,
when flying insects are scarce, swallows find
it more difficult to find enough insects and
have to spend longer feeding. The few
insects which fly in bad weather occur
mainly near ground level and over water,
so this is where swallows concentrate their
hunting. There is a saying that the weather
will be fair when swallows fly high and wet
when they fly low. This is true of House

martins which feed high up in warm weather, but not of Barn swallows which feed low over the ground whatever the weather. When swallows are flying in bad weather they often use a combination of flapping and gliding instead of flapping their wings all the time, since gliding uses up less energy.

Occasionally swallows catch nonaerial prey, especially in bad weather. They may pick up spiders, ants and other insects from vegetation or from the ground. Barn swallows also take certain moth caterpillars.

Swallows usually carry several insects at a time to their nestlings, compressing the insects into a ball which is carried in the throat. Barn swallows may bring some 400 meals a day to a rapidly growing brood of five, about 8,000 insects in all!

Since insects are scarce in winter at high latitudes, swallows of temperate zones have to migrate, whereas tropical species are resident all year. Swallows are unusual among birds in postponing their post-breeding molt until they have reached their winter quarters. Once there, they often form flocks: many hundreds or even thousands of individuals may roost together in reed-beds or, sometimes, on overhead wires in cities. However, they do not breed in their wintering areas.

Swallows usually return each year to their old nesting site, the oldest individuals arriving first. Birds in their first year, how-ever, usually disperse though they remain within a few kilometers of their parents' nest-site. Old nests are often reused; mud nests may be strengthened with fresh mud. Temperate-zone swallows normally only live for about four years, rarely seven or eight, but a nest made of mud may outlast the occupants and subsequently may be used by a different pair. Burrowing swal-lows, however, such as the Sand martin, usually make new nests because of the presence of parasites in the old one and because old burrows sometimes collapse.

Swallows do not hold exclusive feeding territories but they will defend a small area around the nest from other swallows. The radius of this area varies from a few cen-timeters in the colonial Cliff swallow to about 6m (18ft) in the solitary Tree swal-low. Most species are solitary or nest in small groups, although where suitable nesting sites are scarce large numbers may nest together. Only a few species are truly col-onial: colonies of House and Sand martins may number hundreds, and Cliff swallows thousands of pairs, with nests built very close to each other. Nesting in colonies may enable these swallows to detect and deter predators more quickly; individuals may also find distant or scarce sources of food by following successful foragers.

All swallows are monogamous, although promiscuous matings do occur, especially in colonial species. However, the roles of the sexes vary. Usually only the female incubates and broods the young nestlings, but in a few species, mainly those living in colonies, the male shares these duties. Both sexes feed the nestlings. Individuals from the first broods of Barn swallows and House martins have also been known to help their parents feed the second brood.

Swallows start to breed each year when their insect food has become sufficiently abundant in the spring, in temperate areas, or before the period of peak rainfall in the

▲ **A wide gape** is a particular feature of swallows. It provides a large trap for catching insects in flight and a trowel for scooping up mud when nest-building. These are Pearl-breasted swallows (*Hirundo dimidiata*).

◄ **Miners among swallows.** Sand martins nest in chambers at the ends of tunnels, usually about 1m (39in) deep. The locations they select include sand or clay walls, steep river banks and brick factories. Both members of a pair excavate, requiring only three or four days to bore their tunnel. They nest in colonies: their holes en masse can make a bank look like an Emmenthal cheese.

▼ **Examples of swallows' nests** built of mud. (1) A Barn swallow's cup nest built on a pole. (2) A nest of a Red-rumped swallow (*Hirundo daurica*) and (3) a House martin's nest, both built in roof structures.

tropics since very wet weather prevents swallows collecting enough food to raise a brood successfully. Eggs are laid at daily intervals but bad weather may delay laying for a day or more.

Clutches of temperate species are larger than those of tropical swallows. Island species lay the smallest clutches: the Southern martin of the Galapagos Islands has only one or two eggs whereas its close relative, the Purple martin of North America, lays up to eight. Clutch size declines during the breeding season perhaps because the time or good weather available for feeding the nestlings also becomes reduced. Old females also usually have larger clutches than do young birds. There are one or two broods a year depending on the species and locality, occasionally three in a favorable season. Some individuals, especially first-year birds, only have one brood; female House martins rearing one brood have a lower risk of mortality than double-brooded birds.

The growth of nestling swallows is strongly influenced by the prevailing weather and food abundance. Bad weather sometimes leads to nestlings starving to death, although they can survive a few days of adverse weather.

Most swallow populations have probably benefited from their close association with man, as more artificial nesting sites and more open spaces have extended suitable habitat for them. However, intensification of agriculture, the use of pesticides, and industrial pollution have probably contributed to a decline in some areas. In Britain air pollution in towns and cities has decreased since the Clean Air Act of 1956 and numbers of House martins have since increased in urban areas, although the presence of suitable nesting and feeding sites remains crucial. No species of swallow is considered to be a serious pest, although large flocks of roosting swallows, especially the Brown-chested martin in South America, may create local cleaning, health and safety problems. Indeed, swallows are usually welcomed as they eat many insect pests such as greenfly and midges.

The biology of many swallows is still poorly known; the nests and eggs of some species have never been found. One swallow, the White-eyed river martin, was only discovered in 1968 but may already be close to extinction. Ten individuals were originally found at Lake Boraphet in Thailand in a reedbed roost among other swallows. The breeding sites, however, are unknown. Since 1968 a few individuals have been seen but none were found during an intensive search in 1980–81. This species is protected in Thailand and is listed in the *Red Data Book*.   AKT

Varieties of Nest-sites and Nests in Swallows

Swallows are traditionally birds of open habitat: coasts, rivers, grassland and forest clearings, nesting opportunistically in or on any available surface. As a nest-site, many species just use a hole or crevice in a tree, rock, cave or cliff. Blue swallows will nest in the burrows of antbears; Brown-chested martins in the nests of ovenbirds and tree termites; and American rough-winged swallows in the burrows of kingfishers. A few species, such as the Sand martin, excavate their own burrows in sandy banks. Other swallows, particularly *Hirundo* species, construct a mud nest on a vertical or horizontal surface. The mud nest may be open at the top (Barn swallows) or closed (House martins and Cliff swallows). Within the nest cavity the swallow makes a nest of dry grass and twigs, often lined with feathers.

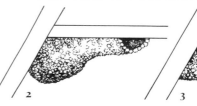

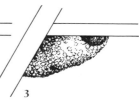

The advent of man and his buildings has increased the number of suitable nesting sites. Houses, barns, bridges, fence posts and nest boxes are all used, as well as some less likely sites, including chimneys, lampshades, old hats left on pegs, the shafts of tin mines, pipes, piles of sawdust, and even moving objects such as boats and trains. Some species now only rarely use natural sites. Purple martins nest mainly in multiple nest boxes ("villages"), Barn swallows and House martins nearly all on buildings and bridges.

Both sexes take part in building a mud nest or burrow, although only the female makes the grass lining. Barn swallows take a week to build a new nest, longer in bad or very dry weather. Over a thousand mouthfuls of mud, as well as dry grass or straw, are needed for a nest. Sand martins spend 5–10 days excavating a burrow, which is 50–100cm (20–40in) long with an enlarged nest chamber at the far end. The burrow usually slopes upward to prevent rain entering.

AKT

LARKS, WAGTAILS AND PIPITS

Families: Alaudidae, Motacillidae
Order: Passeriformes (suborder Oscines—part).
One hundred and thirty species in 18 genera.
Distribution: see map and table.

Larks   Wagtails and pipits

▶ **Representative species of larks, wagtails and pipits.** (1) A Yellow wagtail (*Motacilla flava*) holding an insect. This is the black-headed form of E Europe and Russia. (2) A skylark (*Alauda arvensis*). (3) A Richard's pipit (*Anthus novaeseelandiae*). (4) A Yellow-throated longclaw (a wagtail; *Macronyx croceus*). (5) A Singing bush-lark (*Mirafra javanica*). (6) A Horned lark (*Eremophila alpestris*). (7) A Fischer's finch-lark (*Eremopterix leucopareia*).

▼ **Striking display flights** are a prominent feature of the behavior of the male Bifasciated lark (of North Africa and the Middle East). In these the male takes an upward spiral course and then glides downwards.

Larks are a familiar feature of the bird communities of most open areas within the Old World. They are particularly varied and plentiful in the arid areas of Africa. Many species have evolved elaborate songs which are often given in flight.

Although many species of larks are associated with very arid desert or semidesert areas, this does not mean that they necessarily need hot climates. In the arctic tundras and high on mountain ranges (as well as through much of North America) the Horned lark breeds while a survey found the skylark of Britain to be that country's most widespread breeding bird. Most species are basically brown birds although some have dark markings and white patches on their plumage—in some cases only readily visible when the birds are in flight. For the most part their plumage serves to conceal the birds when they are on the ground and, particularly, when they are incubating. Most species have fairly strong bills although one, the Thick-billed lark, has a monstrous beak similar in size to that of a hawfinch and others, like the Bifasciated lark, have rather long and down-curved bills. Many species have been seen to dig in the ground when feeding—either searching for insects or, more often, for seeds.

In common with many other predominantly ground-dwelling birds larks generally have fairly long legs with long hind claws: these give them additional stability on the ground. Although some species fly at the slightest sign of danger many prefer to escape by walking or running. These species are often masters at using the contours of the ground and any vegetation for concealment during their retreat. Many species have no need of trees or bushes within their area but others regularly perch on posts, bushes or trees. These are often birds of open scrubland and include the varied genus of bush-larks.

Although most species are predominantly seed-eating all take some invertebrate food at times. For example when they are feeding young birds animal protein seems to be essential. In natural habitats the availability of seeds may be severely limited—for instance in desert conditions—and so birds may only be found singly or in pairs. However, where there has been a particularly productive set of seeds, for instance immediately after the rains in a normally arid area or where crops are being cultivated, flocks of dozens or even hundreds of larks may be found. These will normally be of a single species, but flocks of mixed species are not uncommon.

Many species are highly territorial and defend their territories and advertise for their mates, by singing in flight. Many have songs that are very pleasing to man, for example the skylark, woodlark, Bifasciated and Calandra larks. The latter regularly sings from the ground and has often been kept as a songbird in the Mediterranean region. Recognition and warning call notes are also pleasing and more elaborate than those found in some other groups.

In many areas the breeding season of the larks is strongly related to rainy seasons. Breeding starts in time for the young to be in the nest as the weed seed stocks reach their peak. In such circumstances only a single brood may be raised but temperate species often raise two and even three. Almost all species nest on the ground, sometimes in the open but usually at least partly concealed in some vegetation. A few species, mostly from the hottest desert areas, build nests just off the ground in bushes where the circulation of the air may cool the nest slightly. Some incubating birds have been observed spending long periods on the nests standing up and shading the eggs from the sun at its height. Clutch sizes are often low in very hot and dry areas—Fischer's finch-lark generally has a clutch of two and nests in equatorial East Africa. Other temperate species regularly lay four, five or even six

5

eggs—for example the skylark and Crested larks breeding in Europe. A number of desert-dwelling species have been described as building a buttress of stones below the lower edge of their nest which is generally built on a slope. This has been postulated as a method of allowing the nest to drain quickly in the event of a flash flood.

The young always receive some insect food in their first days but many species revert to a vegetable diet well before the chicks move away from the nest, still flightless, within two weeks of hatching. It is thought that this immediate change to vegetable food may lead to the fledglings having rather poor-quality feathers and certainly all lark species so far studied undergo a complete post-juvenile molt. Most other passerines only molt the body plumage at this stage and retain the wing and tail feathers grown in the nest for most of a year.

Modern agricultural techniques within areas where crops are being maximized are probably affecting populations adversely, in some cases through direct poisoning due to misuse of chemicals and in others because weed seeds are gradually being eliminated from cultivated areas and so depriving the birds of their winter food. There is, however, certainly no reason to fear the loss of the familiar song of the skylark and for years to come it will remind people of Shelley's immortal words:

> Hail to thee, blithe Spirit!
> Bird that never wert,
> That from Heaven or near it,
> Pourest thy full heart
> In profuse strains of unpremeditated art.

(From *Ode to a Skylark*, 1819.)   CJM

Although they probably originated in natural grassland in Africa, the **wagtails and pipits** are now one of the most widespread bird families in the world. They must have benefited considerably from forest clearance carried out by man and are now commonly found in farmland of many types. A few species, notably the White wagtail, are strongly associated with man, being common around habitations, parks and golf courses. Several species live in close harmony with domestic livestock, using these animals as "beaters" to flush insect prey from the grassland they inhabit.

All members of this family are essentially birds of open country. Two genera, the longclaws and the Golden pipit, are still largely confined to savanna grasslands in Africa. Wagtails are essentially birds of wet grassland, lakesides and river margins. Several species are resident in Africa, but they are most widespread in Europe and Asia. One species, the Yellow wagtail, has managed to gain a small foothold in Alaska, but each

---

The 2 Families of Larks, Wagtails and Pipits   ▣ Rare.

Larks
Family: Alaudidae
Seventy-six species in 13 genera.
Europe, Asia, Africa, America, Australia. Open country. Size: 12–24cm (5–9in) long, weight 15–75g (0.5–2.6oz). Plumage: most are brown, some with black and white markings; the Black lark is completely black. Voice: melodious songs ranging from short songs to prolonged warbling. Nests: most species build cups of dead grass on the ground; some species build a more complex, partly domed structure. Eggs: 2–6, speckled in most species; incubation period: 11–16 days. Diet: seeds, insects.
Species and genera include:

Bifasciated or **Hoopoe lark** (*Alaemon alaudipes*), **bush-larks** (genus *Mirafra*), **Calandra lark** (*Melanocorypha calandra*), **Crested lark** (*Galerida cristata*), **Fischer's finch-lark** (*Eremopterix leucopareia*), **Horned** or **Shore lark** (*Eremophila alpestris*), **Lesser short-toed lark** (*Calandrella rufescens*), **Razo lark** ▣ (*C. razae*), **Short-toed lark** (*C. cinerea*), **Singing bush-lark** (*Mirafra javanica*), **skylark** (*Alauda arvensis*), **Thick-billed lark** (*Rhamphocoris clotbey*), **woodlark** (*Lullula arborea*).

Wagtails and pipits
Family: Motacillidae
Fifty-four species in 5 genera.
Worldwide except for very high latitudes and some oceanic islands.

Grassland and steppe. Size: 12.5–22cm (5–9in) long, weight 12–50g (0.4–1.8oz). Plumage: wagtails are either black and white or have gray, brown, greenish or bluish upperparts with whitish, yellow or yellowish underparts; in some species there is a boldly contrasting bib or chest band; longclaws and the Golden pipit are mostly brown above (usually heavily streaked) with bright yellow, yellowish or reddish underparts (often with a strikingly contrasting dark pectoral band). Pipits are mostly brown, often heavily streaked, paler below; all species have white or pale outer tail feathers. Voice: sharp call-notes (often repeated when in flight); simple and repetitive song, infrequent in wagtails, elaborate and musical in

pipits and longclaws. Eggs: 2–7, white, gray or brown, typically speckled with brown; incubation period: 12–20 days; nestling period: 12–18 days. Diet: almost entirely arthropods; some mollusks and vegetable matter.

Species and genera include: **Citrine wagtail** or **Yellow-headed wagtail** (*Motacilla citreola*), **Gray wagtail** (*M. cinerea*), **Golden pipit** (*Tmetothylacus tenellus*), **longclaws** (genus *Macronyx*), **Meadow pipit** (*Anthus pratensis*), **Mountain wagtail** (*Motacilla clara*), **pipits** (genus *Anthus*), **Sokoke pipit** ▣ (*A. sokokensis*), **wagtails** (genera *Dendronanthus*, *Motacilla*), **White** or **Pied wagtail** (*Motacilla alba*), **Yellow wagtail** (*M. flava*).

▷ **A wagtail associated with watercourses**
OVERLEAF is the Gray wagtail (*Motacilla cinerea*).
The numbers in wagtail broods vary with
latitude. Species living in equatorial regions
produce two or three young; the Gray wagtail
inhabits most of Europe and the Middle East.

▲ **Bill types of larks.** Several larks inhabit the
veld of southern Africa. They can be divided
into two groups, those that are primarily grain-
eaters (granivorous) and those that are
primarily insect-eaters (insectivorous). Insect
eaters have longish bills (1, 2), grain-eaters
have short, stubby bills (3, 4). (1) Spike-heeled
lark (*Certhilauda albofasciata*). (2) Fawn-colored
lark (*Mirafra africanoides*). (3) Stark's lark
(*Calandrella starki*). (4) Pink-billed lark
(*Calandrella conirostris*).

◀ **A lark of the African savanna**, the Flappet
lark (*Mirafra rufocinnamomea*).

▷ **One of the eight species of longclaws**, the
Pangani longclaw (*Macronyx aurantigula*). They
form a genus of wagtails and pipits.

▼ **Out on the water**, a juvenile White wagtail.
The dark plumage will soon be lost.

autumn these birds return across the Bering
Sea to winter in Southeast Asia, along with
their fellows from the Old World. Members
of the most widespread genus, the pipits, are
almost worldwide in distribution and are
most successful in areas of dry grassland,
subdesert or open woodland. Many species
are strongly migratory, moving from high
latitudes towards or across the Equator in
winter, or from hill and mountain tops
down towards the coast.

Wagtails and pipits are mostly small,
rather slender birds, with characteristically
long tail and long legs. All species have long
toes and often very elongate claws, particularly to the hind toe. In most species the bill
is slim and rather long, but in longclaws it
is rather more robust, so as to deal with the
strong bodies of their mostly beetle prey.

The Golden pipit and the longclaws have
mostly dull, cryptically colored upperparts.
In contrast their underparts are strikingly
colored, often yellow, and usually with a
bold dark breast band. This is used to effect
when in display, during which birds raise
their bill to show off their chin and throat,
and pout their chest.

The wagtails and the pipits have evolved
opposite extremes of plumage patterning
and coloration, which seems to relate to
their reproductive behavior. Pipits are very
inconspicuously colored, mostly brown and
often heavily streaked, but they have usually a very conspicuous song flight and,
though rather simple and repetitive, their
song is often loud and carries far. In contrast, wagtails are brightly plumed with
either striking patterns of black and white
or combinations of bluish, greenish or olive
upperparts and bright yellow or yellowish
underparts. As their name implies, these
birds often wag their tail in a prominent
fashion which may well serve as an effective
territorial signal, to maintain spacing
between neighboring birds. Whilst they
have piercing call notes, their songs are
mostly rather quiet and used much less
frequently than in the pipits. Several wagtail
species exhibit very striking racial differences in plumage pattern. In the Yellow
wagtail these differences have led some
authorities to split the groups into as many
as 14 separate subspecies on the basis of
coloration, largely that of the head. However, at the boundaries between different
races many birds with intermediate
plumage characteristics occur, suggesting a
considerable degree of interbreeding.

Wagtails and pipits are extremely adept
at catching insects, since they form the bulk
of the diet of most species. The most sedentary prey are merely picked from amongst
vegetation or stones, but more mobile prey
may be secured by a sudden lunge, a rapid
running pursuit or by flycatching. The morphology of individual wagtail and pipit species seems to be closely related to the
situation in which they most commonly find
their prey, and hence to the feeding techniques they most often employ. For example, in wagtails the lengths of the tail and
legs appear to be inversely related, associated with the proportions of picking or fly-
catching feeding activity. At one extreme
the Citrine wagtail has very long legs and
a short tail, and spends much of its time
wading in the shallow margins of lakes and

slow-flowing rivers, picking insects and perhaps mollusks from below or on the surface of the water. In contrast the Gray wagtail has a very long tail and rather short legs. It is found by fast-flowing mountain streams, often perching on prominent rocks from which it sallies forth to catch insects in flight above water. Here its long tail probably acts as an efficient rudder, enabling complicated aerial maneuvers to be readily accomplished. However, wagtails and pipits are less agile fliers than, for example, swallows, and hence prefer to feed on the least agile flying insects.

The breeding season of some species is closely linked with the times at which suitable prey emerge. Thus Meadow pipits may feed their young on only one or two species of cranefly which occur in great abundance in some upland grasslands and heaths. Similarly, Gray wagtails may concentrate on the clumsily flying mayflies that emerge seasonally from the waters of the rivers they live beside.

Naturally most wagtails and pipits nest on the ground, making a fairly deep nest, often at the base of a clump of concealing vegetation. Some pipits also use holes in the dry banks of temporary rivers or in small cliff faces, Gray and Mountain wagtails utilize tree roots, holes in riverbanks and bridges, and White wagtails use holes in screes, drystone walls, crevices in buildings and quite often the old discarded nest of another bird species.

Many wagtails and pipits are highly migratory and several species annually traverse the Sahara Desert during journeys between breeding and wintering areas. This may involve them in continuous nonstop flights of over two and a half days' duration and to achieve this they almost double their body weight by accumulating fat reserves (the fuel for the journey) before setting out. In winter many species associate in large flocks, particularly when roosting at night. This has enabled several species to be caught in large numbers for ringing and other scientific studies. Once they have located a suitable wintering area during their first year of life, most birds appear to be remarkably faithful to this in subsequent winters. Thus although their average annual mortality is about 50 percent, which is normal for small birds, at least one Yellow wagtail has been retrapped in its winter roost in West Africa over seven years after it was originally caught and ringed there. This particular bird must thus have successfully crossed the Sahara Desert at least 13 times in its lifetime.   BW

BULBULS

Family: Pycnonotidae
Order: Passeriformes (suborder Oscines, part).
One hundred and eighteen species in 16 genera.
Distribution: Africa, Asia Minor, Middle East, India, Southern Asia, Far East, Java, Borneo, etc; successfully introduced elsewhere.

Habitat: forest thickets, scrubland; many species have adapted to rural cultivated areas and suburban areas.

Size: length 15–28cm (6–11in), weight 20–65g (0.7–2.3oz). In some greenbul species females are much smaller than males.

Plumage: dull brown, gray or green, rarely black, often with bright contrasting patches of red, white or yellow, which is nearly always on the head or under tail coverts. Sexes are normally similar in appearance; females are sometimes a little duller.

Voice: wide range of single and double notes, whistles and chattering calls; many species are exceptionally noisy.

Nests: in the fork of a tree or bush, built of twigs, leaves, spiders' webs and other materials; often lined with fine roots or grass; shallow, usually substantial but some insubstantial.

Eggs: 2–5, pink or white, blotched with various shades of purple, brown or red; about 2.5 × 1.8cm (1 × 0.7in).

Incubation period: 11–14 days.

Nesting period: probably 14–18 days.

Diet: fruit, berries, buds; some species eat insects.

Species and genera include: **Black bulbul** (*Hypsipetes madagascariensis*), **Black-headed bulbul** (*Pycnonotus xanthopygos*), **Brown-eared bulbul** (*Hypsipetes amaurotis*), **Common bulbul** (*Pycnonotus barbatus*), **finch-billed bulbuls** (genus *Spizixos*), **Pale-olive greenbul** (*Phyllastrephus fulviventris*), **Red-vented bulbul** (*Pycnonotus cafer*), **Red-whiskered bulbul** (*P. jocosus*).

▶ **The Black-headed bulbul** of Southeast Asia produces lively, sharp musical chirps. It inhabits stream sides, second growth and coastal scrub.

BULBULS are basically forest dwellers but a number of species have adapted to a variety of other habitats; it is perhaps this adaptability that has made them so popular with man. They make pleasing cage birds and many of them are cheery songsters, which probably explains why they have been introduced to so many parts of the world, either intentionally or accidentally, and why so many of these introductions have been successful. Two species have adapted particularly well, the Red-whiskered bulbul, which has established itself in the USA, southern Malaya, Australia, Mauritius, Singapore, and the Nicobar and Hawaiian Island groups, and the Red-vented bulbul, which has been successfully introduced to several Pacific islands.

Bulbuls are a well-defined, somewhat primitive group of Old World birds. Their most notable feature is a group of hair-like feathers that spring from the nape. These are often long and in many species form a distinct crest.

Bulbuls have short wings, usually rather more curved from front to back than those of most birds, comprising 10 primary feathers, the first of which is very short. The tail, which is made up of 12 feathers, is medium to long and is either square, rounded or slightly forked. They have a short neck and very well-developed bristles around the gape. Almost all species have relatively slender, slightly downcurved bills with longish narrow or oval nostrils. (There are two exceptions: the finch-billed bulbuls.) In size bulbuls vary from that of a House sparrow to that of a large Mistle thrush. One species widespread in North Africa and the Middle East has now been reclassified as two, viz. the Common bulbul of North Africa and the Black-headed bulbul of the Middle East, the latter having yellow undertail covert feathers and a darker head.

Although bulbuls are now probably most familiar in Asia the family apparently originated in the Ethiopian region: it is in Africa and Madagascar where they have attained their greatest development. Here all but two of the 16 genera occur. As one would expect from birds with such short rounded wings they are feeble flyers and not very migratory—the majority of species do not migrate at all, while others only migrate from one altitude to another, especially in Asia, where they occur from 3,000m (10,000ft) up in the Himalayas down to sea level. Only one species appears to be a true migrant, that is the Brown-eared bulbul, which occurs in Japan, and even then it is only the more northern populations that are

migratory, wintering as far south as Korea. They migrate by day, often in large flocks of up to a thousand.

Nearly all bulbuls are active, alert, noisy, gregarious birds, full of character and movement. They often feed in flocks with other species and are almost always the first to give warning of a predator, whether it be a hawk in the air or a snake or cat on the ground, and they often attract the naturalist's attention to rarer birds such as owls which they discover roosting and then mob and torment with shrieks and screams.

The nesting of bulbuls is relatively straightforward. Many are hardly territorial or aggressive to others of their kind, even during the breeding season, though some, such as the Red-vented bulbul, are quite pugnacious. (In Asia they are even kept as fighting birds on which sums of money are placed, fights occasionally continuing until one bird has killed the other.) The nest is usually built in the fork of a tree or bush, often poorly concealed. Because of this many species are often taken by such predators as cats, crows and lizards and are often parasitized by various species of cuckoos. Most nest at a height of 1.5–9m (5–30ft) although the nest of the Black bulbul has been recorded at over 15m (50ft), while the Pale-olive greenbul nests between 0.5 and 1.6m (2–4ft) and conceals its nest in thick undergrowth such as brambles.

The incubation period is usually 11–14 days, with both sexes taking turns on the eggs, which in some species are extremely beautiful; many have unusually thick hard shells for birds of their size. Normally more than one brood is reared in a year, and the young are fed by both parents.

Although bulbuls are not noted for their nuptial displays, these can nevertheless be quite attractive and certainly make the most of what distinctive features they have. The male Red-vented bulbul, whose mating display is one of the best documented, depresses and spreads his tail laterally to show off his bright crimson undertail coverts while fluttering his spread wings up and down above his head. This is not only used to attract females but to warn off rivals when it is accompanied by a series of defiant calls. Many bulbuls are probably cooperative breeders but this is not documented.

Although bulbuls have been introduced to many different parts of the world it is debatable whether this was a wise policy. They damage valuable crops, especially fruit, and probably cause severe damage when liberated where their natural foods are in short supply.   CW

SHRIKES AND WAXWINGS

Families: Laniidae, Campephagidae, Irenidae, Prionopidae, Vangidae, Bombycillidae, Dulidae
Order: Passeriformes (suborder Oscines, part).
One hundred and eighty-seven species in 38 genera.
Distribution: see maps and table.

Cuckoo shrikes   Palmchat

Shrikes   Vanga shrikes

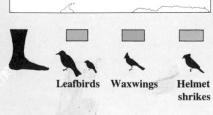

Leafbirds   Waxwings   Helmet shrikes

I N many parts of the world **shrikes** are familiar birds of villages and large towns, being noisy and usually conspicuous because of their bright colors.

The majority of the family (77 percent of species) are endemic to Africa south of the Sahara, and many of these species are probably closely related. Some of the true shrikes occur throughout the northern temperate and Arctic region and some of these are closely related to the African *Lanius* species. The Northern or Great gray shrike is found in North Africa and throughout Europe and the USSR and also occurs in North America south to Mexico. In southern and eastern China the Northern shrike is replaced by the Long-tailed gray shrike. The Rufous-backed shrike also has an extensive range from India through Asia and onto New Guinea. In contrast, the Strong-billed shrike is endemic to the Philippines and the Bornean bristle-head to Borneo. Most African genera have species that either inhabit dense tropical forests, both lowland or montane, or else open deciduous woodland. Thus the puff-back and Sabine's puff-back occur throughout West and Central Africa, the former in savanna and the latter in forest. Some genera are, however, confined to savanna areas (eg the true shrikes, Western long-tailed shrike and the Brubru shrike). Outside Africa shrikes occur in open woodland, orchards and often in pine and oak forests. The African genus *Malaconotus* is remarkable in that pairs of species, one large and one small, that live in the same habitat are color replicas of each other. Thus the Orange-breasted bush-shrike is a small edition of the Gray-headed bush-shrike, both occurring in the savanna of West Africa. Forest species also show this replication and other examples occur elsewhere in Africa. The function of such duplication is uncertain, particularly as the species involved are ecologically separate.

All shrikes have a sharply hooked and notched bill, features that are more prominent in some genera than in others. The powerful beak is used for killing the prey. In the majority of species the legs and feet are strong and the claws sharp for holding prey. The tail is long in many species and often graduated or rounded. Many African shrikes are incredibly beautiful. The gonolek is crimson below and black above apart from a dull yellow crown and under-tail coverts, and other related species are similarly colored. In contrast, the Tropical boubou is black and white and the Sooty boubou is black. The sexes are alike in the first two species but in the case of the Sooty boubou the female is dark olivaceous brown below.

All *Laniarius* species are skulkers in dense habitat and use a variety of contact calls, the sexes duetting, often alternately. The Gray-headed bush-shrike has a green back and yellow underparts and the Gorgeous bush-shrike is similarly colored but has, in addition, a bright red throat bordered by black (less prominent in the female than the male). Other African shrikes are not so brightly colored. Some bush-shrikes have rufous wings, brown backs, pale underparts, patterned heads and black and white tails and in the majority of these the sexes are alike. The Red-backed shrike is well known in Europe but is only one of several *Lanius* species which have rufous or chestnut backs. The male has a gray head and rump, a black eye stripe and a black and white tail; in the female the gray and black areas are replaced by mouse brown. Many *Lanius* species are a mixture of black, gray and white, some have long tails, and the sexes are alike in many. Any differences are confined to flank colors and the presence of some slight barring on the female breast in some species. Two African shrikes, although markedly different in color, are considered closely related, partly because of the social behavior and partly through their distribution. One, the Western long-tailed shrike, is essentially brown above, buff below and is profusely streaked black above and below. Its bill is yellow and on each wing there is a chestnut patch. The other occurs in southern Africa

▲ **The Rufous-backed shrike** (*Lanius schach*) frequents scrub and open country in South and Southeast Asia. Note the large grasshopper impaled in the larder.

◄ **The Red-backed shrike** (*L. collurio*) nests in Europe and western Asia and winters in tropical Africa and Southeast Asia. Its nests are built in bushes and hedges from stalks, roots and twigs. They are lined with grasses.

and is mainly black with white on the wings and flanks.

After breeding in northern latitudes, all populations of the Woodchat shrike and Lesser gray shrike migrate to Africa. Some populations of the Red-backed shrike do also but other populations migrate to Southeast Asia. North–south movements occur in other shrikes that breed at high latitudes but the more southern populations are sedentary. Local movements are suspected for some savanna shrikes in Africa but this has not been proved through ringing. While on migration the *Lanius* species are territorial

and some (Red-backed shrike) defend territories in their winter quarters. In Africa the migrant species are solitary and males return to breeding grounds before the females; in Woodchat shrikes, however, the sexes may arrive already paired.

The Boubou shrikes and smaller bushshrikes are predominantly insect-eaters and feed near and on the ground. The larger species (*Malaconotus*) and puff-backs feed in trees, the former methodically searching the foliage for food, the latter feeding actively like warblers. Small vertebrates and bird eggs make up the diet of the larger species.

The true shrikes characteristically search the ground from a vantage point and pounce on their prey. They may, however, catch insects on the wing and search the ground for food from the air. Many of them store food by impaling their prey on thorns, barbs of wire or else hanging it from the fork of a branch, but not all African *Lanius* species do this. When in Africa the Red-backed shrike does not use such a "larder." The principal food of the Northern shrike is vertebrates, and when dealing with large prey which it could not tear up when frozen it tears the prey into smaller pieces before impaling them, and these may be eaten frozen.

The majority of shrikes breed in pairs; some resident species remain paired for a year or more and maintain their territories outside the breeding season (observed in Boubou shrikes, puff-backs, bush-shrikes). For the majority of species in Africa the breeding season overlaps the end of the dry season and the beginning of the rainy season but in some (Fiscal shrike, Western long-tailed shrike) it is prolonged and ceases during the molting period which is synchronized in a given population. Two or three successful broods are normal for these shrikes. Breeding in northern latitudes is confined to the short summer period (May–July) and one brood is the norm; replacement clutches are quickly laid.

The courtship display of the majority of species has not been described. Male puff-backs puff out their rump feathers and look like puff-balls in their display. Bush-shrikes of the genus *Tchagra* use a display flight accompanied with wing flapping and a duet. The male Woodchat shrike nods his head rapidly up and down while singing to the female and both partners join in a duet, and a similar display is used by the male Red-backed shrike. Courtship feeding of female by the male has been observed in several species of *Lanius* and *Corvinella* and the female's calls (resembling young) quickly reveal the nest location.

Both sexes help build the nest and feed the nestlings. The female alone incubates in *Lanius* and *Corvinella* species but in other genera the limited data available suggest that both sexes incubate. The nests of many of the endemic African shrikes are inconspicuous—neatly formed cups made from tendrils, fiber, grass and spider webs, either secured to a horizontal branch or placed in a fork of a tree. The larger species and the *Lanius* species have more bulky nests of twigs, lined with fibers, tendrils and grass or else (at higher latitudes) with wool, hair

and feathers; these may be placed in trees or thickets.

A good deal of attention has been given in recent years to the study of cooperative breeding, and this occurs in some African shrikes. In southern Ghana, the Western long-tailed shrike lives in groups (average 12 birds) throughout the year and various individuals defend the territory, feed the breeding female, nestlings and fledglings. Breeding in pairs did not occur during a five-year period of study, and two females in their sixth year were still helping in a group.

▲ **Common, intolerant and voracious** is the Fiscal shrike. Its range is Africa south of the Sahara (except for the Kalahari Desert) where it is common in savanna, open country and near human habitations. Birds that come near it are liable to be seized and impaled on thorns or barbed wire. It also frightens birds in cages, especially canaries: they flutter against the bars of their cages where they are seized by the head and killed.

THE 7 FAMILIES OF SHRIKES AND WAXWINGS

Shrikes

Family: Laniidae
Seventy species in 9 genera.
Africa, Europe, USSR, India, Asia, Philippines, Japan, Borneo, New Guinea, N America. Primary and secondary tropical forests, dry and moist savanna woodlands, cultivated orchards. Size: 15–38cm (5.8–15in) long, known weights 10–87g (0.4–3oz). Plumage: many are brightly colored crimson, yellow, green; others are mixtures of black, gray and white; no difference between sexes in most species, but in a few there are marked or slight differences. Voice: some have melodious songs, others have discordant and harsh calls; many species duet, some mimic. Nests: in trees or shrubs, usually supported by twigs, but some are secured to a horizontal branch. Eggs: 2 or 3 in bush shrikes, 4–7 in most other species, ground color ranges from white through blue to pale pink, with brown or purple brown streaks or blotches; incubation: 12–14 days, 15–18 days in some species; nestling period: 16–20 days, 12–15 days in some species. Diet: chiefly insects but some take a variety of invertebrates and the larger species take small vertebrates.

Species and genera include: **Black-headed bush-shrike** (*Tchagra senegala*), **Bornean bristle-head** (*Pityriasis gymnocephala*), **boubous** (genus *Laniarius*), **Brubru shrike** (*Nilaus afer*), **Fiscal shrike** (*Lanius collaris*), **gonolek** (*Laniarius barbarus*), **Gorgeous bush-shrike** (*Malaconotus quadricolor*), **Gray-headed bush-shrike** (*M. blanchoti*), **Lesser gray shrike** (*Lanius minor*), **Long-tailed gray shrike** (*L. sphenocercus*), **Northern** or **Great gray shrike** (*L. excubitor*), **Orange-breasted bush-shrike** (*Malaconotus sulfureopectus*), **puff-back** (*Dryoscopus gambensis*), **puff-backs** (genus *Dryoscopus*), **Rufous-backed shrike** (*Lanius schach*), **Sabine puff-back** (*D. sabini*), **Sooty boubou** (*Laniarius leucorhynchus*), **Strong-billed shrike** (*Lanius validirostris*), **Tropical boubou** (*Laniarius aethiopicus*), **true shrikes** (genus *Lanius*), **Western long-tailed shrike** (*Corvinella corvina*), **Woodchat shrike** (*Lanius senator*). Total threatened species: 2.

Cuckoo-shrikes

Family: Campephagidae
Seventy-two species in 9 genera.
Africa S of the Sahara, Madagascar, India, SE Asia, Philippines, Borneo, Celebes, New Guinea, Australia, some Polynesian and Indian Ocean islands, S and E China, Japan, SE USSR. Dense primary and secondary forest; some species prefer forest edge, cultivated areas and coastal scrub. Size: 14–36cm (5.5–14in) long, known weights 20–111g (0.7–3.9oz). Plumage: many species are pale or dark gray, some black and white, others black and red; females of many species are paler than males; minivets are brightly colored, males being predominantly red and black, females yellow, orange and black. Voice: call notes range from high-pitched whistles (often loud, clear and musical), soft trills to harsh shrike-like notes; the songs of many species are more elaborate versions of the call notes; the Long-billed graybird or cicadabird sounds like a cicada. Nest: high in the fork of a tree or bonded to the top of a horizontal branch, always well concealed; constructed of twigs, roots, mosses, lichens, cobwebs; the nests of some Australian species are occasionally grouped together. Eggs: number varies, 1–5; white, grayish or pale green blotched brown, purple or gray; incubation: where known, 14 days (*Lalage* species), 20–23 days (*Coracina* and *Campephaga* species); fledgling periods: for these two groups, 12 and 20–25 days respectively. Diet: mainly insects, caterpillars, etc; some species take fruit, others take lizards and frogs.

Species and genera include: **Ashy minivet** (*Pericrocotus divaricatus*), **Black-breasted triller** (*Chlamydochaera jefferyi*), **Black cuckoo-shrike** (*Campephaga flava*), **Flame-colored minivet** (*Pericrocotus ethologus*), **flycatcher-shrikes** (genus *Hemipus*), **Ground cuckoo-shrike** (*Pteropodocys maxima*), **Large cuckoo-shrike** (*Coracina novaehollandiae*), **Long-billed graybird** or **cicadabird** (*C. tenuirostris*), **minivets** (genus *Pericrocotus*), **Orange cuckoo-shrike** (*Campochaera sloetii*), **Scarlet minivet** (*Pericrocotus flammeus*), **Small minivet** (*P. cinnamomeus*), **trillers** (genera *Chlamydochaera, Lalage*), **White-winged triller** (*Lalage suerii*), **wood shrikes** (genus *Tephrodornis*). Total threatened species: 2.

Leafbirds

Family: Irenidae
Fourteen species in 3 genera.
From Pakistan through India and SE Asia to the Philippines. Evergreen forest to dry scrub. Size: 14–27cm (5.5–11in) long, about 10–90g (0.4–3.2oz); slight to moderate differences between sexes. Plumage: blue and black or predominantly green; most ioras have white double wing-bars; juveniles resemble females. Voice: strident whistles and melodious mimicking songs. Nest: arboreal open cup. Eggs: 2–3; pinkish speckled and lined red and purple; in Asian fairy bluebird greenish white to stone, streaked brown, gray and purple. Diet: insects, fruit, nectar.

Species and genera include: **Asian fairy bluebird** (*Irena puella*), **Blue-masked leafbird** (*Chloropsis venusta*), **Blue-winged leafbird** (*C. cochinchinensis*), **Common iora** (*Aegithina tiphia*), **Golden-fronted leafbird** (*C. aurifrons*), **Great iora** (*A. lafresnayei*), **Green iora** (*A. viridissima*), **ioras** (genus *Aegithina*), **leafbirds** (genus *Chloropsis*), **Marshall's iora** (*A. nigrolutea*), **Orange-bellied leafbird** (*C. hardwickii*).

Helmet shrikes

Family: Prionopidae
Nine species in 2 genera.
Africa S of the Sahara. Wooded savanna (Red-billed shrike lives in dense lowland forest). Size: 19–25cm (7.5–10in) long, known weights 33–52g (1.2–1.8oz). Plumage: boldly marked black or brown and white, or black and brown with some species having patches of chestnut, gray or yellow; *Prionops* species have prominent crests; most species also have brightly colored wattles. Voice: characteristic sounds are rasping, nasal call notes and bill snapping; some have whistled call notes which sound like those of orioles in the Red-billed shrike. Nests: built on horizontal boughs or in forks high above ground. Eggs: usually 3–5, sometimes 2 or 6; wide range of ground colors (white, pale blue, olive green), blotched or spotted with brown, violet brown and chestnut; incubation and nestling periods: unknown. Diet: insects.

Species include: **Chestnut-fronted helmet shrike** (*Prionops scopifrons*), **Gray-crested helmet shrike** (*P. poliolopha*), **Long-crested helmet shrike** (*P. plumata*), **Retz's red-billed shrike** (*P. retzii*), **Rueppell's white-crowned shrike** (*Eurocephalus rueppelli*), **White-crowned shrike** (*E. anguitimens*), **Yellow-crested helmet shrike** (*P. alberti*).

Vanga shrikes

Family: Vangidae
Thirteen species in 9 genera.
Madagascar (with a subspecies of the Blue vanga occurring on Moheli in the Comoro Islands). Woodland and areas covered in shrubs. Length: 13–32cm (5–12.6in). Plumage: many are metallic black above, white below, some having additional chestnut and gray areas; two species are predominantly blue; sexes differ in some species. Voice: varies between species; loud, tremulous, beautiful whistles in the Rufous and Helmet vangas, drawn out in the Hook-billed vanga, often repeated in the Lafresnaye's vanga; the calls of the Sicklebill falculea are likened to the cry of a playing child. Eggs: 3 or 4; various ground colors (white, cream, pink, greenish blue), profusely marked with brown or gray blotches. Incubation and nestling periods: unknown. Diet: insects.

Species include: **Blue vanga** (*Leptopterus madagascarinus*), **Chabert vanga** (*L. chabert*), **Helmet bird** (*Euryceros prevostii*), **Hook-billed vanga** (*Vanga curvirostris*), **Lafresnaye's vanga** (*Xenopirostris xenopirostris*), **Madagascar nuthatch** (*Hypositta corallirostris*), **Red-tailed vanga** (*Calicalicus madagascariensis*), **Rufous vanga** (*Schetba rufa*), **Sicklebill falculea** (*Falculea palliata*). Total threatened species: 3.

Waxwings and their allies

Family: Bombycillidae
Eight species in 5 genera.
Europe, Asia, N and C America. Woodland and forest. Length: 18–24cm (7–9.5in). Plumage: soft; chiefly brown, gray and black with some red and yellow; sexes similar except in the phainopepla where the male is shiny black and the female olive-gray. Voice: can be noisy, especially when feeding, but songs are poorly developed and are often sung very quietly. The phainopepla sometimes sings in flight. Nests: in trees, built mainly from twigs. Eggs: 2–7; gray, blue or whitish green; incubation: 12–16 days; nestling period: 16–25 days. Diet: berries and insects.

Species: **Black-and-yellow silky flycatcher** (*Phainoptila melanoxantha*), **Bohemian waxwing** or **waxwing** (*Bombycilla garrulus*), **Cedar waxwing** (*B. cedrorum*), **Gray hypocolius** (*Hypocolius ampelinus*), **Gray silky flycatcher** (*Ptilogonys cinereus*), **Japanese waxwing** (*Bombycilla japonica*), **Long-tailed silky flycatcher** (*Ptilogonys caudatus*), **phainopepla** (*Phainopepla nitens*).

Palmchat

Family: Dulidae
Dulus dominicus.
W Indies. Open woodland. Length: 20cm (8in). Plumage: softer than waxwings; upperparts olive, underparts buffy white, boldly streaked with brown. Voice: has a variety of calls but no true song. Nests: large communal nest of twigs. Eggs: 2–4; heavily spotted. Diet: berries, flowers.

Many ideas have been put forward about the usefulness of such behavior and its evolution, and its study will continue to be profitable and worthwhile; the African shrikes are ideal subjects for investigating this behavior. LGG

Although the majority of **cuckoo-shrikes** have shrike-like bills, and colors and plumage patterns resembling cuckoos, they are not related to either shrikes or cuckoos. They are a family of two distinct groups: the cuckoo-shrikes (8 genera, 62 species) which are drably colored in general and range in size from that of a sparrow to that of a dove, and the brightly colored minivets (10 species) which are much more active and gregarious, and wagtail-like in size and shape.

Two genera occur in Africa, one (*Campephaga*, 6 species) is endemic and the other (*Coracina* with a total of 40 species but only 4 in Africa) occurs from East Pakistan through Southeast Asia to New Guinea and Australia. The Ground cuckoo-shrike is endemic to Australia, another (Black-breasted triller) is endemic to Borneo and a third (Orange cuckoo-shrike) to New Guinea. The remainder are distributed throughout the Indian subcontinent, Southeast Asia, Malaysia, Indonesia and northwards to eastern China and Russia.

Cuckoo-shrikes have long pointed wings, moderately long tails (either graduated or rounded), and well-developed rictal bristles which in many species cover the nostrils. Many species (*Campephaga*, *Coracina*, minivets) have spine-like shafts to the feathers of the rump and lower back. These are not normally visible but are raised in defense display. The newly hatched young of some (eg *Campephaga*, *Hemipus*, *Tephrodornis*) are covered with white or gray down which blends in perfectly with the nest and environment. The fledglings are similar to females and differences between sexes are minimal except for *Campephaga* species. In this genus the males are predominantly black with little difference between them and some species have patches of bare yellowish skin at the sides of the gape which is unique in the family. The females are so different from the males that they might easily pass for another species.

In direct contrast the minivets are dainty and strikingly colored with slender narrow wings with a prominent wing bar, and a long strongly graduated tail. There is a marked difference between the sexes. The Scarlet minivet has the whole of the head, throat, back, most of the wings, and central tail feathers black, the rest of the plumage being red. The female is just as striking with yellow replacing the red and also the black on the chin, throat and forehead. In contrast the male Ashy minivet has a gray back and rump, black and white tail, a prominent black nape and crown, and white on the forehead and underparts. The female and juveniles are similarly colored and patterned but not so prominently.

All the family, particularly the minivets, are gregarious and are usually first located in parties of up to 20 or more birds as they move through the tops of trees in search of food. They invariably make up part of any mixed feeding flocks, which are a characteristic of the forests and open woodlands of India and the whole of Southeast Asia. Minivets move through the canopy in noisy parties as they follow each other searching for insects. Flycatcher-shrikes do the same but also catch insects on the wing, and their bills are proportionally shorter and wider at the gape than those of other members of the family. The wood-shrikes are a little more cumbersome and slow moving when feeding but will catch insects in flight and feed on the ground when necessary. The larger *Coracina* species also form loose feeding parties and eat fruit in addition to insects. Most trillers do this as well but the Black-breasted triller, a montane forest species, is thought to eat only fruit. Some trillers in Australia and the Ground cuckoo-shrike feed mainly on the ground. The latter has strong legs well adapted for walking and running. In flight it is much like a cuckoo with black wings and tail contrasting with a gray mantle and head and the finely barred white underparts. The White-winged

repeatedly for some seconds, while calling vigorously; this is then repeated at intervals. However, females also flick their wings (Black cuckoo-shrike) and wing flicking seems characteristic of the group as it is often observed after a bird perches. The male Black cuckoo-shrike performs a moth-like fluttering flight with tail fanned and depressed during his courtship display. In some species (White-winged triller, Large cuckoo-shrike, flycatcher shrikes) both sexes take part in nest building, incubation and feeding nestlings. In others (eg Scarlet minivet, Flame-colored minivet) males feed the nestlings and contribute a little to nest building, whereas in others (Black cuckoo-shrike) the male only helps feed the nestlings, although he may accompany the female while she builds.

Some species are single brooded but others (Small minivet) have two broods in rapid succession, and some (Large cuckoo-shrike in India) have two breeding seasons a year (February–April and August–October). Nest helpers have been recorded at nests of the Small minivet and the Ground cuckoo-shrike. The White-winged triller defends large territories in coastal areas of Australia but in the interior may breed in close proximity to each other.

The Ashy minivet is the only long-distant migrant of the family and leaves its breeding areas in China and USSR to winter in Southeast Asia. Prior to migrating, flocks of up to 150 birds form on the breeding grounds. The rest of the family are mainly sedentary or nomadic but Australian species move north–south over large distances and some Indian species undergo altitudinal migration.　　　　　LGG

▲ **Open forest and forest edge** provide a home for the Large cuckoo-shrike (*Coracina novaehollandiae*) across the enormous expanse of India, South China, Southeast Asia, Australia and New Zealand.

◄ **Parks, gardens and lightly timbered areas** are the preference of the White-winged triller (*Lalage suerii*), which is found in Java, Timor and New Guinea and throughout Australia. This is the female.

triller is a unique member of the family as the male molts from a black and white breeding dress into a nonbreeding dress resembling the female's which is brown above and white (lightly streaked brown) below.

The courtship and breeding behavior of the family have been little studied. The male Scarlet minivet pursues the female into the air from a perch and seizes her tail in his bill. They then spiral down together to the perch and just before landing he releases her tail. Such flights above the tree tops seem to be a feature of all minivets, but some of these may well be territorial in function as a similar spiraling descent has been recorded for a male White-winged triller when defending his territory. In the courtship display of some larger cuckoo-shrikes the male lifts each wing alternately and

The three genera in the **leafbirds** family differ considerably and may not form a natural assemblage. Fairy bluebirds, in particular, need further taxonomic study. Their combination of brilliant blue and black is, nevertheless, repeated in the throat pattern of most male leafbirds (*Chloropsis* species). These two genera also have similar short, thick tarsi with small toes and both shed body feathers profusely when handled—as do bulbuls. It may have escape value in that it may confuse the predator. The intense red eye of adult fairy bluebirds is not shared with others of the family. Leafbirds are otherwise smaller and, as their name implies, green with or without blue on the wing-coverts and tail, and blue, yellow and/or orange on the head and underparts.

Ioras are smaller again, with proportionately long bills and slender legs. They too are basically green or green and yellow with slight to marked plumage differences between the sexes, Great and Common ioras varying in the extent to which males develop a black dorsal breeding plumage. Fairy bluebirds and leafbirds differ significantly in plumage between the sexes, except in the Philippines. There only one species per genus occurs per island. In isolation females of the endemic Philippine fairy bluebird have evolved plumage similar to that of the males and the males of the endemic species of leafbirds have lost their dark head pattern.

Ioras cover the full range of family habitats, from dry acacia scrub (Marshall's iora) through forest edge and cultivation (Common iora) to closed canopy forests (Great and Green). Golden-fronted leafbirds inhabit deciduous monsoon forest; all other species, and the two fairy bluebirds, live in evergreen forest and therefore are of restricted (and shrinking) distribution west of Burma. The Asian fairy bluebird is now extinct in Sri Lanka. Three leafbirds are mountain dwellers: Orange-bellied on the Asian continent, a possible form of the Blue-winged in Borneo and the Blue-masked (with an isolated subspecies of the Golden-fronted in secondary vegetation) in Sumatra.

All species are confined to trees and in forest feed at canopy level. Ioras search foliage for insects, and the Green iora is a regular core member of foraging flocks of mixed species. Fairy bluebirds are fruit-eaters, roaming the forest between scattered sources of food which they may visit in some numbers, advertising themselves with loud, liquid whistles. Leafbirds take both insects and fruit (papped in the bill and the contents sucked out). They also take nectar and may help to pollinate some forest trees. Fairy bluebird songs are inadequately recorded but leafbirds, especially Orange-bellied and Golden-fronted, are fine singers (the latter is also a notorious mimic). Common ioras are conspicuous by their loud, varied calls and the males of at least Common and Great ioras also perform a parachute display flight.

Ioras build compact cup nests felted to branches with cobweb. The few leafbird nests that have been described also incorporate cobweb but are suspended by the rim from twin twigs. Asian fairy bluebirds form a cup of rootlets and moss and liverworts on a platform of twigs in a sapling or small forest tree; only the female builds and incubates but both sexes feed the young. Common ioras may separate their two fledglings, the parents tending one each.

DRW

Many species of tropical birds are gregarious in both breeding and nonbreeding seasons. Such sociability is one of the most important field characteristics of **helmet shrikes**. They always are found in parties of up to 12 or more birds, often with other species.

Although the savanna helmet shrikes have a wide distribution, the ranges of the different species usually do not overlap and when they do overlap are ecologically separate. Thus the Long-crested helmet shrike has several subspecies in its wide range of latitude (15°N–25°S) but is replaced in

Kenya by the Gray-crested helmet shrike, and in the highlands of the eastern Congo by the Yellow-crested helmet shrike. In areas where it occurs together with both Retz's red-billed shrike and the Chestnut-fronted helmet shrike, the Long-crested helmet shrike searches low down on or near the ground while Retz's searches for insects high up in the canopy; the Chestnut-fronted helmet shrike being smaller than the other two is thought to feed on different prey from the others. The insect diet of helmet shrikes is varied (beetles, caterpillars, grasshoppers, mantises) and small geckos are occasionally

▲ **The nest of the Common iora** (a leafbird) is usually built between 2 and 4m (6.5–13ft) up a tree and consists of fine grasses of fibers plastered with cobwebs. The breeding season is mainly July and August when two or three eggs are laid. This species is common in India, Southwest China, the Greater Sundas and Palawan.

◄ **The Chabert vanga** (a vanga shrike) is restricted to Madagascar where it often forms small flocks. They fly from tree to tree, in undulating flight, looking out for small and medium-sized insects.

taken by the Long-crested helmet shrike. The *Eurocephalus* species feed mainly on ground-living prey, pouncing on them from a vantage point.

The bill of helmet shrikes is strong, sharply hooked at the tip, and either black or red. The tail is long and rounded and the feet are strong. As a family they are distinctive in having scales (scutellations) on both the side and front of the tarsus. The Long-crested helmet shrike has a black back, white underparts, gray head and white crest. Most red-billed species are mainly dark slate gray-brown with black head and

breast, the exception being the Chestnut-fronted helmet shrike which has a black back, throat and tail, a white head and chestnut and white underparts. The Yellow-crested helmet shrike is wholly black other than its crest, although this is dull grayish white in young birds. The two white-headed species are distinguished by their brown and white plumage, one (White-crowned shrike) having a brown rump, the other (Rueppell's white-crowned shrike) a white one.

Additional birds, other than the breeding pair, have been recorded as helping in nest construction and/or in feeding nestlings of

the Long-crested helmet shrike, the Gray-crested helmet shrike and the Chestnut-fronted shrike. This cooperative breeding may occur in others but not, apparently, in Retz's red-billed shrike. However, several pairs of this and the other three helmet shrikes may build nests close together, forming a loose colony. Breeding occurs mainly in the dry season, but extends into the wet season, at least for some species. In central East Africa several of the helmet shrikes occur in the same area.   LGG

The **vanga shrikes** or vangas are a good example of what happens when a unique stock of birds (possibly belonging to the helmet shrikes) becomes established on a large isolated island containing only a few other groups of birds. On Madagascar they have filled the ecological niches that, in other parts of the world, are occupied by woodpeckers, shrikes, tits and nuthatches. As a result they differ markedly in size and color, and even more in the shape of the bill: to describe one would draw a picture atypical of the group. But similarity of the skull's shape and of the structure of the bony palate are the basis for placing them in one family. They are found in wet forests (Rufous vanga, Helmet vanga, Madagascar nuthatch), dry forests and open savanna (Sicklebill falculea) and in semidesert

(Lafresnaye's vanga). The size and shape of their bills reflect the size of insect prey taken, their location and the mode of capture. The larger species have shrike-like bills with a characteristic hook at the tip, the bill of the Helmet vanga having a relatively large casque (enlargement) which is bright blue. These search the foliage for large insects and also capture small vertebrates, chameleons and amphibians in the manner of small birds of prey. The three species of *Xenopirostris* have horizontally compressed bills and sit immobile on a twig and catch passing insects like a flycatcher. The bills of the Red-tailed vanga and Madagascar nuthatch are much finer, the former hunting small insects along branches like tits, the latter searching trunks and major branches in the same way as true nuthatches but always moving upwards while searching. The Sicklebill falculea's long curved bill is well adapted for locating prey in crevices in the bark of trees, and this species takes the place of woodpeckers.

In those species studied both sexes help in nest construction, incubation and feeding young; an extra member of the same species has been seen at a nest of a Chabert vanga that was being built. The nests of the majority are neat cups made from small leaves, roots, fibers and bark all bound to the support with spider web but, in marked con-

▲▶ **Representative species of shrikes and waxwings.** (**1**) A Large cuckoo-shrike (*Coracina novaehollandiae*). (**2**) A Northern shrike (*Lanius excubitor*). (**3**) A Red-shouldered cuckoo-shrike (*Campephaga phoenicea*). (**4**) A Golden-fronted leafbird (*Chloropsis aurifrons*). (**5**) A Bohemian waxwing (*Bombycilla garrulus*). (**6**) A Long-crested helmet shrike (*Prionops plumata*). (**7**) A Helmet brid (a vanga shrike; *Euryceros prevostii*) holding prey. (**8**) A palmchat (*Dulus dominicus*). (**9**) A Burchell's gonolek or Crimson-breasted shrike (*Laniarius atrococcineus*).

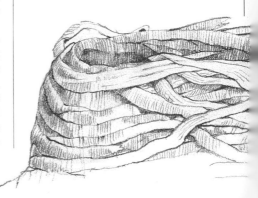

trast, that of the Sicklebill falculea is made from twigs and is like that of a crow.

Most of the vanga shrikes are gregarious in the nonbreeding season, feeding and moving in loose flocks of 4–12 individuals (Chabert vanga, Rufous vanga), but as high as 25 or more in the Sicklebill falculea; others join flocks of mixed species which may include other vangas (eg Blue vanga, Red-tailed vanga). In contrast the Hook-billed vanga and Lafresnaye's vanga are usually solitary.

Of all the endemic groups on Madagascar the Vanga shrikes are the most successful, both in number of species and abundance, but their survival is threatened by the destruction of their forest and wooded habitats.   LGG

The eight species of **waxwings** all depend to a large extent on fruit and are gregarious at some times of year. Although the biology of the true waxwings is quite well known that of their tropical relatives is poorly understood.

The three species of true waxwings are

widely distributed across the coniferous forests of northern Asia, Europe and America. All are similar in ecology and appearance. The name waxwing refers to sealing-wax-like red drops at the tips of the adults' secondary feathers (and more rarely on the tail). The function of these drops is not known. In many other ways too, waxwings are mysterious birds; unpredictable in the timing, numbers and location of their occurrence. They were once thought to be bad omens, which earned them the name "pest-bird" in some parts of Europe.

Waxwings have soft silky plumage, drab colors, short stout bills and legs, long claws and prominent crests. They have relatively long wings which allow them to fly fast. Speeds of up to 46kh (29mph) have been measured for Cedar waxwings. Their flight is characteristically strong and undulating.

All species rely on berries for much of their food, although in spring and summer petals and insects are eaten. Insects are caught on the wing, by fly-catching from high exposed branches, and include such agile prey as dragonflies. Captured insects are brought to a perch to be eaten. The Bohemian waxwing turns to fruits as soon as they appear and will take raspberries, hawthorn, rowan, cedar, juniper, mistletoe and many domestic fruits. These birds will gorge themselves on berries in one place until they seem hardly able to fly, stripping the bushes clean before moving on. An occasional consequence of eating fermenting berries is that waxwings can sometimes be found showing signs of intoxication! Their reliance on fruit and their nomadic habits in winter may make them important dispersers of seeds. However, since seeds can pass through the digestive tract in as little as 16 minutes most seeds will presumably be voided near to where they were eaten.

Waxwings feed mainly in trees, though they will sometimes pluck at groups of berries while hovering at the edge of a bush or tree. They visit the ground to feed, but more often to drink. They are catholic in their tastes and will be attracted to bird tables (feeding stations) by the provision of currants, raisins, dates or prunes. In the wild they will feed on flowing sap. Waxwings are often very tame and will enter cities and feed near the feet of people.

All waxwings are monogamous. Pairing occurs in the winter flocks. A courtship ritual takes place in which a male and female pass an object back and forth between them several times. In Bohemian waxwings the object is sometimes inedible and is not swallowed but in Cedar waxwings

the display ends when one bird eats the berry which the pair have used. It is apparently not known whether it is always one sex or the other that thus terminates the sequence. This display may have its evolutionary origin in courtship feeding of females by males, but has now become highly ritualized.

Pairs do not defend territories, except for the area immediately around the nest. In some areas loose colonies are formed. The nest is built by both parents but the female does most of this work. Nest sites are well away from the main trunk of a tree on a horizontal limb. The height of the nest may be up to 17m (50ft) above the ground. The nest itself is loose and bulky, made of twigs, grass and lichens, and lined with fine grasses, mosses and pine needles. They can often look very similar to loose piles of moss and

◄ **Quick passage.** Waxwings process food at great speed, though it is only half digested when excreted. This feature makes the waxwings important as distributors of the seeds of trees and shrubs. This is the Bohemian waxwing.

► **Annual passage.** BELOW Cedar waxwings of North America breed in southern Canada and the northern USA and migrate to the southern USA and Mexico for winter.

▼ **Head of a phainopepla.** This relative of the waxwing is found in desert scrub from the southwest USA to central Mexico.

twigs that have collected by chance on a branch. Females do all or nearly all of the incubation but are fed on the nest by their mates. Both parents feed the young. Most waxwings are single-brooded but Cedar waxwings are occasionally double-brooded.

Out of the breeding season waxwings are found in flocks which roam widely in search of food. In some years they spread much further south—traveling by day—and in larger numbers than usual. The causes of these invasions are not fully understood but implicated as important factors are food scarcity and population levels. There is some evidence that waxwing numbers grow and fall following a 10-year cycle, independent of food availability, though it is difficult to suggest what other factor could drive such cycles. Waxwings do not seem to return to the same areas to nest every year so it seems that they lead a nomadic existence, probably governed by the availability of berries.

The Gray hypocolius has a restricted distribution in the Tigris-Euphrates Valley. Its biology is little known although it shows some of the characteristics of waxwings (such as flocking outside the breeding season and fruit-eating). It feeds on dates, figs, nightshade and mulberry fruits. A quiet bird with no known song, it spends much of its time hidden in foliage.

The best known silky-flycatcher is the phainopepla whose scientific name means "shining robes". The male is black, with a red eye and white wing-patches. The female is olive-gray. Both sexes have long tails and are crested. Their open cup nest, held together by spider silk, is built largely by the male, who also does much of the incubation during the day.

The biology of the other three silky-flycatchers is less well known. All four species feed on berries, petals and insects. Insects are caught in spectacular flights from high perches. Several insects may be captured on each sortie. All species are loosely colonial.   MA

The **palmchat** is sometimes assigned to the waxwing family. It is similar to them in being a gregarious fruit-eater. It differs from them in having rougher plumage and a heavier bill.

The most striking aspect of palmchat life, as least as we know it at present, is the communal nesting habit. Large nests, over 1m (3ft) in diameter and 3m (about 10ft) high, are built communally by up to 30 pairs (though most nests are probably built by many fewer birds, and some just by pairs). In the lowlands the usual nest-site is in the frond bases of a Royal palm, but conifers are used at higher altitudes. Each pair has its own compartment and entrance to the nest and as far as is known each pair lives independently of the rest. However, it is difficult to observe any interactions which might occur within the nest. The nest is used communally for roosting outside the breeding season. The advantages (and disadvantages) of this communal life-style are not known for this species.

Palmchats live wholly in trees, feeding on berries and flowers. They are common and conspicuous but the details of their biology remain unknown.   MA

DIPPERS AND WRENS

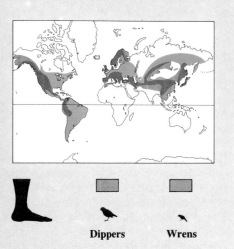

Families: Cinclidae, Troglodytidae
Order: Passeriformes (suborder Oscines, part).
Sixty-four species in 15 genera.
Distribution: see map and table.

Dippers   Wrens

▶ **Desert bird.** ABOVE The spotty Cactus wren
has adapted to desert conditions so successfully
that in the desert areas of SW USA and N and
C Mexico it is often seen and frequently heard
(its song being a distinctive unmusical
monotone of low-pitched notes). It has learnt to
build its nests among the spines of cactus plants
but is famed for its ability to lift and overturn
stones and rocks when out foraging for insects.

▶ **Water bird.** BELOW Like all dippers the
American dipper lives along fast-flowing
streams. Its range stretches from Alaska down
the western flank of North America and
through Central America to Panama; it is often
found in hilly country. The precise locations
and population levels of dippers tend to be
determined by the availability of nest-sites near
rivers and streams.

IPPERS have the remarkable ability to
walk underwater seemingly oblivious of
the current: they are the only truly aquatic
members of the passeriformes. One's first
view of a dipper is often that of a dark bird
flying fast and low, following the twists and
turns of a stream. The Reverend Cotes,
author of Thomas Bewick's *History of British
Birds*, coined the name dipper in 1804: "It
may be seen perched on the top of a stone
in the midst of the torrent, in a continual
dipping motion or short courtsey oft
repeated." The whole body moves up and
down vertically during the dipping motion
and the blinking membrane moves giving
the appearance of a white eye.

Dippers are dark rotund birds like giant
wrens (to which they may be related) with
a thrush-like bill, stumpy tail and brown
legs with strong claws. The five species are
very similar, differing only in range and
plumage color. Species only overlap in
Central Asia; here the White-breasted dipper occupies the higher streams and rivers
while the Brown dipper occurs at lower
altitudes. Dippers swim, dive and walk into
shallow water to obtain their food; they can
remain underwater for 30 seconds but most
dives are much shorter. They have extra
thick body feathers to aid waterproofing and
insulation and can survive winter temperatures down to −45°C (−49°F) if the river
is not completely frozen; they can even feed
under ice.

They are highly territorial in summer and
winter, using a neck-stretching display and
chasing to maintain territorial boundaries.
Territory size is mainly determined by the
extent of stream bed available for feeding.

Dippers breed in early spring when food

is most abundant, and are usually monogamous. Both sexes build the nest (in 14–21
days) although females do most of the building. Nests are placed among tree roots, on
small cliffs, under bridges and in walls and
sometimes behind waterfalls where the
adult must fly through water to the nest.
The bulky nests are often inconspicuous,
either because they are built in crevices or
because the mossy shell closely resembles
the surroundings. The nestling period is
relatively long but nesting success is usually
high (70 percent). If disturbed, nestlings
may explode from the nest after 14 days
(when full body weight is attained); remarkably they can swim and dive expertly before
they can fly. When dippers have second
broods they are perhaps unusual in often
using the same nest (relined); they
frequently use the same nest in successive
years, often for three or four years. Dippers
become very secretive during molt, which
is rapid, and the American dipper can
become flightless. Most populations of dippers are sedentary although some populations move more than 1,000km (625mi)
between summer and winter areas.

Post-fledging mortality is high (over 80
percent in the first six months) but thereafter annual mortality is between 25 and 35
percent. In suitable breeding areas the
habitat is continuously occupied and a non-
breeding surplus of birds either does not
exist or is small and frequents areas unsuitable for breeding. Hence replacement of an
adult which dies in the breeding season is
unusual.   DRL

The Latin word *troglodytes*, from which the
wren family name is derived, means "cave-

The 2 Families of Dippers and Wrens

ⓥ Vulnerable.   ⓡ Rare.   ⓣ Threatened, but status indeterminate.

Dippers
Family: Cinclidae
Five species of the genus *Cinclus*.
Western N and S America, Europe,
N Africa, Asia. Clear running water,
usually among hills and mountains.
Size: 15–17.5cm (6–7in) long, weight
60–80g (2.1–2.8oz). Plumage:
chiefly black, brown or gray,
sometimes with a white "bib", back
or cap; no difference between sexes.
Voice: all species produce a harsh *zit*
call and a rich warbling song. Nests:
large globular structures, about
20 × 20 × 15cm deep (8 × 8 × 6in)
with an opening 6cm (2.5in) in
diameter, usually over running
water; constructed of mosses and
lined with grasses and old leaves.
Eggs: 4–6, usually 5, white;

incubation period: 16–17 days;
nestling period 17–25 days, usually
22–23 if undisturbed. Diet: chiefly
aquatic larvae, especially of stoneflies,
mayflies, caddisflies; also crustaceans,
mollusks; occasionally eat small fish,
tadpoles.

Species: **American dipper** (*Cinclus
mexicanus*), **Brown dipper** (*C. pallasii*),
Rufous-throated dipper ⓣ (*C. schultzi*),
White-breasted dipper or **dipper**
(*C. cinclus*), **White-capped dipper**
(*C. leucocephalus*).

Wrens
Family: Troglodytidae
Fifty-nine species in 14 genera.
N, C, S America, Common wren in
Eurasia and just into N Africa. Dense,
low undergrowth in forest or by

watercourses; rocky and semidesert
localities. Size: most 7.5–12.5cm (3–
5in) long, weight 8–15g (0.3–0.5oz);
the largest is the Cactus wren, 16–
22cm (6.5–9in) long; females are
sometimes slightly smaller than
males. Plumage: brown, cinnamon or
rufous with dark barring above; paler
and sometimes spotted below; no
striking differences between sexes.
Voice: varies from long single whistles
to songs containing hundreds of notes
and melodious and intricate
alternating duets. Nests: suspended in
vegetation, holes or under overhangs;
always roofed with a side entrance
and sometimes with an access tunnel;
typically 8–12cm (3–5in) high,
6–10cm (2.5–4in) wide; Cactus
wrens, however, build structures up
to 60cm (24in) by 45cm (18in). Eggs:

maximum of 10 in northern
temperate species; 2–4 in the tropics;
white with red or reddish flecking;
1.3 × 1.8cm (0.5 × 0.5in) by 1.8–
2.4cm (2.5–4in). Incubation period:
12–20 days; nestling period: 12–18
days. Diet: exclusively invertebrates,
mainly insects, spiders, etc; also
butterfly and moth larvae and adults.

Species include: **Apolinar's marsh-
wren** ⓥ (*Cistothorus apolinari*), **Cactus
wren** (*Campylorhynchus
brunneicapillus*), **Common, European**
or **Winter wren** (*Troglodytes
troglodytes*), **Flutist wren**
(*Microcerculus ustulatus*), **House wren**
(*Troglodytes aedon*), **Long-billed marsh
wren** (*Cistothorus palustris*), **Musician**
or **Song wren** (*Cyphorhinus aradus*),
Zapata wren ⓡ (*Ferminia cerverai*).

dweller"—a reference to the habit of all **wrens** of building elaborate roofed nests which they use not only to house eggs and nestlings but also as communal roosts and as aids to male courtship. In several species prodigious nest-building is matched with fine energetic singing by the males. Field studies of the polygynous wrens of Europe and North America suggest that the form and extent of both these activities may be extreme, perhaps a result of strong sexual selection through female mate choice. Many of the Central American species are thought to be monogamous, while those in the Cactus wren group (genus *Campylorhynchus*) live in family parties and have evolved a cooperative breeding system: independent young help their parents to raise further broods of young. Thus in the wrens we have a passeriform family of exceptional social diversity, despite the fact that virtually nothing is known about the habits of most of its tropical species.

Members of all 14 genera occur in the area between Mexico and the equator in South America. The broad, blunt wings, evident poor flying ability and small size of most wrens have not, however, prevented them from invading some offshore islands. For instance Cuba has an endemic species in the Zapata wren, and distinct subspecies of the Common wren are found, for example, on Taiwan and on St Kilda (off northwest Scotland). This species, known as the Winter wren in North America, is the sole representative of the family in the Old World. It is therefore thought to have migrated west from Alaska to Siberia, and its range now stretches from the eastern USA to Iceland. Another species with a transcontinental distribution is the House wren, which occurs from the eastern USA to Patagonia. These two forms must obviously be very flexible in their habitat preferences and diet, although they and other species breeding at temperate latitudes, such as the Long-billed marsh wren, undertake seasonal migrations to and from wintering grounds with more equable climates. Other wrens, and especially the numerous forms endemic to Central America, occupy much narrower ecological niches and may be very restricted in distribution.

On the basis of behavior and form wrens fall into two distinct groups. The majority are small, cryptically colored, secretive and rather solitary inhabitants of dense forest understory. They flutter and climb among tangled vegetation in search of tiny insects and other animals that make up their diet.

► **Adaptable bird.** Wrens originated in the New World tropics, but 8,000–9,000 years ago the Common or Winter wren managed to cross the Bering Strait. Since then it has colonized northern Asia, Europe and northwest Africa. It can cope with every kind of habitat except extensive open moorland and dense urban areas.

▼ **Courtship in the Common wren.** A male Common wren's courtship is energetic and involved. The mating sequence begins as a male, sitting on an exposed perch (1) or foraging on the ground, sees a female in his territory. He reacts by flying fast and low straight towards her (2). As the male approaches, the female often flies off and a chase ensues, the male pursuing the female in a twisting, rapid flight (3). These chases often end in a "pounce," in which the male attempts, usually without success, to make physical contact (or possibly to mate) with the female (4).

After this episode the male sings his soft and abbreviated courtship songs to the female and then attempts to lead her towards one of his nests (5). When the female is within a few meters of the nest the male sometimes motions her to enter the nest by repeatedly inserting and withdrawing his head (6). The female may then go inside (7), the male singing meanwhile from a nearby perch. She will not usually emerge for at least 10 seconds, and sometimes not for several minutes (8). Some time later the female brings material for lining the nest (9). Copulation takes place outside the nest during or after this elaborate ritual.

In a minority are the much bigger Cactus wren and its allies, living in the more open semidesert habitats of Central America. Although they have a diet similar to that of their smaller relatives, they move much more boldly, perhaps because they are often in small family flocks which should afford them some protection from predators.

All wrens studied in detail seem to be territorial, at least during the breeding season. The role of song in the defense of space is uncertain, but as a family the wrens are renowned as songsters. Several of the monogamous forest-dwelling species live in pairs all year round and some, including the Musician wren, produce melodic and beautifully coordinated alternating duets.

There seems to be little doubt that the song of the males in polygynous species, such as the Common and Long-billed marsh wrens, serves two roles: in defending territory and attracting several mates—trigamy is not uncommon. Neighboring males spend a large proportion of their time each morning answering each other across well-defined territory boundaries. When a female enters a territory she is courted vigorously by the occupant who sings and leads her to a nest he has already built. Common and House wrens may have three or four nests ready simultaneously for use both in these displays and by females making breeding attempts, which they commence promptly after courtship and the collection of some lining materials for the nest cup—their token gesture towards nest construction. Males of these species may build 6–12 nests in the course of a three-month breeding season, but their efforts are paltry beside those of male Long-billed marsh wrens, who construct as many as 25–35 nests over a similar period. They are built in clusters, some even being semidetached, and appear to have a primarily ceremonial role. Males sing vigorously from these collections of nests and lead any female that appears to several of them in succession. Subsequently the male builds yet another nest, in which the female attempts to breed, usually away from his conspicuous courtship center.

Observations suggest that females in these species have a free choice of where to breed, subject to the availability of usable nests. Consequently one can predict that any trait in males that enhances their ability to attract females will be subject to intense sexual selection. Thus it is no surprise to find that males of polygynous species build more nests, have more elaborate courtship displays and songs, and spend more time singing in the breeding season than do those of monogamous species. These adaptations may be seen as the results of an evolutionary

"arms race" driven over the millennia by a combination of male salesmanship and female sales-resistance. Because they spend so much time attempting to obtain mates male Common and Long-billed marsh wrens never incubate and only help feed their nestlings at the end of the season when, presumably, chances of achieving further productive matings are negligible.

In complete contrast, the Cactus wren is monogamous and uses a cooperative system. Parents produce up to four broods a year, later ones being fed in the nest by both the parents and their independent young from earlier broods. All members of these family groups assist the breeding male in territorial defense against other families, but rather paradoxically all but recently fledged juveniles sleep alone in one of the many large nests dotted about in the cacti on their territory.   PJG

MOCKINGBIRDS

Family: Mimidae
Order: Passeriformes (suborder Oscines, part).
Thirty species in 9 genera.
Distribution: New World, from S Canada to
Tierra del Fuego.

Habitat: scrub (often arid), keeping mainly
close to the ground.

Size: 20–30cm (8–12in),
including a fairly long tail in
most species.

Plumage: most are primarily brown or gray
above, usually with pale or white underparts—
often heavily streaked or spotted. A few are
brighter, either rich brown (Black-capped
mockingthrush) or bright gray blue (Blue
mockingbird). Many have strikingly colored
eyes: red, yellow or white. Sexes are similar.

Voice: powerful, complex songs which in some
species include many noises copied from other
birds or animals.

Nest: largish, untidy cup-nest of grass and
twigs, usually fairly close to (or on) the ground,
but sometimes high up in a tree.

Eggs: usually 2–5; color varies from pale,
whitish to dark greenish-blue, often heavily
streaked or spotted with darker markings.

Incubation: 12–13 days.

Fledging period: 12–13 days; may be longer in
some tropical species.

Species include: **Black-capped mockingthrush**
(*Donacobius atricapillus*), **Black catbird**
(*Dumetella glabrirostris*), **Blue mockingbird**
(*Melanotis caerulescens*), **Brown thrasher**
(*Toxostoma rufum*), **Brown trembler**
(*Cinclocerthia ruficauda*), **Curve-billed thrasher**
(*Toxostoma curvirostre*), **Galapagos mockingbird**
(*Nesomimus trifasciatus*), **Gray catbird**
(*Dumetella carolinensis*), **Northern mockingbird**
or **mockingbird** (*Mimus polyglottos*), **Patagonian
mockingbird** (*M. patagonicus*), **Sage thrasher**
(*Toxostoma montanus*).

▶ **The Curve-billed thrasher** ABOVE usually
builds its nest in the fork of a cholla cactus. It
is made of twigs and lined with fine grasses,
rootlets and feathers.

▶ **Master mimic.** The Northern mockingbird,
widespread in the southern USA, is the chief
mimic in the mockingbird family. Mimicry,
however, constitutes little more than 10
percent of total song output.

THE mockingbird family's name is derived
from the ability of several members of the
family, especially the Northern mockingbird, to copy the noises made by other
animals. Although birds of other species are
the main source for their mimicry, mockingbirds have also been recorded mimicking
frogs, pianos and even human voices. Their
songs are clear, powerful and far-carrying.

The mockingbirds (also known as mimic-
thrushes) are a fairly distinct group of New
World birds, thought to be closely related to
thrushes and wrens. They are mostly
thrush-sized, though they tend to have
longer tails and longish beaks, the latter
often strongly downcurved as in the Curve-
billed thrasher. Many are marked rather like
a "standard" thrush, brown above and
paler below with heavy streaking. A number of others are darker and more uniformly
gray. The brightest is probably the Blue
mockingbird which is a bright, grayish-blue
all over except for a black mask. The Gray
catbird is one of the smaller members of the
family and is somewhat aberrantly colored:
it is a uniform gray all over (darker above
than below) with a black cap and bright
chestnut undertail feathers. Many mockingbirds cock their long tail in a conspicuous
manner.

The family occurs over much of North,
South and Central America except for the
northern parts of Canada; only the Patagonian mockingbird occurs in the southern
third of South America. Mockingbirds are
also found in many Caribbean islands and
in the Galapagos and have been introduced
to Bermuda and Hawaii. Many of the birds
in the northern parts of this range move
southwards for the northern winter; for
example, most Gray and Black catbirds and
Brown thrashers leave Canada during the
winter and the large majority of the Sage
thrashers that breed in the USA probably
spend the winter in Mexico or farther south.
However, some Northern mockingbirds
spend the winter in Canada.

The main habitat of the family is scrub or
forest understory; many species inhabit dry,
near-desert habitats. All use the low, often
dense vegetation as cover and most forage
on the ground. Two exceptions are the
Brown trembler of Dominica and nearby
islands which lives in rainforest and the
Black-capped mockingthrush which lives in
dense vegetation in marshes.

Most mockingbirds take a wide variety of
foods; they spend most of their time hopping
through the undergrowth on their long,
powerful legs. Through much of the season
they will eat ground-living arthropods, but,
in season, they will also take many fruits
and berries. The Galapagos mockingbird
also takes small crabs along the shoreline
and, in addition on some islands, especially
Hood (Española) this species has acquired a
reputation for pecking open unattended
eggs of a wide variety of seabird species and
of stealing eggs of the Galapagos dove and
both the Land and Marine iguanas. Most of
their prey is taken from the ground using
their powerful beak which serves either as
a probe or (as in the case of the eggs) for
breaking into a potential food item.

The resident species spend most of the year in their territory which they defend strongly against other members of their species. Usually they live alone or in pairs, but in some species, such as the Galapagos mockingbird, the birds may live in groups of 4–10 individuals, several of which may help in raising the young. While it is not known for certain what the relationships of the birds in a group are, in some cases the extra members helping to raise a second or subsequent brood in a season are known to be young from an earlier brood of the same pair.

As far as is known all species build rather bulky, untidy nests of twigs in dense vegetation. In most cases the nest is either on the ground or within about 2m (6ft) of the ground, though sometimes pairs may build at heights of 15m (50ft) or more. Two to five (rarely six) eggs are laid and these hatch in about 12–13 days and are raised to the point of leaving the nest in about the same length of time. Breeding commences in the spring or, in some arid areas such as the Galapagos, shortly after the start of the rainy season. The breeding season can be prolonged with two or even three broods being raised. Pairs will often remain together in successive seasons, though in the Gray catbird it has been shown that birds are more likely to separate and/or leave the territory and move to another if they fail to raise young than if they succeed. This is thought to be an adaptation against predators; since most nests that fail do so because they are taken by predators, moving after a nest is lost might result in the parent birds being able to find a safer place to nest.

The Brown trembler of Dominica and other islands of the Lesser Antilles is an aberrant species of mockingbird. It is easily recognized by its habit of trembling its wings (which is probably a social signal to others of its species). It also spends much of its time up in the trees of the rainforest where it forages while clinging to the trunk on its rather short legs. It is thought possible that it has taken over the woodcreeper niche of hunting for insect prey on tree-trunks (woodcreepers are absent from these islands).

The Galapagos mockingbird is particularly interesting in that, as with the Galapagos finches (see p404), it influenced Charles Darwin's thinking on evolution by means of natural selection. The mockingbirds in the Galapagos have differentiated strongly on different islands; four well-marked forms are present and some consider them to be four separate species. CMP

ACCENTORS

Family: Prunellidae

Order: Passeriformes (suborder Oscines, part).
Thirteen species of the genus *Prunella*.
Distribution: Europe, Africa N of the Sahara,
Asia except southern peninsulas.

Habitat: mountainous regions, especially scrub.

Size: length 13–18cm (5–7in), weight 18–26g (0.6–0.9oz).

Plumage: upperparts rufous or brownish gray, streaked or striped in most species; underparts grayish usually with rufous markings. Sexes are similar.

Voice: little known; the dunnock has a high-pitched *tseep* call and a complex song structure.

Nest: open cup of plant fragments and feathers, on the ground or in low scrubs or in a rock crevice.

Eggs: 3–6; ranging from light bluish green to blue; unmarked.

Incubation period: 11–15 days.

Nestling period: 12–14 days.

Diet: mainly insects in summer; seeds and berries in winter.

Species include: **Alpine accentor** (*Prunella collaris*), **Black-throated accentor** (*P. atrogularis*), **dunnock** (*P. modularis*), **Himalayan accentor** (*P. himalayana*), **Maroon-backed accentor** (*P. immaculata*), **Robin accentor** (*P. rubeculoides*), **Siberian accentor** (*P. montanella*).

▶ **Hardy mountain bird.** Most accentor species are mountain-dwellers. This species, the Alpine accentor, is found in the mountains of Northwest Africa, southern and central Europe and Asia. Here one is seen in Nepal, at 4,300m (14,000ft), though it is capable of breeding at 5,000m (16,500ft).

ACCENTORS are small plainly colored birds, usually confined to mountainous regions. They are sparrow-like in appearance but with a more slender and pointed bill. The sexes are similar in plumage but males are larger (with longer wings and heavier) and a little brighter. Until recently they were thought to be most closely related to the thrushes. However, recent biological studies suggest that their nearest relatives are wagtails, pipits, sunbirds, sparrows (*Passer* species) and the cardueline and fringilline finches.

The accentors have the rare distinction of being almost exclusive to the Palearctic region (ie Europe, Africa north of the Sahara and Asia north of the Himalayas). Fairly ubiquitous in this region is the Alpine accentor but it occurs only at high altitudes (probably 1,000–5,000m, about 3,300–16,500ft). This may have resulted in the evolution of many races or subspecies: eight or nine subspecies have been described. All species of accentor except the dunnock breed in mountains: the Himalayan accentor can be found breeding at 5,000m (16,500ft) above sea level; the Robin accentor is also found at high altitudes though it prefers to live in dwarf rhododendron and other scrub, or in willows and sedge in damp meadow. The range of the Siberian accentor reaches northwards beyond the taiga region, whereas one subspecies of the Black-throated accentor (*P. atrogularis fagani*), although native to Central Asia, is found further south in winter. The Maroon-backed accentor is found from Nepal to western China and shows a preference for damp areas deep in coniferous forest. Some of the accentors are migratory, others move only to lower altitudes in winter. The dunnock, however, is known to do both.

Unfortunately information about the behavior and breeding biology of the accentors is rare, except for the dunnock, and even this common species has only recently been studied.

During the breeding season (late March to August) members of this species establish several different types of territory: solitary males, pairs of male and female, or male and female plus an additional male. Bigamy and bigamy plus extra males have also been recorded. It is unclear why some territories contain extra males, and suggesting a function for them is made more difficult by the fact that a pair of accentors with an additional male do not seem to produce more offspring than a solitary pair. However, an extra male sometimes feeds the young, mates with the female, and with the other male defends the territory. Pairs with an extra male have significantly larger territories than do solitary pairs.

In all dunnock populations so far examined there has been an excess of males. This may be because fewer females survive the winter because they have a lower place in the dominance hierarchies.

Another fascinating aspect of the behavior of the dunnock is its unusual precopulatory display. During this display the female stands with her body horizontal to the ground, her head slightly raised, her body feathers partly erected, her wings drooped (which she flicks occasionally), and

her tail raised at an angle of 30 degrees which she vibrates rapidly from side to side. In response to the female's display the male makes tentative hopping movements from side to side at the rear of the female. At the same time he also makes pecking movements towards the female's cloaca. The display lasts about 40 seconds and ends with the male jumping at a slight angle towards the female and the pair making contact with their cloacas for a fraction of a second.

The probable reason for such an elaborate display has recently become clear. Because the female can often be mated by either of two males with whom she shares a territory her mate has to be certain that his mating has been successful. The elaborate pre-copulatory display may be a method whereby he can safeguard the paternity of the offspring. The male's pecking behavior appears to stimulate the female to eject any material she has in her cloaca. This material can contain sperm, ie the female's mate can stimulate her to eject sperm from the extra male. (To prevent the extra male from remating the male guards the female during the critical period.) It has been observed that the intensity of the male's display increases with the likelihood of another male having just mated the female.   MEB

▼ **Named for its drabness.** The dunnock's common name is derived from *dunn*, the Old English word for dark or dull. Modern research has revealed that its behavior is exceptionally interesting: it is one of the few temperate species with a cooperative breeding system.

THRUSHES AND THEIR ALLIES

Family: Muscicapidae
Order: Passeriformes (suborder Oscines, part).
One thousand three hundred and ninety-four
species in 255 genera belonging to 11
subfamilies.
Distribution: worldwide.

THE **thrushes** are a large and widespread group of birds with few characters that clearly distinguish them from related groups such as the babblers, flycatchers and warblers. There is thus no easy definition of a thrush, but most of them show the following features: they have 10 primary feathers, of which the outer one is much reduced in length; the tarsus (shank) is "booted" (not divided into separate scales on the leading edge); the juvenile plumage is spotted; they build cup-shaped nests; and they typically forage on the ground for animal food, supplemented with fruits taken from trees and shrubs.

Most of the thrushes that have been well-studied are basically similar in their social systems. Monogamous pairs defend nesting territories in the breeding season; in resident species pairs may remain together all year. In the nonbreeding season thrushes tend to be highly social, feeding in flocks and, especially in cold weather, roosting communally; but some migratory wheatears defend feeding territories in their winter quarters. The larger thrushes may defend their nests pugnaciously, and one among them is apparently unique in the way in which it does so. Fieldfares nest semi-colonially (an unusual habit in the sub-family) and attack predators which approach their nests by flying at them and "bombarding" them with their feces. Hawks have been known to become so plastered with feces in this way that they have been unable to fly and eventually have succumbed to starvation.

With some 60 species the true thrushes constitute far the largest genus in the sub-family. They occupy a central place in that they appear to be unspecialized and to show the basic type from which the various more specialized groups have radiated. Moreover they are familiar to almost everyone, since in every continent except Australia there is at least one common garden species. No other genus of land birds is so widespread. Eurasia is especially rich in species, the Song thrush, Mistle thrush and blackbird being among the best known of European birds. Their place on garden lawns and playing fields is taken by, for example, the Olive thrush in southern Africa, the Rufous-bellied thrush in Brazil, the Clay-colored thrush in Central America and the American robin in North America.

Many of the true thrushes are noted for their songs, which characteristically are composed of a succession of short, richly warbled or fluty phrases; a few species are remarkable mimics. Their substantial cup nests are strengthened by a layer of mud, often mixed with decaying leaves, and are usually finished with an inner lining of grasses or similar material. Northern species are long-distance migrants, and tropical species nonmigratory, while some species from middle latitudes are partial migrants, some individuals moving south in winter and some remaining in their breeding area.

The ground thrushes are closely related to the true thrushes. They have the same general build but relatively longer, stouter bills, and are further distinguished by a striking, usually black and white, under-wing pattern. They are shy birds, living near the ground in forests, and are mainly confined to Asia and Africa. The only exceptions are the widespread White's thrush whose

▲ **One of the most popular birds** in Britain, northern France and Germany, the robin has become the subject of a rich folklore. Of great interest are the origin and purpose of its conspicuous red breast. A Breton legend recounts how the robin's breast was covered with blood as it tried to pull a thorn from the crown of thorns as Christ hung on the cross. The breast in fact serves as a sign of imminent attack. When a male robin has to deal with an intruder to his territory he erects the feathers on his breast and throat, and the invader usually flees.

◄ **From Portugal to China** lives the Blue rock thrush (*Monticola solitarius*), a lively inhabitant of rocky areas.

breeding range extends, uniquely in the sub-family, to Australia, the Varied thrush of western North America and the Aztec thrush of Mexico.

The large group of robins, robin-chats and related species (including the nightingale) are small thrushes of woodland and tropical forest, mainly ground feeders and with proportionately longer legs than the true thrushes. A few, such as the alethes of tropical Africa, are habitual followers of army ants, feeding on insects flushed by the ants. Some have remarkably fine songs. Another group of small thrushes—chats,

wheatears, and their allies—inhabit more open country, nesting in holes or recesses in the ground; among these, the desert wheatears inhabit country as barren as any in which a bird can survive. These two groups of small thrushes have their head-quarters in Asia and Africa. They are entirely unrepresented in the New World, where—apart from many species of true thrushes—the subfamily is represented by a much smaller variety of forms, most out-standing of which are the Hermit thrush and its relatives in North America, blue-birds, nightingale-thrushes and solitaires.

THE 11 SUBFAMILIES OF THRUSHES, FLYCATCHERS AND THEIR ALLIES

Thrushes

Subfamily: Turdinae
Three hundred and four species in 49 genera.

Worldwide (including many oceanic islands). From tropical forest to desert. Size: 11–33cm (4.3–13in) long, weight 8–220g (0.28–7.7oz). Plumage: varied; many species predominantly shades of gray, brown and white, but many (especially males) with bright patches of all colors except yellow; several species all-black; females generally similar to males in species lacking bright colors; in species with bright colors females are usually distinctly duller than males with contrasting patterning reduced or absent. Voice: many species very musical, producing some of the most beautiful of all bird songs; alarm calls usually sharp and staccato, churring or thin and high-pitched. Nests: open cups in various sites, eg trees, shrubs, on ground, in holes in the ground. Eggs: 2–6, rarely 7 (occasionally more in hole-nesters), whitish, blue, greenish or buff, unmarked or with brown or black spots or more diffuse markings; incubation: 12–15 days; nestling period: usually 11–18 days. Diet: invertebrates of many kind, especially insects and earthworms; most species also take fruit.

Species and genera include: **alethes** (genus *Alethe*), **American robin** (*Turdus migratorius*), **Aztec thrush** (*Zoothera pinicola*), **blackbird** (*Turdus merula*), **bluebirds** (genus *Sialia*), **Clay-colored thrush** (*Turdus grayi*), **cochoas** (genus *Cochoa*), **Desert wheatear** (*Oenanthe deserti*), **fieldfare** (*Turdus pilaris*), **forktails** (genus *Enicurus*), **grandala** (*Grandala coelicolor*), **ground thrushes** (genus *Zoothera*), **Hermit thrush** (*Catharus guttatus*), **Island thrush** (*Turdus poliocephalus*), **Mistle thrush** (*Turdus viscivorus*), **nightingale** (*Luscinia megarhynchos*), **nightingale-thrushes** (genus *Catharus*), **Olive thrush** (*Turdus olivaceus*), **robin** or **Eurasian robin** (*Erithacus rubecula*), **robin-chats** (genus *Cossypha*), **Rufous-bellied thrush** (*Turdus rufiventris*), **solitaires** (genera *Entomodestes*, *Myadestes*), **Song thrush** (*Turdus*

philomelos), **true thrushes** (genus *Turdus*), **Varied thrush** (*Zoothera naevia*), **water-redstarts** (genus *Rhyacornis*), **wheatears** (genus *Oenanthe*), **whistling thrushes** (genus *Myiophoneus*), **White's thrush** or **Golden mountain thrush** (*Zoothera dauma*). Total threatened species: 5.

Babblers

Subfamily: Timaliinae
Two hundred and fifty-two species in 50 genera.

Asia, Africa, Australasia, one in western N America. All types of terrestrial vegetation, from desert scrub to swamp, tropical forest to alpine dwarf shrubs. Size: 10–35cm (4–14in) long, weight 5–150g (0.2–5.3oz). Plumage: highly variable, but many species are cryptic browns and grays; species living in dense forest often include bright yellows, reds and blues; no differences between sexes. Voice: great variety of calls, reminiscent of the entire range of songbird vocalizations; some species have group duets, in others there are antiphonal duets. Nests: usually above ground in bushes or trees, open or domed; rockfowl build mud nests. Eggs: 2–6; variety of colors, but often white or blue; unmarked; incubation period: 14–15 days; nestling period: 13–16 days. Diet: predominantly insects and other invertebrates.

Species and genera include: **Arabian** or **Arabian brown babbler** (*Turdoides squamiceps*), **babaxes** (genus *Babax*), **Black-capped** or **Black-headed sibia** (*Heterophasia capistrata*), **chatterers** (two species of the genus *Turdoides*), **Common babbler** (*Turdoides caudatus*), **Fulvous babbler** (*Turdoides fulvus*), **Iraq babbler** (*T. altirostris*), **Jungle babbler** (*T. striatus*), **laughing thrushes** (genus *Garrulax*), **minlas** (genus *Minla*), **scimitar babblers** (genus *Pomatorhinus*), **shrike-babblers** (genera *Pteruthius, Gampsorhynchus*), **tit-babblers** (genus *Alcippe*), **tree babblers** (genus *Stachyris*), **White-crested laughing thrush** (*Garrulax leucolophus*), **wren babblers** (genera *Kenopia, Napothera, Pnoepyga*, 1 species in *Ptilocichla, Rimator, Spelaeornis, Sphenocichla*), **yuhinas** (genus *Yuhina*).

Old World warblers

Subfamily: Sylviinae
Three hundred and thirty-nine species in 56 genera.

Chiefly Europe, Asia, Africa; small numbers in the New World. All types of vegetation, from grassland to forest. Size: most species 9–16cm (3.5–6.3in) long, weight 5–20g (0.17–0.7oz); several large exceptions, eg the grassbird with maximum length 23cm (9in), weight about 30g (1oz). Plumage: chiefly brown, dull green or yellow, often streaked darker; some tropical species (eg White-winged apalis) are brightly colored; in most species sexes are similar, exceptions include: blackcap, kinglets, some tailorbirds. Voice: calls varied, often harsh in the larger species; songs of some species are simple and stereotyped, but in others complex, varied and melodious. Nests: elaborate, carefully woven cup-shaped or spherical structures placed low in dense vegetation; tailorbirds and some other species stitch leaves together with cobwebs to form a cone in which the nest is sited. Eggs: usually 2–7, pale ground colors with dark spots or blotches; incubation period: 12–14 days; nestling period: 11–15 days, though young may fledge earlier (from 8 days), unable to fly, and are then attended by their parents for some days afterwards. Diet: predominantly insects; some species also eat fruit; many take nectar occasionally; kinglets regularly eat small seeds.

Species and genera include: **Aldabra warbler** (*Bebrornis aldabranus*), **Arctic warbler** (*Phylloscopus borealis*), **blackcap** (*Sylvia atricapilla*), **chiffchaff** (*Phylloscopus collybita*), **cloud-scraper cisticola** (*Cisticola dambo*), **Dartford warbler** (*Sylvia undata*), **fernbird** (*Bowdleria punctata*), **Garden warbler** (*Sylvia borin*), **gnatcatchers** (genus *Polioptila*), **gnatwrens** (genera *Microbates, Ramphocaenus*), **goldcrest** (*Regulus regulus*), **grassbird** (*Sphenoeacus afer*), **grass warblers** (*Cisticola*), **Great reed warbler** (*Acrocephalus arundinaceus*), **Icterine warbler** (*Hippolais icterina*), **kinglets** (four species in the genus *Regulus*),

Long-billed crombec (*Sylvietta rufescens*), **Marsh warbler** (*Acrocephalus palustris*), **Oriole babbler** (*Hypergerus atriceps*), **Red-faced crombec** (*Sylvietta whytii*), **Reed warbler** (*Acrocephalus scirpaceus*), **scrub warblers** (18 species belonging to the genera *Bradypterus, Sylvia*), **Sedge warbler** (*Acrocephalus schoenobaenus*), **spinifex-bird** (*Eremiornis carteri*), **tit-flycatchers** (five species belonging to the genus *Parisoma*), **tit-weaver** (*Pholidornis rushiae*), **whitethroat** (*Sylvia communis*), **White-winged apalis** (*Apalis chariessa*), **willow warblers** (genus *Phylloscopus*). Total threatened species: 4.

Old World flycatchers

Subfamily: Muscicapinae
One hundred and fifty-six species in 28 genera.

Europe, Asia, Africa, Australia, Pacific Islands. Chiefly woodlands, forests, shrubs. Size: 10–21cm (4–8in) long. Plumage: varies considerably, some species plain gray or brown, other black and white or bright blue, yellow or red; little difference between sexes in dull species, marked differences in brightly colored species. Voice: produce a wide range of notes; songs vary from the simple and monotonous to the complex. Nests: a few species are hole nesters, though they do not excavate their own holes; most species build cup nests on tree branches. Eggs: usually 2–6, range 1–8, whitish, greenish or buff, most often with spots; in hole-nesting species eggs are bluish without spots; incubation period: 12–14 days; nestling period: 11–16 days. Diet: mainly insects.

Species include: **Ashy flycatcher** (*Muscicapa caerulescens*), **Blue and white flycatcher** (*Ficedula cyanomelana*), **Collared flycatcher** (*F. albicollis*), **Dusky flycatcher** (*Muscicapa adusta*), **Flame robin** (*Petroica phoenicea*), **Mariqua flycatcher** (*Bradornis mariquensis*), **Pied flycatcher** (*Ficedula hypoleuca*), **Spotted flycatcher** (*Muscicapa striata*), **White-eyed slaty flycatcher** (*Dioptrornis fischeri*). Total threatened species: 2.

Fairy-wrens
Subfamily: Malurinae
Twenty-six species in 5 genera.

New Guinea and Australia. From margins of rain forest to desert steppes, salt pans, coastal swamp, heathland, spinifex tussocks, desert sandplains. Size: 14–22cm (5.5–9in) long, weight 7–37g (0.25–1.3oz). Plumage: varies from bright blue in some males to plain brown. Voice: brief contact calls, churrs and sustained reels of song. Eggs: 2–4, whitish with red-brown speckling; incubation period: 12–15 days; nestling period: 10–12 days. Diet: insects and seeds.

Species and genera include: **Black grass-wren** (*Amytornis housei*), **Carpentarian grass-wren** (*A. dorotheae*), **emu-wrens** (genus *Stipiturus*), **Eyrean grass-wren** 1 (*Amytornis goyderi*), **grass-wrens** (genus *Amytornis*), **Gray grass-wren** (*A. barbatus*), **Purple-crowned fairy-wren** (*Malurus coronatus*), **Red-winged fairy-wren** (*M. elegans*), **Superb blue fairy-wren** (*M. cyaneus*), **true fairy-wrens** (genus *Malurus*), **White-throated grass-wren** (*Amytornis woodwardi*). Total threatened species: 3.

Parrotbills
Subfamily: Paradoxornithinae
Nineteen species in 3 genera.

E Asia with the Bearded tit occurring in W Asia and Europe. Reeds, grass, dense thickets, bamboo. Size: 9–29cm (3.5–11.5in) long, weight 5–36g (0.2–1.3oz) except for the largest species, the Great parrotbill (no data available). Plumage: varying shades of cinnamon-buff or gray; some species have whitish underparts, others have small areas of black on the head or throat. Voice: sounds range from twittering and pinging notes to clear musical or mellow whistles, churring or curious wheezy notes, like the twanging of a guitar. Nests: grass and bamboo leaves bound together with cobwebs in a deep, compact cup shape; situated in reeds or low vegetation. Eggs: 2–7, blue or clay in color with irregular reddish brown, lavender or green marks. Diet: mainly insects; also grass seeds and, in the case of larger species, berries.

Species and genera include: **Bearded tit** or **Bearded reedling** (*Panurus biarmicus*), **Black-browed parrotbill** (*Paradoxornis atrosuperciliaris*), **Brown parrotbill** (*P. unicolor*), **Great parrotbill** (*Conostoma oemodium*), **Red-headed parrotbill** (*Paradoxornis ruficeps*), **Three-toed parrotbill** (*P. paradoxus*), **typical parrotbills** (genus *Paradoxornis*), **Yangtse parrotbill** (*P. heudei*).

Monarch flycatchers
Subfamily: Monarchinae
One hundred and thirty-three species in 25 genera.

Africa, tropical and eastern Asia, Australasia. Forest and woodland. Size: 12–30cm (5–12in) long (including tail), weight 15–40g (0.5–1.4oz). Plumage: often metallic black or gray, or chestnut with white underparts; sexes differ in appearance in some species. Voice: harsh or whistling calls. Nests: cup-shaped, often decorated with lichen, moss, bark or spiders' webs. Eggs: 2–4, white with brown spots or blotches. Diet: most species eat insects; a few also take fruit.

Species and genera include: **Frilled monarch** (*Arses telescophthalmus*), **paradise flycatchers** (genus *Terpsiphone*), **peltops flycatchers** (genus *Peltops*), **puff-backs** (genus *Batis*), **Restless flycatcher** or **scissors-grinder** (*Myiagra inquieta*), **Satin flycatcher** (*M. cyanoleuca*), **shrikebills** (genus *Clytorhynchus*). Total threatened species: 3.

Logrunners
Subfamily: Orthonychinae
Twenty species in 9 genera.

SE Asia, New Guinea, Australia. Desert scrub, woodland, rain forest, usually in dense shrub. Size: 10–30cm (4–12in) long, weight 20–80g (0.7–2.8oz). Plumage: most species are brown, black or white; differences between sexes in appearance vary from slight to marked. Voice: calls range from buzzing to whistling and bell-like sounds. Nests: cup-shaped or domed, usually placed in dense shrubs. Eggs: 1–3; white or pale blue. Incubation period: 17–21 days. Nestling period: 12–14 days. Diet: predominantly insects; also invertebrates and seeds.

Species and genera include: **Blue jewel-babbler** (*Ptilorrhoa caerulescens*), **Chiming wedgebill** (*Psophodes occidentalis*), **Chirruping wedgebill** (*P. cristatus*), **quail-thrushes** (genus *Cinclosoma*), **Western whipbird** (*Psophodes nigrogularis*).

Australasian warblers
Subfamily: Acanthizinae
Fifty-nine species in 19 genera.

SE Asia, New Guinea, Australia, New Zealand, Pacific Islands. Arid shrubland, woodland, forest. Size 8–20cm (3–8in) long, weight 7–40g (0.25–1.4oz). Plumage: usually brown, olive or yellow. Voice: twittering and warbling songs and calls. Nests: neat and domed, often with a hood. Eggs: 2 or 3, occasionally 4, white, sometimes with spots, or dark brown; incubation period: 15–20 days; nestling period: 15–20 days. Diet: insects and seeds.

Species and genera include: **Buff-tailed thornbill** (*Acanthiza reguloides*), **Rock warbler** (*Origma rubricata*), **scrub-wrens** (genus *Sericornis*), **whitefaces** (genus *Aphelocephala*).

Fantail flycatchers
Subfamily: Rhipidurinae
Thirty-eight species the genus *Rhipidura*.

India, S China, SE Asia, New Guinea, Australia, New Zealand, Pacific Islands. Woodland and forest. Size: 13–20cm (5–8in) long, weight 7–25g (0.25–0.9oz). Plumage: black, gray, white, yellow or rufous; sexes similar. Voice: chattering or squeaky calls and songs. Nests: cup or goblet-shaped. Eggs: 2–5, white or cream with brown blotches; incubation period: 13–16 days; nestling period: 12–16 days. Diet: insects.

Species include: **Friendly fantail** (*Rhipidura albolimbata*), **Gray fantail** (*R. fuliginosa*), **Willie wagtail** (*R. leucophrys*).

Thickheads
Subfamily: Pachycephalinae
Forty-eight species in 10 genera.

Australasian and Oriental regions. From rain forest to arid scrub. Size: 12–25cm (5–10in) long, weight 15–100g (0.5–3.5oz). Plumage: mostly gray or brown, but males of some species have brighter colors. Voice: melodious whistling or bell-like songs. Nests: made of sticks, bark, grasses and spiders' webs and placed in a low fork in a tree. Eggs: 2–4, white to olive, sometimes with brown blotches; incubation period: about 17 days; nestling period: 13–16 days. Diet: insects and fruit.

Species and genera include: **Golden whistler** (*Pachycephala pectoralis*), **piopio** (*Turnagra capensis*), **pitohuis** (genus *Pitohui*), **Red-lored** or **Red-throated whistler** (*Pachycephala rufogularis*), **Rusty pitohui** (*Pitohui ferrugineus*), **shrike-thrushes** (genus *Colluricincla*), **shrike-tit** (*Falcunculus frontatus*), **whistlers** (genera *Hylocitrea, Pachycephala, Rhagologus*).

Some of these, including the Hermit thrush and solitaires, are among the world's finest songsters, noted for their pure and exquisitely modulated notes.

It seems certain that the main evolutionary radiation of the thrushes took place in East Asia, and it is there that the subfamily is present in greatest variety. The whistling thrushes, which include the largest of all thrushes, live along fast-flowing streams in the Himalayas and other mountains of eastern Asia. They have strongly hooked bills and forage for animal food among rocks at the water's edge. The forktails, slender birds with long tails, and the water-redstarts are also specialists in foraging along the banks of mountain torrents. The grandala, a long-winged and short-legged bird with blue plumage, is so unlike a typical thrush that its inclusion in the subfamily is at first sight surprising. Grandalas are highly aerial, social birds that live above the timberline in the Himalayas and associated mountains, where they feed in flocks on bare mountain slopes. Almost equally unthrushlike are the three species of cochoas. They are wide-billed birds of tropical forest in southeast Asia, with plumage patterned with green, blue and violet. Though little known, they are probably ecological equivalents of the cotingas of tropical America.   DWS

Babblers form a varied assemblage of small to medium-sized songbirds which are an important constituent of the bird populations of tropical Asia. In the middle altitudes of the Himalayas (1,500–3,000m, 5,000–10,000ft) they are the dominant passerines, with 71 species breeding in Nepal alone, out of a resident passerine community of about 350 species. Behavior and feeding ecology within the family are very diverse, with some species of active leaf-gleaners flitting in the forest canopy like warblers and other, robust, heavy-bodied genera rooting like thrushes among leaf litter on the forest floor. The "average" babbler falls between a sparrow and a thrush in size, with short, rounded wings and a longish, rather floppy, tail. They forage in bushes, low vegetation and on the ground.

In Africa the family is represented mainly by the chatterers, which are birds of scrub and savanna. In North Africa, the Middle East and Iran the Fulvous and Arabian babblers and their allies live in sparsely vegetated wadis in open desert. In the Negev Desert of Israel the Arabian babbler is the commonest resident bird, occurring wherever there are a few acacia bushes to provide cover and nest-sites. In contrast, the Iraq babbler inhabits the extensive swamps of the Tigris-Euphrates delta.

At the other extreme of the habitat scale a great diversity of different babblers inhabits the cloud forests of the eastern Himalayas, from tiny wren babblers skulking among rotting logs on the forest floor to the large scimitar babblers, probing with their hoopoe-like bills, and Black-capped sibia, drinking the sap oozing from holes in the trunks of oak trees, after the fashion of North American sapsuckers. Geographically close, but far off in terms of ecology,

◄ ▲ ► **Representative species** of four
subfamilies of thrushes. (1) A Reed warbler
(*Acrocephalus scirpaceus*). (2) A Chestnut-
headed tit-babbler (*Alcippe castaneceps*).
(3) A Pied flycatcher (*Ficedula hypoleuca*).
(4) A Flame robin (*Petroica phoenicea*) holding
an insect. (5) A White-crested laughing thrush
(*Garrulax leucolophus*), (6) An Eastern bluebird
(*Sialia sialis*). (7) A Red-faced crombec
(*Sylvietta whytii*). (8) A Pied babbler (*Turdoides
bicolor*). (9) A White-browed robin-chat
(*Cossypha heuglini*). (10) A Song thrush (*Turdus
philomelos*).

the babaxes inhabit the buckthorn scrub on the southern edge of the Tibetan plateau, in arid high-altitude desert.

In India the Common and Jungle babblers are among the most familiar birds of garden and roadside, moving in noisy bands from tree to tree and sometimes, especially in the early morning, hopping about on tarmac roads. Parties of 5–15 birds are the rule and these normally consist of extended families, with the whole group collaborating to incubate the eggs laid by the dominant female (and presumably fertilized by the dominant male). All members assist in feeding the nestlings, but despite this assistance the young birds grow no faster than other passerines, fledging in about 14 days.

Groups of Jungle babblers defend collective territories; encounters between neighboring groups are very noisy, with most of the birds on each side calling excitedly. Fighting sometimes breaks out in these skirmishes and antagonists can be seen rolling on the ground with their claws locked together, oblivious of the human observer.

The behavior of the more brightly colored laughing thrushes is similar to that of the Jungle babbler, but they often occur in larger groups of up to 100 birds. In the evening these break up into small parties of 2–10 birds which roost separately but within a fairly small area, recombining the next morning. The spectacular White-crested laughing thrush performs a remarkable communal display in which several members take part, prancing together on the forest floor, their white crests raised like helmets, uttering a series of laughing calls that gradually mount to a crescendo. At dawn and dusk these calls are normally answered by neighboring groups, producing a chorus of choruses which echo among the densely forested hills which they inhabit.

In the evergreen rain forests of Southeast Asia and the temperate forests of the Himalayas babblers are important members of the associations of several species of small insect-eating birds that join together for foraging expeditions: a striking feature of the area's bird life. Those involved include minlas, yuhinas, tree babblers, tit-babblers and shrike-babblers, which mix freely with warblers, tits, minivets, treecreepers and woodpeckers to form loosely organized parties, sometimes numbering several hundred, moving steadily through the forest throughout the day and only breaking up in the evening to roost in separate single-species groups.   AJG

Cooperative Breeding in Babblers

Considering the large number of species involved, the babblers are remarkable in being wholly nonmigratory. A few of the high-altitude laughing thrushes move small distances between their summer and winter altitude zones, but this probably entails movements of no more than a few kilometers. Because they are not called upon to do any very sustained flying, and because most species do not take insects on the wing, they tend to be poor at flying, and this is reflected in their short, rounded wings and heavy legs and feet. The fact that they are sedentary has probably contributed to the well-developed social behavior found among many species.

Being poor fliers, babblers tend to remain close to where they were born, giving a good opportunity for young birds to assist their parents in the rearing of their younger siblings. Because groups defend territories year-round there is no annual competition for space and it is more difficult for new territories to become established. In this situation a young bird that remains with its parents until its abilities are fully developed, perhaps after several years, will stand a better chance of reproducing eventually than one that disperses immediately.

In order to form a new territory in the face of strong competition it may be necessary for several birds to collaborate. This is best achieved by groups of siblings, for as all share the same genes derived from their parents any help given to kin thereby benefits the survival of their own genes. In the Jungle babbler groups of sibling males or females sometimes split off from their parental group and roam about in marginal areas. If they encounter a similar coalition of the opposite sex, originating from another group, then they may combine to try to establish a new territory. However, sibling mating has not been recorded and breeding between unrelated individuals seems to be the rule.

The importance of kin associations in setting up new territories provides another incentive for birds to remain in their parental group until they can form a coalition of sufficient strength to attempt to defend their own ground.   AJG

▲ **One of Europe's smallest birds,** the Goldcrest.

◄ **Low-flying forager.** Where several genera of babblers are present each is equipped to exploit a particular section of habitat. The scimitar-babblers of Southeast Asia are active just above ground level. They fly around creepers and bushes with the ease of acrobats, using their long tails for balance. With their long bills they probe for insects. By contrast the terrestrial wren-babblers have long legs, short tails and short bills. This is the Rusty-cheeked scimitar-babbler (*Pomatorhinus erythrogenys*).

▼ **Spectacled warbler** (*Sylvia conspicillata*). The European populations of this species migrate to North Africa for the winter.

For many people the word "warbler" suggests a dull brownish bird singing a gentle, trilling song (ie warbling) from a concealed perch in dense vegetation. Such unobtrusiveness and drabness of plumage are indeed characteristics of many **Old World warblers**, but in fact this large subfamily contains numerous distinctive species to which the above description hardly applies. No fewer than 25 of the 56 genera contain only one species, although clearly many of these and other members of the subfamily are of doubtful affinity and some may not be true warblers at all. The taxonomic confusion surrounding warblers is highlighted by some of the vernacular names; the Oriole babbler, tit-flycatchers and tit-weavers are all currently regarded as warblers.

The great majority of species are Eurasian or African. The New World warblers have nine primary feathers and are not close relatives of the mainly Old World warblers which have ten primary feathers. However, some species of Old World warblers occur in the New World! There are 13 species of gnatwrens and gnatcatchers and 2 kinglets. In addition the Arctic warbler has extended its breeding range from Siberia into western Alaska, although even these birds return to the Old World to winter in southern Asia. Mainland Australia has only 8 resident species, including the distinctive Spinifex bird, and New Zealand only one, the fernbird. The archipelagoes of the Pacific and Indian Oceans contain a variety of unique warblers. The tiny populations of some of these island endemics make them highly vulnerable to extinction. The Aldabra warbler, whose population was fewer than 11 birds in 1983, is a good example of this.

Typical warblers are small birds with fine, narrowly pointed bills. Their feet are strong and well-suited for perching. Some (eg Dartford warbler) have long tails which counterbalance the body as the birds thread their way through dense foliage, carrying out inspections over and under leaves and twigs in their tireless search for insects.

Warblers' dependence on insect prey is the main reason why most warblers of high latitudes are strongly migratory. Most north Eurasian warblers winter in Africa or tropical Asia, some performing prodigious journeys. For example, Willow warblers nesting in Siberia travel up to 12,000km (7,500mi) twice a year, to and from sub-Saharan Africa. These long-distance migrants accumulate substantial reserves of fuel, in the form of fat deposits, before their journeys. It is not unusual for them to double their body weight in preparation for their migration. Those few warblers that remain in cold climates in winter are sometimes badly affected by food shortages in harsh weather. Dartford warblers in Britain, for example, often suffer large population decreases during severe winters.

Warblers are typically monogamous although instances of polygamy are known for a number of species (eg Sedge warbler). Voice has recently been shown to be important in some species for mate-attraction and mate-selection, in addition to being a primary means of advertising the positions of territory boundaries. Male Sedge warblers may cease to sing after pairing and individual Reed warblers with elaborate song repertoires tend to succeed in attracting females sooner than less accomplished singers. Some species (eg Icterine warbler) extend their repertoires by mimicking other bird species, for reasons that are not really understood. The Marsh warbler has gone further: its song consists entirely of imitations of other species. Each Marsh warbler mimics on average 80 species, over half of them African birds heard in the warbler's winter quarters. Voice also plays an important part in distinguishing species. For example, chiffchaffs and Willow warblers look almost identical, but have unmistakably distinct songs. Songs are generally delivered from perches, but warblers of low vegetation often use song flights as a means of broadcasting their songs for long distances. Examples of these include scrub warblers, such as the whitethroat, and many of the *Cisticola* grass warblers, such as the Cloud-scraper.

All warblers seem to be competing for the same basic food: insects. In practice there is often a high degree of spatial separation which minimizes competition for food between species and between individuals. Species that occur at high densities, notably the temperate-zone ones, are characteristically territorial. Typically the males defend territories against members of their own species and sometimes also against members of closely related species. For example, blackcaps and Garden warblers defend territories against each other as well as against other members of their own species. In the first case the territories of both species are large and supply most of the food of the nesting pairs and their broods. In the latter, however, breeding territories are small and perhaps serve mainly to space out nests to make it less profitable for predators to specialize in searching for them. Territorial behavior is not confined to the breeding season nor is it necessarily always directed at other warblers. For example, blackcaps using bird-tables or taking nectar from a particular bush will drive off species of similar or smaller size which try to feed there too.

Some warblers achieve ecological segregation by other means. Vertical separation sometimes occurs; for example, the Long-billed crombec forages lower down in the vegetation, where its range overlaps with that of a close relative, the Red-faced crombec, than it does elsewhere. Sometimes where species cooccur there is dietary specialization. For example, the nestling diets of Reed and Great reed warblers tend to differ where the two species are nesting in the same reedbed, but not where they occur apart from each other. Large warbler species are often found to coexist peacefully with smaller ones. Ecological segregation here may be due to specialization on prey of different sizes and to differences in foraging behavior. For example, blackcap and chiffchaff breeding territories often overlap in Europe since the two species share the same habitat, ie deciduous woodland. Blackcaps take fewer tiny insects than do the smaller chiffchaffs and, in addition, blackcaps feed to a large extent on settled insects whereas chiffchaffs often flycatch, or hover to take insects from the extremities of leaves and twigs where they may be inaccessible to blackcaps.   EFJG

Old World flycatchers are small woodland or forest birds; many can be recognized from their manner of capturing flying insects. They sit on a prominent perch and suddenly dash out, catch the prey in the air and then return to the perch.

Some species of flycatchers live in gardens and parks and are thus well known and provide much of interest to man, but they occur over most of Europe, Africa, Asia, Australia and the Pacific Islands from coastal shrubs to high altitude forests, up to 4,0000m (13,100ft). The majority of species, however, are found in Southeast Asia and on New Guinea. In Southeast Asia, the Fiji Islands and Australia some flycatcher species (those of the three genera, *Petroica*, *Tregellasia* and *Eopsaltria*) are called robins by the Australians although these species look

▲ **The long wings and long tail** of the whitethroat (an Old World warbler) can be clearly seen when the bird is in flight. It breeds in much of Eurasia and migrates to North and tropical Africa for the winter. It is restless and perky.

◄ **Feeding time.** In Old World warblers of the genus *Sylvia* both parents normally care for the young. The range of the Subalpine warbler (*S. cantillans*), seen here, differs substantially from that of the whitethroat. Breeding takes place in southern Europe or northwest Africa, winter is spent in the eastern Mediterranean or North Africa.

like and behave like flycatchers. The name robin is said to have become popular thanks to nostalgia for the red-breasted robin of Europe (a thrush). In Europe flycatchers are popular garden birds, and some species can easily be attracted to nest boxes. Otherwise most flycatchers build small cup nests in forks of branches; among a few southern exceptions are some African species (genus *Muscicapa*) and the Japanese Blue and white flycatcher; these occasionally also use nest boxes.

Flycatchers vary greatly in appearance, from the very colorful to almost uniformly brown or gray. In many species the sexes differ considerably in plumage, but not in size, while in others, most often the duller-colored species, the sexes are very similar. Typical flycatchers have relatively broad,

flat bills with bristles around the nostrils, probably to help in catching flying insects. Their legs and feet are often weak, possibly because their feeding technique demands no more of them than sitting still and waiting. Spotted flycatchers are very fascinating to observe when catching insects on warm days. Then they use a sit-and-wait feeding strategy on low perches from which they sally out to capture prey in mid-air. In this way they may capture, on average, a prey every 18th second. In colder weather, with few flying insects, they have to hover among the foliage in the tree canopy, which is much more demanding of energy. Australian species in general have finer bills than most flycatchers and take most of their food on the ground. Not all flycatchers feed solely on insects; many also take berries and

fruits, for example, the Blue and White fly-catcher in Borneo and the Dusky flycatcher and some of its relatives in Africa. One African species, the White-eyed slaty flycatcher, even takes nestlings of smaller birds.

Most flycatchers are thought to be monogamous. The Pied and Collared flycatchers in Eurasia, however, are polygamous and have a remarkable mating system in which males defend two or more distant territories in succession, to each of which they try to attract a female (see box). The Pied and Collared flycatchers are close relatives, males being black and white. They can easily be distinguished in the field from the white collar and rump of the Collared flycatcher, while the females of both species are gray-brown and almost indistinguishable from each other. In Eastern Europe, where both species occur together, they regularly hybridize and hybrids may locally make up as much as 5–10 percent of all birds present. Male hybrids do not seem to have any disadvantages in attracting a mate but they suffer from reduced fertility. The songs of pure species are very different, but Pied flycatcher males can switch to Collared flycatcher song in areas and situations where the two species are neighbors. In tropical areas some flycatcher species may form

The Deceptive Mating Behavior of Male Pied Flycatchers

The Pied flycatcher is an inhabitant of woodlands. It breeds in holes in trees and can easily be attracted to nest boxes. The male, after arriving in the breeding grounds in spring, sets up a territory around a nest-hole and tries to acquire a female (the "primary" female). If successful he then occupies a second more or less distant territory and attempts to attract another ("secondary") female. He rarely manages to obtain a third. The distance between a male's first territory and his second is on average 200m (about 650ft), but distances up to 3.5km (2.2mi) have been known, and several territories of other males lie in between. By having two distant territories males can hide from arriving females the fact that they are already mated. When trying to attract the secondary female, the male behaves exactly as when he was unmated and tried to attract the primary one. Males desert their secondary females after egg-laying and mainly help their primary female to feed the young. Since secondary females have to raise their young almost single-handed, some of the young may die from undernourishment. Thus males deceive females about their marital status and can increase their number of offspring at cost to the females. Approximately 15 percent of the males succeed in attracting more than one

female. Many more try but fail, while some males stay with their first female all the time.

Most male birds guard their females before egg-laying to prevent other males from copulating with them. Since Pied flycatcher males start visiting the second territory soon after having attracted the primary female, they cannot guard her uninterruptedly, and as a result run the risk of other males inseminating the female and siring some of her young. This has also been seen to happen; while the male is away the nearest neighboring males sneak into his territory and copulate with the female, which leads to shared fatherhood within broods. However, females of monogamous males are also the subjects of extra-pair copulations (there is a considerable risk if the male is more than 10m, 33ft, from the female), since their mates often have to chase intruding males from the territory. This leads to reduced paternity also for monogamous males. Thus, on average, in all broods the attendant male is the true father of only 75 percent of the young. Even though polygynous males may lose relatively more young per nest, due to shared fatherhood, than monogamous males, they in all father more young by having a secondary female than by being monogamous. Bigamy thus is an adaptive feature in the Pied flycatcher.

ALu

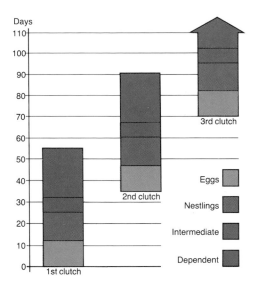

Days

▲ **Breeding with rapidity.** This diagram demonstrates how a female fairy-wren can, with the aid of helpers, reduce the period between successive clutches of eggs. For about 30 days after leaving the nest, young remain dependent on the parents, but after this they become independent and are available to help parents with later broods. For example young of the first clutch take over the care of the young of a second clutch leaving the female free to lay a third clutch.

◀ **The unforgettable bird.** According to Professor David Lack "There is hardly a corner in the world in which the English have not managed to find some red-breasted bird which they could call a robin." In Australia this common Old World flycatcher is known as the Red-capped robin (*Petroica goodenovii*).

▶ **Iridescent miniature** OVERLEAF the Red-winged fairy-wren of southwest Australia.

▼ **The rodent run.** Fairy-wrens are normally found (1) standing or hopping. If one is threatened by a predator it runs along the ground, tail down, squeaking (2–4). As a distraction the display is surprisingly effective.

small flocks in the nonbreeding season, like the Mariqua flycatcher, or may join parties of mixed birds, like the Ashy flycatcher. The Australian Flame robin which also forms flocks in autumn and winter even has communal roosts at night.

Most tropical species are resident, but some perform seasonal movements, and high-altitude species migrate towards lower altitudes in the nonbreeding season. Species in Europe and Asia migrate long distances and spend the winter in Africa, India or Southeast Asia.   ALu

A species of **fairy-wren** can be found in nearly every kind of habitat throughout the 40 degrees of latitude covered by Australia and New Guinea, ranging from dense tall forest in the well-watered southwest Australia (Red-winged fairy-wren) to the spinifex-covered sand dunes of the interior desert (Eyrean grass-wren). Characteristically fairy-wrens have tails longer than their bodies and these are carried cocked, jauntily, most of the time.

The true fairy-wrens are endemic to Australia and New Guinea and wherever they occur the ground cover is generally thick and they hop rapidly through it on their long legs. Their wings are short and rounded and these diminutive birds rarely make prolonged flights. The males in this genus are brightly colored in enameled reds, blues, blacks and white while the females and immatures are usually brown. In the emu-wrens there are clear differences between the sexes, but in the other three genera the sexes are harder to tell apart in the field.

Most of the fairy-wrens depend largely on insects for food but the grass-wrens with their sturdier bills eat large quantities of seeds as well. Foraging is largely done on the ground as they bound along, though some species search through shrubs and even the canopies of tall trees. Because their wings are small and rather inefficient, fairy-wrens only rarely fly sorties after air-borne insects.

Throughout a wide variety of environments most species spend their lifetime within a prescribed area which they defend from trespass by members of their species outside the immediate family and within which they find all their requirements for

feeding, breeding and shelter. Such "territories" cover from 1 to 3h (2.5–7.4 acres) and tend to persist from year to year with little change.

Despite their small size these birds may live for a surprisingly long time (more than 10 years), compared with their counterparts in the northern hemisphere. A long life and residential status seem to have encouraged them to maintain their family bonds beyond the usual period when offspring depend on their parents for food and protection; most fairy wrens tend to live in groups with more than two adults capable of breeding yet only one female lays the eggs. Thus although fairy-wrens of both sexes are capable of breeding in the season after they are hatched, relatively few do so, opting to stay in the relative security of the family territory rather than disperse into the unknown and set up on their own. This "delayed" reproduction is encouraged by there being more males than females in many populations and by suitable breeding habitat often being in short supply: where young birds do disperse it is generally the females that leave.

In most species of fairy-wren the female builds the nest, lays and incubates the eggs and broods the young when they first hatch. Her mate may call her off the nest and escort her while she forages hurriedly before returning to brood. The young fledge after ten days or so in the nest and at first are unable to fly, though they will scuttle fast over the ground and hide. If a predator approaches a nest the parents (and other group members) perform a frenzied "rodent run" display: instead of hopping, which is their usual mode of progression, they run, keeping close to the ground, trailing their tails and squeaking, hence the name of the performance. This performance is surprisingly effective in distracting a variety of predators, from snakes to man.

The young are fed for several weeks after they have left the nest. Fairy-wrens nest several times during a season and the non-breeding members of the group may take over the raising of an early brood and so allow the breeding female to start a second (or third) nest. Later in the season young hatched earlier will attend their nestling-siblings and help to raise them, so that the

habit of "helping" is formed early in life.

Emu-wrens live deep in dense heathland: it is hard to catch more than a fleeting glimpse of them. Grass-wrens are birds of the deserts, arid shrublands and rocky plateaus and they, too, are rarely seen. In the last 35 years one new species has been discovered (the Gray grass-wren) and four others have been rediscovered after being unseen for 50 years or more (the Eyrean, Carpentarian, White-throated and the Black grass-wrens).

Most of the fairy-wrens have survived the environmental impact of European settlement and the accompanying exotic pests, the feral cat and the fox. However the Purple-crowned fairy-wren does seem to be particularly vulnerable and to have decreased in numbers recently. This species lives in the gallery forest that lines a dozen tropical river-systems. Often only a few meters in width, this fringe vegetation is easily damaged by overgrazing and by stock trampling it down as they seek access to water. Hopefully this situation has been recognized in time, and adequate reserves will be maintained.

One of the great attractions of this family of small birds is that some species have thrived alongside the mushrooming of suburbia. In particular the Superb blue fairy-wren is common in the parks and gardens of six capital cities and brightens the lives of those who live there.   IR

Parrotbills are thought to have originated in China, as most species occur in that country. Though they have spread, their distribution remains basically Asiatic; there is just one exception: the Bearded tit. This species occurs in Europe, reaching as far west as Britain. It should be regarded as a somewhat aberrant representative of the subfamily as it differs from the typical parrotbills in having a more conventionally shaped bill. In this species, moreover, the sexes differ in appearance and the young resemble the female. The male has conspicuous erectile black moustaches and beautiful plumage in cinnamon-buff, gray and vinaceous rose. The Bearded tit produces "pinging" notes, which are frequently encountered in the extensive reed beds where the species breeds.

The typical parrotbills comprise the largest genus with 15 species, which range in size from 11 to 22cm (4.5–8.5in). Their distinguishing feature is the peculiarly shaped yellowish bill, which is shorter than the head—broad, highly compressed with an extremely convex outline to both

mandibles. They also have longish tails, which give them a superficial tit-like appearance.

Parrotbills are mostly found in hilly or mountainous regions, in mixed secondary forest and bamboo and in the dwarf rhododendrons of the Himalayas. Some species are found up to 3,700m (12,000ft), while other species extend to lowland areas. However, bamboo appears to be necessary for most species.

All species of parrotbills are gregarious, occurring in small restless flocks, which forage through the lower trees of forests, tall grasses and bamboos. There are also seasonal vertical movements by those species that breed at high altitudes. The Great parrotbill, which breeds between 3,000 and 3,700m (10,000–12,000ft), moves down to 1,850m (6,000ft) in the winter. This, the largest of parrotbills, is uniform mousy-brown with a heavy but normally shaped bill. The Yangtse parrotbill, which is superficially marked in such a way that it looks like a large version of the Bearded tit, has a massive yellow beak. It also has the most restricted range of any parrotbill, being recorded only along an 80km (50mi) stretch of reedbeds bordering the lower Yangtse. It is now considered an endangered species, particularly in view of cutting and reclamation and increase in navigation by powered vessels along the river during the last 50 years.

The uniformly brownish Three-toed parrotbill ranging from the Himalayas to Southwest China is unique in having its outer toe reduced to a clawless stump, adhering to the middle toe. Surprisingly enough the Brown parrotbill is barely distinguishable from the Three-toed parrotbill, and their ranges overlap slightly. Another pair of species are the Black-browed and Red-headed parrotbills, both of which have ginger-colored heads, pale brown backs and white underparts. However, the Red-headed parrotbill has a massive yellow bill twice the size of that of its sibling partner and presumably tackles much heavier seeds or insects.

PRC

Monarch flycatchers attract attention by their activity, quivering tail, harsh calls and metallic plumage. The paradise flycatchers are the most spectacular species with their 15cm (6in) long tail feathers. A range of closely related species is found from southern Africa across tropical Asia to Japan.

Africa, south of the Sahara, has many genera, as do Indonesia and New Guinea.

The subfamily extends as far as the Himalayas, Korea and Japan and has successfully colonized many of the islands of the Indian and Pacific Oceans, though not New Zealand.

Supposed species hybridize frequently and many species show several colors, the male having varying amounts of white, black and chestnut. New Guinea is the center of diversity of the monarchs with five or six species known to occupy one small area of forest. The peltops flycatchers sally from trees that extend above the forest canopy while other species occupy the canopy itself, subcanopy and understory. The sexes of the Frilled monarch differ strikingly in behavior. The rufous female, which has a long tail and wide beak, often sallies after insects in the subcanopy. The black and white male, on the other hand, gleans from trunks, branches and vines. As one would expect he has longer, more curved claws than the female.

Although most species have a long tail and plumage of chestnut, black or gray (glossed with blue or green), some species

differ from this pattern. The African puff-back flycatchers are small, short-tailed, dumpy birds with a conspicuous breast band. Typically, monarch flycatchers have flat, broad beaks and small feet and often steep foreheads with a slight crest. Several species have brightly colored flaps or patches of bare skin around their eyes.

Although most monarch flycatchers sally after flying insects, several species are gleaners and the shrikebills occasionally take fruit. The Restless flycatcher hovers above the ground making a strange grinding noise, which has given rise to its other name, the scissors-grinder. The New Guinean and Australian species nest in

▲ ► **Representative species** of seven subfamilies of thrushes. (1) A Gray-headed parrotbill (*Paradoxornis gularis*). (2) A Yellow-rumped thornbill (*Acanthiza chrysorrhoa*). (3) A Gray fantail (*Rhipidura fuliginosa*) sitting on its nest. (4) An African paradise flycatcher (*Terpsiphone viridis*) holding an insect. (5) A Black-backed fairy-wren (*Malurus melanotus*). (6) A Golden whistler (*Pachycephala pectoralis*). (7) A Northern logrunner (*Orthonyx spaldingi*).

spring (September to December) and build neat nests on horizontal branches, often beautifully camouflaged with lichen. The Satin flycatcher often nests close to Noisy friarbirds—bold, aggressive honeyeaters.

HAF

The **logrunners** are a group of secretive birds, more often heard than seen. Most species are consequently rather poorly known—indeed the wedgebill was recently split into two species based on calls: the Chirruping wedgebill calls "tootsie-cheer" and the Chiming wedgebill "did-you-get-drunk." The wedgebills and whipbirds perform duets, the male eastern whipbird giving a characteristic whipcrack to which the female replies "cher, cher."

The name quail-thrush describes the genus *Cinclosoma* well, as they are thrushlike in proportions and plumage yet are ground-dwelling and eat seeds and insects. They mostly live in desert or eucalypt or acacia woodlands in Australia whereas most of the other logrunners occupy the understory of rainforest in eastern Australia and New Guinea, where they are chiefly insectivorous. Although most species are cryptically colored the Blue jewel-babbler male is blue and white. Most are dumpy birds with rather long tails; they have strong feet, which are used for digging. Logrunners often dig in areas from which Brush turkeys have removed the leaf litter for their mounds.

Logrunners may engage in noisy territorial battles in the breeding season, and perhaps most species are monogamous and territorial. Nests of dry sticks, bark, roots and grass are placed in thick foliage or on the ground, in winter and spring, but occasionally in the fall. Though quail-thrushes mostly nest between August and November, the desert species have been recorded breeding in all months of the year.

The Western whipbird was at one time considered rare or even endangered, but once its haunting, ventriloquistic call was learnt it was discovered in several places in southern Australia. Several species of logrunners have been affected by the clearing of forest or the overgrazing of shrubland in Australia, though none is currently threatened.

HAF

To many people the **Australasian warblers** are just dull little brown birds. However they are of great scientific interest because they display a variety of complex breeding biologies.

The *Gerygone* warblers are the most widespread members of the group occurring in

Australia, New Guinea, Indonesia, Malaysia, Burma, New Zealand and many Pacific Islands. They are delicate attractive birds with tinkling songs that flitter through the foliage after tiny insects. Scrub-wrens inhabit the understory of forests in Australia and New Guinea and thornbills are principally Australian, where they forage in a range of sites from the ground to the treetops.

Most Australasian warblers are small, even tiny, with short tails and wings and fine bills. Although many are dull brown or olive, many thornbills have contrasting rumps and the *Gerygone* warblers often have bright yellow underparts. The Rock warbler, which nests in caves in sandstone around Sydney, NSW, is dark gray above and reddish brown beneath. In appearance the sexes and ages are similar, often identical.

Insects are the primary food, but the whitefaces, which live in dry habitats, eat a lot of seeds. Where several species of thornbill occur in the same place each usually forages at a different level in the vegetation.

Evidence is slowly emerging that thornbills, despite their tiny size (7–10g, 0.25–0.28oz) are long-lived, with 10-year-old birds being quite frequent in populations studied. Perhaps due to this they often do not breed in their first year. Breeding takes place from late winter to summer, and although some species breed as pairs cooperative breeding is more typical of the group.

The Buff-tailed thornbill lives in clans of about ten birds for most of the year. At the beginning of the breeding season these break up into pairs, trios and quartets which attempt to breed. Those that fail in their own breeding attempt help a neighboring pair or group, until the clan comes together again in the fall. A change in foraging coincides with the breakup of the clan. Larger groups feed more on the ground, pairs more on bark or among foliage.

Australasian warblers frequently join and may lead feeding flocks of mixed species in the nonbreeding season, a habit that does not help the bird-watcher confronted with a host of species of little brown birds.

HAF

Fantails frequently fly straight at human observers and hover a meter or two from them. Consequently they are regarded with great affection, to the extent that one species is called the Friendly fantail. In truth they are probably more interested in our flies than in us.

▲ **The deep nest** of the shrike-tit (a thickhead) is made of strips of bark woven together, felted with cobweb and decorated with moss and lichen.

◄ **The Black-throated wattle-eye** (*Platysteira peltata*), a monarch flycatcher, lives in southern Africa, from eastern Kenya south to Angola and Natal. It is almost always found near water.

► **One of the most extraordinary songs** in New Guinea is that of the Crested pitohui (*Pitohui cristatus*), a species of thickhead. It starts as a series of repeated identical notes but gradually the notes become shorter and the pitch falls. In one recorded example the song lasted almost 3 minutes. At the start there were 5 notes per second, at the end 13. During the song the pitch fell by half an octave.

New Guinea has the most species of fantail and here three or four species coexist in small patches of rain forest, foraging at different levels. Four species occur on the Asian mainland from India through Southeast Asia to southern China. Australia has three species, with the Willie wagtail occupying much drier and more open habitats than the other fantails. They have successfully invaded the Indonesian and Pacific Islands and spread as far east as Fiji and Samoa.

The most striking character of the group is the very long tail, which can be spread into an impressive fan and waved from side to side. The body is surprisingly small, legs are delicate, and the bill is short but broad, typical of a flycatcher. The Willie wagtail is black and white, other species are all black, gray and white or rufous and white.

Flies, beetles and other insects are snapped up in acrobatic sallies from perches in the understory or canopy. The Willie wagtail often uses a sheep's back as a perch, and frequently takes insects from the ground. The fanned tail and hyperactivity of these birds probably help to flush insects into the air.

The breeding biology of the Willie wagtail and of the Gray fantail in New Zealand have been well studied. Fantails suspend delicate nests of bark and moss from a low, thin branch. They breed from August to February and may have several successive clutches, with nests sometimes reused and later nests being built faster than early ones. The nestlings are often preyed upon by introduced weasels and mice. Willie wagtails place a nest of hair, wool, thistledown,

bark and dead leaves on a horizontal branch or often a man-made structure. Nests are sometimes parasitized by Pallid cuckoos; despite this, young are reared from about 65 percent of nests.

All fantails seem common and popular and most adapt well to human disturbance, though some of the Pacific species have small distributions.   HAF

The popular name **thickheads** is hardly a complimentary one; preferable, for the largest genus, is whistlers as these include some of the finest songsters in a region not noted for its richness of birdsong.

Whistlers are found from Indonesia and Malaysia, through New Guinea and Australia to Fiji and Tonga. Most other genera occur in New Guinea or Australia. Only the piopio comes from New Zealand, and the taxonomic position of this species is confusing; it is often placed in its own family. The Golden whistler superspecies spans the range of the subfamily: some 70 forms are found, differing in plumage and in the extent of different appearances of the sexes. Shrike-thrushes and female whistlers are predominantly gray or brown, whereas male whistlers often have black and white heads and yellow or reddish breasts. Both sexes of shrike-tit have black and white striped heads, yellow breasts and green backs. Shrike-tits have massive beaks, hooked on each mandible. Other species have strong, slightly hooked beaks and strong feet.

Whistlers capture insects among foliage, whereas shrike-tits forage on bark and most of the other genera fossick among debris on or near the ground. Several species occasionally eat fruit, the pitohuis do so frequently.

The breeding season is from July to January and most species (including migratory species) are very faithful to their breeding territories from year to year. Nests are made of sticks, bark, grasses and spiders' webs, usually placed in a low fork. So far only the shrike-tit is known to be a cooperative breeder though the pitohuis live in groups. The Rusty pitohui associates with babblers, honeyeaters, cuckoo-shrikes and drongos in New Guinean lowland rainforests. Such mixed flocks are remarkable in that all members are a similar rufous color.

The piopio of New Zealand is possibly extinct, not having been seen since 1955. The Red-lored or Red-throated whistler from mallee-scrub on the borders of Victoria, New South Wales and South Australia is very rare and possibly endangered. Its habitat is rapidly being cleared.   HAF

TITS

Families: Paridae, Aegithalidae, Remizidae
Order: Passeriformes (suborder Oscines, part).
Sixty-two species in 10 genera.
Distribution: see map and table.

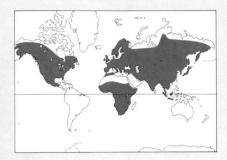

▶ **Representative species of the three families of tits.** (1) A Rufous-bellied tit (*Parus rufiventris*). (2) A Black-eared bushtit (*Psaltriparus melanotis*), one of the long-tailed tits. (3) Seven Long-tailed tits (*Aegithalos caudatus*) roosting. (4) A Yellow-cheeked or Chinese yellow tit (*Parus spilonotus*). (5) A Blue tit (*Parus caruleus*). (6) A verdin (*Auriparus flavifrons*), one of the penduline tits. (7) Head of a Bridled titmouse (*Parus wollweberi*) holding a worm. (8) An Azure tit (*Parus cyanus*).

TITS are small, active woodland and scrub dwellers: many are well-known visitors to bird feeders in gardens. Most are gregarious and vocal. The word "tits" derives from "titmice", the name for "true" tits (family Paridae) or, in North America, one group of *Parus* species (another group is called the chickadees). Other, unrelated, bird species are called tits, but here we include only members of three families currently thought to be closely related; they form a group probably closely allied to the nuthatches and creepers.

The **true tits** are by far the largest and most widespread of the three families, occurring from sea level to high mountains wherever there are trees: apart from treeless areas and offshore islands, only South America, Madagascar, Australia and the Antarctic are without true tits. Ten species are confined to North America, 10 to Africa south of the Sahara and the remainder are primarily Eurasian, though some of these spread into North Africa and one into Alaska. The North American and European species include some of the most "popular" of all birds, nesting in boxes in summer and common at bird-feeders in winter. They rarely cause any damage but provide hours of interest and enjoyment to home-bound observers.

In form and general appearance most of the true tits are fairly uniform and easily recognized as "tits" all over the world—a generalization borne out by the fact that all but two species are in the single genus *Parus*. Many have pale or white cheeks contrasting with black or dark caps; a number are

The 3 Families of Tits

True tits

Family: Paridae
Forty-six species in 3 genera.
Europe, Asia, Africa, N America (just into Mexico; also introduced to Hawaii). Chiefly woodland and forests. Size: 11.5–14cm (4.5–5.5in) long, weight 6–20g (0.2–0.7oz), except Sultan tit which reaches 22cm (8.7in), weight more than 30g (1oz). Plumage: chiefly brown, white, gray and black; some with yellow; three species have bright blue; only slight differences between sexes—females duller than males in some species. Voice: wide range of single notes, chattering calls and very varied complex songs, many whistled. Nests: all in holes, excavated in soft wood by some species. Eggs: usually 4–12, whitish with reddish-brown spots; incubation period: 13–14 days; nestling period: 17–20 days. Diet: chiefly insects but also seeds, berries; some species store food for later retrieval.

Species include: **Black-capped chickadee** (*Parus atricapillus*), **Black tit** (*P. leucomelas*), **Blue tit** (*P. caeruleus*), **Bridled titmouse** (*P. wollweberi*), **Coal tit** (*P. ater*), **Crested tit** (*P. cristatus*), **Great tit** (*P. major*), **Marsh tit** (*P. palustris*), **Plain titmouse** (*P. inornatus*), **Siberian tit** (*P. cinctus*), **Sultan tit** (*Melanochlora sultanea*), **Tufted titmouse** (*P. bicolor*), **Willow tit** (*P. montanus*), **Yellow-browed tit** (*Sylviparus modestus*).

Long-tailed tits

Family: Aegithalidae
Seven species in 3 genera.
Europe to Asia, N America (just into C America). Mainly forest and woodland. Size: 9–14cm (3.5–5.5in) long, weight 5–7g (0.25oz). Plumage: chiefly black, gray, white and pink in the Long-tailed tit. Voice: churring contact calls and subdued songs. Nests: purse-like structure of moss, feathers and lichens. Eggs: usually 6–10, white speckled with red spots in many species; incubation period: 13–14 days; nestling period 16–17 days. Diet: mainly insects.

Species include: **bushtit** (*Psaltriparus minimus*), **Long-tailed tit** (*Aegithalos caudatus*), **Pygmy tit** (*Psaltria exilis*).

Penduline tits

Family: Remizidae
Nine species in 4 genera.
N and C America, Africa, Eurasia. Open country in trees and bushes; reedbeds. Size: 10–11cm (4in) long. Plumage: mostly pale grays, white and yellows, but striking black mask and rich chestnut "saddle" in adult Penduline tit; a few species with bright yellow or red. Voice: fairly quiet, *ti-ti-ti*, thin whistles. Nests: purse-like with prickly twigs in verdin. Eggs: white except verdin (bluish-green) with red spots; incubation period: 13–14 days; nestling period: about 18 days. Diet: chiefly insects; some species also take small seeds.

Species include: **Fire-capped tit** (*Cephalopyrus flammiceps*), **Penduline tit** (*Remiz pendulinus*), **verdin** (*Auriparus flaviceps*).

crested. They have short sturdy bills and short legs. All spend most of their time in trees and bushes, though they will forage on the ground. They are extremely nimble and readily hang upside down on small twigs. Although they can fly long distances, they commonly only flit from one tree to the next.

True tits are monogamous in temperate areas, the male defending a territory against all comers. These territories are usually established in winter and early spring and break down when the young become independent, though in some species there is a brief resurgence of territorial behavior in the fall after the molt. Some species maintain their territories throughout the year. In Scandinavia the Willow tit may winter in groups of up to four in one territory; mortality in winter can be high and some territories do not have a pair by spring. In other species the birds may join up in flocks for much of the year, roving over large areas of woodland. Parties of mixed species of tits, often together with other small woodland birds, are a common feature of woodlands in Europe, Asia and North America. The behavior of tropical and African species is less well known. However, in the African

Black tit, territories are occupied by 3 or 4 birds during the breeding season and all help to raise the brood. The "extra" birds are usually males which have been raised in the same territory the previous year.

Of the two Southeast Asian species in separate genera, the Sultan tit is an enormous bird for a tit, about 22cm (8.7in) long, and weighing perhaps well over 30g (1oz). It is predominantly a glossy blue-black (the female is a little duller) with a bright yellow crown, an erectile crest and a yellow belly. It lives in rich forests and is not well known. Even less is known about the rather drab, greenish Yellow-browed tit, which lacks the distinctive patterning of most tits. It lives in high-altitude forests above about 2,000m (6,000–7,000ft). It was not until its nest was found in a hole in a rhododendron tree in 1969 that its breeding habits were known to be like those of other tits.

Many species have extensive ranges, the Great tit, Coal tit and Willow tit breeding from the British Isles across to Japan. The Marsh tit also breeds at both ends of this range, but has a gap of some 2,000km (1,250mi) in its range in Central Asia. The Siberian tit ranges from Scandinavia across Asia into Alaska and Canada. The Willow tit of Europe and Asia is very similar to the North American Black-capped chickadee; probably in prehistoric times a single species encircled the Northern Hemisphere; only later did they diverge into two species.

Most tropical and many temperate species are resident. Some, such as the Siberian tit, remain on their breeding grounds throughout the year despite very low winter temperatures (as low as −45°C, −49°F overnight); they roost in cavities in trees or even in mouse-holes in the snow, and go slightly torpid during the night, regaining their normal temperature at dawn. Some temperate species may migrate over long distances, especially when there are failures of the seed crops on which they are dependent in winter. Great tits from northern Russia have been known to winter as far afield as Portugal.

Most tits are primarily insect-eaters. Many also take seeds and berries, particularly species in colder climates where seeds are the main item of the winter diet. An abundance of an alternative food source is the reason why tits are so common in gardens and at bird feeders in winter. Some tits store food, primarily seeds, but sometimes also insects; such items are usually put behind cracks in the bark, but may also be buried under moss. The cache may not be used for some time, or the bird may store

▲ **An insatiable brood** of Coal tits begs for food from a returning parent. The white patches on the nape and crown of the adult distinguish this species from other similarly colored tits, such as the Marsh tit. The Coal tit prefers conifer wood habitats and nests in holes in banks and tree stumps.

◄ **The Southern black tit** (*Parus niger*) from Africa is one of the largest of true tits.

► **Frozen in flight,** a Marsh tit rises from a waterside feeding site. Its common name is a misnomer: this species has no particular preference for marshes. It is often seen in deciduous woods, hedges and sometimes in gardens. Its range is somewhat unusual. It is found in most of Europe, between the Black Sea and Lake Baikal, and in northern and eastern China and Hokkaido, Japan. There are no Marsh tits in the area between 52°E and 85°E.

food and collect it within hours. In the warm breeding season all species feed insects to their young. A pair of Blue tits may feed caterpillars to their nestlings at the rate of one a minute while the young are growing most rapidly, and bring well over 10,000 such items while the young are in the nest. Tits have been thought—although the evidence is not convincing—to be important in the control of forest pests, and large numbers of nesting-boxes have been put up for this reason. Tits are very versatile and quick to learn from one another. In 1929 some tits in Southampton were observed to remove the tops from milk bottles and drink the cream. This habit spread very rapidly throughout England by tits copying the skills from each other.

As far as is known, all *Parus* species are hole-nesters. A few nest in nesting-boxes in gardens; these species are well known and have been studied extensively (see pp388–89). The majority probably search for a hole which is suitable, because they do not seem to enlarge it in any way. However some, including the Crested tit, Willow tit and Black-capped chickadee, excavate their own nest-chamber in a soft piece of dead timber. This habit seems so fixed that they will excavate a new chamber even if the previous year's chamber is standing unused in the same tree. These species will normally not use nesting boxes, although if the boxes are filled with wood chippings they may then "excavate" them and find them acceptable! When suitable tree sites are in short supply, holes in the ground may be used.

Most species line their nests with moss, some adding hair or feathers; the female does the work, though the male may accompany her on trips to collect material. The eggs are laid at daily intervals. Clutches tend to be large, 4–5 in tropical species and more in temperate areas; as with other hole-nesting species, large clutches are thought to be related to the safety from predators of nests in holes, enabling large numbers of young to be raised. The average clutch of Blue tits in oak woodlands is about 11 eggs

Tufted Titmouse

Some of the 10 New World species of true tits are well known to the casual birdwatcher. The Black-capped chickadee and the Tufted titmouse (here illustrated) are a common sight at bird feeders, and the latter is particularly familiar since, unlike the chickadee, it will readily use a nesting box.

Although never reaching population densities as high as those of the Blue and Great tit in the Old World, the Tufted titmouse is very common throughout much of the eastern USA. It is rather scarcer in the northern States, perhaps largely because, for this resident species, the winters are too severe.

However, in recent years it has gradually become more common in these States, especially in urban areas. Since its first appearance in Ontario in 1914, the Tufted titmouse had gradually established itself along the southern edge of this Canadian province. It seems almost certain that the widespread provision of food at bird-feeders is the key to this species being able to survive in such cold areas.

The Tufted titmouse is the only crested member of the family found in the eastern half of the United States. However, it has a crested counterpart to the west, the Plain titmouse, which lacks the rich orange-brown flank and the black above the beak. There is also a Bridled titmouse in the States bordering northwest Mexico, which people consider a separate species. All these North American crested birds are called "titmice" as opposed to the chickadees that make up the other members of the family. At one time the crested titmice of North America were put in a genus of their own, *Baeolophus*.

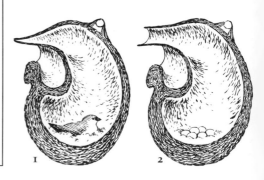

species and probably for much longer in some tropical species.

Long-tailed tits are very small birds, their tail being perhaps half of their length. All seven species are highly social and live in flocks of 6–12 birds for much of the year. The Long-tailed tit and the bushtit roost in little groups, huddling together for warmth on cold nights. In Europe many Long-tailed tits die in very cold weather.

They build elaborate purse-like nests of feathers and moss—more than 2,000 feathers have been counted in a single nest. The beautifully constructed nest is bound together with spider's web and camouflaged with a covering of lichen; it may be 18cm (7in) or so deep in Long-tailed tits and up to 30cm (12in) or more in the bushtit, and it takes many days to complete. Although both members of a pair may roost in the nest at night, probably only the female incubates, acquiring a bent tail from sitting in the tiny nest. The Pygmy tit in Java also lives in flocks and builds similar nests, but little else is known of the behavior of this species.

In both the European Long-tailed tit and the bushtit, one or more "helpers" may assist the parents to feed the young at the nest. The helpers usually arrive after the nest has been built and the eggs laid: they may be birds that have lost their own nest to predators.

Penduline tits are named for their hanging nests. All are very small and have finer, more needle-pointed bills than the other tits. All the species are primarily resident. The Penduline tit has by far the greatest range, stretching from southern Europe across to eastern China. In Europe its range is extending slowly west and north. Penduline tits live in small parties for most of the year, many species in rather open, scrubby woodland, but the Penduline tit lives in small trees such as willows and tamarisks in marshes and spends much of its time hunting for its food amongst the reeds.

The Penduline tit and all *Anthoscopus* species build purse-like nests, of a strong felt-like construction. Indeed some nests are occasionally used as purses by certain tribes in Africa. *Anthoscopus* nests have a dummy entrance which is blind. The parents close the real one when they leave, thus making it hard for would-be predators to find their way in. The verdin builds a more normal domed nest with many thorns woven into it, and the Fire-capped tit nests in holes in trees like the true tits (it is arguable that it should be placed in the family Paridae).

▲ **Putting the final touches,** a male Penduline tit hangs from its miraculous purse-like nest.

◄ **The Long-tailed tit's nest** ABOVE is constructed of feathers, mosses and spiders' webs.

◄ **An entrance leading nowhere** is built into the nest of the Cape penduline tit (1). The blind chamber to which it leads is thought to mislead predators. The true entrance lies above (2). It closes after the bird has entered or left the nest.

(exceptionally birds may lay as many as 18 or 19); these are probably the largest clutches of any song bird and only a few non-passerines such as gamebirds and ducks (which do not bring food to nestlings) lay larger clutches. In some species clutch size has been shown to vary with a number of factors: first-year birds lay smaller clutches than older, more experienced ones; clutches are smaller in the poorer habitats of gardens than in woodland; they are smaller later in the season when caterpillars are scarcer; and smaller when breeding density is high. Most species have a single brood, but some raise two broods in favorable seasons. Incubation is by the female alone. After leaving the nest the large brood is cared for by both parents for a week or so in temperate

The Great Tit

The World's Most Studied Bird?

The Great tit is perhaps the most studied wild bird in the world. The first person to realize the usefulness of the Great tit for purposes of study was H. Wolda in the Netherlands, who kept careful records for many years. Many of his results were published, together with new data, by H. N. Kluijver in 1951. This classic work in bird biology has inspired many other studies.

The Great tit is a common species over much of western Europe and Asia: except in the very coldest areas the birds are usually resident. In the wild it nests in holes in trees, but it readily accepts nest-boxes and often seems to prefer them to natural sites; all the birds within an area may nest in boxes. It is these characteristics that have made the Great tit (and to a lesser extent the Blue tit) such a convenient bird to study.

Great tits eat a wide variety of food. Although primarily insect-eaters they readily turn to seeds and nuts in winter when insects become scarce. The Great tit has a powerful beak with which it can hammer open seeds as large as hazel nuts, something that most of the smaller tits cannot do. Outside the breeding season, the birds often go about in small parties of perhaps 4–6 birds among other species of tits, each bird keeping an eye on where the others are feeding and what they are taking. As soon as one bird finds a new source of food the others will change their foraging technique to include the new item in their searches.

Great tits tend to settle in broadleaved deciduous woodland at densities of around one pair per ha (2.5 acres) and in coniferous woodland at about one pair per 2–5 ha (5–12.5 acres). Long-term studies show that although the numbers of breeding pairs are relatively stable, there is a tendency to "see-saw" up and down from year to year. The most important factor in this is the presence or absence of beech mast. The beech tree tends to produce a rich crop of seeds at intervals of two years (or more) and tit numbers increase after a winter when the crop has been available, and decrease when there is no crop then. In northern populations the presence of beech crops also influences whether or not the birds will winter in the same area.

Birds emigrate ("irrupt") southward in years without a crop, but are more likely to remain on the breeding grounds in years when there is a good crop. Birds also come to bird feeders in gardens less often when beech mast is abundant, which leads some people to conclude that tits are very scarce in years when the reverse is in fact true.

Great tits stake out their territories in late winter and early spring, taking up the best areas first so that latecomers may have to settle in marginal areas. Some birds are even excluded from obtaining a territory at all; this can be demonstrated by removing established territory holders; the empty territories are usually filled by newcomers within 24 hours. The replacement pairs take up much the same areas as the original occupants, except that some occupants of adjacent territories expand their domain into the territory temporarily left vacant. If a tape-recording of Great tit song is played in the vacant territory it apparently "fools" would-be immigrants, as reoccupation by new owners is delayed. Territorial behavior breaks down when the birds have young, when they are too busy collecting food to be able to defend their territory.

In Central Europe Great tits start to build nests in early to mid April. Each egg weighs about 10 percent of the female's body weight and she may lay 10 eggs. She needs a plentiful supply of food in addition to her

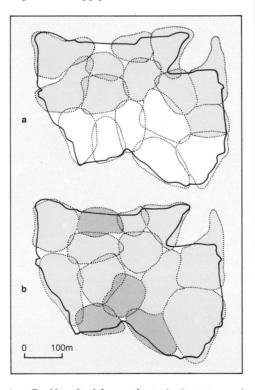

▲ **Rapid territorial expansion** in the Great tit. These maps show the distribution of Great tit territories in a small wood (18ha, 45 acres). (a) Six pairs of birds were removed from their territories. (b) Within three days four new pairs had taken up residence (amber), while other residents of the wood had expanded their territories where their neighbors had been removed.

▶ **Head down, wings open,** a male Great tit threatens an intruder.

normal requirements, to form her own body weight in eggs over a period of just 10–14 days. The male brings food to the laying female. She also needs to lay as early as possible, since young born early in the season stand a better chance of surviving than those of later nests. However, the female's requirement for food is such that she cannot always lay at the time which would be best from the chicks' point of view; she has to wait until food is sufficiently abundant for her. Evidence for this is the fact that where food is put out for them just prior to laying the Great tits lay earlier than in adjacent areas where the birds are not fed. Great tits breeding in gardens also tend to lay earlier than those in woodland, probably again because the food put out for them by people enables them to do so.

After 13–14 days the eggs have hatched. Now the parents have to work exceedingly hard to feed their large and hungry brood. In the first days, the female may need to brood the young to keep them warm, but once they are 4–5 days old both parents spend almost all the daylight hours bringing food to the nest. Caterpillars collected from the trees are the main item. If caterpillars are sufficiently plentiful, between them the parents may bring them at a rate of one every minute; at the height of the nestling period 1,000 feeding visits may be made in one 16-hour day. In spite of this, the young beg for more. In a large brood the young leave the nest lighter in weight than those of smaller broods, showing that they have not received sufficient to bring them to full weight. This has important consequences, as the heavier young have a better chance of surviving to the next breeding season. The higher survival rate comes about not merely because of better nutrition in the nest, but because the heaviest chicks (and the earliest fledged) become dominant in the feeding flocks and so have the best opportunities for displacing their weaker comrades in disputes over food. In many species of tit only one brood is raised each year, but the Great tit may raise two if feeding conditions are good when the first brood leaves the nest.

Few of the very large number of young produced survive. About 1 in 10 of the eggs laid or about 1 in 6 of the newly fledged young end up as breeding adults. Roughly 50 percent of adult birds survive the winter to breed the following summer. Thus, on average, about one bird per pair survives to breed and one egg per brood does also. Of a thousand adult Great tits entering their first winter in Central Europe, perhaps one will live to reach the age of ten.   CMP

NUTHATCHES

Family: Sittidae
Order: Passeriformes (suborder Oscines, part).
Twenty-one species in 4 genera.
Distribution: N America, Europe, N Africa,
Asia, New Guinea, Australia.

Habitat: woodlands, parks, rocks.

  Size: length 9.5–20cm
(4–7.5in), weight 10–60g
(0.35–1.75oz).

Plumage: upperparts blue-gray; two species
have a bright blue back (Azure and Velvet-
fronted nuthatches); some species have a black
stripe through each eye; underparts grayish
white to brown. Little difference between sexes
except in the Chestnut-breasted nuthatch:
males chestnut underparts, females cinnamon.

Voice: repeated piping phrases, chattering calls.

Nests: the two sittellas build open nests in trees;
all other species use holes in trees or rocks.

Eggs: 4–10; white with reddish spots; weight
1–2.5g (0.04–0.09oz).

Incubation period: 15–18 days (19 days in
Wall creeper).

Nestling period: 23–25 days (28–29 days in
Wall creeper).

Diet: insects and spiders, also seeds in autumn
and winter (except in Wall creeper).

Species and genera include: **Azure nuthatch**
(*Sitta azurea*), **Chestnut-breasted nuthatch**
(*S. castanea*), **Corsican nuthatch** (*S. whiteheadi*),
Eastern rock nuthatch (*S. tephronota*), **Eurasian
nuthatch** (*S. europaea*), **Kabylian nuthatch** Ⓡ
(*S. ledanti*), **Red-breasted nuthatch** (*S.
canadensis*), **Rock nuthatch** (*S. neumayer*),
sittellas (genus *Neositta*), **Velvet-fronted
nuthatch** (*S. frontalis*), **Wall creeper** (*Tichodroma
muraria*), **White-breasted nuthatch**
(*S. carolinensis*), **White-tailed nuthatch**
(*S. himalayensis*).

Ⓡ Rare

NUTHATCHES are the only birds able to
climb not only up trees but also down
them, headfirst. No other bird can move on
trees with such versatility. The method
employed differs from that of woodpeckers
and treecreepers in that the tail is not used
for support. When climbing the nuthatch's
feet are not parallel but one is placed high,
from which to hang, and the other low, for
support. The word "nuthatch" is derived
from the fondness of the Eurasian species for
hazel nuts.

The species belonging to the main genus,
Sitta, are so similar in form and habits that
they are easily recognized as nuthatches.
They are mostly gray-blue above (blue in
some tropical species) with long bills and
short necks. All except the Rock nuthatch
and the Eastern rock nuthatch forage on
trees, climbing around on trunks and thick
branches. The two sittellas, which are confined to Australia and New Guinea, are similar to the true nuthatches except that they
build open nests in trees, never using holes.
The Wall creeper is similar to the true
nuthatches in color but has a bill shaped
more like that of the treecreepers. It also
lives in the high mountains of Europe and
Asia whereas nuthatches generally prefer
woods from high altitudes down to sea level.

The Eurasian nuthatch has the most
extensive range of all nuthatches, being distributed from North Africa and Spain across
to Japan. The White-breasted nuthatch
breeds in North America and the Chestnut-
breasted nuthatch, whose behavior is similar to that of the Eurasian species, throughout the Indian subcontinent. Other species
have smaller, often isolated ranges. The Wall
creeper, however, has a restricted habitat
but is found in high mountains from Spain
across Eurasia to the eastern Himalayas.

Only a few species are known to undertake migrations. The Red-breasted nuthatch
migrates from the woods of Canada as far
as the southern montane woodlands of
North America. In some winters the east
Siberian subspecies of the Eurasian
nuthatch moves west as far as Finland.

Most nuthatches eat insects and spiders;
the Rock nuthatch also takes small snails.
Nuthatches from more northern areas and

▶ **Descending nuthatch.** The Pygmy nuthatch
(*Sitta pygmaea*) is the smallest species of
nuthatch. It lives in the western USA, from the
Rockies to the Pacific. Its plumage and habits
are matched in the eastern USA by the
Brown-headed nuthatch (*S. pusilla*).

▼ **Nuthatch postures.** (1) A solitary Corsican
nuthatch feeding. The foot takes the weight of
the bird, the right provides support.
(2) Courtship feeding in Corsican nuthatches.
(3) A Eurasian nuthatch in a threatening
posture. (4) A Eurasian nuthatch making a
defensive posture.

also some of the small species, for example the Corsican nuthatch, take tree seeds from the fall onwards and store them in bark crevices or under moss for later consumption. One pair of Eurasian nuthatches made a daily average of 921 collecting flights over three days, each time taking one or two sunflower seeds. The seed is hidden by covering it with bark or moss. When young hatch they are fed, in all species, by both parents on insects and spiders.

The true nuthatches are monogamous, each pair living in a territory which it will often defend throughout the year. The formation of new pairs takes place in the fall and through the winter, often in February. (In winter nuthatch pairs often associate in feeding flocks with parties of tits.) All nuthatches of the genus *Sitta* are hole-nesters, some excavating their nest-chambers in rotten wood. Rock nuthatches make a nest-chamber by closing up a rock niche with a hemispherical mud wall and entering through a specially constructed tube. Some nuthatches (eg the Eurasian nuthatch but also the Chestnut-breasted and White-tailed nuthatches) use mud to reduce the size of an entrance: the hole is covered until there is just enough space left to accommodate the width of the bird's body. Using a similar technique all cracks and small openings in the cavity are sealed. In dry periods Rock nuthatches (and also other species in Asia) use animal dung as building material, and also caterpillars, other larvae and insects which are squashed with the bill. Berries have also been found in walls made by Rock nuthatches. The White-breasted nuthatch rubs insects round the entrance hole while the Red-breasted uses smeared resin as a protection.

Inside their holes nuthatches construct nests. Various materials are used. The Eurasian nuthatch and its Asiatic relatives (such as the Chestnut-breasted and White-tailed nuthatches) make a nest of thin flakes of bark (mainly pine). Some species use fine grasses and feathers. The rock nuthatches use exclusively mammal hair and filaments, often fragmented owl pellets. North American nuthatches also use bark and animal hair.

Most pairs produce just a single brood during the breeding season, which is incubated by the female alone. During the incubation period the male brings food for the female. Both adults feed the young. The young can fly and climb well by the time they fledge. At this point they require just one week to become independent.

HL

TREECREEPERS

Families: Certhiidae, Climacteridae, Rhabdornithidae
Order: Passeriformes (suborder Oscines, part).
Fourteen species in 4 genera.
Distribution: See map and table.

▶ **At the nest-hole,** a female White-throated treecreeper (an Australasian treecreeper). Treecreepers' life is centered on trees, with different species sometimes concentrating on trunks or branches.

▼ **Fan-like wings spread,** a Common treecreeper (an holarctic treecreeper) returns to its nest.

TREECREEPERS are small, mostly brown birds which are usually seen climbing steadily up the trunk of a tree and along its branches, then planing down to the base of another tree to repeat the process. They have long toes with deeply curved claws for climbing, and a slightly downcurved bill for probing into crevices and under flakes of bark in search of insects. Apart from these adaptations to their niche, however, the members of the three families of treecreepers have little in common. Even their climbing techniques differ. In the Holarctic treecreepers the feet are held parallel and are moved simultaneously, whereas in the Australasian treecreepers one foot is always held in front of the other and the lower foot is brought up to the level of the upper before the latter is moved higher. Moreover most species of Australasian treecreepers spend much time on the ground.

The five species of Holarctic treecreepers belonging to the genus *Certhia* are unique among treecreepers in possessing pointed tail feathers with stiffened shafts, which are used as a prop when climbing. This adaptation is also seen in the unrelated woodpeckers and woodcreepers. The five *Certhia* species are very similar in appearance and habits, being mainly solitary. The circumpolar Common treecreeper, known as the Brown creeper in America, overlaps the range of all four of the other species to some extent. In Britain, where it is the only treecreeper, this species inhabits open deciduous woodlands, but in Europe this habitat is occupied by the Short-toed treecreeper and the Common is confined to coniferous forests. Four species occur in the Himalayas up to the timberline (about 3,500m)11,500ft), all moving down to the foothills and adjacent plains during winter. The Himalayan treecreeper apparently favors conifers and avoids pure oak forest, where it is replaced by the Brown-throated treecreeper. The Stoliczka's treecreeper has the most restricted distribution of all, but it is not known how this bird differs from the others in its habitat or niche requirements.

Although the Spotted creeper is included in the Holarctic treecreepers it lacks the modified tail of the main genus *Certhia* and differs markedly from all other treecreepers in its nest, which is built on a horizontal branch usually in a fork. It is beautifully camouflaged, being decorated externally with spiders' eggs bags, lichen and caterpillar frass (excrement). This peculiarity suggests that it may have closer relatives in other nonclimbing families. Similarly, though once considered allied to the Australasian treecreepers, the Philippine creepers lack the sexual differences and modifications of the foot of the latter and may instead represent a branch of the diverse Asian babblers (Timaliinae). Little is known about these birds. They reputedly gather at times to visit flowering plants in open areas but their tongue is not particularly specialized for nectar-feeding. Of the two Philippine creepers the larger Plain-headed creeper prefers the higher montane forest regions, while the Stripe-headed creeper occupies lower areas.

The six species of Australasian treecreepers are all found on the Australian mainland, but one also occurs in New Guinea. They overlap little in their distribution except in southeastern Australia, where the White-throated often coexists with the Red-browed in eucalypt forests, and with the Brown in woodlands and partly cleared areas. The larger Brown is often found on the ground but the other two are similar in size and live almost entirely in trees. However, the White-throated uses rough-barked trees more than the Red-browed, preferring the fibrous bark of the trunk, while the latter concentrates on the smooth branches of such trees.

The White-throated treecreeper is the only species that occurs in rain forests and possibly had a different ancestor to the other

Australasian treecreepers. It differs in many respects, including patterns of sexual differences, juvenile plumage and egg coloration. In the White-throated, females have an orange spot on the cheek while females of the other species are characterized by rufous stripes on the chest. Juvenile White-throated treecreepers have whitish streaks on the scapular feathers (above the shoulders) and a bright chestnut patch on the rump (in females), features lacking in the other species. In contrast with the other species, the White-throated has relatively unmarked eggs, and only the female builds the nest. It has a much longer incubation period, a special territorial display, and calls specific to each sex. Moreover, it roosts externally whereas the other species generally sleep inside hollow spouts.

Social organization varies greatly among the Australasian treecreepers. The White-throated breeds in pairs but is normally solitary during the nonbreeding season. By contrast, the Red-browed and Brown treecreepers live in pairs or groups of up to six. These groups usually consist of the breeding pair and their male offspring, females tending to disperse in their first year. Both species breed communally, nonbreeding birds feeding the incubating female and young. In the Brown, however, birds sometimes attend two nests in different territories contemporaneously. This unique behavior results from, firstly, some birds continuing to attend nests in their natal territory even after they have become breeders with their own separate territory, and secondly some nonbreeders attending the young of their brothers or stepbrothers, as well as their father. The parents benefit from this "help" from these extra attendants but the latter may also benefit in the future from the help of the young they attend.   RAN

The 3 Families of Treecreepers

Australasian treecreepers
Family: Climacteridae
Six species of the genus *Climacteris*.
Australia and New Guinea. Forest and woodland. Size: 12–19cm (5–7.5in) long, weight 20–40g (0.7–1.4oz). Plumage: upperparts brown to black, underparts striped or rufous; broad, pale wing-bar. Voice: loud piping notes, trills, chatters; harsh grates, rattles. Nest: cup in hole of tree or hollow branch. Eggs: 2–3, white with sparse brown dots (White-throated treecreeper) or pinkish, densely marked with red-brown and lilac-gray; incubation period: 16–23 days; nestling period: 25–26 days.

Diet: insects (especially ants).

Species include: **Brown treecreeper** (*Climacteris picumnus*), **Red-browed treecreeper** (*C. erythrops*), **White-throated treecreeper** (*C. leucophaea*).

Holarctic treecreepers
Family: Certhiidae
Six species in 2 genera.
Eurasia to Indo-China, Africa, N America. Forest, woodland. Size: 12–15cm (5–6in) long, weight 7–16g (0.25–0.6oz). Plumage: upperparts brown, underparts paler in *Certhia*; blackish spotted white in *Salpornis*. Voice: high-pitched, thin whistles and songs. Nest: cup on a loose platform of twigs, usually wedged against a tree trunk behind a flap of loose bark in *Certhia*; cup cemented to a horizontal branch with cobwebs, decorated on the outside in *Salpornis*. Eggs: in *Certhia* 3–9 (usually 5 or 6), white with red-brown dots; in *Salpornis* 2 or 3, pale turquoise with black and lilac markings; incubation period: 14–15 days; nestling period: 15–16 days. Diet: insects and spiders.

Species include: **Brown-throated treecreeper** (*Certhia discolor*), **Common treecreeper** or **Brown creeper** (*C. familiaris*), **Himalayan treecreeper** (*C. himalayana*), **Short-toed treecreeper** (*C. brachydactyla*),

Spotted creeper (*Salpornis spilonotus*), **Stoliczka's treecreeper** (*C. nipalensis*).

Philippine creepers
Family: Rhabdornithidae
Two species of the genus *Rhabdornis*.
Philippine Islands. Forest, second growth. Size: 13–15cm (5–6in) long. Plumage: upperparts brown, underparts white with blackish streaks on flanks. Voice: unknown. Nest: holes in trees. Eggs: unknown. Diet: unknown.

Species: **Plain-headed creeper** (*Rhabdornis inornatus*), **Stripe-headed creeper** (*R. mystacalis*).

WHITE-EYES AND THEIR ALLIES

Families: Zosteropidae, Dicaeidae, Pardalotidae, Nectariniidae
Order: Passeriformes (suborder Oscines, part).
Two hundred and fifty-five species in 24 genera.
Distribution: see maps and table.

White-eyes   Flowerpeckers

Pardalotes   Sunbirds

▶ **Extremely common and very well known**
ABOVE in eastern Africa (Abyssinia to South Africa) is the Pale white-eye (*Zosterops pallida*). Here one is seen taking pollen from a Bird of paradise flower (*Strelitzia reginae*) in South Africa. Otherwise this species eats mainly soft fruit and berries.

▶ **Pardalotes are confined to Australia** BELOW with the Spotted pardalote (*Pardalotus punctatus*) being restricted to eastern Australia. It is a fairly sedentary species which lives in forests and woodlands, but its habits are both arboreal and terrestrial. Here a male is seen looking out of his nest-hole.

WHITE-EYES—small greenish birds with white eye-rings—forage in gardens and forest edges, and flock around bird tables in parts of Africa, Asia, New Guinea, Australia and South Pacific islands. They have short, pointed bills and brush-tipped tongues, with which to collect nectar. They also hunt insects and spiders by gleaning foliage, probing into small crevices and hawking. They appear in orchards and eat fruits as well as aphids. With versatile feeding habits they exploit a variety of resources to survive, and breed even on small wooded islands where most other passerines fail to establish themselves.

Some white-eyes on continents migrate regularly in winter to lower latitudes, though part of the population remains resident in the cold region. They also disperse in flocks to remote islands. In the 1850s white-eyes from Tasmania colonized New Zealand across 2,000km (1,200mi) of sea. Successive generations on oceanic islands and isolated mountains differentiated into new forms by becoming large (eg the Black-capped speirops) and/or losing certain pigments from plumage (eg the Cinnamon white-eye) or even the white eye-ring (eg Olive black-eye). As such differentiations take place in a relatively short geological time, successive invasions of original stock have led to the present coexistence of two or three species on some islands. Yet the similarities between some distant species, resulting from convergence, are so remarkable that it is often difficult to establish true affinities among them.

Most white-eyes pair for life and breed in small territories. Members of a pair often perch together and preen each other. On Heron Island, Great Barrier Reef, where the Gray-breasted white-eye maintains a very high density with more than 400 adults in 16ha (40 acres), they attempt to nest two or three (occasionally four) times between September and March (southern summer). From a clutch of three eggs, two young usually fledge after 11 days of incubation and 12 days of feeding in the nest by both parents. Birds nesting in their first year produce fewer young than older birds (they have fewer clutches); when an adult loses its mate it tends to pair with another bird of similar age rather than a first year bird. Very few change partners. Juveniles suffer a higher mortality than adults, but for those that survive the first year the mortality rate remains constant thereafter and the oldest birds die in the 10th or 11th year. In cyclone years the population is reduced considerably, but it recovers in the following year

after an extended breeding season.

The same ritualized form of aggression used in territorial defense is used in winter when fighting over food. Aggressive birds flutter their wings at their opponent. Equally matched birds may take to the air to fight, after a period of mutual display. Sometimes they supplant a feeding bird or attack and chase an approaching bird with beak clatter or challenge calls.

Some specialized species on islands are in danger of extinction as their population size is small and their available habitats are being destroyed through local development. The Norfolk white-throated white-eye of Norfolk Island, the largest member of the genus *Zosterops*, is one such species. White-eyes are kept as cage-birds in some Asian countries because of their attractive songs. However, they do not breed in aviaries.

Although they are considered pests by orchard-keepers they also consume large quantities of pest insects wherever they occur.   JKi

Flowerpeckers are small dumpy birds, associated with mistletoes, berry-bearing shrubs, trees and vines. They also visit flowers for small insects and possibly nectar. Hence they are called flowerpeckers, berry-peckers and the Mistletoe bird. Thirty-five species belong to the main genus *Dicaeum*, distributed in southern Asia and the islands, east and south to New Guinea and Australia. Many of them are notable as seed dispersers. The Mistletoe bird in Australia excretes a mistletoe seed within half an hour of ingesting a berry. It occurs wherever mistletoes grow, be it the arid center of the continent or the rain forest of the tropical coast. It is only absent from Tasmania, where mistletoe is absent. The greatest variety of flowerpecker species is seen in New Guinea where there are eight species of berrypeckers belonging to four genera. In some berrypeckers the sexes have a different appearance with females duller and larger (an unusual character for passerine birds). The Crested berrypecker is the only crested member of the family and is much larger than the others. It was once placed in a separate family of its own (Paramythiidae).

Flowerpeckers and berrypeckers generally nest in pairs and outside the breeding season they form small flocks or sometimes congregate in large numbers on fruiting shrubs.   JKi

The **pardalotes** are often grouped with flowerpeckers because they have small bodies with stumpy bills and short tails, and plumage having some bright colors and 9 instead of 10 primary flight feathers. These features are now considered to be a result of convergence rather than revealing affinities with flowerpeckers. Biological analysis showed that they are not members of the flowerpeckers as was once thought. Unlike flowerpeckers they forage in outer foliage for small insects and nest in hollows or burrows. Strictly endemic to Australia, the pardalotes probably evolved in association with eucalypts and acacia from among the old passerine colonizers of Australia. Their distinct territorial calls and displays at nest-sites are features of the Australian bushlands (they are absent from rain forest in the breeding season, which starts in winter in the subtropical region and extends to spring and summer in southern parts of the range. The Striated pardalote has several

distinct geographical subspecies which were once treated as separate species. However, where their ranges overlap they hybridize.

JKi

Sunbirds are small, brightly colored, nectar-feeding birds of the Old World tropics. As the ecological counterparts of hummingbirds of the New World, sunbirds are closely associated with flowers that depend on them for pollination and offer large quantities of nectar as the tempting reward.

Africa and its islands are the home of most sunbirds (76 of 116 species), but other species inhabit the Middle East, India, Ceylon, the Himalayas, Burma through Malaysia, the East Indies, New Guinea and Australia. The Palestine sunbird alone is found in Israel and Palestine. Many colorful, long-tailed species of the genus *Aethopyga* occur in India and the Himalayas, while spider-hunters are restricted to Malaysia.

The largest sunbird is the Giant sunbird, which is restricted to the island of Sao Tomé in the Gulf of Guinea. Other large, spectacular species, the Golden-winged sunbird, Scarlet-tufted malachite sunbird and Tacazze sunbird live in the mountains of East Africa. Three medium-sized species of West Africa, the Superb sunbird, Splendid sunbird and Johanna's sunbird, and several Himalayan species are renowned for their spectacular colors. Most highly colored species in Africa are found in open habitats while plain-colored species inhabit shady forests.

Spider-hunters lack the bright plumage colors of other sunbirds and their bills are larger, stronger and downcurved. They feed primarily on spiders as their name implies. Their nests are cup-shaped like those of many passerine birds, not hanging, bag-like structures. Both sexes incubate, unlike other sunbirds where this is the job of the female.

Sunbirds are small to very small birds with long, thin, curved bills. Fine serrations on the edges of the delicate bill help to capture and hold insects. The nostrils are covered by flaps (opercula) which keep out flower pollen. The tongue is mostly tubular except for its split tips. Sunbirds have strong feet with short toes and sharp claws that aid difficult perching while feeding at flowers.

▶ **Sunbird feeding territories** in central Kenya. Golden-winged sunbirds feed at flowers of the mint *Leonotis nepetifolia* during months when flowers and nectar are scarce in their mountain habitats. The number of flowers in a territory is predictably close to the number required to supply a sunbird's daily energy needs. As the number of new flowers on a site changes from day to day the boundaries of the territory expand or contract.

Territorial defense requires constant vigil and also investment of energy in frequent chases and eviction of intruders of several species of sunbirds, which try to feed at the same nectar-rich flowers. Golden-winged sunbirds invest energy in territorial defense when they expect to recover that investment plus some "profit." Return on the investment derives from being able to obtain more nectar from undefended flowers and being able to rest rather than feed as a result. When Golden-winged sunbirds can get adequate nectar from flowers that are common property they do not defend a territory but instead share flowers with others.

▶ **A Greater double-collared sunbird** (*Nectarinia afra*), an African species.

The 4 Families of White-eyes, Flowerpeckers and Sunbirds ⓡ Rare.

White-eyes and allies
Family: Zosteropidae
Eighty-five species in 11 genera.
Africa, Asia, New Guinea, Australia, Oceania (introduced to Hawaii). Woodland, forest, gardens. Size: 10–14cm (4–5.5in), weight 8–31g (0.3–1.1oz); in some species females are smaller than males. Plumage: greenish with yellow, gray, white and brown parts; most species have a conspicuous white ring round the eye; in some species males are brighter than females. Voice: males produce a rich warbling song at dawn; a high-pitched plaintive note is produced for keeping contact across long distances; other distinct notes used in alarm, distress and for courtship; beak clatter also used in aggression. Nest: cup shape, slung in a tree fork under cover. Eggs: 2–4, whitish or pale blue without spots (2 species have spotted eggs); size: 1.4 × 1cm to 2 × 1.5cm (0.5 × 0.4in to 0.8 × 0.6in); incubation period: 10–12 days; nestling period: 11–13 days. Diet: insects, nectar, berries; fruits in winter.

Species include: **Black-capped speirops** (*Speirops lugubris*), **Gray-breasted white-eye** (*Zosterops lateralis*), **Cinnamon white-eye** (*Hypocryptadius cinnamomeus*), **Norfolk white-throated white-eye** (*Zosterops albogularis*), **Olive black-eye** (*Chlorocharis emiliae*). Total threatened species: 4.

Flowerpeckers and allies
Family: Dicaeidae
Forty-nine species in 6 genera.
Southern Asia, New Guinea, Australia. Woodland, forest. Size: 8–15cm (3–6in), weight 5–20g (0.2–0.7oz); Crested berrypecker is 21cm (8.3in) long, weight 42g (1.5oz). Plumage: upperparts dark and glossy, underparts light; in species with dull plumage no difference between sexes, in others males have patches of bright colors. Voice: faint metallic notes and high-pitched twittering; some species produce series of rapid oscillating notes. Nests: open, cup-shaped or pendant with a side entrance. Eggs: 1–3, white with or without brownish blotches; 1.5 × 1cm to 3 × 2.1cm (0.6 × 0.4in to 1.2 × 0.8in); incubation period: 12 days; nestling period: about 15 days. Diet: berries (swallowed whole), insects, spiders.

Species include: **Crested berrypecker** (*Paramythia montium*), **Mistletoe bird** (*Dicaeum hirundinaceum*).

Pardalotes or diamond birds
Family: Pardalotidae
Five species of the genus *Pardalotus*.
Australia. Woodland and forest. Size: 8–12cm (3–5in) long, weight 8–13g (0.3–0.5oz). Plumage: back is slate to olive, head and wings black with white spots or stripes, bright yellow or orange patches; females duller than males in some species. Voice: 2–5 distinct notes, repeated. Nests: cup-shaped or dome-shaped, placed in tree hollow or at the end of a tunnel 40–70cm (16–28in) long dug in a bank or down from the surface of sand. Eggs: 3–5, white; 1.6 × 1.3cm to 1.9 × 1.5cm (0.6 × 0.5in to 0.7 × 0.6in); incubation period: 14–16 days; nestling period: about 25 days. Diet: small insects and spiders.

Species include: **Striated pardalote** (*Pardalotus striatus*).

Sunbirds and spider-hunters
Family: Nectariniidae
One hundred and sixteen species in 6 genera.
Old World tropics, from Africa to N Australia including Himalayas. Lowland forest, second growth, gardens, thornscrub, moorlands, rhododendron forest. Size: 9–30cm (3.5–12in) long including the tail, which accounts for about a third of length; weight 5–20g (0.2–0.7oz). Plumage: males are bright iridescent blue and green, often with bright red, yellow or orange underparts; females usually duller—olive green, gray or brown with tinges of yellow below and some streaks or spots; the colors of some males are highlighted by yellow or red display tufts at the bend of the wings and by long central tail feathers; male spider-hunters lack metallic colors as do some forest sunbirds of Africa. Voice: produce sharp and metallic songs—loud, high pitched, fast and tinkling. Nests: purse-shaped structure, embedded or suspended; side entrance is often covered with a porch-like projection; often decorated or held together by spider webs; nests of spider-hunters are cup-shaped. Eggs: 2, sometimes 3, whitish or bluish white with heavy dark spots, blotches or streaks; incubation period: 13–15 days; nestling period: 14–19 days. Diet: flower nectar and insects especially spiders; rarely fruit.

Species and genera include: **Amani sunbird** ⓡ (*Anthreptes pallidigaster*), **Giant sunbird** (*Nectarinia thomensis*), **Golden-winged sunbird** (*N. reichenowi*), **Johanna's sunbird** (*N. johannae*), **Palestine sunbird** (*N. osea*), **Scarlet-tufted malachite sunbird** (*N. johnstoni*), **spider-hunters** (genus *Arachnothera*), **Splendid sunbird** (*N. coccinigastra*), **Superb sunbird** (*N. superba*), **Tacazze sunbird** (*N. tacazze*).

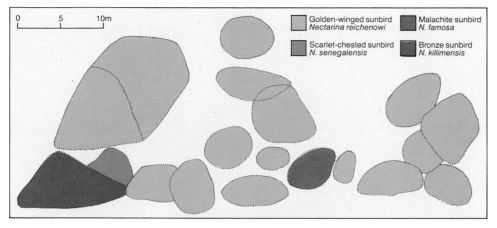

The variable tail shapes include long central feathers in males of some species.

Although many sunbirds aggregate in large numbers at suitable flowers, they rarely form cohesive flocks. Some species, especially insect-eating species of *Anthreptes*, participate in parties of mixed species. Many species are highly nomadic and are know to wander great distances in search of nectar.

Sunbirds feed on insects and nectar. Even subtle differences in sunbird bill sizes affect abilities to feed at different kinds of flowers. Small, short-billed sunbirds find insects in the foliage and extract minute volumes of nectar from small insect-pollinated flowers. Large, long-billed species depend more on nectar in large, conspicuous red or orange flowers with long corollas that should exclude short-billed species. Short-billed sunbirds, however, often pierce the bases of these flowers to obtain the nectar. Sunbirds normally perch while feeding at flowers; they rarely hover like hummingbirds. Typical sunbird flowers in Africa include species of the following: *Erythrina*, *Spathodia* and *Symphonia*.

Many mistletoe flowers depend on sunbirds for pollination. They literally explode when a sunbird visits them. A new mistletoe flower houses spring-like filaments and anthers bearing pollen. When a sunbird pokes its long bill into one of the slits on the side of the flower, the trap is sprung and the flower bursts open to spray a cloud of fresh pollen onto the forehead of the sunbird for transport to another flower.

Studies in Kenya of sunbirds feeding at one mistletoe (*Loranthus dshallensis*) revealed that whereas young sunbirds exploded flower after flower in their own faces and became covered with pollen, adults often ducked quickly after they tripped the trigger.

Nesting by sunbirds is related to rainfall and in turn to peaks in the availability of flowers and insects. Some species may breed at almost any time of the year, and pairs may renest up to five times in succession. In contrast to hummingbirds, which are promiscuous, sunbirds are monogamous. Male sunbirds feed their young, but do not help with nest-building or incubation. Instead they often defend flowers which are their mate's energy supply.

Breeding male sunbirds have a reputation for being extremely pugnacious. Subordinate species in East Africa may breed successfully only when large dominant species do not usurp their nectar supplies.

FBG

HONEYEATERS AND AUSTRALIAN CHATS

Families: Meliphagidae, Ephthianuridae
Order: Passeriformes (suborder Oscines, part).
One hundred and seventy-four species in 40 genera.
Distribution: see map and table.

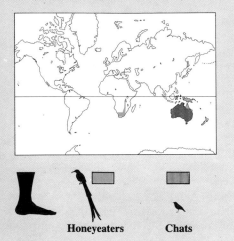

Honeyeaters   Chats

► **The Orange chat** ABOVE is a brilliant inhabitant of a dull, arid habitat.

► **Sweet tastes** BELOW are evident in the diet of Lewin's honeyeater (*Meliphaga lewini*). Here one is eating a paw-paw fruit. The species eats mostly fruit but also honey and insects. It inhabits rain forest in eastern Australia.

▷ **Dining on waratah** OVERLEAF a Noisy friarbird (*Philemon corniculatus*). Another species of eastern Australia and southeast New Guinea it is a raucous bird. Its bare head has earned it the alternative common name of leatherhead.

H ONEYEATERS all have a long protrusible tongue with a brush-like tip which they use to extract nectar from flowers. They are important pollinators of Australian flowers and many have co-evolved with certain species of plants. Otherwise they are extremely variable in size and habits. They are one of the dominant passerine families in Australasia and represent a very successful adaptation to a wide variety of food-types. Almost all feed on nectar and many on insects and fruit, some predominantly so.

Honeyeaters are often the most numerous species present in an area and there may be more than 10 different honeyeater species in 1ha (2.5 acres). None are truly terrestrial or found in arid country, unlike their close relatives the Australian chats, and only the Singing honeyeater occurs in open country and coastal dunes.

In general they are longish, streamlined birds with long, pointed wings and undulating flight. Bold and vigorous, they have strong legs and sharp claws which enable them to clamber agilely around flowers and foliage as they feed, sometimes upside-down. Nearly all have rather long, down-curved and sharply-pointed bills, with many variations on this shape associated with differences in diet. Most honeyeaters are drab but a few are brightly colored, resembling their counterparts, the sunbirds of Africa and Asia and hummingbirds of America.

There were once at least five honeyeaters in Hawaii but the kioea and one moho became extinct about 1840 and two other

mohos were last seen earlier this century. Only the ooaa still lives in the forests of Hawaii, feeding on insects and some nectar. Bellbirds and the starling-like tui are found throughout New Zealand, especially in or near forest, but the stitchbird disappeared from mainland New Zealand around 1885 and is now confined to one offshore island.

The sugarbirds of South Africa resemble large honeyeaters but opinion is divided as to whether they are really members of the family Meliphagidae or merely convergent in appearance and habits. Recent evidence suggests that they are not true honeyeaters.

Honeyeater diversification has been so great that 14 of the 38 genera in this family contain only a single species, and 10 genera only two species each. The largest group, the "typical" honeyeaters (*Meliphaga*), contains 36 of the 169 honeyeater species. Olive in color and very similar in appearance, their relationships are complex. Most are smallish, foliage-gleaning insectivores with relatively short, straight bills.

No honeyeater is truly solitary and some are very gregarious. Cooperative breeding occurs in the White-naped honeyeater and is widespread in the miners. Species such as the Noisy miner live in dense colonies—up to 10 birds per hectare (4 per acre)—broken into territorial, family groups which forage together and unite to mob predators and other birds. Only the female incubates and meanwhile the males in a group may help feed the nestlings of neighbouring groups. Over 20 different males may help a female with the nest and feed nestlings during a season and the feeding rate may exceed 50 visits an hour. Even the fledglings from one brood may feed their siblings in the next. The groups have a clear-cut hierarchy and sometimes indulge in elaborate communal displays called "corroborees."

Only the two *Ramsayornis* honeyeaters build nests with domes; all others have cup-shaped nests. In most species the female

Honeyeaters as Pollinators

Many Australian flowers rely on honeyeaters for pollination and reward them with copious nectar. Some plants have only generalized flowers (eg eucalypts), which are also visited by insects, but others have flowers adapted to birds, especially in the families Proteaceae and Ericaceae. Long, narrow tubular corollas, sometimes defended by hairs, deter insects but not birds and are often yellow or red—a color insects see badly. Bird-pollinated flowers are often clumped and a banksia inflorescence 20–40cm (8–16in) long may contain over 5,000 flowers.

Bird pollination probably developed from insect pollination, as honeyeaters evolved from insectivorous birds. All honeyeaters still eat insects to obtain essential nutrients although some have become very reliant on nectar for energy.

Pollen deposited on the forehead, face, chin and beak of a honeyeater, often visible as a yellow patch, is transferred to the stigmas of the next flowers visited. Honeyeaters typically carry thousands of pollen grains from several

different plant species at a time and their relationships with Australian flowers are much less specific than those between hummingbirds and flowers in tropical America. However, a process of co-evolution has produced some elaborate mutual adaptations such as the long, curved beak which Western spinebills use to probe the long tubular flowers of kangaroo-paws and jug-flowers.

Some plants produce only a few flowers at a time, albeit over prolonged periods, which forces honeyeaters to move between plants and promotes cross-fertilization, a genetic advantage. Indeed, many bird-pollinated plants are probably incapable of self-pollination. The greater mobility of birds makes them more effective at outcrossing than insects and they are less affected by adverse weather. The unpredictable climate and flowering patterns in much of Australia results in many honeyeaters being migratory or nomadic as they follow the nectar flow opportunistically.

The 2 Families of Honeyeaters and Australian Chats

E Endangered.   V Vulnerable.

Honeyeaters

Family: Meliphagidae
One hundred and sixty-nine species in 38 genera.
Australia, New Guinea, New Zealand, SW Pacific and Bonin Islands, Hawaii, Indonesia, S Africa. Mostly forest and woodlands containing nectar-producing plants such as eucalypts and banksias; some species in heathlands and open country but none fully terrestrial. Size: 8–45cm (3–18in) long (including tail of longest sugarbird), weight 6.5–150g (0.2–5oz). Plumage: most species dull green, gray or brown, some with black, white or yellow markings.

Sexes similar in most species but different in some. Voice: small species often musical, larger ones raucous. Nests: cup-shaped, built by the female. Eggs: 2 (1–4), white, pinkish or buff with reddish-brown spots; incubation period: 13–17 days; nestling period: 10–16 days (17–21 days for sugarbirds). Diet: nectar, insects and sometimes fruit.

Species and genera include: **Noisy miner** (*Manorina melanocephala*), **ooaa** E (*Moho braccatus*), **Painted honeyeater** (*Grantiella picta*), **Singing honeyeater** (*Meliphaga virescens*), **stitchbird** V (*Notiomystis cincta*), **tui** (*Prosthemadera novaeseelandiae*), **wattlebirds** (genus *Anthochaera*), **Western spinebill** (*Acanthorhynchus superciliosus*), **White-naped honeyeater** (*Melithreptus lunatus*), **Yellow-faced honeyeater** (*Meliphaga chrysops*), **yellow-winged honeyeaters** (genus *Phylidonyris*).

Australian chats

Family: Ephthianuridae
Five species in 2 genera.
Australia. Open scrubland, dry woodland, desert and margins of water. Size: 10–13cm (4–5in) long, weight 10–11g (0.4oz). Plumage: red, yellow or black and white; males

more brightly marked than females. Voice: metallic twanging contact calls, aggressive chattering calls and high-pitched whistles. Nest: cup-shaped nest in a bush close to the ground or on ground. Eggs: usually 3–4, white or pinkish white with reddish brown spots; 17 × 14mm. Diet: insects taken on ground.

Species: **Crimson chat** (*Ephthianura tricolor*), **Gibber chat** (*Ashbyia lovensis*), **Orange chat** (*Ephthianura aurifrons*), **White-fronted chat** (*E. albifrons*), **Yellow chat** (*E. crocea*).

incubates alone but in some both sexes incubate; both parents feed the young. Most honeyeaters breed in the spring but some also breed in the fall or have protracted breeding seasons. They have a typical passerine molt after the spring breeding attempt.

Most honeyeaters are very generalized feeders, with few anatomical specializations for extracting nectar from particular types of flowers. They differ greatly in their dependence upon nectar and insects, although all take insects for the essential nutrients not present in nectar and some are almost entirely insectivorous. The widespread Singing honeyeater balances its diet between nectar, insects and fruit, while the Painted honeyeater is almost entirely fruit-eating—it is nomadic in its search for mistletoe berries.

Ecologists often divide honeyeaters into long-billed and short-billed forms. The small to medium-sized honeyeaters with rather short, straight bills (eg *Melithreptus*, *Meliphaga* and *Manorina* species) are more insectivorous in their habits and tend to segregate by habitat.

The long-billed honeyeaters eat more nectar than insects, and the small red honeyeaters and spinebills use their long, curved bills to feed from tubular flowers. This group also includes the medium-sized yellow-winged honeyeaters, which are generalized nectar-eaters visiting a wide range of flowers, and the wattlebirds which tend to prefer eucalyptus and banksia flowers.

How can several species of long-billed honeyeaters live in the same area when they are competing for a limited nectar supply? The answer seems to lie in a balance between small, efficient honeyeaters and large, aggressive ones. The larger species, such as wattlebirds, aggressively exclude other honeyeaters from dense clumps of flowers where nectar levels are highest, but cannot defend all the flowers over a wider area. This allows the smaller honeyeaters, which can still feed profitably on the poorer nectar sources, to co-exist with larger species. Thus a hierarchy of aggression based on size maintains a diversity of birds even where nectar abundance varies greatly.

If nectar is really scarce some honeyeaters probably switch to a more insectivorous diet but most move to areas richer in nectar. In the tropical rain forests of New Guinea and northeastern Australia most honeyeaters are sedentary but in the more arid areas they are markedly nomadic. Even in the mediterranean and temperate coastal areas many honeyeaters show extensive movements. In southeastern Australia, the Yellow-faced honeyeater and the White-naped honeyeater regularly migrate northward each fall and return in spring, although some birds remain in the south during winter and elsewhere movements are purely local.

The **Australian chats** are colorful birds whose brush-tipped tongues and egg coloration suggest they may be related to honeyeaters. Males are red, yellow, or black and white, but females are duller in four of the five species. Chats live in open country, usually in groups, taking insects on the ground. They nest in low bushes, often in loose colonies. Most are well-adapted to dry, even desert, conditions.

Crimson chats and Orange chats occur throughout the semi-arid saltbush, samphire and savanna of the inland plains. Highly gregarious, they sometimes form large flocks. Both species, but especially Crimson chats, are very nomadic and occasionally erupt coastwards in adverse seasons. Both sexes build the cup-shaped nest, incubate the eggs and feed the young. The rare Yellow chat is known only from swamps near the north and northeast coasts and from reeds around water in the interior.

White-fronted chats are fairly common throughout southern Australia in samphire, saltbush and the edges of swamps. Most birds breed in the south of their range. Tasmanian birds and some mainland populations are sedentary but others move northwards when not breeding.

In the more robust Gibber chat the sexes are similar in color. Their name comes from the stony Gibber plains around Lake Eyre in central Australia where they live. Some birds are sedentary but others make local movements. Breeding occurs whenever conditions are suitable, the nest being placed on the ground.   RDW

BUNTINGS AND TANAGERS

Family: Emberizidae
Order: Passeriformes (suborder Oscines, part).
Five hundred and fifty-two species in 136 genera.
Distribution: Worldwide except extreme SE Asia and Australasia.

▶ **Reed bunting** ABOVE, widespread from Europe to East Asia. Female (here) has black and whitish moustache streaks—males have distinctive head markings in breeding season, as do males of most Eurasian buntings of the genus *Emberiza*.

▶ **Male Lapland longspur** or bunting BELOW by nest. Females do all the incubating but males share the feeding of young. The "long spurs" are the elongated toes of this species.

▼ **Unique coloration** of male Painted bunting (*Passerina ciris*), from the southern USA to Central America: no other bird has a blue head and red underparts. The female Painted bunting is a brilliant yellow-green.

THE term **bunting** is derived evidently from an old English word "buntyle," the original meaning of which is somewhat obscure. Whatever its meaning, the name was given to several grain-eating, ground-feeding birds in western Europe. The name was later carried by early settlers and pioneers from Britain to other parts of the world and there applied to some not particularly closely related birds: in North America, for example, to some members of the subfamily Carduelinae, the cardinal grosbeaks. Ironically, most true buntings of the New World are called sparrows.

The true buntings almost certainly evolved in the New World. More than three-quarters of the world's species are found in the Americas, and there occupy a diverse and broad range of habitats. Of the 60 or so species in North America, for example, we find species inhabiting arctic tundra, boreal forest, prairies and meadows, deserts, alpine meadows, salt and freshwater marshes, and oak and pine woods. Probably, ancestral open-country buntings crossed the Bering Sea into Asia, the genus *Emberiza* evolving in temperate Asia where it is best represented, and spreading westward into Europe and Africa. Interestingly enough, there are only a couple of buntings breeding in tropical Asia, the Crested bunting and the Chinese blue bunting, and the group has failed to penetrate or persist in the East Indies–Australasia region, although the Cirl bunting and the yellowhammer have been introduced with some success into New Zealand.

The true buntings are characterized by a stout, conical bill adapted for crushing and taking the husks off seeds. The upper and lower parts of the bill can be moved sideways in some species; juncos for example are particularly adept at manipulating, cracking, and discarding the husks off seeds with their bills. True buntings show considerable diversity in plumage and voice—somberly plumaged species such as the Corn bunting, dull grayish-brown with heavy streaks, contrast with the more brightly-plumaged ones, such as the yellowhammer with bright yellow underparts and streaked yellow head, and the Lapland longspur with black, chestnut and white head markings.

In temperate and arctic regions, buntings are mostly monogamous, with a few males attracting more than one female in some species studied. The Lark bunting and Corn bunting, however, are usually polygamous, with some males reportedly attracting up to seven females at a time, and other males within a population attracting no female at all. It is generally supposed that this mating system occurs when there are large differences in quality of territory among males, so that a female is better off pairing with an already mated male in a good territory rather than with a bachelor male in a poor territory.

Most species are territorial. In migratory species, the male arrives before the female and defends the territory against other males. Often the male reoccupies the same territory he held the year before. Most breeding activities—courting, pairing, nesting, and raising young—occur within the territory. Collecting food for young may or may not occur within territory boundaries—American tree sparrows defend large territories, usually more than 1ha (2.5 acres), within which food is collected, whereas Clay-colored sparrows defend small territories of usually less than 1,000sq m (11,000sq ft) and forage exclusively outside the territory, often on communal feeding grounds. Once the breeding season is over, territorial boundaries break down and adults and young gather together in loose flocks.

Courtship in buntings usually involves a male advertising his presence by singing. When a female approaches, the male dives and chases her through the vegetation. These courtship chases frequently involve the male buffeting the female, and end with both birds tumbling to the ground in a mass of feathers. Song flights occur in open-country species; males of Lapland longspurs, Snow buntings in the Arctic and Chestnut-collared longspurs and Lark buntings on the

North American prairies, for example, typically rise a few meters above ground and then slowly circle back to earth, holding their wings at an angle above the body, and uttering their song.

Nests are usually placed on the ground or low in a bush, and tend to be neat compact cups built of dried vegetation (grass, weeds) and lined with hair, mosses, fine vegetation fibres, wool and/or feathers. Females are usually solely responsible for incubating eggs and brooding young, and males usually contribute substantially to feeding young, at both the nestling and the fledgling stages.

The **Plush-capped finch** is somewhat of an enigma. Little is known of its reproductive biology, vocalizations, foraging or social behavior; most of what we do know comes from collecting trips in South America and from museum specimens. Adults measure about 15cm (6in) in length, and have a striking plumage: dark gray upperparts, chestnut underparts, black nape, and yellow crown of stiff, erect, "plush-like" feathers—hence the name. In overall appearance, this bird resembles the tanagers, except that it has a short, thick, stubby bill more akin to the buntings—indeed, it appears to be a link between these two groups.

Plush-capped finches inhabit forest edges and clearings in the cloud forests of the Andes from Venezuela to northern Argentina. Reports from Colombia and Ecuador indicate that it forages close to the ground, eats insects, and occurs primarily on its own or in pairs, but will join mixed-species flocks.

RWK

THE 5 SUBFAMILIES OF BUNTINGS AND TANAGERS

Old World buntings and New World sparrows
Subfamily: Emberizinae
Two hundred and eighty-one species in 69 genera.

Practically worldwide; absent from extreme SE Asia and Australasia (introduced to New Zealand). Almost cosmopolitan in the New World: open woodlands, grasslands, arctic tundra and alpine meadows, and desert regions; primarily open country, hedgerows, parkland, "edge" habitats in Eurasia. Size: 10–22cm (4–8.5in) long; weight 11–40g (0.4–1.4oz). Plumage: ranges from dull brown and gray to bright blue-green, yellow and red; several groups have sharply patterned plumages. Voice: alarm calls usually loud and easily localized, anxiety calls frequently ventriloquial; songs short and simple to long and melodious, containing whistles, chatters and trills. Nests: woven, cup-shaped nests usually well-concealed on ground or in low bush. Eggs: usually 4–6, base color off-white, light brown or light blue, usually with brownish, reddish or blackish marks; incubation period 10–14 days; nestling period 10–15 days. Diet: primarily grains; adults eat seeds and berries; nestlings are fed almost exclusively on arthropods.

Species and genera include: **American tree sparrow** (*Spizella arborea*), **Black-headed bunting** (*Emberiza melanocephala)*, **Black-throated finch** (*Melanodera melanodera*), **Chestnut-collared longspur** (*Calcarius ornatus*), **Chinese blue bunting** (*Latoucheornis siemsseni*), **Cirl bunting** (*Emberiza cirlus*), **Clay-colored sparrow** (*Spizella pallida*), **Corn bunting** (*Emberiza calandra*), **Crested bunting** (*Melophus lathami*), **Galapagos finches** (*Geospiza, Camarhynchus, Certhidea, Pinaroloxias*), **Gough Island bunting** (*Rowettia goughensis*), **grassquits** (*Tiaris*), **Lapland longspur** (*Calcarius lapponicus*), **Lark bunting** (*Calamospiza melanocorys*), **Red-headed bunting** (*Emberiza bruniceps*), **Reed bunting** (*E. schoeniclus*), **Rock bunting** (*E. cia*), **Rustic bunting** (*E. rustica*), **Savanna sparrow** (*Passerculus sandwichensis*), **seedeaters** (*Sporophila*), **Snow bunting** (*Plectrophenax nivalis*), **Yellowhammer** (*Emberiza citrinella*), **Zapata sparrow** (*Torreornis inexpectata*). Total threatened species: 3.

Tanagers and honeycreepers
Subfamily: Thraupinae
Two hundred and thirty-three species in 56 genera.

Western hemisphere from Canada to northern Chile and central Argentina, including Antilles; nearly all tropical. Forests, scrub, thickets, plantations, parks, gardens; lowlands to high mountains. Size: 9–28cm (3.5–11in) long; weight 8.5–40g (0.3–1.4oz). Plumage: exceedingly varied; many bright colors to gray, olive, black and white. Sexes alike or very different. Voice: on the whole, poorly developed, some species songless, a few persistent and pleasing songsters. Nests: usually well-made open cups in trees and shrubs, rarely in crannies. Euphonias build covered nests with side entrance. Eggs: usually 2, up to 4–5 in euphonias and the few species that breed in temperate zones; blue, blue-gray, gray or white, spotted, blotched and scrawled with lilac, brown or black; incubation period 12–18 days, nestling period 11–24 days. Diet: mainly fruits and arils, also nectar, insects.

Species include: **Blue-and-yellow tanager** (*Thraupis bonariensis*), **Blue-gray tanager** (*T. episcopus*), **chlorophonias** (*Chlorophonia* species), **Crimson-backed tanager** (*Ramphocelus dimidiatus*), **dacnises** (*Dacnis* species), **Diademed tanager** (*Stephanophorus diadematus*), **Dusky-faced tanager** (*Mitrospingus cassinii*), **flower-piercers** (*Diglossa* species), **Green honeycreeper** (*Chlorophanes spiza*), **orangequit** (*Euneornis campestris*), **Paradise tanager** (*Tangara chilensis*), **Red-legged honeycreeper** (*Cyanerpes cyaneus*), **Rose-breasted thrush tanager** (*Rhodinocichla rosea*), **Sayaca tanager** (*Thraupis sayaca*), **Scarlet tanager** (*Piranga olivacea*), **Scarlet-rumped tanager** (*Ramphocelus passerinii*), **Silver-throated tanager** (*Tangara icterocephala*), **Spot-crowned euphonia** (*Euphonia imitans*), **Summer tanager** (*Piranga rubra*), **Yellow-rumped tanager** (*Ramphocelus icteronotus*). Total threatened species: 3.

> ### Island Species
> Island species are of special interest, for their rarity, or relationship to mainland species. Among buntings, the Zapata sparrow is confined to a few marshes in Cuba. The Ipswich (a subspecies of the Savanna) sparrow, occurs only on the shifting sands of windswept Sable Island, some 160km (100mi) east of Nova Scotia. The Gough Island bunting is a recent offshoot of the South American Black-throated finch, but the origins of the Tristan da Cunha species are obscure. On the Pacific Galapagos Islands, 6 of the 13 species are seed eaters, 6 insect eaters, and one insectivore occupies a woodpecker-type niche (a 14th species occupies Cocos Island, 965km/600mi northeast). In this classic adaptive radiation, mainland buntings found their way to the Galapagos Islands and in the absence of competitors evolved to fill various unoccupied niches.
>
> RWK

Cardinal grosbeaks
Subfamily: Cardinalinae
Thirty-seven species in 9 genera.

Central Canada to central Argentina. Temperate zone woodlands, tropical rain forests, thickets, arid scrub, plantations, gardens, fields. Size: 11.5–24cm (4.5–9.5in) long. Plumage: brilliant and varied, or olive, gray, blue-black. Males and females either alike or very different. Voice: Many are superb and persistent songsters. Nests: massive or loosely built open cups in trees and shrubs, rarely on ground. Eggs: 2–5, white, greenish, bluish, or blue, unmarked or speckled or scrawled; incubation period 11–14 days, nestling period 9–15 days. Diet: seeds and grains, fruits and insects.

Species include: **Black-headed grosbeak** (*Pheucticus melanocephalus*), **Blue-black grosbeak** (*Passerina cyanoides*), **Buff-throated saltator** (*Saltator maximus*), **cardinal** (*Cardinalis cardinalis*), **dickcissel** (*Spiza americana*), **Indigo bunting** (*Passerina cyanea*), **Painted bunting** (*P. ciris*), **pyrrhuloxia** (*Cardinalis sinuata*), **Rose-breasted grosbeak** (*Pheucticus ludovicianus*), **Yellow-green grosbeak** (*Caryothraustes canadensis*).

Swallow-tanager
Subfamily: Tersininae
Tersina viridis.

S America from eastern Panama to northern Argentina. Open woodland, clearings with scattered trees, and suburban gardens. Size: about 13cm (5in) long; weight 28–32g (1–1.1oz). Plumage: male largely iridescent turquoise blue with a black mask, black-barred sides and white abdomen; female bright green. Voice: a pebbly twitter of up to 7 syllables. Nests: a shallow cup of vegetable materials in long tunnels in masonry, cliffs or earthen banks. Eggs: 2 or 3, shiny, unmarked white, weight 2.8g (0.10z); incubation period 13–17 days; nestling period 24 days. Diet: fruit, insects.

Plush-capped finch
Subfamily: Catamblyrhynchinae
Catamblyrhynchus diadema.

Western S America. Biology little known (see text).

► **Rainbow or Orange-breasted bunting** (*Passerina leclancherii*) of Mexico.

To contemplate the colorful, constantly changing throng of **tanagers**, peaceably eating in a tree laden with berries, is one of the delights of bird watching in the tropics. From warm lowlands to high, cold mountains, their amazingly varied plumage adds touches of warm color to the foliage of trees and shrubs. The small tanagers of the genus *Tangara* display every bright color in the most varied patterns: one of them, the Paradise tanager, is splendidly attired in scarlet, golden yellow, shining apple green, purplish blue, turquoise, and black.

Tanagers are compactly built, with short to medium-length and often rather thick bills, generally notched or hooked at the tip. Their tails are short to medium-length, and their wings have only nine primary feathers instead of the usual 10.

With one known exception (see box), even the most brilliant tropical tanagers wear the same colors throughout the year. Of the four species that nest north of Mexico, the Scarlet tanager, which performs the longest migration, shows the greatest seasonal color changes in the male—from scarlet to yellowish; male Western and Hepatic tanagers travel less far and change only slightly; male Summer tanagers winter in the tropics in their full coats of red. At the other extreme of the family's range, the three partly migratory species—Diademed, Blue-and-yellow, and Sayaca—that breed as far south as central Argentina change

◄ ▼ ► **Representative species of buntings and tanagers,** males in breeding plumage.
(1) Swallow tanager (*Tersina viridis*) catching insects. (2) Black-headed bunting (*Emberiza melanocephala*). (3) Corn bunting (*E. calandra*) in middle of "bunch-of-keys" rattling song (plumage of both sexes similar). (4) Rose-breasted thrush tanager (*Rhodinocichla rosea*) foraging in leaf litter. (5) Buff-throated saltator (*Saltator maximus*) eating a banana. (6) Rose-breasted grosbeak (*Pheucticus ludovicianus*) male in winter. (7) White-throated sparrow (*Zonotrichia albicollis*). (8) Plush-capped finch (*Catamblyrhynchus diadema*). (9) Red-legged honeycreeper (*Cyanerpes cyaneus*) feeding on nectar.

little. Wholly tropical tanagers are nonmigratory but may wander up and down the mountains with the changing seasons. In the small tanagers of genus *Tangara*, and many other tanagers that are paired throughout the year, the sexes are nearly or quite alike. Among tanagers that travel in small flocks in which pairs are not obvious, the female may be much duller than the male, as in the Scarlet-rumped tanager and the Yellow-rumped tanager.

Largely fruit-eating, the tanagers are probably by far the most important disseminators of tropical American trees and shrubs, as they do not digest the seeds that they swallow. Tanagers vary their diet with insects gleaned from foliage or caught in the air. Some work along horizontal limbs, bending over now on this side and now on that to pluck insects and spiders from the lower side. Species other than honeycreepers (see box) occasionally sip nectar. Summer tanagers, expert flycatchers, tear open wasps' nests to eat larvae and pupae. Gray-headed tanagers regularly accompany the mixed flocks of small birds that follow army ants to capture insects that the ants drive up from the ground litter. The Rose-breasted thrush-tanager is one of its few members that forage on the ground, flicking aside fallen leaves with its bill.

Although tanagers are nearly always monogamous, bigamy is occasional in the Blue-gray tanager and Scarlet-rumped tanager. Males of many species feed their mates. The open, cup-shaped nest, high in a tree or low in a shrub, rarely on the ground, is built by both sexes in many species, by the female only, attended by a songful partner, in others. The eggs, most often two in the tropical species, are laid early in the morning and incubated by the female alone, even when she is no less colorful than her mate. He frequently escorts her when she returns to her eggs. The incubation period varies with the form and situation of the nest. In low, open, thick-walled nests, such as those of the Scarlet-rumped and Crimson-backed tanagers, it is 12 days. In the smaller, usually higher, less conspicuous mossy nests of Silver-throated tanagers and other species of *Tangara*, it is usually 13 or 14 days. In the covered nests with a side entrance that euphonias hide in crannies, it is prolonged to 15 or 18 days.

The insides of the hatchlings' mouths are red. Nearly always, their father helps to feed them and to clean the nest, but only their mother broods. Sometimes a young Golden-masked tanager in immature plumage helps its parents to feed a later brood; and in this and other species of *Tangara*, as also in the Dusky-faced tanager three or four adults may attend one or two nestlings. The nestling period varies in the same way as the incubation period; 11 or 12 days in species with low, open nests, 14 or 15 days in those whose nests are usually higher, 19 to 24 days in the covered nests of euphonias and chlorophonias.

The 25 species of euphonias differ in many ways from other tanagers. Among the smallest tanagers, they are mostly blue-black above and often also on the throat, with yellow on the forehead and sometimes also crown, and yellow underparts. Although not brilliant songsters, many utter bright, clear notes which make them attractive pets and, unhappily, sometimes lead them to be confined in miserably small cages. In addition to insects and many kinds of fruits, they eat so many mistletoe berries that they are among the chief disseminators of these abundant parasites on tropical trees. The tiny, nearly downless nestlings are fed by regurgitation rather than directly from the bill, as is usual among tanagers. When the parents arrive together with food, the male regularly feeds them first. Spot-crowned euphonias sleep singly in snug pockets in moss, instead of roosting amid

► **The cardinal.** Seen here beside Roosevelt Lake, Arizona, the cardinal may be found from the eastern and southern USA to Mexico, and is common in wood margins, hedgerows and suburbs. The more yellowish-brown female also has a crest and pink bill.

▼ **Electric breeding plumage** of the male Red-legged or Blue honeycreeper—the only tropical species of the subfamily whose males are known to shed their breeding plumage (for the green of the female). Long, downcurved bill points to its nectar staple diet, but honeycreepers take a wide range of other foods.

Honeycreepers

The 27 species of honeycreepers, dacnises, flower-piercers, and allies, here included with the tanagers, are often classified with the bananaquit (*Coereba flaveola*) in a separate family, the Coerebidae. With the exceptions of the Red-legged honeycreeper in Cuba and the orangequit of Jamaica, all are confined to the tropical American mainland and closely adjacent islands. Mostly under 14cm (5.5in) long, they wear varied plumage. Most colorful are the lowland honeycreepers, whose males are clad in blue, turquoise, purple, green, and yellow. Their bills are long and slightly downcurved in the four species of *Cyanerpes*, intermediate in the Green honeycreeper, short and sharp in the nine species of *Dacnis*. More frequently than tanagers with thicker bills, these birds probe flowers for nectar. They also eat much fruit, catch insects in the air, or pluck them from foliage; they come readily to feeders where fruit is displayed. They are almost or quite songless.

The 11 species of the less colorful but more tuneful flower-piercers of the genus *Diglossa*, attired largely in blue, cinnamon, olive, and black, prefer cooler regions where flowers abound, from the upper levels of the tropical zone to the chilly *páramos*. Their queer, uptilted bills are efficient instruments for extracting nectar from tubular flowers. The tip of the upper mandible hooks over the tube and holds it while the sharp lower mandible pierces the corolla, and the two tubes of the tongue suck out the sweet liquid. Thus, they take nectar from the flower without pollinating it. Small flying insects balance their diet. They lay two eggs in thick-walled open cups at the same time as their neighbors the hummingbirds do, at a season when few other birds are breeding. Also like hummingbirds, whose diet closely resembles theirs, they feed their nestlings by regurgitation instead of directly from the bill, like other honeycreepers.   AFS

foliage like other tanagers. The chlorophonias of wet mountain forests are essentially, as their name implies, green euphonias (adorned with blue and yellow), and have quite similar habits. AFS

Among the **cardinal grosbeaks** are familiar birds of suburban gardens in temperate North America and little-known species in tropical rain forests. A favorite is the high-crested, black-throated cardinal, who wears his warm red plumage amid winter's snow. His mate is much duller. Thanks largely to people who provide seeds in winter, during the last century the cardinal has extended its breeding range from the Ohio Valley to above the Great Lakes in southern Canada. Along the USA–Mexican border, it coexists

with the equally high-crested and thick-billed pyrrhuloxia, more gray than red.

The lovely little buntings of the genus *Passerina* live chiefly in the USA and Mexico. One of the most elegant, the Painted bunting, has a blue head, yellow-green mantle, red rump and underparts, and dark wings and tail. The almost solid-blue male Indigo bunting, which nests in bushy places through much of the eastern half of the USA, wears a brownish dress much like the female's in its winter home in southern Mexico and Central America. Also highly migratory is the Rose-breasted grosbeak, which after nesting in woodland edges and similar habitats in the northeastern USA and southern Canada travels as far as Venezuela and Peru. In winter plumage, males retain enough red on their breasts to distinguish them from the browner females. Equally migratory is the dickcissel, which sings its name in open fields chiefly in the Mississippi Valley and winters as far south as Venezuela and Trinidad, in vast numbers where rice is grown, sometimes causing heavy losses. Huge numbers roost on sugarcane leaves in neighboring fields.

Among the nonmigratory tropical members of this subfamily are the Blue-black grosbeak and his brown mate, both of whom sing beautifully in rain forests and bushy clearings. They eat maize, whether in the milk or dry, but, not being gregarious, they do only slight damage to the crop. More closely confined to mid and upper levels of

rain forests is the Slate-colored grosbeak, whose nearly uniformly dark bluish gray plumage contrasts with his heavy, bright red bill.

Most cardinal grosbeaks consume many insects and soft fruits as well as weed seeds and grains. More closely allied to the tanagers in their preference for fruits, although least like them in their largely grayish and olive-green plumage, often with a white eyebrow, are the dozen species of saltators, which inhabit semi-open and scrub country through much of tropical America. The widespread Buff-throated saltator is a frequent attendant at feeders where bananas are offered. Never having learned to hold food with a foot while they prepare it for eating, these birds and some of their relatives rest a fruit precariously on a horizontal branch while they bite off pieces.

The social habits of cardinal grosbeaks vary greatly. Solitary and pugnacious in the breeding season, lovely male Painted buntings may occasionally wound and even kill their adversaries. At the other extreme are Yellow-green grosbeaks, who at all seasons travel in loose flocks through rain forests and shady clearings, displaying no territorial exclusiveness. Parents feeding nestlings are joined by one or more helpers.

The cup-shaped nest is usually built by the female, but male cardinals and Blue-black grosbeaks share the task. Although in most species only the female incubates, male Rose-breasted and Black-headed grosbeaks take turns on the eggs, often singing while they sit. Male cardinals, Buff-throated saltators and Blue-black grosbeaks bring food to their incubating partners. Nearly always the father helps to feed the young, but male Painted buntings are unreliable attendants, and the polygamous male dickcissel neglects his offspring. AFS

In plumage the **swallow-tanager** resembles tanagers, but differs in its broad, flat bill and pointed, swallow-like wings. Like tanagers, they eat much fruit; like swallows, they catch many insects in flight. From warm lowlands where they live when not breeding, they ascend into the mountains of northern south America to nest at 800–1,800m (2,600–5,900ft). The female, with token assistance by an attentive mate, builds the nest. She alone incubates but both parents feed the nestlings. Highly social birds, Swallow-tanagers engage in mass displays, all simultaneously "curtseying" or bowing deeply down and up, while facing one another or perching close together.

AFS

WOOD WARBLERS

Family: Parulidae
Order: Passeriformes (suborder Oscines, part).
One hundred and twenty species in 26 genera.
Distribution: N and S America, the West Indies.

Habitat: forests and brushlands.

Size: 10–18cm (4–7in) long, weight 7–25g (0.2–0.9oz), sexes similar.

Plumage: among the brightest of North American birds. Female plumage usually similar to male's but duller.

Voice: distinct musical songs, often more than one per species; a wide variety of call notes.

Nest: well built, in tree or on ground.

Eggs: 2–8 (usually 4–5); white to green, usually with brown spots or splashes.

Incubation period: 10–14 days; nestling period: 8–12 days.

Diet: invertebrates, especially insects; some fruit.

Species include: **American redstart** (*Setophaga ruticilla*), **Bachman's warbler** E (*Vermivora bachmanii*), **Black-and-white warbler** (*Mniotilta varia*), **Blackpoll warbler** (*Dendroica striata*), **Kirtland's warbler** E (*D. kirtlandii*) **Olive warbler** (*Peucedramus taeniatus*), **ovenbird** (*Seiurus aurocapillus*), **Semper's warbler** E (*Leucopeza semperi*) **Tennessee warbler** (*Vermivora peregrina*), **Yellow-rumped warbler** (*Dendroica coronata*).

E Endangered.

▶ **Bill-full of grubs** from mother Yellow warbler (*Dendroica petechia*) for her young, as father looks on. Females are responsible for incubation at the well-constructed nest, and for most feeding of the newly hatched young; males make greater feeding contributions as the young grow. After fledging, some of the young may disperse with their mother, the rest with the father. They may be fed for up to two weeks after leaving the nest. Warblers are typically single-brooded in the temperate zone, but will nest again if the nest is broken up—as quite frequently happens—by other birds, mammals or snakes.

WOOD warblers are of great interest to birders and professionals alike, because of their bright plumage and large number of species. They are the most diverse and abundant family of forest-dwelling birds breeding in eastern North America: five to six nesting species of a single genus, *Dendroica*, may constitute as much as 70 percent of the birds occupying the region's spruce forests.

Western North America has a poorer wood warbler fauna, which declines as one proceeds into Mexico, Central America, and South America. High-latitude breeders migrate to warmer climes for the northern winter, the majority wintering within the tropics. Numbers of migrants also decline markedly as one moves from Mexico and northern Central America southward. Few winter south of the Equator.

With few exceptions, wood warblers are small foliage-gleaners. Their bill is generally narrow and pointed, although species that capture much of their food on the wing have a broad bill like that of the tyrant flycatchers. The ovenbird and waterthrushes are largely ground foragers, with a life-style similar to that of thrushes. The Black-and-white warbler has even adopted a nuthatch-like life-style, and moves about easily on trunks and large limbs.

As a group, the warblers have some of the brightest and most variable plumages of North American passerine families. Colors include yellow and blue in abundance, with red and orange as well. Males and females often have similar plumage, but in migratory species males are brighter than females. Many have conspicuous wing and tail markings of white, or, less frequently, yellow. Young usually resemble females until their first breeding season, when they molt into adult plumage. However, the American redstart and the Olive warbler have subadult male plumages and do not molt into the adult male plumage until their second breeding year. Ground-dwellers, such as the ovenbird and waterthrushes, have plumage of olive, brown and dull white, spotted below (hence "-thrush").

The life spans of warblers are poorly known. The oldest bird known in the wild is a Black-and-white warbler that lived at least 11 years and three months. However, most warblers that fledge are unlikely to breed more than once. All species probably breed the year following their birth, although first-year males of some species have lower opportunities of breeding than older individuals.

Warblers are first and foremost insect feeders, and this habit accounts for their strongly migratory habit at high latitudes. Some feed partially on fruit outside the breeding season, a few on nectar or pollen. The Yellow-rumped warbler, subsists on fruits, largely bayberry or wax myrtle, during the winter. Elsewhere, a few will feed on nectar or pollen at this time. In fact, the faces and throats of many Tennessee warblers, otherwise white, olive, and gray, become yellow or red from pollen as a consequence of feeding at flowers during the tropical winter.

Some warblers have elaborate courtship maneuvers, consisting of intricate flight patterns. Prior to mating, the songs of some species differ from the songs usually sung after breeding, which suggests the importance of song in courtship. A well-constructed nest is built either in trees or on the ground. Females are largely or totally responsible for brooding, and the newly-hatched young are fed mainly by the females, but males make greater feeding contributions as the young grow. After fledging, some of the young may disperse with the female, the others with the male. They may be fed for as much as two weeks after leaving the nest. Warblers are typically single-brooded in the temperate zone, but will nest again if their nests are broken up. Predation on nests by birds, mammals or snakes appears to be heavy.

Warblers are intensely territorial during the breeding season, but later in the year may join flocks led by chickadees and titmice. Yellow-rumped warblers frequently form large, unstable, single species flocks, which move about rapidly. Many warblers join flocks of other species on their tropical wintering grounds, often one per flock, suggesting that they are aggressive towards their own species at this time.

Although some warblers are among the most abundant of North American birds, a few species are rare or endangered. The Kirtland's warbler has declined to a few hundred known birds, which breed in a few Michigan counties.

In fact, habitat destruction on the wintering grounds may provide a serious threat to many species of wood warblers. Neotropical forests are being destroyed at an alarming rate, to the point that few will remain by the year 2000, unless unforeseen changes occur. This area includes Mexico and northern Central America, where a high proportion of warblers winter. Some thrive in second-growth vegetation, but others appear dependent on the pristine forest, and are likely to disappear with those forests.

DHM

VIREOS

Family: Vireonidae
Forty-three species in 4 genera.
Order: Passeriformes (suborder Oscines, part).
Distribution: N, C and S America, West Indies
(Vireoninae only).

Habitat: scrub, woodlands, forests.

Size: Vireoninae (true vireos
and greenlets): 10.2–15.3cm
(4–6in) long, weight 9–22g
(0.3–0.7oz); Cyclarhinae
(pepper-shrikes): 12.7–16.5cm
(5–6.5in) long, 20–39g (0.6–
1.3oz); Vireolaniinae (shrike-
vireos): 12.7–16.5cm (5–6.5in)
long, 22–36g (0.7–1.2oz);
males and females similar in
size.

Plumage: chiefly green above, but some species
of *Vireo* are gray or brown on the back; yellow
or white on belly. Males and females similar but
male Black-capped vireo has a black crown
(female gray), and male Chestnut-sided shrike-
vireo much wider and brighter barring on
throat, breast and "face" than females.

Voice: rarely musical, repetitive song of the
same or different whistled or "burry" notes (a
gravelly roll to certain syllables); up to 15
different calls in some species.

Nest: bag-like, suspended by rim from fork.

Eggs: 2 in tropical species to 4–5 in northern
species; whitish with brown spots at the broad
end; incubation period 11–13 days; nestling
period 11–13 days.

Diet: arthropods and some fruit in summer and
winter.

Species include: **Bell's vireo** (*Vireo bellii*), **Black-
billed pepper-shrike** (*Cyclarhis nigrirostris*),
Black-capped vireo (*Vireo atricapillus*), **Black-
whiskered vireo** (*V. altiloquus*), **Blue mountain
vireo** (*V. osburni*), **Chestnut-sided shrike-vireo**
(*Vireolanius melitophrys*), **Cozumel vireo** (*Vireo
bairdi*), **Gray-headed greenlet** (*Hylophilus
decurtatus*), **Gray vireo** (*Vireo vicinior*), **Hutton's
vireo** (*V. huttoni*), **Jamaica vireo** (*V. modestus*),
Philadelphia vireo (*V. philadelphicus*), **Red-eyed
vireo** (*V. olivaceus*), **Rufous-browed pepper-
shrike** (*Cyclarhis gujanensis*), **Scrub greenlet**
(*Hylophilus flavipes*), **Solitary vireo** (*Vireo
solitarius*), **Warbling vireo** (*V. gilvus*), **White-
eyed vireo** (*V. griseus*), **Yucatan vireo**
(*V. magister*).

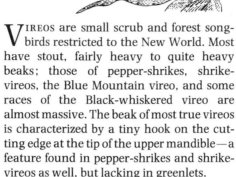

Vireos are small scrub and forest songbirds restricted to the New World. Most
have stout, fairly heavy to quite heavy
beaks; those of pepper-shrikes, shrike-
vireos, the Blue Mountain vireo, and some
races of the Black-whiskered vireo are
almost massive. The beak of most true vireos
is characterized by a tiny hook on the cutting edge at the tip of the upper mandible—a
feature found in pepper-shrikes and shrike-
vireos as well, but lacking in greenlets.

Greenlets are more uniform in color—
greenish on the back with varying amounts
of yellow buff and white on the face and
underparts—than are vireos, which have
plumage of these colors as well, but also
include species which are brown (Cozumel
vireo) or gray (Gray vireo) above. True
vireos differ further from greenlets by the
presence of whitish or yellowish eye-stripes
or eye-rings and all but the Red-eyed vireo
and its closest relatives also have faint to
strongly marked wing bars. Wing bars are
lacking in greenlets, pepper-shrikes and
shrike-vireos, but the pepper-shrikes have a
distinctive, reddish stripe above the eyes and
shrike-vireos have strongly patterned facial
and crown markings of yellow, bluish-
green, or chestnut.

To a varying degree all vireos appear to
eat some fruit. Arthropods are taken mostly
from leaves and twigs by Red-eyed and
White-eyed vireos; Red-eyed, Solitary and
Yellow-throated vireos forage mostly in
treetops, whereas White-eyed vireos and
other closely related scrub-dwelling species
forage low in vegetation. Out of the whole
family, only the Gray vireo takes prey from
the ground and then only in about 5 percent
of its foraging bouts. Greenlets generally
either take arthropods in low scrub or forage
high in the canopy. Vireos also flycatch, taking insects on the wing. Pepper-shrikes and
shrike-vireos apparently only glean prey
from leaves, twigs, branches, trunks and
flower parts. Other than on migration,
vireos are not noted for long distance flights;
the Gray vireo, however, may fly several
hundred meters at a time within its
territory—up to 8ha (20 acres)—in the
desert scrub and canyon country it favors.

Tropical and subtropical vireos and their
allies, as far as is known, are territorial all
the year round, gathering in pairs or family
groups. The temperate zone resident, Hutton's vireo, forms winter flocks with chickadees, nuthatches and kinglets. Red-eyed
vireos and their close relatives form small
flocks in winter moving from one fruiting
tree to another. The remaining migrant species maintain winter territories which are
defended against other individuals of the
same species. Distance of migration varies
from as little as 160km (100mi) in Gray
vireos to more than 4,800km (3,000mi) in
Red-eyed vireos.

Solitary and White-eyed vireos and their
close relatives sing throughout the year. In
summer, Red-eyed and Bell's vireos are
among the most persistent singers of all New
World songbirds. Although as a rule members of the vireos are not known for their
beautiful voices, individual pepper-shrikes
often have pleasant warbled, albeit repetitive, song types within their repertoires.
Such song stands in sharp contrast to the
police-whistle trill of the Blue Mountain
vireo and the monotonous chatter song of
several Caribbean and circum-Caribbean
scrub-dwelling species. Female song has
only been documented in the Gray vireo in
which it is a regular feature of nest
changeover by incubating or brooding
adults. Males of most vireos sing when on
the nest, probably as a reminder to the
female of the nest location and as a stimulus
for her to return to it once her hunger is
satisfied.

In tropical and temperate regions in the
Northern Hemisphere nesting begins
between late April and mid-May and in all
except the Red-eyed, Black-whiskered, the
Yucatan and the Philadelphia vireos nests
are built by both sexes. In the aforenamed
species a singing male accompanies his
female as she builds, but does not actually
participate in construction. Nest building
requires from 4–5 days in Bell's vireos and
most other temperate zone species and up
to 25 days in the Chestnut-sided
shrike-vireo.

The nest has an outer layer of coarse strips of bark and leaves, or in some species moss, bound together by spider silk and decorated with whitish spider egg cases, and an inner layer of fine grass stems carefully coiled around the bowl of the nest. In species in which both sexes build, males are capable of building rough bag nests by themselves, but the lining is done by the female.

In temperate zone species eggs are laid within a day of nest completion. Males of all species except the Red-eyed vireo and closely related forms sit on eggs at intervals during the day when the female is not incubating. When hatching occurs the male Red-eyed vireo and his Black-whiskered and Yucatan vireo close counterparts finally participate in the care of young and share with the female feeding of arthropods to nestlings. Upon fledging individual young appear to be fed exclusively by one parent or the other for up to 20 days after leaving the nest.

Some vireos are highly susceptible to nest parasitism by the Brown-headed cowbird, and their breeding success is accordingly reduced. Bell's vireo, a heavily parasitized species, often buries cowbird eggs laid in its nest by adding additional nesting material to the interior of its nest thereby effectively walling in eggs of the social parasite. Solitary vireos have been observed tossing cowbird eggs from the nest, although cowbird young may also be raised by this species.

JCB

◄ **Typical vireo nest** is bag-like and hangs from the crotch of a thin branch. Two is a typical brood size in the tropics, but clutches in the temperate zone may be twice as large.

▼ **Most common bird of deciduous forests** in the eastern USA, the Red-eyed vireo (male illustrated) has a persistent robin-like song.

AMERICAN BLACKBIRDS

Family: Icteridae
Order: Passeriformes (suborder Oscines, part).
Ninety-four species in 24 genera.
Distribution: N and S America.

Habitat: grasslands, savannas, marshes,
woodlands, and forests

Size: 15–53cm (6–21in) long, weight 20–454g
(0.7–16oz).

Plumage: chiefly black with bold patches of
yellow, orange or red; brown common among
both sexes of grassland species and females of
many others. Differences between males and
females pronounced in temperate, migratory
species and among polygynous species at all
latitudes.

Voice: a wide range of single notes and
chattering calls. Songs range from simple and
harsh to long, complex and musical.

Nests: trees, shrubs, on ground, and in
emergent aquatic vegetation; occasionally on
cliffs.

Eggs: variable in background color and amount
of spotting; weight 2.1–14.2g (0.07–0.5oz);
incubation period 12–15 days; nestling period
9–35 days.

Diet: arthropods, seeds, fruit, nectar, and small
vertebrates.

Species include: **Bay-winged cowbird** (*Molothrus
badius*), **bobolink** (*Dolichonyx oryzivorus*),
Brown-headed cowbird (*Molothrus ater*), **chopi**
(*Gnorimopsar chopi*), **Common grackle** (*Quiscalus
quiscula*), **Giant cowbird** (*Scaphidura oryzivora*),
Melodious blackbird (*Dives dives*), **Jamaican
blackbird** (*Nesopsar nigerrimus*), **Martinique
oriole** (*Icterus bonana*), **Montserrat oriole**
(*I. oberi*), **Montezuma oropendula** (*Psarocolius
montezuma*), **Red-eyed** or **Bronzed cowbird**
(*Molothrus aeneus*), **Red-winged blackbird**
(*Agelaius phoeniceus*), **Scarlet-headed blackbird**
(*Amblyramphus holosericeus*), **Scarlet-rumped
cacique** (*Cacicus uropygialis*), **Screaming cowbird**
(*Molothrus rufoaxillaris*), **Shiny** or **Common
cowbird** (*M. bonariensis*), **St Lucia oriole** (*Icterus
laudabilis*), **Tricolored blackbird** (*Agelaius
tricolor*), **troupial** (*Icterus icterus*), **Yellow-headed
blackbird** (*Xanthocephalus xanthocephalus*).
Total threatened species: 1.

THE American blackbirds are common
and conspicuous birds over much of
North and South America, and their habit
of forming large flocks outside the breeding
season attracts the attention of even casual
observers of birds. The family also includes
the cowbirds, most of which are brood
parasites, laying their eggs in the nests of
other species. Sometimes very closely
related blackbirds have strikingly different
social systems.

The majority of species are tropical. There
are centers of species richness in southern
Mexico (24 species) and in Colombia (27
species), both regions with diverse habitats.
Many species are found in temperate areas
with an abundance of marshes, such as
northern Argentina and adjacent Uruguay
(19 species), and the Midwest of the USA (10
species). Blackbirds breed in all habitat types
but especially in open environments such as
grasslands, savannas, marshes. Forest species favor edges and disturbed sites rather
than mature forest, but a few tropical species breed in primary forest. Blackbirds are
generalized foragers, eating a wide variety
of invertebrates and plant materials. Many
species are insectivorous during the breeding season but seed-eaters during the
remainder of the year.

Blackbirds are medium-sized birds, ranging in size from that of a large sparrow
(females of some orioles and tropical marsh-
nesting species) to that of a crow (tropical
oropendolas). Bills and eyes are brightly colored in many species but legs are dull. In
many tropical species, males and females
are alike in plumage; striking sexual differences are found among high latitude
migratory species and among species in
which males hold harems (polygynous) at
all latitudes. Females of all species achieve
adult plumage within one year, but males
of many polygynous species retain a
subadult plumage until they are two years

old. Juvenile plumages are always female-
like and subadult plumages of males are
intermediate between those of females and
adult males.

During the nonbreeding season blackbird
flocks may be extremely large. Social groups
during the breeding season are much smaller, but the Tricolored blackbird of California
breeds in dense colonies that may contain
over 100,000 birds. Territorial blackbirds
breed in all habitat types occupied by the
family. Colonial breeders are found
principally among marsh-nesters, species
that breed in isolated trees in open savannas
where nesting sites are limited but feeding
areas are widely dispersed, and among the
partly fruit-eating tropical oropendolas and
caciques that form conspicuous colonies in
isolated trees in forest clearings.

Among the blackbirds can be found most
of the social systems of the avian world.
Most species breed as mated pairs on large
territories, but there are also colonial species, species with highly clumped territories,
and monogamous, polygynous and promiscuous species. A few species live in year-
round flocks and up to eight individuals may
attend a single nest.

Among the brood-parasitic cowbirds are
two species (Brown-headed cowbird of
North America and Shiny cowbird of South
America) that lay their eggs in the nests of
hundreds of other species of birds. Two
others (Red-eyed cowbird and Giant cowbird) parasitize primarily other members of
the blackbird family, especially orioles,
caciques and oropendolas. The Bay-winged
cowbird takes over active or inactive nests
of other species of birds but incubates its
own eggs and feeds its own nestlings.
Finally, the Screaming cowbird is known to
parasitize but a single host, the Bay-winged
cowbird. Adaptations of cowbirds for brood
parasitism include short incubation times,
the habit of throwing out an egg of the host

▲ **Yellow-headed blackbirds** of western North America. During the nonbreeding season, most blackbirds gather into flocks. In the southern USA winter roosts of Red-winged blackbirds, Common grackles and Brown-headed cowbirds have been estimated to contain up to 50 million individuals!

▶ **Gaping for food.** American blackbirds obtain much of their food by inserting the closed bill into some potential food source, and then forcibly opening it. Blackbirds "gape" into rotting wood, flowers, curled leaves, clumps of grass, soil, and objects lying on the surface of the soil. In all cases, gaping exposes food, usually arthropods, not available to a bird gleaning prey from the surface.

◀ **Common grackle** may be a pest in ricefields and cornfields. The species flocks with Red-winged blackbirds, cowbirds and starlings. Open-country blackbird species have become more, tropical forest species less, numerous since the arrival of European settlers.

for every egg they deposit and a tendency towards mimicry of the eggs and nestlings of their hosts.

Regardless of the form of breeding social organization, male and female blackbirds assume very different roles. Nests are built exclusively by females in every species that has been studied except two. Incubation of eggs by males has never been reported, even

among species with identical males and females. Males do not bring food to their incubating spouses but many stand guard near the nest. Males of most monogamous species feed nestlings and fledglings, but males of only about one-third of the polygynous species do so. Polygynous males feed preferentially at the nest containing the oldest nestlings. Among monogamous species, males and females have about the same number of vocalizations, but males of polygynous species utter a greater variety of sounds than do females.

Among West Indian species, several of which are restricted to single islands where their populations were never very large, those considered threatened (but not yet listed by the ICBP) include the St. Lucia oriole, the Martinique oriole, the Montserrat oriole and the Jamaican blackbird. In South America the troupial, the chopi, and the Shiny cowbird are often kept as caged birds because of their beautiful songs.   GHO

FINCHES

Family: Fringillidae
Order: Passeriformes (suborder Oscines, part).
About 153 species in 33 genera.
Distribution: N and S America, Eurasia, Africa
(except Madagascar); introduced to New
Zealand, Hawaiian finches confined to
Hawaiian Islands

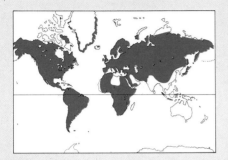

▼ **Commonest finch in Europe,** the chaffinch breeds in all kinds of woodland, making its nest usually quite low down in a tree or bush. Male (here) and female feed the young with caterpillars, which they bring one at a time. Most other finches bring their young seeds, which they carry in large quantities in the crop, prior to regurgitating the meal at the nest.

Finches of one kind or another are familiar to everyone. Not only do they breed commonly in our parks and gardens, they are also frequent visitors to feeding trays in winter. However, few people are familiar with more than a handful of species.

Finches have stout bills, strong skulls, large jaw muscles and powerful gizzards, all for coping with hard seeds. Other seed-eating birds share these features, but the Fringillidae are distinguished by the presence of 9 instead of 10 large primary feathers in each wing. 12 large tail feathers, and the fact that the female is responsible for building the cup-shaped nest and for incubating the eggs.

The three species of fringilline finches have fairly long tails, peaked heads and prominent shoulder patches and wing markings. Chaffinches breed in all kinds of woodland, and over much of Europe are one of the commonest birds, usually comprising between one-fifth and two-fifths of the total woodland bird population. The brambling replaces the chaffinch as a breeding bird in the subarctic birch woods of northern Europe, and also extends across Asia to Kamchatka, migrating south for the winter, and concentrating in areas with beechmast. The rare Blue chaffinch occurs only in high-altitude pine forests of the Canary Islands.

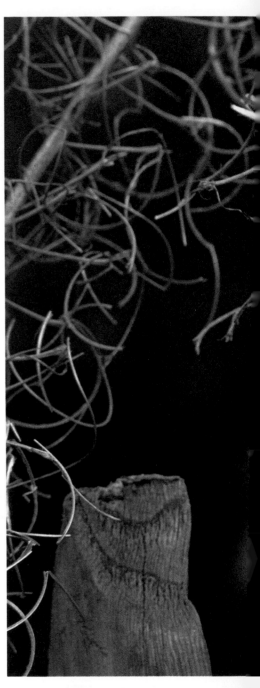

The fringilline and cardueline finches differ in the way they feed their young, and the dispersion system that results from this. Although the main food of all species is seeds, fringilline finches feed their young entirely on insects (especially caterpillars), while cardueline finches feed their young either on a mixture of seeds and insects or on seeds alone. The raising of young entirely on a seed diet is comparatively rare among birds, but has been recorded for crossbills, siskins, redpolls and linnets. Also, while fringilline finches carry insects to their young one or a few at a time in the bill, cardueline finches carry large quantities of

▲ **Greenfinch on dried flowerhead** of willowherb (*Epilobium* species). Greenfinches breed through most of spring and summer, changing their diet as different plants come into seed.

seeds in their gullets and regurgitate them to the young. Some species, including the bullfinch, have special throat pouches for this purpose.

The fringilline finches defend large territories while breeding, and pairs spread themselves fairly evenly through the habitat. The food is obtained from the territory itself, and the young are fed at frequent intervals (about every 5–10 minutes). The carduelines nest solitarily or in loose colonies, within which each pair defends only a small area around its nest; they forage away from the colonies in flocks, wherever seeds happen to be abundant at

the time. They pack large amounts of seeds into their crop, and feed their young at infrequent intervals (about 20–60 minutes). The pair forage and visit the nest together.

The fringilline finches sing only on their territories, and the song serves to advertise the occupation of the territory and to attract a mate. The cardueline finches sing anywhere they happen to be, and the song serves as a form of self advertisement. Many cardueline finches have special song flights over their breeding areas.

Like other birds, all these finches breed when their food is most plentiful, but the timing varies between species, according to what they eat. The chaffinch, which eats caterpillars, has a short breeding season in late spring, while the cardueline finches, which need seeds, have long and varied seasons, in which individual pairs often raise more than one brood. The greenfinch, linnet and bullfinch, which eat a variety of seeds, breed for almost the whole growing season, continually changing their diet as different plants come into seed. The European goldfinch, which likes the seeds of thistles and related plants, breeds later in summer, while the American goldfinch, which depends even more on thistles, breeds later still. The regular start of its breeding season is the latest in North America. The crossbills nest in any month, whenever conifer seeds are sufficiently available; in larch forests this is mainly in late summer or early fall, in spruce forests in fall to winter, and in pine forests in spring. If spruce and pine are available in the same area, breeding can occur continuously for 10

▼ ► Representative species of finches.
(**1**) Kauai akialoa (*Hemignathus procerus*) of Hawaii. (**2**) Common or Red crossbill (*Loxia curvirostra*). (**3**) Pine grosbeak (*Pinicola enucleator*). (**4**) Hawfinch (*Coccothraustes coccothraustes*). (**5**) Maui parrotbill (*Pseudonestor xanthophrys*). (**6**) European goldfinch (*Carduelis carduelis*). (**7**) Siskin (*C. spinus*). (**8**) Two-barred crossbill (*Loxia leucoptera*). (**9**) Ou (*Psittirostra psittacea*). (**10**) Apapane (*Himatione sanguinea*). (**11**) Parrot crossbill (*Loxia pytopsittacus*).

The Finch's Bill

The beak of a finch is modified internally for shelling seeds. Each seed is wedged in a groove on the side of the palate and crushed by raising the lower jaw onto it. The husk is peeled off with the aid of the tongue and discarded, while the kernel is swallowed.

The cardueline finches can extract seeds from the seed-heads of plants. Species differ in the size of seeds they prefer, and in the types of seed-head they can best exploit, corresponding with differences in the size and shape of their bills. Hawfinches have big powerful bills for crushing large hard tree fruits, such as cherry stones. Goldfinches have long tweezer-like bills for probing into thistles, and other composite plants; they are the only species able to eat the seeds of teasel, which lie at the bottom of long, spiked tubes. The male European goldfinch has a slightly longer beak and can reach teasel seeds more easily than the female, which in consequence rarely feeds from this plant. Siskins also have tweezer-like bills, and feed largely from seeds in small cones, such as alder.

Bullfinches and Pine grosbeaks have rounded bills adapted for eating buds and berries, the bullfinch in general taking smaller items than the grosbeaks. The crossbills use their crossed mandibles to help them extract seeds from hard closed cones. The three species in Europe have different-sized bills and feed primarily from different conifers: the slender-billed Two-barred crossbill eats seeds mainly from the small soft cones of larch, the medium-billed Common crossbill feeds mainly from the medium cones of spruce, and the large heavy-billed Parrot crossbill mainly from large hard cones of pine.

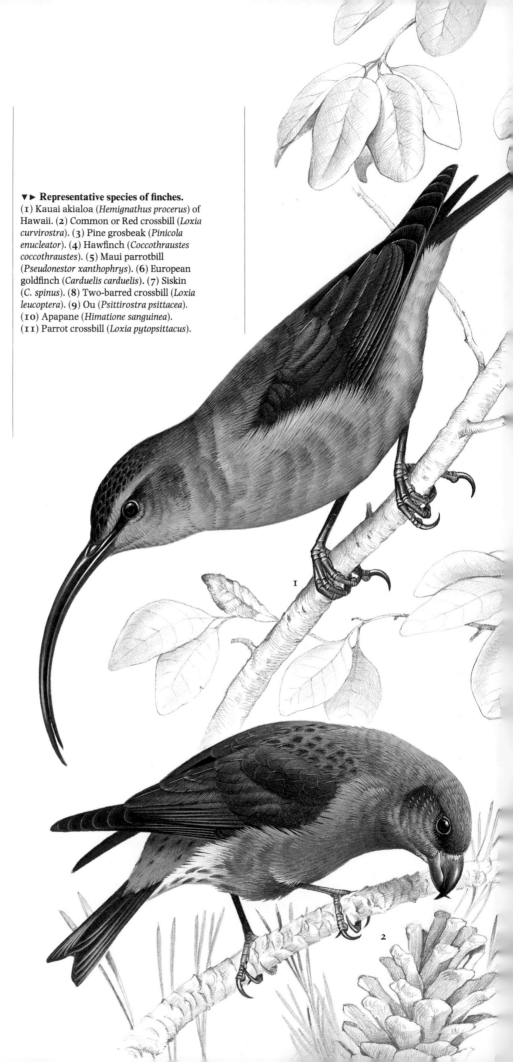

months. Thus crossbills are often forced to nest when days are short and cold, and the ground is snow covered. In the Moscow region, some nests were found in February, when air temperatures were −19°C (−2°F); inside the nest the temperature was as high as 38°C (100°F) while the female brooded.

Another major event in the annual cycle of finches is migration, and here again food plays an overriding role. The main distinction is between species which feed from low herbaceous plants and those which feed high in trees. Herbaceous plants produce an abundance of seeds every year, but at times of snow these seeds may be unavailable. Most finches that depend on such seeds migrate south for the winter, and in Europe many thousands winter in the Mediterranean region. Such species have fairly fixed migration routes and show strong homing tendencies, returning to the same areas for breeding and wintering in successive years. Examples include the European goldfinch and linnet.

The tree feeders have a different problem because, although their food is generally available above the snow (enabling them to winter much further north), in any one locality the seed crops vary enormously from one year to the next. In some years the trees and bushes are laden with fruits but in other years they are barren. In different parts of a continent, however, the crops are not necessarily in phase with one another, so in a year when the crops may fail in one region, they may be good in another. With such a fluctuating food supply, there would be little point in individuals migrating to the same places every year. In consequence, the migrations are highly variable both in direction and distance travelled. When seed crops are good in the north most of the birds stay there. However, when the northern crops fail, most of the birds move further south. As band (ring) recoveries testify, individuals of such species may breed or winter in widely separated regions in different years. Enormous year-to-year fluctuations of populations may be seen at any one locality, but the continental population as a whole probably does not fluctuate to such a large extent. This system applies particularly to siskins and redpolls, but also to bullfinches, Pine and Evening grosbeaks.

The most famous of all eruptive finches are the crossbills. Every few years these birds move out of their breeding areas and occur in enormous numbers outside the normal range. Sometimes, the movements are so spectacular as to attract general attention; as long ago as 1251, the English chronicler, Matthew Paris, wrote about these strange birds which invaded his homeland in great numbers, and caused devastation to the apple crop (for the birds are often forced on to unusual foods when away from their favorite conifers). Eruptions of crossbills have since been recorded from all their main centers, including parts of North America, Japan and the Himalayas, but have been best documented in Europe. On this continent between 1800 and 1965, crossbills erupted at least 67 times at intervals of up to 17 years. Only recently have band recoveries confirmed that some birds return to their regular range in later years. From a batch of birds banded in Switzerland on migration, some were recorded the following fall and winter in southwest Europe, having continued their journey; others were recorded in later years, 4,000km (2,500mi) northeast, in the northern USSR.

Because of their song, bright colors, engaging habits and simple seed diet, finches have for centuries been kept in cages as pets. Some species breed readily in captivity, and from the wild serin of the Canary Islands all the various strains of domestic canary were derived. Certain finches are also important as pests, notably the bullfinch which eats buds of fruit trees, sometimes devastating orchards.

In the past, man must have had an enormous influence on the distribution and numbers of the different finches. Deforestation must have greatly reduced the habitat available to certain species, but the spread of cultivated and urban environments provided new habitats for others. One adverse trend in recent decades has been the increasing use of herbicides in agriculture. These chemicals kill the weeds on which several species depend, and in the long term deplete the "seed bank" in the soil. Plowing and other soil disturbance turns buried seeds to the surface, where they are available to certain finches, but farmland offers much less food for finches than in times past.

IN

▲ **Heavy-billed Parrot crossbill** male regurgitating a meal of seeds for its young.

◄ **The Common or Red crossbill** of Europe, North Africa, Asia and North to Central America reveals its whereabouts by the presence on the ground of open fir cones, from which it has taken the seeds. Male crossbills are brick red in color, the females and young are greenish.

Hawaiian finches (also known as Hawaiian honeycreepers) are thought to be derived from a single finch-like species that crossed more than 3,000km (1,860mi) of ocean to colonize the Hawaiian Archipelago. In the near absence of competition, these immigrants, resembling the Nihoa finch, evolved specialized feeding behavior and remarkable bills to exploit highly diverse island ecosystems—from shrubby coral atolls and rocky islets to mountain rain forests receiving more than 1,000cm (400in) of rain per year.

Many seed-eaters retained finch-shaped bills; an extinct, unnamed Oahu species had one of the most massive known. In contrast, the insectivorous creepers have thin warbler-like bills. The Kauai akialoa's decurved bill, 6.6cm (2.6in) long (one-third the bird's length), is used for seeking insects in thick mosses or deep cracks. The Maui parrotbill chisels into branches for insects with its broad lower mandible. Most remarkable is the akiapolaau, which chips into soft wood with its stout lower mandible while holding its curved upper mandible, with which it later probes for insects, out of the way.

Nectar-sipping species such as the Black mamo and iiwi have bills that closely match the flower corollas that provide their food, and possess tubular tongues to aid in sucking nectar.

Other members of the group eat berries, fruit, snails and seabird eggs. The colorful red apapane and dazzling orange iiwi fly many kilometers each day in their search for nectar-bearing flowers, and their evening flights in the thousands can be very spectacular.

The Hawaiian finches have extended breeding seasons beginning in January and continuing through July or August. Because many species are rare and frequent rugged, wet terrain, nests of only half of them are known. Their nests are open, constructed of twigs and lined with fine fibers, and are well concealed in terminal leaf clusters. The Nihoa finch nests in rock cavities, while the Laysan finch, which belongs to the same genus, prefers to nest in grass tussocks on its sandy island.

These amazing birds have been decimated by changes in their island homes. At least 15 species, known from undescribed fossils, survived until Polynesians, beginning about 400AD, converted their dry lowland forest habitats to agriculture. Of the 28 species known from records made in more recent times, 8 are extinct and 12 are endangered. Habitat destruction by man and ungulates (primarily cattle, goats and pigs) and introduced predators and diseases have greatly reduced the numbers of all surviving species. It is hoped that ambitious conservation programs currently under way will protect most of those species that still survive.

CBK

The 3 Subfamilies of Finches

E Endangered. V Vulnerable. R Rare. Ex Extinct. Ex? Probably Extinct.

Fringilline finches
Subfamily: Fringillinae
Three species of the genus *Fringilla*.
Eurasia, Canary Islands. Woodland and forest. Size: about 15cm (6in) long, weight 26–30g (0.9–1.0oz). Plumage: males very colorful: in chaffinch, blue head, greenish back, and pink breast; in brambling, black and buffish back and orange underside; in Canary Islands chaffinch, mainly bluish; females generally duller, and in chaffinch mainly pale green. All species have conspicuous shoulder patches, wing and tail markings.
Voice: chaffinch has "spink, spink" call, and loud musical song, lasting 2–3 seconds and consisting of a succession of "chip" notes, followed by a flourish. Brambling has a harsh "tswark" note, and a softer "tchuck," mostly used on the wing and a long drawn-out "dwee" note, which constitutes the song.
Nests: mainly of grass, moss and other vegetation, usually in a tree or bush. Eggs: 3–5, dark greenish-blue with purple-brown streaks and spots that have a paler rim; incubation period 12–14 days; nestling period: 11–17 days. Diet: seeds; young fed on insects, especially caterpillars.

Species: **brambling** (*Fringilla montifringilla*), **Canary Islands chaffinch** (*F. teydea*), **chaffinch** (*F. coelebs*).

Cardueline finches
Subfamily: Carduelinae
About 122 species in 17 genera.
N and S America, Eurasia, Africa (except Madagascar). Woodland and forest. Size: 11–19cm (4–7.5in); weight up to 100g (3.5oz). Plumage: varied in color but generally with prominent wing and tail markings, many species streaked, especially in juvenile plumage. Voice: very varied, but most have pleasant, musical songs of pure notes; a few, such as the bullfinch, have rather coarse, creaky songs. Nests: built mainly of grass, moss and other vegetation, usually in a tree or a bush. Eggs: 3–5, whitish with brown spots; incubation period 12–14 days; nestling period 11–17 days. Diet: seeds; young fed on seeds and insects or seeds alone.

Species include: **American goldfinch** (*Carduelis tristis*), **bullfinch** (*Pyrrhula pyrrhula*), **Common or Red crossbill** (*Loxia curvirostra*), **European goldfinch** (*Carduelis carduelis*), **Evening grosbeak** (*Hesperiphona vespertina*), **greenfinch** (*Carduelis chloris*), **hawfinch** (*Coccothraustes coccothraustes*), **linnet** (*Acanthis cannabina*), **Parrot crossbill** (*Loxia pytopsittacus*), **Pine grosbeak** (*Pinicola enucleator*), **redpoll** (*Acanthis flammea*), **Two-barred** or **White-winged crossbill** (*Loxia leucoptera*). Total threatened species: 3.

Hawaiian finches
Subfamily: Drepanidinae
Twenty-eight species in 15 genera.
Hawaiian Islands. Native forests and shrublands. Size: 10–20cm (4–8in) long, weight 10–45g (0.4–1.6oz). Plumage: green, yellow, brown, black, red, and orange. Males and females usually similar; males brighter than females in some. Voice: variable, from musical trills to fragmented squeaky phrases and whistled notes. Nests: open cups, occasionally in tree cavities. Eggs: normally 2–3, whitish with gray to reddish-brown scrawls; incubation period 13–14 days; nestling period 15–22 days. Diet: mainly insects and nectar, but also snails, fruit, seed-pods, and seabird eggs.

Species include: **akiapolaau** E (*Hemignathus munroi*), **apapane** (*Himatione sanguinea*), **Black mamo** Ex (*Drepanis funerea*), **iiwi** (*Vestiaria coccinea*), **Kauai akialoa** Ex? (*Hemignathus procerus*), **Kauai creeper** R (*Oreomystis bairdi*), **Laysan finch** (*Telespyza cantans*), **Maui parrotbill** V (*Pseudonestor xanthophrys*), **Molokai creeper** E (*Paroreomyza flammea*), **Nihoa finch** (*Telespyza ultima*), **ou** E (*Psittirostra psittacea*), **poo-uli** R (*Melamprosops phaeosoma*). Total threatened species: 12.

WAXBILLS AND WEAVERS

Families: Estrildidae, Ploceidae
Order: Passeriformes (suborder Oscines, part).
Two hundred and sixty-seven species in 45 genera.
Distribution: see map and table.

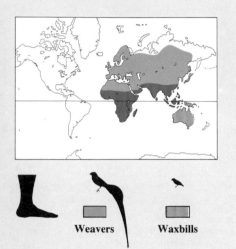

Weavers | **Waxbills**

▶ **Plague-like flock** of Red-billed queleas ABOVE threatens serious damage to grain crops in the vicinity. Attempts at pest control south of the Sahara have so far failed. Flocks may number over a million birds.

▶ **Spectacular Gouldian finch** BELOW (male illustrated) is a popular cage bird in its various color forms; it is now protected by the Australian Government's ban on import and export of fauna.

▼ **Blue-capped cordon bleu** (*Uraeginthus cyanocephala*) of East Africa is another cagebird favorite. The colorful waxbills are probably the single most important family for aviculturists.

THE **waxbills** are notable for their extraordinary diversity of plumage. Some species are relatively somberly clad in grays, browns and white but many of them make up for their lack of bright coloration with attractive markings. The Double-bar finch, Pictorella finch and Zebra finch all illustrate this tendency. Other species are richly colored, including the blue of cordon bleus, reds of firefinches and green and yellow of the Green avadavat. The most colorful of them all is, however, the Gouldian finch, whose combination of green, yellow, cobalt-blue, turquoise, purple and white give it a bizarre, and perhaps (depending on taste), beautiful appearance. This species also shows an interesting variation in head coloration: the heads of roughly 75 percent of Gouldian finches in the wild are black but most of the remaining 25 percent are red. There is another so-called yellow-headed form (in reality it is orange in color), which occurs in about one in every thousand or so wild birds.

Most waxbills are social and occur in flocks in the nonbreeding season, sometimes aggregating in large mixed species groups. The behavior of individuals within flocks tends to be synchronized; they feed together, take-off simultaneously, show coordinated flight movements and perform acts, such as preening and bathing, at the same times. Experimental work on captive birds, and recordings made from flocks living under natural conditions, have shown that both calls and visual stimuli are important in synchronizing behavior. Flight move-

ments, for instance, are coordinated, at least in part, by so-called "flight calls" which are given by birds taking-off and in flight. The acts of preening and flying down from perching places to the ground in order to forage are, on the other hand, synchronized by the sight of other birds performing these acts. There is greater emphasis on coordination by calls in forest-inhabiting species, in which members of flocks may have difficulty in maintaining visual contact with one another, than in species which inhabit open country.

The Mouse of the Avian World

The relative ease with which the Zebra finch can be kept and bred in captivity recommends it as a laboratory animal. Indeed, it is widely used in experimental work in many parts of the world, particularly in laboratories in Europe and the USA. Some research workers have even predicted that it will become as familiar in laboratories as the mouse.

One significant line of research in which the Zebra finch has been involved illustrates the ways in which early experiences of an animal can affect the development of patterns of behavior which are not performed until it reaches maturity. It is possible to alter the normal nestling environment of the Zebra finch and therefore its experiences during development, by allowing it to be foster-reared by Bengalese finches. Adult pairs of the latter species will incubate Zebra finch eggs and rear the nestlings, as if they were their own. Young Zebra finches which have been reared in this way, however, become sexually imprinted on their foster-parents, and as a consequence, show abnormal mate choice when they

become adult. If they are given access to both Bengalese and Zebra finch females, they prefer to court, and pair with, members of the foster species, rather than their conspecifics. The effects of imprinting are remarkably stable. Foster-reared male Zebra finches can be persuaded to pair, and nest, with females of their own kind, if they are caged with them alone, in the absence of Bengalese finch females. But even this experience does not affect subsequent mate choice. When such males are separated from their Zebra finch mates and given the choice between unfamiliar Zebra finch and Bengalese finch females, they still prefer the latter species. Similar experiments have shown that the male Zebra finch also learns features of its courtship song during its early development. It does so by listening to the songs of its father. Birds reared by their natural fathers imitate their songs and consequently have typical song repertoires of the Zebra finch; males foster-reared by Bengalese finches, sing like members of this species.   SME

Pair-bonds are strong in most species and members of pairs keep together during the nonbreeding season. They indulge in gestures, such as clumping (perching in contact) and preening one another, which probably serve to maintain and strengthen bonds between them. Breeding occurs in the wet season, when the food on which the nestlings are reared, mostly seeding grasses and insects, is abundant. Predators, including hawks, snakes and small mammals, take a heavy toll of eggs and nestlings and breeding success is often poor. Records of several African species show that only 18–30 percent of the eggs laid survive to produce fledglings; most of the rest are destroyed by predators. Nestlings possess conspicuous marks on the palate and tongue which are revealed whenever they gape for food. There are additional luminous spots at the base of the bill in some species. These markings probably stimulate parents to feed their young and also help them to locate the nestlings' mouths in the semi-darkness of the nest.

Waxbills adapt well to life in captivity and have become popular cage birds. Two species in particular, the Bengalese finch and the Zebra finch, are now thoroughly domesticated and are available in a number of different color varieties. Together with other species, they are kept by aviculturists throughout the world. Unfortunately, the demand for most African and Asian finches is met by trapping them in the wild. Dealers in these two continents export enormous numbers of finches worldwide. It has been estimated, for example, that Europe alone imports $7\frac{1}{2}$ million birds a year, a very large proportion of which are wild-caught waxbills. The extent to which the trade is depleting natural populations is unknown, but other aspects of it, such as severe mortality of birds in transit, caused by overcrowding or insufficient food, are undesirable. In fact, it is questionable whether the trade is necessary at all. Aviculturists faced with the non-availability of certain species from the wild have been highly successful in breeding and maintaining captive strains. The Australian Government's ban on the import and export of fauna in the 1960s, for example, meant that new stocks of African and Asian species were no longer available to Australian aviculturists, and of Australian finches to aviculturists in other parts of the world. Serious bird breeders in Australia have nevertheless established strains of many non-native species, including cordon bleus, firefinches and waxbills, while European aviculturists still keep and breed viable stocks of at least thirteen of the Australian species.   SME

The Waxbills and 4 Subfamilies of Weavers   Ⓡ Rare.

Waxbills
Family: Estrildidae
One hundred and twenty-four species in 27 genera.
Africa, Asia and Australia. Dry savanna, thorn scrub, open grassland, reedbeds, tropical forests, semideserts. Size: 9–14cm (3.5–5.5in) long. Plumage: a great variety of color patterns and markings. Males and females distinctly different in some species, similar in others. Voice: a range of calls in social situations, eg flock synchronization, contact; a quiet song during courtship and in a solitary context by males. Nests: mostly built of grasses, domed with a side entrance; some species nest in holes. Eggs: usually 4–8, white, length 13–17mm (0.5–0.7in). Diet: mostly grass seeds. Some species take insects, particularly when rearing young.

Species include: **Beautiful firetail** (*Emblema bella*), **Bengalese finch** (domesticated) or **White-backed munia** (*Lonchura striata*), **Double bar finch** (*Poephila bichenovii*), **Golden-breasted waxbill** (*Amandava subflava*), **Gouldian finch** (*Chloebia gouldiae*), **Green avadavat** (*Amandava formosa*), **Pictorella finch** (*Lonchura pectoralis*), **Pink-billed parrotfinch** Ⓡ (*Erythrura kleinschmidti*), **Red-billed firefinch** (*Lagonosticta senegala*), **Red-cheeked cordon bleu** (*Uraeginthus bengalus*), **Zebra finch** (*Poephila guttata*).

Weavers
Family: Ploceidae
One hundred and forty-three species in 18 genera.

Buffalo weavers
Subfamily: Bubalornithinae
Three species in 2 genera.
Africa south of the Sahara. Semi-arid areas, thorn-bush scrub, savanna and acacia country. Size: 22–24cm (8–9.5in) long. Plumage: two species black, one white and brown with scarlet rump. Voice: noisy when breeding (colonial), harsh chattering and guttural calls. Nests: large, untidy domed nests of thorny twigs. Eggs: 3–4, length 25–28mm (1.1in), pale blue or grayish, marked with olive. Diet: seeds, fruits and insects.

Species: **Black-billed buffalo weaver** (*Bubalornis albirostris*), **Red-billed buffalo weaver** (*B. niger*), **White-headed buffalo weaver** (*Dinemellia dinemelli*).

Parasitic viduine weavers and whydahs
Subfamily: Viduinae
Nine species of the genus *Vidua*.
Distribution: Africa south of the Sahara. Savanna and open plains; also villages and gardens. Size: 11.5–41cm (4.5–16in) long. Plumage: mainly black or steely-blue, some with some white or yellow; many females with sparrow-like plumage.

Voice: chirping and soft warbling songs. Males mimic the song of host species. Nests: parasitic in their nesting habits. Eggs: white, length 15–19mm (0.6–0.7in). Diet: seeds and insects.

True weavers
Subfamily: Ploceinae
Ninety-four species in 7 genera.
Distribution: mainly Africa, some extending to Arabia, India, China and Indonesia. Habitat: savanna and forest. Size: 11.5–65cm (4.5–25.5in) long (longest is Long-tailed widow bird *Euplectes progne*). Plumage: many bright yellow, red or glossy black. Females of most *Ploceus* species have sparrow-like plumages, males brighter. Voice: loud chattering, various chirpings and twittering. Nests: often nesting colonially; domed nests suspended from branches. Eggs: 2–4, length 18–25mm (0.7–1in), vary greatly in color and markings: white, greenish, bluish or pink. Diet: seeds, vegetable matter and insects.

Species include: **bishops** (9 species in the genus *Euplectes*), Cuckoo weaver (*Anomalospiza imberbis*), **fodies** (genus *Foudia*), **Grosbeak weaver** (*Amblyospiza albifrons*), **Red-billed quelea** (*Quelea quelea*), **Village weaver** (*Ploceus cucullatus*), **Yellow bishop** (*Euplectes capensis*). Total threatened species: 4.

Sparrow weavers, sparrows and snow finches
Subfamily: Passerinae
Thirty-seven species in 8 genera.
Distribution: Africa, Europe, Asia, introduced to the Americas, Australasia and many islands. Dry bush to full desert, savanna, forest, rocky mountain sides. Also villages and towns. Size: 10–18cm (4–7in) long. Plumage: mainly brown and gray, but sometimes with black or bright yellow. Snow finches show varying amounts of white. Voice: loud chirpings, twitterings and some simple trilled songs. Nests: many species gregarious, breeding in colonies in trees or bushes, making grassy domed nests. Also in holes in trees, rocks or buildings. Eggs: 3–7, length 18–22mm (0.8in), whitish, creamy or pinkish suffused with mauve-brown, grayish or lilac markings. Diet: mainly seeds, vegetable matter and some insects. True sparrows (*Passer*) largely seed-eaters with marked preference for cereals; House sparrows can exist mainly on bread and household scraps.

Species incude: **House sparrow** (*Passer domesticus*), **Pale rock sparrow** (*Petronia brachydactyla*), **Rock sparrow** (*P. petronia*), snow finches (*Montifringilla*), **Tree sparrow** (*Passer montanus*), **Yellow-throated sparrow** (*Petronia xanthocollis*).

The weaver family can be divided into four subfamilies. Most **true weavers** are thick-set seed-eating birds with strong short bills and many have the ability to construct elaborately woven nests. Some forest species have less robust bills and are mainly insectivorous.

The majority of the true weavers are confined to Africa and its neighboring islands and can be separated into two groups. The first group are exclusively tree dwellers, nearly all with bright yellow or red plumage, and build elaborately suspended nests which are tough, with the entrance on the underside, or protected by a tunnel. The tunnel may be as much as 60cm (2ft) long and the nests are often built at the tips of twigs or palm fronds, often sited near water. In a nesting colony, the tree-top is often filled with their nests, slung on branches very close together. The Village weaver may build several nests, advertising each to any interested female. He hangs upside down at the entrance, located in the bottom of the nest, with much wing flapping and chattering.

The second group comprises the fodies and bishops, which build globular nests and except for the fodies, often place them in grass or herbage instead of suspending them in trees. Territorialism is highly developed in these birds and in a grassy area of a flood plain several species may have their territories. The Yellow bishop can have several females nesting in his territory, so that he spends a great deal of his time patrolling his boundaries giving aggressive calls.

Among the three species of diochs, the Red-billed quelea has been known from its earliest recorded history as a menace to

▲ **Representative species of waxbills and weavers.** (1) Golden palm weaver (*Ploceus bojeri*), male displaying at nest. (2) White-backed munia (*Lonchura striata*), wild form of the domesticated Bengalese finch. (3) House sparrow (*Passer domesticus*), in flight. (4) Golden bishop (*Euplectes afer*) male courtship flight. (5) Pin-tailed whydah (*Vidua macroura*). (6) White-headed buffalo weaver (*Dinemellia dinemelli*). (7) Social weaver (*Philetairus socius*) with nests in background.

▷ **Trapeze-like foundation** OVERLEAF of nest laid by male Red-headed weaver (*Anaplectes rubriceps*).

crops of small grain. This species is completely colonial in its habits and is often found in concentrations of over a million birds. Large-scale efforts at control, coupled with research, began in the Sudan in 1946, and by 1953 had become necessary in other territories, but in spite of immense slaughter the plague continues.

There are also two species in separate genera outside the two main groups, the Grosbeak weaver, which has a very heavy bill and weaves a superior globular nest of extremely fine fibers, and the Cuckoo weaver which is a small yellow bird that parasitizes grass-warblers.

The **viduine weavers and whydahs** parasitize species of waxbills. The young of each host species carry distinctive colors and markings on their palates, which serve to release the feeding behavior of the parents. Chicks of the parasitic whydahs mimic these markings with extraordinary accuracy.

The **buffalo weavers** inhabit the drier areas of Africa, feeding on the ground in the manner of starlings. They have a mixed diet, and build large untidy nests of thorny twigs, which are highly protective.

The **sparrows** have a tendency to associate with man, and at least eight of the species regularly nest in the eaves of inhabited buildings. The House sparrow is the most persistent of all and is only rarely found breeding away from man. The Tree sparrow fills the same niche in the eastern parts of its range, where the House sparrow is absent. Despite the close association with man, House sparrows are extremely wary birds and not easily kept in captivity. Many of the sparrows are gregarious and breed in colonies, although the nests do not form communal structures as do those of some other species of weavers.

The Rock sparrows are mainly gray and brown birds with a yellow patch on the throat. However, the African species, including the Yellow-throated sparrow, which extends to India, are birds more of trees than rocks. The remaining two species, the Rock sparrow and the Pale rock sparrow, are more typical "rock" sparrows, as they typically nest in holes in rocks or walls.

The snow finches spend their lives almost entirely on the ground and are among the highest-nesting of living birds, since they occur at from 1,800 to 4,600m (5,900–15,000ft). They are gregarious in winter, forming flocks, which may descend to lower altitudes in severe weather, although they do not leave the mountains altogether.

PRC

STARLINGS, ORIOLES AND DRONGOS

Families: Sturnidae, Oriolidae, Dicruridae
Order: Passeriformes (suborder Oscines, part).
One hundred and fifty-four species in 26 genera.
Distribution: see maps and table.

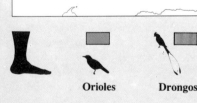

Starlings

Orioles　　　Drongos

▶ **Returning to the nest,** a male European starling pauses on his perch before flying the last few feet to feed his young in their tree-hole nest. Jaunty, loquacious and gregarious, the European starling is at once one of the most successful and most damaging of birds. It is a fearsome competitor and will oust other birds, such as woodpeckers and hoopoes, from their holes.

The male European starling sometimes mates with a second female while his first mate is still incubating her clutch of 4–6 eggs. In such cases, the male goes on to help feed the chicks of his first mate, rarely those of the second. Some females lay their eggs in nests of other starlings rather than in one of their own, in cuckoo-like fashion.

THROUGHOUT history, one of the greatest scourges of man's crops has been the locust and the delectation for this pest of several species of **starling**, such as the Rose-coloured starling, the Common mynah and the Wattled starling brought them to man's attention many centuries ago. Other species are better known as pests.

Most species of starling are resident but some migrate. The Violet-backed starling and the Blue-eared Glossy starling undertake local migrations in Africa and the Brahminy starling makes similar movements in India. The Gray starling migrates from its breeding areas in eastern USSR, northern China and Japan to winter in southern China and the Philippines. Northern populations of the European starling migrate to milder climates for the winter, those from Siberia heading south towards the northern shores of the Indian Ocean while Scandinavian birds migrate southwest towards the Atlantic seaboard. Some starlings are nomadic. This applies particularly to the Wattled starling, which settles to breed where locusts abound but moves on when the insects disappear, and the breeding sites of the Rose-coloured starling, which winters in India, are determined by the abundance of insects—an area that has a large colony of birds one year may be deserted the next.

Starlings are small- to medium-sized birds that make their presence felt near human habitations by their ceaseless activity, loud calling and squabbling. In general appearance, they are rather variable since forest-dwelling forms, like the African glossy starlings, tend to have broad, rounded wings whereas those species that live in drier, more open habitats, such as the European starling, have longer and more pointed wings. The legs and feet are fairly large and strong and the birds tend to walk, rather than hop. In the oxpeckers, the toes are also long and sharp to enable them to cling to the pelts of large mammals. The bill is rather stout and usually straight and reasonably long. Such a bill allows starlings to be catholic in their choice of food, and most eat invertebrates and fruit. Some are more omnivorous and include nectar and seeds in their diets. The tongue of the Brahminy starling bears a brush-like tip which is used for collecting pollen and nectar and the brush-like crests of some of the mynahs are believed to be important in pollination.

Some of the south-east Asian starlings have areas of bare skin on the head, especially around the eye; these areas are yellow in the Andaman starling, blue in Roths-child's mynah and red in the Sulawesi starling. The amount of naked skin reaches its maximum in the Bald starling, where feathering is restricted to a narrow strip of bristles running down the crown. The Hill mynah and the Wattled starling develop fleshy wattles on the head; in the latter species the wattles appear, and head feathering is lost, mainly by birds coming into breeding condition but the wattles are subsequently resorbed and feathers grow anew. The Rose-coloured and Brahminy starlings have long feathers on the head that can be raised into a crest, and the Sula starling has a stiff crest that is permanently erect.

Most starlings breed in holes in which they build a bulky nest. Holes in trees and cliffs are commonly used, while close to human habitation nests may be made inside buildings. The Thin-billed chestnut-winged starling nests in holes behind waterfalls, and several species use holes made by other birds. Some starlings bore their own holes, such as the Bank mynah in river banks and the Woodpecker starling in dead trees. A few species do not nest in holes, however: the Superb starling builds a domed nest in bushes and the Shining starling builds hanging nests, weaver fashion.

In many of the species that have been studied, both sexes incubate the eggs but the male usually plays the lesser role. In the Spotless starling the male does not incubate at all and yet in no species are males known to feed the female on the nest. Nestlings are fed by both parents but the role of the male can be variable. Cooperative breeding, where three or more fully grown birds may feed a brood of chicks in one nest, has now been demonstrated in some African starlings.

Most starlings are gregarious, breeding in colonies, feeding in flocks and roosting communally at night. Several species of starling may roost together and they may also roost among other birds. Roosts are usually in trees but the European starling has recently adopted a habit of roosting in cities in flocks that can contain over a million birds.

During the last 400 years four species are known or thought to have become extinct, two from Indian Ocean islands and two from islands in the Pacific. Rothschild's mynah survives in a small population in a forest nature reserve on Bali, Indonesia. The European starling, on the other hand, is one of the most successful birds, with a world population running into hundreds of millions. The most dramatic example of the species' success, however, comes from its introduction to North America: about 100

individuals were released in New York in 1890—only 90 years later it is now one of the most numerous birds in North America.

The European starling causes extensive damage in Eurasia and North America by eating grapes, olives, cherries, germinating wheat and cattle food, while in northern Europe and central Asia and in New Zealand it is held to be useful on account of its destruction of insects. Many species are kept as cage birds, especially those, like the Hill mynah, with a capacity to mimic speech. The feathers of some African glossy starlings are used for human adornment and several species are killed for food, including the European starling in southern Europe. The Wattled starling's ability to resorb its wattles has been studied in cancer research, while its ability to re-grow feathers has been investigated by optimistic seekers of cures for human baldness!   CJF

The name **oriole** appears to have been derived from the Latin *aureolus*, meaning golden or yellow. Most of the orioles are yellow and black, although some are crimson and black. They are not closely related to the

---

The 3 Families of Starlings, Orioles and Drongos

E Endangered. V Vulnerable. R Rare.

Starlings

Family: Sturnidae
One hundred and six species in 22 genera.
Africa, Europe, Asia, Southeast Asia, Oceania (just into Australasia), introduced to North America, New Zealand, southern Australia and many tropical islands. Forest, savanna, steppes and temperate grassland. Size: 16–45cm (6–18in) long, weight 45–170g (1.5–6oz). Plumage: chiefly dark but usually with iridescent sheens of green, purple and blue; some with brilliant orange and yellow, some with dull gray, some with bare skin or fleshy wattles. Males and females usually similar but with males brighter than females in some. Voice: vociferous, with wide range of whistles, squawks and rattles. Some mimic other animal sounds, including human speech. Nests: most in holes in which a bulky nest of dried grass is built; usually natural holes in trees, cliffs, or buildings or holes made by other species, but some excavate own; some build domed or pendulous nests; many colonial or loosely so. Eggs: usually 1–6, pale blue with brownish spots, but some genera without spots; incubation period 11–18 days; nestling period 18–30 days. Diet: most eat fruit and insects, some also seeds, nectar and pollen; oxpeckers specialize on insects parasitic on large mammals.

Species include: **Andaman starling** (*Sturnus erythropygius*), **Bald starling** (*Sarcops calvus*), **Bank mynah** (*Acridotheres ginginianus*), **Blue-eared glossy starling** (*Lamprotornis chalybaeus*), **Brahminy starling** (*Sturnus pagodarum*), **Chestnut-bellied starling** (*Spreo pulcher*), **European starling** (*Sturnus vulgaris*), **Glossy starling** (*Aplonis panayensis*), **Golden-breasted starling** (*Spreo regius*), **Gray starling** (*Sturnus cineraceus*), **Hill mynah** (*Gracula religiosa*), **Ponape mountain starling** V (*Aplonis pelzelni*), **Red-winged starling** (*Onychognathus morio*), **Rose-colored starling** (*Sturnus roseus*), **Rothschild's mynah** E (*Leucopsar rothschildi*), **Santo mountain starling** R (*Aplonis santovestris*), **Shining starling** (*A. metallica*), **Spotless starling** (*Sturnus unicolor*), **Sula starling** (*Basilornis galeatus*), **Sulawesi starling** (*B. celebensis*), **Superb starling** (*Spreo superbus*), **Thin-billed chestnut-winged starling** (*Onychognathus tenuirostris*), **Violet-backed starling** (*Cinnyricinclus leucogaster*), **Wattled starling** (*Creatophora cinerea*), **Woodpecker starling** (*Scissirostrum dubium*), **Yellow-billed oxpecker** (*Buphagus africanus*).

Orioles and figbirds

Family: Oriolidae
Twenty-eight species in 2 genera.
Africa, Asia, the Philippines, Malaysia, New Guinea and Australia. One species present in Europe. Most species present in the eastern quarter of the family's range. Woodlands and forest. Size: 20–30cm (8–12in) long, weight about 70g (2.5oz). Plumage: predominantly yellow, and yellow and black, occasionally crimson and black in orioles; female orioles, with few exceptions, are less brightly colored than males and in a number of species, are also streaked. The figbirds are duller olive green, gray and yellow, with bare red skin around the eyes in the male. Voice: orioles have clear liquid calls and a growling or bleating call; some orioles are capable mimics. Figbirds have peculiar chattering calls. Nests: open cup-shaped nests high in trees. Eggs: 2–4 in orioles, usually 3 in figbirds; apple to dull olive-green, with red, reddish-purple, purplish-brown and brown markings. Diet: fruit, insects.

Species include: **African golden oriole** (*Oriolus auratus*), **Black-naped oriole** (*O. chinensis*), **Black oriole** (*O. hosii*), **Black-winged oriole** (*O. nigripennis*), **Eastern black-headed oriole** (*O. larvatus*), **figbird** (*Sphecotheres vieilloti*), **Golden oriole** (*Oriolus oriolus*), **Green-headed oriole** (*O. chlorocephalus*), **Maroon oriole** (*O. traillii*), **Sao Thomé oriole** (*O. crassirostris*), **Yellow figbird** (*Sphecotheres flaviventris*).

Drongos

Family: Dicruridae
Twenty species in 2 genera.
Africa, S Asia, Philippines to Solomon Islands, Malaysia, N and E Australia. Open country, cultivation, second growth, edges of rain forest, coastal scrub and mangroves. Size: 18–64cm (7–25in) long. Plumage: black with greenish or purplish gloss, gray or some white; hair-like feathers on crest and elaborate tail shape, forked or racket-tipped. Sexes alike. Voice: jumble of harsh metallic notes, musical calls and whistles; some accomplished mimics. Nests: frail structure, placed in fork of branch. Eggs: 2–4, often white, speckled with brown. Diet: predominantly insects, some nectar.

Species include: **Black drongo** (*Dicrurus macrocercus*), **Crested drongo** (*D. forficatus*), **Fork-tailed drongo** (*D. adsimilis*), **Great Comoro drongo** (*D. fuscipennis*), **Greater racket-tailed drongo** (*D. paradiseus*), **Mayotte drongo** (*D. waldenii*), **Mountain drongo** (*Chaetorhynchus papuensis*), **Shining drongo** (*Dicrurus atripennis*), **Spangled drongo** (*D. hottentottus*).

New World orioles or American blackbirds, which are an entirely different family (p414).

All orioles are remarkably similar in shape and size. The figbirds are less bright in plumage than the orioles, and are more heavily built and more sluggish. In the orioles the bill is slightly decurved, while the figbirds have short, stout bills, hooked at the tip. All the species occur in woodland or forest, where they are restricted to feeding in trees, although both the Golden oriole and the Eastern blackheaded oriole will feed on the ground on fallen fruits or insects in the grass layer. Figbirds commonly occur in small parties or flocks, even in mixed flocks with other oriole species, but most of the orioles are solitary, or found in pairs or family parties. The African orioles, African golden, Eastern black-headed and Green-headed orioles occasionally join mixed-species foraging flocks, and, when they do so, move slowly through the forest or woodland with the other birds. When foraging alone, orioles often fly long distances, as much as 1–2km (0.6–1.2mi), from fruiting tree to tree or other food sources. The rather flapping flight in all orioles is heavy, fairly swift and undulating, rather similar to the flight of woodpeckers.

It is on the islands of Indonesia and New Guinea where the greatest diversity of species has developed, and the greatest range of plumage colors may be seen here. In contrast to the African orioles, in which the plumage is yellow and black, or in one species only, clear yellow and olive green, the plumages of orioles in Australasia range from the completely black, with chestnut under tail coverts of the Black oriole, through the crimson and black of the Maroon oriole to the dull yellowish and greenish of the Australian orioles.

Oriole nests are neatly woven, deep baskets of fine material including grass and beard lichens. The lining is of softer, finer material. Nests, particularly those built from beard lichens, often have material trailing down which serves to camouflage the nest to a great extent. In the African orioles, nest sites are more often inside the tree and seldom on the outer edge of the canopy. Figbird nests are shallower and more flimsy than oriole nests, and are placed in the canopy of trees, in forks at the ends of slender branches. Figbirds construct their nests of twigs and grass and do not weave the materials together as the orioles do.

Although orioles are widespread and usually common or frequently seen where they do occur the nests and eggs of several species

remain to be discovered.   WRJD

The **drongos** are generally solitary, tree-dwelling birds, usually encountered resting on some convenient tree-perch from which they sally forth to snap up some suitable passing insect. Many of them make spectacular swoops, curves and twists in pursuit of their prey.

The adoption of this kind of feeding technique in woodland calls for a much greater maneuverability than is necessary when hawking in open country, hence many drongos have acquired long and often lyre-shaped tails. The shape and structure of the tail varies greatly, from cut-off and shallow-forked to very deeply forked. The outer tail

feathers may be extremely long, curled or denuded of barbs and ending in spoon-shaped rackets, as is found in the Greater racket-tailed drongo of India and Southeast Asia, which has a tail length of 31cm (12in) or more. African drongos are conventional in appearance compared with some of the Asiatic species, which have conspicuous crests as well as racket-shaped tails.

Seven species of drongo occur in Africa, Madagascar, the Comoros and on the island of Aldabra, the remainder being found in the Oriental region. The Spangled drongo has the most extensive range of any drongo, extending from the northern Himalayas to China and through the whole of Indo-Malaysia to the Austral-Papuan regions, as far as the eastern Solomons, and in eastern Australia, with some 30 recognized races.

The Black drongo is one of the most abundant and familiar birds of India and is often seen perched on the earth banks surrounding the fields near villages. It often accompanies grazing cattle, snatching insects disturbed by the animals' movements through the grass, or riding upon their backs. Black drongos are considered to be of great usefulness to agriculture, in destroying vast quantities of insect pests. They are bold and pugnacious birds with piratical habits, setting upon foraging birds with great speed and determination, pursuing them relentlessly with agile twists and turns, forcing them to give up their prey. The Black drongo often retrieves the prey in mid-air, then calmly flies back to its perch, where it tears the insect to pieces with its hooked bill, while holding it in its feet. Fired

grassland will attract considerable numbers of Black drongos to hunt and catch the escaping insects. They also have a great liking for winged termites, hunting them till well into dusk, when they are frequently seen flying up vertically to snatch them on the wing.

A nesting pair of Black drongos will fearlessly attack any crow or raptor which crosses its nesting territory, with great ferocity. During the winter, numbers will congregate to roost in company in bamboo clumps. The Black drongo ranges in seven subspecies from southeastern Iran through India to China, and to Java and Bali.

The Fork-tailed drongo of Africa is very similar to the Black drongo, and is sometimes regarded as being the same species. It also shows the same tenacity, often harrying much larger birds than itself. It is widely distributed south of the Sahara in savanna wherever there are trees.

The Shining drongo of West Africa ranges in lowland forest and is difficult to distinguish from the Fork-tailed drongo. However it is more given to joining the mixed bird parties of the forest, preferring the sunlight of the high tree-tops and the edges of the forest clearings.

The drongos of Madagascar, the Comoro islands and Aldabra are closely related to the Fork-tailed drongo. The Crested drongo of Madagascar and Anjouan islands can be distinguished by its small crest, and the Great Comoro drongo is larger with brownish wings and tail. The Mayotte drongo of Mayotte Island is also larger with a more deeply forked tail.   PRC

▲ **Common mynah feeding its young.** The Common mynah (*Acridotheres tristis*) is as common a sight on the roadsides of pastoral New Zealand (where it has been introduced, as in Australia, South Africa and elsewhere) as it is in the dry hills of India. The species is a good mimic, but the Yellow-wattled Hill mynah is even better and therefore more popular as a cage bird.

▶ **Golden oriole nest,** high up in a horizontal fork of a tree. Both parents share incubation of the eggs and care of the young.

◀ **A Crested drongo in Madagascar** awaits its insect prey. The long, forked tail helps the bird to perform the aerobatics required in the pursuit.

NEW ZEALAND WATTLEBIRDS AND AUSTRALIAN MAGPIES

Families: Callaeidae, Corcoracidae, Grallinidae, Artamidae, Cracticidae
Order: Passeriformes (suborder Oscines, part).
Twenty-six species in 8 genera.
Distribution: see maps and table.

New Zealand wattlebirds   Australian mud-nesters   Magpie-larks

Bell magpies   Wood swallows

THERE are relatively few species of birds confined to New Zealand, and many of these have found it difficult to cope with the loss of habitat due to massive clearing for forestry and agriculture, and the efficient introduced predators that accompanied European settlement. The **New Zealand wattlebirds** exemplify this conflict; all have declined in abundance over the past 100 years and one, the huia, has almost certainly become extinct since it was last seen alive in 1907.

The three species that make up this family were all forest-dwellers that spent a proportion of their time foraging at ground level: this and their readily accessible nests are thought to have made them very susceptible to predation by cats and rats. However, it would seem that collecting by both Maoris and the early European settlers significantly hastened the demise of the huia, which, unfortunately, was sought for ornamentation by both cultures.

The family gains its name from the conspicuous hanging face wattles that adorn each species. These are orange colored except for the Northern Island race of the kokako which has blue wattles. The huia is one of the very few birds in which there is a pronounced difference in bill shape between the sexes.

The kokako and saddleback both eat a wide variety of fruits, berries and insects gathered at all levels of the forest. Their legs are well developed and their wings, while not large, are quite adequate for short flights. Breeding is usually in the spring and early summer. The female builds the nest and she alone incubates the eggs. The male feeds the female on the nest and escorts her when she leaves it to forage. Both parents feed the nestlings. Young stay with their parents for several months after leaving the nest but there is no evidence of longer term associations such as might lead to cooperative breeding groups.

Both living wattlebirds have been the subject of much concern to ornithologists in New Zealand, and the Wildlife Service has been active to prevent either following the huia into possible extinction. The establishment of the saddleback on predator-free islands forms one of the few major success stories in the management of endangered species. It is hoped that efforts with the kokako along similar lines will be as successful.   IR

How did the first mud-nest builder recognize that wet mud was a good material to use? Although wet sloppy mud seems to be a most unpromising material no less than 16 different families of birds ranging from flamingos to swallows have recognized that mud dries to a firm shape and use it regularly to build their nests. In Australia and New Guinea two endemic families have been linked in the past solely on the basis of building their nests with mud. But recently, the two magpie-larks have been placed in a family of their own (Grallinidae), leaving the White-winged chough and the apostlebird as the family of Australian mud-nesters (Corcoracidae).

They are neither magpies nor larks, but the **magpie-larks'** pied plumage suggests the former, their feeding the latter. Alternative names include pee-wee, from their call, and mudlark, from their nests. Both the magpie-lark and the Torrent lark are black and white with slight differences between the sexes. The former is starling-like in build and terrestrial gait, but has a slow flapping flight. The Torrent lark is smaller, very active, and an inhabitant of fast-flowing

▲ **Family of apostlebirds at roost.** Young of this east Australian species often stay with their parents and others of the family group for three or four years, rather than dispersing in their first year like most other birds. All family members help to build the nest, incubate the group's single clutch, and care for and feed the young.

▲ **Endangered species,** the kokako ABOVE LEFT or Blue wattlebird of North Island, New Zealand.

◄ **Insect caught on the wing** is brought back by this male Masked wood swallow to the nest. The species inhabits drier parts of Australia, where it rarely breeds in the same place two years running.

streams in upland New Guinea. It persistently wags its tail from side to side. Magpie-larks often feed around the edge of ponds, frequently eating snails.

Magpie-larks have a call-and-response "pee-wee" call, usually initiated by the male. It maintains contact between male and female and proclaims the territory. They are aggressive, attacking other black and white birds, even their own reflections. Breeding starts in late winter and the mud nests are strengthened with wool and grass. Both parents incubate and feed the young, which are dependent for several weeks after fledging. Flocks of young birds gather in late summer.   HAF

Both **Australian mud-nesters** are confined to eastern Australia and since neither has reached Tasmania or shows any signs of different forms throughout its range, this suggests that they are relatively recent arrivals. The plumage of these birds is soft and fluffy (as in many babblers) compared with the smooth, glossy feathering of most passerines (including the magpie-larks). Both spend most of their time foraging on the ground and have well developed legs in consequence. The White-winged chough has a long slightly curved bill (remarkably similar to that of the unrelated chough of Europe, hence the name) with which it probes into tussocks, digs in soft earth and turns over twigs and pieces of bark to search for insects, its main source of food. Apostlebirds have shorter chunkier "finch-like" bills and although they, too, eat insects they consume a wide variety of seeds as well.

The Australian mud-nesters are very rarely found in simple pairs but in groups of up to 15–20 members, the result of young from earlier years retained within the family group instead of dispersing. Usually, only one female lays in a nest though occasionally two may do so, resulting in a very large clutch.

All members of these groups help to build the nest, to incubate and brood the nestlings and to feed the young in and out of the nest. Sexual maturity is not reached until three or four years from hatching, and during this time the eye color of the birds changes. This feature provides a very useful guide to a bird's age.

Sometimes groups aggregate into large flocks at a localized source of abundant food such as a stubble field recently harvested, or a recently sown cereal crop. This has sometimes caused conflict with farmers in the past but is sufficiently rare that in these days of more enlightened thinking about conservation matters, the species are unlikely to be slaughtered on this account. Most farmers and their families enjoy the presence of these birds which with encouragement may become adapted to man and with their often amusing social interactions add to the variety of country life.

IR

Wood swallows are a distinct group of small birds with strong well-developed wings that enable them to stay aloft for hours scooping up insects in their broad bills. Besides hawking high in the sky, wood swallows have been seen feeding among the blossoms of trees and since they have brush-like tips to their tongues they may gather nectar as well as insects. They have short legs and hop clumsily on the ground. The triangular wing-silhouette closely resembles that of the Common starling and has led to the name in German of Schwalbenstare ("swallow-starling"), which is very apt.

Both members of the pair build the nest, incubate the eggs and feed the young for at least a month. In the Dusky, Little, Black-faced and White-breasted wood swallows groups have been known to attend the nest.

Species in temperate regions breed in spring, those in the tropics during the wet season. Species of the arid inland, such as the Black-faced wood swallow, may breed at any time, responding very rapidly to heavy falls of rain; nests have been built and eggs laid within 12 days of such a downpour. Wood swallows generally nest in loose colonies with their flimsy, stick, cup-nests

▶ **A telegraph pole in Queensland** provides this magpie-lark with a high horizontal "branch," its preferred nest site. "Mudlarks" nest high up, but forage on the ground.

▶ **Pied currawong** BELOW of the Great Dividing Range. Currawongs take insects and other small creatures, and also quantities of fruit. They are named for their gong-like calls.

▼ **Mud nest of a White-winged chough takes shape.** The initial "saddle" of mud (1) is enlarged to a platform (2), raised into a saucer (3), and finally a bowl (4).

In the social White-winged chough and apostlebird, all members of the family group help build the mud nest. Butcherbirds and currawong pairs build their nests without such assistance.

The 5 Families of New Zealand Wattlebirds and Australian Magpies

E Endangered. Ex? Probably Extinct.

New Zealand wattlebirds
Family: Callaeidae
Three species in 3 genera (one probably extinct).

Endemic to New Zealand. Dense forest. Size: 22–50cm (9–20in) long, weight 77–240g (3–8.5oz). Voice: a variety of whistles, clicks, mews and pipes. Plumage: gray, black and white in kokako, black and reddish in saddleback. Eggs: 2–4, whitish with purplish-brown blotches and spots; incubation period 18–25 days; nestling period 27–28 days. Diet: fruit and insects.

Species: **huia** Ex? (*Heteralocha acutirostris*), **kokako** E (*Callaeas cinerea*), **saddleback** (*Philesturnus carunculatus*).

Magpie-larks
Family: Grallinidae
Two species of the genus *Grallina*.
Australia, Timor, Lord Howe Island, New Guinea. Woodland and forest.

Size: 20–50cm (8–20in) long, weight 40–350g (1.5–12oz). Plumage: gray or black and white. Voice: harsh, buzzing and piping calls. Eggs: 3–5, white to pink in color, blotched with red, brown or gray. Incubation period 17–18 days; nestling period 19–23 days. Diet: insects, other invertebrates, including snails, some seeds.

Species: **magpie-lark** (*Grallina cyanoleuca*), **Torrent lark** (*G. bruijni*).

Australian mud-nesters
Family: Corcoracidae
Two species in 2 genera.
Eastern Australia. Woodland and grassland. Size: 33–47cm (13–19in) long, weight 110–425g (4–15oz). Plumage: soft and fluffy; sooty black in White-winged chough, gray and black in apostlebird. Voice: piping whistles. Eggs: 2–5, creamy white with brown, gray or black blotches; incubation period 18–19 days;

nestling period 18–25 days. Diet: seeds and insects.

Species: **White-winged chough** (*Corcorax melanorhamphos*), **apostlebird** (*Struthidea cinerea*).

Wood swallows
Family: Artamidae
Ten species of the genus *Artamus*.
India, SE Asia, Melanesia, New Guinea and Australia. Woodland, shrubland and grassland. Size: 12–23cm (5–9in) long, weight 14–73g (0.5–2.5oz). Plumage: gray and brown, piebald, multi-colored gray, white, reddish and black; juveniles: mottled or speckled. Voice: brisk "preet preet." Eggs: 2–4, creamy white, spotted red brown; incubation period 12–16 days; nestling period 16–20 days. Diet: insects.

Species include: **Ashy wood swallow** (*Artamus fuscus*), **Bismark wood swallow** (*A. insignis*), **Black-faced wood swallow** (*A. cinereus*), **Dusky**

wood swallow (*A. cyanopterus*), **Little wood swallow** (*A. minor*), **Masked wood swallow** (*A. personatus*), **White-backed wood swallow** (*A. monachus*), **White-breasted wood swallow** (*A. leucorhynchus*), **White-browed wood swallow** (*A. superciliosus*).

Bell magpies
Family: Cracticidae
Nine species in 3 genera.
Australia and New Guinea; one introduced to New Zealand. Woodland, shrubland and grassland. Size: 25–50cm (10–20in) long, weight 80–140g (3–5oz). Plumage: gray, white and black. Voice: loud varied carolling. Eggs: 3–5, blue or green, blotched and streaked brown; incubation period 20 days; nestling period 28 days. Diet: omnivorous but mainly insects.

Species include: **Australian magpie** (*Gymnorhina tibicen*), **Louisiade butcherbird** (*Cracticus louisiadensis*), **Pied currawong** (*Strepera graculina*).

rarely within 3m (10ft) of another nest. Family parties remain together long after the breeding season and are very sociable, frequently preening each other and huddling together for roosting even when the night temperature remains above 30°C (86°F); these associations sometimes lead to cooperative breeding. In cold weather, wood swallows may even cluster during the day, and as many as 200 have been seen to gather like a swarm of bees on a tree trunk. A male may courtship-feed his female; copulation is preceded by a characteristic display in which both birds flutter their part-open wings and rotate their half-spread tails.

Some wood swallows remain as residents all the year around while others are regular migrants, returning to the same place to breed each year. The truly nomadic species,

the White-browed and the Masked wood swallows, form mixed flocks which annually travel thousands of kilometers between breeding attempts. They rarely breed in the same place two years running even if there appears to be plenty of food.   IR

Australia is widely supposed to be a "land of song-less birds," but the **bell magpies** give the lie to this. They comprise three genera of basically black and white robust birds that are chiefly insectivorous. They differ in the way they catch the bulk of their insect prey: butcherbirds live a shrike-like existence flying from perches well above the ground and even impaling their prey in "larders" as shrikes do. Magpies are heavier birds with longer legs: they spend much more time on the ground foraging, probing into the ground and under branches, cow-pats etc with their bills. Currawongs are larger still and although they too may spend a lot of time on the ground they are adept at foraging in the forest, searching the canopy for phasmids or probing into the bark of living trees.

One butcherbird is endemic to New Guinea: the Louisiade butcherbird; three other species are shared between New Guinea and Australia and the Gray only occurs in Australia. They all have long massive bills, blue-gray with a black, hooked tip which enables them to capture and dismember prey as large as small birds. Usually found in resident pairs or family parties, they all have beautiful piping or carolling calls that are often performed by the pair or group, with calls and responses creating a magnificent performance.

The Australian magpie is the best known of the family. Its social life is complex but basically territorial. Food is varied and ranges from small seeds and ants, through scarabs, ground weevils and grasshoppers to worms, frogs, lizards and mice. This illustrates the versatility of the species, explains the value of a varied territory and the need for the experience of a long-lived resident to exploit it fully.

Currawongs are named from their call, which is loud and ringing. Their bills are large, pointed and very strong; they are skillful predators of other birds' nests and tend to forage over much larger areas than the other two genera. The Pied currawong nests in the forests of the Great Dividing Range and makes annual nomadic movements towards the plains and cities, in large flocks. They may be significant predators of stick insects which at times defoliate large areas of eucalypt forest.   IR

BOWERBIRDS AND BIRDS OF PARADISE

Families: Ptilonorhynchidae, Paradisaeidae
Order: Passeriformes (suborder Oscines, part).
Sixty-one species in 26 genera.
Distribution: see map and table.

Birds of paradise   **Bowerbirds**

Bowerbirds are the supreme artists among birds. Not only do the males construct elaborate structures decorated with colorful objects—fruits, berries, fungi, tinfoil and bits of plastic—but some even paint them with natural pigments applied with a tool or "paintbrush" held by the bill.

Nine bowerbirds live only in New Guinea, seven only in Australia and two are common to both. Most inhabit wet forests, up to 4,000m (13,000ft) above sea level in the case of the little-known Archbold's bowerbird, discovered as late as 1940. Many are extremely localized, like the Adelbert bowerbird, confined to the Adelbert Mountains of Papua, New Guinea, and the Golden and Tooth-billed bowerbirds, found only in rain forests above 900m (2,950ft) on and around the Atherton Tableland of Queensland, Australia. Other species, notably New Guinea's Flamed bowerbird and Australia's Spotted and Great Gray bowerbirds have extensive continuous ranges, while most others have patchy broken distributions.

Bowerbirds have long been considered close relatives of birds of paradise and recently several ornithologists placed both groups in the family Paradisaeidae. Anatomical and behavioral studies, and the analysis of genetic characters indicate very strongly, however, that the two groups form distinct families. Some genetic studies have

► **Gray-green plumage** of the female Satin bowerbird has its counterpart in the male's glossy black. Those bowerbird species with the greatest color difference between the sexes tend to have the more elaborate bowers.

The Bowerbird and Bird of Paradise Families

Bowerbirds
Family: Ptilonorhynchidae
Eighteen species in 8 genera.
New Guinea, Australia. Tropical, temperate and montane rain forests; riverine and savanna woodland, grassland; dry, arid zones. Size: 21–38cm (8.5–15in) long, weight 70–230g (2.5–8oz); males larger than females except Regent bowerbird, in which the male is smaller. Plumage: nine species predominantly camouflaged brown, gray or green; males of remaining species with yellow or orange crest or cape; or generally gaudy iridescent yellows, reds or blue and their females drab brown, gray or green with barring underneath. Voice: bird mimicry, mechanical noises, cat-like wails. Nests: bulky cup of twigs, leaves, tendrils in fork, vine or crevice. Eggs: 1–2, rarely 3; plain off-white to buff or blotched and scrawled with color about large end. Incubation period

about 19–24 days, nestling period approximately 18–21 days. Diet: fruit, insects, other invertebrates, lizards, other birds' nestlings.

Species: **Adelbert bowerbird** (*Sericulus bakeri*), **Archbold's bowerbird** (*Archboldia papuensis*), **Fawn-breasted bowerbird** (*Chlamydera cerviniventris*), **Flamed bowerbird** (*Sericulus aureus*), **Golden bowerbird** (*Prionodura newtoniana*), **Great gray bowerbird** (*Chlamydera nuchalis*), **Green catbird** (*Ailuroedus crassirostris*), **Lauterbach's bowerbird** (*Chlamydera lauterbachi*), **MacGregor's gardener** (*Amblyornis macgregoriae*), **Regent bowerbird** (*Sericulus chrysocephalus*), **Satin bowerbird** (*Ptilonorhynchus violaceus*), **Spotted bowerbird** (*Chlamydera maculata*), **Spotted catbird** (*Ailuroedus melanotis*), **Striped gardener** (*Amblyornis subalaris*), **Tooth-billed bowerbird** (*Scenopoeetes dentirostris*), **Vogelkop gardener** (*Amblyornis inornatus*), **White-eared catbird**

(*Ailuroedus buccoides*), **Yellow-fronted gardener** (*Amblyornis flavifrons*).

Birds of paradise
Family: Paradisaeidae
Forty-three species in 18 genera.
Moluccas, New Guinea, Australia. Tropical and montane forests, savanna woodland. Size: 15–110cm (6–44in); males larger than females. Plumage: most males colorful with iridescing ornate feather structures; females camouflaged, often barred underneath. Some monogamous species black or iridescent blue-black all over. Voice: varied, including crow-like notes, gunfire or loud bell-like sounds. Nests: bulky leaf and tendril cup on stick foundation in tree or vines. Several build domed nests, and the King bird of paradise is a hole nester. Eggs: 1–2, rarely 3; pale often pinkish base, colorfully spotted, blotched and, typically, smudged mainly at larger

end. Incubation period: about 17–21 days; nestling period 17–30 days. Diet: most are largely fruit-eaters, some insectivorous; also leaves, buds, flowers, animals.

Species include: **Blue bird of paradise** (*Paradisaea rudolphi*), **Brown sicklebill** (*Epimachus mayeri*), **King bird of paradise** (*Cicinnurus regius*), **Lawes' parotia** (*Parotia lawesii*), **Long-tailed paradigalla** (*Paradigalla carunculata*), **MacGregor's bird of paradise** (*Macgregoria pulchra*), **Magnificent bird of paradise** (*Diphyllodes magnificus*), **Magnificent riflebird** (*Ptiloris magnificus*), **Paradise crow** (*Lycocorax pyrrhopterus*), **Paradise riflebird** (*Ptiloris paradiseus*), **Raggiana bird of paradise** (*Paradisaea raggiana*), **Ribbon-tailed bird of paradise** (*Astrapia mayeri*), **trumpetbird** (*Manucodia keraudrenii*), **Victoria riflebird** (*Ptiloris victoriae*), **Wallace's standardwing** (*Semioptera wallacei*).

▲ **Maypole bower** of the Golden bowerbird. The male adds moss, flowers and fruit to the attractions of the bower, which may attain 2m (6.6ft) in height.

▷ **Avenue and mat bower** OVERLEAF of the Satin bowerbird. A blue plastic lid is part of the show, together with blue feathers and green leaves. The male solicits the female with grating, cackling and squeaking calls, as it dances about with its tail cocked high, jumps over the bower, and points its bill to the decorations. Having entered the bower and mated, the female leaves to build a nest and raise young on her own.

the females' concern. Recent studies of the Satin bowerbird indicate that bower building is not innate but is learned behavior. Young males start with inferior bowers but gradually improve them as they gain experience. Males of bower-tending species are promiscuous, attracting many females to their bower by calls and mating with as many as possible. Most such males are very brightly colored; glimmering gold, or orange, and black as in the Flamed, Adelbert, Regent and Archbold's bowerbirds; iridescent blue-black in the well known Satin, completely brilliant yellow and golden-olive in the Golden or generally brown with contrasting orange or yellow crest like most of the Gardener bowerbirds. The "avenue" bower building Spotted, Great Gray, Fawn-breasted and Lauterbach's bowerbirds of grasslands and more arid woodlands are generally drab gray or brownish with small pinkish nape crests.

An important generalization is that species with more colorful males build modest bowers while drabber ones build bigger complex structures (see box). Females of promiscuous species wear drab camouflage, being predominantly brown, olive or gray, often with barring or spotting. The sexes of White-eared, Spotted and Green catbirds are similar, being generally green with white spotting on breast, wings, tail and about the head or throat. Sexes of the presumed promiscuous Toothbilled bowerbird are also identical, being olive brown above and heavily streaked brown on dirty white below. Male Toothbills clear a forest floor "court" of litter and lay decorative green leaves on it, and they call almost continuously at it to attract females.

Males of promiscuous species are long lived, taking up to seven years to attain adult plumage from their initial female coloration, whereas females may breed after two years. Some Satin bowerbird bower sites have been used for nearly 50 years.

Most bowerbirds are predominantly fruit eaters, but insects, vegetable matter and some animals are also taken. In winter some of the avenue-building bowerbird species regularly form flocks which may be serious pests to commercial fruit crops, and Satin bowerbird flocks will ground feed on grasses. Most other polygamous species appear to be sedentary and probably solitary. Toothbilled bowerbirds eat considerable amounts of leaves and succulent stems in winter, having a stout "toothed" bill for tearing and chewing leaves. Until recently, promiscuous male bowerbirds were presumed to form breeding colonies or leks,

indicated closer relationships between bowerbirds, lyrebirds and Australian scrubbirds than previously acknowledged.

Bowerbirds are stout, strong footed, heavy-billed birds ranging in size from that of a starling to that of a medium crow. As much a part of the physical appearance of adult male bowerbirds is the court or bower. These remarkable external secondary sexual characters—only discovered in 1870—are created to impress females, and possibly also to intimidate rival males, and have nothing to do with nesting, which is entirely

their bowers being clustered in associated congregations, but no confirmation of this exists. Recent studies show that the Regent, Satin, Fawn-breasted, MacGregor's and Golden bowerbirds certainly do not, their bowers being evenly distributed throughout suitable habitat. In those promiscuous species which have been studied, females defend only their nest site and males only the immediate vicinity of the bower. In the monogamous catbirds an all-purpose territory is maintained year round.

Birds of paradise are so named because of the bizarre appearance of most males, which have fantastic feather and plume structures and wonderful coloration, much of which is iridescent.

Most species are confined to New Guinea where the family doubtless originated, but the Paradise crow and Wallace's standard-wing are confined to the Moluccan Islands and the Paradise and Victoria's riflebirds to eastern Australia. The Magnificent riflebird and the trumpetbird ranges also just reach Australia from New Guinea. Some New Guinea species have extensive lowland distributions but most have restricted and/or patchy ranges in the mountains at definite altitudinal zones. A few are confined to offshore islands. Most species are wet forest birds although a few occur in sub-alpine woodlands, lowland savanna or mangroves.

Birds of paradise are stout crow-like or starling-like, round-winged, very strong-footed birds. Plumage is extremely varied, from black with brilliant areas of metallic iridescence in some to brilliant combinations of rich yellows, reds, blues and browns, with rich pastel areas of specialized display plumes or weird head or tail "wires" of modified feathering in others. Each genus of the polygamous species has a basic male plumage structure peculiar to it which is manipulated in certain ways during ritualized display sequences.

The five generally uniform blue-black manucodes (*Manucodia* species), and the generally black MacGregor's bird of paradise, show no sexual differences in plumage and are monogamous, and the similarly dull-plumaged Paradise crow and the two paradigallas are presumed to be likewise. The other more colorful and sexually dimorphic species are known or presumed to be polygamous, males being promiscuous and females raising the young alone.

Bills of birds of paradise vary enormously, from short stout crow-like generalized bills, and finer starling-like ones, to very long fine sickle shapes specialized for probing under moss and bark for insects and larvae. While most species are predominantly fruit eaters that also take a variety of insects, animals, leaves and buds, the sicklebills and riflebirds

▲ **Bowerbirds without a bower.** The Spotted catbird's plumage is similar in both sexes. Catbirds do not build a bower.

▶ **Raggiana bird of paradise.** Males display to establish their precedence over other males at the breeding ground where females gather. In this species the performance may include the bird hanging upside-down.

The Transferral Effect

In bowerbirds, the gaudy display plumage of the males has been progressively transferred to the bower "displays" that they build. There are various stages of this "transfer"—birds that have retained colorful plumage build dull bowers and the most elaborate bowers are built by dull-looking birds.

There are four basic types of bower: the "court" of the Toothbilled bowerbird, merely a cleared area of forest floor decorated with green leaves; the "mat" of Archbold's bowerbird, being a carpet of mosses and ferns; the "avenue" bowers of the Flamed bowerbird, the Satin bowerbird (**1**) and the Spotted bowerbird, which have two parallel upright stick walls forming a central avenue; and "maypole" bowers of the Yellow-fronted gardener and the Golden bowerbird, consisting of stick accumulations about sapling trunks. Three maypole builders build bowers so complex they look just like small towers or thatched buildings, decorated with moss or lichen "lawns," colored flowers, fruits and insect castings.

Maypole, or gardener bowerbirds clearly demonstrate the transferral effect. Within these four species, bowers vary from the simple stick tower of MacGregor's gardener (**2**) to the complex hut-like structure of the Vogelkop gardener (**3**). The males of each species differ in the extent of a colorful crest relative to bower complexity. MacGregor's gardener builds the simplest bower and has a large orange crest. The Striped gardener has a more complex bower (**4**) but a reduced crest, and the Vogelkop gardener builds the most complicated bower and completely lacks a crest. When the relationship between luxuriance of crest and bower was first noticed, about 30 years ago, the home, bower, and the female of the beautifully crested

fittest males are able to maintain their place in the breeding community and that only the most vigorous immatures "inherit" display areas or places in leks. Interestingly, captive young male birds of paradise have been noted to breed at a relatively early age in the absence of adult plumage males, suggesting hormonal activity may be restricted by the presence of dominant adult males. No such inhibition however acts on females, which are capable of breeding at two to three years old.

While a breeding system in which few males fertilize many females has brought about evolutionary rapid divergence in the appearance of the males of the various birds of paradise, they remain genetically close. Thus species markedly different in male appearance are nevertheless not genetically isolated and as a result hybrids are a common phenomenon. Not only do species within a genus hybridize, but species of many different genera do so; in which the males of the two parent species are utterly different in appearance. In the case of male offspring from such hybridization the characters of the two contributing species mingle to produce different looking birds, many of which were described as new species to science prior to our understanding of the hybrid situation.

The fact that some birds of paradise, and bowerbirds, are monogamous and territorial, and that some of the polygamous species have displaying areas (leks) where males congregate while others display solitarily, raises the question: how did these different systems arise? It seems that the predominance of tropical forest fruits in the diet is important to the development of polygamy in these bird groups and that the quality of fruit and/or its dispersion in the forest in space and time may dictate the kind of breeding system and/or the way in which males disperse and display.

Several distributionally restricted species may be threatened by habitat destruction but, unfortunately, some species populations, such as several in Irian Jaya (Indonesian New Guinea), are still unknown and urgently require objective assessment. Perhaps the most striking of all species, the Blue bird of paradise, is presently considered to be threatened because the mid-mountain forests vital to it have been reduced by encroaching agriculture. It may be further threatened by potential competition from the Raggiana bird of paradise, which tolerates a wider range of habitats and abuts the lower distributional limits of the Blue bird. CBF

Yellow-fronted gardener remained undiscovered and it was postulated, therefore, that its bower would prove to be simple in accordance with the inverse relationship exhibited by the other species. Recently, the Yellow-fronted gardener has been discovered in remote mountainous Irian Jaya, and the bower is similar to MacGregor's gardener, as predicted.

Sexual selection, through "female choice," has apparently caused this transfer of visual sexual signals from crest to bower; females select males with superior bowers and thus enhancing bower architecture because only males with superior bowers reproduce. As discerning females selected for improved bowers, males lost their bright plumage: it became disadvantageous, attracting predators.

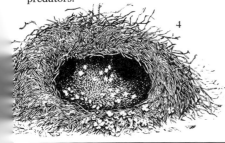

are highly specialized insectivores that eat only some fruit. In the latter, longer billed species, the bill of the female is larger in most species. This is noteworthy as many birds of paradise appear to suffer from limited resources in nonbreeding seasons, when the females move lower down the mountains than the males in order to limit intraspecific competition.

The incredible displays of promiscuous male birds are to impress females or, in birds such as the typical or plumed birds (*Paradisaea* species), which congregate on breeding grounds (leks) to establish a male dominance hierarchy. The six-wired birds (*Parotia* species), like many promiscuous species, display as solitary males at traditional courts or perches which young males eagerly wait to occupy at the first opportunity. Meantime, like young male bowerbirds, they must spend years, perhaps as many as seven, in immature female-like plumage. This situation, with adult males mating promiscuously with many females, means that there are few breeding males in the population relative to females or immature males. Pressure by the latter, in addition to that from rival adult males, ensures that only the

CROWS

Family: Corvidae

Order: Passeriformes (suborder Oscines, part).
One hundred and sixteen species in 23 genera.
Distribution: worldwide, except for the high
Arctic, Antarctic, southern S America, New
Zealand and most oceanic islands.

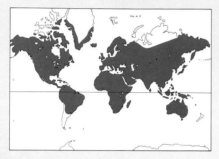

Habitat: varied, including forests, farmland,
grasslands, desert, steppes and tundra.

Size: 15–65cm (6–26in) long
(including long tails of some
magpie species), weight 80–
1,500g (2–50oz).

Plumage: often all black, or black marked with
white or gray; many jays brightly marked with
blue, chestnut, buff or green. Sexes usually
similar.

Voice: varied range of harsh or more musical
calls; some species capable of mimicry.

Nests: typically bowl-shaped structures of twigs
with lining of fine materials, placed in tree;
some species have domed nests or nest in holes.

Eggs: usually 2–8; ground color whitish, buff,
cream, light blue or light green, often marked
with dark spots or blotches; incubation period
16–22 days; nestling period 20–45 days.

Diet: varied in most species, including fruit,
seeds, insects, small vertebrates, often eggs of
other birds or carrion; many species store food.

Species include: **Alpine chough** (*Pyrrhocorax
graculus*), **American crow** (*Corvus
brachyrhynchos*), **Australian crow** (*C. orru*),
Australian raven (*C. coronoides*), **Biddulph's
ground jay** (*Podoces biddulphi*), **Blue jay**
(*Cyanocitta cristata*), **Carrion crow** (*Corvus
corone*), **chough** (*Pyrrhocorax pyrrhocorax*),
Clark's nutcracker (*Nucifraga columbiana*), **Fish
crow** (*Corvus ossifragus*), **Gray** or **Canada jay**
(*Perisoreus canadensis*), **Green magpie** (*Cissa
chinensis*), **Hawaiian crow** E (*Corvus tropicus*),
House crow (*C. splendens*), **Hume's ground jay**
(*Pseudopodoces humilis*), **jackdaw** (*Corvus
monedula*), **jay** (*Garrulus glandarius*), **Jungle
crow** (*Corvus macrorhynchos*), **Little crow**
(*C. bennetti*), **magpie** or **Black-billed magpie**
(*Pica pica*), **Marianas crow** E (*Corvus kubaryi*),
Mexican crow (*C. imparatus*), **nutcracker**
(*Nucifraga caryocatactes*), **Pied crow** (*Corvus
albus*), **raven** (*C. corax*), **Red-billed blue magpie**
(*Urocissa erythrorhyncha*), **rook** (*Corvus
frugilegus*), **Scrub jay** (*Aphelocoma coerulescens*),
Sinaloa crow (*C. sinaloae*), **Steller's jay**
(*Cyanocitta stelleri*), **White-necked raven** (*Corvus
albicollis*).

E Endangered.

R AVENS, crows and magpies have often
been seen as birds of ill-omen, perhaps
because of their color and size, their
perceived intelligence and their raucous
cries. The raven especially was believed to
have the power of foretelling death. In
Marlowe's words: "The sad presaging raven
tolls the sick man's passport in her beak."

The crow family contains the largest of all
passerines, the ravens, as well as a wide
variety of smaller jays, magpies, and others.
Some of them are regarded as the most intelligent and highly evolved of all birds. Many
of the species are woodland or forest birds,
and most of the jays and magpies of Asia and
South America are almost confined to forests. However, most of the familiar species
of Europe and North America prefer more
open habitats, and there are no forest birds
among the African or Australian representatives.

The most widespread and familiar group
comprises the typical crows and ravens of
the genus *Corvus*. These are large birds with
tails of short or medium length and plumage
that is all-black, black and white, black and
gray or entirely sooty-brown. Because they
diverge further from the typical types of
songbird than most other members of the
family, they are usually regarded as the
most highly evolved of the crows.

In Europe the genus is represented by the
raven, Carrion and Hooded crows, rook and
jackdaw; in southern Asia by the House
crow and Jungle crow among others; and
in Africa by the Pied crow, White-necked
raven and others. In North America and
again in Australia there are a number of all-

▲ **Quick to exploit** any opportunity, crows will seize on an unexpected food source. Here Carrion crows at carrion, the carcass of a calf on a hillside. Crows (genus *Corvus*) are the largest of the passerines and are considered the most evolutionarily advanced of all birds.

◄ **The Azure-winged magpie** (*Cyanopica cyana*) has actions like a magpie's. The species is unusual for its patchy distribution, for it is found in Spain and Portugal and the Far East (chiefly China, Korea, Japan) but not in-between. The tree-fork nest site is typical for the species.

black crows that resemble each other rather closely in structure and appearance but differ in their voices. Thus the American crow, Fish crow, Sinaloan crow and Mexican crow are more readily separable by voice than appearance, and in Australia the Australian crow, Little crow, Australian raven and others are difficult to identify except by their calls. The genus *Corvus* has been more successful than others of the family in colonizing remote islands, resulting in development of species with local distributions in the West Indies, Indonesia, the southwest Pacific and Hawaii.

The chough and Alpine chough resemble *Corvus* in their glossy all-black plumage, but differ in having more slender downcurved bills colored red or yellow. They are mainly mountain birds, extending to elevations of nearly 9,000m (27,000ft) in the Himalayas, but also occurring near rocky sea-cliffs in some regions.

Two species of nutcracker inhabit Eurasia and North America, respectively. The European nutcracker is mainly chestnut with white streaks, whereas the American Clark's nutcracker is mainly gray. Both feed largely on seeds of nuts and rely on hidden supplies during the winter.

The magpies include not only the familiar piebald magpie of Europe, Asia and North America, but also a number of more brightly colored species from southern Asia such as the Green magpie and Red-billed blue magpie. They all have short strong bills and very long graduated tails. The dividing line between the Asian magpies and jays relies mainly on the length of the tail, but the American jays include both short-tailed and rather long-tailed forms. Among the American jays there is a large proportion of species of rather small size, some of them no bigger than large thrushes, and also a large proportion with much blue in the plumage.

Among several atypical groups placed in the crow family, the ground-jays of central Asia are unusual in being predominantly ground-dwelling. They inhabit dry semi-desert and steppe regions and usually run from danger rather than taking to the air. Hume's ground jay is particularly small and lark-like and there is uncertainty about whether this species rightfully belongs in the crow family.

However, allowing for this and a very few other exceptions, the crow family is fairly well defined. The combination of large to very large size, robust build, a strong bill with the external nostrils covered by bristle-like feathers, and strong legs, serves to distinguish most crows from other songbirds, although certain starlings, drongos and birds-of-paradise share some features.

The adaptability and versatility of crows shows most clearly in their diets and feeding behavior. Most species take both animal and plant foods, and many are quick to exploit new and artificial food sources. The manipulation of food is made easier by the robust, generalized bill widespread in the family, and in most species also by use of the feet to hold food while it is dismembered. Many species have been recorded "dunking" or washing food, and this may be an adaptation to counter stickiness. Food-hiding is also prevalent in the family (see pp446–47). It has often been suggested that crows can survive on almost any food, but the poor physical condition of many captive birds strongly implies that their nutritional requirements are similar to those of most other birds.

The longevity of crows has probably been overestimated by casual observers because of the tendency for them to persist from generation to generation in suitable territories. Thus we have the old folk saying that "a crow lives three times as long as a man, and a raven lives three times as long as a crow." However, the maximum age recorded in captivity for a raven was 29 years, and that bird died of senile decay, suggesting that wild birds do not often live as long. Recoveries of ringed birds of several crow species show that one-third to one-half of young birds may die in the first year, and that few adults live to be older than 10 years. Nevertheless, some of the larger crows would thus appear by passerine standards to be long-lived.

Several studies of marked birds have shown that individuals do not start to breed until they are two years old, although in the Carrion crow and magpie they may be paired and holding territories during the second year of life. This deferment of sexual maturity may allow the young birds to gain additional experience before attempting to breed.

Crafty Corvines

The quick-wittedness and great adaptability of many of the typical black crows (genus *Corvus*) may partly account for their wide distribution over four continents. At any event, intelligence accounts for the versatility in feeding behavior that has allowed them to survive in such harsh environments as deserts, tundra and cities.

Experimental studies with ravens have suggested that under some controlled conditions they can "count" up to five or six. This species and the jackdaw performed better than parrots, pigeons and chickens in simple experiments designed to test intelligence.

Wild crows appear to use their intelligence to good effect in obtaining food. For example, Carrion crows learned to drop freshwater mussels from the air onto land surfaces so as to break them open and obtain the soft body of the animal within. Accompanying Herring gulls would repeatedly drop the mussel onto soft mud, but the crows were much quicker in learning to select hard surfaces.

Another example was reported by a gamekeeper who had been checking on the location of pheasant nests with clutches of eggs. On returning to several of the pheasant nests he found they had all been robbed by crows along several hundred meters of hedgebank. Later observations showed that a Carrion crow had learnt to watch the gamekeeper in order to obtain information on the location of the nests.

Other instances have been reported of ravens, Carrion crows and jackdaws being quick to rob nests of gulls or birds of prey during brief periods when they were left unattended owing to presence of birdwatchers in the vicinity. Indeed, nests of some of the scarcer birds of prey such as eagles are less likely to be deserted as a result of human disturbance than they are to be robbed by crows while the parent birds have been frightened away from the nest.

A majority of members of the crow family defend exclusive breeding territories in which they nest. As examples, the raven, jay and Blue jay all defend territories from which both birds of the pair threaten intruders. A few species nest colonially, notably the jackdaw, which has rather loosely spaced colonies nesting in holes, and the rook which nests in denser colonies in the tops of trees. The colonial nesters are gregarious throughout the year, and many of the species that hold breeding territories flock outside the breeding season, some of them occupying large communal roosts. Studies of marked birds of several species have shown that the same territories are occupied year after year and that the pair-bond often lasts for life.

Several different species of crows are known to have breeding seasons that are timed to take advantage of peak food supplies for the nestlings. Thus, in England the rook lays in March to take advantage of the peak in earthworm abundance in April, whereas the jay lays in late April or May to take advantage of the late May and early June peak in abundance of defoliating caterpillars on trees.

Incubation is carried out by the female alone in most species (by both sexes in nutcrackers), and the female is usually fed on the nest by the male. Because incubation often starts when the first egg of the clutch is laid, the nestlings differ in size as they hatch over a period of several days. When food is short the smallest of the brood often dies. Both parents feed the young on food that is mostly carried to the nest concealed in the throat of the adult bird. The fledglings of most if not all species are fed by their parents for some weeks after they leave the nest, and in at least some species they may remain in the parents' territory for many months after they become independent. Florida Scrub jay young may stay for a year or more. This species is known to breed cooperatively.

Several species of crows are significant pests of agriculture. The rook makes severe inroads as a pest because of its depredations on cereal sowings in winter and early spring. During World War II it was estimated that rooks in Britain caused damage costing £3 million per annum, but no recent estimates of this damage are available.

DTH

◄ **The Pied crow** FAR LEFT is common throughout most of tropical and southern Africa and is the only corvid found in Madagascar.

◄ **Displays of the rook** BELOW. In late winter and early spring, the cawing that accompanies the territorial bowing and tail-fanning display (1) is the characteristic sound of a rookery. In males, the display may develop into the pre-copulatory display (2), especially early during the breeding season. In fighting over food, rooks and other corvids adopt an aggressive "take-off" posture (3).

▲ ▼ **Representative species of crows.**
(1) White-necked raven (*Corvus albicollis*).
(2, 2a ABOVE, in flight) Jackdaw (*Corvus monedula*). (3, 3a) Chough (*Pyrrhocorax pyrrhocorax*). (4, 4a) Magpie (*Pica pica*). (5, 5a) Raven (*Corvus corax*). (6) Nutcracker (*Nucifraga caryocatactes*). (7) Jay (*Garrulus glandarius*). (8) Steller's jay (*Cyanocitta stelleri*). (9) Green magpie (*Cissa chinensis*). (10) Red-billed blue magpie (*Urocissa erythrorhyncha*).

Squirreling crows

How crows cache food

Most members of the crow family that have been studied in detail in the wild have been seen to hide food. In captivity, many ravens, magpies and jays appear to have a compulsion to hide food. Often the food is carried inside the throat of the bird, so that it is only when the bird is seen to regurgitate or when the food caches are discovered that the extent of food-hiding becomes clear.

Food-hiding behavior is usually not seen when the food consists of such small, well-hidden, living items as insects or earthworms. However, when a surplus of bread is supplied to wild jays or crows they quickly begin to hide away supplies. They typically use small holes in the ground, under debris or vegetation, but sites above ground on trees or buildings may also be used. A deliberate effort is usually made to cover the hidden food by raking loose material on top of it, or by walking a short distance to find a stone or other object to place on top.

Several instances have been reported of very hungry ravens and crows, when suddenly faced with an abundance of food, taking the trouble to hide a large quantity before beginning to eat. However, the extent to which food is deliberately stored for later use varies widely between species. Where there are no seasons of major shortage the hiding and later recovery of food is on a small scale, as for example with magpies and jackdaws in England. Other species use stored reserves of food to allow survival through harsh winter conditions when only scanty food supplies remain available.

The Gray jay inhabits forests of spruce and other conifers over large areas of northern Canada. During the winter, food supplies are very scarce in these forests and the thick and extensive snow cover would prevent the jays from recovering food hidden in the ground. Instead, spruce seeds and other food are stored in the foliage of the conifers stuck to the leaves with saliva. For this purpose, the Gray jay has evolved especially large salivary glands.

Food-hiding may serve two functions in addition to, or instead of, the provision of a food supply during periods of shortage. One suggestion was that the extensive transport and surface-burial of acorns by jays and of hazel-nuts by nutcrackers was aimed at the spreading and perpetuation of these trees.

The second suggestion was that the Blue jay may carry and hide food in order to remove surplus food from its territory. This was argued to have the effect of discouraging other Blue jays from trespassing in search of food, and hence perhaps of competing for food later when it may be scarce. Despite these possible explanations, several studies have suggested that at least some members of the crow family derive a significant part of their diet from stored reserves

▲ **Hard times** for the gregarious rook of Eurasia. It is less common for such social species to cache food for the winter—mates and other flock members are watching! But for some corvids squirrel-like provisioning appears to be an important aid to surviving the winter.

◄ **Acorns are a major food** of the European jay, which makes large stores in the fall for use in the following winter and spring.

► **The Gray or Canada jay** favors coniferous and spruce forests in its North American home. The species caches food in conifer foliage, not on the ground as most other corvids do, because this becomes too deeply covered with snow in winter.

during a season of food shortage. Hence it seems likely that this is the main function of food-hiding.

The crows' memory for the whereabouts of hidden food is good. European nutcrackers spend much of the fall hiding hazel nuts or pine seeds in holes in the ground, often carrying them for over a kilometer. During the winter, the diet of the nutcrackers includes a high proportion of this stored food, and they can excavate food from beneath 20cm (8in) or more of snow cover. There are records of nutcrackers feeding hazel nuts to their nestlings in the late spring and these nuts were presumably hidden the previous fall. Nonetheless, some of the hidden nuts and pine seeds are not recovered and these may germinate, having been both dispersed and "planted" by the nutcrackers.

By comparison with the European nutcracker, a study of jays in Holland suggested they were less efficient at recovering acorns, relying in part on the development of a growing shoot to reveal the hiding place. However, jays also recover many acorns before they germinate, and there is one instance recorded of them digging through snow to find them.

Social crows such as the rook may have difficulty in hiding food where it will not be discovered by other members of the flock. There are several observations of the mate or other birds of the flock watching food being hidden and then quickly trying to find it. In these instances the bird often appears to have difficulty in locating the exact spot, whereas the bird that hid the food may be immediately successful in recovering it.

DTH

Bibliography

The following list of titles indicates key reference works used in the preparation of this volume and those recommended for further reading. The list is divided into two sections: general and regional books about birds and books dealing with particular families or groups.

General and Regional

Ali, S. (1977) *Field Guide to the Birds of the Eastern Himalayas*, Oxford University Press, Delhi.

Ali, S. and Ripley, S.D. (1983) *A Pictorial Guide to the Birds of the Indian Subcontinent*, Bombay Natural History Society/Oxford University Press, Delhi.

Ali, S. and Ripley, S.D. (1984) *Handbook of the Birds of India and Pakistan*, Oxford University Press, Delhi.

Baker, R.R. (1984) *Bird Navigation—the Solution of a Mystery?* Hodder and Stoughton, Sevenoaks, Kent.

Baker, R.R. (1978) *The Evolutionary Ecology of Animal Migration*, Hodder and Stoughton, Sevenoaks, Kent.

Blake, E.R. (1977) *Manual of Neotropical Birds, Vol I. Spheniscidae to Laridae*, University of Chicago Press, Chicago.

Blakers, M., Davies, S.J.J.F. and Reilly, P.N. (1984) *The Atlas of Australian Birds*, Melbourne University Press, Melbourne.

Bock, W.J. and Farrand, J. (1980) *The Number of Species and Genera of Recent Birds: a Contribution to Comparative Systematics*, American Museum of Natural History, New York.

Bond, J. (1979) *Birds of the West Indies: a Guide to the Species of Birds that Inhabit the Greater Antilles, Lesser Antilles and Bahama Islands*, Collins, London.

Brown, L.H., Urban, E.K. and Newman, K. (1982) *The Birds of Africa*, vol I, Academic Press, London.

Brudenell-Bruce, P.G.C. (1975) *The Birds of New Providence and the Bahama Islands*, Collins, London.

Campbell, B. and Lack, E. (1985) *A New Dictionary of Birds*, T. and A.D. Poyser, Stoke-on-Trent.

Clements, J. (1981) *Birds of the World: a Checklist*, Croom Helm, London.

Cramp, S. (1978–85) *Handbook of the Birds of Europe, the Middle East and North Africa: the Birds of the Western Palearctic*, vols I–IV, Oxford University Press, Oxford.

Dementiev, G.P. *et al* (1966) *Birds of the Soviet Union*, vols I–VI, Jerusalem.

Dorst, J. (1962) *The Migration of Birds*, Heinemann, London.

Dunning, J.S. (1982) *South American Land Birds: a Photographic Aid to Identification*, Harrowood, Pennsylvania.

Eastwood, E. (1967) *Radar Ornithology*, Methuen, London.

Ehrlick, P. and A. (1982) *Extinction*, Gollancz, London.

Elkins, N. (1983) *Weather and Bird Behavior*, T. and A.D. Poyser, Stoke-on-Trent.

Falla, R.A., Sibson R.B. and Turbott, E.G. (1979) *The New Guide to the Birds of New Zealand*, Collins, Auckland and London.

Farner, D.S., King, J.R. and Parkes, K.C. (1971–83) *Avian Biology*, vols I–VII, Academic Press, New York and London.

Farrand, J.J. (1983) *The Audubon Society Master Guide to Birding*, 3 vols, Knopf, New York.

Ferguson-Lees, J., Willis, I. and Sharrock, J.T.R. (1983) *The Shell Guide to the Birds of Britain and Ireland*, Michael Joseph, London.

Finlay, J.C. (1984) *A Bird Finding Guide to Canada*, Hurtig, Edmon.

Flint, V.E., Boehme, R.L., Kostin, Y.V. and Kuznetzov, A.A. (1984) *A Field Guide to Birds of the USSR*, Princeton University Press, Princeton, N.J.

Gallagher, M. and Woodcock, M.W. (1980) *The Birds of Oman*, Quartet, London.

Glenister, A.G. (1971) *The Birds of the Malay Peninsula, Singapore and Penang*, Oxford University Press, Kuala Lumpur.

Godfrey, W.E. (1966) *The Birds of Canada*, National Museum of Canada, Ottawa.

Gotch, A.F. (1981) *Birds—their Latin Names Explained*, Blandford Press, Poole, Dorset.

Gruson, E.S. (1976) *A Checklist of the Birds of the World*, Collins, London.

Halliday, T. (1978) *Vanishing Birds: their Natural History and Conservation*, Sidgwick and Jackson, London.

Harris, M. (1982) *A Field Guide to the Birds of Galapagos*, revised edn, Collins, London.

Harrison, C.J.O. (1975) *A Field Guide to the Nests, Eggs and Nestlings of British and European Birds, with North Africa and the Middle East*, Collins, London.

Harrison, C.J.O. (1978) *A Field Guide to the Nests, Eggs and Nestlings of North American Birds*, Collins, London.

Harrison, C.J.O. (1982) *An Atlas of the Birds of the Western Palaearctic*, Collins, London.

Harrison, C.J.O. (ed) (1978) *Bird Families of the World*, Elsevier-Phaidon, Oxford.

Harrison, P. (1983) *Seabirds—an Identification Guide*, Croom Helm, London.

Howard, R. and Moore, A. (1980) *A Complete Checklist of the Birds of the World*, Oxford University Press, Oxford.

Irby Davis, L. (1972) *A Field Guide to the Birds of Mexico and Central America*, Texas University Press, Austin.

King, A.S. and McLelland, J. (1975) *Outlines of Avian Anatomy*, Baillière Tindall, London.

King, B., Woodcock, M. and Dickinson, E.C. (1975) *A Field Guide to the Birds of South-East Asia*, Collins, London.

Krebs, J.R. and Davies, N.B. (1981) *An Introduction to Behavioral Ecology*, Blackwell Scientific Publications, Oxford.

Lack, D. (1968) *Ecological Adaptations for Breeding in Birds*, Methuen, London.

Leahy, C. (1982) *The Bird Watcher's Companion: an Encyclopedic Handbook of North American Birdlife*, Hale, London.

McFarland, D. (ed) (1981) *The Oxford Companion to Animal Behavior*, Oxford University Press, Oxford.

McLachlan, G.R. *et al* (1978) *Roberts' Birds of South Africa* (4th edn), Struik, Cape Town.

Moreau, R.E. (1972) *The Palaearctic–African Bird Migration Systems*, Academic Press, London.

Murton, R.K. and Westwood, N.J. (1977) *Avian Breeding Cycles*, Oxford University Press, Oxford.

National Geographic Society (1983) *Field Guide to the Birds of North America*, NGS, Washington.

Newman, K. (1983) *The Birds of Southern Africa*, Macmillan, Johannesburg.

O'Connor, R.J. (1984) *The Growth and Development of Birds*, Wiley, New York.

Penny, M. (1974) *The Birds of the Seychelles and the Outlying Islands*, Collins, London.

Perrins, C.M. (1976) *Bird Life: an Introduction to the World of Birds*, Elsevier-Phaidon, Oxford.

Perrins, C.M. and Birkhead, T.R. (1983) *Avian Ecology*, Blackie, London.

Peters, J.L. *et al* (1931–) *Checklist of Birds of the World*, Museum of Comparative Zoology, Cambridge, Massachusetts.

Peterson, R.T. (1980) *A Field Guide to the Birds East of the Rockies* (4th edn), Houghton Mifflin, Boston, Mass.

Peterson, P.T., Mountford, G. and Hollom, P.A.D. (1983) *A Field Guide to the Birds of Britain and Europe* (4th edn), Collins, London.

Pizzey, G. (1980) *A Field Guide to the Birds of Australia*, Collins, Sydney.

Schauensee, R.M. de (1982) *A Guide to the Birds of South America*, Academy of Natural Sciences of Philadelphia.

Schauensee, R.M. de and Phelps, W.H. (1978) *A Guide to the Birds of Venezuela*, Princeton University Press, Princeton, N.J.

Schauensee, R.M. de (1984) *The Birds of China Including the Island of Taiwan*, Oxford University Press, Oxford, Smithsonian Institution Press, Washington D.C.

Serle, W., Morel, G.J. and Hartwig, W. (1977) *A Field Guide to the Birds of West Africa*, Collins, London.

Sharrock, J.T.R. (1976) *The Atlas of Breeding Birds in Britain and Ireland*, British Trust for Ornithology, Tring, Hertfordshire.

Simms, E. (1979) *Wildlife Sounds and their Recording*, Elek, London.

Skutch, A.F. (1975) *Parent Birds and their Young*, University of Texas Press, Austin, Texas.

Slater, P. (1971, 1975) *A Field Guide to Australian Birds*, vol I, Oliver and Boyd, Edinburgh; vol II, Scottish Academic Press, Edinburgh.

Stresemann, E. (1975) *Ornithology from Aristotle to the Present*, Harvard University Press, Cambridge, Mass.

Tyne, J. van and Berger, A.J. (1976) *Fundamentals of Ornithology* (2nd edn), Wiley, New York.

Warham, J. (1983) *The Techniques of Bird Photography* (4th edn), Focal Press, Sevenoaks, Kent.

Watson, G.E. (1975) *Birds of the Antarctic and Sub-Antarctic*, American Geophysical Union, Washington, D.C.

Weaver, P. (1981) *The Bird-Watcher's Dictionary*, T. and A.D. Poyser, Stoke-on-Trent.

Wild Bird Society of Japan (1982) *A Field Guide to the Birds of Japan*, Wild Bird Society of Japan, Tokyo.

Williams, J.G. and Arlott, N. (1980) *A Field Guide to the Birds of East Africa*, Collins, London.

Wilson, E. (1967) *Birds of the Antarctic*, Blandford Press, Poole.

Families or Groups

Brown, L. and Amadon, D. (1968) *Eagles, Hawks and Falcons of the World*, 2 vols, Country Life Books, Feltham, Middlesex.

Delacour, J. (1977) *The Pheasants of the World* (2nd edn), Spur Publications, Hindhead, Surrey.

Delacour, J. and Amadon, D. (1973) *Curassows and Related Birds*, American Museum of Natural History, New York.

Forshaw, J.M. (1978) *Parrots of the World* (2nd edn), David and Charles, Newton Abbot.

Forshaw, J.M. and Cooper, W.T. (1977) *The Birds of Paradise and Bower Birds*, Collins, Sydney and London.

Fry, C.H. (1984) *The Bee-eaters*, T. and A.D. Poyser, Stoke-on-Trent.

Goodwin, D. (1976) *Crows of the World*, British Museum (Natural History), London.

Goodwin, D. (1982) *Estrildid Finches of the World*, British Museum (Natural History), London.

Goodwin, D. (1983) *Pigeons and Doves of the World* (3rd edn), British Museum (Natural History), London.

Greenwalt, C.H. (1960) *Hummingbirds*, American Museum of Natural History, New York.

Hancock, J. and Kushlan, J. (1984) *The Herons Handbook*, Croom Helm, London.

Hayman, P., Marchant, J. and Prater, A. (1985) *Shorebirds: an Identification Guide to the Waders of the World*, Croom Helm, London.

Johnsgard, P.A. (1983) *Cranes of the World*, Croom Helm, London.

Johnsgard, P.A. (1978) *Ducks, Geese and Swans of the World*, University of Nebraska Press, Lincoln, Nebraska.

Johnsgard, P.A. (1983) *The Grouse of the World*, University of Nebraska Press, Lincoln, Nebraska.

Johnsgard, P.A. (1981) *The Plovers, Sandpipers and Snipes of the World*, University of Nebraska Press, Lincoln, Nebraska.

Keer, J. and Duplaix-Hall, N. (eds) (1979) *Flamingos*, T. and A.D. Poyser, Stoke-on-Trent.

Lack, D. (1956) *Swifts in a Tower*, Methuen, London.

Mikkola, H. (1983) *Owls of Europe*, T. and A.D. Poyser, Stoke-on-Trent.

Newton, I. (1972) *Finches*, Collins, London.

Newton, I. (1979) *Population Ecology of Raptors*, T. and A.D. Poyser, Stoke-on-Trent.

Nørgaard-Oleson, E. (1973) *The Tanagers*, Skibby Books, Denmark.

Perrins, C.M. (1979) *British Tits*, Collins, London.

Ripley, S.D. (1977) *Rails of the World*, M.F. Feheley, Toronto.

Short, L.L. (1982) *Woodpeckers of the World*, Delaware Museum of Natural History, Greenville, Delaware.

Simpson, G.G. (1976) *Penguins*, Yale University Press, New Haven, Connecticut.

Snow, D.W. (1982) *The Cotingas*, British Museum (Natural History), London.

Soothill, E. and R. (1982) *Wading Birds of the World*, Blandford Press, Poole, Dorset.

Wyllie, I. (1981) *The Cuckoo*, Batsford, London.

Picture Credits

Artwork

GLOSSARY

Adaptation features of an animal that adjust it to its environment. NATURAL SELECTION favors the survival of individuals whose adaptations adjust them better to their surroundings than other individuals with less successful adaptations.

Adaptive radiation where a group of closely related animals (eg members of a family) have evolved differences from each other so that they occupy different NICHES and have reduced competition between each other.

Adult a fully developed and mature individual, capable of breeding but not necessarily doing so until social and/or ecological conditions allow.

Air sac thin walled structure connected to the lungs of birds and involved in respiration; extensions of these can occur in hollow bones.

Albino a form in which all dark pigments are missing, leaving the animal white, usually with red eyes.

Alpine living in mountainous areas, usually above 1,500m (5,000ft).

Altricial refers to young that stay in the nest until they are more or less full grown (as opposed to PRECOCIAL). See also NIDICOLOUS.

Aquatic associated with water.

Arboreal associated with or living in trees.

Avian pertaining to birds.

Beak see BILL.

Bill the two MANDIBLES with which birds gather their food. Synonymous with beak.

Blubber fat, usually that lying just beneath the skin.

Bolus a ball (of food).

Boreal zone the area of land lying just below the north polar region and mainly covered in coniferous forest.

Broadleaved woodland woodland mainly comprising angiosperm trees (both deciduous and evergreen), such as oaks, beeches and hazels, which is characteristic of many temperate areas of Europe and North America.

Brood group of young raised simultaneously by a pair (or several) birds.

Blood-parasite a bird that has its eggs hatched and reared by another species.

Call short sounds made by birds to indicate danger, threaten intruders or keep a group of birds together. See also SONG.

Canopy a fairly continuous layer in forests produced by the intermingling of branches of trees; may be fully continuous (closed) or broken by gaps (open). The crowns of some trees project above the canopy layer and are known as emergents.

Carpal the outer joint of the wing, equivalent to the human wrist.

Casque bony extension of the upper MANDIBLE.

Cecum diverticulation or sac of the hind-gut.

Class a taxonomic level. All birds belong to the class Aves. The main levels of a taxonomic hierarchy (in descending order) are Phylum, Class, Order, Family, Genus, Species.

Cloaca terminal part of the gut into which the reproductive and urinary ducts open. There is one opening to the outside of the body, the cloacal aperture, instead of separate anus and urinogenital openings.

Clutch the eggs laid in one breeding attempt.

Colonial living together in a COLONY.

Colony a group of animals gathered together for breeding.

Comb a fleshy protuberance on the top of a bird's head.

Communal breeder species in which more than the two birds of a pair help in raising the young. See COOPERATIVE BREEDING.

Congener a member of the same genus.

Coniferous forest forest comprising largely evergreen conifers (firs, pines, spruces etc), typically in climates either too dry or too cold to support DECIDUOUS FOREST. Most frequent in northern latitudes or in mountain ranges.

Conspecific a member of the same species.

Contact call CALLS given by males in competition.

Contour feathers visible external covering of feathers, including flight feathers of tail and wings.

Convergent evolution the independent acquisition of similar characters in evolution, as opposed to the possession of similarities by virtue of descent from a common ancestor.

Cooperative breeding a breeding system in which parents of young are assisted in the care of young by other adult or subadult birds.

Coverts the smaller feathers that cover the wings and overlie the base of the large FLIGHT FEATHERS (both wings and tail).

Covey a collective name for groups of birds, usually gamebirds.

Creche a gathering of young birds, especially in penguins and flamingos; sometimes used as a verb.

Crest long feathers on the top of the heads of birds.

Crop a thin-walled extension of the foregut used to store food; often used to carry food to the nest.

Crustaceans invertebrate group which includes shrimps, crabs and many other small marine animals.

Cryptic camouflaged and difficult to see.

Deciduous forest temperate and tropical forest with moderate rainfall and marked seasons. Typically trees shed leaves during either cold or dry periods.

Desert areas of low rainfall, typically with sparse scrub or grassland vegetation or lacking vegetation altogether.

Dimorphic literally "two forms." Usually used as "sexually dimorphic" (ie the two sexes differ in color or size).

Disjunct distribution geographical distribution of a species that is marked by gaps. Commonly brought about by fragmentation of suitable habitat, especially as a result of human intervention.

Dispersal the movements of animals, often as they reach maturity, away from their previous HOME RANGE. Distinct from **dispersion**, that is the pattern in which things (perhaps animals, food supplies, nest-sites) are distributed or scattered.

Display any relatively conspicuous pattern of behavior that conveys specific information to others, usually to members of the same species; often associated with

Display contd.
courtship but also in other activities, eg "threat display."

Display ground the place where a male (or males) tries to attract females.

DNA deoxyribonucleic acid; the key substance of chromosomes—important for inheritance.

Dominance hierarchy a "peck-order"; in most groups of birds, in any pair of birds each knows which is superior and a ranking of superiors therefore follows.

Double-brooded (also triple or multiple brooded) birds which breed twice or more each year, subsequent nests following earlier successful ones, excluding those when the first or all earlier nests fail, in which case the term **replacement nests** applies.

Echolocation the ability to find one's way around by emitting sounds and gauging the position of objects by timing the returning echo.

Erectile of an object, eg a crest, that can be raised.

Facultative optional. See also OBLIGATE.

Family either a group of closely related species, eg penguins, or a pair of birds and their offspring. See CLASS.

Feces excrement from the digestive system passed out through the CLOACA.

Fledge strictly to grow feathers. Now usually used to refer to the moment of flying at the end of the nesting period when young birds are more or less completely feathered. Hence **fledging period**, the time from hatching to fledging, and **fledgling**, a recently fledged young bird.

Flight feathers the large feathers of the wing, which can be divided into PRIMARY FEATHERS and SECONDARY FEATHERS.

Fossorial burrowing.

Frontal shield a fleshy area covering the forehead.

Frugivore eating mainly fruits.

Gallery forest a thin belt of woodland along a riverbank in otherwise more open country.

Generalist an animal whose life-style does not involve highly specialized strategems (cf SPECIALIST), for example, feeding on a variety of foods which may require different foraging techniques.

Genus the taxonomic grouping of species. See CLASS.

Gizzard the muscular forepart of the stomach. Often an important area for the grinding up of food, in many species with the help of grit.

Gregarious the tendency to congregate into groups.

Guano bird excreta. In certain dry areas the guano of colonial sea birds may accumulate to such an extent that it is economic to gather it for fertilizer.

Gular pouch an extension of the fleshy area of the lower jaw and throat.

Habitat the type of country in which an animal lives.

Hallux the first toe. Usually this is small and points backwards, opposing the three forward-facing toes.

Harem a group of females living in the territory of, or consorting with, a single male.

Hatchling a young bird recently emerged from the egg.

Helper an individual, generally without young of its own, which contributes to the survival of the offspring of others by behaving parentally towards them. See COOPERATIVE BREEDING.

Herbivore an animal which eats vegetable material.

Holarctic realm a region of the world including North America, Greenland, Europe and Asia apart from the Southwest, Southeast and India.

Homeothermic warm-blooded, having the ability to keep body temperature constant.

Home range an area in which an animal normally lives (generally excluding rare excursions or migrations), irrespective of whether or not the area is defended from other animals.

Hybrid the offspring of a mating between birds of different species.

Hypothermy a condition in which internal body temperature falls below normal.

Incubation the act of incubating the egg or eggs, ie keeping them warm so that development is possible. Hence **incubation period**, the time taken for eggs to develop from the start of incubation to hatching.

Insectivore an animal that feeds on insects.

Introduced of a species that has been brought from lands where it occurs naturally to lands where it has not previously occurred. Some introductions are natural but some are made on purpose for biological control, farming or other economic reasons.

Irruption sudden or irregular spread of birds from their normal range. Usually a consequence of a food shortage.

Keratin the substance from which feathers are formed (and also reptile scales, human hair, fingernails etc).

Krill small shrimp-like marine CRUSTACEANS which are an important food for certain species of seabirds.

Lamellae comb-like structures which can be used for filtering organisms out of water.

Lanceolate (of feathers) referring to lance-like (pointed) shape.

Lek a display ground where two or more male birds gather to attract females. See DISPLAY.

Littoral referring to the shore-line.

Mallee scrub small scrubby eucalyptus which covers large areas of dryish country in Australia.

Mandible one of the jaws of a bird which make up the BILL (upper or lower).

Melanin a dark or black PIGMENT.

Metabolic rate the rate at which the chemical processes of the body occur.

Migration usually the behavior in which birds fly (migrate) from one part of the world to another at different times of year. There is also local migration and altitudinal migration where birds move, eg on a mountain side, from one height to another.

Molt the replacement of old feathers by new ones.

Monoculture a habitat dominated by a single species of plant, often referring to forestry plantations.

Monogamous taking only a single mate (at a time).

Monotypic the sole member of its genus, family, order etc.

Montane pertaining to mountainous country.

Montane forest forest occurring at middle altitudes on the slopes of mountains, below the alpine zone but above the lowland forest.

Morph a form, usually used to describe a color form when more than one exist.

Morphology the study of the shape and form of animals.

Natural selection the process whereby individuals with the most appropriate ADAPTATIONS are more successful than other individuals, and hence survive to produce more offspring and so increase the population.

Neotropical originating in the tropics of the New World.

Nestling a young bird in the nest, hence **nestling period**, the time from hatching to flying (see FLEDGE).

Niche specific parts of a habitat occupied by a species, defined in terms of all aspects of its life-style (eg food, competitors, predators and other resource requirements).

Nidicolous young birds which remain in the nest until they can fly. See ALTRICIAL.

Nidifugous of young birds that leave the nest soon after hatching. See PRECOCIAL.

Nomadic wandering (as opposed to having fixed residential areas).

Obligate required, binding. See also FACULTATIVE.

Oligotrophic of a freshwater lake with low nutrient levels; such lakes are usually deep and have poor vegetation.

Omnivore an animal that eats a wide variety of foods.

Opportunistic an animal that varies its diet in relation to what is most freely available. See GENERALIST, SPECIALIST.

Order a level of taxonomic ranking. See CLASS.

Organochlorine pesticides a group of chemicals used mainly as insecticides, some of which have proved highly toxic to birds; includes DDT, aldrin, dieldrin.

Pair bond the faithfulness of a mated pair to each other.

Palaearctic a zoogeographical area roughly comprising Europe and Asia (except the Indian subcontinent and Southeast Asia).

Pampas grassy plains (of South America).

Parasitize in the ornithological sense, usually to lay eggs in the nests of another species and leave the foster parents to raise the young. See BROOD-PARASITE.

Passerine strictly "sparrow-like" but normally used as a shortened form of Passeriformes, the largest ORDER of birds. (See notes on Classification pxiv.)

Pecten a structure lying on the retina of the eye.

Pigment a substance that gives color to eggs and feathers.

Pod a group of individuals, especially juvenile pelicans, with a temporary cohesive group structure.

Polyandry where a female mates with several males.

Polygamy where a male mates with several females.

Polymorphic where a species occurs in two (or more) different forms (usually relating to color). See MORPH, DIMORPHIC.

Polygyny where a bird of one sex takes several mates.

Population a more or less separate (discrete) group of animals of the same species.

Prairie North American steppe grassland between 30°N and 55°N.

Precocial young birds that leave the nest after hatching. See ALTRICIAL.

Predation where animals are taken by a predator.

Predator birds that hunt and eat other vertebrates hence "anti-predator behavior" describes the evasive actions of the prey.

Preen gland a gland situated above the base of the tail. The bird wipes its bill across this while preening feathers, so distributing the waxy product of the preen gland over the feathers. The exact function of this is not known; some groups of birds do not possess preen glands.

Primary feather one of the large feathers of the outer wing.

Primary forest forest that has remained undisturbed for a long time and has reached a mature (climax) condition; primary rain forest may take centuries to become established. See also SECONDARY GROWTH.

Promiscuous referring to species where the sexes come together for mating only and do not form lasting pair bonds.

Pyriform pear-shaped.

Quartering the act of flying back and forth over an area, searching it thoroughly.

Race a subsection of a species which is distinguishable from the rest of that species. Usually equivalent to SUBSPECIES.

Radiation see ADAPTIVE RADIATION.

Rain forest tropical and subtropical forest with abundant and year-round rainfall. Typically species rich and diverse.

Range (geographical) area over which an organism is distributed.

Raptor a bird of prey, usually one belonging to the order Falconiformes.

Ratites members of four orders of flightless birds (ostrich, rheas, emu and cassowaries, kiwis) which lack a keel on the breastbone. (See notes on Classification, pxiv.)

Relict population a local group of a species which has been isolated from the rest for a long time.

Resident an animal that stays in one area all the year round.

Roosting sleeping.

Sahara-Sahelian zone the area of North Africa comprising the Sahara Desert and the arid Sahel zone to its south.

Savanna a term loosely used to describe open grasslands with scattered trees and bushes, usually in warm areas.

Scrape a nest without any nesting material where a shallow depression has been formed to hold the eggs.

Scrub a vegetation dominated by shrubs—woody plants usually with more than one stem. Naturally occurs most often on the arid side of forest or grassland types, but often artificially created by man as a result of forest destruction.

Secondary feather one of the large flight feathers on the inner wing.

Secondary forest an area of rain forest that has regenerated after being felled. Usually of poorer quality and lower diversity than PRIMARY FOREST and containing trees of a more uniform size.

Sedentary nonmigrating. See RESIDENT.

Sequential molt where feathers (usually the wing feathers) are molted in order, as opposed to all at once.

Sexual selection an evolutionary mechanism whereby females select for mating only males with certain characteristics, or vice versa.

Sibling group a group containing brothers and sisters.

Sibling species closely related species, thought to have only recently separated.

Single-brooded birds which only make one nesting attempt each year, although they may have a replacement clutch if the first is lost. See DOUBLE-BROODED.

Solitary by itself.

Song a series of sounds (vocalization), often composed of several or many phrases constructed of repeated elements, normally used by a male to claim a territory and attract a mate.

Specialist an animal whose life-style involves highly specialized strategems, eg feeding with one technique on a particular food.

Species a population, or series of populations, which interbreed freely, but not with those of other species. See CLASS.

Speculum a distinctively colored group of flight feathers (eg on the wing of a duck).

Spur the sharp projection on the leg of some game birds; often more developed in males and used in fighting. Also found on the carpal joint of some other birds.

Staging ground/place an area where birds may pause to feed during migration.

Steppe open grassy plains, with few trees or bushes, of the central temperate zone of Eurasia or North America (prairies), characterized by low and sporadic rainfall and a wide annual temperature variation. In cold steppe temperatures drop well below freezing point in winter, with rainfall concentrated in the summer or evenly distributed throughout the year, while in hot steppe, winter temperatures are higher and rainfall concentrated in winter months.

Stooping dropping rapidly (usually of a bird of prey in pursuit of prey).

Strutting ground an area where male birds may display.

Subadult no longer juvenile but not yet fully adult.

Sublittoral the sea shore below the low-tide mark.

Suborder a subdivision of an order. See CLASS.

Subspecies a subdivision of a species. Usually not distinguishable unless the specimen is in the hand; often called races. See CLASS.

Subtropics the area just outside the tropics (ie at higher latitudes).

Taiga the belt of forests (coniferous) lying below (at lower latitudes to) the TUNDRA.

Tarsus that part of the leg of a bird which is just above the foot. Strictly the tarso-metatarsus, bones formed from the lower leg and upper foot.

Temperate zone an area of climatic zones in mid latitude, warmer than the northerly areas but cooler than the subtropical areas.

Terrestrial living on land.

Territorial defending an area, in birds usually referring to a bird or birds which exclude others of the same species from their living area and in which they will usually nest.

Territory area that an animal or animals consider their own and defend against intruders.

Thermal an area of (warm) air which rises by convection.

Thermoregulation the regulation and maintenance of a constant internal body temperature.

Torpor a temporary physiological state, akin to short-term hibernation, in which the body temperature drops and the rate of METABOLISM is reduced. Torpor is an ADAPTATION for reducing energy expenditure in periods of extreme cold or food shortage.

Totipalmate feet feet in which three webs connect all four toes. (Most birds have only two webs between the three forward pointing toes, with the hind claws free.)

Tribe a term sometimes used to group certain species and/or genera within a family. See CLASS.

Tropics strictly, an area lying between 22.5° and 22.5°S. Often because of local geography, birds' habitats do not match this area precisely.

Tundra the area of high latitude roughly demarcated by its being too cold for trees to grow.

Upwelling an area in the sea when, because of local topography, water from deep down in the sea is pushed to the surface. Usually upwellings are associated with rich feeding conditions for birds.

Vermiculation (on feathers) fine markings.

Wattle a fleshy protuberance, usually near the base of the BILL.

Wetlands fresh- or salt-water marshes.

Wing front limb of a bird transformed into an organ for flight.

Wing formula statement of relative lengths of wing feathers, especially of primary feathers. Used as a defining characteristic for many species.

Wing spur a sharp projection at or near the bend of the wing. See SPUR.

Wintering ground the area where a migrant spends the nonbreeding season.

Zygodactyl having two toes directed forwards and two backwards.

INDEX

A **bold number** indicates a major section of the main text, following a heading; a **_bold italic_** number indicates a fact box on a single species or group of species, usually a family or subfamily; a single number in (parentheses) indicates that the animal name or subjects are to be found in a boxed feature and a double number in ((parentheses)) indicates that the animal name or subjects are to be found in a spread special feature. _Italic_ numbers refer to illustrations.